Tinclads
in the Civil War

D1200152

ALSO BY MYRON J. SMITH, JR.,
AND FROM MCFARLAND

The Baseball Bibliography, 2d ed. (4 vols., 2006)

*Le Roy Fitch: The Civil War Career of a
Union River Gunboat Commander* (2007)

The Timberclads in the Civil War: The Lexington,
Conestoga *and* Tyler *on the Western Waters* (2008)

Tinclads
in the Civil War

Union Light-Draught Gunboat
Operations on Western
Waters, 1862–1865

MYRON J. SMITH, JR.

McFarland & Company, Inc., Publishers
Jefferson, North Carolina, and London

LIBRARY OF CONGRESS CATALOGUING-IN-PUBLICATION DATA

Smith, Myron J.
Tinclads in the Civil War : Union light-draught gunboat operations
on western waters, 1862–1865 / by Myron J. Smith, Jr.
p.   cm.
Includes bibliographical references and index.

ISBN 978-0-7864-3579-1
softcover : 50# alkaline paper ∞

1. Mississippi River Valley — History — Civil War, 1861–1865 — Riverine operations.
2. Mississippi River Valley — History — Civil War, 1861–1865 — Campaigns.
3. Gunboats — Mississippi River Valley — History —19th century.
4. United States. Navy — History — Civil War, 1861–1865.
5. Gunboats — United States — History —19th century.
6. United States — History — Civil War, 1861–1865 — Riverine operations.
I. Title.
E470.8.S65   2010   973.3'5 — dc22   2009042186

British Library cataloguing data are available

©2010 Myron J. Smith, Jr. All rights reserved

*No part of this book may be reproduced or transmitted in any form
or by any means, electronic or mechanical, including photocopying
or recording, or by any information storage and retrieval system,
without permission in writing from the publisher.*

On the cover: Tinclad *Argosy* watercolor by Acting Ensign D.M.N. Stouffer, ca. 1864–1865
(David Dixon Porter Papers, Library of Congress); Iron borders ©2010 Shutterstock

Manufactured in the United States of America

*McFarland & Company, Inc., Publishers
Box 611, Jefferson, North Carolina 28640
www.mcfarlandpub.com*

For the Tusculum College Library Staff

CENTRAL ARKANSAS LIBRARY SYSTEM
LITTLE ROCK PUBLIC LIBRARY
100 ROCK STREET
LITTLE ROCK, ARKANSAS 72201

Table of Contents

Abbreviations

There are several different ways to cite military rank. Below are the abbreviations used herein for both the Union and Confederate military.

Army

Army Rank

Pvt.	Private
Cpl.	Corporal
Sgt.	Sergeant
Lt.	Lieutenant
Capt.	Captain
Maj.	Major
Gen.	General
Lt. Gen.	Lieutenant General
Maj. Gen.	Major General
Brig. Gen.	Brigadier General
Col.	Colonel
Lt. Col.	Lieutenant Colonel

Navy

Navy Rank

Acting Rear Adm.	Acting Rear Admiral
Rear Adm.	Rear Admiral
Cdr.	Commodore
Capt.	Captain
Cmdr.	Commander
Lt. Cmdr.	Lieutenant Commander
Lt.	Lieutenant

Introduction

By the spring of 1862, the American Civil War was nearly a year old. At that time, United States troops were making significant inroads into the seceded Upper South, mostly in the undeveloped area west of the Allegheny Mountains. Major victories were won and, consequently, large swaths of land and several sizeable towns were returned to Federal control. A logistical chain maintained the viability of these gains, one run through largely unpacified territory or via rivers, many of which were then natural communication arteries.

Interdicting this Union logistical cord was a big problem for the South, one seldom directly met by regular Rebel field armies. To disrupt the flow of Federal supplies, the Confederacy very early on began to rely upon mobile cavalry forces (regular and partisan), supported by foot volunteers (variously uniformed if at all) from the indigenous population. This in turn resulted in growing Federal frustration and increasingly harsher counterinsurgency policies and initiatives.

Initially, the Federals had too few fast gunboats to halt or deter a large number of Southern antishipping attacks from the river banks. Those available, whether led by Navy or Army officers, could not operate far from the main shipping channels at certain times of the year due to low water depth. As Rebel assaults intensified, new Union weapons, strategy, and leadership were required.

Northern naval commanders leading the Western Flotilla began to find the necessary ingredients to combat the scourge of the Rebel irregulars during the summer of 1862. Several light captured steamers were converted into gunboats and employed on the Tennessee and Ohio rivers, but initiation of a comprehensive riverine anti-guerrilla mission was slow in development.

Numerous attacks upon river traffic stimulated the Union military to create a new "mosquito squadron" to catch or frustrate partisans operating against traffic on those streams. It would provide convoy and other protections for Union shipping and sympathizers, while also engaged in patrol and flag-showing missions.

At the same time, new casemated light-draught gunboats were added. Altered from purchased river steamers and covered with thin sheets of iron, they were nicknamed "tinclads." More than 60 were eventually ordered and were modified in shipyards from Cincinnati to St. Louis and Cairo.

It was the fall of 1862 before these initiatives began to bear fruit and the initial units could be allocated to what Navy leaders came to call their "upper flotilla." The river levels were initially down and it took time to convert and crew the boats.

The War Department's Western Flotilla, responsible for riverine forces since the start of the conflict, became the U.S. Navy's Mississippi Squadron in October. Its new commander, Rear Adm. David Dixon Porter, happily pushed tinclad acquisition, largely viewing the craft as reinforcements for his main fleet. As had been the case since summer, he was first and foremost committed to working with the U.S. Army for the reduction of the Confederate bastion of Vicksburg, far down the Mississippi. The new additions, he reasoned, would serve admirably in support, as dispatch and light replenishment vessels, towboats, patrol boats, swift raiders, minesweepers, troop ship guardians or anchorage pickets, and gunfire support vessels.

Acting without U.S. Navy consultation, the War Department continued to maintain or foster some militarized riverine assets, including a special anti-guerrilla force under Col. Alfred Ellet. The Union Army's Quartermaster Department, together with several states such as Indiana, also operated *ersatz* gunboats. These were usually chartered steamers protected by cotton bales and armed with field pieces. Needless to say, the U.S. Navy, as well as cannon-equipped Confederate regulars and guerrillas, had little regard for these units, particularly the "gotten-up" armed steamers.

As they became increasingly available, it was fully understood that the little Northern tinclads could not stand "in the line of battle," or go toe-to-toe with large emplaced or mobile cannon. Still, they were extensively employed on dedicated military operations aimed at flanking the great Confederate fortress town. Save for two sent to the Ohio, the first purpose-altered units were all rushed down to the Yazoo River in December 1862 and provided anti-torpedo (mine) and gunfire support during the Chickasaw Bayou campaign.

From January to July 1863, the tinclads attached to Porter's lower fleet played significant support roles in most of the amphibious schemes designed to outflank and capture Vicksburg. The small craft took direct combat roles in the campaigns against Arkansas Post and into the Yazoo Pass. The number of tinclads assigned to the Vicksburg campaign increased after March. Once the heavy units of the Mississippi Squadron ran past Vicksburg in April, the little boats continued to provide support and conduct feints above the town as the Navy tackled Grand Gulf and Yankee soldiers crossed over the Mississippi from west to east to launch the climactic campaign.

Although a few more light draughts were allocated in these months to the "upper flotilla" for the protection of shipping on the Cumberland, Tennessee, and Ohio rivers, the majority were not turned loose for participation in the anti-partisan war until after the fall of Vicksburg in July. At that point, the Mississippi Squadron was subdivided into ten, later eleven, geographical sections (or "districts") to which its vessels were assigned. By patrolling these areas and offering convoy, the speedy tinclads were able to maintain Union supply lines and guard Federal interests.

With only one or two exceptions when they were diverted to provide escort and gunfire support for purely military ventures (such as the Red River Campaign of 1864), the light draughts maintained an aggressive but sometimes mundane counterinsurgency and logistical protection effort on the Western waters for the remainder of the conflict.

Still, as Union forces drove deeper into the South and Trans-Mississippi West, Confederate raiders continued their own efforts to slow down their enemy. Cavalrymen like Nathan Bedford Forrest, Jo Shelby, and Colton Greene saw that it might still be possible to disrupt Northern progress if they warred upon logistics.

Unable to defeat the Federals on "its streams," the Confederacy collectively resorted to operating both an organized and a disorganized ("guerrilla") antishipping campaign in the West, hoping to dissuade the enemy. As one writer noted, these "tactics caused the Union some concern, but did little more than increase the barbarity of an already vicious war."[1]

Despite hundreds of attacks by Southerners on river transport during the war (only a fraction of which are reviewed within these pages), the overall number of U.S. civilian and commercial steamboats sunk by military action was surprisingly small. Bvt. Brig. Gen. Lewis B. Parsons, USQMD river transport czar, later reported that direct "guerrilla" action against river transports on all of the Western streams from 1861 to 1865 resulted in 28 vessels of 7,065 tons sunk for a loss of $355,000. Regular Confederate forces sank another 19 craft of 7,925 tons valued at $518,500. Confederate secret agents using incendiaries sank double the tonnage (18,500) of either Rebel cavalry or irregulars, 29 boats worth $891,000.[2]

As part of their often mundane patrols and occasionally spirited actions in direct support of military activities, the 60 tinclads protected all Western river steamers either compelled to or willing to have their cover. This duty was often performed with very slight naval concentrations, whether of tinclads or other craft, including *ersatz* Army gunboats.

For most of the time after August 1862, for example, Lt. Cmdr. Le Roy Fitch operated all Cumberland River escort and patrol with fewer than eight light draughts and often stretched this slight chain into the Ohio and Tennessee rivers as well. Often there were no more than four boats available to Lt. Cmdr. S. Ledyard Phelps and Lt. George Bach on the White River of Arkansas.

The presence of the light draughts with convoys or individual transports was decisive. Most of the steamers lost to river bank attacks were steaming independently when hit or captured.

The tinclads also interrupted Confederate communications, blockaded the huge Trans-Mississippi area, and sailed into harm's way in the bays and rivers surrounding New Orleans. There were far fewer mundane moments aboard a light draught than a larger ironclad. Rowland Stafford True, who served aboard the *Silver Lake,* remembered how the time passed: "One day lying peacefully at anchor, and the next, off on some expedition up or down the river." He continued: "Up the Cumberland today, up the Tennessee tomorrow, down the Mississippi the next — here and there wherever needed."[3]

It should also be noted that a few tinclads were acquired with oceangoing modifications and were transferred to the West Gulf Coast Blockading Squadron for use in the lakes and bayous at the mouth of the Mississippi. One of these, the *Stockdale,* participated in the August 1864 Battle of Mobile Bay; others were sent into Mobile Bay in the spring of 1865 to lend logistical and torpedo-sweeping support during the final push on the Alabama town.

In order for our story to be complete, we shall review in some detail the Confederate resistance mounted against waterborne commerce, military and civilian, on the Western rivers between the end of 1862 and early 1865. It is a tale often overlooked.

To accomplish this goal, we will not only review the evolution of the Mississippi Squadron's tinclad gunboats, but look at the streams upon which they operated, and the tactics of their regular and irregular Southern opponents. We pay particular attention to Confederate attacks upon Federal shipping, gunboat countermeasures (effective and ineffective), and specific counterinsurgency activities outside the reporting found in the usual histories of the Western river war.

In order to concentrate upon this irregular war and detail the work of some of the many converted vessels, we will forgo detailed discussion of several purely military campaigns in which the boats participated along with (usually behind) the big ironclads, e.g., Chickasaw Bayou, Arkansas Post, Yazoo Pass, and the Red River Campaign. This is not to say that all mention of tinclad activities during these operations will be omitted. Occasionally, the little boats were involved in quite spirited, unique, or unsupported fights during those larger campaigns and those are stories worth retelling.

In three years of conflict, surprisingly few tinclads (13) were lost, though many were damaged by nature or gunfire. One was burnt out (*Glide I*), one was snagged and lost (*Linden*), and one was destroyed by a storm (*Rattler*). Nine were direct or indirect victims of Confederate shore batteries (*Covington, Elfin, Key West, Petrel, Queen City, Signal, Tawah, Undine,* and *Wave*) and one was sunk by an underwater torpedo (*Rudolph*).

Due to their success, the tinclads were among the most important vessels of the Civil War. Their activities continuously reinforced the claims of the North to an undivided Union through incessant probes into the heartland via the Western rivers that helped to keep open the great Midwestern communication lines by convoy, patrol, and direct support of national military action.

Years later, a British historian stated the worth of the tinclad in a single long sentence. "All in all these tinclad river gunboats were ungainly, slow and unprepossessing," wrote Angus Konstam in 2002, "but without them the Union would never have managed to supply its field armies in the West, or keep them in communication with each other."

Perhaps Acting Volunteer Lt. George W. Brown, the first commander of the light draught *Forrest Rose*, has summed up the spirit and contribution of the tinclad better than most, and we ask him to launch our tale of their service:

> Like cavalry, we, the light-draft fleet, were kept on the go, never at rest. Our duties on the river were severe; we were never out of rifle-range, and often our men were picked off by sharpshooters from behind the levee. There seemed to be something about us, perchance it was our activity, that made the army like to have us around; and I believe, if they could have put us upon wheels, "Uncle Billy" would have taken us on his "March to the Sea."[4]

All of the engagements between Yankee tinclads and Confederate troops (regular and irregular) reveal the determination and courage of the officers and men fighting on both sides. Many of these actions were previously labeled by historians or writers as miscellaneous and escaped telling in the naval histories of the war (even those devoted to the river war).

As I gathered materials over the past decade for a biography of Lt. Cmdr. Le Roy Fitch (McFarland, 2007), the intensity and breadth of the tinclad war constantly amazed me. Looking farther south than the Hoosier officer's beat on the Tennessee, Ohio, and Cumberland rivers, I found it easy to determine that the scope of action and challenge faced by Fitch on the upper rivers was encountered by other Federal naval leaders on the Mississippi itself, as well as its lower tributaries and even along the Gulf Coast.

Largely absent from works designed to foster common memory, accounts of light-draught action, as they exist and regardless of location involved, have mostly languished in dusty archival records, diaries and personal letters; old newspaper reports; or pages of the *Official Records*. Incidents once called minor or otherwise ignored have a berth within these pages and will hopefully no longer be minimized.

Personnel at a number of libraries and archives helpfully provided insight and information during the research and writing stages of this outing. Among them were the kind folks manning the libraries and collections of the U.S. Navy Department , Library of Congress, National Archives, University of Tennessee, University of Arkansas, East Tennessee State University, Kentucky Historical Society, U.S. Army Historical Center, Missouri Historical Society, Tennessee State Library and Archives, West Virginia Department of Archives and History, Illinois State Library, Chicago Historical Society, Ohio State University, Nashville Public Library, Greeneville-Greene County (TN) Public Library, and Tusculum College.

I would like to tip my hat in thanks to Tennessee state historian Walter T. Durham and West Virginia state archivist Fred Armstrong for their encouragement, as well as *North and South* magazine editor Keith Poulter.

Myron J. Smith, Jr. • Chuckey, Tennessee

1

Rivers and Steamboats

The Civil War was just beginning when Union officials were challenged by the need to make a startling strategic decision: location of the fight. For the North to win the conflict, it would have to control not only the seacoasts and Eastern interior, but the Mississippi Valley as well, including its great rivers.

Despite something of a confused military start, Federal leaders from President Abraham Lincoln on down recognized the need to feed resources into this vital theater. As Charles Boynton wrote in 1867:

> It was clear that the whole seaboard might be regained, even to Florida, and yet the rebellion remain as dangerous as ever, if the rebels could hold the Mississippi River and the valley up to or near the Ohio.

Physical reoccupation of the seceded South in the area west of the Appalachian Mountains required that the war be waged on the Mississippi River itself, plus the Ohio, Tennessee, Cumberland, Arkansas, White, Yazoo, and Red. Many lesser tributaries such as the Green, Black, Little Red, and Ouachita would also be affected.[1]

Travel by land in the South and Midwestern states was at that time usually arduous and sometimes quite expensive, particularly for the shipment of goods. As Adam I. Kane points out in his recent study, there were, through most of the first half of the 19th century, two primary means of transportation in the region, roads and rivers. To these were added railroads in the decade or so before the Civil War.

For thousands of years, the Western rivers were natural communication arteries little controlled by man. Since the early decades of the 19th century, these streams had served as commercial highways, linking the Midwestern section of the United States with eastern markets and southern ports.

Prior to and during the Civil War, it was more economical to transport goods by river than road or rail. Indeed, that remains the case for certain bulk material even today. After all, some 5,000 miles of river were open to 200-ton boats for six months of the year; craft of lesser draft could navigate additional mileage for longer periods.

Prior to the advent of viable regional railroads, wagons traveled poor roads, dispatch riders carried only the lightest items, and where they had been strung, the wires of the newfangled telegraph were often down. It was left to the steamboat to provide much of the lift in the Mississippi Valley, accounting for a huge segment of its bulk logistics and

the fastest connections for travelers. Indeed, steamers were "the first man-made apparatus to radically interrupt the Arcadian wilderness, collapse vast distance, and discharge
the artifacts of distant cultures into remote places." They "galvanized and connected"
outposts cities from New Orleans to St. Louis and Cincinnati and thus "reshaped much
of America, economically and structurally."

The majority of the Mississippi Valley commercial vessels, whether strictly cargo or
packets (cargo and passengers operating to a schedule), were owned in the North and
were removed from southern rivers at the outbreak of the conflict. Consequently, the
Confederacy had many fewer available bottoms to fill and a huge logistical disadvantage.

After Fort Sumter, the Confederacy employed those portions of the Western rivers
under its control to transport supplies from the fertile Trans-Mississippi West to its armies
and people in the east. Those steamboats that were available to the Rebels were used as
efficiently as possible as long as possible, even if their life spans before capture or destruction were relatively short.

A direct relationship existed during the conflict between the available transport modes
and the conduct of successful military operations. Without full control of all lines of
communication, neither side would be able to "operate in anything but the most static
of fashions."[2]

To better understand the military requirements demanded of the great rivers of the
Mississippi Valley, one must first and foremost realize something of the mid–19th cen-

By the time of the Civil War, Western railroads provided increasingly formidable transport
competition for steamboats, but like the steamers, they would become tempting targets for
Confederate raiders. Trains were regularly derailed and their track and other supporting
infrastructure torn up. Steamboats, though often shot up, usually completed their trips, particularly after the introduction of the tinclad gunboat (*Miller's Photographic History of the
Civil War*).

tury geography and peculiarities of that watery system. It is then useful to review the development of the steamboats created to gain maximum advantage from it.

In his delightful early 20th century illustrated children's work *Paddle Wheels and Pistols*, Irvin Anthony wrote of the great rivers during the war. The Mississippi, he remarked, "remained neutral in the Civil War." While its steamboats became gunboats and engaged in deadly struggle, "the great river paid no heed." In its various hazards, it was not partisan, a "respector of causes." Often the streams "seemed to mock the efforts of the warriors" by snag, current, or low-water. "The malice of the river was like that, it was ever so impartial," Anthony concluded, adding the wry thought that: "Perhaps, after all, it smiled."

Hot, cold, wet, and dry weather, usually seasonal, fashioned the volume, speed, and depth of the Western rivers. These key factors determined nautical access for steam-powered vessels at any given time. Some of the larger streams, such as the Mississippi, Ohio, and Tennessee, were, except at certain blocking points like Muscle Shoals, usually wide and blessed of year-round deep channels scoured by fast water. These streams were home to large, usually side-wheel, merchantmen not unlike those associated with the famous Broadway musical *Showboat*.

The hydrology of most of the tributaries for both the Mississippi and the Ohio, like the Cumberland and White, was less magnanimous. Narrow channels, curves and steep rock banks, slow water and buildups of silt and loose logs caused low water and navigational risk.

From the beginning of the Western steamboat period to its end in the 20th century, all riverboat activities were governed first and foremost by the moisture or lack thereof at various times of the year. Wet and dry seasons varied in different parts of the Mississippi River system, depending upon geographical location. It was generally recognized that river depth increased as one moved from a stream's headwaters to its mouth or from tributary to main river.

Rains, snow, floods, and drought determined the river depths and thus the size of vessel which could operate in any given stream at any given time. In the words of famed steamboat historian Louis Hunter: "Each part of the river system rose and fell almost continuously according to a variety of controlling conditions, many of which were not shared by other parts at the same time." Usually beginning in the early spring, melting snow and ice plus rain swelled streams. These ran into the smaller rivers, like the Nolichuckey in Tennessee, which, in turn, ran into the intermediate tributaries like the Tennessee River, and then eventually raised the levels of the trunk rivers, Mississippi, Ohio, etc. This annual "spring rise" marked the opening of the steamboat navigation season, the duration of which was different for every river depending upon its ecology and physical characteristics, particularly shoals. The steaming period on the larger rivers depended not only on this one rise, but on various rises or "freshes," which were, in turn, determined by the weather.

Generally, the hotter summer months saw a drop in the river stages of the tributary streams in the Mississippi Valley; water levels could fall so far as to greatly restrict navigation or prohibit it entirely in all or portions of the Ohio, Cumberland, White, and Red Rivers. The low-water period usually began sometime in June and ended in October.

Hot, cold, wet and dry weather, usually seasonal, fashioned the volume, speed, and depth of the Mississippi River and its tributaries. The Father of Waters is shown here at high stage, a dangerous time for snags and other floating debris (*Harper's New Monthly Magazine*, December 1855).

Severe summer thunderstorms could result in a "fresh," which might, at least briefly, allow intensification of previously restricted activities. Skilled river men aboard both naval and civilian steamers could tell a river's stage, rising or falling, by using a lead or even watching driftwood.

In practice, the maxim became: the smaller the river or the lower the stream, the lighter the boat draft required. The key to commercial — and later, military — success on such waters came to be centered upon very light boats, craft requiring very little water in which to float. These were often powered by a single paddle wheel mounted in the stern.[3]

By the 1850s, Western river steamboat evolution was essentially complete; the vessel's form, retained into the early 20th century, was that of lightly-constructed, flat-bottomed craft with multiple decks rising high above their waterlines. The boats had an average length of 120 to 250 feet and were usually 18 to 33 feet wide, though this beam, if you will, could be increased significantly (almost doubled) aboard side-wheelers by the guards hung over the hull to the outboard edges of the paddle boxes. These, in the words of one student of steamboat architecture, "effectively masked" the hulls.

Mark Twain remembered a side-wheeled steamboat which appeared at his hometown of Hannibal, MO, as being a "handsome sight, too."

> She is long and sharp and trim and pretty; she has two tall, fancy-topped chimneys, with a gilded device of some king swung between them; a fanciful pilot-house, all glass and "gingerbread," perched on top of the "texas" deck behind them; the paddle-boxes are gorgeous with a picture or with gilded rays above the boat's name; the boiler-deck, the hurricane-deck, and the texas deck are fenced and ornamented with clean white railings; there is a flag gallantly flying from the jack-staff....

The Mississippi River and its tributaries were also challenging waters during those periods when their stages were low. Sandbars and shoals were a constant challenge. For Union Civil War gunboatmen fighting their elusive Southern foes along the banks, the increased height of cliffs made shipboard defense all the more problematic (***Harper's New Monthly Magazine***, December 1855).

In general, the appearance of these commercial passenger-carrying "packets" changed little from the antebellum days of Mark Twain to that of one visited by George Ward Nichols in 1870:

> From her keel to the roof of the upper cabin she includes forty feet. Above that is the "Texas," as it is called, which is an upper row of cabins where the officers' quarters are, and upon the top of which is imposed the pilot-house. The main cabin is plainly but well furnished, with large staterooms on either side. Below it is the main deck, where the big boilers and furnaces and engines are. Below this deck again there is a deep, spacious hold, where a thousand or fifteen hundred tons of freight may be stowed away.... Perhaps the most ornamental and most needful parts of this noble creature, as we see her from the outside, are the two big black smoke-stacks.

The same detail was earlier provided by a *Philadelphia Inquirer* correspondent who used the pen name "Alex," but who may have been their ace reporter Henry Bentley. Writing from Quincy, IL, on August 29, 1861, "Alex" described the layout of the new 394-ton side-wheeler *Sucker State*. Constructed at McKeesport, PA, in 1860 and homeported at Galena, IL, the St. Louis and Keokuk packet was, like other Western boats, quite different from the steamers his readers might have "seen in the East." Marine features originally present at the beginning of the inland steamboat era were stripped away in favor of lighter, more practical construction. Shallow, flat-bottomed hulls with "flimsy" superstructures, constructed to avoid "topheaviness," were now commonplace.

Built atop of the hold of the boat's spoon-shaped hull was an inch-thick main deck, where the machinery was placed, which extended the entire length of the craft. Passengers, livestock, and light freight not placed into the hold was carried here. The forward portion of the deck was occupied by the deck hands. In front of the boilers, a staircase led to the Saloon deck or second story of the steamer. The clerks' office was located toward the front of this deck, and behind was a social hall and the main saloon, which extended the balance of the boat's length. Staterooms were built on either side.

Wandering higher, "Alex" found the third story, or Hurricane deck, that offered a fine promenade by extending the roof and guards of the boat. He might have been surprised to know that it was only ¾ of an inch thick. Up a flight of steps, one found the Texas deck, where the officers' quarters, staterooms, and mess deck were located.

The final stairs led to the fifth story or pilot house, located between the two tall chimneys. Therein the pilots worked a large wheel that was connected by a series of ropes and chains to the rudder. Looking forward through large windows to the center of the bow, they could see the jackstaff and employ it as a sight.

Official terminology for the decks in the colorful layout descriptions of Nicholas and "Alex" were, in fact, slightly different. Borrowing from the detail provided in Adam Kane's excellent recent *The Western River Steamboat*, let us elaborate. Directly above the cargo hold was the open Main deck which hosted all of the machinery, a blacksmith's shop, deck passenger berths (bunks, actually), heads, and hatches covering stairs into the hold. Most passengers were accommodated in cabins on either side of a deck-long central hallway, often called "the saloon," on the boiler, Saloon, or "upper" deck.

This next deck up from the main deck was equally as wide as the one below it and also contained washrooms, a bar and a saloon, a pantry, and a baggage room. The saloon hallway was also the dining and social area. The after part, closed off at night by folding doors, was set aside for ladies and children and was usually equipped with a piano. The clerk's or business office was located in the forward part of the saloon hallway. The exterior of the boiler deck was largely surrounded by a covered walkway, also called a gallery or a guard; sometimes, the bar and a barbershop were located on this area.

The largely-open roof of the boiler or Saloon deck was known as the Hurricane deck. The open portion usually had skylights to illuminate the saloon on the boiler deck directly below.

Forward and covering about a third of the deck was "a long narrow house" with cabins for officers, clerks, pilots and overflow passengers. It was known as the "Texas." It was constructed of quarter- and half-inch boards "fastened with small nails" and light framing." Sometimes the structure looked like an elongated shed; given that it first appeared about the time of the Mexican War, the unknown derivation of the name may have been some kind of reference to Texas' annexation.

The pilothouse was located atop the "Texas" and was ringed with windows for the pilots; it was either somewhat centered or built on the forward edge. On civilian boats, ladies and gentlemen in escorted groups were often allowed to visit the pilothouse to enjoy the steamer's best view of the surrounding countryside.

Built from multiple sections of sheet iron, the smokestacks Nichols and "Alex" referenced above were actually known, per Mark Twain, as "chimneys" in everyday parlance. The pair came up through the superstructure from the forward end of the boilers below and were essential, as in the case of a fireplace, to the provision of an air supply or draft that aided fuel combustion. These chimneys were tall, usually between 75 and 90 feet above water, and were often viewed as an aesthetic necessity.

It required approximately 30 years for the Western steamboat to evolve into the general form familiar during the second half of the 19th century. As navigational problems and commercial demands were addressed by technological innovation, it remained only to build boats marrying the plentiful wood supply available with hardware and power plant manufacture.

Steamboat construction was informal, to say the least, more of a "craft tradition" than a documented matter of naval architecture. The major construction and repair locations were the towns along the upper tributaries of the Mississippi (Tennessee, Ohio, Kanawha, Wabash, Missouri), plus St. Louis. Some firms specialized in hull or cabin building, while others supplied machinery. Written plans were seldom employed and such deviations from standard as occurred (as in the case of the tinclad conversions) were largely a matter of negotiated handshake. Such contracts as there were emphasized delivery times and boat finish.[4]

Two or more engines and three or more boilers per vessel were common. Imprecisely-built and easily repaired, the engines powering Western riverboats were of the lighter-weight, high-pressure variety rather than the low-pressure condensing engines employed elsewhere. Very fuel inefficient, the horizontally-oriented poppet-valve engines, with their relatively small but long horizontal cylindrical fire-tube iron boilers, were located on the main deck, and, indeed, occupied a large part of it. The boilers were, as former Acting Assistant Paymaster E.J. Huling remembered, "provided with places where the sand and sediment from the water can be blown out at short intervals when the boat is running."

The location of the machinery on the main deck over the hold was interestingly described by "Alex" for readers of his "Western Letter" in the August 30, 1861, issue of the *Philadelphia Inquirer*:

> Upon the deck, immediately over the hold, was placed the boilers, on iron legs, the furnaces being below the boilers, without any surroundings whatever.... The engines, two in number — one working each wheel — are placed upon heavy timbers upon a crank axle, with which each wheel is provided, no shaft being required.

The engine cylinder was about one foot to 20 inches in diameter with a three- to eight-foot piston stroke. The fuel employed was wood or, when available, anthracite coal. The latter fuel was not provided by the ton or hundredweight, as might be expected. Rather, it was obtained by the bushel or the box. In July 1863, Master's Mate Symmes E. Browne of the *Tyler* wrote that 500 boxes of coal —1,000 bushels — was sufficient to power his timberclad from Memphis to Cairo.

Given the manner of construction, with various rough approximations in valve, flue, and head fittings, the engines, particularly when overly stoked to obtain speed or poorly maintained, were dangerous. Hot combustion furnace gases were shoved from the rear of the boilers through the boiler water to the front of the boilers, creating a significant amount of steaming water under very high pressure, usually over 100 pounds per square

Transports nestled together at Alexandria, Louisiana, in 1864. This scene might have been familiar to any traveler along the Western rivers in the 1850s through the 1870s. The steamers connected cities from New Orleans to St. Louis and Cincinnati and "reshaped much of America, economically and structurally." During the Civil War, they also carried thousands of soldiers (sometimes whole regiments on a single boat) to battle (U.S. Army Military History Institute).

inch. The *Sultana* disaster of 1865 provides the worst example of the resulting vulnerability, but steamboat explosions were common. Although the use of more sophisticated engines or valve mechanisms had been possible for over 20 years, their introduction "was successfully resisted by riverboat engineers until well after the Civil War."[5]

The steamboat's power plant provided the energy to turn paddle wheels, which were uncomplicated and fairly easy to repair if damaged. True, the water thrown up with each turn was a waste of fuel, but that was not a significant concern when wood was easily available and did not detract from the restoration advantage. Obstructions, snags, logs, and ice caused much damage, which could often be readily fixed by the boat's carpenters.

During the first half of the 19th century, most Western river craft were powered by side-wheels of fairly significant diameter and width (30 foot diameter and 12 foot width was common), which were mounted about one-third of the length forward from the boat's

During the first half of the 19th century, most Western river craft were powered by side-wheels. Completed at Pittsburgh, Pennsylvania, in 1852, the 287-ton *Ben Campbell* is a perfect example. Though lost by fire in 1860, she continued to live on as her equipment went to a stern-wheeler by the same name (Library of Congress).

stern. Each was driven by at least one dedicated engine. These big wheels, located in special housings, were particularly helpful in steering the vessels, and at those times, as was very common, when it was necessary to back out into a stream after making a bow-on landing. This was the same arrangement as was employed by steamers on the Hudson River and elsewhere in the east.

It has been recorded that side-wheel packet boats, which could also haul cargo on their main decks and in a shallow hold, were much longer on the Mississippi River than on the Ohio, while the latter tended to have their wheels located further aft. This difference occurred because of the need for those plying between Cincinnati and the west to get through the locks of the Louisville and Portland Canal, which had been built around the Falls of the Ohio at Louisville.

In contrast to the side-wheel boats, stern-wheelers had a more difficult time in getting established in the years before the Civil War. They were seen as slower and harder to handle. However, rear propulsion did make significant technical gains and was beginning to win larger acceptance by operators. This trend would continue, particularly in the two decades after Appomattox. Pilots and captains, and during the war, the U.S. Navy, recognized that these rear-wheeled boats, generally smaller in size than the side-wheeled packets, had some major advantages over their two-wheeled rivals.

Stern-wheelers were less prone to hit things in the water or to need to stop to avoid

This photograph, taken at Memphis ca. 1906, clearly shows the differences in rig between the stern-wheel steamer on the left and the side-wheeler on the right. Both types had their advantages and disadvantages, both were widely employed on the Western rivers, and both would be chosen for conversion into Federal light-draught gunboats (Library of Congress).

ramming floating objects. The rear wheel location offered a built-in advantage to those needing to get boats off bars or over shoals. Most importantly, the removal of the propulsion wheels from the sides to the rear meant that builders, on about the same hull tonnage, could do away with the heavy side wheel houses and provide these types with greater beams, thereby lightening draft. The square-sterned boats each had at least three rudders, which were connected by rods "in a rude sort of way, but very strong." Approximately the same size cargo could be carried by stern-wheelers, but the craft could operate in drier seasons, earning more return.

"To obtain lightness of draft in relation to tonnage and cargo capacity became the primary object of steamboat builders from an early date," wrote Louis C. Hunter in 1949, "and remained so throughout the steamboat era. The true western river steamboat was first and last a shallow-water boat." Indeed, as one observer put it, a good boat was one "built so that in a low river her first mate could tap a keg of beer and run his vessel four miles on the suds."

Another advantage was a certain convenience in the use of the vessels as towboats. Instead of towing barges or other boats astern, connected by long lines (towlines), stern-wheelers could lash their tows forward and push them. This practice allowed for greater control over the tows in crooked channels or swift currents.

When it came to the handling of the two different types when employed as warships, side-wheelers also had advantages. As Gary Matthews wrote in a message on the Civil War Navies Message Board:

> In order for a stern-wheeler to come about in a narrow river, the pilot had to put the boat's bow or stern into the bank and then allow the current to swing the opposite end around, whereas a side-wheeler could simply go ahead on one wheel and back on the other. The independent side wheels could also be used to steer a boat if her rudder or steering ropes were damaged, which was a fairly common occurrence.

Rear Adm. David Dixon Porter, when he came on the scene in the fall of 1862, definitely voiced an opinion in favor of side-wheelers that did not employ tubular boilers. If given a choice, he would have his boats constructed new with extra-large boilers and large cylinders. He, like those before him, beginning with Cmdr. John Rodgers in July 1861, would also pay tribute to the saying: "the smaller the river or the lower the stream, the lower the boat draft required."[6]

2

Insurgents and Gunboats

In the early months of 1862, after the Union victories at Forts Henry and Donelson and Shiloh, Federal gunboats and transports regularly carried bluecoat infantry with ease up and down the streams of the Mississippi Valley. Numerous Dixie citizens were forced to accept a new understanding of the changing strategic position even while pondering local resistance to this ominous invasion.

As Southerners watched fortifications fall or become invested, control over portions of "their" rivers, to say nothing of important communities, was lost to "the Cause." Memphis and Nashville were occupied and turned into forward depots. Corinth was abandoned, Vicksburg was placed under siege, and large parts of the Upper South appeared ripe for Union consolidation. While Maj. Gen. Henry Halleck's Federal troops fanned out over parts of Missouri, Arkansas, Tennessee, Alabama, Mississippi, and Kentucky, Confederate troops regrouped. Major campaigning by regular troops in the West slowed almost to a standstill.

This is not to say that the fighting ceased. On the contrary, in the words of historian Benjamin Franklin Cooling, "The conflict became a 'war in the shadows' in which rebel horsemen garnered most of the honors." According to Daniel E. Sutherland, "Large numbers of common folk assumed from the earliest days of the Confederacy that guerrillas would be an important component of the nation's military force." The potential for this sort of contribution to the war effort was recognized by Confederate leaders and opinion makers early on. State governors were also urged to authorize irregular activities. A.O.W. Lattern wrote to Tennessee Governor Isham G. Harris on June 14, 1861, strongly suggesting that he authorize "armed men to repel the enemy at every point" in a Volunteer State guerrilla war. Lattern stressed his belief that a "more deadly and destructive antagonism could not be raised to repel the invaders."

Writing in the July 1861 issue of *De Bow's Review*, George Fitzhugh urged the South to supplement its regular armies with "that desultory partisan method of warfare before which invading armies gradually melt away." If the war dragged on and Federal forces captured Rebel territory, then, he believed the "chief reliance must be placed on irregular troops and partisan warfare."

In Arkansas, destined to be a hotbed for irregular activity, Little Rock's leading newspaper, the *Arkansas True Democrat*, put out a call the same month for volunteers, "inclined to go into guerrilla or independent service" to rendezvous at the capital, ready for action.

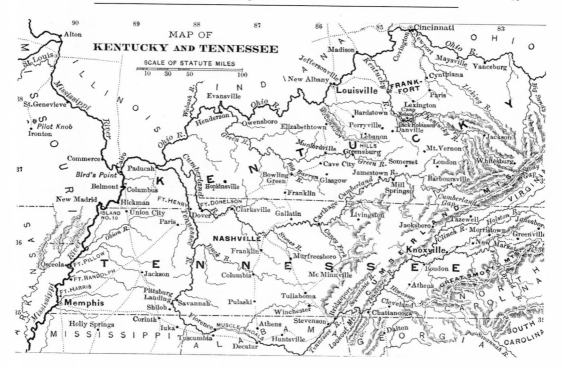

The vast logistical challenge facing Federal forces on the upper rivers can be seen from this map. Supplies for "down the river" started out at Cincinnati and Louisville and continued, either passing down the Cumberland to Nashville for redistribution by rail, or going down the Mississippi to Memphis and below (*Battles and Leaders*, vol. 1.).

Every man (Caucasian only and no women) should arrive possessing "a good horse, a good double-barrel shot gun, and [be] as well supplied with small arms as possible." Editorial sentiment like this could be read regularly in all of the Southern newspapers over the next few months. A few even emphasized attacks on river shipping.

For example, on February 26, 1862, the editors of the *Memphis Avalanche* published a report concerning preparations being made by guerrilla home guardsmen to attack steamers, and especially gunboats, on Tennessee's rivers. The newsmen recognized, along with others, that communications disruption was, as historian Noel Fisher wrote, "the least risky and most common activity" irregulars could perform. Squads of five or six men, the journal told its readers, were going out to live off the land and, when the opportunity presented itself, to "pick off the Lincoln pilots." Firing from "behind trees, logs, and in the narrow bends of the river," they hoped to cause Yankee-employed pilots to "refuse to ascend a steam where death awaits behind any big tree." Amounting almost to an endorsement of guerrilla warfare, the sentiment expressed by the newspaper would increasingly be seen in volunteer actions of the sort over the months and years ahead.

In some quarters, it came to appear as though Southern men were fighting to stem in an irregular manner that loss of ground they were so far unable to directly prevent on the battlefield. As Fisher later noted, there were basically three typical forms of low-intensity activity: ambushes of small Northern military parties; intimidation of Yankee sympathizers and Unionist civilians; and raids on communication lines.

Southern units — military raider, partisan, and guerrilla — struck back at the Yankee invaders, hitting Union outposts, small or isolated contingents, supply dumps, loyalist leaders and homesteads, and most especially, rail and water transport and telegraph communications.

By late spring 1862, Southern steamboats plying the streams of the Upper South were mostly captured, sunk, or forced to flee. The stern-wheelers and side-wheelers now seen were no longer innocent merchantmen; the overwhelming majority of those chugging the currents, whether contract steamers or independents, were transporting either soldiers or war goods aimed at the South. It became painfully obvious to those tasked with holding back the Yankees that all river traffic had become a legitimate target. Civilians aboard these vessels, including women and children, rode in harm's way at their own risk. There were no neutral trading vessels.

If you were a Yankee invader or sympathizer in Tennessee, Kentucky, Arkansas, or some other Southern state, the differences between the types of insurgents shooting at your steamer, destroying your home, burning your supplies, killing your straggling troops or foraging parties, tearing up railroad tracks, or pillaging in some other fashion probably did not matter any more to you than did the destruction of homes, theft of livestock, destruction of railroad rolling stock, cotton bale looting, overly ambitious foraging, or murders committed upon Southerners by Union troops or supporters. The noted British military historian, John F.C. Fuller, once wrote: "The Federal soldier was semi-regular and the Confederate semi-guerrilla." Yet, in fact, there was, as Dr. Robert M. Mackey notes, a real difference between the various kinds of Southern attackers, if not the outcome of their assaults.

In the spring and summer of 1862, as the Rebel irregular menace became more fully appreciated by the Union army in the West, Maj. Gen. Halleck asked the German immigrant jurist Francis Lieber, whom he had met in the aftermath of Shiloh, to give his legal opinion on the matter, and of potential countermeasures. Guerrillas, a 19th century term first applied to Spanish irregulars in the Napoleonic Wars, were seen by Lieber as unpaid volunteers who were not part of an army but who joined together in self-constituted bands to take up arms against (or also who had faded away from) invaders. They often wore no uniform and quarter was seldom given or expected in combat or after capture. Partisans, on the other hand, were elite military groups — special forces, if you will — who wore uniforms and undertook unconventional activities, like stealthily capturing opposing generals. Lieber, whose thoughts were contained in his *Guerrilla Parties Considered with Reference to the Laws and Usages of War*, also known as the "Lieber Code," noted that raiders were regular cavalry units usually sent to attack targets of substance, like railroads, supply centers, and river shipping, rather than political or "soft" targets such as farmers or shopkeepers.

As the war continued, "guerrilla" became the epitaph usually employed by Northerners to mean groups, primarily of Southerners, engaged in any type of unconventional or irregular warfare from cavalry raids to bushwhacking. On the Western waters, the Federal gunboatmen labeled as a "guerrilla" anyone, in uniform or not, who shot at them from a river bank, whether barricaded in a fort or hiding behind a tree. Usually — but not always — these raiders melted away when bombarded or when troops were put ashore in pursuit. In the eyes of the Western sailors, this insurgent conflict, as Cmdr. John A. Winslow put it in June, was "barbarian warfare" and those Rebels participating in it deserved the derogatory title given them. Such irregular warfare was considered just as barbarous as if it were conducted by Native Americans riding ponies on the Great Plains and was worthy of the most direct retribution without quarter.

This irregular Southern resistance was seen as a full scale "pestilence" by Northerners over the summer months of 1862. By now, the names of raiding regular Confederate cavalrymen like John Hunt Morgan and Nathan Bedford Forrest caused panic in Union circles, but so, too, did those of regional partisans. Lesser-remembered irregulars, like Captains Adam Rankin Johnson of Kentucky and T. Alonzo Napier of Benton County, Tennessee, to name two of hundreds, inspired fear. Throughout large swaths of the mid–South, unconventional small-scale combat became more than just a part of the war; to its victims and perpetrators, it became the war itself. All of the evils we've come to know in insurgent and counterinsurgent warfare in our own time, save possibly suicide bombings, were experienced during the Civil War.[1]

As 1862 passed, the true differences between cavalry operating as special-force raiders and small bands of unorganized bushwhackers was more fully recognized. It also came to be understood that in many areas, such as Middle Tennessee, "civilian animosity and guerrilla marauding ... were," as historian Steven V. Ash has put it, "two sides of the same coin." Indigenous guerrilla bands, in addition to fighting within provincial, hometown boundaries, were also of major assistance to regular CSA cavalry raiders. Forrest, Morgan, and others received intelligence, food, horses and forage, and recruits from these sometimes informal, always irregular people. As Union Brig. Gen. James S. Negley later wrote: "The wealthy secessionists ... are undoubtedly aiding and sympathizing with these guerrilla parties. Many of their sons are with them."

There was at least one high-level systematic and organized Rebel effort to create and harness guerrilla bands, "in the proper sense of the term," to a state's defense. This measure was, in effect, to quote irregular warfare historian Robert Mackey, an attempt "to give the Yankee army a taste of what Napoleon's army experienced in Spain." As commander of the new Trans-Mississippi District, Maj. Gen. Thomas C. Hindman immediately set to work building up in Arkansas as much resistance as possible to halt an expected Northern influx. Building up regular military forces to replace those sent east would take time, and to help buy that time, Hindman authorized the raising of independent guerrilla companies to fight behind enemy lines. He may have guessed that command and control difficulties would spell failure.

Hindman's attempt to set up a formal irregular force soon passed, but unconventional warfare, especially against steamers plying "our rivers," did not, despite often very harsh examples of Federal retribution. The Southern view on steamboats as enemy solidified throughout the Western theater in the weeks after Shiloh. As Donald Davidson put it years later, whoever was willing could "stand behind cottonwoods or at any other convenient point" and blaze away "at boats of all sorts." After all, each was a direct threat and "a Federal boat — in one way or another a ship of war — and it ought to be stopped, captured, burned, or driven back."[2]

As the second spring of war neared summer, the surge in Southern irregular warfare, coupled with the annual drop in the depths of the rivers, affected the logistical chain of the entire Federal Western military establishment, especially the steamboat industry employed in its behalf. Fewer craft were able to ascend streams such as the Cumberland, and those that could were often attacked. The *Louisville Democrat* in mid–June reported one of many ambushes. We cite it here as an example.

When passing the narrows 20 miles above Duck River on her return down the Tennessee River from Pittsburg Landing to her Paducah home port, the side-wheeler *Autocrat* was fired into by unknown riflemen on the river bank. In the noise and confusion of the moment, it was believed that the 255-foot-long steamer was subjected to "about 900 shots." Of those, some 60 hit the cabin, passing through it, while another nine balls struck the pilot house. Four persons were wounded, one, a fireman, seriously.

This Confederate philosophy and approach to Northern logistical interdiction occurred not just along river banks, but inland, and intensified in the months ahead into late 1864. Wherever Union colors appeared, horsemen or wagons traveled, or locomotives whistled, Southern fighters appeared, often without uniform and attacking from ambush.

As historian Mackey notes in his coverage of the White River campaigns, by summer 1862, attacks on Federal steamers upon that stream had escalated and were as troublesome as those occurring at the same time on the Ohio, Mississippi, Cumberland, or Tennessee. This land and water assault, though often localized both in goal and commission, was all part of a pattern of irregular resistance growing increasingly dangerous.[3] The principal problem for Federal authorities in combating this low-intensity offensive seemed to lie with accepting the truth about just how widespread the underlying local support was for the insurgents and in developing measures to deal with both the fighters and with those actively assisting them. The challenge existed not only in Tennessee and Kentucky, but in Mississippi, Louisiana, Arkansas, and wherever Union troops inserted themselves in the South.

Federal anti-guerrilla policy was

Maj. Gen. Thomas C. Hindman (1828–1868) served briefly during 1862 as commander of the Confederate Trans-Mississippi Department. A staunch believer in unconventional and irregular warfare, Hindman attempted to employ his partisans to cut off Federal supply efforts on the White River. Whether under his direction or that of another officer, the antishipping war on the White would become among the most ferocious struggles of the Civil War (*Battles and Leaders*).

initially one of conciliation. An effort was made to shield Dixie's civilians from the harsh realities of conflict. As Mark Grimsley later wrote, "Northern commanders expected to woo Southern civilians back to their former allegiance." This policy, despite mounting evidence that wooing did not work, remained the official U.S. approach till summer 1862. Union soldiers became increasingly frustrated with the ineffective approach.

As Morgan and Forrest continued to gain publicity and unnamed irregulars shot up trains and steamers, the germ of a counterinsurgency position was considered by a number of influential Union generals. Leniency, the unpopular concept of "winning hearts and minds," gave way to what Prof. Grimsley calls "the pragmatic policy." The Northern aim remained battlefield success with the least harm to Southern civilians possible. They or their economy were not yet to be the direct targets of attack. This policy remained in place until approximately February 1864. At that point a final "hard war" approach was put into place, directed at the destruction of the Southern economy. Under this pragmatic approach, far harsher responses would face those abetting or participating in "guerrilla" warfare. Responses to perceived attacks — whether by legitimate soldiers or unregulated bands, and regardless of location — were increasingly standardized by Federal military units and warship commanders. Homes, farms, or towns were burned or sometimes ransomed; prisoners were taken and often jailed or exiled beyond the lines.

Both Maj. Gen. Ulysses S. Grant and William T. Sherman, as well as Rear Adm. David D. Porter, certainly drew the line, offering little protection to non-uniformed and unorganized irregulars. The former's General Order No. 60 of July 3 authorized Union commanders who suffered losses from guerrillas to seize personal property from Rebel sympathizers in the immediate vicinity of attack. Grant saw local residents as responsible for policing their areas and suppressing unregulated incidents "being so pernicious to the welfare of the community where it is carried on."

The pragmatic and total-war policies took a serious toll on the civilian population and contributed to the continuing disharmony between occupier and resident. Southern irregulars continuously harassed their neighbors who might be Union sympathizers and forcibly impressed soldiers from among them. Federals, for their part, engaged in widespread foraging activities as a means of supplying their own needs and denying substance to their enemy. "Rural women left alone in cabins and on farms were repeatedly robbed of livestock and food items as troops looked for food to feed their armies."

Employing often harsh measures, Union soldiers afloat and ashore came to wage a continuing and intense struggle against the irregulars and guerrillas, as well as uniformed raiders, and those viewed as sympathetic to them. Protecting communication lines in a war of logistics was now viewed by the Federals as vital. Maintaining control of the rivers, rail routes, and roads had become a paramount mission for all Yankee land forces, as well as the gunboats.

If the guerrillas and partisans could not be beaten off, it would be impossible for the North to guarantee a dependable flow of supplies and munitions to its field armies. At this point and for some time to come in the West, there would be few real front lines, enemy or friendly, save around Nashville, Memphis, Helena, and a few other communities. "Large areas," wrote the modern British observers Cornelia and Jac Weller, "were not and could not be totally controlled by either side save for short periods." "Without an adequate naval force to challenge the Union naval activities, the Confederates could only resort to guerrillas," wrote several well-known Civil War historians just a decade ago. To win that war against the Southern irregulars, at least from a riverine viewpoint, required new strategy and tactics, as well as equipment.[4]

Having so far governed largely with tolerance and restraint, Union occupation forces grew disillusioned. The guerrillas were not a few hardcore infiltrators coming in from outside to insert their will upon local townsfolk; they were home-grown. Those who ambushed Union personnel "were men and boys who killed by night and hid among their kinfolk and neighbors by day." The support given them, for the most part, was not coerced but freely provided. The attempt to win these people to the Union by forbearance and even some good deeds did not succeed; the policy, which Rear Adm. David Dixon Porter later called one of "milk and water," was replaced with increased harshness.

As we shall see, the U.S. Navy adopted this policy. Historians like Ash have suggested that this form of brutal civilian treatment, coupled with other similar policies such as sympathizer banishment or the arrest of guerrilla family members, had some impact on defusing the irregular war. If so, that was late in the war. In the summer of 1862, as would be the case for another two years, the lands transversed by the Western rivers were not only battlegrounds for uniformed armies, but "a turbulent arena of civil strife where every man and woman was a combatant, every neighborhood a battleground."

The ongoing Southern raider/guerrilla campaign in the West resulted in additional reprisals against the populace and deepening enmity on both sides. The internecine North-South struggle was no less ferocious on the rivers and river banks than it was on dry land. For sailors and those ashore alike, the accessibility of one combatant or victim to another, often separated by only a few yards between boat and shore, had both physical and psychological consequences that helped to spark fear and hatred on both sides.

The proximity of Northern steamboat operators, passengers, and Navy bluejackets allowed for frequent and sharp exchanges with Confederate raider and guerrillas which were not always decisive for either side. Additionally, Southern civilians and slaves were increasingly startled and downright frightened to find light-draught gunboat tars the first Yankees in areas where good roads did not exist.

A clergyman named George R. Browder, a Kentuckian who lived on the shores of the Cumberland north of Clarksville, recorded the sentiments of others when he noted the many "small bodies, called guerillias [sic], coming in and scouring the county, and yet not in force enough to hold it." He went on to confess to his diary: "I fear guerilla warfare more than the shock of vast armies in battle array" because the irregulars "are never still — life, liberty and property are not safe an hour." Over a hundred years later, Michael J. Bennett gave further voice to a sentiment which was obvious to many riverside citizens of the Confederacy. "Southerners viewed gunboats and their crews," he concluded, "as akin to a Viking invasion, spreading fear and instability...."

This realization of vulnerability on both sides, occasionally bordering on helplessness, coupled with apprehension and abhorrence, helps to explain the upsurge in animus and in attacks upon Western river steamers. Employing speed, tricks, and surprises, plus armament ranging from masked cannon batteries to shotguns, guerrillas increasingly pelted both civilian craft and naval warships, in addition to the various forms of land communication.

The geography of the largely undeveloped region made these attacks relatively easy. Speaking specifically of the Cumberland, but with equal emphasis upon the high points of Tennessee and Mississippi, the editor of the *New York Times* wrote in April 1863 that "it is the easiest thing for armed men to hide themselves in the glades crowning these cliffs and fire down on passing boats. To return the fire effectively from boats, with any sort of cannon, is simply impossible."

Twin Morgan-Forrest summer raids led the Yankees to begin fortifying their outposts, rail bridges, some river crossings, and even the city of Nashville. The raider triumphs, encouraged by already sympathetic local populations in Tennessee and Kentucky, also held up bluecoat campaigns, particularly toward Chattanooga. They also emboldened irregulars to mound an increased number of attacks on easy or soft targets, most especially transportation. "Western commanders," the *New York Times* suggested, should understand "the impracticability of dislodging guerrillas from ... banks so long as a disloyal population remains in the country bordering on the river, and armed bands from the rebel army are able to reach that population and stimulate it with the hope of eventual rebel success."

Severe problems for the Western Flotilla (later the Mississippi Squadron) were also occasioned as a result of the dismal science of economics, specifically in a thriving contraband trade in goods and with cotton seizures. This was a problem that involved not only Southern regular and irregular forces, but corrupt Union military officers and merchants, traders, and speculators. From the earliest days of the conflict, the Federal policy toward commercial intercourse on the Western rivers was ambiguous. "By summer of 1862," E. Merton Coulter wrote in 1919,

> rules were in force that all trade on the Ohio River, below Wheeling, excepting Louisville, and on the Mississippi River below the mouth of the Des Moines, excepting St. Louis, should be allowed only by permit. The license or permit system was a failure from beginning to end.

Part of the difficulty arose from the Union government's constant alteration of nonintercourse policy. Everyone seemed to have a hand in writing it, either in its proclamation, or in composing rules and regulations offering interpretation: President Lincoln, the U.S. Congress, Secretary of the Treasury Salmon P. Chase and Treasury Department officials, and U.S. Army and Navy officers on the ground or afloat. The rules were often hard for the gunboatmen, whether regular Navy or volunteer, to interpret and apply. "It requires a nice distinction on the part of an officer," wrote Acting Rear Admiral David Dixon Porter, "to discriminate in these matters and not run against the regulations of the Treasury Department."

Under whatever rules were in place, the opportunities for dishonest trading were manifest, particularly as the Federal army occupied additional Southern territory. One official believed that elements within the Union army were not paying enough attention to

> the persistent efforts of persons in the loyal states, who sympathize with those engaged in the rebellion, and by peddlers and corrupt traffickers, many of whom have come

from disloyal states and sections for this purpose — to smuggle goods, medicines, and other supplies through to the insurgents.

Economic warfare resulting in armed confrontations began after "Grant's troops had reached the northern part of Alabama and were in the midst of the cotton area." Coulter continues the previous quote: "Immediately a mad scramble for cotton set in. Everything seemed to be prostituted toward that end."

Federal military commanders at Memphis attempted to regulate this trade by issuing specially-signed licenses to trading vessels, at a $100 fee, Boats were not allowed below Helena without being in possession of this special permit. If they sailed without one, they were subject to confiscation if caught. Armed with their permits and often escorted by Federal gunboats, private speculators led Union cotton expeditions out along the Mississippi almost daily after June 1862. Eliminating or capturing the South's most valuable commodity, its "white gold," became official Northern policy and organized confiscation missions were common.

Under protection, private confiscation steamers were allowed to put into shore and "collect" bales just inland of the rivers. Soldiers and sailors, mostly the former, usually participated in some way or another, though largely as pickets, sometimes as wagon drivers. In time, Federal sailors were able to claim "prize money" when they seized this pro-

Unauthorized trading in cotton and goods along the river banks proved difficult to prevent during the Civil War. Customs regulations, permits, and other arrangements to control contraband changed often and were often difficult to interpret. When the Union gunboatmen found private steamers engaged in landings, such as this depicted in an 1870 Currier and Ives print, at points unauthorized or suspect, they often seized the vessels and sent them off to prize courts for adjudication (Library of Congress).

duce. It was during one of these missions, on September 14, 1862, that soldiers from the 33rd Illinois would destroy the town of Prentiss, MS, in response to "guerrilla" attacks.

"Probably the most harmful variety of this fraudulent trade in cotton," A. Sellew Roberts has observed, "was that carried on by the trade-boats plying up and down the rivers." These were the vessels that caused the most difficulty for the Mississippi Squadron. Unlike the cotton expeditions accompanied by Federal warships, these craft plied their trade without supervision. "They would clear from some town," Roberts continues, "loaded with supplies and stay out for as long as 40 days, renewing their cargo from passing boats, entertaining Confederates, and trading with anybody and everybody."

Even though certain zones were to be off limits (for example, the area below Helena in late 1862), tinclads and other naval craft constantly encountered these private trading boats. Like today's U.S. Coast Guard, Federal commanders usually boarded the steamers. If anything was suspected of being improper (manifests, permits, cargoes), the craft were seized and sent to Cairo for determination of legitimacy.

Adding what he considered to be a little naval discipline to the resolution of the contraband problem, Acting Rear Adm. Porter, in December 1862, penned a general order that quite simply forbade commerce from being carried out at any point not occupied by U.S. troops. His gunboat captains were not to honor any permits from any authority, unless they came from Porter directly. This approach was overturned by Navy Secretary Welles in March 1863 by a Washington order requiring that any Navy-seized property be turned over to Treasury agents, some of whom accompanied cotton-gathering speculation missions. Porter revised his three-month-old directive.

The capture of Vicksburg and the complete reestablishment, by December 1863, of the old river trade between New Orleans and ports as distant as Louisville and Cincinnati made policing the rivers for the cotton and contraband rogues even more difficult. Constant complaints continued to come in concerning the abuse of trading licenses and "the provisioning of Confederate forces near the Mississippi River." All variety of steamers felt free to visit wherever they could, "up every bayou and creek" to "trade and traffick" as desired. Lafayette C. Baker, head of the Federal detective service, observed: "It seems incredible that in the midst of the most tragical scenes that war has ever created, the very arena of conflict should be the busy field of mercenary and lawless trade."

There was not a great deal that the U.S. Navy's Western gunboatmen could do to put an end to illegal trade in cotton and goods that it was not already doing. So, in October 1863, Porter, however inconsistent with his superior's March directive, issued yet another general order concerning these economic questions. He ordered that whatever enemy property came into the possession of his captains was seized as a prize of war and was, under naval prize law of the time, sent to Cairo for adjudication at a prize court. This principle, which applied to all manner of property, including cotton, was no different from that which had covered the capture of vessels on the high seas since before the time of the Revolution.

In May 1864, Maj. Gen. Cadwallader C. Washburn, new commander of the Federal District of West Tennessee, determined to end illegal trade on the Mississippi. All of the abuses and confusion of the previous three years would, he hoped, be ended by military intervention. Henceforth, steamboats were prohibited from landing at any location

Cairo, at the very tip of Illinois, was a major Federal ground and naval command center from the beginning of the Civil War. On numerous occasions, rumors were spread of imminent Confederate attack. In July 1862, Flag Captain Alexander Pennock, commanding a got-up task group of steamers and tugboats, steamed in its defense, while also providing assistance to Indiana soldiers seeking to redress a Rebel attack on Henderson, Kentucky. The nature of the vessels comprising Pennock's only waterborne offensive gave a further boost to the call for light-draught gunboats. In this photo, Cairo is seen from its Ohio Street and Ohio River side, ca. 1864 (Miller's *Photographic History of the Civil War*).

between the mouth of the White River and Cairo, except where garrisoned by U.S. soldiers. Any boat foolish enough to trade anyway would be seized if spotted by patrolling tinclads. Even this draconian act was insufficient to complete close off illegal trade.

The Confederate government, which benefited greatly from the wishy-washy trading policies of the Lincoln government, reacted to the post–July 1862 economic assault by specifically legalizing the burning of cotton to keep it from Union marauders, as well as direct attacks upon the interlopers. Federal navy commanders considered such income-lowering resistance to be guerrilla terrorism. Despite the weakness of the logic, they also linked it to partisan assaults on waterborne logistics.

Insurgent forces led by lesser-known heartland partisans also executed pinprick raids on river bank communities. Leading a group later known as the 10th Kentucky Partisan Cavalry, Adam R. Johnson defeated a group of Union soldiers at Madisonville, KY, and captured the Ohio River town of Henderson on July 17, 1862. Johnson, a surveyor by profession, operated from sanctuaries in Union County, KY, that allowed easy access to Federal posts and transportation on the Ohio, Cumberland, and Tennessee Rivers.

Employing a pair of ersatz cannon fashioned from stovepipes, Johnson next crossed the Ohio and scared many defenders away from Newburg, IN. Johnson, thereafter known as "Stovepipe" Johnson, did not dally, quickly ending his demonstration and returning to Kentucky. Meanwhile, two companies of Indiana volunteers, armed with a pair of real cannon, had departed for Newburg from Evansville aboard a steamer as soon as the first distress wire arrived.

Indiana Governor Oliver P. Morton, on July 19, wired Cairo naval base chief Cdr. Alexander M. Pennock: "Henderson, Ky., taken by rebels. Evansville and Newburg are threatened." Although Morton wanted a gunboat sent, Pennock, running activities on the upper rivers in the absence of Flag Officer Charles H. Davis, who was down the Mississippi, had none. Over the next two days, he scraped together a makeshift fleet, comprising the receiving ship *Clara Dolsen,* armed with four howitzers; the *Rob Roy,* aboard which were 125 base sailors and 200 men from the 63rd Regiment of Illinois Volunteers; and the tugboat *Restless,* also armed with a howitzer. Led by Pennock in person (his only fleet command of the war) on the *Dolsen,* aboard which "the greatest enthusiasm was manifested by all," the little armada steamed up to Evansville, arriving on July 21.

Next day, U.S. forces, taken across the stream by Pennock's boats, reoccupied Henderson. The day was far more peaceful here than it was hundreds of miles down the Mississippi.

Captured up the Tennessee by U.S. timberclads in February, the 256-ton *Sallie Wood*[5]

Col. Adam "Stovepipe" Johnson (1834–1922) was among the earliest and most famous of Confederate irregular cavalry leaders to actively pursue steamboat interdiction. Employing both muskets and cannon, his men would regularly prey upon transports plying the upper tributaries of the Mississippi (Johnson, *The Partisan Rangers of the Confederate States Army,* 1904).

was taken into the Western Flotilla to serve as a fleet auxiliary transport and ammunition boat. In that capacity, the stern-wheeler often made the long return run down past Memphis from Cairo. Returning upstream on July 21 with sick soldiers, the *Wood* steamed into the sharp turns of the Mississippi adjacent to Chicot County, AR, and Washington County, MS. Here the Mississippi swerved in a series of bends: Rowdy, Miller's, Spanish Moss, and Batchelor's. Several islands (80, 81, and 82) dotted the center of the great river here, narrowing the main channel.

The level country adjacent to this stretch of the Mississippi was, as a reporter from the *New York Herald* put it, "admirably adapted to the purpose to which the enemy occupies it." Indeed, their artillery could sweep the river not once but twice in the same assault. Confederate raiders could cross at this point or mount attacks on passing steamers. If Rebel artillery on one side of a bend failed to sink a craft during its initial bombardment, it could limber up and race across country to a second firing position before the target could steam the same distance by river. For Federals, the most worrisome population centers, from or near which several attacks would be made in the months ahead,

Fleet captain of the Western Flotilla and Mississippi Squadron, Alexander Pennock (1814–1876) handled the logistical and repair operations of those units, and stood in for the fleet commander in his absence. His improvised response to the Newburg, Indiana, raid of Adam "Stovepipe" Johnson in July 1862 led directly to the creation of both of an anti-guerrilla Mosquito Flotilla for the upper rivers and the first tinclad gunboats. It was Pennock who oversaw the operations of the former and arranged the latter (Library of Congress).

were Greenville and Argyle Landing on the Mississippi side, and Eunice and Gaines Landing opposite in Arkansas.

The *Sallie Wood* was taken under fire by masked batteries at Carolina Landing, at Princeton, and at several other points above. Escaping on, the *Sallie Wood* was attacked next morning by concealed cannon on the eastern bank at Argyle Landing, some three miles above Greenville, MS. Pushing out of danger for a third time, she was hit by a fourth group of Rebels who fired upon her from a location near Gaines Landing, not far from Island No. 82. During this ambush, a round entered her steam drum, leaving her dead in the water.

Pilot Lucas, a Memphis native, was able to employ the current to run the vessel aground on the foot of the island, but could not put her in to shore out of cannon range. Consequently, Rebel shot continued to smash into the *Sallie Wood*, forcing her 35 officers, crew and passengers to abandon ship. Most were captured, including the boat's chief engineer, George Gracy, his wife and their daughter, and sent to Jackson, MS, some 60 miles inland. The pilot was able to escape and get word to a passing Federal ironclad. Lt. L.H. Wing of the 4th Wisconsin wandered in the woods for four days before he was rescued.

Having removed all desired items, the attacking Southern soldiers burned the *Sallie Wood* to the waterline, leaving her wreckage to be seen from passing steamers. At low water over the next several weeks, ox teams were sent out to her and "everything valuable in her" was removed.

On July 23, reports arrived at Evansville indicating that "guerrilla" forces had taken over Uniontown and were poised to cross over the Ohio to Mount Vernon, IN. Pennock's craft and troops under Maj. Gen. John Love, Indiana Legion, next secured Uniontown. The little task group was near Shawneetown, KY, on July 23, patrolling against attack from the Kentucky side of the river, when a wire was received from Quartermaster George D. Wise.

Irregulars, the logistics man noted, were poised to attack Cairo from the Kentucky shore opposite. Splitting his force and dispatching the troop-laden *Rob Roy* back to Henderson, Pennock pushed back down to Cairo with the *Clara Dolsen* and *Restless*. By the time they arrived, the enemy had withdrawn. Maj. Gen. Love wrote to the commander expressing the "gratitude with which the citizens of this locality will regard the prompt cooperation of yourself and your officers in this emergency, which threatened their security."[6]

The need for a viable Union naval counterinsurgency capability was fully demonstrated by Capt. Pennock's Evansville expedition in late July. Not only were regular patrols required, but so too was aggressive mid-level leadership and new weapons systems. Indeed, the fleet captain, in his report of the Ohio River cruise, had two closing observations: (1) there was "but little Union feeling on the Kentucky shore"; and (2) "the interests of government and the safety of steamers navigating the Ohio require that light-draft gunboats should be kept moving up and down the river."

Pennock's actions and reports were lauded in writing to Navy Secretary Gideon Welles by Western Flotilla commander Davis on August 6. They were independently complemented by continuing newspaper reports of how "guerrilla warfare was becoming more serious and travel on the Ohio River was extremely hazardous," and "the bold manner in which guerrilla warfare is carried on at the present time on the Tennessee River."

Employing three light and refurbished captured steamers, Flag Officer Davis, while still off Vicksburg, made the decision to create a "squadron of small vessels to suppress the active guerrilla movements on the Ohio and Tennessee Rivers." He also pushed the development of a whole new class of light river gunboats with his superiors. In this, he was aided by colleagues from the army and the fleet who were already on the scene.

Looking at the situation from afar a few months later, the *New York Times* prophesied: "With the best intentions and the best service it is possible for men to give, it will be found impracticable to suppress the system of guerrilla warfare by attacking it from the water. The disease is in the body politic in the country through which the river runs. It must be purged from the interior before it ceases to break out upon the rivers." Whether or not this was point of view was accurate remained to be tested. Davis for his part was determined that, first and foremost, he would have light draughts and trained crews dedicated to stamping out the Confederate irregular "disease" along the banks of all accessible Western streams. It was understood that they might be engaged in a protracted struggle — but the effort had to be made. Little successes were better than none.[7]

Rear Adm. Charles H. Davis (1807–1877) commanded the Western Flotilla between May and October 1862. It was he who pushed the Navy Department to sanction the acquisition of light-draught ("tinclad") gunboats and established a special Mosquito Flotilla to employ the premier units on the upper tributaries of the Mississippi River (Library of Congress).

Upon his return to Cairo from below, Flag Officer Davis fell ill with the same fever which had touched so many of his officers and men near Vicksburg and Helena since July 4. For three weeks in early August, he slowly convalesced in a bed in Pennock's quarters. Upon his recovery and prior to his departure back down the Mississippi, the Western Flotilla commander made good upon his resolve to do something about combating Rebel irregulars on the upper rivers. The need for fast reaction along the rivers was now absolutely vital.

For example, the Union suffered two significant losses on the Cumberland between sunup and sundown on Monday, August 18. In a combined guerrilla-regular cavalry operation, Adam "Stovepipe" Johnson's 10th Kentucky Partisan Cavalry and Thomas G. Woodward's 2nd Kentucky Cavalry, together with two companies from Forrest's 1st Kentucky Cavalry, captured Clarksville, TN, and six defending companies from the 71st Ohio Volunteer Infantry. The Rebels would hold the seat of Montgomery County for 29 days. In taking the town, Woodward's men captured the steamer *Fisher* as she appeared from upriver. Bringing her to the bank, the riders tossed her cargo of corn and oats into the Cumberland, but then, surprisingly, held an auction, selling off the remainder of the stores to the town's Confederate sympathizers.

That evening, three additional steamers were targeted over on the Tennessee River, between Waggoner's and Walker's Landings in Benton County, TN. Survivors reported that upwards of 500 partisans under Capt. T. Alonzo Napier captured and burnt the *Skylark* and *Callie*; the third unnamed vessel escaped.

Near the foot of Island No. 8 in the Mississippi during the day, the steamer *Champion No 3*[8] (also called the *New Champion*), en route to Memphis from Cairo, was fired into by men hiding along the shore. She ignored an order to halt and kept on, taking a second volley. Her officers later reported, "About 40 bullets struck her. No one was hurt."

The same evening, perhaps just after dinner, Flag Officer Davis, probably with only limited if any information on the day's events, told his fleet captain of his plans to create an anti-guerrilla division of the gunboat flotilla. He informed Secretary Welles of his executive intention on August 19. That night, the Union lost its fifth steamer on Western waters in three days and nearly lost a sixth.

The 198-foot stern-wheeler *Swallow*, the squadron's floating armory and blacksmith shop, had gone aground on the bar near Carr Island, about 20 miles south of Memphis, over a week before. Having received no assistance for whatever reason, she was unable to get off. After dark, a party of guerrillas supposedly snuck aboard and set her afire. Only the clerk escaped capture, and that because, as he told the captain of the rescuing *City of Alton* before dawn, "he had jumped to save himself without waiting to ascertain how the fire originated."

Meanwhile, on the eastern side of the Mississippi River, irregulars struck again. About a mile and a half from Helena, a party fired several times into the six-year-old, 133-ton stern wheel ferry *Hamilton Belle*,[9] but she escaped with little damage.

Flag Officer Davis officially created the new special light draft squadron on August 21. Newspapermen would call it a "Mosquito flotilla." Later sailors and historians would sometimes nickname it the "mosquito squadron."

With energy and unflappable devotion to the Union, a relatively small group of regular U.S. naval officers, backed up by numerous volunteers, participated in the war-long anti-guerrilla, anti-partisan, and anti-raider operation now started on the Western waters. The majority of these nautical counterinsurgency operations were conducted from the decks of tinclad gunboats. When not actively engaged in such conflict, these vessels offered support to the U.S. Army, convoyed steamers, served as coast guard, and engaged both in and against an insidious trade war in cotton.

Allowing that the "gunboat service of the upper rivers has suddenly acquired a new importance," Davis placed the new command under Pennock's "special care." Lt. Cmdr. Le Roy Fitch was made squadron executive and gunnery officer, which, in effect, gave him on-scene operational control of the unit subject to direction from his seniors, Davis and Pennock. Fitch was to send his reports to Cmdr. Pennock, who would read them and react, giving any necessary orders, and then detail the highlights to Davis "from time to time."

Fitch was given the *General Pillow*, largest of the three available small warship conversions, as his flag boat. It became his duty to enforce naval discipline upon the men of the entire mosquito group and, employing a recognized expertise with small ordnance, to take "pains to render the officers and men efficient in the use of the howitzers and small arms." In his orders to the Hoosier officer, Davis put on paper his hope for the new unit and its commander: "I rely upon your zeal and ability, already well known to me, to conduct this service in such a manner as will result in the suppression of this barbarous warfare and the chastisement of those engaged in it." Fitch would undertake his first patrol in just two days.[10]

3

The Coming of the Tinclad

It was dogwood time in Tennessee and the second spring of the internecine American Civil War. Late April 1862 was a time of magnificent color and beauty on the Tennessee River, just as it is today. The devastating effects of a great flood a few weeks earlier could no longer be seen. As the earth began its annual cycle of renewal, a various-hued season greeted man and beast alike.

Out on the river, two large black steamers chugged and puffed slowly upstream, approaching Florence, AL, and the Muscle Shoals. Great clouds of sooty coal smoke escaped from their chimneys as their wood-covered side wheels thrashed the muddy water of the great tributary. With oak bulwarks, giant cannon and willing hands, the craft searched for activity along the shoreline, but only flowering trees, great flocks of birds, and the occasional homestead were revealed.

The United States steam gunboats *Lexington* and *Tyler*, together with the absent and smaller *Conestoga*, were the first vessels in the Union army's Western Flotilla and were always busy. Presently they were on patrol, guarding the river flank of the Federal army as it moved toward northern Mississippi. Peering from the decks, officers and men alike were struck by the sensual views that greeted them from the largely unpopulated river banks.

Lt. Cmdr. William Gwin, skipper of the *Tyler*, and his colleague, Lt. Cmdr. James W. Shirk of the *Lexington*, heroes of the recent Shiloh battle and veterans of the February dash to Florence led by Lt. Cmdr. S. Ledyard Phelps of the *Conestoga*, marveled at the flora and fauna before them. Redbud and dogwoods and many varieties of hardwood trees, flowers of every description, ferns, berry bushes, and brambles of many types demonstrated glorious new hues. Beaver, heron, and turtles were seen in the water and ashore, countless species of birds, including turkeys, hawks, bald eagles, robins, and woodpeckers, spoke from the growth or sky, and deer, wolves, and bear may have been seen as well. In the evening, bats, owls, fox and other nocturnal denizens were plentiful.[1]

As the Federal sailors appreciated the scenery around them, they also kept a lookout for Rebel steamers. It was widely believed that the last Rebel-owned boats on this river were run to ground during the first quarter, but rumors persisted that one or two might have been hidden. Which ones might be tied to the bank under protective foliage and their appearance was a matter of keen speculation.

In the weeks after the Battle of Shiloh, the two naval steamers were the major instru-

The *Lexington* and *Tyler* at Shiloh, April 1862. Although the timberclad gunboats, the first units in the Western Flotilla, performed well, there were too few of them to accomplish all the missions required: Army support, counterinsurgency, convoy protection, patrol, communications, and coast guard. Acquisition and conversion of the *Alfred Robb* and several prizes from the Battle of Memphis led to a light-draught ("tinclad") gunboat acquisition program (Library of Congress).

ment of Union nautical force projection on the Tennessee River. Even as the stream continued a fall begun in mid-month, their vigilant patrols, running between the mouth of the stream and the head of navigation, continued. The side-wheeled *Lexington* and *Tyler* not only provided convoy of Federal steamers, but actively sought to disrupt Confederate ferry operations and irregular attacks. They were also prepared to intercept any Southern steamers foolish enough to show themselves. On April 21, the *Tyler* discovered a scuttled fugitive and then made one of the most important captures of her career.

While inspecting river banks and adjoining creeks near Florence, AL, Lt. Gwin came across the sunken hull of Gus Fowler's steamer, the *Dunbar*.[2] Not destroyed as was believed back in February, the transport of the notorious Southern captain lay largely undamaged on the bottom of Cypress Creek, some two miles below Florence. Although water covered the *Dunbar* up above her wheel guards, it would have been possible to raise her. The engines could have been restored and, as was occasionally the fashion with other sunken steamers, she could then have been returned to service. Gwin's crew could not raise her with the resources available. So a boarding party went aboard and put her exposed works to the torch.

A second Rebel transport, also believed lost two months earlier, was taken at the mouth of Crane Creek later in the day. The 86-ton *Alfred Robb*,[3] a stern-wheeler, was

While in command of the timberclad *Tyler*, Lt. Cmdr. William Gwin (1832–1863), one of the rising stars of the Western Flotilla, captured the steamer *Alfred Robb* up the Tennessee River on April 21, 1862. He would soon thereafter dispatch her to Fleet Captain Pennock at Cairo for conversion into the first tinclad. Fresh from the Battle of Shiloh, Gwin would go on to fight the Confederate ram *Arkansas* in July before dying in action aboard the giant ironclad *Benton* in December (Naval Historical Center).

captured in good running order. Next day, the *Robb* arrived at Pittsburg Landing. In reporting her seizure, *Philadelphia Inquirer* newsman Henry Bentley, who saw her there, also remembered to add a note that the "weather is rather more pleasant."

At the urging of Maj. Gen. Halleck, who was deeply impressed by the sterling roles played by the *Tyler* and *Lexington* in the April 6 Battle of Shiloh, the two timberclads remained on the Tennessee River into May, continuing to provide Army assistance. As he continued his deliberate, weeks-long approach to Corinth, Halleck was informed by Lt. Cmdr. Gwin on May 17 that his warships would have to depart the Tennessee due to its rapidly falling water. "Old Brains" was not pleased by this development. In fact, Halleck asked the gunboatman to remain as long as it was deemed safe. Still, he recognized that a boat with a draft much lighter than the 420-ton side-wheeler *Tyler* or her compatriot, the 362-ton *Lexington*, was required. Each of them, after all, sat six foot deep in the water.

Writing to Lt. Cmdr. Gwin from his camp on the Corinth Road the same day, the top Federal general in the west stated his view simply: "I think the *Robb* should be fitted up to render us all the assistance possible on the [Tennessee] River." Halleck's message to Gwin was forwarded to Capt. Charles H. Davis three days later.[4]

During the next week, that portion of Davis's fleet engaged on the Mississippi invested Fort Pillow and fought an engagement with the Confederate River Defense Force at Plum Point Bend. During the remainder of the month, the Union's Western Flotilla, despite some Confederate resistance, smashed Rebel defenses on the big river above Memphis.

Maj. Gen. Henry W. Halleck (1815–1872) was the U.S. Army Western theater commander until July 1862. Deeply appreciative of the support provided by the U.S. Navy timberclads on the Tennessee River prior to and after the Battle of Shiloh, he was deeply disappointed when informed that low water would cause their withdrawal in late May due to low water. When apprised of the capture of the *Alfred Robb*, a vessel of significantly lighter draft, Halleck asked that she be "fitted up to render us all the assistance possible." This message was employed by Flag Officer Davis to support his efforts to obtain permission from the Navy Department to construct light-draught ("tinclad") gunboats (*Battles and Leaders*).

While operational activities occupied Davis downstream, Cmdr. Alexander M. Pennock, in his capacity of fleet captain and Cairo, Illinois, naval base commander, daily attended to the mired of administrative matters behind the lines. Simultaneously, he attempted to keep an eye on Southern activities in the areas bordering the Ohio, Tennessee, and Cumberland Rivers.

On May 20, Lt. Cmdr. Gwin wrote to Capt. Davis, via Cmdr. Pennock, advising that the timberclads would momentarily have to depart the Tennessee River. In forwarding the communication to Davis next day, the Cairo station chief asked that they might be permitted to remain at the tip of Illinois in order to protect public property at the town and serve as a mobile strike force that could "go up the Ohio, Mississippi, and Tennessee rivers whenever it may be required."

Among Pennock's responsibilities was supervision of the construction, repair, and outfitting of new or captured warships as well as the coaling and supply of these and others. Thus it was that the *Alfred Robb* came into his care when she arrived at the Cairo river base from up the Tennessee. In the same May 21 letter to Davis in which he asked to retain the *Tyler* and *Lexington*, the fleet captain advised "in accordance with the suggestion of General Halleck in his letter of May 17, I shall prepare the *Robb* so as to protect her pilot house, etc., against rifle shots from the shore."

On the night of June 2, Pennock again communicated with his distant chief in one of a series of detail-laden reports he would compose on what was often called "general matters." In addition to a variety of miscellaneous flotilla detail, the fleet captain explained that the renovation of the *Robb* was well underway. "She will carry four howitzers," Pennock wrote, "and be well supplied with small arms, etc." For protection, the Cairo man revealed that he had ordered a "bullet-proof bulkhead around her forecastle and also iron-plated the pilot house." Lt. Cmdr. Gwin, who had originally captured her, thought that the new little light-draught gunboat would be "equal to any emergency that may occur." A total of 30 officers and men under the command of First Master Goudy were detailed to the boat.

That Tuesday evening, acting under Pennock's orders, the *Alfred Robb* departed Cairo for Pittsburg Landing on the Tennessee River. Master Goudy would be expected to employ his rebuilt craft, in actuality the first "tinclad," to protect Union interests in a stream considerably more shallow than when the timberclads left it days earlier.[5] "Tinclad" was a misnomer born of the popular press and the need in some quarters to differentiate these small, shallow-bottomed, swift, and lightly armed Western river boats from the larger, ponderous ironclads and monitors. Tinclads, of which the *Alfred Robb* was the first, were not clad in tin.

Although most of the riverboats extemporized into this heterogeneous group had some light protection, mostly metal, several, like Master Goudy's command, had wooden bulkheads and only some iron for protection. "Some people do not understand what the Yankees mean by calling some of their Mississippi gunboats 'tin clad,'" wrote the editor of the *Macon Weekly Telegraph* in late 1864. The craft were so named, he told his readers, "because they are sheathed with iron only to resist rifle shot and light artillery," iron with a thickness "about equal to that of a steamboat boiler."

For compactness of location, let us here complete our review of the weapons system that dominates the remainder of this book.

The light-draught inland river U.S. Navy gunboats nicknamed "tinclads" were all converted from former merchant boats, some brand new. No two of the vessels were exactly alike and photographs do not exist for most of them. Of the 72 total, 49 were stern-wheelers chosen, like the *Alfred Robb*, for their capabilities in shallow streams; the other 23 were highly maneuverable side-wheelers. Some had their original names shortened or changed altogether while in naval service. As a whole, the group averaged 150–175 feet in length and carried between six and eight cannon, mostly brass Dahlgren howitzers.[6]

The success of the *Alfred Robb*'s makeover, coupled with the failure of a joint Army-Navy relief expedition up the White River in June, drove home in Union naval circles the necessity for light-draught gunboats. The White River effort, designed to bring support to Federal troops attempting to exit Missouri, was defeated as much by low water in the upper reaches of the stream as by determined Confederate resistance. The poor river stages occurred throughout the Western theater and made it easier for irregulars to attack river traffic.

Finding that the water level made it impossible for him to complete much of the mission of his command, Flag Officer Davis put into writing the Western Flotilla's need for light-draught gunboats. In a missive famous in the annals of tinclad history and directed to Navy Secretary Gideon Welles, the Union river commander wrote:

> Our recent experience in the navigation of the White River has made it apparent that in order to acquire control of the tributaries of the Mississippi, and to maintain that control during the dry season, it will be necessary to fit up immediately some boats of small draft for this special purpose. These boats will be sufficiently protected about the machinery and pilot houses against musketry. They will be selected for their light draft and their capacity to receive a suitable armament of howitzers, field pieces, or other light guns, and to accommodate the requisite number of men; and, finally, for their susceptibility of protection.

Davis ventured a guess, in his opinion to the cabinet officer, that boats could be had for between $8,000 and $10,000 apiece, provided, of course, that their purchase was entrusted to an officer or someone who knew how to obtain the most for the department's money. A copy of the letter was also sent to Quartermaster General Montgomery C. Meigs in hopes that it would be taken seriously and considered by War Secretary Edwin Stanton, who still controlled the purse strings of the Western gunboat squadron. For comparison purposes, it might be noted that the least expensive Union river ironclad was the *Chillicothe*: $92,960.

A week later, from the Vicksburg vicinity, the flag officer again wrote to Secretary Welles, providing a brief overview of the recent White River expedition, which closed with the strong suggestion that:

> If it is the intention of the Government to make use of the rivers as a means of communication, I will venture again to suggest that it can only be done by means of suitable vessels of small draft lightly, but sufficiently protected against rifle muskets.

While the Western Flotilla awaited word from Washington on permission to begin creation of a light-draught fleet, Davis and Pennock pushed ahead with the renovation of the former Confederate vessels *Little Rebel* and *General Pillow*, both of which reached Cairo in July. When the Mississippi Squadron uniquely ordered numbers painted on the pilothouses of its tinclads in June 1863, the former would become Tinclad 16 and the latter Tinclad 20. The other Memphis-captured Rebel gunboats, *General Bragg* and *General Sterling Price*, were also turned into gunboats, but they were not classified as tinclads.[7]

Following the initial depression in trade caused by Fort Sumter and Rebel activities in 1861, the traffic in Union civilian steamboat services on the upper Mississippi and its tributaries gradually resumed, beginning in the spring of 1862. Not only was it relatively safe, save for Confederate guerrillas and the occasional snag, for boats to visit Nashville or Memphis, but hundreds were chartered by the U.S. government to support its western armies. Into the logistical pipeline served by both river and rail, but served best bulk-wise by the former, were pumped all manner of necessities from troops and their animals to arms and munitions, food, medicines, equipment, and forage, to wounded Yankee soldiers, Confederate POWs, men on leave, captured goods and equipment, refugees, and various kinds of seized contraband, the most contentious cargo of all.

The number of steamer bottoms required to handle the massive increase in river business in 1862–1863 was significantly more than was available. New riverboats were built by private investors and even the government. One newspaper reported about the time that Flag Officer Davis was seeking support for the acquisition of light draughts:

> The mania at present is for investment in floating property. Everybody wants an interest in a steamboat. We learn of many happy possessors of cash in sums of from one hundred dollars up, who eagerly desire to be steamboat owners. Youth and men who hardly ever saw a steamboat are tremblingly eager to invest.

Riverfront shipyards, primarily along the Ohio River, but on other streams as well, which had been idle in late 1861, were a year later working at full capacity. Mound City, Pittsburgh, Cincinnati, Wheeling, Evansville, and so on all had men in construction or the equally necessary three Rs: repair, renovation, and refitting. Louis Hunter, quoting the *Cincinnati Gazette* of June 13, 1863, notes that in the spring of 1863, a total of 105 steamboats were abuilding on the Ohio between just Pittsburgh and Wheeling.

These boats, including several which would be turned into tinclads, became a hot

Known as the "Queen City," Cincinnati, Ohio, on the Ohio River was a major center of both steamboat building and commerce. Numerous shipyards were located here and nearby, where all manner of warcraft were built or outfitted. Beginning in November 1862, most of the steamers converted into light-draught ("tinclad") gunboats were modified here at the facilities of Joseph Brown. Once converted, they were dispatched to Cairo or Mound City to take aboard their crews, furniture, and ordnance (*Harper's Weekly*, Sept. 27, 1862).

Commodore Joseph B. Hull (?–1890) went to sea as a midshipman in 1813. He assumed his duties as Superintendent of Gunboat Construction at St. Louis in July 1862 and, together with Naval Constructor Edward Hartt, for the USN construction program on Western waters. It was Hull who found and oversaw the purchase and conversion of the first two purpose-modified tinclads, the *St. Clair* and the *Brilliant*. Once they were finished, they were sent to Cairo to receive their crews and ordnance (Library of Congress).

and expensive commodity. Those with stock in new construction made fortunes while those with new craft to sell also did extremely well. "So great was the demand for any kind of bottoms that steamboats six or eight years old, or older, which normally would have been destined only for the breaking-up yard brought prices close to or even equally their original cost." Those private companies or persons who owned the boats could liquidate their entire costs in several months of government service or in six or eight safely made trips down and upriver.[8]

The gentleman who was initially tasked with answering Flag Officer Davis's plea of June 28 for "an officer of judgment and experience" to purchase and equip the light-draught fleet was Capt., soon Com., Joseph B. Hull, who had been in the U.S. Navy since 1813. Hull was named by Secretary Welles as Superintendent of Gunboat Construction at St. Louis in May, but did not take up his post until summer. The aged sailor, who had spent most of his 47 nautical years on sea duty, would be assisted by Naval Constructor Edward Hartt, who was sent out from the New York Navy Yard. Hartt would actually superintend the work "in all matters pertaining to the hull, cladding, equipment, and accommodations," making certain that all work was done and inspected in conformity with the let contracts, and certifying bills for payment.

That we may dock all of the tinclad creation story within this chapter, we must move ahead in time, delaying launch of the strict operational chronology that might at this point be expected.

Upon his return from his June–July visit to Vicksburg, Flag Officer Davis received a telegram from Com. Hull on August 12 indicating that a pair of good new shallow-draft boats had been found not far from his St. Louis office. If Davis could use them, the gunboat superintendent was inclined toward their purchase. They drew 18 and 20 inches respectively and could be quickly fitted up for service. Davis wanted both vessels and quickly got this word orally to Hull.

The *St. Clair* was purchased next day from R.D. Cochran, Robert Finney, C.A. Dravo, Jane and Mary A. Nimick of Allegheny County (Pittsburgh), PA, for $19,750; her total costs of repairs would come to $7,554.53. Slightly more expensive, the *Brilliant* was simultaneously acquired from Albert G. Mason, Joshua Michem, and William Cock of Brownsville, PA, for $20,000. Conversion of both began at Carondelet, MO.

On August 15, the flag officer sent Hull a formal response to his telegram via Quartermaster George Wise. Wise had agreed to drop it off and to discuss with Hull the Davis recommendations, which Wise supported, for modifications to the two steamers. The flag officer was convinced that if he, Hull and Wise could fully agree on the desired boat configurations and Hull was fiscally authorized, under Davis's sanction, that of Wise, or whomever, the resultant anti-partisan warcraft would "render valuable aid to the public service." From his Cairo office, the navy chief opined that neither boat should cost more than $10,000 each as they stood, "without the removal of anything belonging to them whatsoever."

In the same communication, Davis went on to indicate that Fleet Captain Pennock, having already outfitted the *Alfred Robb* and *Little Rebel*, had plans "for strengthening and protecting these vessels in a manner suited to the service" anticipated for them. We do not have copies of these and so such plans were probably mostly mental. At best, there may also have been some unofficial notes and sketches. No major changes in vessel configuration were anticipated; the overriding requirement for any of them was that they have a shallow draft.

Also during the day, Davis had a long and productive meeting in his Cairo office with Naval Constructor Hartt. The two talked exclusively on the topic of light-draught design and renovation per the Pennock model, which included provision that the boat cabins be left on and light protections built. Davis was completely convinced that Hartt left possessed of "all of the information I can give him on the subject." The flag officer reiterated his urgent want for the vessels, needed to aid in the "suppression of the guerrilla warfare now raging on the Upper Ohio and Tennessee."

What became the third tinclad was captured on August 18. A joint Army-Navy expedition under Lt. Cmdr. Phelps captured the Confederate transport *Fairplay* at Milliken's Bend, Louisiana, before she could offload a large cargo of rifles, cannon, and ammunition. A prize crew then took her to Cairo.

Next day, August 19, the flag officer was shocked to receive a message from Capt. Wise indicating that, while Hull intended to purchase the steamers noted a week earlier, he was also planning major changes to them. These included putting the officers' apartments below and protecting the boilers and machinery with double six-foot-high bulkheads filled with coal and lightly plated. Davis wrote Hull bluntly:

> My plans were founded upon a knowledge of the manner in which guerrilla warfare is conducted on the banks of the rivers. I trust that in the preparation of these vessels for the service for which at the moment they are so urgently required, no speculative notions are to supplant views founded upon actual experience of war and that these vessels be fitted in the manner I have requested.

Refurbishment of the two vessels at Carondelet now proceeded in the manner the flag officer had requested.

Upon her arrival at Cairo from Helena on August 31, the *Fairplay* was converted within days into a tinclad along these same lines. The earliest light-draught for which a photo exists, the side-wheeler was constructed in 1859 at New Albany, IN, to participate in the cotton trade. She was 138.8 feet long, with a beam of 27 feet and a draft of 4.9 feet. Her two engines and two boilers permitted a top speed of 5 mph upstream. A pair of 12-pounder smoothbore howitzers were placed aboard, along with two rifled 12-pounder howitzers.[9]

On Saturday, September 6, Com. Hull at St. Louis learned that Washington was sending authorization for the purchase of five additional "small boats," and wrote a note to Constructor Hartt asking that he be prepared to "find such as are wanted at Cincinnati or Louisville." Simultaneously, Fleet Captain Pennock at Cairo grew concerned with the delay being experienced with delivery of the two August 12 light-draughts being remodeled at Carondelet. He wired Hull pointing out how important was their need and also asked when he should "send officers and men for them." As was often the case with Civil War electronic mail, the telegram was delayed and Hull did not receive it until sometime on Monday.

By the afternoon of the 9th, Pennock, not knowing his earlier message was delayed, decided to push the commodore with another telegram. After all, irregulars were nearly "at all points on the Ohio and Tennessee" and "the need of armed boats is extremely urgent." Davis's deputy knew of two light-draught steamers at Cairo that were suitable for conversion and told the St. Louis construction boss that if the boats were purchased, the naval workforce at the tip of Illinois could have them protected and manned within five days.

Also during the day, naval officers in the West officially learned in a message from Secretary Welles that the Western Flotilla in which they had served during the past year would be transferred from Army control to the Navy on October 1. At the same time, a new commander, Acting Rear Admiral David Dixon Porter, would take over. During the next three weeks, all preparations were to be completed for a successful handover.

Com. Hull received Pennock's Tuesday wire just before suppertime. It was still daylight when, after his meal, he wrote out a reply to send aboard the Cairo mail boat next day. Completion of the two Carondelet craft was delayed, he reported, by non-receipt of the sheet metal needed for their sides. They would be available within a week of its delivery.

Hull also informed Pennock that his St. Louis office had received authority to acquire five more light-draughts to be "fitted as Commodore Davis desires for the river service." To make certain that there was no repetition of the August misunderstandings, Hull asked Pennock to tell him "as definitely as you can what kind and size [of boat] you desire and also the manner in which you wish them to be fitted for the service they are intended for." Constructor Hartt had already been briefed and could leave on a selection trip up the Ohio as soon as Pennock's response was in hand.

The fleet captain received Hull's missive late on Thursday and spent the evening specifying in detail Davis's wishes regarding the next five light-draughts. Pennock knew his boss's desires on this matter intimately and expressed those desires to Hull as though the flotilla leader was a co-author in the room and not hundreds of miles away at Helena.

The document sent to St. Louis on September 12 gives us the most complete published contemporary description of the manner in which these "tinclads" were to be worked up. It is worth reviewing the salient parts of that report here with comments on actual practice.

First, it was imperative that the boats be of the lightest draft possible. They were to be armed with a pair of 24-pounder and a pair of 12-pounder or four 12-pounder brass howitzers, an armament which would later be augmented. Each howitzer was manned by eight men plus a powder boy or "monkey." Later, heavier cannon were placed at the bow, where they proved superior to the short-range howitzers; indeed, one veteran of the U.S.S. *Hastings*, No. 15, remembered them as "the only effective guns." Those employed were usually either 32-pounder smoothbores, 9-inch Dahlgrens, or 30-pounder rifled Parrotts.

It was important that the engines and boilers be protected against light fieldpieces and the space between them against Minie rifle balls. The protection was to be carried up from the main deck, which was to be used as the gun deck and which was therefore strengthened to accommodate the extra weight of cannon. The shielding was to be sufficiently high as to prevent Rebel troops from firing between it and the hurricane deck from their roosts on high banks.

In general, this defensive requirement meant that an enclosed thick wooden case-mate made of planking, vertical on the sides and usually sloping at the bow and perhaps the stern, was constructed. Sheets of boiler plate were then attached to the forward part of the casemate and on each side adjacent to the engines. It would not be uncommon, as time wore on, for cotton bales and large rope hawsers to bolster weak points. The case-mate front and sides were pierced for gun ports.

The thickness of the metal protection on the enclosed casemate gave the ship type its nickname of "tinclad." Everyone seemed to appreciate almost from the start that these craft were not ironclads; they could not battle shore batteries, heavy field artillery, or other warships or rams. If they did get into a serious fight, casualties aboard might be high.

"The fact is," Ensign Symmes Browne of the *Signal*, No. 8, later wrote home, "none of these light draft gunboats are fit for anything except to drive off guerrillas where they have no artillery." A veteran of the *Naiad*, No. 53, remembered: "This kind of a gun-boat was ingeniously contrived so that, while a solid shot would go clear through it, tak-ing only what came in its way, a shell would be carefully and safely nursed on the covered deck until it fully exploded." Browne shared this lack of confidence. "I will guarantee to whip the whole tinclad fleet"—his fleet, he confided—"with one good battery of rifled field pieces placed behind the levee on the bank of the Misspi [*sic*]."

"If, to preserve light draft, it became necessary to take off a portion of the hurricane deck cabin," Pennock cautioned, Davis desired that at least four rooms on a side be retained, in addition to the small apartment usually found at a commercial boat's stern, for use by the captain and officers. If the required draft could be had by placing the quar-ters amidships, then Hull was to have that done while also fitting up a pair of small rooms on each side of the gun deck. In general, protection for these quarters was minimal, usu-ally about ½ inch of wood. A guard or gallery surrounded the officers' quarters, upon which doors opened from the staterooms. The "quarterdeck" was located forward of the officers' quarters and here the "officer of the watch" was stationed.

In general practice, the "Texas," if present, was removed along with the civilian pilot-house; a new and heavily protected (iron plate backed by thick wood) pilothouse was located atop the second deck. Beginning on June 19, 1863, numbers were painted on the tinclad pilot houses, each the approximate height of a man.

In any event, whether retrofitting stern-wheelers or side-wheelers, Hull was to be certain that all officers' quarters were located on the upper decks of the boats and that their main boiler decks be kept "clear of everything except the battery." To help accom-modate the changing out of cannon, swinging doors were to be located at each end of the casemated gun deck so that "artillery can be taken on board at one end and off at the other." In fact, the boiler/gun decks also housed the crew (who slept in hammocks slung from hooks in the overhead deck timbers), their galley, and coal used to fuel the boilers. The ammunition magazine and storerooms, or lockers, were in the hold, nearly below the waterline. All decks and internal portions of the vessels were reinforced wherever pos-sible with extra timbers and beams.

"In action," wrote former Acting Assistant Paymaster E.J. Huling in 1881, "all the officers and crew were stationed below, excepting the pilots and the commander, with a single aide, who were in the pilot house." From the pilothouse, the tinclad's captain could see what was transpiring and relay orders through a speaking pipe to the executive officer on the gun deck, who, in turn, relayed the commands to the men.

We would be remiss if we did not digress for a few sentences to acknowledge the role of tinclad pilots. As had been the case since before the time Mark Twain learned the piloting craft from the famous "Mr. [Horace] Bixby," the riverboat pilot was, in the words of Flag Officer Davis, "an essential, intrinsic, and indispensable part of the ship's complement." The navy chief, who thought so highly of these men as to recommend to his superiors that those serving the Western Flotilla all be made officers, went on to point out that "no one ever takes the wheel on board of a Western steamboat for a moment except the pilot, such is our dependence upon them ... they always remain attached to a vessel, and the latter never moves without them at any time." James Edwin Campbell, later governor of Ohio, recalled the lot of the tinclad pilots from his time on the *Naiad*:

> The only men who knew their business were the pilots to whose indispensable service, cheerfully rendered, justice has never been done. The pilot house was known as the "slaughter-pen" and on the tinclads — upon which it was my unhappy lot to serve — it was preeminently the post of danger. It was a matter of history that they freely volunteered for this perilous service knowing that they would be targets for every sharpshooter on the bank, and it was not unusual for a single shell to wound or kill both pilots and to blow the steering wheel in their hands into a thousand fragments; yet they were poorly paid and never had either rank or rating as officers of the navy, nor a recognized share in the memory of its glories.

Armed with Pennock's instructions, Naval Constructor Hartt selected the first of the five steamers on September 17. The *Marmora* was located at St. Louis and acquired from C. Brennan, William Nelson, and James McDonnell for $21,000. Another stern-wheeler, the *Signal*, was purchased in the same port five days later from Thomas C. & Andrew J. Sweeney for $18,000. Like the *St. Clair* and *Brilliant*, both were sent to the Carondelet boatyards of James B. Eads for modification.[10]

Work on reconfiguring the stern-wheelers into tinclads continued to lag as the third week of September closed. Exasperated, Fleet Captain Pennock wrote to Flag Officer Davis on the matter on September 18. Next day, Com. Hull, for his part, reported to Navy Secretary Welles that neither he nor Eads were at fault. Rather, the work was retarded by the delivery failures of the iron mills and by a local requirement that boatyard employees enroll in the militia. Far away at Helena, a disgusted Davis, who did not have Hull's full explanation, confided in a note to Pennock on September 21 that he had "given up in despair any further efforts in regard to the small steamers."

Even as the flag officer's message floated upstream by dispatch boat to Memphis and on to Cairo, Com. Hull, working independently of Cmdr. Pennock, was pleased to find contractor Eads making great progress after all. On the morning of September 23, the aged naval officer wired the fleet captain announcing that the two boats would be ready six days hence. Anyone viewing them could, as Bruce Liddell did years later, compare each of them to "a two-story flat-roof boarding house...."

Flag Captain Pennock responded immediately, detailing Master Jacob S. Hurd and Master Charles G. Perkins and their officers to take the noon mail steamer to St. Louis.

Their crews and a week's provisions would follow. All had bunks at Barnum's Hotel by 5 P.M., at which time Hurd wired Hull at Carondelet announcing their availability and asking if the craft were ready to sail. "We are ready to leave," he noted, as soon as the men came up from Cairo.

Hurd, Perkins, and the officers met their men at Carondelet next morning. There, in an ancient ceremony, the *St. Clair* became the first purchased tinclad to be formally placed into commission. With preparations completed, both Hurd and Perkins received steaming orders for Cairo from Com. Hull early on September 25.

With Constructor Hartt watching intently from the wharf that Thursday afternoon, the *Brilliant*, under Master Perkins "departed the waters of Carondelet," at precisely 12:40 P.M. Master Hurd's *St. Clair* left simultaneously. Within a few days of their arrival off the tip of Illinois, both steamers would receive their guns and operational outfits, making this a good time for a closer look at both.

Slightly heavier than her consort, Master Perkins's 227-ton *Brilliant* had been constructed at Brownsville, PA, earlier in the year. She measured 154.8 feet in length, with a beam of 33.6 feet. When departing Carondelet but before her cannon were shipped, her draft was 1.10 feet forward and 2.4 feet aft, though official records would show her with an overall five-foot draft. Employing two engines and three boilers, *Brilliant* could make 6 mph steaming against the current. Her initial armament consisted of two 12-pounder rifles and two 12-pounder smoothbores.

The 203-ton *St. Clair*, also an 1862 model, was built at Belle Vernon, PA, and measured 156 feet long by 32 feet wide; her draft both forward and aft was 2.4 feet. Master Hurd's command was powered to an unknown speed by two boilers and probably two engines. Her 66-man complement worked two 12-pounder rifles and two 12-pounder smoothbores. Both boats were sold out in 1865 and enjoyed short postwar careers, the former as the merchant *John S. McCune* and the latter as *St. Clair*.

The *Brilliant* was commissioned at Cairo on October 1. Together, the two stern-wheelers reported to the new Mosquito Flotilla at Evansville on October 14. From this point, we will discuss individual vessel features as we note their operational debut.[11]

The Western Flotilla of the U.S. Army was officially transferred to the U.S. Navy the day the *Brilliant* was commissioned and was renamed the Mississippi Squadron. Planning for the shift had been underway for weeks. Jumped several grades, Cmdr. David Dixon Porter was appointed acting rear admiral and ordered to relieve now Acting Rear Admiral Davis. The changeover in top squadron leadership did not actually occur on October 1, as Porter was still in transit from Washington, D.C., conducting inspections requested by Secretary Welles at Pittsburgh, Cincinnati, Mound City, and St. Louis while en route. Davis, meanwhile, availed himself of his remaining tenure to clean up as much squadron business at Cairo as was possible.

After reviewing matters in Pennsylvania, the freshman fleet commander stopped off at Cincinnati to check progress on the new ironclads *Chillicothe*, *Indianola*, and *Tuscumbia*. Under construction at the river-front yards of Joseph Brown, the three were found to have serious defects in need of correction.

By telegram, Porter attempted to get his recommendations past Com. Hull, who would have none of it without express authorization from Secretary Welles. "I was quite wild" over this rebuff, the new naval chief informed Assistant Secretary Gustavus Vasa Fox on October 12, but he was able to work out arrangements for the changes with the Navy's on-site inspector Lt. George Brown and the amenable contractor.

Continuing down the Ohio to Mound City and then on up to St. Louis, Porter arrived at Carondelet on October 13 to meet with James B. Eads, Edward Hartt, and Com. Hull to review the ironclads and tinclads under construction or modification at the former's complex. Eads, rightfully famous as prime contractor for ironclads built or building at both Carondelet and Mound City, had two river monitors and two giant ironclads on his ways, to say nothing of smaller craft being outfitted at the wharf.

Taken past cheering workmen to the banks of the "Big Muddy," the Mississippi Squadron commander-designate found himself as delighted with the Davis-Halleck-Pennock tinclad concept as he had been disappointed in the fitness of Joseph Brown's hulking iron monsters. A tour had been laid on by Eads, Hartt, Hull and others to demonstrate not only the building of the ironclads, but the modifications to the *Signal*. Showing off the smallest warship present, its former owners, Thomas C. and Andrew J. Sweeney, told the admiral that the new gunboat, when finished, "would float on a heavy dew."

Porter came away from this inspection impressed and with the belief that "tinclads" were "admirably adapted for ascending shallow rivers." That night he wrote to Secretary Welles asking that the number available be boosted by ten, all to be armed with 24-pounder howitzers. While publicly endorsing the light-draught idea, he remained cautious regarding their berth in the St. Louis yards. Wanting as many of these little vessels in service as quickly as possible, he made a mental note to order the next several from Joseph Brown at Cincinnati.

Beginning in April, Brown, using his own plans, had demonstrated some skill in his construction of the ironclads *Tuscumbia* and *Indianola*, though they would later be judged inferior. His Queen City facility could, it was believed, easily handle the rapid modification of light-draughts. Additionally, the work could be overseen by Porter's own newly-appointed supervisors rather than Com. Hull and Constructor Hartt, whose primary emphasis remained the large—and delayed—St. Louis ironclads *Choctaw* and *Lafayette*.

On October 14, the first two purpose-modified tinclads, the *Brilliant* and *St. Clair*, reported to Lt. Cmdr. Le Roy Fitch at Evansville. There the men would be reviewed, the boats and crews worked up to battle proficiency, and various flotilla strategies discussed.

After finishing the day further west at Carondelet, the enthusiastic David Porter arrived at Cairo on October 15 and, in full admiral's regalia, assumed his new command. His predecessor retired east to a new assignment and the "stalled" Mississippi Squadron could now to be recharged for action.[12] When he took over the Mississippi Squadron, Acting Rear Adm. Porter found himself with a mountain of administrative and operational concerns and ploughed straight into these with zeal.

Recruitment was a long-standing critical issue. Manning the inland river navy had been a problem ever since June 1861, when Cmdr. John Rodgers commissioned the timberclads. Although recruiting rendezvous (stations) were opened throughout the Midwest, volunteers were limited. Drafts of men from either the eastern fleets or the Army were equally hard to obtain. By the fall of 1862, over 400 of the available sailors were ill, many with diseases contracted near Vicksburg during the summer.

The men present for duty throughout the Western navy were a mix of old-timers and new recruits. As more and more African-Americans ("contrabands") came into Federal lines along the rivers, some were shipped individually and others in small groups, with most assigned duties as firemen or coal-heavers. From this point, contrabands were actively and increasingly signed on to help fill the continuing manpower shortage of the expanding flotilla. A significant majority of these men were posted to the new tinclads joining the squadron.

While Porter energetically addressed the huge variety of operational and administrative matters facing his gunboat fleet, his letter from Carondelet requesting additional light-draughts reached the Washington desk of Secretary Welles. The cabinet member responsible for an unprecedented expansion of the U.S. sea service was inclined to approve its content. Noting that Constructor Hartt had already purchased four tinclads, Welles authorized Porter on October 24 to obtain six more. If the type was truly considered indispensable, authorization was also given to add four more, "making 14 in all." Porter's light-draught acquisition project was overseen by Fleet Captain Pennock and several deputies, including Lt. Cmdr. Watson Smith and, briefly, Acting Master George W. Brown. Both Smith and Brown had recently served in divisions of Porter's mortar flotilla at New Orleans.[13]

Meanwhile, Acting Rear Adm. David G. Farragut had informed the Navy Department that the Confederates had placed batteries on the Mississippi River below the Red River. In relaying this news on November 12, Secretary Welles informed his Western river commander that it devolved upon him "to open the Mississippi to Baton Rouge and New Orleans." Appreciating that Porter had only a few weeks' tenure in his current post and would need more boats if he was to achieve this new directive, the navy secretary authorized the Cairo naval leadership to purchase and arm 12 to 15 more light-draughts for use on the rivers emptying into the Gulf of Mexico. There was a caveat: someday, they might all be transferred to the West Gulf Coast Blockading Squadron. As Welles put it, the boats would form a part of the Mississippi Squadron "until required in the Gulf." Above all, "that they are for any squadron but your own will be known only to yourself."

By the time the navy secretary's communication was received in Cairo, Porter had already contracted with Joseph Brown for the conversion of river steamers. It was quickly learned at the beginning of November that the overall demand for civilian steamboats, particularly from the U.S. Army, was driving up prices. Still, only new boats would be acquired, with their invoices forwarded to the Bureau of Construction. The admiral was able to obtain from Joseph Brown what he believed to be very competitive alteration rates of $8,000 per boat, including "outfit of every kind." Indeed, he was pleased that the modification cost was actually $2,000 per boat "cheaper than Mr. Hartt said he could do it for."

On November 16, a requisition was sent to Capt. John A. Dahlgren, Chief of the Bureau of Ordnance at Washington, asking that 72 more 24-pdr. howitzers be supplied for 12 tinclads in addition to the 90 guns already ordered, This is the first, albeit informal, indication we have that Porter had received Welles's authorization for Gulf Coast tinclads.

Three days later, a lengthy message was mailed to Washington detailing Cairo's

The 12-pdr. and 24-pdr. Dahlgren brass howitzer was the principal ordnance employed upon the light-draught ("tinclad") gunboats and was normally mounted in broadside. It was soon, however, found that these guns alone were inadequate, and so the armament of the boats was enhanced by the addition of more powerful cannon, usually Parrott rifles. The boat howitzers could be (and were) employed ashore on wheeled carriages, as depicted in the lower illustration (*Naval Ordnance Instructions,* 1866).

approach to tinclad acquisition in accordance with the Department's purchase authorizations. It specifically detailed certain of the light-draught alterations made and as such serves as augmentation to the Pennock descriptions of September 12 noted above. "These boats have been covered with iron all around and 11 feet high," Welles was informed. This made them "perfectly rifle proof and proof around the boilers against light cannon shot." The new tinclads had "every comfort and accommodation" and carried "eight 24-pounder howitzers in smooth water without any trouble." The boats were all "of good size" and could "carry comfortably 200 men for an expedition and accommodate a great many officers."

This official acknowledgement of Welles's orders lumps both of his directives together and does not directly differentiate between that applicable to the Upper River sent on October 24 and that relative to the Gulf of November 12. There was, however, subtle information provided that Welles and his officers or confidants would understand. In his report of November 19, for example, Acting Rear Adm. Porter hesitated to say what the new boats would "do at sea or where there is any motion." He thought "they would not suit to go far from the coast." Still, "any of these boats will do to go into salt water with trifling alterations" and they were being fitted "for such an emergency."

The vessels in question and others besides were purchased and altered without much fanfare over the next two years. A few additional physical changes were undoubtedly requested. For example, on December 15, Porter detached Acting Volunteer Lt. Robert K. Riley from his command of the ironclad *Louisville* off Cairo and ordered him to report to Lt. Cmdr. Smith for command of one of the new light-draughts. "If it can be done without delay in Cincinnati," the squadron commander asked, "tell Captain Smith that I wish the ports on these steamers cut up 1 foot higher; that the guns have no elevation."

It is true that, at least initially, there was some difficulty in adequately paying Joseph Brown's alteration claims. On December 20, 1862, Fleet Captain Pennock informed Porter that the Mississippi Squadron's chief bursar, Paymaster William B. Boggs, had previously sent the Cincinnatian "all the money he could spare" and had just received another $56,000 from Washington to complete payment. Acting Rear Adm. Porter, anxious for receipt of additional tinclads, attempted to make certain that his people stayed on top of payments. On January 14, 1863, he wrote to Pennock from Arkansas Post inquiring whether sufficient funds were being regularly received to pay for the steamers "as they are bought." It was important, the commander continued, that as soon as Brown altered a steamer, he was to be paid for her at the rate of $8,500, plus extra charges for special modifications.

Also, earlier in January, Pennock dispatched the squadron ordnance officer, Lt. Cmdr. Joseph P. Sanford, to Cincinnati, along with Master Carpenter Charles F. Kendall, to assume responsibility for affairs at that city from Lt. Cmdr. Smith, including the supervision of tinclad alterations. Additionally, the two were to seek out reasonably priced additional steamers for conversion.

Although the time of alteration from purchase to commissioning soon accelerated to a period as short as five weeks, the conversion process during these early months of the new year was deliberate. Much consideration was given to vessel selection and the USN officers tasked with steamboat acquisition had yet to develop a practiced eye for their assessment. The men acted carefully and wrote detailed reports and observations on their choices, some of which have come down to us. So it was that we have greater information on the pre-purchase configuration for at least three of these early 1863 squadron additions than we have for many obtained before or later.

After reviewing the large number of boats available along the Cincinnati wharf for over a month, Lt. Cmdr. Sanford located a pair of side-wheel ferry boats that he believed well-suited for alteration into tinclads. The *Covington No. 2* and the *Queen City No. 3* were strong, sound, and reportedly swift. It was initially believed that, following their conversion, they would most likely draw less than 36 inches. On February 16, arrangements were completed to purchase the pair from their owner, Samuel Wiggins, for $19,000 and $16,000 respectively. Payment for the latter would be made first; a check for the *Covington* would not, however, be handed over until she dropped anchor off Cairo.

A day or so after the purchase, the boats were in the hands of contractor Joseph Brown, who "commenced on them with a large force" and pushed the work even on "nights and Sundays." As the laborers pounded away, Master Carpenter Kendall and others observed their work, expecting that, because they were larger and stronger, the two boats, whose names would drop the numbers upon commissioning, could "give much better satisfaction and be a great deal more serviceable than the others" [read: *St. Clair* and *Brilliant*]. It was emphatically hoped that Porter, who preferred side-wheelers anyway, would "be much better pleased with them than with the stern-wheel boats."

Kendall, in a February 23 report to Pennock, gave a very detailed view of the new craft as they lay in the boatyard, perhaps as good or better than any we have for any of the light-draughts. The conversion was progressing quickly and it was expected that, if the iron work progressed as fast as the woodwork, at least one of the vessels could be away to the tip of Illinois within a few days.

Constructed at Cincinnati in 1862, the 224-ton *Covington* was 126 foot long, with a beam of 37 feet and a depth of hold of 6 foot, 6 inches. Although her dimensions are unknown, the month-old *Queen City* weighed just 12 tons less than her consort.

The stern-wheelers were each being cleared to have a gun deck, forward of the engines and boilers, that was 50 feet long by almost 40 feet wide, with space for two 24-pdr. howitzers in broadside, plus two 30-pdr. Parrott rifles aimed out of forward gun ports. Abaft the power plant on board each was a large deck, about 35 × 40, that could support a pair of Parrotts and still leave room for an armory, dispensary, galley, and gangway stairs.

Below the main deck in the hold of the *Covington* and *Queen City* were two magazines, a shell room, a bread room, rooms for the yeomen, boatswains, sail makers, and carpenters, eight general storerooms, and a pair of coal bunkers, each with a capacity for 2,000 bushels. As their conversions progressed, expectations rose that, when finished and coaled, both would draw but 30 inches.

The upper hurricane deck forward of the cabin was strengthened to accommodate the firing of wheeled 12-pdr. howitzers and was made large enough to accommodate up to 100 men under its roof. The spar deck had hammock nettings 3 foot high around the front and 40 foot down each side.

As we saw with Com. Hull and Flag Officer Davis and shall see again below, the matter of vessel protection was a subject of continuing interest with the naval establishment and builders, as well as the sailors who were expected to man the craft. The casemates were much heavier than, for example, on the *Brilliant*, *St. Clair*, or *Signal;* there were 5-inch-square oak stanchions with 2½- and 3-inch planks.

Lt. Cmdr. Sanford originally asked Joseph Brown to extend the casemates around the bows of the sisters in an angular circle. After due deliberation and consultation with his supplier, the contractor reported the task insurmountable. Cutting, shaping, and bending the iron per Sanford's requirement was impossible given time constraints. In the end, the forward casemate of the *Covington* and *Queen City* was each built across the bow at a 50-degree angle.

Although their appearance was superficially similar and we actually have photographs of each tinclad, we have no physical evidence from either the *Covington* or *Queen City* (both of which were destroyed during the conflict) for review. The wrecked remains of two other tinclad war casualties, one each stern-wheeler and side-wheeler, have been found and checked.

The *Key West* (the stern-wheeler) and *Tawah* (also a one-time ferryboat named *Ebenezer*) joined the squadron in May–June 1863 and were later lost at Johnsonville, TN, in November 1864. In the early 1990s, divers from R. Christopher Goodwin and Associates, working with the Tennessee Division of Archaeology and the private Raise the Gunboats foundation, examined the suspected wrecks of the two off the former Tennessee River port, now a submerged bottom area of the great TVA project of the 1930s.

This recent research, when coupled with Master Carpenter Kendall's report on the *Queen City* and *Covington*, suggests that, in general, tinclad casemates were perhaps even more unsophisticated structures than initially depicted, with "walls constructed of 6-inch planks of various widths," which "merely enclosed the main deck without substantially altering the form of the upper works." Prefabricated sections of the casemates, built in whole or in part to the required specifications of individual vessels, could be bolted into the existing boiler deck structures. In order to lighten ship to make repairs or get over obstacles, light-draught captains could, among other measures, simply order their casemates, or parts of them, unbolted and held aboard an accompanying barge until reshipped.

Once a tinclad's casemate was constructed and hung, ½-inch to 1-inch-thick sheets of boiler plate were riveted to its forward part and adjacent to the engines on each side. Admiral Porter later wrote that his light draughts were "well-protected, except in the hull, with an inch of iron all around the boilers, and an inch in the bulwarks abreast and in front of the boilers, making two inches of iron and eight inches of wood, besides the coal." Gun ports were mounted in the front and cannon ports on the sides. In April 1863, Acting Rear Admiral Porter ordered that his light-draught captains "paint the hull and casemates of their vessels black, leaving the cabins a buff color."

Two days after sending his extraordinarily detailed report on the *Covington* and *Queen City* to Fleet Captain Pennock, Master Carpenter Kendall sent another. This one, for the *Champion No. 4*, was announced as yet another side-wheeler. Owned by Amos and Vincent Shinkle of Covington, KY, the little boat has been the subject of some disagreement as to her propulsive rig. Kendall (initially), ORN II, and Frederick Way Jr. state that she was a side-wheeler, while Paul Silverstone tells us that she was a stern-wheeler. Although the number of her wheels is in dispute (most likely because of scribes incorrectly copying reports back and forth), we discuss the *Champion* here because carpenter Kendall provides an excellent description of the boat.

Built at Cincinnati at the beginning of 1860, the 115-ton *Champion* was 145 feet, 8 inches in length, with a beam of 26.5 feet and a depth of hold of just three feet, six inches. Forward of the power plant was a "roomy" main deck, with a large deck room aft. She had a large hurricane roof over the boiler deck, but no cabin or cabin outfit.

Disputing his opening line (upon which later observations are doubtless made), Carpenter Kendall describes the tiny steamer as having two engines, each with 15-inch cylinders and a five-foot stroke. She had one 24-foot water wheel, with a six-foot length of bucket. That would have been mounted at the back of the boat, making her a stern-wheeler, as Silverstone tells us. The owners were anxious to sell the *Champion*. If a sale was not completed, they would send her to Nashville "with a tow of coal." The asking price was $16,000.

At the beginning of March 1863, Lt. Cmdr. Phelps, perhaps the most experienced officer in the Mississippi Squadron, was detailed by Cmdr. Pennock to review the Cincinnati acquisitions, as well as several under purchase consideration in the St. Louis area. He was provided with the usual tips on what to look for, including a new requirement that the chimneys be hinged for lowering.

A month earlier, Phelps had been commissioned by Porter to review progress on the ironclads building at St. Louis. Phelps, whose *Lexington* was fired upon from the river banks during a January 1862 mission up the Cumberland River, was a fervent believer in the need for additional craft to help stem the "guerrilla menace."

By this time, the market for available steamers was severely inflated; as Phelps put it in a letter to Porter: "People have gone mad in regard to steamboat stock." The veteran soon concluded that the government should just seize the number of boats needed, have them appraised, and pay the owners without negotiation. Writing from Cincinnati about the same time, Lt. Cmdr. Sanford echoed the same sentiment. "If it is imperative to buy boats," his March 12 telegram to Pennock read, "will have to pay exorbitant prices [as] Individuals are buying at same rates and paying cash."

While traveling up the Ohio from Cairo, Phelps halted at Jeffersonville to consult with contractor Brown regarding the *James Thompson*, a ferryboat identified as "just the boat for a staunch light clad." In December, a month after her construction, the side-wheeler's Louisville-based owners H. Marbury, *et al.*, were asking $25,000, a markup of about $5,000 over her building cost. A commitment for the vessel, known eventually as the *Fort Hindman*, was made and she was ordered to Cincinnati for conversion. She was officially purchased on April 16 for $35,000, though Phelps believed her worth at least $11,000 less.

Continuing up to Cincinnati quite probably with Brown, Phelps consulted with Sanford, Brown and Kendall and, on March 10, purchased the *Champion No. 4*. The following day he approved Sanford's acquisition of the stern-wheeler Argosy and made an offer for the *Emma Duncan*. On March 12, arrangements for the *Emma* were completed and she was ordered down to Cairo, where she would be officially acquired from J. Batchelor on March 24 for $39,000. Later, she would be called *Hastings*. Writing from the mouth of the Yazoo River on March 14, Acting Rear Admiral Porter notified the Navy Department of his *Covington* and *Queen City* acquisitions; other personal purchase notifications would follow for other vessels.

Having completed his inspection and review trips to Cincinnati and St. Louis, Lt. Cmdr. Phelps reported his activities to Porter from Cairo on April 19. Given that Lt. Cmdr. Sanford had already acquired "a number of stern-wheel and other river steamers," he was able to add three suitable boats to the total, the only ones that could be purchased "at anything like a fair and proper price."

In addition to paying the fee asked for by the owners of the *Champion No. 4*, he also bought the St. Louis-based ferryboat *Fanny* for $8,000 from her Chicago owner J. Van Vortwick. The vessel would later be commissioned as the *Paw Paw*. An $11,000 deposit was also placed on an initially unnamed St. Joseph, MO, ferry. Her acquisition would be finalized if her machinery stood up to close inspection. She, too, was purchased in May, and retained her civilian name of *Peosta*. When he learned of the $35,000+ cost of these vessels in May, Porter wrote to Phelps pointing out that, although the vessels were economically purchased, they may might turn out to be "too cheap — I never buy a cheap thing. I am always afraid of it."

When he took over the Tennessee River division at the beginning of May 1863, Phelps, who was not known for his bashfulness, was bitterly disappointed in the quality of the entire tinclad acquisition and modification program. Poor calking of the *Queen City* and of his own *Hastings* was the immediate cause of concerned comments made on May 14 to Rear Adm. Porter. "Mr. Joseph Brown's work on these vessels is of the most worthless description," Phelps complained, adding, "Mr. Kendall seems not fit for his position." Poor hull calking caused the *Hastings* to take on "tons of useless weight," dropping to a point where her wheel guards touched the water.

When they got to Cairo, there remained much work to be done. Aboard the receiving ship *Clara Dolson* on June 11, new recruits James A. Dickinson and Eratus Sherman ("Mac") McCellan found time to idle at the rail and watch the workmen "building a turtle-boat near the wharf. It used to be a middle-wheel ferry boat called the *Fanny*. She is not a very large boat."

Rear Admiral Porter and his subordinates continued their aggressive tinclad acquisition program throughout the remainder of his time in the West. The requirement for light draught continued to be the paramount criterion upon which all vessel selections were made, although two outsized vessels, or "large tinclads," were added: the flag boat *Black Hawk* and the prize *Ouachita*.

In practice, the boats were selected and altered, usually by Brown at Cincinnati. When the deck and casemate arrangements were complete, they were then sent to Cairo, or later Mound City, for their furniture, armament, and crews. When several vessels were purchased close together, it was usual practice to send one of them awaiting her turn for alteration ahead to Cairo or Mound City loaded with furniture and other needs acquired in the Queen City. She would then return empty to Brown's yards for conversion.

Landsmen Dickinson and McCellan, along with 12 other men and boys, were assigned to the new tinclad *Tawah* on June 16, followed by 46 more plus firemen and coal-heavers two days later. Their introduction to navy life and shipboard routine, begun on the *Dolson*, was intensified, though hardly different from thousands of other Mississippi Squadron bluejackets. To quote from the former's diary:

> June 16th, 1863 — We pumped all the bilge water out of the hold. June 17, 1863 — Been hard at work all day. Cleared the decks of all rubish and scraped the decks of pitch, tar and paint. Our boat is a stout looking wittle craft with the sides 14 inches thick. The bow [illegible] is 18 inches thick with rolled plates of iron 2½ inches thick with an inch of iron. There is no iron on the sides. We have two 30-pounder Parrott cannon, four 24-pounder smooth-bore shell guns, and two 12-pounder rifled Wiard steel guns. The Wiard guns were not mounted so we had to mount them ourselves.

On Friday, June 19, steam was raised and a stakedown cruise ensued up the Ohio River to within two miles of Mound City. After rounding to, the *Tawah* paddled back to Cairo and tied up at the wharf boat, where her officers reported "the boat went bully."

The tinclad's rookie crew spent all day Saturday loading small arms (including cutlasses), cannon and rifle ammunition, ordnance equipment, fire buckets, and all other supplies. Occasionally, sweat running down their backs, the men paused to refresh themselves. "The Mississippi is awful muddy," Dickinson recorded, "and it made all of us sick to drink the water."

The *Tawah*, under her new skipper Acting Master Alfred Phelps — brother of Lt. Cmdr. S. Ledyard Phelps — was commissioned on June 21 and her crew was actually if not officially in the fighting Navy. It being Sunday, the men were, per regulations, subjected to their first formal Sabbath inspection. Speaking of shipboard procedure, "we have come to strict rules now," Dickinson told his diary. These gist of these rules have been digested for modern readers in the social histories of naval historians Bennett and Ringle.

In November 1863, Navy Secretary Welles received a report from his Mississippi chief alluding to additional physical alterations and precautions that were being taken with at least some of the new tinclads. Particular reference was made to several soon to be transferred to the West Gulf Coast Blockading Squadron. The light-draughts then being fitted were, in the admiral's opinion, well protected except in their hulls. They were in most respects "completely musket-proof."

Shielding of the boilers, however, remained of great concern on all the Western gunboats, and protection of the power plants on board the new squadron acquisitions was ordered beefed up. Consequently, an extra inch thickness of iron plate was placed "all around the boilers and an inch on the bulwarks abreast and in front of the boilers, making 2 inches of iron and 8 inches of wood, besides the coal, between a shot and the boilers." In addition to strengthening their protection, Porter required some alterations in the fastening of boilers and machinery aboard those tinclads slated for the salt water of the Gulf. Additionally, upon their arrival at New Orleans, these light-draughts would be taken in hand and their bottoms coppered in much the same fashion as ocean going warships.

Argosy No. 2 (later renamed *Wave*) was the first of the Gulf-class tinclads to be commissioned, on November 14, 1863. She was followed by the *Glide 2* (November 30), *Nyanza* (December 21) and *Stockdale* (December 26). With skeleton crews, they were delivered from Cairo to New Orleans at the beginning of 1864 and were in action by spring.

Though regretting that so few officers could be retained, Com. Henry H. Bell, in command of the West Gulf Coast Blockading Squadron, acknowledged receipt of two light-draughts on January 6, 1864. At this point, he informed Rear Adm. Porter of a new requirement in his area, namely tinclads for the Texas blockade. Would it be possible, in furtherance of this objective, Bell asked, if the newer vessels might be of deeper draft (3–4 feet) and be "stauch enough in top hamper, boiler, chimney, hog braces, and wheels to stand a moderate sea in running down the coast to their destinations?" This vessel class could not be obtained at New Orleans, Bell informed his colleague, "while the upper waters within your command abound with them." If Porter could send several down, "you would do a good public service," the commodore concluded.

The initial quartet was joined by five tinclads in the spring of 1864, with the latter units strengthened to meet Com. Bell's requirements: *Meteor* (March 18), *Tallahatchie*

(April 19), *Carrabasset* (May 12), *Rodolph* (May 18), and *Elk* (June 6). The *Elk* and *Carrabasset* were, like the *Nyanza*, side-wheelers.

A year after Joseph Brown started converting light-draughts, a reporter from the *Chicago Daily Tribune* reviewed wartime industry in the Queen City. As he told his readers on December 1, 21 gunboats of all classes had been rebuilt and fitted out in the previous twelve months, including "a number of sternwheel boats ... tinclads as the naval men call them." At the same time, the Cincinnati recruiting rendezvous had the Mississippi Squadron at over 1,800 enlisted seamen and 200 petty officers.

Aside from comments upon individual units joining the squadron, little more is heard about tinclad acquisition for almost a year, save for a special arrangement with the War Department for a quartet of light-draughts for the lower Tennessee River.

The Federal army at Chattanooga, besieged and in need of succor in October 1863, opened an emergency "Cracker" supply line at the end of the month. With the Union victories on the Alabama-Tennessee border, the logistical requirement continued. The decision was taken to construct a fleet of transport steamers to ensure deliveries. On November 4, the influential and on-scene Assistant Secretary of War Charles A. Dana, in a letter to War Secretary Edwin Stanton, in reviewing the transportation situation, also commented upon a need for its protection: "I suggest that gunboats of very light draught should be provided for this part of the Tennessee."

With support and commitment from Union army officials from Stanton to Grant to Quartermaster General Montgomery Meigs and Western river transportation czar Col. Lewis B. Parsons, it was agreed that four tinclads be built in time to take advantage of the spring rise. As we extensively review in our biography of Lt. Cmdr. Le Roy Fitch, these were to be assembled at the steamboat-building yard set up by Capt. Arthur Edwards at Bridgeport, AL, after the Chattanooga siege. The army would pay for their construction and lease them to the navy, which would provide officers, crews, and armament.

Asked for an opinion, Rear Adm. Porter, no fan of stern-wheelers, advised that the new boats be side-wheelers, equipped with very large boilers and large cylinders. To coordinate and oversee the project for the navy, Porter ordered Lt. Cmdr. Fitch to work with Capt. Edwards. Fitch was given the authority to recommend specific gun deck configurations and other adjustments necessary to turn the steamers into fighting ships.

The Edwards-Fitch enterprise required that Edwards, who initially had neither mechanics nor local material with which to work, obtain all of his propulsion machinery and most of his other material from manufacturers on the Ohio or in St. Louis. The orders had then to be transported 600 to 800 miles overland by already overtaxed railroad trains.

For his part, Fitch assisted from his Evansville headquarters, traveling frequently down to Alabama to confer with Edwards and ensuring the delivery of recruits and ordnance. After the Confederates launched their spring offensive against places like Paducah and Fort Pillow, Acting Volunteer Lt. Henry Glassford often filled in, exercising the same authority and concern as his commander.

Progress on the Bridgeport gunboats, each of which would cost the government $19,000, continued all spring. Named the *General Grant*, *General Thomas*, *General Burnside*, and *General Sherman*, all four had approximately the same dimensions and same

Outfitted for the West Gulf Coast Blockading Squadron in May 1864, the *Elk* was active in the waters off New Orleans and Mobile and on the lower Mississippi River over the next year. Her photo is entered here to provide perspective on the size of Civil War light-draughts relative to the officers and men (Naval Historical Center).

To support its supply requirements on the Upper Tennessee River, the U.S. Army, with assistance from several Mississippi Squadron officers, constructed a fleet of steamboats and four light-draught ("tinclad") gunboats at Bridgeport, Alabama, from late fall 1863 to spring 1864. When completed, the four military steamers were leased to the Navy, which provided crews and ordnance. When the war was over, the quartet was returned to the Army, with proper receipts received (National Archives).

armament. The 201.5-ton General *Burnside* was 171 feet long, with a beam of 26 feet and a 4.9-foot depth of hold. The 204-ton *General Grant* possessed identical specifications. With the same beam, a length of 168 feet, and a depth of hold of 4.6 feet, the 187-ton *General Sherman* was slightly smaller, while the *General Thomas*, with the same hold depth and beam, was three feet shorter and three tons lighter than the *Sherman*. Except for the Grant, which had two 30-pounder instead of 20-pounder Parrott rifles, all had three 24-pounder Dahlgren howitzers in broadside.

The *General Grant* was commissioned on July 20, a month after the four were turned over to USN administration by order of Maj. Gen. Sherman. The *General Sherman* was commissioned on July 27, while the *General Burnside* and *General Thomas* followed on August 8. Acting Volunteer Lt. Glassford was appointed interim commander of the upper Tennessee flotilla, a post he held until September 29, when Lt. Moreau Forrest came over to take over the new 11th District of the Mississippi Squadron.

The feat of building gunboats and especially the tinclads at Bridgeport won wide acclaim in Union logistical circles. Col. Parson regarded the achievement as "worthy of record among the remarkable incidents of the war." The Mississippi Squadron would return the four leased boats to the War Department for disposal on June 1, 1865.

Conversions and tinclad deliveries continued apace. However, it was not until Acting Rear Adm. Samuel Phillips Lee, Porter's successor, requested additional light-draughts in October 1864 that we learn more about the tinclad acquisition process or desired boat configurations. Secretary Welles, in response to Lee's request, sent authorization to Cairo on November 9, 1864, for the purchase, arming, and equipping of ten more light-draughts. Lee, who was then concerned with events that would culminate in the Battle of Nashville, was delayed in implementing the order.

On November 23, the Marylander wrote out a lengthy light-draught acquisition order for Lt. Cmdr. James A. Greer, commander of the squadron flag boat *Black Hawk*. In these instructions, the admiral set out his preferences, adding a few more that offer further enlightenment on tinclad configuration. If possible, Lee wanted only new side-wheelers purchased, though strong, fast stern-wheelers with a "good-sized wheel" were acceptable. Once a boat was selected, it was to be purchased at the lowest possible price and a clear title obtained.

Lt. Cmdr. Greer was to avoid any vessels not already inspected by U.S. government officers or any outfitted "with second-hand engines or boilers or any engines or boilers that have been much used." Lee wanted to avoid any that required "considerable and expensive alterations or repairs after we have purchased them, in addition to the fitments necessary for naval service." Selected craft were to have all of the pumps necessary to keep them afloat, "also good donkey engines."

No boats were to be selected in which the boilers were set so far forward that 30-pounder Parrotts could not be worked after the boiler casemates were fitted. Indeed, the reason Lee wanted only side-wheelers was to be able to fit two 30-pounder Parrotts forward and two aft. This could not be done aboard stern-wheelers. Lee's orders represent the first time that space for extra firepower was actually cited in writing over maneuverability as a reason for obtaining side-wheelers rather than stern-wheelers.

When these vessels were eventually acquired, they were the last light-draughts added to the Mississippi Squadron.[14]

4

Early Rounds, August–December 1862

Mid–19th century summers on the Western rivers were long, hot, and because of low water, often transport-poor. On August 23, two days after Flag Officer Charles H. Davis created the "upper" division of his Western Flotilla, its new executive officer, Lt. Cmdr. Le Roy Fitch, took the *General Pillow* from Paducah, KY, up the Tennessee River, intent upon conducting the unit's first anti-guerrilla sweep. Unhappily, this inaugural mission was scuttled by low water above Duck River, about 100 miles above the river's mouth. Low water in the Tennessee and Cumberland rivers was common at this time of year and would remain so for several months more.

About this same time, the Confederate Army of Tennessee, rebuilding for some time, started north from southern Tennessee and from Knoxville toward the Ohio River, via Kentucky. Although its campaign would capture many newspaper headlines, it would have no direct bearing on the Confederate anti-shipping war, which continued unabated and hot over the next several weeks.

The 175-ton stern-wheeler *W.B. Terry*,[1] under Master Leonard G. Klinck, left Paducah five days after Fitch, hoping to independently rendezvous with the Federal gunboat upstream. She, too, could not pass the Duck River shoals and so Klinck, like Fitch, rounded to and returned. The retreat of the seven-year-old Vernon, Pennsylvania-built craft was halted at sundown on August 30 when she ran aground.

While trying to free herself next morning, the steamer was attacked by Rebel troops under Captains T. Alonzo Napier and James B. Algee from positions on an adjacent hill not far from Napier's house. Although she was protected by two 12-pounder field howitzers and 17 men from the 81st Ohio Volunteer Infantry, the 200 determined men in gray quickly forced a surrender. Once the Confederates had achieved their goal of being transported across the river, the *Terry*'s passengers were put ashore, where three free African-Americans taken in the attack were sold into slavery "on the spot." Master Klinck, his crew and the soldiers were forced into a raft and the steamer was run onto a bar and burned.[2]

Rumors being rife that Paducah would be attacked, the *General Pillow* was left to guard the Bluegrass community while Lt. Commander Fitch returned to the squadron anchorage at Cairo, IL, aboard a commercial steamer to bring up the repairing *Alfred*

Robb. Upon reporting, he was pleasantly surprised when Capt. Pennock pointed out that the newly-captured steamer *Fairplay*, which had arrived at Cairo from Helena on August 31, was already being converted into a tinclad.

The earliest light-draught for which a photo exists, the side-wheel *Fairplay* was constructed in 1859 at New Albany, IN, to participate in the cotton trade. She was 138.8 feet long, with a beam of 27 feet and a draft of 4.9 feet. Her two reciprocating steam engines and two boilers permitted a top speed of 5 mph upstream. A pair of 12-pounder smoothbore howitzers were placed aboard, along with two rifled 12-pounder howitzers.[3]

Reports continued to circulate about various real or imagined raids, which were now "very annoying along" the Ohio River. The most pressing alarm concerned a supposed foray by troops under Brig. Gen. Simon B. Buckner, CSA, against the locks at Spottsville, KY. Not all rumors were alarms. On September 3, Southern irregulars took and burned the 170-ton side-wheeler *Silver Lake* at Linn Creek on the Osage River some distance from St. Louis.

The *Fairplay* weighed for Paducah in the predawn darkness of September 6 with two companies from the 2nd Michigan Cavalry

Lt. Cmdr. Le Roy Fitch (1835–1875) was chosen in August 1862 by Flag Officer Charles Davis to serve under Fleet Captain Alexander Pennock as operations officer for the Mosquito Flotilla formed to pacify the upper tributaries of the Mississippi River. Fitch would become the longest-serving tinclad commander and the most active of all, commanding his unit from ship and shore throughout the entire war (Naval Historical Center).

embarked hoping to prevent serious harm to the Spottsville regulatory machinery. Shoal water held her up at Cumberland bar for a week.

Fortunately in this case, Evansville officials and Indiana Legion officers, led by Col. John W. Foster, had already taken the initiative to convert the locally-built side-wheeler *Lue Eaves* (sometimes spelled *Lou Eaves*)[4] into a harbor defense vessel. Under the command of a civilian "commodore," she was armed with a brass cannon and possibly protected by hay bales.

Foster's Hoosier troops, assisted by the *Eaves*, drove the Confederate marauders away from the Spottsville gates before the tinclads arrived, but not before several tons of rocks were dropped on the upper gate. It was also learned during this time that Fort Heiman commander Col. William Lowe and his 5th Iowa Cavalry, with a mixed brigade, was able to retake the Cumberland River town of Clarksville on September 7.

Lt. Cmdr. Fitch "impressed" for hire Capt. William Thompson's brand-new *Cordelia Ann*[5] on September 1. Arming her with a spare howitzer and placing her under command of the *Fairplay*'s second master, George J. Groves, Fitch sent his auxiliary up to Caseyville,

Captured prior to her conversion into a light-draught gunboat, the *Fairplay* was photographed on the Cumberland River, ca. 1864, by Bell & Sheridan of Franklin Street, Clarksville, Tennessee. The earliest tinclad for which an image exists, the side-wheeler joined the Mississippi Squadron in September 1862 as flag boat of the Mosquito Flotilla operated by Lt. Cmdr. Le Roy Fitch. She would remain on the upper rivers throughout the war, serving as a stalwart convoy escort and participating in numerous shootouts with Confederate regular and irregular forces (Naval Historical Center).

KY, to punish irregulars reportedly firing at passing steamboats. The Hoosier's instruction to his subordinate required both stealth and firmness:

> In approaching Caseyville, be particular to keep your men hid from observation and
> use every precaution to disguise the true character of the boat and expedition. Should
> you be fired into at Caseyville, or any resistance offered, destroy the place at once.

The outcome of the Caseyville gambit is unknown, with no contact the probable result.

The Northern "mosquito squadron" could not be everywhere at once. When the gunboats were at one or more Ohio River locations, irregulars would attack elsewhere. Sometimes their targets were lucky and escaped without harm; occasionally, they offered to fight. Making a return trip to Evansville from Cairo, the *Mattie Cook*,[6] built at Madison, IN, during the fall of 1860, and Capt. J.T. Hugo's 91-ton *Ollie Sullivan*[7] were both fired into by Rebel batteries on the bank near Caseyville, KY. Initially reported sunk, they were only grazed by rifle bullets and made port without difficulty.

On September 10, the *Henry Fitzhugh*,[8] in a gamble that would have made "Stovepipe" Johnson proud, twice faked out partisans with a Quaker gun. Just before reaching Curlew, KY, officers aboard the unarmed *Fitzhugh* learned that a party of Confederates were waiting to board them. The steamer's fast-thinking but unknown master ordered that a piece of timber, about five feet long and a foot in diameter, be painted up to resemble a cannon barrel. This was mounted on a truck and covered with a tarpaulin.

Arriving at Curlew, the *Fitzhugh* did indeed find 50 Rebels lined up on shore; the boat's surrender was demanded. Thereupon, members of the crew brought up from the hold a number of small sacks, containing pieces of limestone about the size of grapeshot, and laid them on the deck next to the ersatz cannon. The log masquerading as a weapon was then slowly turned toward the Southerners and just as the "gun crew" began to remove the protective tarpaulin, the graycoats ran off.

Continuing on, the *Fitzhugh* was hailed by another group of irregulars, numbering about 40, from Battery Rock on the Illinois shore. They too demanded the boat put in and they too were scared off by the imposing black "bit of wood." When the steamer reached Cairo on the morning of September 13, her officers and men were all proclaimed heroes. The story of their adventure amazed many, from Capt. Pennock on down, and was happily celebrated in local waterfront establishments.

The *Fairplay* passed the Cumberland bar on September 12 and steamed up toward Shawneetown, IL. Near that location, the Navyman spied a small band of 50 or 60, perceived as guerrillas, and quietly attempted to put a landing force behind it, thereby trapping those people on the bank between the bluejackets and the tinclad. Unfortunately, due to low water, this ploy didn't work; as the sailors prepared to go ashore, they were spotted and the Confederates fled. The *Fairplay* threw "a few shell after them" and went ahead with the landing. Once ashore, the 20 sailors pushed inland some three miles and ransacked their enemy's camp at Cypress Lake. They also took over a river-bank house and made five men captive; as nothing could be proved against them, they were released.

Historian Donald Davidson later summed up what became for gunboat commanders both a common observation and usual claim. "Guerrillas," he wrote, "never made a stand against superior forces. When the gunboats landed troops, the guerrillas withdrew or dispersed, and hence gunboat commanders were always able to say that they had 'driven off' or 'broken up' guerrilla parties."

Continuing a flag-showing cruise, Fitch made it a point to make his presence known at all the intermediate towns en route to Evansville. For example, stopping at Uniontown, KY, on September 16, the Hoosier sailor informed the mayor and local citizens that he was the new man representing the Union on the Ohio River and that he "would hold them and their property responsible for all guerrilla depredations within 10 miles either up or down the river."

Low water, ship repairs, and the need to allow his men to recuperate now forced Fitch to pace the Evansville river bank until September 29. All he could do was ensure by wire that the *Alfred Robb* guarded Paducah while the *General Pillow* cruised between that city and Smithland.

During the first month of tinclad Mosquito Flotilla operations on the Ohio River, many of the tactics and obstacles to be employed or encountered in the years ahead were demonstrated. Low water, poor communications, equipment failures, fleet opponents, and failed traps were certainly challenges, but civilian cooperation, relatively quick response when conditions allowed, and interservice cooperation held promise.[9]

While Lt. Cmdr. Fitch and his new naval unit were attempting to slow irregular depredations on the Ohio, Maj. Gen. William T. Sherman, Union commander at Memphis since July, had his hands full attempting to dissuade the "guerrillas" in his vicinity. As was demonstrated in August, insurgents continued to snipe away at Mississippi River steamers; or, as the garrison commander put it in an unalarmed September letter to his wife Ellen Ewing Sherman: "The boats coming down are occasionally fired on." At the same time, larger bands and military units also conducted various sized raids in the interior.

The red-haired Buckeye field commander quickly found that regular counterinsurgency operations yielded no positive results. Infantry regiments on foot were no match for speedy horsemen or locals who could quickly fade into the wooded shadows. Sherman, like Fitch, concluded that attempts to run down those directly responsible for partisan attacks was a fruitless task. Reprisals against the populace and its possessions might prove more beneficial.

While in command at Memphis, Maj. Gen. William Tecumseh Sherman (1829–1891) was particularly incensed by Confederate attacks upon steamers plying the Mississippi above and below his garrison. He instituted a number of measures to check the Rebel plague, including deportations behind the lines, anti-guerrilla sweeps, and riverborne attacks upon towns suspected of providing refuge. Always appreciative of the supportive effort of the Union gunboats, he would call upon them for assistance on numerous occasions (Library of Congress).

The regular mail packet *Eugene*,[10] en route to Memphis from St. Louis, put in toward Randolph, TN, about 25 miles upstream from her destination, on September 23. As she approached the levee, a band of insurgents, estimated to number between 25 and 40, pumped a volley into her from the bank. The guerrillas were part of a band of about 400 based at Huntington, TN, and led by Capt. W.W. Faulkner, who "claimed all of West Tennessee and the Purchase area of Kentucky as his haunts." Possible plans for her capture were foiled when the steamer backed out and headed down the river. It was later reported that the craft was making a stop because she was laden with stores for local families, many of whom had family members in Rebel arms.

When Maj. Gen. Sherman heard of the attack he was outraged to think "that people there or in connivance with them [guerrillas] should fire on an unarmed boat." Cooling down, he determined to retaliate. Col. C.C. Walcutt and companies from the 46th Ohio Volunteer Infantry were quickly ordered to board the *Eugene* and another boat quickly chartered and return to Randolph.

At daybreak the next morning, the Yankee soldiers stormed ashore. Walcutt explained to Randolph's citizens that the soldiers who had come in "deeply deplored" vengeance and that the townspeople must flee, to protect themselves and their boats, the Federals were making a draconian example of the town. Randolph was burned, leaving, at Sherman's direct order, but "one house to mark the place." Once the deed was finished, the soldiers that had come from Memphis aboard the *Eugene* were embarked aboard the contract steamer for the return trip; the *Eugene*, herself, continued upriver past Cairo to St. Louis.

Upon the regiment's return, Sherman wrote to Grant that "Randolph is gone." "It is no use tolerating such acts as firing on steamboats," he added. "Punishment must be speedy, sure, and exemplary." It was vital that Union commanders do everything possible to protect the craft in order to stop "such acts as decoying them to the shore and firing on them regardless of the parties on board."

Writing home, Sherman reviewed his pragmatic approach. "We cannot reach the real actors, but cannot overlook these acts of outrage. Therefore, we punish the neighbors for not preventing them."

The number of assaults on steamers in the Memphis area briefly slowed; they did not stop for long. On Friday morning, September 26, two separate attacks were made on steamers near Ashport, TN, 160 miles below Cairo and a dozen miles above Fort Pillow, by Capt. W.W. Faulkner's large guerrilla band.

In the first, the *Forest Queen*,[11] under Capt. C. Dan Conway and Pilot John H. Meeker, en route up from Memphis to Cairo, was almost caught during a scheduled stop. In order to put off a passenger and pick up a shipment of cotton for which she was contracted, the boat landed at Ashport not long after sunrise. The cotton was piled on the river bank and, as the crew was putting out the line to shore, a band of 80 to 100 guerrillas, led by Capt. Faulkner, sprang from behind the bales and demanded the *Queen's* surrender. The Rebel chief and about a dozen men clamored aboard while the others opened fire on the pilothouse.

Pilot Meeker later reported that 29 balls passed through, two of which wounded him slightly, but did not prevent him from turning the wheel and the boat from her levee-bound course. Despite further tussles in both the engine room and the pilothouse, Capt. Conway and loyal hands were able to get the boat off shore, thereby preventing additional boarding.

As the *Queen* was turning away, the 354-ton side-wheeler *Sunshine*[12] hove in sight, carrying a battalion of the 1st Wisconsin Cavalry en route to Memphis from St. Louis, via Cairo. The sight scared Faulkner and his men into making a rapid escape. Although a few passengers were robbed in the process, Clerk Billy Blanker was able to secret away most of the $30,000 in government money Faulkner knew was aboard and had come for.

En route from Cairo to Memphis, the *John J. Roe*[13] passed Ashport about 11 A.M. There a dozen horsemen were seen riding up to the bank. These quickly dismounted and leveled their rifles across their horses' backs, pouring a fusillade into the boat. Two balls passed directly through the pilothouse, but the pilot, who had recently installed iron plates in this area, was unhurt. As the vessel ran out of musket range, a meeting was held between the boat's officers and male passengers. It was decided that, in case of another attack, all would now arm themselves with carbines from a supply of arms being shipped to the 16th Illinois Cavalry.

It was a wise choice. When the *Roe* passed within 150 yards of shore near Randolph Bluff about 12:15 P.M., she was attacked again. This time 100 of Faulkner's men came with a 6-pdr field gun, which they fired at the steamer. Riflemen aboard the *Roe* dropped two of the cannoneers and their deadly aim forced the insurgents to abandon their big gun. A brisk musketry exchange continued for some miles as the horsemen pursued the steamer along the bank, firing at her from behind trees and fences. Eventually the seven-year-old Cincinnati-built *Roe* gathered sufficient speed to escape.

Undoubtedly sounding her whistle, the *John J. Roe* reached Memphis that evening before sundown. Her arrival brought Maj. Gen. Sherman, officers, newsmen, and others to the wharf to hear of her escape and inspect her damage. Believing they had killed 4 or 5 guerrillas, the survivors admitted to only one casualty, a wounded porter. The boat, on the other hand, was badly shot up. Exclusive of those that perforated her chimneys, 80 to 100 bullets had struck the side-wheeler. No fewer than 23 balls hit her Texas deck and pilothouse. One ball passed through the escape pipe and several others through state-rooms occupied by ladies, none of whom were hit.

Although the passengers and crew aboard the *John J. Roe* were undoubtedly terrified, they were also lucky. First and foremost, Confederate partisans and guerrillas were not yet sufficiently sophisticated to adequately employ cannon. And barring a lucky shot, a steamboat was too big a target to stop with rifle fire. Once regular troops began employing field guns against transports and gunboats, the story would change.

It was equally impractical to burn another town in reprisal for these assaults or "send parties of infantry to chase these wanton guerrillas." Maj. Gen. Sherman now published a banishment decree. Henceforth, for every steamer shot at, 10 known Memphis secessionist families would be sent beyond the lines. Additional reprisal raids were not ruled out.[14]

On October 1, the Western Gunboat Fleet, brought into being under jurisdiction of the War Department for operations on the western waters, was officially transferred to the Navy Department and renamed the Mississippi Squadron. Cmdr. David Dixon Porter was jumped several grades to be appointed acting rear admiral and ordered to relieve Rear Admiral Davis, who had commanded the force since June. The changeover in top squadron leadership did not occur that day as Porter was still on his way from Washington, D.C., conducting inspections en route.

Rear Adm. Davis, meanwhile, availed himself of his remaining tenure to clean up as much squadron business as possible. Among the details not overlooked, as noted in an October 2 report to Navy Secretary Welles, was rank title revisions. In the shortly-to-be-approved Davis list, for example, all first masters in the Western Flotilla were appointed USN acting volunteer lieutenants, third masters became acting ensigns, etc.

Launched in August, the Confederate advance into Kentucky was halted by a Union victory at Perryville on October 7. An enterprise begun with hope of glory ended in hesitancy and withdrawal. Still, the Bluegrass incursion caused great consternation in Union circles. Maj. Gen. William S. Rosecrans took command at Nashville on October 23 and within five days, the Rebel Army of Tennessee was back at Murfreesboro. There it would wait while "Old Rosy," under orders to advance, built up and supplied the Army of the Cumberland.

Although the story of the irregular anti-shipping war as reported in the newspapers of the day seemed to shift back and forth from the Memphis area in late September to the Ohio River in October and thereafter to the Cumberland and Tennessee, the truth is that it was pervasive on the Mississippi and all of its major tributaries. Convenient Confederate attack points seemed to be everywhere.

For example, "The most sustained and serious threats to the Union hold on the lower Cumberland," wrote Richard Gildrie in 1990, "originated south of the river." Specifically, the most worrisome points were the Yellow Creek district in southern Montgomery County, TN (about 13 miles southwest of Clarksville bordering Dickson County), and the Dickson County seat of Charlotte. To the northeast and northwest of the town were the two main "attack positions" from which Confederate forces would plague Cumberland river traffic and the Union Navy over the next months: Harpeth

Rear Adm. David Dixon Porter (1813–1891) commanded the Mississippi Squadron from October 1862 till October 1864. During that time, the colorful leader not only endorsed the light-draught concept, but vastly expanded the number of tinclads available, including some sent to the West Gulf Coast Blockading Squadron. Working closely with the U.S. Army, Porter most notably participated in the siege and capture of Vicksburg in 1862–1863 and the Red River expedition of 1864. During the latter adventure, he briefly took over the tinclad *Cricket*, guiding her out of a dangerous Confederate trap (Library of Congress).

Shoals and the bluffs overlooking the community of Palmyra. The Navy tinclads, with Army quartermaster help, would be responsible for ensuring Rosecrans's supply convoys negotiated those chokepoints.

On October 14, the first two purpose-modified tinclads, the *Brilliant* and *St. Clair*, reported to Lt. Cmdr. Fitch at Evansville. There the crews were reviewed, the boats and men worked up to battle proficiency, and various flotilla strategies discussed.

When he took over the Mississippi Squadron on October 15, Acting Rear Adm.

Porter found himself with a mountain of administrative and operational concerns and ploughed straight into these with zeal. It was common knowledge that his goal was a renewed campaign against Vicksburg, for which he now prepared. *New York Herald* reporter Thomas Knox informed his readers on October 28 that the new flotilla would "soon move down the river to clear away all Rebel obstructions, including guerrillas, movable batteries, and formidable works on the bluffs of Vicksburg."

Almost as soon as he started his new duties, the colorful bearded seadog found the guerrilla menace to be one of his command's most troublesome problems. These irregulars were "firing on unarmed vessels from the river banks and at places not occupied by United States troops, when the steamers stopped...." It was also widely believed that "large quantities of goods were intentionally landed [along the river banks] for the rebels and shipped from St. Louis" by unscrupulous businessmen and agents. Porter would deal harshly with irregular warfare, authorizing or condoning blockades, port closures, aggressive convoys and patrols, and retaliations.[15]

By mid–October, "nearly every boat ... which landed at the Evansville wharf told of encountering guerrillas." The *Evansville Daily Journal* ran frequent stories of steamer encounters with irregular Confederate forces. The unsuccessful attempt to take the *Eugene* at Randolph, TN, was covered in its pages, largely because the Ohio River packet was built at Parkersburg, VA, and, as flagboat of Capt. Anson Ballard's Louisville & Henderson Mail Line, was a frequent visitor. An attack upon the *D.B. Campbell*[16] near Uniontown, KY, was also reported in this newspaper. The *Campbell* was familiar to local readers because she was home-ported at Evansville.

Almost as if to insult Acting Rear Adm. Porter upon his taking command of the Mississippi Squadron, irregular forces stepped up the number of steamboat attacks. Assaults were made on three boats in two widely separated locations over a two–day period.

On Wednesday, October 15, men from Adam "Stovepipe" Johnson's command forcibly boarded, with shots exchanged, the U.S. mail steamer *Hazel Dell*[17] at Caseyville, KY, and robbed her of post and a quantity of goods. Several African-Americans aboard were abducted from the unarmed stern-wheeler.

Out on the Mississippi, Capt. Faulkner's men reappeared on the Arkansas shore on October 16, this time with a 12-pdr. howitzer. As the side-wheelers *Continental*[18] and *John H. Dickey*[19] passed their masked location "at a point near the boundary line of Missouri" at the foot of Island No. 21, the Southern gunners opened fire. The 282-foot Pittsburg-built *Continental* was hit once in her hull, but suffered no serious damage.

A later report indicated that the *Dickey* was also struck. All were relieved that no passengers were hurt. The ironclad *Pittsburg* would be sent to investigate the Island No. 21 incident on October 17; at Memphis, Maj. Gen. Sherman expelled 20 families.

Word arrived at Evansville on October 16 of the strike against the *Hazel Dell*. Lt. Cmdr. Fitch was ready to pounce when the attack was reported. The energetic sailor quickly had his two new gunboats and the flagship *Fairplay* steaming to the scene, but once again, low water, coupled with thick fog, slowed his response.

While Fitch waited on nature, Confederate raiders struck again, stopping Capt. Thompson's *Cordelia Ann* near Smithland, KY. Although the craft was not sunk, she was stripped of her cargo and 15 African-American deckhands.

Unable to proceed as quickly as desired, Fitch wrote his own blockade orders from the middle of the Ohio River that Friday. These regulations, which were sent by passing steamers or other craft to river communities on both banks, suspended all ferries on the Ohio between Evansville and Paducah (except at the Kentucky towns of Henderson and Smithland).

Additionally, masters of all freight and passenger steamers plying between Evansville and Cairo were prohibited from taking aboard passengers and cargo for or, unless absolutely unavoidable, landing at any point on the Kentucky shore not garrisoned by U.S. forces. Further, all boats, skiffs, scows, or flatboats found along the Kentucky shore at unguarded locales were subject to destruction along with all goods, merchandise, or other articles of traffic sold or sent to the Kentucky shore which had not been authorized by a port or other U.S. official.

Meanwhile, overland runners were able to reach Caseyville ahead of the Union tin-

The *Signal* was the first of the purchased and purpose-altered light-draught ("tinclad") gun-boats sent to war. Fresh from her outfitting in early November 1862, the stern-wheeler was ordered to Helena, Arkansas, to support the activities of the lower unit of the Mississippi Squadron, then assembling craft to assist a Federal expedition to the Yazoo River (*Miller's Photographic History*).

clads, sounding a warning which permitted Johnson's *Hazel Dell* attackers "and many of the most prominent aiders and abettors" to escape. When the *Fairplay, Brilliant*, and *St. Clair* rounded to off the community on the morning of October 18, detachments from the three, under the command of Second Master Groves, went ashore, surrounded the town, and detained all the Caucasian men they found.

Upon inspection, Lt. Cmdr. Fitch found that a few "good" Union men were in town during the raid, but these had been forcibly restrained and prevented from warning off the mail steamer. "The worst and most rabid persons," the sailor later reported encountering, were "the farmers living a mile or so from town. They are the ones who have been feeding and keeping Johnson's men, and the ones also who shared the spoils of the late robbery."

Taking a leaf from Maj. Gen. Sherman's book, the Mosquito Flotilla commander posted a notice of warning to local inhabitants that they were being held accountable for the assault. The naval officer demanded, on his own authority, that the citizens of Caseyville and those 10 miles inland in surrounding Union County collectively pay reparations of $50,000 by 10 P.M. that evening. If the "good current money" was not forthcoming, women and children would be ordered out of town and the whole place burned to ashes.

While Fitch was putting an economic squeeze on Caseyville, Acting Rear Adm. Porter, two days into his new job, appealed for reinforcements. Already he was concerned with his need for additional light-draught vessels for his other regions of responsibility. Urgent requests from the Army for light boats to provide convoy on Arkansas's White River were stacking up. On the 18th, the fleet commander wrote to Com. Joseph B. Hull in St. Louis asking that he forward the tinclads *Signal* and *Marmora* to the tip of Illinois, regardless of whether or not they had yet received their guns.

Porter also dispatched his most famous fighting captain, Henry Walke, to Helena to assume operational control over naval activities on the Mississippi below Memphis. Taking station off Helena, the captain of the famous Pook turtle *Carondelet* found the water level in that area nearly as low as Fitch was encountering on the Ohio.[20]

Meanwhile, the insurgents on the Mississippi continued their work as though the "object lesson" of Randolph had not occurred. On the morning of October 19, the side-wheeler *Gladiator*[21] became the latest target.

En route through Council Bend to Helena from Memphis, this veteran of the St. Louis-to-New Orleans service touched at Bledsoe's Landing, on the Arkansas shore about 45 miles above her destination. As her stages were lowered, a party of guerrillas, pistols blazing, stormed aboard. In the following melee, the engineer and a passenger were killed. Simultaneously, a rush of passengers sought the safety of the shore and, as they were escaping, distracted the raiders. Her veteran captain, John Simpson Klinefelter, ordered the *Gladiator* to back off and make steam for Memphis. When the undamaged steamer reached Memphis, Klinefelter reported to the Federal army on the attack and the MIA status of 32 of his crew and passengers. Several of these later turned up in a shanghaied yawl.

Not long after the *Gladiator* assault, in another bend of the Mississippi some nine miles below Memphis, the side-wheeler *Catahoula*[22] was fired into by bushwhackers hiding along the river bank. Two aboard the Helena mail boat were killed and several others were wounded in the fusillade. Her captain ordered more speed and the vessel soon reached Memphis with details of her misfortune.

Upriver at Caseyville later that day, Lt. Cmdr. Fitch perhaps realized that his ferocious order did not differentiate between those pledging support to the Union and those who did not. Consequently, his ransom order was modified. Payment was reduced to $35,000, due in a week. If the cash was not ready, "the property of all secessionists or sympathizers ... will be confiscated and their houses, furniture, grain, and produce of all kinds destroyed." A guard was posted who ensured that, over the next seven days, nothing was removed; meanwhile, a number of men who could not explain themselves were clapped into irons and sent off to Cairo, via Smithland, for further interrogation and processing.

Implementing his duly-announced policies, Maj. Gen. Sherman, down at Memphis, reacted strongly to the attacks on the *Gladiator* and *Catahoula*. In addition running 20 more secessionist families out of his town, the city's commander once again sent soldiers to the scene in retaliation. Within a day or so, Col. Walcutt's Buckeye soldiers, protected by the ironclad *Baron de Kalb*, destroyed all of the houses and crops of the plantations stretching along the river bank for seven miles in every direction of the *Catahoula* strike.

Meanwhile, 300 men were transported to Elm Grove, just beyond Bledsoe's Landing, escorted by the ironclad *Louisville*, to punish the town's perceived guerrilla supporters for the *Gladiator* attack. After landing and giving the populace half an hour to evacuate, the Federals burned the town. The village of Hamblin, two miles further down the Mississippi, "was similarly served."

Demonstrating a pragmatic yet determined response to the *Hazel Dell* attack, Navyman Fitch acted against the Ohio River town of Caseyville without knowledge of Acting Rear Adm. Porter's position on irregular containment. His retribution was far less direct than Sherman's.

The first counterinsurgency operation by the new upper river Mosquito Flotilla could have ended badly for its 28-year-old executive officer if Porter had chosen to disavow the action. Communications being what they were, Fitch did not know the impact of his action up the command chain until October 21.

That Tuesday a mail sack arrived for the *Fairplay*'s skipper at Caseyville with a communication from the admiral, who enclosed a copy of his newly-issued General Orders Nos. 2 and 4 regarding warship operations and anti-guerrilla precautions. "I had already acted according to my own judgment," Fitch recorded, and was quite possibly relieved and "happy to say, nearly in conformity" to orders. In fact, Porter, who saw guerrilla warfare as "an outrageous practice," actually wanted a fee 10 times greater than that levied by Fitch and the arrest of all white male citizens not known to be of "good, loyal" character.

Under Porter's orders, retribution for attacks on steamers or Federal posts or men was expected. The squadron commander's view, shared by Generals Grant, Sherman, and several other Northern political and military leaders in the Western theater, bears quoting as it both grants a permission and sets a tone for actions which followed:

When any of our vessels are fired on it will be the duty of the commander to fire back with spirit, and to destroy everything in that neighborhood within reach of his guns. There is no impropriety in destroying houses supposed to be affording shelter to rebels, and it is the only way to stop guerrilla warfare. Should innocent persons suffer it will be their own fault, and teach others that it will be to their advantage to inform the Government authorities when guerrillas are about certain localities.

Despite the grimness of Porter's message, "the countermeasures taken by the Federal commanders," wrote historian Davidson, "never had more than a local effect." As Alfred T. Mahan put it:

The ruling feeling in the country favored the Confederate cause, so that every hamlet and farm-house gave a refuge to these marauders, while at the same time the known existence of some Union feeling made it hard for officers to judge, in all cases, whether punishment should fall on the places where the attacks were made.

Frank Cooling summarized the dilemma a century later as a vicious circle: "Supply route interruption followed by local foraging, succeeded by civil disobedience and rising partisan activity, followed ultimately by harsh retribution."

Assaults on Mississippi and Ohio River shipping did not cease after the Caseyville, *Gladiator*, or *Catahoula* incidents. About two miles above Curlew, KY, on October 21, guerrillas, attacking from a thick cluster of woods and brush, shot up Capt. P.K. Barclay's stern-wheeler *Nashville*;[23] one man aboard was killed and another wounded. When the pride of the Pioneer Line reached her next port, Shawneetown, witnesses could see 16 bullet holes in her pilothouse.

Lt. Cmdr. Fitch received word of the *Nashville* attack that evening via a messenger from Capt. Barclay. The *Fairplay* immediately steamed down to Shawneetown, and next day convoyed the *Nashville* up to the head of Mississippi Bend, above Uniontown. En route, the steamer was fired into at the foot of Cincinnati Bar; however, the tinclad was close behind and shelled the attackers off.

The continuing Confederate assault on riverborne shipping threatened to cut communications between certain towns and points. To counteract the partisans on the Mississippi, Acting Rear Adm. Porter instituted a thrice-weekly convoy system for that stream on October 28, announced days earlier in handbills posted at landings located between Cairo and Helena. Steamboat captains, military and civilian, desiring naval protection were instructed to make application of the squadron commanders at Helena, Memphis, or Cairo. Three hours before setting out, the escort commander would hoist a white flag with a blue cross and fire a gun as assembly notice.

Protection was also to be made available, assuming there was advance notice, for cotton speculators wishing to stop en route and pick up cotton. Its export prohibited by the Confederacy and its import banned under the blockade, cotton, the "white gold" of the Civil War, was in great demand for New England textile mills.

The initial escort duties were handled by the timberclads *Lexington*, *Conestoga*, and *Tyler* and by other auxiliaries. As time went on and the tinclads entered the picture, this naval escort of merchantmen in organized groups became an essential element of the Mississippi Squadron's counterinsurgency effort. It was practiced with regularity throughout the remainder of the conflict.

There were drawbacks to the convoy system. In order for the boats to complete their up and down turnarounds, it was necessary for shipping to idle — often for as long as a week — at river towns waiting for the escorts to return and scheduled convoys to assemble. At main ports like Nashville, the arrival of large quantities of goods at one time made offloading dispersal to terminals and other land locations confusing and difficult. Still, this inland river convoy system became so efficient that requests for convoy from army quartermasters stacked up at every port-of-call on the Mississippi and its tributaries.[24]

The Evansville-based Mosquito Flotilla was hampered by low water for the remainder of the year. The same problem plagued units out on the Mississippi as far down as Helena. On the plus side, additional light-draught reinforcements for the Mississippi Squadron were received from the river-front boat yards in Missouri and Ohio. Most of these initial reinforcements were not tasked to the anti-guerrilla war. Rather, they directly augmented the main fleet as it once more steamed against Vicksburg.

On October 22, Naval Constructor Edward Hartt at the Eads yards at Carondelet wired good news to the St. Louis headquarters of Com. Hull. Following a brief commissioning ceremony, the *Signal*, which Acting Rear Adm. Porter had personally inspected two weeks earlier, had departed for Cairo that morning at 7 A.M. Upon leaving, she drew 21 inches forward and 22 inches aft. The *Marmora*, with an equal displacement and a similar brief acceptance, left in her company. The former was captained by First Master John Scott and the latter by Acting Volunteer Lt. Robert Getty.

It would take approximately three weeks for the first purpose-modified tinclads to complete their outfit at Cairo. Guns, coal, and stores were taken aboard, men were shipped, and the boats were worked up in much the same manner as the vessels in the flotilla of Lt. Cmdr. Fitch.[25]

On November 2, Maj. Gen. Ulysses S. Grant led the Army of the Tennessee south from Bolivar, TN, on a campaign into central Mississippi designed to not only capture a huge portion of that state, but to reopen the Mississippi River. Hoping to reach Granada and attract all regional Confederate defenders, the Buckeye general believed that Maj. Gen. William Tecumseh Sherman, with Navy support, could move out of Memphis and capture Vicksburg from the rear. Although Acting Rear Adm. Porter declared himself ready to participate, Grant's month-long military campaign was fought out of sight of the vessels of his Mississippi Squadron. In a speedy advance, Northern troops acquired Holly Springs, where a supply base was established, and reached Oxford.

November was administratively busy for Porter and his officers. Due to the falling river stage, there was little action on the Mississippi, save the continuing war on irregulars and the government-sanctioned effort to obtain Rebel cash crops.

The picture on the Ohio River was much the same as it was on the Mississippi. By November 2, it was necessary for Lt. Commander Fitch to inform Cairo that the water stage in the Ohio had reached a point where it was "impossible for the gunboats to get either up or down the river." The situation was so bad that it would injure the little warships if they were dragged over the sandbars and, consequently, no more trips could be made downriver until it rose. This was a big regret as Confederate irregulars were reported as being "very bad between Wabash Island and Ford's Ferry, below Caseyville."

This is not to say, however, that Fitch was without either his increasingly famous initiative or resources. Borrowing back the leaf first demonstrated by Indiana Legion Colonel Foster with the *Lou Eaves* in September and simultaneously imitated by himself, the Logansport sailor put an officer, a gun crew, and a 12-pounder howitzer aboard several ultra-light-draught mail steamers plying the river. The practice began with the *May Duke* and some men under Master Groves. Some months later, the Lt. Commander was able to recall the results with pride:

> Guerrillas on several occasions made so bold as to present them-selves on the banks and hail the steamers in, but receiving rather unexpected and severe lessons from the howitzers, soon learned to let the vessels pass unmolested.

On November 4, Porter ordered Capt. Walke to offer convoy to vessels from Helena to Memphis and to protect them "while they are picking up cotton and tobacco on the way up." The tall and gaunt-looking Walke, upon receipt of the directive four days later, agreed to do so "if there is a sufficient depth of water." He added: "A few of the light-draft armed steamers would be very convenient for this service."

The admiral, on November 14, ordered Lt. Cmdr. James W. Shirk of the timberclad *Lexington* and First Master Scott of the *Signal* to provide protection to a civilian boat, owned by a Mr. Tucker and with soldiers embarked, about to engage in the confiscation of cotton along the river banks south of Helena. Although this was to be the first Mississippi River operation for any of the new tinclads, the *Signal* and her consort were not to land their men or engage in any direct acquisition on their own.

With Hunter delayed, the *Lexington* and *Signal* steamed to Helena. A message was found there from Capt. Walke ordering any arriving light-draughts sent below to join him off Montgomery Point, at the mouth of White River, as he covered a planned waterborne army expedition into Arkansas. Reacting to his subordinate's report of conditions, Acting Rear Adm. Porter advised him not to risk getting aground just because the military "had the White River fever." There would soon be "seven light drafts for that business."

The *Signal*, meanwhile, was dispatched downstream and found the *Carondelet* struggling against the current. The campaign had been aborted and Walke was slowly paddling toward his Helena headquarters. The *Signal* towed the big ironclad back upstream, demonstrating her tugging capabilities — yet another tinclad attribute often shown in the months ahead.

In the middle of November, Maj. Gens. Grant and Sherman, in collaboration with Porter, initiated plans for a second effort to overwhelm Vicksburg and "liberate" the last 250 miles of the Mississippi held by the Confederacy. While Grant came in from the east, Sherman and Porter would undertake an amphibious operation up the Yazoo River. If the strategy worked, the Southern citadel would be squeezed between the Federal forces and the wide river.

The commander of the Mississippi Squadron wrote Sherman of his desire to cooperate in any downriver enterprise on November 12. From that point on, almost all of the newly arriving tinclads were assigned, for the duration, to direct amphibious support, in some fashion or another, of the Vicksburg campaign. Their slight drafts would make them invaluable close-in vessels, much as their destroyer descendants that served off Normandy and the Pacific beaches in World War II.

Meanwhile, low water also continued to plague naval operations on the Ohio River, giving guerrillas and contraband traffickers continued opportunity for mischief. Toward the middle of November, all steamers with government contracts were summarily prohibited from ascending Kentucky's Green River, across the Ohio from Evansville.

For some time, another expedition against Vicksburg was the talk of the river — and of newspapermen reporting from its local towns. Frank Knox of the *New York Herald* revealed the idea at the end of October and, on November 11, Junius Henri Browne of the *New York Tribune* told his readers that there was considerable doubt in his mind — and Acting Rear Adm. Porter's, he presumed — that a waterborne campaign could get "fairly under way before a rise occurs in the river."

Before any ascent could be made up the Yazoo, the Northern commanders had to be certain that no masked batteries or other obstructions were present to block their progress. If any were found, they had to be isolated or removed. At the same time, waterways and possible landing areas had to be secured. To handle these requirements, Porter, on November 21, ordered Capt. Walke to take a force of ironclads and several lighter vessels from Helena down to the mouth of that river. Additionally, a message was sent to the *Marmora*, then off Cairo, to proceed downstream at flank speed and join Walke's division, hopefully before it departed Helena. It would, in fact, fall to the tinclads to make the initial reconnaissance into the Yazoo. Such scouts in advance of military action would become a common duty for the little warships.

Elsewhere on November 23, the *Evansville Daily Journal* reported that no mail could be sent from Indiana to any Kentucky town on the Ohio River except Henderson, Smithville, and Paducah due to "guerrilla problems." The Green River mails had to go by way of Owensboro. Lt. Cmdr. Fitch found it necessary to issue the edict because he could not get up that stream and unarmed steamers from Evansville and Louisville were transporting their freight right into the guerrilla sanctuaries. "I must say," he later wrote, "I was very much surprised at the loose manner in which surveyors of customs permitted cases of boots, clothing, and the like to pass into the Green River country, it being at the time almost entirely under the control of organized guerrilla bands." The ban could hopefully be lifted when the rivers rose.

Having weighed from Helena on November 25 in company with the tugboat *Laurel*, the *Mound City*, *Signal* and *Marmora*, the *Carondelet* dropped anchor off Milliken's Bend, above the mouth of the Yazoo River, three days later. Two coal barges towed down by the tinclads were anchored nearby under guard. While the newest tinclads and their ironclad consorts push south, let us review the end of the month with the Ohio River mosquito flotilla.

Back in the spring of 1862, following the triumphs at Fort Henry and Fort Donelson, Maj. Gen. Don Carlos Buell had optimistically written to his superiors that, with Nashville as a springboard, his Union army could "operate east, west, or south. All our arrangements should look to a centralization of our forces [in the city]." Now with his successor, Maj. Gen. William S. Rosecrans, in charge, this axiom was seen as truer than ever from Tennessee to Washington, D.C.

The Cumberland River was the largest road into the city for the vast and necessary quantities of goods needed to equip the Army of the Cumberland. Soldiers, animals, food, forage, wagons and harness, clothing and dry goods, camp or garrison equipment, hospital supplies, and even items down to stationery were taken down gangplanks from the boats and dispersed from a large landing. A careful and deliberate man, Maj. Gen. Rosecrans was appalled at the damage done to the city's northern railroad artery by Rebel raiders over the past weeks and early in his tenure as Nashville's new military chief "came to rely upon the Cumberland River as his principal transportation artery to the North."

Aware that John Hunt Morgan in particular had been and probably would continue to be effective against his land lifeline, Rosecrans recognized that keeping the Cumberland functioning without Southern interference — when water levels permitted — was a matter to be accomplished at all costs. For the 46 days after his arrival, Rosecrans would wait in Nashville, "a Union island in a Confederate sea," building up his troops and supply strength and calculating the proper moment to advance.

On November 14, Rosecrans wired Maj. Gen. Henry Halleck in Washington, D.C., seeking additional troops and took the occasion — the first of several — to ask his superior to intercede with the leadership of the Navy Department to request "some provisions for gunboats to patrol the Tennessee and Cumberland Rivers." These patrols, he explained, could help keep down attacks by Rebel irregulars upon river traffic and even go so far as to prevent expected guerrilla attempts to blockade the river by blasting rocks into it.

It was now about time for the Cumberland to begin its fall rise. Late on November 20, the winds shifted and the clear nights enjoyed earlier gave way to rains so heavy they flooded Nashville's streets. Early next morning, mist covered the riverfront and the Cumberland was up over an inch. Despite this welcome news, the week that followed saw Morgan and his men again sowing confusion against Union rail and road transport and stalling the promised advance by the Army of the Cumberland. It was in this time of confusion that Rosecrans's mid-month petition reached Acting Rear Adm. Porter.

The fire-eating Mississippi Squadron CO on November 27 ordered Lt. Cmdr. Fitch to begin active patrols of the Tennessee and Cumberland Rivers. Claiming that he did not need to give his subordinate "precise instructions," he did just that, requiring that no means was to be left for Rebels to cross the rivers — "all small boats likely to carry intelligence" were to be destroyed and all Rebel property captured. Although Porter believed Fitch knew his views on counter-guerrilla warfare "pretty well by this time," these thoughts were summarized in two pithy sentences: "You can never go wrong in doing a Rebel all the harm you can.... I am no advocate for the milk and water policy." A hundred years later in another place of riverine conflict, "milk and water" would be reborn as "hearts and minds."

The Navy boss anticipated that the Evansville-based light-draught flotilla would soon have "water enough" to navigate in Tennessee waters. In closing his written command, Porter, who was at that time also concerned with Army plans for Vicksburg, gave Fitch a "left-handed" compliment. Acknowledging a continued belief in the young tar's ability to engineer success largely on his own hook, he closed simply: "I look to you to see that quiet is maintained there."

The call for action downstream reached Lt. Cmdr. Fitch at Evansville three days after it was written, just as the *Brilliant* was returning from Owensboro. As Porter had surmised, the winter "rise" was beginning.

Writing from a troop boat far below, the *New York Times* correspondent Franc B. Wilkie, known as "Galway" to his readers, now took the time to describe the local geography of the Vicksburg region. He noted that a line of hills ran from the Rebel citadel and struck the Yazoo about 20 miles above its mouth. The country between the river and the bluffs was alluvial, with swamps and lakes. It was known as the "Bottoms" of Mississippi. At the northern intersecting point of hills and waterway on the Yazoo, there was a fort of eight or nine guns called Haynes Bluff. All the way back down to Vicksburg, "the slope of the hills toward the river is fortified to command every accessible avenue of approach." The rich land up to the river bank was home to "a half dozen plantations scattered here and there, while along the river and around the lakes are built broad, high levees."

Capt. Walke, still suffering from the malaria he had contracted when last above Vicksburg in July, was well familiar with the area's physical features, though he was professionally quite interested in finding any defensive improvements made by the Rebels during the intervening months. Late on the afternoon of November 28, Capt. Walke ordered Pilot Joseph Smith, a Yazoo pilot who had come down aboard the *Marmora* at Acting Rear Adm. Porter's instruction, and Acting Ensign H.H. Walker from that tinclad to take the *Laurel* and make a reconnaissance down toward the entrance into the Yazoo. Within an hour, she returned, Ensign Walker having been wounded (not dangerously) by a volley from shore.

Acting upon orders received the previous evening, Acting Volunteer Lt. Getty's *Marmora*, followed closely by the *Signal*, weighed anchor at 10 A.M. on November 29 on a Yazoo reconnaissance. Pilot Smith, who knew that the Confederates were building a fort upstream, urged caution over the initial bars and shoals and the two vessels steamed slowly, taking soundings. Having penetrated five miles, Getty found a consistent five-foot river depth and so continued on up without opposition from White House Shoals to Twelve Mile Bayou. Shortly after noon, butternut cavalry on picket duty were seen, but these dispersed. A bit later, a log shanty serving as a picket station was discovered; all nearby fled after firing at the boats. The tinclads halted in midstream and the *Marmora's* gunners destroyed the structure.

The scout continued, with Confederate outriders seen frequently. Approximately an hour after the picket cabin was destroyed, men on shore at Anthony's Ferry, about 21 miles up the Yazoo, volleyed the light draughts. Howitzers, Parrotts, and carbines fired in reply.

The *Marmora* and *Signal* continued on for another mile and a half until batteries were discovered at Drumgould's Bluff. These were the fortifications Pilot Smith had reported earlier. A careful examination, mostly by spyglass, was conducted, and Getty and Scott both concluded the guns a formidable obstacle. The tinclads rounded to and returned down the river, reaching the Mississippi about 4 P.M.

Getty quickly went aboard the *Carondelet* to report his findings. Although there was more water in the Yazoo than Walke had expected, it was still insufficient for his ironclad or the *Mound City* to enter.

The *Chicago Daily Tribune* noted on December 1 that the water in the Yazoo River was rising and was higher than that in the Mississippi. Indeed, any boat drawing more than eight feet could not cross the bar off Helena. The same day, Capt. Walke wrote to his superior indicating that he would be sending the *Marmora* and *Signal* on another Yazoo reconnaissance within a day or two.

Meanwhile, to the north, the Evansville fleet, carrying all of the property acquired from the "Rebels" at Caseyville, departed for Cairo. It would return to Paducah within three days.

During this time, the *Signal* and *Marmora* returned up the Yazoo as promised, indeed, becoming regular visitors. Soon they were engaged on a dangerous assignment to sweep the river clear of underwater mines (then called "torpedoes"). Even as this drama began to unfold on the Yazoo, the antishipping and anticontraband war out on the Mississippi and up on the Ohio, Cumberland, and Tennessee continued, sometimes netting a success for one side and sometimes for the other.

As the reader will remember from our discussion of contraband trade in Chapter 2, private trading vessels, sometimes operating with local licenses, busily plied the Mississippi, exchanging forbidden items with Confederates for cotton. This was a serious problem by early December. On December 3, one H.J. Brooks at Cairo sent an intelligence report to Acting Rear Adm. Porter informing him that, since at least November, a number of steamers had been permitted to pass Helena with full or partial contraband cargoes down into Rebel-controlled territory. Among the five boats named were the *Blue Wing No. 2*[26] and the *Lake City*.[27] Some had permits from U.S. Army generals or the Helena or Memphis boards of trade.

Acting Rear Adm. Porter decided that the Mississippi Squadron would put an end to waterborne contraband trade "with the Rebels." In General Order 21 of December 3, he required his commanders to board suspicious steamers, including any encountered below Helena, especially those named by Brooks. If the stopped craft were found with prohibited items, they were to be seized. Porter's vessels were to halt all commerce "carried on at any points not occupied by United States troops, no matter what permits they may have unless they are mine."

Having repositioned to an anchorage off Paducah, the *Fairplay*, *Brilliant*, *St. Clair*, *General Pillow*, and *Alfred Robb* made a trip up the Tennessee River beginning on December 4. The five could not ascend beyond Duck River due to the shoals and so returned north. The *Pillow* and *Robb* were left at Paducah and the three larger craft hop scotched back to Evansville.

Upstream at Louisville, the rise which had assisted Fitch to reach Duck River continued to increase in volume. Deepening levels in the Ohio were seen in the Cumberland and Tennessee. As the streams inched slowly up their banks, a preacher of Confederate persuasion in Shelbyville was heard to pray: "O Lord, let the rain descend to fructify the earth and to swell the rivers, but O Lord, do not raise the Cumberland sufficient to bring upon us those damn Yankee gunboats."

As the rivers rose, Lt. Cmdr. Fitch, acting with his usual independent zeal, once more stopped all steamers not in U.S. employ from passing up Green River. By now, Fitch, like Porter with the contraband traders steaming out of Memphis, had lost patience with U.S. surveyors of ports who would, in the absence of Navy units, pass contraband articles up the waterway, failing for whatever reason to discriminate between forbidden and legitimate trade articles. It was hoped that this action would prevent guerrillas from getting supplies from the Green River area.

To further ensure that nature's semiannual beneficence did not aid the Confederates as the streams continued to swell, Maj. Gen. Rosecrans would issue his own proclamation on Christmas Eve prohibiting all steamboats not under U.S. contract from trading up the Green or Cumberland rivers.

On December 8, as a squadron of Col. Wirt Adams's 1st Mississippi Cavalry was scouting the northern end of Washington County, MS, locals near Carson's Landing, 65 miles below Helena, informed it of a familiar Memphis-based trading vessel approaching from up the river. Often engaged in an illegal ("contraband") commerce with Confederate citizens, providing goods for cotton, the *Lake City* was a tempting target.

The Rebel squadron commander determined to take the stern-wheeler by ruse. A number of cotton bales were hauled to the river bank where they could be clearly seen, after which the dismounted horse soldiers hid themselves behind the levee. Sure enough, and by and by, the "Yankee hucksters," as they were called in Southern newspaper accounts of the event, saw the valuable produce and were decoyed to shore.

Immediately after the steamboat was made fast, the Rebel charge sounded. The butternut riders swarmed over the bank and quickly and bloodlessly secured their prize. In addition to the passengers and crew, plus 42 Northern soldiers, all made POW, the vessel was transporting an astonishing amount of goods. One eyewitness reported that the haul included:

> ...several hundred pairs of boots and shoes, clothing of all kinds, calicos, domestics, flannel, tobacco, fifteen barrels of whiskey, cheese, soda, salt, pepper, cotton and wool cards, and a great many other useful articles.

Twenty wagons from the surrounding countryside were pressed into service to haul the booty to the regimental camp near Greenville, on Deer Creek. As the offloading continued, another boat was heard above. Fearing that it might be a Federal gunboat, the cavalrymen, having obtained the most useful commodities, decided to abandon 200 bales of cotton and 40 sacks of salt remaining aboard. The *Lake City* and her remaining cargo were burnt to the water's edge.

At Helena later in the day, Lt. Cmdr. William Gwin, captain of the ironclad *Benton*, seized Capt. Samuel Saunders's *Blue Wing No. 2* as she eased into the Helena wharf. Basing his action upon December 2's written orders from Acting Rear Adm. Porter, the acting station chief had the vessel searched from stem to stern, finding 30 or more bales of cotton obtained in exchange for bags of salt. Gwin had the vessel anchored in the stream with a guard aboard and wrote to his superior for orders concerning her disposition.

Mississippi Squadron units anchored at the small Arkansas enclave now suspected that the *Lake City* was missing. Not yet possessed of a sizeable tinclad fleet and with heavy demands in hand for support of the Yazoo expedition, Lt. Cmdr. Gwin decided to improvise a search. The nefarious trading reputation of the absent steamer, plus several others, was as well known to the Federal Navy as to the Confederates. This would be an excellent opportunity to crack down on the misconduct of several private traders.

Gwin had one asset that could do the job, the 300-ton side-wheel fleet auxiliary transport *General Lyon*. Captured as the *De Soto* at Island No. 10 in April, she was rechristened on October 24. Built at New Albany, IN, in 1860, the craft had a draught of seven feet; she was 181 feet long and 35 feet wide. Armed with two brass 12-pdr. rifled howitzers, she was under the command of Acting Master John R. Neeld.

Calling Neeld aboard the flag boat, Gwin explained to him, and to his own XO, Acting Volunteer Lt. George P. Lord, that a sweep was required down to a point some 80 miles below Helena. Several private trading vessels were, contrary to law and regulation, making unauthorized stops at points not held by U.S. forces, and trading with the enemy — or at least the enemy population. The two junior officers, leading a party of 20 armed sailors, returned aboard the *General Lyon* and proceeded downstream.

At the foot of Islands No. 62 and 63, the ersatz gunboat came upon the steamer *J.R. Williams*, one of several not mentioned in the compilations of Lytle or Way. Before a small prize crew from the *General Lyon* departed with her for Helena, the trader's captain revealed the fate of the *Lake City*, reporting that her crew and passengers were being held by Adams's cavalry.

The naval vessel steamed on down the river and, upon approaching Hudson's Landing, encountered the 139-foot long side-wheeler *Clarabel*.[28] A review of her papers showed her many miles from her normal Missouri River routes and an acting master's mate was placed in charge. As the two vessels approached the landing, a rider was seen marking their progress. Lt. Lord ordered one of the howitzers to chase him with a shell.

At this point, several of Master Neeld's officers reportedly implored him to turn back, The *General Lyon* was only lightly armed and was steaming in dangerous waters a long way from support. She would not be able to withstand any kind of attack from sizeable Rebel horse cannon. Neeld supposedly addressed their petition in words worthy of John Paul Jones: "I'll go to hell or find the *Lake City* or her crew and passengers, provided they are north of Napoleon."

The *General Lyon* and *Clarabel* were greeted at Carson's Landing by a party of nine African-American men waving a flag of truce. The *Lyon*'s gig was lowered and Master Neeld, together with his chief engineer, were rowed ashore. The visitors provided the navymen with further details concerning the destruction of the *Lake City*. One of the informants, named Joshua, warned Neeld that Confederate irregulars and maybe some of Adams's horsemen still lurked about, but that some of the passengers from the steamer might be found in town.

All of the remaining armed party put aboard the transport by Lt. Cmdr. Gwin were

Captured by the Federals at Island No. 10 in April, the 300-ton *De Soto* was renamed the *General Lyon* in October 24 and assigned duties as one of the Mississippi Squadron's ordnance, stores, and dispatch boats. Because she mounted a pair of wheeled 12-pdr. howitzers (one of which is shown here with a sailor, giving size perspective) in that period before the Western navy possessed a large light-draught ("tinclad") fleet, she was pressed into combat service in December. In a sweep of the river below Helena, Arkansas, made in search of private trading vessels caught in non-permit landings, the 28-man ersatz gunboat prized four vessels, freed passengers from a captured boat, and destroyed a reported 42 buildings. "Not bad," concluded a reporter for the *Milwaukee Daily Sentinel* who summarized the *General Lyon*'s cruise for his readers (Naval Historical Center).

ordered to surround the town and a search was made of its relatively few buildings. With Joshua's assistance, five of the *Lake City* passengers were soon found in a warehouse, together with their baggage. It and they, together with the former slaves, were removed to the *General Lyon*. The remaining prisoners in Confederate hands would be exchanged by the end of the month.

Believing themselves justified in taking stern action, Acting Master Neeld and Acting Volunteer Lt. Lord called all of the little community's inhabitants together and advised them that Carson's Landing would be put to the torch. The citizenry had 15 minutes to remove their property. Hardly had the sailors finished setting fire to the prisoner warehouse, a couple of houses, and some slave quarters than they were taken under fire from the woods at the edge of the clearing.

The Federals retreated aboard the *Lyon* and dropped downstream a short distance to Concordia Landing. The inhabitants of this hamlet had already fled. After a few shells were thrown into the couple of warehouses and houses back of the bank, another landing party went ashore and turned them into blazing ashes. A reporter later testified that prior to setting the homes alight, the bluejackets removed their contents to the single street.

The cruise of the *General Lyon* continued for several more days, moving above Helena as well. During this time, Neeld and Lord freed not only the five passengers and nine African-Americans, but destroyed a reported 42 buildings. Their makeshift cruiser also fell in with and captured two more craft suspected of non-permit trading.

The first was the *Lottie*, another steamer not mentioned in the usual sources, which was taken at Blue Point, about 40 miles above Helena. The second, prized at Helena itself, was the Memphis-Cincinnati Dean Line packet *Lady Pike*.[29] When Master Neeld's boarding party inspected the stern-wheeler, they found, in the words of Lt. Cmdr. Gwin, "a large quantity of contraband articles, salt, shoes, etc." Lt. Cmdr. Gwin sent a prize crew aboard and ordered the steamer to "proceed without delay to Cairo."

The exploits of the *General Lyon* were reported upon at length in the *Milwaukee Daily Sentinel* on December 17. "This for an A-2 dispatch boat carrying 28 men and two 12-pounder brass howitzers," concluded the correspondent, "is not so bad."

The fluid situation concerning trading regulation and licensure changed again on December 10 when Acting Rear Adm. Porter received a new set of regulations from Treasury Secretary Salmon P. Chase concerning internal and coastwise intercourse. After reading them, the Mississippi Squadron chief wrote out another order for his Memphis-Helena commanders explaining the latest development. By Chase's appointment, Thomas H. Yeatman was now the Treasury Department agent at Memphis and would henceforth be issuing trading permits through boards of trade, collectors, or surveyors of ports authorized by himself or his deputies. These would allow private vessels with accurate manifests to clear from Memphis, as well as Helena, Columbus, Hickman, and smaller towns on the river.

The new objective, Porter digested, was not to stifle trade, but to "permit steamboat captains to carry small quantities of family stores to be exchanged for cotton." Even salt, though still classified as a contraband good, could pass "on proper permit."

Naval officers were called upon to assist the Treasury agents and representatives in carrying out this new interpretation, even to "giving protection whenever they can do so." If a vessel were suspected of violating these regulations, it was to be stopped and searched; if a legal permit were found, the vessel was to be freed. If none could be produced, a prize crew was to be sent aboard to take the vessel to the nearest district attorney for adjudication.

The *Blue Wing No. 2* was subsequently allowed to return to Memphis, where she was temporarily chartered by the U.S. Quartermaster Department. Another arrested steamer, the *Catahoula*, was also temporarily detained at the Tennessee port. Treasury agent Yeatman vouched for both craft on December 12 and they were subsequently released. Almost immediately the *Blue Wing No. 2* received orders to return to Helena and take a tow to the main fleet below.

Also on that Friday, Maj. Gen. Grant, writing from Oxford, Mississippi, informed Acting Rear Adm. Porter that a large cavalry force was reported to be moving from Columbia, TN, toward Savannah, TN. These were troops under Brig. Gen. Nathan Bedford Forrest, who had departed for a sojourn into West Tennessee the day before. "Can a light-draught gunboat get up there at this time?" he wondered. Porter informed the Army leader that two tinclads were going up the Tennessee, but could not get above Cuba Ford.

The next day, Porter wrote his man Le Roy Fitch at Evansville imploring him to ascend the Tennessee with all of his force. The Tennessee was reported to be rising and Fitch had to get his boats up it "as far as you can." It was of vital importance to get possession of the whole stream before Forrest got across it, but if he were too late, the Hoosier was to cut off the Memphis native's retreat by stationing his vessels at the different fords. Although Fitch duly departed up the Tennessee the next evening with all of his boats, he was unable to prevent Forrest's crossing and thereby interfere with what turned out to be a very successful Rebel raid.

Down the Mississippi, Confederate riflemen still continued to shoot up Yankee steamers. En route to Vicksburg from Helena on December 20, Capt. John Wolf, Jr.'s stern-wheel dispatch boat *Rocket*[30] was fired into from the Arkansas shore by a large group of irregulars. As *Chicago Daily Tribune* reporter F.C. Foster told his readers on January 5, 1863, this veteran of the Shiloh campaign was struck over 100 times in her cabin and pilothouse, but no one was injured. Instead of meekly pouring on steam to escape, the angered master, whose boat carried a field piece on each deck, rounded to and "replied with grape, canister, and musketry from a detachment of the 11th and 24th Indiana volunteers."

Also out west, a Confederate force under Maj. Gen. Earl Van Dorn destroyed Maj. Gen. Grant's supply base at Holly Springs, MS, on December 20, along with goods valued at between $500,000 and $1.5 million. This attack would prevent Grant's joining in the Porter-Sherman assault upon Vicksburg.

There still not being sufficient water in the Cumberland for the Federal tinclads to ascend, Lt. Cmdr. Fitch and Col. William W. Lowe, post commander at Forts Henry and Heiman, came up with the idea of an amphibious raid from the Tennessee which might be able to get behind Forrest's raiders.

The Fitch-Lowe expedition shoved off on December 20, the same day the *Rocket* was shot up and Holly Springs was hit. The *General Pillow* was left behind to guard the forts. The tinclads and the troop ships proceeded as high as Duck River Sucks, where the soldiers were disembarked. Leaving the *Alfred Robb* and *St. Clair* with Lowe's transports, the *Fairplay* and *Brilliant* attempted to steam further up the river. The latter two did not get very far before the flagship grounded on Duck River Bar; once she was off, both returned without getting higher.

Lowe's men made no contact with the enemy. The colonel abandoned his fruitless quest and returned to Fort Henry, freeing the tinclads on December 24 for service elsewhere. Also on Christmas Eve, Maj. Gen. Sherman and Acting Rear Adm.

Porter, leading a giant troop convoy from Memphis, arrived off the mouth of the Yazoo River.

Thereafter, with other newly arriving light-draughts, the *Signal* and *Marmora* played an important role in what was known as the Chickasaw Bayou campaign. During the holiday period of 1862–1863, it failed, with many Federal casualties.

Although the overall goal of securing Vicksburg was ultimately a winning Federal mission, its actual accomplishment would require nine more months and considerable trial and error. In that period, tinclads continued to join the Mississippi Squadron above the Rebel bastion and to see some of the operation's toughest fighting, most often against Confederate regular forces.

At the same time, Brig. Gen. Morgan conducted his famous 400-mile Christmas raid, striking at Maj. Gen. Rosecrans's rail lines north of Nashville. Although Morgan put the trains off schedule for another five weeks and destroyed almost $2 million in Yankee supplies, the Cumberland was now sufficiently high to ensure that needed Federal supplies and soldiers could be safely, quickly, and directly gotten through no matter how much damage was done to the railroad.

On December 21–22, the Army of the Cumberland reached full strength with the arrival in Nashville of 13,500 more soldiers under Maj. Gen. George H. Thomas and by Christmas Day, Rosecrans had sufficient supplies on hand to sustain his army until February 1.[31]

On Boxing Day, December 26, even as men under Acting Rear Adm. Porter and Maj. Gen. Sherman vainly attempted to get at Vicksburg via Chickasaw Bayou, the Army of the Cumberland quit Nashville and marched south. No one at that time could know that the seizure of a trading vessel, cleared for a voyage down the Mississippi that day, would later lead to a Federal victory.

Recently freed from contraband charges and taken into USQMD service, the *Blue Wing No. 2* departed Helena that day en route to Milliken's Bend, LA, with a sizeable load of ordnance, a large shipment of government mail, and two coal barges in tow. As she turned into Cypress Bend, eight miles below Napoleon, AR, on December 28, the side-wheeler was attacked by horse artillery from an independent Louisiana artillery company, under Capt. L.M. Nutt, firing from the Arkansas shore.

Quick-thinking deck hands were able to cut one barge loose before the captain was forced to heave to and surrender his boat and its 30-man crew. Acting Rear Adm. Porter later described the skipper as "a great rascal" who, immediately upon interrogation, pointed out and turned over the mail sacks destined for Maj. Gen. Sherman.

The pleased Confederates not only gained much-needed coal and ammunition, but what Acting Rear Adm. Porter confessed was an additional valuable prize, 16 bags of army (not navy) mail. The *Blue Wing No. 2* was sent up the recently-risen Arkansas River to the Post of Arkansas, where the South had constructed a fort to protect that stream against Yankee incursion. The insecurity of the Union's Mississippi River supply line from Helena to Milliken's Bend was amply demonstrated and a decision would soon be made to do something about it.

Three days later, on December 31, Maj. Gen. Rosecrans's soldiers engaged the Confederate Army of the Tennessee at Stones River, just north of Murfreesboro. The great battle, fought in very rainy weather, see-sawed back and forth across fields and cedar brakes until January 4, 1863, when the Army of Tennessee, out of supplies and initiative, retreated southward in the direction of Shelbyville and Tullahoma. Rosecrans's exhausted troops held fast in its hard-won winter quarters at Murfreesboro as the Northern government and press lauded the Pyrrhic victory as a great triumph. It was not great, but unlike the Porter-Sherman campaign up the Yazoo, at least it did not end in Federal retreat.[32]

5

Tinclad River Guardians, January–April 1863

It was impossible to know on January 1 that 1863 would be the decisive year of the Civil War. The great battle at Stones River, near Murfreesboro, TN, raged without decision on that day, while in the vicinity of Vicksburg, MS, Federal forces were repulsed at Chickasaw Bayou. As Federal naval commanders in those areas reviewed events, they could take some solace.

To the south, squadron commander Acting Rear Adm. David Dixon Porter provided every waterborne assistance to the amphibious operation by Maj. Gen. William T. Sherman's army. That the bluecoat soldiers could not penetrate the defenses of Vicksburg north of the city was not, in the end, viewed as a naval failure.

Although it would be a few days before the outcome of the Tennessee battle was known for certain, Fleet Captain Alexander Pennock, Mississippi Squadron deputy in charge of the convoy and anti-partisan war on the upper rivers, together with his operational executive, Lt. Cmdr. Le Roy Fitch, could take pride that their work helped Maj. Gen. William Rosecrans stockpile sufficient supplies in the depot city of Nashville to permit the offensive.

By January 4, the Federals were able to announce a victory in the fighting at Stone's River. The costly but strategically insignificant battle did, however, bring, in the words of historian James M. McPherson, "a thin gleam of cheer to the North."

Both the flanking move against Vicksburg and the buildup of forces at Nashville were facilitated, in no small part, by the arrival on the scene of an increasing number of small Federal warships known as tinclads. Following the *Linden*, commissioned on January 3, 18 more light-draughts entered service during the first half of 1863. Space does not permit a discussion of their specifications and commanders here; however, each will be profiled in footnotes following its first textual mention.

The Confederate war against Union shipping continued in the snow, rain and cold of the new year. Along the Mississippi, bands of cavalry took up the challenge from the commander of the Trans-Mississippi department to "scout and burn" cotton found on the river bank and to "annoy" any steamers encountered. From hiding spots between northern Louisiana and Missouri, Rebels shot up vessels, occasionally seizing and destroying vulnerable boats.

At the mouth of the Yazoo River, Federal military and naval leaders, licking their wounds after the Chickasaw Bayou defeat, elected to use the *Blue Wing* incident as cover for a short campaign against the Post of Arkansas. On January 4, Acting Rear Adm. David D. Porter and Maj. Gen. John S. McClernand set off to subdue the Arkansas River fortress. Rather than leave soldiers to "idle at Milliken's Bend," the two, plus Maj. Gen Sherman, elected to occupy this gateway to Little Rock from "which hostile detachments were constantly sent forth to obstruct the navigation of the Mississippi River and thereby our communications."

The capture of the *Blue Wing* and Southern attacks upon river boats in general were irritating and sometimes embarrassing, but were not vital to the success of the war effort and certainly did not require such a large-scale reaction. Still, as Frank Knox, the *New York Herald* correspondent covering the expedition, told his readers, it was hoped that "following so soon on our [Chickasaw Bayou] reverse," such a victory would be a "partial atonement for our recent defeat."

Meanwhile, in Tennessee, two brigades of cavalry under Brig. Gen. Joseph ("Fighting Joe") Wheeler were dispatched to damage lines of communication supporting the Army of the Cumberland. If Maj. Gen. Rosecrans could be convinced that his logistics were threatened, he would probably abandon pursuit of Gen. Braxton Bragg's retreating Army of Tennessee.

Despite the dangers, the beginning of the new year saw an even greater demand for steamboats "in the government service." Defending the increasing number of steamers the USQMD had contracted to shuttle troops and supplies to Nashville on the Cumberland River was vital to the war effort, both from an operational point of view and to the political-emotional orientation of the Union theater commander. The task would not be an easy one because the water levels were so low that gunboats could not ascend the Tennessee nor get up the Cumberland to within 35 miles of Nashville. Any supply steamers from Louisville would have to stop at Harpeth Shoals and offload some their cargoes to lighters sent down from Nashville. Several ersatz Army gunboats could then provide cover into the city. If these craft could not pass, wagons would be required for the rest of the trip.[1]

Maj. Gen. Joseph ("Fighting Joe") Wheeler (1836–1906) was ordered to take two brigades of Confederate cavalry in January 1863 and disrupt Federal communications support for the Nashville-based Army of the Cumberland. His units attacked steamers on the river and attempted a month later to capture the town of Dover, near the ruins of Fort Donelson (U.S. Army Military History Institute).

At 4 P.M. on January 5, the year's first big Cumberland River supply convoy departed Evansville with rations for Rosecrans's army. The 14 steamers, later increased to 18, picked up their naval cover while passing Smithland next morning. As usual, the larger and faster boats towed the less fleet or smaller craft, often by lashing them alongside. The gunboats interspersed themselves to offer cover. The owners of the boats, to help save themselves and their machinery from sharpshooters along the shores, usually piled cotton bales around their boilers and engines. For the most part, these essential cargoes reached the Nashville landing on January 8, the same day Acting Rear Adm. Porter steamed into the White River en route to Arkansas Post.

The passage upon the Volunteer State waterway was the most challenging. En route, Confederate riders were constantly seen on bluffs and in the woods. The sailors aboard the escorting tinclads *Brilliant* and *St. Clair* fired at them with their Enfield rifles, while shells were sent after the grayclads from the tinclads' bow guns. Aboard both boats, most of the officers usually congregated in the open on the hurricane decks forward, according to Acting Assistant Surgeon William H. Howard of the *Brilliant*. Howard had joined the navy the previous October 1 and would, despite several threats to resign, remain on duty until November 9, 1865.

On one occasion during this trip, as the *Brilliant* was turning, a noise was heard coming from the direction of the left bank of the Cumberland. It was a volley of what was believed to be over 100 Minie balls that made all exposed crewmen rapidly dive for cover. Howard, in writing home about the incident some time later, believed it a miracle that the men on his craft were not hit. "One ball went directly over my head and through the chimney — and then through the other chimney, and two struck the pilothouse." The potentially disastrous attack, which the healer labeled "vicious," had been a surprise because the Rebel perpetrators had left their horses behind and crept up to the edge of the river bank before shooting.

About four of the convoy's steamers, lighter than the others, had paddled on ahead, hoping to get to and over Harpeth Shoals before dark. They were shot into along the way and, being unable to get over, were considered fortunate not to be captured before the tinclad group arrived. As the two light-draught gunboats hovered at the head of the shoals that evening, crews from the heavily-laden steamboats unloaded or cross loaded freight to sufficiently lighten their craft to pass over the obstacle and continue on to Nashville. Cargoes left behind would be strongly guarded until they could be retrieved by other steamers or wagons sent from the capital city

In this cold, damp January, Rosecrans's entire logistical apparatus hinged on the Cumberland River, the depths of which were becoming daily more navigable. Although it was true that foraging Yankee forces could try to live off items taken from the local countryside, Southern commanders knew that, if they could damage the Federal supply and evacuation convoys, both success and opportunity might be their reward. Attacking boats steaming up and down the Cumberland could not only divert Northern forces from his pursuit but cause notable supply hardship for units and organizations in need of replenishment in Nashville and Murfreesboro. Brig. Gen. Philip H. Sheridan, as quoted by William Lamers, summed up the logistical problems that challenged the Army of the Cumberland:

Though taken on another river a year later, this photograph of an actual Civil War Western rivers convoy gives the reader some idea of the regular processions organized and escorted by the light-draught ("tinclad") gunboats of the Mississippi Squadron. As most naval officers were quick to explain, particularly in the dangerous days of 1862–1864, escorted vessels usually had a far better chance of reaching their destinations unharmed than those steaming independently (Miller's *Photographic History of the Civil War*).

> The feeding of our army from the base at Louisville was attended with many difficulties, as the enemy's cavalry was constantly breaking the railroad and intercepting our communications on the Cumberland River at different points that were easily accessible to his then superior force. The accumulation of reserve stores was therefore not an easy task....[2]

Capt. James H. "Jim" McGehee, commander of an independent, unnumbered, and unattached Arkansas partisan cavalry company, was one of those responding to Confederate Maj. Gen. Edmund Kirby Smith's New Year's call to burn river bank cotton and harass Federal Mississippi River shipping. An industrious soul, McGee wasted no time in striking, sending several of his men across the Mississippi to lie in wait, hoping to make a capture on January 8.

Having provided succor for Mississippi Squadron units off the mouth of the White River and now returning to St. Louis, the 144-ton stern-wheeler *Jacob Musselman* had just passed Memphis when, in sight of the city bluffs at a point known as the Hen and Chickens, the engineer reported her cylinder head thrown out. As she eased into the Tennessee bank, the two-year old Paducah-built craft was boarded by Lt. R.H. Barlow plus six other "white men and three Negroes armed to the teeth."

Quickly in control of the *Musselman*, Barlow ordered repairs completed and then instructed her pilot to back out and continue upstream to Bradley's Landing, 15 miles above Memphis. There the boat was run into the shore and met by Capt. McGehee's party of 50 or 60 mounted men, whom witnesses later swore wore "military buttons, but not uniforms." It was later observed that "since river traffic was so heavy, the movement of the rebel steamer attracted no attention."

While not robbing the crew or passengers, the guerrillas quickly removed all of the bedding aboard, along with the furniture and private property in the possession of clerk W.S. Spalding, the total later valued at $8,500. As the Rebel horsemen labored, a flatboat loaded with chickens and stock (28 head of cattle and 50 hogs) drifted by and it, too, was seized. The stock was quickly taken off and the boat was burned.

Once all of value was in hand from the steamboat, Capt. McGehee ordered the officers and crew paroled. They, together with the wife of the captain and the wife of one of the owners, taking passage, were then ordered into the vessel's lifeboat and yawl and permitted to return to Memphis. As they rowed away, the butternut partisans departed, leaving a few men behind to set fire to the *Musselman*.[3]

Over the next several days, finishing on January 11, Federal forces under Acting Rear Adm. Porter and Generals McClernand and Sherman attacked and captured Arkansas Post in a set-piece engagement with regular Confederate forces.[4] The tinclads *Rattler*[5] and *Glide I*[6] were directly involved in supporting Union troops during the engagement which, due to its strictly military flavor, is not reported in detail here. We might mention that the steamer *Blue Wing No. 2*, taken to the Confederate fort after her December capture, escaped upriver to St. Charles next day, hauling a pair of 8-inch cannon for emplacement at that point.

As an owner, steamboat captain Thomas Chester was not having a good war. The previous April at Island No. 10, he was able to reclaim the wreck of his 100-ton sternwheel towboat, the *Grampus*, which Confederate elements stole in 1861 and turned into a two-gun reconnaissance vessel. Prior to her destruction, the vessel had plagued the timberclads and other vessels of the Western Flotilla.

In early 1862, he constructed a replacement craft, 17 tons larger, at Brownsville, PA, and named her *Grampus No. 2*.[7] Not much is known about the second stern-wheeler. On January 10, the *Grampus No. 2* arrived just above Memphis, towing five barges of coal. Visibility being slight on the cold winter evening, she anchored 50 yards off the Tennessee shore a little above the mouth of Wolf River at Little Chicken Island. Around midnight, with the crew asleep, Capt. James McGehee and a dozen armed men quietly rowed out from shore in several skiffs and boarded. The night watchman had a pistol placed at his head and, in ones and twos, the crew was taken captive, being warned, upon pain of death, to make no shout or signal to shore or passing vessels.

The towboat was not only towing coal, but had an on board cargo of 3,500 bushels of the black fuel. McGehee ordered the engineers to get up steam, while lines to the coal barges were cut, and back away from the bank into deep water. The departure by Chester's vessel upriver early on January 12 was actually witnessed by lookouts aboard the timberclad *Conestoga*, "but as steamers are constantly passing up and down during the night, there was nothing suspicious in the movement."

The *Grampus No. 2* ran up to the regular ferry landing at Mound City, AR, five miles above the city. Here they were met by additional semi-uniformed riders from the captain's partisan band, who had, when planning to take another boat, remembered to have a wagon and six-horse hitch, brought in to carry plunder.

In no position to protest the loss of another vessel, Capt. Chester had earlier given up without resistance. Now McGehee added damage to insult by relieving the steamer's master of a valuable gold watch and almost $1,000 in greenbacks in a money belt. He supposedly bragged that it was his people who burned the *Jacob Musselman* and warned that more Yankee shipping would be torched. Indeed, he brazenly asked Chester to take a verbal request to Memphis area commander Brig. Gen. Stephen Hurlburt to please "have his bed big enough, for he would find one of them sleeping with him some night."

During the one-sided exchange between McGehee and Chester, guerrilla horsemen stripped the *Grampus No. 2* of everything remotely useful and piled it into their wagon: furniture, lanterns, rope, poles, navigational aids, bedding, crockery and dishes. The Southerners were particularly pleased to remove the boat's bell, said to have value. When all that was desired had been removed, Capt. Chester and his crew were paroled. Although offered accommodation for the remainder of the night in an empty house once owned by one of the raiders, Chester and his men walked down the shoreline and were rescued at 7:30 A.M. by an armed boat crew from the *Conestoga*.

In the meantime, the *Grampus No. 2* was set alight and cut adrift. She floated down to the foot of the island opposite the landing, where she and her coal continued to burn for a day or so. McGehee and his men made their escape hours before the Navy rescued Chester and his men.[8]

After dropping off Chester and his men, Lt. Cmdr. Thomas O. Selfridge Jr. of the *Conestoga*, ranking naval officer at the Tennessee city, ordered his subordinate, Lt Joshua Bishop, to take the new tinclad *Linden*[9] up that afternoon and visit the places where the *Jacob Musselman* and *Grampus No. 2* were burned. The tinclad took aboard several companies of the 89th Indiana Volunteer Infantry.

The *Linden* passed Mound City, seeing no movement, and continued up to Bradley's Landing, where she dropped anchor after dark in the stream offshore. About 7 A.M. on January 13, a landing party was put ashore to look around. It did not take the men long to ascertain that there were many partisans in the area, undoubtedly intent upon "destroying steamers." From African-American contrabands and others, it was learned that the riders made their headquarters not only at Bradley's Landing, but at Marion and Hopefield.

Two hours later, the tinclad began back down the river, dropping howitzer shells at intervals into the woods "as it was supposed there were guerrillas thereabouts." The Hoosier soldiers were sent ashore at Mound City, where they made prisoners of several citizens suspected of harboring bushwhackers. Several vacant homes, believed recently occupied by partisans, were burned after quantities of small arms were found. Meanwhile, pickets shot at several mounted men seen riding beyond their perimeter. The Federal soldiers next marched down the Arkansas shore the short distance to Hopefield and made another house-to-house arms search. Early in the afternoon, the *Linden* put in to shore, reembarked the bluecoats, and returned to Memphis.[10]

The first mission of the new light–draught ("tinclad") *Linden* in mid–January 1863 was to search for the perpetrators responsible for destroying the steamers *Jacob Musselman* and *Grampus No. 2* near Memphis. As was often the case, by the time the gunboat reached the area where the depredations occurred, the Confederates were long gone. In this photo, the upper works of the *Linden* can be seen behind the ironclad *Tuscumbia* and a mortar boat of the type used to bombard Vicksburg. The *Linden* spent most of her short career in the Lower Mississippi; she struck a snag and sank in the Arkansas River on February 22, 1864 (Naval Historical Center).

Several of the steamboats to reach Nashville in the inaugural convoy earlier described were fitted up as hospital ships for the turn around trip north. When the first evacuation convoy left the city for Louisville on January 11, these craft carried approximately 2,000 wounded Union men. Other boats carried hundreds of Rebel prisoners from Stones River and Arkansas Post up both the main rivers and the Green River. Before long, a huge fleet of some 66 steamboats was chartered to haul provisions upriver to Rosecrans. "What few boats were permitted to run on private account," wrote Evansville steamboat historian Milford Miller in 1941, "carried capacity cargoes. Of the steamboats that passed down the river, few returned, for the government pressed them into service...."[11]

While Acting Rear Adm. Porter and Maj. Gen McClernand considered their Arkansas options, the Confederate raider war in Tennessee blazed. To the north of Nashville, Brig.

Gen. John Hunt Morgan and his men rode toward Kentucky after crossing the Cumberland above Gallatin. His aim was not only to forage, but to further damage the Louisville and Nashville Railroad. Further south, "Fighting Joe" Wheeler and two cavalry brigades hit the Nashville and Chattanooga Railroad and attacked wagon trains slogging between Murfreesboro and Nashville.

Rebel insurgents also had significant success in attacking Union vessels in the area around the Harpeth obstruction. The winter weather, in addition to the navigational difficulties of the river, may have played a role. All around the weather was freezing and blowing and the towns and countryside were covered with snow. In the words of Kentucky soldier Marcus Woodcock, "Everything wore a dreary aspect." It was little different throughout the Mississippi Valley as far down the Mississippi as Arkansas Post.

En route to Nashville on January 13, the transport *Charter*,[12] loaded with hay, corn, and commissary stores, was jumped by Capt. Dick McCann's guerrillas at a point near Ashland, five miles on the Nashville side of the Harpeth Shoals. The cargo was destroyed and the boat was burned. Her crew was paroled, except for six captured African-American contraband deckhands. These, according to a report in the *Chicago Daily Tribune*, were led "out on the bank and shot."

The exact whereabouts of Rebel cavalry units led by Morgan and Wheeler were unknown in Nashville at this time and so it was deemed safe that Tuesday to resume unescorted medical evacuation sailings. Early in the morning, three hospital boats, the *Hastings*,[13] *Parthenia*,[14] and *Trio*,[15] departed down the Cumberland, each flying hospital flags for identification. In fact, it was no more safe on this snowy day for these vessels than it had been for the *Charter*. Operating near the shoals was an entire brigade of "Fighting Joe's" troopers, under Col. William B. Wade.

First in line, the *Hastings* had aboard 260 wounded bluecoats under the protection of Chaplain Maxwell P. Gaddis, 2nd Regiment, 2nd Ohio Volunteer Infantry. Spied from shore at a point at the head of the shoals, some 30 miles from Nashville and 35 miles from Clarksville, the boat was ordered to halt by a number of Confederate Wade's men brandishing arms. Unable or unwilling to respond, the *Hastings*'s civilian pilot turned the boat over to the parson, the military's senior representative aboard.

Gaddis called over to the shore that his ship was loaded with Murfreesboro casualties and couldn't stop. The Rebels responded with musket fire. Resigned to compliance, Gaddis ordered the boat put into the river bank, but its slow turn in the swift current was mistaken by Wade's men as an effort to escape. Two rounds from the Confederate's horse artillery slammed into the vessel before it could ground. As the *Hastings* touched, Wade's men, many intoxicated, jumped aboard and set to looting from both the boat and its passengers.

On June 17, 1862, Capt. Perry Brown's *Parthenia* was the first private packet to steam from Pittsburgh for Memphis since the war had started. The stern-wheeler's independence lasted only a few months before she was impressed by charter by the USQMD. Prior to her required hire, Capt. W.B. Russell's stern-wheeler *Trio* had spent most of her career trading from that Kentucky town to St. Louis. She and the *Parthenia* were now also taken as they came upon the *Hastings*, stopped, their captains believed, to take on wood for fuel.

Unbeknownst to both Chaplain Gaddis and Col. Wade, the three seized steamers

Despite the severe weather, troops from the command of Maj. Gen. Joseph Wheeler captured and destroyed a number of steamers on the Cumberland River in January 1863, including the *Hastings, Parthenia,* and *Trio* here depicted. An ersatz U.S. Army gunboat, the *W.H. Sidell* was also captured, and initial reports of her loss led some Union leaders to believe the steamer was a U.S. Navy tinclad (*Annals of the Army of the Cumberland*, 1864).

were also transporting cotton. When this was discovered, Wade, who had been inclined to parole at least one of the boats, ordered all of their passengers ashore so that he could burn the three and their baled cargoes. Gaddis, with pistols leveled at him, stood up to Wade and refused to order his men off, demanding that Wade first get an order signed by Wheeler. Somewhat surprisingly, Wade agreed to consult his superior concerning actions to be taken next and a messenger was sent off to find the boy leader. Meanwhile, according to an eyewitness quoted in an Illinois newspaper account, numerous wounded soldiers were sent ashore and laid on damp ground, "stripped of their blankets, great coats, shoes, and in many instances, of their money."

The Confederate cavalry general sent Wade's courier back with orders to parole the *Hastings* and all of the Yankees, provided Gaddis promised to burn the cotton when he reached Louisville. Gaddis agreed, but before the *Hastings* could depart, yet another strange incident occurred.

As Wade and Gaddis were concluding their parole discussions and preparations to get the *Hastings* underway were being made, the U.S. Army steamer *W.H. Sidell*, an old shallow-draught ferryboat outfitted with two or three field pieces and minimal protection, rounded a bend and headed toward them. Named for a Nashville assistant quartermaster and commanded by infantry Lt. William Van Dorn, the *Sidell* was one of several ersatz gunboats fitted up to provide cover for cargoes on the Cumberland stretch between Harpeth Shoals and Nashville.

The *Sidell* might have been able to change the outcome of the Wade capture — if Van Dorn had been able to fight. As the Rebels ran to their cannon, the impromptu warship swung into the Cumberland's opposite bank and, shortly thereafter, signaled its intention to surrender. The amazed Col. Wade ordered the boat to come across and, once under his control, had her cannon thrown in the river.

Van Dorn's men were sent aboard the *Hastings*, which was finally permitted to cast off after her surgeon, Luther D. Waterman of the 39th Indiana Volunteer Infantry, had signed a written parole for all 400 of the Caucasian passengers and crew. The black deckhands, two captured aboard the *Hastings* and "one poor fellow who was found clinging to the water wheel of the *Parthenia*," were executed at the river's edge.

As the *Hastings* gathered way, torches were placed to the *Parthenia*, *Trio*, and *W.H. Sidell*. A witness reported that "the flames soon spread to all parts of the steamers and not many moments elapsed until all were in full blast, causing such an intense heat as to fire the then-dry stubble on the opposite side of the river."

As might be imagined, a considerable hurrah of glee or public uproar, depending upon one's allegiance, was occasioned over Col. Wade's success. Gen. Bragg reported that Wheeler had been "hotly pursued by a gunboat [*W.H. Sidell*], which he attacked and captured, and destroyed her with her whole armament." A local Tennessee lady, Lucy Virginia French, wrote in her journal: "The late raid of Wheeler and Forrest on the Cumberland below Nashville is the talk now — cavalry capturing 5 transports and a gunboat is as good as Forrest's men taking a battery at Murfreesboro last summer with shot guns!" Nashville post commander Brig. Gen. Robert B. Mitchell, on the other hand, hurriedly wrote to Maj. Gen. Rosecrans at Murfreesboro: "The rebels are burning everything on the river. There are at least four more freight boats destroyed...."

Acting Rear Adm. Porter first heard of the incident, since labeled the "Affair at Harpeth Shoals," while reading captured Confederate newspapers downriver near Vicksburg. He was hopeful that it was not one of his gunboats or a squadron-protected convoy that had been lost. If it were and Lt. Cmdr. Fitch had gone up with only one vessel, he had "disobeyed his orders as I directed him never to let one vessel go alone, and always to have two vessels together." As Rebel accounts were known to not always be reliable, Porter wisely elected not to place confidence in the report.

On January 14, the commander of the Army of the Cumberland telegraphed Secretary of War Edwin M. Stanton admitting that Rebel cavalry had done "great mischief" (because, he suggested, his own was out numbered four to one), and launched a verbal campaign seeking additional horsemen. Rosecrans went on to say that he also required "some light-draught transports, with bullet-proof boilers and pilot-houses, immediately."

Many Northern newspapers reported the Rebel success, amplifying the details of the admittedly horrific black murders into atrocities. Even U.S. Navy Secretary Gideon Welles, from his office on the other side of the Allegheny Mountains, felt compelled to inquire of Porter concerning the burning of the gunboat on the Cumberland River. The Western naval CO, who knew how his military colleagues were prone from time to time to arm steamers, wrote back to his boss on January 29 assuring him that the boat was not one from the Mississippi Squadron. With a certain amount of intra-service glee, Porter noted that "the army undertakes sometimes to get up an impromptu navy, which generally ends up getting them into difficulty."[16]

When, at the end of the Battle of Arkansas Post, the captured steamer *Blue Wing No. 2* escaped up the White River, a joint Federal army and navy force was sent to capture the boat and to take Confederate positions at St. Charles. When the invaders arrived on April 14, they found the steamer gone, along with two 8-inch cannon and a field piece, to a railhead above.

It was decided to push on after the guns and the renegade steamboat next morning. Followed by troop transports, the ironclad *Baron de Kalb* came to off Devall's Bluff in late afternoon just, it was subsequently learned, about 15 minutes after the *Blue Wing No. 2* escaped. The cannon, being loaded onto railroad flatcars, were captured, as were the mail sacks (now empty) that were aboard the *Blue Wing No. 2* when she was taken in December.[17]

By this time, Acting Rear Admiral Porter, anticipating the further Northern advance, had dispatched three tinclads to provide assistance, as well as to examine numerous bayous off the main stream where other paddle wheelers could be "stowed away." The *Signal* and *Romeo*[18] were sent first, with the *Forest Rose*[19] following with dispatches.

Following the Devall's Bluff arrival of the *Forest Rose* on the morning of January 17, the naval commander on scene, Lt. Cmdr. John G. Walker, assembled a light-draught task group. With the *Rose* in the lead, followed by the *Romeo* and a troop transport, Walker's unit started up the White River. Keeping a sharp lookout into the woods and small clearings along the snow-covered bank, the three proceeded 34 miles without incident (other than running afoul of overhanging branches) to the village of Des Arc. When armed parties from the tinclads were landed, they found that, once more, the *Blue Wing No. 2* had escaped. A total of 39 wounded Confederate soldiers were found in (and paroled from) a small hospital and a small quantity of ammunition was captured. No Rebel resistance was encountered by the soldiers from the transport.

Walker's tinclad unit returned to Devall's Bluff the next morning, Sunday. Before a new expedition could be mounted to seek out the *Blue Wing*, White River withdrawal orders were received from the squadron commander. All of the Federal units committed to the taking of Arkansas Post were being recommitted to a new and larger riverborne campaign against Vicksburg.[20]

Also on January 18, a 19-boat supply flotilla departed Evansville for Nashville, picking up its Cumberland River escorts *Brilliant* and *St. Clair* as it passed Smithland. Among the merchantmen in the convoy was the brand-new steamer *Mary Crane*,[21] which had been loaded by the quartermaster at the Indiana port with a cargo that included 134 barrels of beans, 50 barrels of sugar, 448 barrels of flour, 10 barrels of molasses; 226 barrels of pork, 35 boxes of candles, 50 boxes of soap, and 300 bags of corn.

At Betsy's Landing, near Harpeth Shoals, next day, she dropped out of formation to refuel. While the needed cords of wood were being taken aboard, the boat was captured by men from a partisan ranger battalion captained by D.W. Holman. Within minutes, the pilot was dead, the cargo was destroyed, and the *Mary Crane* was ashes.

Because steamers were at this time free to assemble for protection or operate independently, their safety could not be guaranteed. The two tinclads and the 28 survivors made it to Nashville later on Monday without further losses. This is not to say that there was no opposition. Horsemen and men in the trees fired on the boats from the banks, forcing the tiny warships to shoot back several times with their howitzers. Sailors on the vessels used rifles as well. Surgeon William Howard on the *Brilliant* noted: "Saw one of our men drop a 'grill' out of his saddle very prettily. He was just on the rise of the bank...."

In reporting the loss of the *Crane*, the Nashville-based correspondent of the *New York Herald* told his readers that the Cumberland was now sufficiently high to permit vessels to pass over the shoals; indeed, it was still rising. On the other hand, it was, because of the river's topography, "almost as difficult to keep the river open as it is to preserve the railroad." Was it possible that the newsman had spoken with the gunboatmen about places like the bluffs near the Harpeth Shoals, for example, those near Betsy's Landing or Palmyra? In something of a premonition, he wrote:

> The only safety is for boats to go under the guardianship of gunboats, and even these may be of no avail against a battery planted on some of the bluffs, from whose summit they can drop their shot upon the decks of the boats immediately beneath them.[22]

The weather remained friendly near Nashville during the next several days as the earlier convoy unloaded and preparations for a voyage downriver were completed. As Surgeon Howard wrote home from the *Brilliant*, it was "like spring—birds singing, clear sky, etc." On January 22, the small steamer *Millboy*[23] was attacked by guerrillas, probably from Capt McGehee's band, on the Mississippi above Memphis. Although surprised, she was able to escape.

Also that Thursday, Lt. Cmdr. Le Roy Fitch began to upgrade the organized operational tactics of Cumberland river convoys, while simultaneously overseeing the work of his subordinates engaged in reconnaissance patrols up the Tennessee River. It was during this time that he perfected a process for naval convoy which would be followed, with modifications, by the U.S. Navy in later conflicts.

According to historian Rod Paschall, U.S. Army officers have planned convoys for nearly 200 years. In the 1800s, these were essentially infantry and cavalry escorts provided for wagons or river craft that traveled back and forth between a logistical base and the rear area. Because of the locations served, these supply convoys were different from supply trains, transport that accompanied troops. The army mission was one of protection, and doctrine advised dividing the escort into advance, main-body, rear, and flank guards. In World War I, Paschall writes, the Allied navies also employed convoy. In these, escort craft surrounded the merchant or troop ships; the most important vessels were centered inside the defensive ring, and the whole convoy proceeded at the pace of its slowest ship. The process was refined in World War II. Escort tactics in the 19th and 20th centuries, as now, are "essentially defensive." In and of themselves, "they do not win wars."

Borrowing somewhat from army doctrine and inventing some of his own, Fitch's plan envisioned lengthy water parades that were majestic, often noisy, but usually well-organized entities designed to ensure "perfect safety" by keeping all transports within covering distance of the escorts' cannon. He was, in fact, establishing what the 1944 War Instructions of the United States Navy, in its Chapter 6, called "Cruising Dispositions." These largely defensive arrangements had as their requirements: (a) protection against surprise in any form; (b) security for the whole force and component parts thereof through mutual support; (c) ready transition to approach, contact or battle disposition; and (d) provisions for rapid and certain transmissions of orders and information. This regiment was not then an easy process — just as it wasn't in the world wars of the 20th century. The Cumberland River was "very narrow, crooked, and swift," the young convoy commodore later reported; it was impossible to put more than two steamers abreast.

For increased power and protection should one become disabled, it was not unusual for the protected Cumberland steamers to be lashed together "two and two." Fitch placed the slowest vessels (usually towboats with barges) in the van of his columns, with the most valuable cargoes in the center, and the swiftest boats in the rear. The gunboats were dispersed along the line, always with one in the lead and one in the rear. Sometimes in strong current, one or more of the lighter escorts might be lashed to heavy transports.

As noted above, in the wake of the *Hastings* affair, Acting Rear Adm. Porter required a minimum of two tinclads for the escort of any merchant group. In his letter, Fitch did not mention a common practice remarked upon by Surgeon Howard in a letter home — towing slower vessels and other dirty work, such as helping to free stuck boats. As the *Brilliant*'s medical man put it: "If there does happen to be any slow boat without power enough to draw a sitting hen off her nest, we offer her aid, comfort, and support."

The time required to complete a naval convoy cycle was one week. The days were taken up with actually achieving the round trip, coaling the escorts, cleaning boilers and making small repairs, and finalizing arrangements for starting the next fleet down.

Over the next month, this action scheme would be refined, permitting the Mosquito Flotilla to offer convoy protection, anti-ferriage patrols up beyond Nashville, and a weekly visit to the Tennessee River. By the beginning of February, Capt. Pennock, Fitch's Cairo-based superior, was able to confidently inform Maj. Gen. William S. Rosecrans that arrangements were in place that allowed the Cumberland River tinclads to "leave Smithland or Fort Donelson every Monday to convoy loaded transports and to return with those which have discharged cargo."[24]

At noon on January 23, a 22-boat return convoy, "with a large mail," weighed from Nashville for Smithland, accompanied by the *Brilliant* and *St. Clair*. As it approached Betsy's Landing that evening, Confederate raiders, with three light field pieces, fired down on Capt. John Bradley's *R.B. Hamilton*[25] from low hills, just as the *Herald*'s special had predicted was possible. A 6-pdr. shot entered the port side of the steamer, passed close to its machinery, and lodged in a starboard side beam. Before any of the other vessels could be damaged, Acting Volunteer Lt. Charles G. Perkin's *St. Clair* steamed up quickly and "engaged the enemy," driving them "off into the woods." The entire fleet anchored at Clarksville sometime after dark. It remained off that town next day, because of heavy rains that continued into January 25 and caused the Cumberland to rise six inches more. Meanwhile, naval reinforcements were on the way from far and near.[26]

For some time in the past and continuing into the months to come, differences existed between Federal army and navy commanders in the West concerning the quantity of nautical support provided by the latter to the former. Army men like Grant, Rosecrans, and Parsons were not backward in voicing their concerns to Washington, D.C., and these usually ended up on the desk of already-stressed Navy Secretary Welles. Although appreciative of Pennock's work, Secretary Welles on January 23 wired the fleet captain at Cairo reminding him that it was "imperative that more gunboats should be sent in the Cumberland and Tennessee Rivers to protect the transports." Another message, even more forceful, was sent next day. Meanwhile, newspaper stories continued to appear suggesting the river banks were swarming with "guerrillas" armed with "heavy field artillery."[27]

As the Nashville return convoy waited at Clarksville on January 24, Fleet Captain Pennock made an effort to do what he could to enhance the Cumberland naval effort. Early that Saturday morning, he wired Maj. Gen. Rosecrans that he was sending the new tinclad *Silver Lake*,[28] "lightly-manned"—she had 28 men aboard, as well as "a case of smallpox"—to the Cumberland River that day. The fleet captain's move anticipated, by two days, an order from Acting Rear Admiral Porter: "As fast as the light-draft steamers are finished, take one out of every three vessels for the defense of the upper rivers."

At the same time, Pennock, because of his pressing duties, was unable to make a personal inspection of the Cumberland River. Lt Cmdr. Seth Ledyard Phelps was dispatched with the *Lexington* on January 25 to conduct a survey and provide a non-biased assessment about what else might be done to help the Army. The heavily armed timberclad, which had been active on the western rivers for over a year, had arrived at Cairo four days earlier as escort to a convoy of Confederate prisoners taken in at the Post of Arkansas.[29]

Having departed from Smithland for Nashville aboard the *Fairplay* on January 23, Lt. Cmdr. Fitch, guarding a big convoy of 31 steamers and eight or 10 barges, encountered the *Brilliant* and *St. Clair* in the area near Dover. After departing soggy Clarksville, the tinclads of Acting Volunteer Lt. Jacob S. Hurd and Charles G. Perkins were coming down with a return fleet from the foot of Harpeth Shoals. Both convoys halted while their shepherds communicated and revised their steaming plans.

Fitch now directed that the warships of his two subordinates break off and join him. The transports, en route to Louisville from Nashville, were now below significant risk of danger. Thus they moved down out of the Cumberland unescorted. With enhanced cover, the big Nashville-bound fleet resumed churning toward the intermediate port of Clarksville.

As the fleets got upsteam and prepared to depart in opposite directions, time permitted the convoy commodore to run ashore to the telegraph office and wire Capt. Pennock. The lengthy communication reported that the Nashville-bound convoy had some 30 vessels, "which makes a very long line to be convoyed with only three boats." Believing that he would, at some point, have to contend with enemy batteries placed where the river channel was most narrow, Fitch asked if he not have more escort craft. He did not know that the *Silver Lake* and *Lexington* were steaming to his aid.

While the protected steamboat parade ascended towards Clarksville, great billows of smoke pouring from its collective chimneys, Lt. Cmdr. Phelps's *Lexington* was also in the Cumberland on January 26. There she met a steamer sailing independently—the same vessel fired upon by Confederate artillery at Betsy Town Landing three days earlier.

It was sometimes the case that the light howitzers of the tinclads were insufficient to suppress the attacks made by regular and irregular Confederate forces upon the Union supply convoys. During the spring of 1863, the timberclad *Lexington*, one of the first three vessels of the Mississippi Squadron, was transferred to the upper tributaries of the Mississippi River in order that her big 8-inch cannon could assist in getting vital supplies to their destinations. The *Lexington* had participated in the sweep resulting in the capture of the first tinclad, the *Alfred Robb*, in April (*Official Records of the Union and Confederate Navies*).

Phelps determined to extract satisfaction for the affront. Pushing on up past Clarksville in the dark, the timberclad, early the following morning, reached the river bank location described by the civilian craft's pilot. There a landing party went ashore and burned a storehouse supposedly used by Rebels as a "resort and cover."

With his armed reconnaissance completed, Phelps was returning to Clarksville when Rebel cannoneers, firing a couple of Parrott rifles from shore, hit the *Lexington* three times "without injury." She quickly returned fire with her big 8-inch guns and, as Nashville post commander Brig. Gen. Mitchell put it in his telegram on the event to Maj. Gen. Rosecrans, "we succeeded in driving the rebels out." The offending Confederate artillerymen were among those handling the six field guns of Maj. Gen. Wheeler's combined regular army division tasked by Bragg with the interruption of Union navigation of the Cumberland. It was made up of an 800-man brigade led by Brig. Gen. Nathan Bedford Forrest and another, with 2,000 soldiers, under Brig. Gen. John Wharton.

Observed from the *Lexington* as well as from shore, the Fitch convoy reached Clarksville toward dusk on January 27 and anchored for the night. There the Indiana-born convoy commander met Acting Volunteer Lt. Hurd and Perkins, as well as many of the steamer captains, explaining that the rest of the trip was potentially dangerous. To lessen the chances of Confederate attack, the convoy would leave at midnight and proceed under cover of darkness. It would be closely maintained and the three escorts would always be available, with one in the van, one in the center, and one in the rear. Lt. Cmdr. Phelps, joining in the discussions, not only learned the tactical situation from Fitch and his lieutenants, but agreed to lead the convoy into Nashville.

Col. Sanders D. Bruce of the 20th Kentucky Infantry, post commander at Clarksville, reported the fleet's arrival to Maj. Gen. Rosecrans. One steamboat, he added, had continued on toward Nashville without stopping. It was noted that Confederate raiders were on the south side of the Cumberland, near the shoals; their force was reckoned at 5,000, with eight pieces of artillery.

Brig. Gen. Mitchell reported to Maj. Gen. Rosecrans on January 28: "Fleet passing Shoals at 1 P.M. without interruption." The convoy made Nashville at midnight without, as Phelps put it in his report to Capt. Pennock, "so much as a musket shot having been fired upon a single vessel of the fleet."

Early on the morning of January 29, and throughout the day, citizens lined the Nashville wharves, enjoying the sight of so many vessels. Large numbers of African-Americans were pressed into unloading freight, as well as the wagons, pontoon boats, and lumber, coal, and miscellaneous cargo on the accompanying barges. The *Lexington* remained only long enough to coal before returning to Cairo, leaving the tinclads to assume protection of the next return convoy.

As if anticipating at least one of the findings of the Phelps review, Acting Rear Adm. Porter wrote to his fleet captain earlier in the day concerning the matter of escort on the Cumberland and Tennessee. Pennock, Porter directed, was to inform the tinclad skippers of the mosquito fleet that they were never to permit any vessels to proceed independently up the rivers. Any boats refusing convoy must be forced to participate and while under navy protection, all boats had to conform to any rules the convoy commodore deemed necessary to enforce.

After conferring with Capt. Pennock early on January 30, Phelps wrote out what he told his superior verbally. The main points of his report were exactly those Pennock, Fitch, Porter, and others had known for some time, but which the army and the civilian contractors had been unwilling to recognize or appreciate. Rebel forces were thick on both the Cumberland and Tennessee Rivers. They had a number of guns "with considerable covering force" along the eight to 10 miles of Harpeth Shoals, as well as near Savannah on the Tennessee River.

The remedy Phelps saw was not exactly in keeping with Fitch's request of Pennock for more boats, but was held a happy substitute. The captain-designate of the *Eastport* believed the Confederates would not stay away from attacking howitzer-equipped tinclads, but would back off from assaulting any fleet guarded by the big guns of a heavier boat. He recommended that the *Lexington* be sent to Fitch and, further in reinforcing Porter's order, reiterated just how important it was that no steamer be permitted to run on either of the twin rivers without a naval escort. In conclusion, Phelps had no doubt that, "with the aid of the *Lexington*, Captain Fitch will be able effectually to protect all the government vessels in those rivers." And so the big-gun timberclad was temporarily detached to bolster the tinclads.[30]

The return convoy being assembled, Fitch and his gunboats led it downriver on January 30. The voyage to the confluence of the Cumberland and Ohio was, as the escort leader later remembered, quite heated: "We were greatly annoyed by rebel sharpshooters from behind the trees."

It was correctly reported in Northern newspapers that Nathan Bedford Forrest, backed by a thousand men and four cannon, had a particular interest in negating Fitch's progress and was planning a "stupendous effort for the capture of the boats on the Cumberland." "Fighting Joe" Wheeler was also believed to be involved, also contemplating nautical mischief. On February 3, the *Raleigh Weekly Register* reported — erroneously, as it turned out — that Confederate cavalry "destroyed five more transports on the Cumberland River" on January 30. No transports were lost, though bullet holes appeared in many before the Rebels were, as Fitch reported, "soon dispersed." His escort vessels rounded to off Smithland on January 31, as the civil steamers continued toward Louisville.[31]

For the Federal tars of the Smithland escort group, the final day of the month began with the welcome news that, despite earlier Union suspicion concerning batteries, "nothing very serious" was going on up the Tennessee River. Word was also received by wire from Capt. Pennock concerning another big convoy coming from Louisville to take on to Nashville and one to bring back down, as well as a smallpox epidemic reported at Paducah.

During the last two weeks of January, the 12,000 men of Maj. Gen. Gordon Granger's Army of Kentucky were assembled at Louisville. This was a huge command, in fact a division of the Department of the Ohio, which was destined to become the Reserve Corps of the Army of the Cumberland. It comprised 20 infantry regiments, four cavalry regiments, and four artillery batteries. At the city's wharf, an armada of 28 transport steamers was ready to receive these men and their equipment. Early on the morning of January 31, soldiers started to clamor aboard their assigned vessels while wagons, once they were taken apart, "were lugged on board and packed in the hold and between decks." Many of the untried men may, as they boarded, have had expectations akin to those of John M. King of the 92nd Illinois Volunteer Infantry:

> We were to have a long boat ride down the Ohio and up the Cumberland Rivers, where we could ride by day and night, view all the beautiful scenery and catch a glimpse of four or five states, one of which would be our dear old state of Illinois. We could watch the sunbeams, stars and moonlight sparkle, glitter, and dance on the waves of those beautiful rivers.

It took two days to get everything and everybody aboard the grand fleet. Starry-eyed, a few of the thousands of recruits could "dream of what would follow."

Those soldiers and commanders "in country," as well as many elsewhere, had some ideas — or fears — as to what might be expected as the transports steamed up into Kentucky and Tennessee, with the chief concerns being weather and navigation plus Confederate opposition. Department of the Ohio commander Maj. Gen. Horatio G. Wright wrote Capt. Pennock from Cincinnati and specifically noted "the importance to the army service of keeping the line of the Cumberland River between its mouth and Nashville constantly open to the use of our steam transports...."[32]

As February began, the center of action, if not operations, for the Union Navy's tinclads remained the upper rivers, where frigid weather made the interiors of their casemates among the warmest places of refuge. With most of the mosquito boats stationed on the Mississippi at or below Helena for the next Federal campaign against Vicksburg, only one or two remained on that river above Memphis. The half dozen available to Capt. Pennock and Lt. Cmdr. Fitch to safeguard the Ohio, Cumberland, and Tennessee continued their yeoman's work in protecting convoys and battling Confederate raiders.

Following its recent convoy attacks, Brig. Gen. Forrest's contingent traveled over to Palmyra, TN, located at a great vantage point overlooking the Cumberland that all convoymen feared. There his men were concealed and his guns masked. A rendezvous was to be affected near the town with Maj. Gen. Wheeler, who sought the most favorable position from which he, Wharton, and Forrest could challenge Yankee shipping.

There did not appear to be a good attack location for the Rebels. Wheeler was now convinced that his enemies had divined his intentions and had also stopped dispatching transports up or down the Cumberland. In this, he was only partially correct. The bluecoats did by this time know he was loose in the area, but their reactions did not extend to the river. Steamers still plied the waterway, but now most were under naval protection and convoys sailed far more infrequently than independent steamers. On top of this, gunboats and army patrols had eliminated all of the miscellaneous ferryboats above the Tennessee-Kentucky border near Fort Donelson, making a Rebel river crossing impossible.

Additional problems for the Confederate raiders were the weather, forage, and intelligence on local defenses. The former was bad and the latter two absent. The most difficult challenge facing Wheeler was a lack of rations and ammunition. Forrest's cavalry had only about 15 small arms rounds per man with a total of 45 cannon rounds; Wharton's brigade fared only slightly better: 20 shots per man and 50 artillery rounds. Cumulatively, these adversities were seen by Wheeler as necessitating a fast decision either for action in or retreat from the area. Despite a strong protest from Forrest, Gen. Bragg's cavalry chief elected to launch an assault on Fort Donelson, or, more correctly, the fortified nearby hamlet of Dover. If, as he postulated, the place could be captured and held, his people might better interdict Federal shipping.[33]

On February 2, the Confederates started their movement toward Dover, with Forrest traveling along the river from Palmyra by way of the Cumberland Iron Works. The same day, Col. Abner C. Harding, whose 83rd Illinois Regiment had garrisoned Dover since the fall, sent a telegram to his superior, Col. William C. Lowe of the 5th Iowa Cavalry commanding at Fort Henry. Lowe, who had also fed men into the Dover defenses, was told that Forrest, with 900 men and cannon, was at Palmyra intent upon blocking the Cumberland.

Harding felt himself ready. Four 12-pounder cannon were available, courtesy of Battery C, 2nd Illinois Artillery, along with an ex–Confederate 32-pounder brought over from Fort Donelson's unused water batteries. All the big guns and most of the 750 soldiers were assigned to prepared rifle pits or battery emplacements dug south and east of the town; Dover itself was 600 feet south of the Cumberland and was surrounded by deep natural ravines on its north side.

Just to be certain as to the accuracy of his intelligence, Harding proposed an amphibious expedition be run up toward Palmyra the next morning. The transport *Wild Cat*[34] would be employed, and the rest of the day was taken up with reinforcing her decks with hay bales and placing two 12-pounders aboard.[35]

As Confederate raiders and Dover defenders gathered or prepared down on the Cumberland, troops, animals, and supplies from Maj. Gen. Granger's corps were meanwhile being loaded aboard the transports at Louisville on February 1 as the weather grew colder and colder. One of the vessels was home to 92nd Illinois diarist John M. King. The men were packed on the boiler decks with animals and coal, while officers were given the cabins above. Cotton bales were employed as bulkheads to protect boilers and engines, while boiler iron was secured around vulnerable pilothouses. "These shields," King remembered, "were about the size of half a hogshead, but longer and so thick that a musket ball could not penetrate them."

Granger's boats were, in the words of diarist King, "loosed from the shore" at two A.M. on February 2 and steamed down the Ohio. One of the winter's coldest nights was clear, King later wrote, with a bright moon. Looking aft, the observer noted that the water in his steamer's "track glistened in the moonlight and its resembled fire so much that it was hard to believe it was not." Granger himself would write Maj. Gen. Rosecrans reporting that his column was finally away: "After perils by land and water, negroism and abolitionism, worthless quartermasters, and vexation of every kind and description."

Sometime before dawn on February 3, the great procession of Yankee army troop boats reached Smithland. The craft hauled up to take on additional coal at first light for the arduous journey up the Cumberland, and King of the 92nd Illinois was able to record his impressions of those he saw ashore. "Here," he wrote, "sailors and loafers congregated to lounge and loaf, tell vulgar stories, chew, smoke, drink, and talk politics!"

The few hours of coaling were completed and it was time to shove off under the protection of all six of Lt. Cmdr. Fitch's gunboats: *Lexington, Fairplay, Brilliant, St. Clair, Alfred Robb,* and *Silver Lake.* Notwithstanding the navy, many of the green soldiers aboard were fearful of roving bands of Rebel riders. They were afraid that the riders would attack individual boats by aiming "first to kill the pilot." After that, the enemy could "let the vessel run aground, then after pillaging it, they would burn it."

While Granger's fleet refueled at Smithland, Maj. Elijah C. Brott of the 83rd Illinois, with two infantry companies, boarded the *Wild Cat* at Dover for an excursion up the Cumberland toward Palmyra to check on reports of Rebel raiders. Earlier, a small group of 5th Iowa cavalry was sent up by road toward the iron works to act in conjunction with Brott. Before the steamer could shove off, however, a civilian rode into the town warning Col. Harding that Wheeler was at the works; the warning was too late to save the cavalrymen, who were captured.

By 1:30 P.M., Confederate forces surrounded Dover and sent Col. Harding an ultimatum from Maj. Gen. Wheeler demanding unconditional surrender. Harding refused.

He was also able to send away the town's noncombatants aboard two steamers, simultaneously dispatch the *Wild Cat* with orders to seek out and return with gunboats, and send messengers to Fort Henry for reinforcements.

Once it started, the combat, which is described by Cooling and other historians and is captured in the pages of the army and navy *Official Records*, continued throughout the afternoon. Wheeler's men mounted determined attacks, skillfully employing their cannon and limited ammunition. Although Yankee infantry was pushed back and the Confederates, at one point, occupied the entire western half of Dover, the Rebel assaults were, in the end, repulsed by the determined Northern defenders.

As dusk fell that cold, snowy winter evening, the Confederate leadership met to consider options. Given his lack of ammunition and the fact that Col. Harding would not surrender (a second ultimatum was sent and refused — Harding did not reveal that he was nearly out of ammunition as well), and realizing that Federal relief was en route, Wheeler decided "that it would be better to retire." In darkness, his men undertook an orderly withdrawal to a bivouac area some four miles south of Dover.[36]

"We could faintly hear the cannonading away up the river at a great distance," diarist King recalled. He and the 92nd Illinois men aboard the transport *Tempest*, as well as soldiers on the other boats being convoyed by Lt. Cmdr. Fitch's six gunboats, were aware of the Dover fight early in the afternoon of February 3. Entirely by dint of Yankee luck, the Granger fleet was only 24 miles downstream from Dover when it was located by the *Wild Cat*. As the procession continued, Harding's steamer and the flagship *Fairplay* made rendezvous, and Fitch received the colonel's message sent some hours earlier at the beginning of the battle. Harding's note was brief: his pickets had been driven in, he was being assaulted in force, and he needed immediate assistance.

The young convoy commodore instantly made signal to the other gunboats, ordering that they all push on up toward Dover "with all possible speed." The transports were left to follow "as fast as possible." Twenty-four miles is not a great distance by 2010 standards. That is the round-trip distance daily commuted by the author in about 40 minutes' total driving time (admittedly on rural roads in Greene County, Tennessee). But in 1863, in the current of the Cumberland River, aboard gunboats with a speed of 4–6 knots (5–8 mph), 24 miles was a long way off. Still, Lt. Cmdr. Fitch was determined to mount a rescue and signaled his warships to steam up at forced draught, with coal shoveled into the boilers as quickly as possible.

The trip to Dover took Fitch's flotilla about five hours. A short distance below the town, the *Fairplay* spoke to another steamer, the captain of which cried that the place had been entirely surrounded and could not hold out much longer. Pushing on up, the gunboats arrived off Dover about 8 P.M. The encircled Col. Harding and his men were found, Fitch later remembered, holding off overwhelming numbers from small breastworks back about 300 yards from the river bank.

In composing his report next morning, the Indiana-born sailor offered a rare insight into the command difficulties of those first post-arrival moments. "For a minute or so, I was at a loss as to where to begin," he confided to paper, "as I could not get word from our forces, the enemy then holding the ground between them and the river...." With no intelligence at all as to Confederate dispositions, he decided he could at least "let off a gun up the ravine" to give Union forces "encouragement by letting them know that assistance was at hand."

Two other pieces of luck now fell the Federal way. "Just then the moon shone out bright," Fitch recalled. At the same time, an officer from the 83rd Illinois arrived at the river bank, having secreted himself through Rebel lines at the sound of the *Fairplay's* howitzer. The man was taken aboard and pointed out the enemy positions. The main body of Confederates were formed in line of battle through the graveyard at the west end of the town, about 700–800 yards from Federal positions, with its left wing resting in a ravine leading down to the river and possibly extending almost to the river bank.

It was perfectly obvious to the men aboard the gunboats that Rebel forces were not expecting them. While moving close inshore to make it easier to rake nearly the entire length of the enemy line, the sailors could hear Confederate soldiers talking in the darkness. In position, all six gunboats opened fire up the exposed ravine, into the graveyard, and into the valley beyond — almost every location known or suspected of holding Southern troops, active or reserve, and horses. "The rebels were so much taken by surprise," Fitch reported, "that they did not even fire a shot, but immediately commenced retreating."

"I was enabled to throw shell right in their midst," Fitch rejoiced. Once the main body was dispersed, the *Alfred Robb* and *Silver Lake* were stationed abreast of Dover to throw random shells and to prevent Confederates from returning to carry off their wounded. The *Fairplay* led the *Lexington*, *St. Clair*, and *Brilliant* above to shell the roads leading out toward the east. Believing that other retreating Rebel units would follow the river for some distance, the *Lexington* and *St. Clair* were sent on up to shell the woods along the river bank, primarily to harass and annoy any Southerners choosing that exit. The *Fairplay* and *Brilliant*, meanwhile, lay opposite the upper ravine and tossed howitzer shells up the various roads. Except for harassment fire, the gunboats ceased fire at 10 P.M. An hour later, Col. Harding sent word that the Confederates were completely gone from around the town. The gunboats were then positioned to provide night guard over the roads approaching Dover.

Fitch honestly believed that, in the words of Admiral Mahan, his arrival had occurred with the Union garrison *in extremis* and that his intervention turned the tide in favor of Dover's defenders. Thereafter the naval officer — and the U.S. Navy — always maintained that his men were right to "claim the honor of dispersing" Maj. Gen. Wheeler's forces "and saving Fort Donelson." Indeed, his officers and men "were very glad to have a shot at these river infesters, having been somewhat annoyed by them on previous occasions." The gunboatmen were happy to know — or believe — that, by their actions, the Confederates were "cut up, routed, and despoiled of its prey by the timely arrival of the gunboats and that Col. Harding and his gallant little band were spared to wear the honors they had so fairly won." It would be left to others over the next century to debate the effectiveness of Fitch's tinclads on this occasion.

The night of February 3–4 was very cold with considerable snow in the Dover area. The Union transports, which had made their way up in the absence of naval cover — some racing one another — arrived at the landing about noon on February 4. Union soldiers and sailors policed or visited ashore in the Dover area over the next several days congratulating themselves on the stout defense.

Meanwhile, Maj. Gen. Wheeler and Brig. Gen. Forrest retreated south, through Charlotte and on over the next days to Centerville, on the Duck River. The ground pursuit by the men from the commands of Colonels Lowe, Harding, and others was ineffective in the snow and cold; the nearly frozen Confederates were able to escape across the icy stream after volunteers swam over and returned from the far side with a ferry.

Although the regular Rebel riders had gone, partisans and guerrillas, among them the 2nd Kentucky Cavalry (CSA) of Col. Thomas Woodward, remained behind to harass and annoy Union communications. For the next month, Woodward hovered around Cumberland Furnace and joined with local men in making attacks at both Palmyra and Harpeth Shoals. The area from which these people operated was considered not only a safe spot for irregulars, but a protected river crossing point. Wheeler, Forrest, and Wharton may have failed to take Dover, "but the Rebels still effectively controlled the southerly banks of the lower Cumberland River and thereby remained a potent threat to Union supply lines."

On the morning of February 6, Maj. Gen. Granger's troop convoy, guarded by the navy tinclads, steamed slowly up the Cumberland River toward Nashville. The size of the group had been increased the previous day by the addition of 17 late-arriving transports. The civilian boats were "lashed together two by two," one passenger recalled, a formation held as the craft passed Clarksville. Although it was "a pretty town," it was notorious in the eyes of 92nd Illinois soldier John King as home to a group which, besides being "secessh," had made "the world nastier and filthier by raising and shipping large quantities of that weed called tobacco," a product that "boys love to eat, chew, and smoke and they learn to swear and become lazy, filthy loafers." The convoy reached Nashville about 4 P.M. on the afternoon of February 7, though many of the transports were not unloaded until the next morning.

A concise evaluation of the battle was rendered some years later by Cumberland River historian Douglas. "It is doubtful if the capture of Fort Donelson [Dover] could have resulted in a complete blockade of the river, but it would have had a tremendous psychological effect upon the people of the South." At the same time, it would have had "a most depressing effect at this particular time upon Rosecrans, who thought he was facing a disruption of his entire line of supplies and communications."[37]

While the eyes of many were focused were on the Dover battle and the convoy of the Army of the Kentucky, events on the Mississippi also occupied the attention of numerous tinclad commanders. On February 3, six light-draughts assigned to the Lower Mississippi Squadron began participation with two ironclads, two rams, and 21 troop boats in a large Vicksburg bypass campaign known as the Yazoo Pass Expedition. This effort to yet again get behind the Confederate fortress city via interconnecting streams from the north was a regular military enterprise and its combat is outside the scope of this narrative. The scheme was not a success and ended in mid–March.[38]

The great levee of the Yazoo Pass was hardly breached when, on February 7, the new tinclad *Glide* was accidentally destroyed by fire at Cairo. The light-draught was moored astern of and to the wharf boat and outboard of several other boats and the blaze aboard this early cold morning quickly got out of control. Arriving on the scene, Captains Pennock, Phelps, and Woodworth speedily summoned the tug *Dahlia* and the *Glide* was towed out into midstream, away from the naval station. She slowly drifted to the Kentucky shore near Fort Holt and burned to the water's edge, the first tinclad lost during the war.[39]

Normally serving as a dispatch boat and transport, the tinclad *New Era*,[40] under Acting Master Frank W. Flanner, assumed the responsibilities of guard ship at Island No.10 toward the end of January. In relieving the ironclad *Carondelet* stationed there previously, she was ordered to prevent Confederate assembly and to interdict contraband trade.

On February 7, the *Wisconsin State Register* told its readers of an engagement between the *New Era* and a large group of Rebel raiders that attacked her with three cannon from the Tennessee shore at 11 P.M. on February 1. The tinclad replied with shell and the ensuing battle "was kept up without cessation until nearly daylight" on Monday. The Confederates having gotten the worst of it, the journal reported, they "beat a hasty retreat down the river."

There are no reports or other records to show the event ever happened. On the other hand, the *New Era*, beginning on February 4, bagged four contraband steamers in less than a month, setting something of a record in the tinclad war against illegal shipping. Although a bit out of chronological sequence, we review all of the captures here.

At mid-morning on February 4, the 55-ton side-wheeler *William A. Knapp*,[41] under a Capt. Day, was intercepted while passing downstream and boarded by a party under the tinclad's executive officer Acting Ensign William C. Hanford. A review of the boat's papers immediately revealed tampering and an inspection of various suspicious boxes and trunks was ordered. When the *New Era*'s carpenter's mate pried these open, all manner of contraband was found: revolvers, quinine, morphine, sundry cloth, and other valuable goods all on the proscribed list of the U.S. Treasury Department. All of the merchantman's crew and passengers were taken prisoner and, together with the prize vessel, were sent to Cairo for adjudication.

On February 13, the side-wheeler *White Cloud*[42] was halted on the Mississippi below Memphis and boarded. A large Confederate mail, en route from St. Louis for the army of Maj. Gen. Sterling Price, was uncovered and the steamboat was confiscated. A prize crew was detailed aboard and the packet was sent off to Cairo.

Later that day, at Hale's Point on the left bank in the vicinity of Island No. 10, Capt. James Cass Mason's *Rowena*,[43] owned by Capt. John T. Dozier and named for his daughter, was overhauled by the *New Era* and boarded. Hale's Point was a transfer point for goods and produce brought down the Obion River, but it was not garrisoned by Federal troops and was consequently "heavily infested with rebels." Acting Ensign Hanford and his men reviewed the *Rowena*'s manifests and searched the 225-foot-long side-wheeler, finding large amounts of contraband, including 2,900 pairs of Rebel uniform pants, medicines, saddles, etc. When Acting Master Flanner was informed, he ordered the *New Era*'s gunner to take a prize crew aboard the vessel and move it to Cairo. Later, Navy Secretary Welles would disavow the capture.

Intent on landing at Fulton Bend below Fort Pillow on the last day of the month, Capt Paul F. Semonin's 150-foot stern-wheeler *Curlew*[44] was intercepted by the *New Era* before she could do so. Acting captain Hanford's boarding party once more uncovered unpermitted goods, along with $1,587.15 in Confederate money and counterfeit Union greenbacks. The confiscated steamer was also sent to Cairo.[45]

In the weeks following the Battle of Dover, TN, the Upper Rivers Mosquito Flotilla, under Lt. Cmdr. Le Roy Fitch, ran several more convoys up to Nashville. Patrols were also operated to the Upper Cumberland River and to the Tennessee. It was during a scout up the latter stream that the gunboat men had a chance to participate in some "Yankee" horse soldier activity.

About this time, a small Union force mounted a daring little raid, gaining one of the North's few successful military surprises that month in the Federal anti-insurgency conflict. On February 19, intelligence was received by a scouting party from the 3rd Michigan Cavalry, headquartered at Lexington, TN, that noted guerrilla leader Col. John F. Newsom and his men were staying across the Tennessee at Clifton. Having found and refloated a sunken flatboat and mounted a small deception designed to convince local spies that they had returned to base, Capt. Cicero Newell took 60 of his fellow Grand Rapids troopers across after midnight and surrounded Clifton before dawn, February 20, doing in the weary grayclad pickets.

In a furious dawn attack upon the sleeping but fast-responding Rebels at Clifton, 3rd Michigan Cavalry Capt. Newell was wounded and succeeded in command by Capt. Frederick C. Adamson. After a short time, 54 Confederates were captured, including Col. Newsom, who had been shot in the left arm. Horses and small arms were also taken and the rest of the "guerrillas" had fled. When the battle was done, the town was set ablaze.

As smoke rose from several burning structures, U.S. Navy tinclads on patrol from Fort Henry came around the bend. Looking through his telescope, Lt. Cmdr. Fitch saw Capt. Adamson signaling him to land. Once ashore, the navy leader and the army officer conferred on the Michiganders' raid. Adamsom feared a Rebel counterattack and asked the navy to get his force, the Confederate prisoners, and the captured property, including the horses, back across the river. Fitch agreed to all the soldier's requests before inspecting what was left of the community and taking time to interview a number of prisoners. While Fitch and others from the gunboats reviewed the area trying to learn of other local enemy activities, Surgeon Howard dressed the wounds of Adamson and also of Col. Newsom, who was paroled and released.

Later that afternoon, all of the prisoners, whom Howard described in a letter home as "the most ragamuffin collection that can be found," were distributed around the gunboats. Lt. Cmdr. Fitch next took Capt. Adamson and 40 Michigan cavalrymen aboard and steamed up to Eagle Nest Island seeking another reported group of Rebels and a cache of stores. Neither was found, and, after dark, the tinclads landed Adamson's people on the west bank of the Tennessee.

Fitch's gunboats continued on upstream on their armed reconnaissance. Eyes were peeled for enemy guns and men along the shores. "They are good marksmen," the *Brilliant's* Surgeon Howard admitted of the Confederates, "and if they fire from planted guns, we stand a chance to be well pounded as a ball from a 12-pounder would go through us like so much paper."

The Mosquito Fleet's Tennessee River review took another week. When it was over, Surgeon Howard summed up the entire trip in one sentence of a letter home: "We have gone up the Tennessee River to Florence and some 60 miles above to the Muscle Shoals and we have seen no batteries."[46]

Convoys to Nashville and patrols up the Tennessee occupied the Upper River tinclad fleet throughout March. To grow the fleet needed on the Cumberland and for the Tennessee River enterprise, Fleet Capt. Pennock sent the *Springfield*[47] back from Illinois to Smithland. The tinclad had been employed at the Cairo station for the last month.

Over on the Mississippi, at Island No. 10, Acting Vol. Lt. Henry Glassford relieved Acting Ensign Hanford as commander of the *New Era* on March 4. The tinclad's war against Confederate communications and smugglers, as well as contraband shippers, continued unabated. Under recommendation of Brig. Gen. Asboth, now commanding the post at Columbus, KY, the giant side-wheeler *Ruth*[48] was boarded and seized on the morning of March 12. The vessel, famous for magnificent paintings of the Biblical Ruth on her wheelhouses, had been identified by Federal detectives as secreting both contraband goods and a Confederate mail. A prize crew took her to Memphis. During the remainder of March, the *New Era* intercepted or otherwise overhauled all downward-bound vessels not in government service, making arrests and seizing contraband goods and thousands of dollars in Southern funds.

Acting Volunteer Lt. A.R. Langthorne's tinclad *Cricket*[49] departed downstream from Memphis on April 14 searching for two steamers, the *Delta*[50] and *Forest Queen*,[51] reportedly engaged in "the contraband business." Coming upon them lying at the bank, the gunboat sent boarding officers to inspect the pair. The manifests and other papers were found to be in order and no illegal goods were uncovered. Upon inquiry as to their business laying in a prohibited location, the captains informed Langthorne that they were guarding abandoned cotton to prevent Southerners from burning it.

The men sought naval protection as they loaded it, hinting that such help was suggested when they cleared the Memphis customs house. The tinclad captain refused, indicating that the only way he could help was if the produce was turned over to the U.S. government. The men readily agreed, and the abandoned bales were taken aboard the *Cricket*. Upon her return to Memphis next day, the cotton was landed at the navy yard to await a decision on whether it would be returned to the captains or forwarded on to Cairo.

Dealing with abandoned cotton, tobacco, rice and other articles became something of a problem as the month wore on, occasioning a General Order from Rear Adm. Porter in early April demanding that naval officers refrain from stopping along river banks to pick up such loose booty, leaving it to Treasury Department agents "appointed for this purpose."[52]

As the month closed, Army of the Cumberland chief of staff and future U.S. president Brig. Gen. James A. Garfield, south in Murfreesboro, informed Maj. Gen. Granger, at Franklin, of emerging Tennessee River developments. His review was closed with an ominous suspicion: "There seems to be a considerable force at Palmyra." Before the navy could get back up the Tennessee, the fleet slated for the trip would have to return to the Cumberland and deal with the town Lt. Cmdr. Fitch had earlier called a "noted guerrilla haunt." Palmyra, Tennessee, is located on the Cumberland River 27.2 miles upstream from Dover and 10 miles below Clarksville. Host to an important prewar steamboat landing, it was founded as Blountville in 1797. That year the U.S. Congress designated the town the "first official point of entry in the West."

Elements of Maj. Gen. Wheeler's force had congregated in the little town, population about 200, before the February attack on Dover. The place, one of the highest to overlook a straight portion of the river, offered a wonderful position to shoot down from its bluff into approaching Union shipping. At the beginning of April, Col. Thomas Woodward's 2nd Kentucky Cavalry (C.S.A.), plus local irregulars and at least three cannon, were once again located there to interdict Yankee transport.

By this time, Northern logistics officials, military and civil, had grown complacent with the operation of their Louisville-Nashville-Louisville supply chain. After all, some 180 steamers and 30 barges had been safely escorted up the river from Smithland or Fort Donelson in seven convoys to Nashville between January 24 and March 15.

Having stood out from Smithland on March 31, the gunboats *St. Clair* and *Fairplay* arrived at Fort Donelson on April 1, where they took several waiting transports in hand and proceeded upriver, reaching Gower's Island on the morning of April 2. Guessing there was no danger ahead, Acting Volunteer Lt. Jacob Hurd, the escort commander, signaled the steamers to go on to Nashville while he took his two warships back to Fort Donelson to pick up additional incoming transports and towboats. From the site of the ferocious February battles, Hurd gathered up the new group and headed up the Cumberland late in the afternoon, with the *St. Clair* at the head of the column and the *Fairplay* at the rear. Unhappily, Hurd, a "brave and efficient" officer, miscalculated his convoy's cruising disposition. He would also fail tactically in the fight which followed.

Mosquito Flotilla commander Fitch had instructed his subordinates to always place their slowest vessels in the van, with the most valuable in the center and the fastest in the rear. This allowed for the line to be kept closed up and for one gunboat to always be within supporting range of another. Acting Volunteer Lt. Hurd did not observe this doctrine and, instead, placed his most valuable boats up front and his slowest at the rear, making it impossible for the pokey *Fairplay* to remain within support distance. The line as it proceeded up the Cumberland included the steamers *Eclipse*[53] and *Lizzie Martin*[54] lashed together, the *St. Clair*, the transport *Luminary*,[55] the towboats *Charles Miller*[56] and *J.N. Kellogg*[57] each with a barge drawing 7.5 feet of water, and the *Fairplay*. Hurd, who had encountered no enemy activity while passing Palmyra on earlier trips, was concerned about his deeply-laden barges and did not anticipate an ambush.

At 10:30 P.M. Hurd's fleet approached Palmyra. When off the bluff immediately above that town, it was fired into by an elevated enemy battery comprising a depressed 6-pounder Parrott rifle and a 12-pounder smoothbore cannon. Paired as they were, the *Eclipse* and *Lizzie Martin* should have been an easy target for the Confederate gunners — who missed, badly damaging neither one of the two, largely because they were already too far upstream in the dark to be easily targeted.

Unhappily, the *St. Clair* and the *Luminary* were only about 400 feet from their attackers, who now gave them their full attention with cannon and some 60 muskets. The *Luminary* was struck by numerous Minie balls; however, it was the *St. Clair* which took the brunt of the assault. Acting Volunteer Lt. Hurd, his guns run out, was unable to elevate his howitzers sufficiently in his location to hit the guns up on the bluff. Still, he fired away and, as he put it in his official report, "the contest was spirited for a short time."

The fight was also all one-sided, with the *St. Clair* struck by small arms, canister, and at least six shells, one of which went through her deck and struck her supply pipe, letting all the water out of her boilers and making the boat unmanageable. *St. Clair* went dead in the water, but fortunately, the undamaged *Luminary* heeded Hurd's hail, came alongside, and took the warship under tow.

Hurd's executive officer, Acting Master George W. Fouty, one of the Mosquito Fleet's most popular and devoted officers, rose from a sickbed to go to his battle station as soon as the fighting began. During the largely one-sided battle, he was badly hurt when a 6-pdr. elongated shot came through the *St. Clair*'s bulkhead and shattered his right knee. When the wounded tinclad, under tow of the *Luminary*, reached Fort Donelson, Fouty was, after examination aboard by the post surgeon, immediately transferred ashore to the hospital.

The convoy leader was unable to get a wire through to Lt. Cmdr. Fitch at Smithland as the telegraph lines to that post were down. Hurd did get a message through to

One of the first two stern-wheelers converted by Commodore Hull at St. Louis into light-draught ("tinclad") gunboats, the veteran *St. Clair* was roughly handled by Col. Thomas Woodward's 2nd Kentucky Cavalry (C.S.A.) at Palmyra, Tennessee, on April 2, 1863. She was towed out of danger by one of the steamers she was protecting and eventually repaired. The attack upon her caused the Cumberland River town to be burned to the ground in retaliation (Naval Historical Center).

Fleet Capt. Pennock while Col. William P. Boone, in command at Clarksville, informed Nashville and Murfreesboro of the attack. There was genuine relief that the two vessels were not captured. The repairs made to the *St. Clair*'s supply pipe were so imperfect that she could not safely steam on her own. It was necessary for the *J.N. Kellogg* to tow the gunboat back to Smithland.

Several days later, Acting Volunteer Lt. Hurd was forced to accept the displeasure of his superior, whose guidance included a catalog of the volunteer lieutenant's battle mistakes: poor convoy arrangement; a decision (made after his supply pipe was cut) not to anchor and fight back until the *Fairplay* could come up, and then use the combined firepower of the two to drive out the Rebels; and a failure to understand that, had he again been compelled to drop down, the current and the availability of towing assistance would have aided him.

Following his perceived success at Dover in February and the work of the gunboats at Arkansas Post a month before that, Fitch had supreme confidence in the day-and-night superiority of naval tactics against river bank cavalry and cannon. He would later come to appreciate their limitations.[58]

Fleet Captain Pennock and Lt. Cmdr. Fitch did not at first realize what had happened at Palmyra. The former received Hurd's Fort Donelson wire and immediately sent one of his own to Smithland asking Fitch, who had just returned to that rendezvous, whether he had heard anything of the attack. He had not.

When Fitch at Smithland finally received word from Acting Volunteer Lt. Hurd late on April 3, he immediately called his captains together and gave them the news. Their boats were already coaled and were, in fact, completing last-minute preparations for another patrol up the Tennessee in the morning. Rushing ashore to the telegraph office, Fitch wired Capt. Pennock: "I leave in 10 minutes for Palmyra with all the boats. Will whip them out." The Cairo station chief quickly messaged back his approval to "Go ahead and whip them out."

Overnight, the *Lexington, Brilliant, Alfred Robb, Silver Lake,* and *Springfield* steamed upriver intent upon retaliation for the convoy attack by Col. Woodward's force. Downriver from Dover, the warships encountered the *Fairplay* and the crippled *St. Clair,* under tow of the *J.N. Kellogg.* During the ensuing mid-river rendezvous, Hurd made a preliminary report concerning the particulars of the attack as he knew them, the enemy's positions and guns, and of the wounding of Mr. Fouty.

As the *St. Clair* continued on to Cairo for repairs, the *Fairplay* joined the avenging fleet. The latest intelligence was sought at Fort Donelson, where the gunboats arrived on the morning of April 4, and arrangements for a visit to Palmyra were completed, including the placement of hay bales around the boilers of the five tinclads.

When ready, the Union fleet proceeded on up, arriving at Palmyra — Surgeon Howard called it "the cursed spot" — late that Saturday afternoon. Several transports, which had been waiting at Fort Donelson for escort to Nashville and perhaps with soldiers aboard, were allowed to accompany the fleet to within a safe distance of the town, being closely guarded by three of the tinclads. Although the men on the warships were "beat to quarters" and every cannon was ready, no enemy battery or forces were found.

Lt. Cmdr. Fitch was one of the few naval officers who remained opposed to the more draconian aspects of Federal anti-guerrilla policy then being employed, including "the wanton destruction of property." Many of the men of his command, having experienced a constant peppering from the river banks for weeks and now having learned of the fate of "poor Fouty," had no such qualms. Surgeon Howard on the *Brilliant* seemed to speak for most of the bluejackets now off Palmyra: "Every town harboring Rebel sympathizers should be burned" because the irregulars did not believe in a fair fight — "they hide in the bush, shoot and run." If it were left to Howard and his fellow tars to set Federal counterinsurgency policy, they would "make this accursed Reb country a howling wilderness, and trust in the goodness of the Lord that it might be peopled by a better race in the future."

As it was, Fitch agreed that, in this instance, the total destruction of Palmyra was justifiable. The *St. Clair* attack confirmed for him the village's reputation as "one of the worst secession places on the river." Every Federal believed that "unarmed transports had been fired into from doors and windows of the houses in the town." The *Lexington* landed opposite the town and a detachment was sent on shore, in charge of Acting Master James Fitzpatrick from the timberclad, with orders to burn every building in the town. Fitzpatrick was to make certain that his men did not "remove or pillage a single article," because everything was to be torched as an object lesson. Beforehand, the inhabitants were given a specified time to evacuate.

As Fitzpatrick and his landing party spread out, several men, perceived as stragglers from the enemy battery, broke from their concealment and tired to run away. They were fired upon and one was killed, with a second wounded and others taken prisoner. Once the work of retribution was completed, the gunboats "left the town of Palmyra by its own light" at moonrise. There was real satisfaction among the sailors; as Howard put it, "it was clean work — every building was in flames and falling."

Lt. Cmdr. Fitch, in a mission-ending telegram to Capt. Pennock from Nashville a few days later, was matter-of-fact: they had "burned the town; not a house left; a very bad hole; best to get rid of it and teach the rebels a lesson." Writing more than 130 years later, Nashville judge Robert Brandt reaffirmed what many Middle Tennesseans had long been taught: Fitch's raid "ruined" Palmyra. The town, as the *Chicago Daily Tribune* reported, was "now numbered among the things that were and now are not."[59]

Anticipating Union Navy retribution, Woodward's Confederates, according to those captured at Palmyra, hitched up their guns and retreated toward Harpeth Shoals shortly after the *St. Clair* attack. The exact destination, as the bluejackets learned, was Betseytown Landing, another notorious guerrilla hangout, some 32–33 miles upstream beyond Clarksville and Hinton.

Determined to catch the bushwhackers, Fitch continued up the Cumberland. At Clarksville on April 5, the mosquito boat chief and local post commander Col. Boone agreed to make the pursuit amphibious. A number of infantry and cavalry from the post, led by the colonel personally, were loaded aboard the tinclads, and the expedition, again with the civilian transports trailing at a safe distance under escort, steamed upstream.

The bluecoats were landed a few miles below Harpeth Shoals in the forenoon of April 6 and moved on their suspected enemy while the gunboats steamed up to Betseytown Landing to attract attention with a bombardment from the river. If Fitch could keep the grayclads occupied, it was hoped that Boone's men could sneak up behind them and capture the offending cannon or that they would withdraw directly into the path of the arriving Federals. The scheme, now the familiar plan of Northern ground-sea attack, was foiled in the end because Fitch's opponents learned of his approach and retreated again, this time from their camp, two miles back from the river, toward Charlotte. Cavalry landed from the gunboats pursued about six miles up the Charlotte road, but elected not to go deeper into hostile country.

The Cumberland River was rapidly falling and Lt. Cmdr. Fitch believed he had accomplished all that was possible in pursuit of the Palmyra ambushers. The accompanying transports were sent up to Nashville under protection of the *Brilliant, Alfred Robb,* and *Silver Lake* as the *Lexington, Springfield,* and one transport returned Boone's command to Clarksville. Nothing but smoldering ruins were seen by the two latter warships as they passed the rubble of Palmyra en route back to Smithland.[60] Immediately upon his return to the main Cumberland gunboat rendezvous, Lt. Cmdr. Fitch reported to Capt. Pennock, who replied: "Congratulations on your success.... Keep the Cumberland clear of the enemy. Go ahead and clear the banks of the Tennessee."

The burning of Palmyra and the reported departure of Col. Woodward's force to join Forrest's main body near Columbia occasioned no relaxation in the Confederate war on Federal river transport in Middle Tennessee — primarily because the Kentucky horsemen were not actually gone.

At some point on April 9, a pair of small steamers, the 60-ton propeller *Saxonia*[61] and the 100-ton stern-wheeler *R.M.C. Lovell,*[62] both transporting sutler's stores, arrived at Fort Donelson. The *Brilliant, Alfred Robb,* and *Springfield* were away, taking a return convoy to Smithland. Refusing to wait for the tinclads to come back and thus to join in the next escorted passage, the two set off together next day up the river to Nashville. Both were captured as darkness fell at a point about 15 miles north of Clarksville by Woodward's men and local guerrillas. Once the crews of the two boats were secured, it was later reported, the Confederates "took out eight negroes and shot them, by the light of a lantern." When the captain of the *Lovell* protested, he, too, was murdered.

Only Col. Parsons and two Southern newspapers, including the *Granada* (MS) *Appeal* (formerly the *Memphis Daily Appeal*), reported this incident. The latter, portraying the *Lovell* as a "gunboat," confirmed that her commander was killed and that both craft were destroyed. When he heard of the matter, Lt. Cmdr. Fitch was frank in his summation. "As far as the boats were concerned," he wrote to Rear Adm. Porter on April 15, "there was no one to blame but themselves." Their captains "paid the penalty of disobedience of orders by having their boats burned."[63]

As April's spring blossomed, it was at last determined that Federal efforts to reach and take Vicksburg from the Yazoo region would not succeed. The grand strategy was revised and the U.S. Army camped above Vicksburg would now make an assault crossing of the Mississippi below the Confederate fortress. To that end, Maj. Gen. Grant marched his men about 50 miles down the west side of the river from Young's Point, stopping first at New Carthage before continuing down to Hard Times Landing.

For his part, Rear Adm. Porter agreed to take the ironclads and transports necessary to ferry the troops directly downstream past the Vicksburg batteries. Most of the Pook turtles, the *Lafayette*, *General Price*, *Tuscumbia*, and the *Benton* would make the trip. The Eads ironclad *Baron de Kalb*, the new *Chocktaw*, all of the locally-assigned light-draughts and the timberclads would remain behind as guard ships and to provide diversions in the streams above the fortress.

The April 17 Vicksburg passage was a grand success. Only one transport was sunk. A few nights later, additional transports ran the gauntlet.[64]

Even as the Cumberland River flotilla guarded convoys and tried to pacify the river-bank guerrillas and while Maj. Gen. Grant and Rear Adm. Porter looked for a new way into Vicksburg, another, larger Federal enterprise, with a far less happy ending, was beginning to unfold: the Streight Raid. The first mounted incursion of Confederate territory by a large force of mounted bluecoat infantry would be supported by units from the Mississippi Squadron.

Maj. Gen. Rosecrans, still under continuous pressure from Washington, D.C., to move south, badly wanted to advance, but as bloodlessly as possible. "It occurred to his fertile mind," John Wyeth later wrote, "that if he could secure the destruction of the two important railroads leading from Chattanooga — one to Atlanta and the other to Knoxville — about the time he could force Bragg" south out of Tullahoma, Chattanooga would be cut off.

Col. Abel D. Streight, commander of the 51st Indiana Volunteer Infantry, was an energetic, original thinker who, like others in his army, was disappointed that the Union had, thus far, been unable to match in effectiveness — or glory — the raids of such Confederate saddle wizards as John Hunt Morgan and Nathan Bedford Forrest. Like others familiar with the region, he knew that Dalton, GA, was a key Confederate rail hub, where tracks met connecting Chattanooga and Atlanta, and was vulnerable to a large mounted party riding east through the local mountains. If other Northern troops took Tuscumbia and he, with help from pockets of Union sympathizers behind in the rough country of north Alabama, could then take Dalton, easy Rebel transportation into Tennessee would be terminated.[65]

Col. Streight's newly-formed, 2,000-man "Independent Provisional Brigade," that others derisively labeled "the Mule Brigade," was loaded on steamers and, under convoy of the Army gunboat *Excelsior*, sent down to Palmyra on April 11. There, near the "black and charred ruins" of the town, training exercises were held. The empty transports were, meanwhile, sent downstream and around via the Ohio into the Tennessee and up to Fort Henry. There they met Streight's command, which had come overland.

While the Indiana colonel and his men moved toward Fort Henry, the Mississippi Marine Brigade, another unusual group, prepared to play a role in this story. Led by Brig. Gen. Alfred W. Ellet, it was originally a War Department amphibious outfit that fought in the June 1862 Battle of Memphis. The command had been transferred to the U.S. Navy the previous November. In an April 9 report to Secretary Welles, Porter noted that Ellet's force and several gunboats under Lt. Cmdr. Fitch were en route to the Tennessee to co-operate with Streight. "This is all we can do for General Rosecrans," he concluded, "and it is all he should require, or would require, if he will advance his troops as far as the Mussel Shoals."

By mid-month, the 2nd Division, under Brig. Gen. Granville Dodge, from the U.S.

XVI Army Corps, was ordered to capture Tuscumbia. As cover for the real mission, Streight's brigade would join in the Dodge endeavor, before peeling off to "go directly to its main object — the destruction of the railroads." All the U.S. Navy vessels that could be spared were assigned to support this enterprise. Fitch's orders from the admiral were, as he put it in a note delivered to Dodge on April 16, "Go down as the river falls." Conversely, "of course, I ascend as it rises." The Tennessee had been low for some time and it remained impossible to say whether a rise would occur.

In addition to the big-gun *Lexington*, Fitch had available the new tinclads *Argosy*,[66] *Covington*, and *Queen City*,[67] "four of my best boats," that together could also carry about 2,000 infantry. The *Covington* and *Argosy* were left at Fort Henry to convoy Ellet and Streight's transports, while the *Lexington* and the *Queen City* pushed up. Although the Hoosier commodore left the remainder of his Mosquito Fleet in the Cumberland to convoy transports back and forth to Nashville, he knew that his combinations were such that reinforcements from their number could be quickly called in for a short period if necessary.

Despite a spirited Confederate defense, Tuscumbia Landing fell to the Union about noon on April 23, with Florence captured shortly thereafter. All of the noise along the Tennessee, from Streight, Ellet, Dodge, Fitch, and others, did not go unnoticed at Gen. Bragg's headquarters. In the evening of this Thursday, the Confederate leader wired Brig Gen. Nathan Bedford Forrest at Spring Hill and directed him to put an end to the Streight-Dodge incursion.

On Sunday, April 26, Streight and Dodge separated at Tuscumbia. Streight and his men slipped away into north Alabama, headed toward Georgia. Dodge began an attempt to deceive Forrest's men by acting as though he were headed toward a linkup with Maj. Gen. Grant.

The arrival of the famed Confederate raider into the story was a fatal stroke of bad luck to befall the Streight project. Forrest and his men were not fooled by the Dodge ruse and weaved into a relentless pursuit of the Hoosier colonel that did not end until the 1,446 surviving officers and men of the Independent Provisional Brigade were all cornered and taken on the Alabama-Georgia line on May 3. Neither Dodge, nor Ellet, nor Fitch were in any position to assist, and Streight could not get free of his dogged pursuer who, in one of his most celebrated exploits, captured an entire Yankee force three times his size.[68]

A day after Dodge and Streight took Tuscumbia Landing, Brig. Gen. Ellet and Lt. Cmdr. Fitch were themselves drawn into a fight with Confederates secreted on the banks of the Tennessee River. Among the enemy units now unleashed against the Union river invaders was a battery of four fieldpieces belonging to Maj. Robert M. White's 6th Texas Cavalry (CSA). White, a native of the area, placed his guns at Green Bottom Bar, on the Duck River Shoals just above Waverly Landing, intent upon catching Union steamers coming his way and maybe even shooting up a gunboat or Mississippi Marine Brigade ram. River pilots had long considered this stretch "one of the worst in the river navigation," making it an ideal spot for an ambush.

Maj. White's first target was the brand-new USN light-draught *Emma Duncan*, later known as the *Hastings*, or Tinclad No. 15.[69] Hiram H. Martin was one of the new crewmen aboard, recruited with his friend Robert Wheeler at Chicago on April 1. Both men were sent to the receiving ship *Clara Dolson* at Cairo and hence to the *Emma Duncan*, which Martin later recalled was a "mosquito boat, only protected against bullets."

Within a fortnight, the former packet was altered and ready to go to war. Actually, "ready" is not the correct word; "available" might better suit. The *Emma Duncan*, like most of the new tinclads, was, in the words of First Class Fireman Martin, "hardly in condition for service and the crew consisted mostly of green men unaccustomed to service of that kind." Captain Griswold, who had briefly skippered the *Argosy*, was placed in command. It would be his responsibility, with assistance from men like chief engineer "Mr. Watson, an old River Engineer and a very fine man," to turn his crew into fighting bluejackets.[70]

On April 22, Acting Master Griswold's new command was ordered to reinforce Lt Cmdr. Fitch. After departing Illinois, she paddled east along the Ohio River to Paducah and then up the Tennessee. The *Emma Duncan* was at general quarters, engaged in its first-ever general exercise in "enemy country," as it approached Green Bottom Bar about 2 A.M. on Friday, April 24, her second night out.

As the tinclad slowed in anticipation of the obstruction, she was fired into by the four guns of Maj. White's Texas battery. The enemy, as Fireman Martin recalled, "was peppering it into us hot and heavy." The *Emma Duncan* "commenced turning around so that the guns first on one side and then the other could be used."

One early shot (shrapnel) came in forward through the iron sheathing, struck the No. 1 Parrott gun portside, and exploded, mangling the arms of three men so badly that their hurt appendages had to be immediately amputated. The men were all new hands who had shipped at Chicago with Fireman Martin; all would recover at the Memphis naval hospital.

The *Emma Duncan* engaged by the light of gun flashes in the dark for a short time. That was the only way the men aboard the gunboat could guess where their enemy was. "But we were a good target for them," Fireman Martin remembered, "as they could see the lights from our furnaces and on the boat." The cannonading continued for about 45 minutes until the river-bank force ceased firing. The gunboat went to full steam and shelled the woods at every nearby suspicious point, but there was no return fire, as the Confederates had withdrawn.

Losing touch with the Rebels, Griswold's bloodied command proceeded upriver, checking damage. Upon examination, it was found that the *Emma Duncan* had been hulled seven times. In addition to the terrible first shell, it was determined that another had come in aft and burst over the heads of the second division. No one was hurt, but the hammock carline and the cabin floor were torn away. Others hit the wheelhouse, but did little damage. Still others did badly cut up the light work of the cabin and wardroom.

Late that Friday afternoon, the *Emma Duncan* met the *Lexington*, coming down ahead of Brig. Gen. Ellet's fleet, and Griswold reported his shot-up craft for duty. Taking a boat over to the timberclad, the master reported his encounter with the unknown Rebel force. Lt. Cmdr. Fitch immediately ordered the newcomer to take station astern as the two ran down toward Green Bottom Bar "in hopes of catching the rebels at or near the same place." The Yankee warships reached the bar toward dusk, but there was no enemy activity to be seen. With the *Lexington* short of fuel, the two put down to Fort Henry where the big-gun unit spent most of the 25th coaling.

Following supper on April 25, the *Lexington* and *Emma Duncan* steamed back up to the foot of Green Bottom Bar, where they anchored about midnight. Guards were posted and a sharp lookout was maintained until dawn.

Just after first light on April 26, a search for the enemy was made, but again, nothing was found. Lt. Cmdr. Fitch then directed that the two proceed upriver to meet and communicate with Brig. Gen. Ellet. As the pair paddled on, the tinclad kept station about a mile behind the timberclad.

At one point after the *Lexington* had passed, a ferry flat attempted to run out of a hidden creek and make it across the river. Too late. The *Emma Duncan* came upon it and destroyed it just as its occupants jumped out and scurried off into the woods. The Federal cruise, made rather leisurely because a good lookout was kept for the enemy along the right bank, proceeded without incident until the two gunboats came within about a mile of Duck River Shoals, where they met the Ellet ram *Monarch*.

The same gunners who had fired into the *Emma Duncan* were now taking aim on the other Ellet rams *Autocrat*, *Diana*, and *Adams* as they maneuvered their way into and through the swift current of the shoal's narrow channel. Fieldpieces and rifles raked the wooden boats with canister and Minie balls, sending splinters flying into the air but doing remarkably little damage to their heavy oak planking. The rams, unable to round to or back out of the channel, pushed on over the bar, taking punishment. It was later reported that, while running this gauntlet, the pilothouse of the *Autocrat* was struck 80 times by rifle balls, while six entered the bulwarks of the *Diana*. Canister shot struck, but fell harmlessly into the river.

Coming upon this fiery duel, Lt. Cmdr. Fitch pushed over the Green Bottom Bar and met Ellet's fleet at the head of the shoals, where it was engaging the Texan battery, firing back at it with its onboard fieldpieces and small arms. The *Lexington* moved into good range and opened fire with her 8-inch guns. Fitch took the battery side of the river to cover Ellet's craft while raking the bank. "The brush was so thick I could not see the enemy's guns, yet the smoke enabled me to fire directly at them," he later recorded.

As soon as the big timberclad, followed by the *Emma Duncan*, rounded the point, the Confederate gunners went into something of a panic. After sending a parting shot toward a brigade boat, Maj. White ordered his gunners to limber up and make off. A few sharpshooters were left behind to take potshots at the boats and attempt to impede any Yankee response.[71]

The gunboat task force of Lt. Cmdr. Fitch remained up the falling Tennessee for three more days, but was unable to provide any significant assistance to scattered Union military forces. On April 29, the boats, guarding a number of transports, descended the river to Fort Henry "to return no more." The five gunboats were back at Smithland two days later.[72]

6

Guerrilla Attacks and Morgan's Raid, May–December 1863

By the beginning of May 1863, the number of tinclads available to the Mississippi Squadron had grown significantly. Twenty-one units, some recently added, were listed in the monthly report made by Acting Rear Adm. David Dixon Porter to Secretary of the Navy Gideon Welles. Of these, eleven were up the Tennessee and Cumberland Rivers convoying transports, with the remaining 10 guarding key points on the Mississippi or stationed above Vicksburg in support of the main fleet effort against that city. Porter and his fleet captain, Capt. Alexander M. Pennock, who both championed the light-draughts, were busily buying and outfitting every one Welles authorized.

Flowers and dogwood trees were not the only things blooming throughout the Western theater in the spring of 1863. Plans were advanced or renewed for great military achievements on both sides, and Confederate raiders, regular and irregular, were out in force busily visiting points in the countryside and on the rivers. In Nashville and other Southern towns garrisoned by Northern troops, civilian oaths of allegiance and a closer scrutiny of citizens became more common. Counterguerrilla activities by Yankee forces were enhanced, and this included the Union's Mississippi Squadron.

A month before the Streight Raid stepped off, Fleet Captain Pennock suggested to Acting Rear Adm. Porter that the upper Mosquito Flotilla be divided in half. Not only was he rapidly adding additional light draught boats, but Army requirements for military and logistical support on both the Cumberland and Tennessee was stretching his command to its limit. Pennock's idea was to have one task force under the current upper fleet commodore, Lt. Cmdr. Le Roy Fitch, protect the Cumberland and continue to guarantee the Nashville supply convoys. The other unit, under an experienced but as yet unnamed officer, would take over the boats operating military cover up the Tennessee.

Porter was not unfamiliar with divisional commands, having employed them on several occasions since taking over the squadron. Capt. Henry Walke was in command of the lower division of the fleet off the Yazoo from October to December 1862 when the admiral arrived to take direct command during the Chickasaw Bayou campaign. Lt. Cmdr. Watson Smith skippered a light-draught division during the same campaign and later during the operation against Arkansas Post. Several units from the main battle fleet and all of the light-draughts were left behind north of Vicksburg when the ironclads ran past the city's batteries earlier in the month. Additionally, numerous *ad hoc* task groups were stationed at various strategic points, particularly near Island No. 10 and at Montgomery Point, opposite the mouth of the White River.

So it was that Pennock's upper river plan found favor with Porter, and may, indeed, have influenced his decision, announced the following month, to go ahead and divide the entire Mississippi Squadron into districts. The rear admiral directed Lt. Cmdr. S. Ledyard Phelps to head up the new Tennessee River division, at least temporarily, on April 15. Upon his return from supporting the Streight mission — if not before — Lt. Cmdr. Fitch was advised of his change in responsibilities.

On May 4, Phelps and Fitch met at Paducah to discuss the admiral's divisional instructions, to compare assets and possibilities for cooperation, and to amicably divide the 12 available gunboats (11 tinclads and the *Lexington*). When the latter departed that evening for the Cumberland, his force consisted of the *Lexington* (flagship), *Fairplay, St. Clair, Brilliant, Silver Lake,* and *Springfield.* The *Covington, Alfred Robb, Argosy, Hastings, Queen City,* and the newly-arrived *Silver Cloud*[1] remained with Phelps.[2]

While Phelps and Fitch were configuring their commands on the Tennessee, Cumberland and Ohio, the Confederate war on Union shipping continued full-bore out on the Mississippi. Confederate Brig. Gen. Samuel W. Ferguson, commander of the cavalry units supporting Vicksburg, had earlier battled Rear Adm. Porter's attempt to get behind the bastion via Deer Creek and Brig. Gen. Frederick Steele's efforts into the Delta via Greenville, MS. When the latter withdrew from the county seat of Washington County at the end of April, Ferguson's men moved back in, intent upon harassing Federal shipping on the swervy bends of the Mississippi above the town.

En route north from Milliken's Bend, LA, on the morning of May 3, the captain of the 249-ton side-wheel troop transport *Golden Era* (sometimes referred to as just the *Era*)[3] spied a number of Confederate horsemen moving along the Mississippi shore not far above Greenville. Then, about a mile and a half further on, a cannonball from a masked three-gun battery splashed into the water ahead of her. Determined to avoid danger, the Golden *Era* stood toward the Arkansas shore. Her captain decided to run past Ferguson's battery and ordered up a full head of steam. When the grayclad cannoneers saw this move, they opened with every gun, firing in all about 13 shots.

The *Golden Era* paddled on as cannonballs splashed into the muddy water around her. She was hit eight times "without material damage, except the tearing away of parts of the cabin." Fortunately none of the Confederate bolts hit any vital spots. Seeing that their target would escape, the horsemen moved their battery across the point of the bend. As she came within range off Argyle Landing, the troop boat was again fired upon. This time, the civilian captain sent a small boat rowing quickly back to seek help from the tinclad *Cricket,* stationed off the town to protect it from Brig. Gen. Ferguson. The warship, under Acting Volunteer Lt. Amos R. Langthorne, quickly raised anchor and steamed up toward the attack point.

As the *Golden Era* moved up and tied to the bank out of danger, the Confederates, rather than pulling back, attacked the *Cricket* as she came up. An inconclusive engagement continued for the next three hours. Before the Southerners withdrew, they succeeded in sending a shot through the light-draught's wardroom and exploded a second on her forecastle. When the firing stopped, the *Cricket* moved up to the *Golden Era*'s location and convoyed her, with three other halted boats, on to Island No. 82. The day's proceedings resulted in no casualties on either side.[4]

Early the following morning, the side-wheeler *Champion No. 3* (also called the *New Champion*), one of a series of vessels of that name built for the Shinkle family of Covington, KY, appeared off Greenville and asked Acting Vol. Lt. Langthorne for convoy. Although he had strict orders not to leave his station, the *Cricket*'s captain, believing that Confederate irregulars might try to hit this steamer as they had the *Golden Era*, agreed to escort the 160.6-foot steamer safely below. Unfortunately for the Union, the gunboat's departure left defenseless the Greenville area below Island No. 82.

Just after noon on May 2, the 142-ton stern-wheeler *Minnesota*,[5] unaware of the *Golden Era*'s ordeal, arrived off Argyle Landing towing three barges, two containing coal and another with sutler's stores. The captain, pilot, and African-American crew of the vessel were completely surprised when Brig. Gen. Ferguson's gunners opened fire upon them. Even though the *Minnesota*'s pilot reportedly deserted the pilothouse at the first shot, the captain and crew attempted to escape, but they were unsuccessful. The boat was sunk off the river bank and her crew escaped ashore, leaving the Confederates to plunder and burn the wreck.

That morning the *Golden Era* arrived off the mouth of the White River and reported the previous day's action to Lt. Cmdr. Thomas O. Selfridge Jr., station chief and commander of the timberclad *Conestoga*. That officer, who had positioned the *Cricket* off Greenville earlier, departed immediately to reinforce Acting Volunteer Lt. Langthorne. When the *Conestoga* came to off Argyle Landing late Sunday afternoon, Selfridge found the *Cricket* absent and the Rebel "rascals" looting the smoking ruins of the *Minnesota*. The timberclad chased off the plunderers and picked up many of the *Minnesota*'s African-American crew. As the wooden gunboat moved to an anchorage off Greenville, the steamer's captain was debriefed.

The *Cricket* returned to her station around 9 P.M., and Acting Volunteer Lt. Langthorne was summoned aboard the *Conestoga* to explain why he was away. Selfridge was not pleased by what he heard and made Langthorne aware of his displeasure. The timberclad's captain later informed Rear Adm. Porter that the *Cricket*'s escort was made against his orders and was a "case of mistaken judgment" on Langthorne's part.[6]

The *Conestoga* steamed off Greenville for a day, during which time Acting Master Walter Fentress's[7] tinclad *Rattler* arrived. The timberclad and the two tinclads coaled on Monday, during which time their captains discussed antipartisan contingencies. Intelligence reports came in suggesting that Brig. Gen. Ferguson's force comprised some 1,500 men and half a dozen pieces of artillery. Another Rebel force was believed headed toward Gaines Landing. At sunset, the *Conestoga* and *Rattler* departed for up the river, with the latter detailed to a new station off Island No. 82, from which she could command two of the Greenville bends.[8]

Those living on the river banks up and down from Greenville suffered greatly in the Civil War due to their location and the actions of combatants on both sides. The Confederates saw the many bends as splendid locations from which to attack river shipping.

Federals, adhering to their antipartisan policies, several times destroyed houses, outbuildings, and livelihoods along those shores in retribution for the attacks.

In order to chastise and instruct those in the Greenville region suspected of aiding and abetting continuing Confederate attacks upon Union river transport, a punitive expedition was, on May 8, ordered to destroy housing and plantation support buildings in a stretch between Argyle Landing and the Washington County seat. The expedition was placed under the command of Lt. Joshua Bishop, captain of the gunboat *General Bragg*.[9] Late that day, the former Confederate gunboat, accompanied by the *Cricket* and *Rattler*, steamed down to and anchored just above Chicot Island, not far from Argyle Landing.

At 4 A.M. on May 9, with mist visible over the river and the sounds of nature just beginning to stir, Lt. Bishop organized a landing party under Acting Ensign William Ferguson[10] of the *Rattler*. The force comprised 67 marines, led by Lt. J.N. Gillham, Company D, 101st Illinois Volunteer Infantry, and a mixed force of 30 sailors chosen from the three naval vessels. Ten of the latter were detailed to serve as "scorchers," or the men who would actually put the torch to buildings and facilities.

As the sun rose, it was discovered that the initial Federal disembarkation point was impracticable. The 97 men were reembarked aboard the *Cricket* and were landed a second time on the main shore at the foot of Chicot Island above Greenville. The big guns of the *General Bragg* and *Rattler* were run out, prepared to offer support.

Acting Ensign Ferguson personally led the "scorchers," while Lt. Gillham's men provided cover. Confederate resistance was light and fires burned brightly by 8 A.M. from buildings of the Blandonia and Roach plantations. Costly furniture and a "splendid library" were among the items in the main homes "enveloped in flames." An hour after the Federals landed, they were reembarked aboard the *Cricket*. At that point, the *Rattler* steamed back to her permanent station off Island No. 82.

The *General Bragg* and *Cricket* then paddled a short distance upstream and the raiders were again sent ashore to burn the buildings on Chicot Island and at Argyle Landing. A dozen houses, cotton gins, a large barn containing 5,000 bushels of corn, Negro quarters, outbuildings and stables were "scorched." Again, opposition was slight.[11]

The attack by the landing party from the three Federal gunboats did not deter Rebel Brig. Gen. Ferguson. On May 18, his gunners assaulted its biggest target yet — Brig. Gen. Jacob G. Lauman's entire U.S. 4th Division, XVI Army Corps, en route to join General Grant's army below Vicksburg.

Five steamers, led by the huge *Crescent City*,[12] the very same vessel upon which Samuel "Mark Twain" Clemens stood his first piloting watches, turned into the bend at Island No. 82 just after lunch. It was noted at the time that the spot was 15 miles from Greenville by river and seven across the land. The side-wheeler was taken under fire by a masked battery and dismounted horsemen hidden on the Mississippi shore. Cannonballs from three fieldpieces and musket balls slammed into the troop boat, wounding 14 soldiers of the 3rd Iowa Volunteer Infantry.

This convoy was escorted by the U.S. tinclad *Linden*, commanded by Acting Volunteer Lt. Thomas E. Smith. She immediately steamed up and opened fire on the Confederates with both shell and canister, optimistically claiming the destruction of two horses. More importantly to the convoy's safety, the *Linden*'s 25 rounds caused the enemy to fall back out of sight.

Brig. Gen. Lauman ordered his boats to land all of their soldiers and an effort was made to pursue the perpetrators. Infantry chasing cavalry never ended well, and so the bluecoats settled for torching every building in the vicinity of the attack. "The troops," Smith later reported, then "marched across the point to Greenville and burned that place."[13]

Spring on the Western rivers brought not only nicer weather and the blooming of blackberries, honeysuckle, and other vegetation, but what Surgeon William H. Howard of the *Brilliant* called "the sickly season." His boat's commander, Acting Volunteer Lt. Charles G. Perkins, took ill at Fort Donelson and had to be sent home. The Cumberland was specifically, in the doctor's opinion, "a fearfully poor place for a sick man." Many sailors wished to transfer away from the terrible climate of the Mississippi Valley and some officers, failing that, wished to resign. Rear Adm. Porter, with continuous manpower problems, refused to grant furloughs or accept resignations while the fate of Vicksburg remained unresolved.[14]

As days lengthened, so did the opportunities for Confederate attacks upon Federal shipping up and down the Western rivers. The regularity of assaults at certain points on the Mississippi reached a point where a correspondent from the *Chicago Daily Tribune* was able to offer a catalog of dangerous locations. Island No. 10 and the stretch of the Mississippi about 20 miles below New Madrid, MO, remained a hot spot, as did the country between Helena and the mouth of the White River on both the Arkansas and Mississippi sides. Later, he added the area near the mouth of the Red River and the river banks along the west side of the stream between Baton Rouge and Donaldsonville.

On May 20, Porter, "with characteristic energy," issued General Order No. 20, the inaugural official decree outlining his divisional administrative plan for the Mississippi Squadron. Perhaps refined from Capt. Pennock's original March suggestion for the upper rivers, this blueprint created six geographical sections, each, as the admiral later wrote, "extending between specified points." The admiral's divisions were "filled up with light-draft vessels, to cruise up and down the river and carry dispatches." The light-draughts in this chain were intended to be "strung along the river between ironclads." Lookouts aboard were "to watch the shore very close and capture every strolling party they may come across." Boats and skiffs encountered along the banks were to be taken and "every available method" taken to break up and disperse guerrillas.

The new geographical units, initially called "sections," were led by divisional officers, all trusted regular navy officers, who commanded a certain number of named vessels. For example, Division Five was the Tennessee River (later expanded to include the Mississippi from Cairo to Helena) under Phelps; Fitch had Division Six, comprising the Cumberland and Ohio Rivers from Cairo to the mouth of the Kanawha River; Selfridge remained in command off the mouth of the White River. These leaders were also charged with the maintenance of "strict discipline," for cooperation with various U.S. Army officers, and were to employ all of their spare time directly or by mandate to their subordinates "exercising the men with the great guns and small arms."

The vessels in these new districts were responsible for patrol, convoy, and other work within the assigned boundaries. It was understood that vessels within a district could not leave station without the authority of the district leader, who would also approve all acquisitions (except money) and forward on all communications from his subordinates to Cairo. This decentralized district plan worked well, though from time to time over the next year as the squadron grew in size, it had to be amplified by later General Orders, all of which are printed in the Navy *Official Records.*

Having provided these general rules, Rear Adm. Porter did not often interfere with the routine work of his district commanders. All of his officers, particularly such battle-tested leaders as Selfridge, Phelps, Breese, and Fitch, were given the necessary authority to carry out their responsibilities, were supported in their actions, and, for the most part, were not second-guessed.

"It is difficult to determine the importance of Porter's district policy in Union naval control of the rivers," wrote a group of distinguished scholars in 1986, "but the evidence strongly suggests that it was effective and efficient." Writing in 2007, Gary D. Joiner stated that this "district system worked as planned." He continued:

> The rivers were never without a well-armed patrol, and the gunboats appeared along the same stretch of river often, but at irregular intervals. The greatest burdens went to the tinclads because they were more numerous and were able to navigate narrow streams with shallower depths than the ironclads.[15]

In mid–May, Fleet Captain Pennock received a strange request from Maj. Gen. Ambrose Burnside's Cincinnati office. Would it be possible for the commander of the District of Ohio to use one of the tinclads being modified at Cincinnati for a few days for a "special purpose?" Although he did not know what this mission was, the Cairo base commander readily agreed, sending orders that the new *Exchange*[16] be detailed.

Ohio Congressman Clement L. Vallandigham had, for several years, held the reputation as the Union's most prominent "Peace Democrat." Gerrymandered out of his Washington seat, the legislator continued to speak out against the war and against the Lincoln administration. His agitation reached a point where Maj. Gen. Burnside had him arrested in early May, tried by military court, and sentenced to prison. In the face of some mob reactions, rather than make Vallandigham a martyr to his cause, the chief executive suggested he be banished.

The Confederacy was not anxious to take the Ohioan and officially refused to accept him when, under a flag of truce, negotiations were conducted on the matter. So it was that Maj. Gen. Burnside called upon the Navy.

The naval officer in charge of the Cincinnati rendezvous made certain that a commander and a skeleton crew were sent aboard the nearly-ready *Exchange.* Burnside, for his part, placed a field gun and a small guard aboard. On the evening of May 19, Vallandigham was rowed out to the middle of the Ohio River and put on board the tinclad.

The politician's transfer to the gunboat was "very quickly done and attracted no crowd," a Cincinnati dispatch to the *Boston Daily Advertiser* reported. "Those who saw him," the message continued, "say he looked sober, sad, and much broken down." The

Exchange conveyed Vallandigham to Louisville, from whence he was taken by train and wagon to Murfreesboro, TN, where he and his valise were dumped near the Confederate picket lines.[17]

As the Vallandigham mission unfolded in secret, the war between the gunboats and Confederate riders noisily continued, though high level attention to it would wax and wane over the crucial next month and a half. Three days after the Ohio politician was sent across the Ohio, Maj. Gen. Ulysses S. Grant launched the climatic siege of Vicksburg. Hoping to regain the South's initiative in the war, Robert E. Lee's Army of Northern Virginia began a move toward Pennsylvania on June 3 that would end a month later at a little town called Gettysburg. The outcome of the titanic battle fought there, together with the outcome at Vicksburg, would completely overshadow the lesser events of the river war.

Clement L. Vallandigham (1820–1871) was a leading "Peace Democrat" or "Copperhead" from Ohio, who was arrested for treason at Cincinnati in May 1863. Rather than cause him to become a martyr to the Confederate cause, President Abraham Lincoln ordered him exiled behind Southern lines. The first step in that forced removal came when the prisoner was rowed out to the new light-draught ("tinclad") *Exchange*, anchored in the middle of the Ohio River, and subsequently taken to Louisville, from where he was sent overland to Tennessee (Brady-Handy Collection, Library of Congress).

While steaming down the Mississippi from Island No. 76 toward her station off Eunice, AR, on the night of June 13, the light-draught *Marmora* was fired into about a mile above the town by a party of some 30 irregulars. No damage was done to the boat and, despite a few howitzer shells tossed in their direction, so far as is known no Rebels were hurt either. Rounding to, the *Marmora* continued down to Eunice, anchoring off the home of one Martin.

At first light on June 14, a fleet of steamboats came down and passed Eunice. After most were by, one of the trailing craft, the giant 683-ton Cincinnati-built side-wheeler *Nebraska*,[18] was fired upon, supposedly by the same Rebels that had attacked the *Marmora* the night before. Once again, rifles and muskets only were employed by the Southerners, who had no artillery. The *Nebraska* steamed on with a few bullet holes in her latticework.

The reaction of the *Marmora* was

draconian. Getting underway, she stood across the river and shelled the town and woods on the western side of the Mississippi for some two miles' distance up and down. With the fleet long gone, the tinclad landed at the town and armed parties spread out to destroy it. Every building was torched, including the railroad depot (with a locomotive and car inside), a large warehouse, and every house and shed within a mile of the landing.

When "not a vestage [sic] of the town of Eunice" could be seen, the *Marmora* went below and shelled the woods on the eastern side of the river where it was understood that the enemy generally crossed from one side to the other. No Rebel forces were seen, and since the previous evening, not a single bluejacket was injured.

On the morning of June 15, the *Marmora* visited Gaines Landing, AR, where her captain was prepared to "inflict the same punishment on it as I did the latter" if he were attacked. While lying at the coal barges at that point, the light-draught was, sure enough, fired into by unknown assailants from shore. As a result, a landing party was sent ashore and more houses went up in flame. Indeed, all were destroyed except one.

Late in the afternoon, the tinclad *Prairie Bird* arrived off Gaines Landing convoying the steamer *Ohio Belle*.[19] Speaking the *Marmora*, her captain learned that the Eunice-based gunboat had been fired into and that only one dwelling had been missed in the retribution that followed. An agreement was reached for the *Prairie Bird* to return and assist in applying the final torches.

At 3 A.M. on the morning of April 16, 65 men from the *Marmora* and *Prairie Bird* were assembled into a landing force that went ashore at daylight. Although there was some reason to believe an organized Confederate force waited inland, only four men were actually seen before the house was reached. After it was found that there were more beds than could be occupied by even a large family, the place was burned.

En route upriver, the big *Platte Valley*,[20] built at Jeffersonville, IN, in 1857, approached a point some 15 miles above Memphis on the evening of June 17. There, Rebel horse artillerymen struck, as the steamer was attacked by Col. Leonidas C. Campbell's gunners and dismounted riflemen from the 3rd Missouri Cavalry (C.S.A.) of Col. Colton Greene. Five cannonballs and over 300 musket balls struck the *Valley*, killing three of her crewmen and wounding two others. The badly damaged side-wheeler put across the river and rode up on the bank, too crippled to proceed.

At approximately the same time, the steamer *Golden Era* attempted to pass Campbell's battery. She too was fired upon, and turned back and returned to Memphis to report the assaults.

On the morning of June 19, as Campbell maintained his blockade, the giant 309-foot-long, 1,681-ton *Ruth*, displaying giant biblical paintings on her paddle-wheel houses, hugged up the river. Unlike the *Platte Valley* and *Golden Era*, she mounted a 12-pounder cannon on her bow. When the Confederates opened upon her, the *Ruth* returned fire and also crossed the stream. From the safety of the east bank, the side-wheeler lobbed shells at the Confederates for, Col. Campbell later remembered, something like three hours.

While the grayclad gunners and the *Ruth* were exchanging compliments, the Federal gunboat *Covington* arrived from Memphis and joined in the ball, shelling the woods on the western side of the Mississippi. Campbell's men limbered up their guns and withdrew, having suffered no casualties during their 24-hour adventure.[21]

Despite the falling river stage, Lt. Cmdr. Phelps left Acting Volunteer Lt. Goudy with three vessels about Clifton and Savannah and Acting Volunteer Lt. Hurd with three others in the lower river. In addition to their normal antipartisan patrols and convoy work, these provided succor to various Army units raiding Rebel targets of opportunity west of the stream.[22]

Having recovered his health somewhat in the wake of his earlier service aboard the tinclad *New Era*, Acting Ensign William C. Hanford was currently commander of the light draught *Alfred Robb*, the first tinclad. She was on patrol in the Tennessee River, near the village of Cerro Gordo.

At the beginning of the second week of June, bands of Confederate horsemen with artillery, including several active with and returning from Brig. Gen. Forrest's pursuit of Col. Streight, busily crossed the river west to east near Cerro Gordo. When the light Federal gunboats under Acting Volunteer Lt. Hurd attempted to interfere, they were fired upon from the river banks. Nevertheless, it was reported that his tinclads were able to disperse Rebel parties at Saltillo on the 14th and at Beech Creek Island on the 17th.

Brig. Gen. Dodge, meanwhile, had stationed a "sort of home guard" at Cerro Gordo to monitor and protect the river crossing. These were regularly taken under fire by Confederate bands on the opposite bank. Whenever a gunboat approached in response, the butternuts faded into the woods.

On the evening of June 18, Acting Ensign Hanford presented his superior with a bold plan. Two of the Robb's 12-pdr. howitzers could be mounted on field carriages and with picked crews, hidden ashore to open upon the advancing butternut soldiers. The *Robb* and Hurd's *Silver Cloud*, five miles downstream at Saltillo out of sight, could then charge to the rescue and in the surprise, defeat the Confederate scheme.

Acting Volunteer Lt. Hurd quickly gave his approval. At dusk, Hanford took one of the horses — kept on board for just such a purpose — ashore and rode down to Cerro Gordo to reconnoiter. There he personally picked out a good location for his battery.

Back aboard the *Robb*, Hanford told off 16 men to form his battery and instructed them closely concerning his plan. At 10 P.M., the *Robb* eased into the bank at his chosen location and the guns were placed ashore. Special care was taken to make certain that all incoming roads were double-picketed to guard against surprise. Once everything was hidden, the tinclad backed out into the river and steamed down to Saltillo.

Only a few hours had passed when, at about 4:30 A.M. on June 19, Hurd and Hanford heard the little USN battery firing upstream. Casting off, the two ready gunboats steamed up the river. As they paddled at flank speed, some 400 dismounted Confederate horsemen charged the two Union cannon four abreast, voicing the Rebel yell. Scared but undeterred, the seamen opened into their ranks with grape shot and canister. Even though the Southern charge reportedly came within 20 yards of the two boat howitzers, it was not successful and was called off. When the *Robb* and *Silver Cloud* arrived, the fight was over and the enemy horsemen were gone, supposedly with 50 casualties. In the engagement, one Federal sailor was killed and two wounded.[23]

The Rebels were also busy on the Mississippi in the area of the Greenville Bends.

Early on June 27, a Confederate battery was posted on the Arkansas bank below Gaines Landing to wait for Federal transports. Towards dusk, a five-boat convoy, escorted by the tinclad *Prairie Bird*, came within sight of the *Kenwood*,[24] a new squadron addition, anchored above. As they passed her, the latter took over the group, relieving the *Prairie Bird*.

Moving down, the *Kenwood* went alongside the steamer *Silver Moon*,[25] leaving the *Crescent City*, a short distance ahead, to take the van. As a result, that huge floating target was the first to be attacked by the masked Rebel battery, which put several balls into her, killing one man and wounding another. With her men still on alert, the *Prairie Bird* charged down ahead of the *Kenwood* and commenced shelling the enemy. The *Kenwood* followed her into action, firing off 33 shells. The Rebels "fired but a few rounds," her log reported after the action. Once the shooting stopped, the *Prairie Bird* retired to anchor off Gaines Towhead. The *Kenwood* resumed the convoy escort, taking her charges down below Greenville in the wee hours of Sunday morning.[26]

Far down the Mississippi at a point six miles below Donaldsonville, LA, Confederate horsemen unlimbered their 6-pounder fieldpieces on the evening of July 2. Lying in wait, they were soon rewarded by the appearance from up the river of the 368-ton *Iberville*.[27] Carrying a cargo of stores and cavalry mounts, the big side-wheeler was an easy target and paid a severe price for being in the wrong place at the wrong time.

A shell ploughed into the *Iberville*'s saloon, cutting everything into pieces before passing through a stateroom, where it cut up a pillow, scattering feathers over the floor, and then exploded. A 6-pounder rifle shot passed through the boat's steam drum, while another cut down her bell. Two shots smashed into her hull below the waterline, causing leaks, while another passed through the wheelhouse. Musket balls peppered the boat from stem to stern. The damage to the *Iberville* caused her to lose power. She was adrift and helpless when Capt. Dyas Power's 267-ton side-wheeler *Sallie Robinson*[28] hove in sight, also bound downstream under escort of the tinclad *Romeo*.[29] While the gunboat entertained the Rebel flying artillery with shot and shell, the *Robinson* took the *Iberville* under tow and helped her to withdraw out of danger.

The escape of the transports did nothing to discourage continuing Confederate harassment. The very next evening, the express boat *Zephyr* was caught as she approached the same place. Her flag was riddled by Minie balls and two men were wounded before she could round to and flee.[30]

Victory was achieved by the Union at both Gettysburg and Vicksburg on July 4, a day on which salutes rang from every vessel in the U.S. Navy. Although the navy was not in the Pennsylvania fight, it had had a major role at Vicksburg. The Mississippi Squadron also turned in another noteworthy performance during the day. Eight-inch projectiles from the U.S. timberclad *Tyler* helped the Union Army win a convincing triumph in the Battle of Helena, Arkansas.

In Kentucky, meanwhile, Confederate Brig. Gen. John Hunt Morgan started a raid that few then understood was en route to the Ohio River. Morgan reasoned that a diversion north of that stream could stall the everywhere-anticipated move south by Maj. Gen. Rosecrans, and another, aimed at Knoxville and East Tennessee, by Maj. Gen. Burnside. The secretly-developed scheme called for a sweep from the Blue Grass State across the Ohio River at Brandenburg, 38 miles below Louisville, then a long ride across the southern counties of Indiana and Ohio, and a return to Kentucky through Virginia.[31]

As the raid developed, many believed Morgan would attack Louisville. Upon hearing of this Rebel push, Lt. Cmdr. Le Roy Fitch, then in Cincinnati, knew that his gunboats could not prevent the enemy from coming into the Kentucky city from its rear or land side. Thus he prudently moved to protect the Louisville and Portland Canal, at the Falls of the Ohio. By his direction, Acting Master Joseph Watson's[32] tinclad *Springfield* did not complete her patrol down to Brandenburg, but rather moved up to and lay off Portland, KY, at the foot of canal. There she was to remain unless her captain heard of enemy activity at some point within his patrol area. If he did, Watson was to move to that hot spot immediately.

John Hunt Morgan (1825–1864) was perhaps the most famous Confederate cavalry commander in the Western theater when he mounted his raid into Indiana and Ohio in July 1863. Captured when the light-draught ("tinclad") gunboats of the Mississippi Squadron prevented his return to Southern soil, Morgan later escaped from the Ohio State Penitentiary. While commanding troops in the Rebel Department of Southwest Virginia on September 4, 1864, he was surprised and killed at Greeneville, Tennessee (National Archives).

Just after midnight on July 8, Morgan, his horsemen, and their artillery began pouring into Brandenburg. Confederate artillerymen immediately placed their big Parrotts on a commanding hilltop location not far from the county courthouse and smaller guns lower down the hillside. At about the same time, two steamers were captured to ferry Rebel troopers and their horses across the Ohio.

These developments did not go unnoticed across the Ohio. Lt. Col. William J. Irvin, an Indiana Home Guard officer in charge of 100 militiamen from Mauckport, IN, the next downriver town three miles west, was able to send off reports of the Confederate buildup just across from him in Kentucky.

Morgan's captured steamboats started their troop transfer not long after dawn. About that time, Acting Master Watson received word on the *Springfield* of the Confederate appearance on the river. His dark warship, wearing the number 22 on her pilothouse, moved down to investigate. As he neared the town of Brandenburg around 9 A.M., he was fired on by butternut infantry already over on the Indiana shore, but did not return the compliment. Her progress was watched by Brig. Gen. Morgan and others, and Col. Duke later described her approach:

Suddenly checking her way, she tossed her snub nose defiantly like an angry beauty of the coal pits, sidled a little toward the town, and commenced to scold. A bluish-white, funnel-shaped cloud spouted out from her left hand bow and a shot flew at the town, and then changing front forward, she snapped a shell at the men on the other side.

When she was about a mile away from the town landing, the *Springfield* came under fire from Morgan's Parrotts, followed by his lesser cannon. Morgan was determined to sink the tinclad as rapidly as possible because her arrival jeopardized his entire plan. Every minute she survived, his ferry was halted and pursuing Federal cavalry neared. The crossing could not be abandoned; if it were, half the Rebel force would be stranded on the Indiana shore.

Acting Master Watson was just as aware of the stakes as was John Hunt Morgan, then watching the gun duel from the high vantage point of the back yard behind the old Buckner house. Morgan's host, Col. Robert Buckner, was a War of 1812 veteran and a relative of Maj. Gen. Simon B. Buckner, commander of the Confederate Department of East Tennessee. For the next hour and a half, the small howitzers of Watson's craft deliberately bombarded enemy troops on both sides of the Ohio River, while also engaged in a running duel with the larger Rebel field guns. The navy boat could not harm the Parrotts because of their greater range and elevation, but it could make them expend precious ammunition. Watson skillfully handled his stern-wheeler and avoided being hit, and, in the process, managed to delay the Confederate river crossing.

Everyone on both sides of the river who dared watched in utter fascination as the tinclad unloaded her wrath on the Confederates, primarily in and around Brandenburg. One of her shells hit the levee and killed three horses. Another went through the kitchen of a local judge, hit the town stable, and buried itself in a hill. Yet a third plunged down through the Meade Hotel to its first floor. It was later estimated that, in all, more than 50 rounds were fired into the town.

Running low on powder and shell, the *Springfield* withdrew above Brandenburg to wait for infantry support. Two boatloads of bluecoats, some 500 in number, duly arrived. Expecting that the Northern troops would engage from the land side, Watson returned and began firing upon Morgan's embarkation just before the noon hour. Once more the Parrotts replied. Unsupported by the army and within a few shells of ammunition exhaustion, the scrappy Watson realized that he could not alone break up the Rebel crossing.

Minutes after starting his second Brandenburg sweep, Watson retired a second time and steamed up toward New Albany to contact Lt. Cmdr. Fitch. Between them, Watson aboard his tiny gunboat, along with the army steamers, stopped the forward progress of Morgan's great enterprise for several hours.[33]

Alerted to the Morgan threat, Cincinnati's ranking naval officer sprang into action, quickly putting together a blockade strategy that eventually led to the successful containment of the Rebel raiders.

Morgan, meanwhile, completed his troop transfer and over the next several days rode across southern Indiana, skirted Cincinnati, and headed toward Portland on the river in southeastern Ohio. Years later in his *The Naval History of the Civil War*, Adm.

Porter offered his thoughts on the Morgan chase. "It was a novel sight," he wrote, "a flotilla of gunboats (very 'gallinippers') in pursuit of a land force. It was in every respect a new feature of the war."

As they approached the Ohio River on July 15 and the planned reentry into Dixie somewhere near Pomeroy, the Confederate raiders were overconfident. Although they knew that Union troops were somewhere behind in hot pursuit, no new intelligence was obtained. Morgan continued to believe what he had been told when his gambit began: the Ohio would be too shallow for gunboats. Besides, if any showed up, they would be at a terrible disadvantage when matched against his Parrotts. Fitch, for his part, had no first-hand information on the location of either Morgan or his Federal pursuers.

At Cincinnati, the U.S. Army had hastily gotten up an ersatz gunboat, the *Magnolia*,[34] to assist in guarding the waterfront of that town. That vessel mounted a single Parrott rifle at her bow and was protected with captured Southern cotton bales. Maj. Gen. Burnside offered the boat to Fitch, who, upon inspection, determined that her draft was too deep and that she would not do to augment his fleet.

Another steamer, the much lighter *Allegheny Belle*,[35] was available and her captain, Master Nat Pepper, and pilot, John Sebastian, were most eager to join the hunt. With military approval, the cotton and cannon were transferred to her from the *Magnolia*. Fitch now had five tinclads and an auxiliary with which to continue the chase. "This might have been considered an extravagant use of boats," he later wrote, "but the river was so low and fords so numerous that a less number might not have met with such a favorable result."

About ¼ mile at its widest point by 1.2 miles long, oval-shaped Buffington Island, unlike Island No. 10 in the Mississippi, survived both nature and the Civil War and today is still located close to the Ohio shore opposite the mouth of Little Sandy Creek, between the communities of Sherman, WV, and Portland, OH. Located 43 miles below Parkersburg and 35 below Marietta, the island served as a station on the Underground Railroad prior to the Civil War.

Union defenders correctly divined that Morgan's goal was Buffington Island and began to draw closed the great net which had been cast around the invading Southerners from land and water. Increasing their own pace, pursuing Yankee riders chased the Confederate horsemen relentlessly.[36]

Building largely upon his own information and planning, Lt. Cmdr. Fitch made his final strategic deployment of the pursuit, establishing a blockade some 40 miles in length around Pomeroy. Steaming north against the increasing current of a fortuitous rise, his six warships were "distributed" at those transit locations which might prove most inviting to the raiders.

In all, four major and a number of minor fords were patrolled. The *Victory*[37] and *Springfield* were posted to guard Pomeroy, Wolf's Shoals, and the crossing at Belleville. The ford at Eight Mile Island was covered by the *Naumkeag*,[38] while the *Reindeer*[39] watched over the crossing at Goose Island. The *Moose*[40] and *Allegheny Belle*, in company with the dispatch steamer *Imperial*,[41] patrolled even further upstream.

On the evening of July 18, a few hours before the hotly-pursued Confederates reached the crest of the nearby shore, the *Moose*, towed up by the *Imperial*, anchored off Little

Sandy Creek Bar, below Buffington Island on the West Virginia shore. Here it was sighted by Rebel outriders sometime later. It was dusk and a night crossing of the bar at the foot of the island would have been risky. Fitch elected to pause; neither he nor Morgan knew that the five- to six-foot-deep Buffington ford was clear of any enemy presence. As was the practice under long-established squadron standing orders, steam was kept up so that the vessels could move quickly if necessary. In the predawn darkness, the *Allegheny Belle*, the packet outfitted at Burnside's order and placed under naval authority, also came up and dropped anchor.

Hastily-made Confederate plans to get across the Ohio at daybreak now began to unfold. Leaving their horses behind, 110 men were first sent across in a flatboat and four skiffs in the wee hours to the West Virginia side. In the new state, they were organized into two companies and ascended the river bank, up the bluff and into the bushes from which they were to cover and protect the rest of Morgan's command as it came over. These men would see the entire ensuing battle over on the west bank and later escape.

Unwilling to ford his command, including his wounded in horse-drawn ambulances and wagons, in the dark, Brig. Gen. Morgan found himself entirely surrounded about six in the morning of the nineteenth and outnumbered nearly four to one. He had only two choices: fight or surrender. In addition to the *Moose* and *Allegheny Belle*, advance elements of the Federal land forces were closing in from Ohio's interior. The Battle of Buffington Island ensued when Morgan, refusing to quit, fired on them.

Lt. Cmdr. Fitch, uninformed except in general of bluecoat movements, knew nothing of the impending battle until the officer-of-the-deck awoke him at 7 A.M. with news that musketry was rampant a little ahead off the port bow. The Indiana-born sailor quickly ran from his cabin to the pilothouse and ordered the *Moose* and *Imperial* to get underway. Fitch also hailed Pilot Sebastian on the *Allegheny Belle*, ordering that, in going through the chute ahead, the auxiliary remain close to the flag boat in case the *Moose* was disabled. If she were, Sebastian was to take hold of her and pull her out, or tow her through. The *Imperial*, third in line, already had such orders.

Sounding along the way, the Federal tars were able to con their vessels over the bar "fairly into" the chute between the island and the State of Ohio. Churning slowly ahead through white mist toward the head of the island, the steamers were soon greeted by a hail from shore. Easing in, the *Moose* picked up a stranded Union officer. He was able to give Fitch his first indication of what was going on ashore, as well as the relative positions of the opposing forces. As the two men spoke, the fog suddenly started to dissipate.

It was at this point that the men aboard the Yankee river craft saw butternut soldiers headed toward the northern river bank so quickly that Fitch thought they must be charging him. They had a couple of pieces of artillery (a 20-pdr. Parrott and a 12-pounder military howitzer) with them and the sailor quickly imagined that the Rebels were about to plant them on the bank at the head of the chute to block his progress. To disabuse the Rebels of any such idea, the *Moose* immediately opened fire on the squad with her two bow guns. The Confederates, who were not able to load and sight their fieldpieces in time, wheeled and ran for cover, firing their rifles as they fled.

With the *Imperial* behind, the *Moose* pushed on through the chute and got above the head of the island, nearly opposite Morgan's left flank. From that spot, she yawed just enough to open fire over the high river bank with her three port broadside howitzers, which were elevated to their maximum angle. The relocated Rebel field guns threw a few shells at the two boats, "but their aim was very bad. The rounds either went over or burst short and a little ahead." Thick smoke mixed with the last evaporating mists.

Back from the river, the battle intensified when bluecoat soldiers, mainly cavalry, encouraged by the navy cannonade, joined the attack, rushing onto the plateau between the river and the high ridges which rise a mile inland. By 9 A.M., the fog was gone and Northern units, with a big numerical advantage, began to pummel the Confederate defensive line.

The Confederates were not the only ones discomforted that morning. Without gunfire spotters and unable to see what was occurring so as to direct his green gunners, Lt. Cmdr. Fitch was never quite sure where his own 24-pdr. shells were landing. Both Yankee and Rebel soldiers later agreed on the confusion the shells caused as they roared in overhead. One Federal, Lt. Henry C. Weaver of the 16th Kentucky (U.S.A.), wrote some years afterwards that "a shot or two caused a hasty transfer of headquarters." Unaware of just where the shells were landing, a newspaperman aboard the *Imperial* later recorded simply that "an extensive scattering took place." Although Fitch remained basically ignorant of the changing bluecoat maneuvers ashore, his fire upon the Rebels was deadly. Col. Duke cursed what he believed was more than one tinclad and "heartily wished that their fierce ardor, the result of a feeling of perfect security, could have been subjected to the test of two or three shots through their hulls."[42]

Overwhelmed by the Union cavalry charges and subjected to bombardment by the *Moose*, the Southerners were now getting the worst of it. Although Col. Duke was able to hold the line, just barely, the fight was going so badly that a large group of raiders tried to make a break. Shielded by Duke's gallant rear-guard, plus the howitzer and Parrott on the north bank, many of Morgan's men speedily descended a steep ravine toward the river at a point about a mile and a half above the head of Buffington Island. From here they tried to escape along the stream over a pathway Yankee scouts believed impassable. This hasty and desperate push was, however, exactly the event Fitch had dreamed about throughout the 10-day, 500-mile pursuit.

On the enemy's left flank at a narrow place along the river road, the *Moose* opened on the protective Confederate cannon. After a few shots from the bow pieces, the Rebel gunners fled, allowing her to turn her attention toward the men on foot and horseback. The trailing *Allegheny Belle* also opened on the Confederates as soon as the flag boat had cleared the chute and the auxiliary had room to fire clear of her. Her contribution was provided by gunners from the 11th Michigan Battery, employing a few of their embarked 6-pdr. fieldpieces in addition to the Parrott strapped to the bow back in Cincinnati.

Ashore, Col. Duke despaired. "A shell struck the road throwing up a cloud of dust," he remembered. His men panicked as the "gunboats raked the road with grapeshot." Lt. Henry Weaver observed that "the thundering tones of those monsters, together with the terrifying shriek of the shells as they came over the heads of the enemy, completed the rout already begun." Ridding themselves, in many instances, of both clothes and arms, numerous Confederate soldiers tried to make it across the "swift waters rippling over the sand shallows of Buffington Bar and plunged into the angry and powerful currents of the flooded Ohio River."

Seeing Morgan's column about one-third over the crossing, Fitch called down the voice pipe ordering his portside gunners to shift fire to the men in the water. Their first shell landed at the head of the column, which immediately began to turn back. As it did so, the tinclad moved in so close that the Rebels could not retreat back up the ravine. "Finding our shell and shrapnel too uncomfortable for them," the Southerners broke into a rout up the beach in a line which led directly away from the *Moose*. About 30 Confederates made it across in the confusion.

Hemmed in by the high bank on one side and the river on the other, many men threw down their arms and clawed their way up the bank and headed for the woods. The escape was difficult as the whole area was covered in trees, shrubs, and other brush, some prickly. Col. Duke later remembered that "the hiss of the dreaded missiles increased the panic." Left behind on the beach were the two cannon, transport, camp equipage, "and the like." One of the carriages, "in which Morgan was said to be riding," was upset by a shell and its two horses were wounded.

In all, according to the tinclad's logbook, the navy was responsible for making prizes of two artillery pieces, 20 horses, six carriages and buggies, a quantity of dry goods, four kegs of powder, plus canister, shot and small arms. During her part of the action, the *Moose* had expended 29 HE shells, 10 shrapnel, one canister, and 100 rounds of small arms cartridges.[43]

After what seemed like hours of fighting but really was not, Basil W. Duke, Morgan's brothers Richard and Charlton, and about 700 from the weary rearguard gang of "horse-thieves, cut-throats, and nondescripts" were POW by noon. A number of men were captured on the West Virginia side of the river. Another 57 Rebels were killed in the fighting, with 63 wounded; three Union officers and eighteen enlisted men paid the ultimate price, with an unknown number hurt.

The Battle of Buffington Island, which some still wrongly regard as a "naval battle," was, however, nothing less than a disaster for the outnumbered Confederate raiders. Still, a naval "mop-up" was required as Morgan and his remaining effectives retreated eastward, seeking to cross the Ohio River. Only about 300 graycoats made it across, while the remainder rode or walked inland, dogged by Union cavalry. Morgan and his few followers surrendered near East Liverpool, OH, on July 26.

The importance of this Confederate foray north was portrayed differently in various locales and in succeeding years. Following upon the disasters at Gettysburg and Vicksburg, the "bold raid" was portrayed in the July 16 issue of the *Richmond Enquirer* as "the only actively aggressive operation in which our forces are engaged." According to Morgan's adjutant, S.P. Cunningham, the Southern riders wounded 600 Federal soldiers, paroled another 6,000, destroyed 34 vital bridges and 60 different stretches of railroad tracks, burned army depots and military and civilian warehouses, and tied down over 120,000 militia in Indiana and Ohio. The estimated value of the burned bridges, destroyed railroad equipment, telegraph wires, and military stores was placed at $10 million. On July 28, the *Chicago Daily Tribune* told its readers that the raid had cost the Confeder-

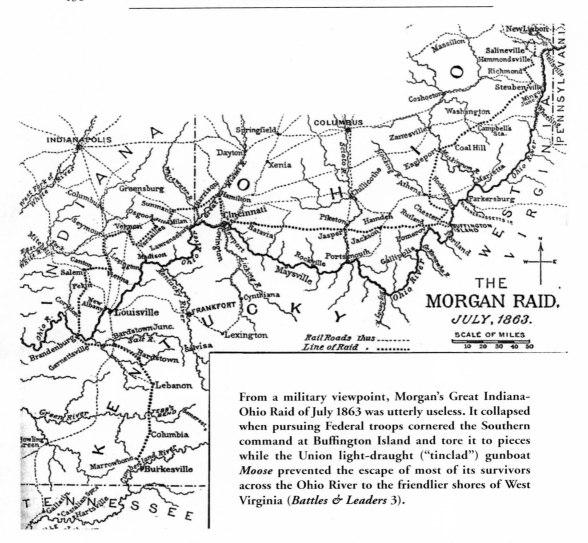

From a military viewpoint, Morgan's Great Indiana-Ohio Raid of July 1863 was utterly useless. It collapsed when pursuing Federal troops cornered the Southern command at Buffington Island and tore it to pieces while the Union light-draught ("tinclad") gunboat *Moose* prevented the escape of most of its survivors across the Ohio River to the friendlier shores of West Virginia (*Battles & Leaders* 3).

THE MORGAN RAID. JULY, 1863. SCALE OF MILES. Rail Roads thus .... Line of Raid ....

acy over 4,000 men and horses, but had released for other duties over five times that many Federal troops, not counting Hoosier and Buckeye minutemen. The most recent historian to profile Ohio's history, Andrew R.L. Cayton, dismisses the Morgan episode as doing "little serious damage beyond frightening people." The naval historian Bern Anderson was more blunt: "Except for the alarm and consternation it caused, his raid was pointless."[44]

Disturbance of regular and irregular Rebel ambitions and commercial intercourse in the interior portions of those Southern states adjacent to the great natural waterways remained a cornerstone of Federal naval policy in the West even as the tinclads entered their second summer of service. Gunboat patrols were stepped up, but water levels and a wily enemy proved frustrating. The tinclad patrols and convoys past known Confederate chokepoints caused the Southern antishipping raiders to watch their chances and to elude the noisy black vessels.

On the other hand, unhappy was the lot of many transient merchant steamers outside the protection of the naval craft. In the words of one newspaperman, "They were pounced upon without mercy."

Despite falling waters, the need for naval counterinsurgency to lessen attacks grew. Endeavors by the thinly-protected tinclads in this mission were continuously demonstrated.

Immediately after the fall of Vicksburg, Rear Adm. Porter ordered a series of raids up the Yazoo, Red, White, Black, and Tennessee Rivers. Specifically, these were designed, in the words of Lt. Cmdr. Thomas O. Selfridge Jr., "to make such captures of cotton and other stores as might prove practicable and to drive Confederate forces away from the vicinity of" river mouths.

Two of these 1863 cruises, one up the Red, Black and Tensas Rivers and the other on the White River, are of interest here. The first, led by Selfridge in the *Conestoga*, in company with the tinclads *Forest Rose*, *Petrel*,[45] *Manitou*,[46] and *Rattler*, departed the mouth of the Red River on July 12 en route to Trinity, LA. Interestingly, the task group flag boat towed a raft with a 100-pounder Parrott gun mounted.

The path chosen for ascent was, in fact, a waterline that ran parallel with the Mississippi and featured at its furthest extent a large region of navigable waters, Tensas Lake and Bayou Macon. This head of navigation for the Tensas River was at a point but 30 miles from Vicksburg and only five miles from the Mississippi. The group's specific mission was to capture cotton and fugitive steamers and to interrupt irregular Rebel attacks on Mississippi River transports by men firing from the shores of the intervening narrow strip of land.

Moving from the Red into the Black, Selfridge's gunboats steamed with some care up the narrow channels of that stream and the connecting Tensas. Navigating the difficulties of the water approaches without incident, the timberclad and tinclads suddenly emerged that afternoon on the lake and Bayou. As the Federals arrived, it was dusk, but lookouts aboard the gunboats spied a pair of transports in the distance, the *Dr. Batey*[47] and *Nelson*.[48] The keen-eyed Confederates, momentarily taken by surprise, succeeded in escaping up a maze of uncharted channels. Still, the Federals scored a success in seizing a large quantity of ammunition recently arrived from Natchez on the lake shore.

The little task group anchored about 8 P.M. and Lt. Cmdr. Selfridge called his light-draught captains together to plot the next day's activities. The night of July 12–13 was dark and rainy, but before sunrise on Monday, the gunboats were further divided into task units, with two tinclads sent up the Tensas and two up the Little Red River, a tributary of the Black River. The *Manitou* and *Rattler*, after groping their way carefully up the twisty Little Red River, returned at noon with a prize, the *Louisville*.[49] She was one of the largest vessels remaining in Confederate service anywhere. Indeed, the noted 227.6-foot-long side-wheel Mississippi packet would be converted into the 40-gun *Ouachita*.

About the same time, the *Petrel* and *Forest Rose* exited from the Tensas River with the 139-ton stern-wheeler *Elmira*[50] in custody. The four-year-old vessel had been caught with a cargo of Confederate sugar, rum, and military stores. A further tinclad reconnais-

The huge steamer *Louisville* was captured up the Little Red River on July 13, 1863, by the tinclads *Manitou* (later *Fort Hindman*) and *Rattler*. Taken to Mound City, she would be converted by the end of the year into the largest light-draught gunboat of all, the 40-gun *Ouachita* (Muller painting, Naval Historical Center).

sance was conducted up the Tensas that afternoon, but no captures were made. Great quantities of burning cotton were observed on shore, along with a few miscellaneous Confederate troops that were apparently surprised to see the Federal craft.

The *Conestoga* led the *Rattler*, *Forest Rose*, and *Manitou* up the Ouachita River on July 14 on a reconnaissance towards a fort reportedly being built near Harrisonburg, a town of about 800. Meanwhile, the *Petrel* convoyed the prizes to the mouth of the Red River. The Harrisonburg task group anchored slightly below the wooden Confederate bastion for the night, its gun crews at their stations.

At 5 A.M. on Wednesday, July 15, the *Conestoga* and *Manitou* cruised up to within two miles of the fort. Lt. Cmdr. Selfridge, aboard the *Conestoga*, elected to test the fort's strength by firing three shells toward it from the 100-pounder Parrott mounted on the raft the timberclad was towing. There was no response. A thick fog came on about an hour later that required the gunboats to withdraw. The scout, Selfridge later wrote, did, however, reveal that the enclave "contained guns too heavy to be trifled with by wooden gunboats."

The Selfridge group returned to Trinity later that evening, its mission completed to the great satisfaction of Rear Adm. Porter. The capture of the ammunition from Natchez left the Confederate river raiders without the bullets and powder needed, the squadron commander later wrote, and so they "moved his forces into the interior and troubled the Mississippi no more."

Four days later, on July 19, Maj. Gen. Grant, from Department of the Tennessee headquarters at Vicksburg, took the opportunity to write to Rear Adm. Porter. It was his suggestion "that the gunboats between here and Cairo be instructed to let all boats pass until further orders, without convoy." This recommendation was not welcomed aboard the *Black Hawk*.[51]

Despite the utmost vigilance on the part of the Federal Navy, Confederate irregulars continued to take every opportunity to attack Northern river traffic. Quoting from the "Memphis-Granada-Jackson-Atlanta" *Appeal* on August 8, the Cairo correspondent of the *New York Herald* reviewed the call by the Rebel paper's editors for a "systematic plan of [guerrilla] operations on the banks," one which would "see travelers on the Father of Waters bushwacked from every canebrake and bluff below Memphis."

Toward dusk on Sunday evening, August 9, the *Rose Hambleton*,[52] en route from Cincinnati, was steaming close to the Tennessee shore, approaching the head of Island No. 37 in the Mississippi River some 35 miles above Memphis. At that point, she was greeted by a volley of musket fire from approximately 20 guerrillas hiding along the bank. Several shots struck the boat and one passed through the clerk's office. No one aboard was injured. A Rebel sprang forward and demanded that the vessel put into shore, but her captain ordered her to steam on and she escaped further damage.[53]

The next tinclad sweep was more than just a pinprick. The capture of Vicksburg freed thousands of Union troops for other duty and one of the places they would now attempt to visit was Little Rock. Before the end of July, Maj. Gen. Frederick Steele, a West Point classmate of Maj. Gen. Ulysses S. Grant, had arrived at Helena to take command of all Federal troops in Arkansas and to mount an assault on its capital. Rear Adm. Porter was contacted for gunboat support on the White River and a task group was readied to provide assistance. The admiral, away on a New Orleans inspection trip, called upon Lt. Cmdr. Phelps to provide overall naval direction in the area below Memphis.

At this time, Lt. George M. Bache was operating interdiction missions off the mouth of the White River. Alerted that elements of the Federal army would soon be headed his way, his task group congregated in support near Montgomery Point, MS, across from the White's entrance.

As the naval vessels gathered, plans were finished for a ground attack on Little Rock. The first Federals underway to participate were a large contingent of cavalry from St. Louis under the command of Brig. Gen. John Davidson. From Memphis, XVI Corps commander Maj. Gen. Stephen A. Hurlbut, upon orders from Grant, was orchestrating the expedition against the Arkansas capital. Marching overland from Helena, the assigned VII Corps infantry would halt at Clarendon or Des Arc to join the cavalry from Missouri.

Naval cooperation was desired at the final rendezvous point. While supply depots were established, Bache's gunboats were to scout as far up the White as possible, hopefully to Jacksonport.

After a 350-mile ride, Davidson's 6,000 "sabers" reached the L'Anguille River at

Crowley's Ridge, AR, from St. Louis on August 1. In a letter to Maj. Gen. Grant, he indicated that he was headed for Clarendon and needed the protection of a pair of gunboats while a bridge was thrown across for his horsemen.

Five days later, Lt. Bache received a communiqué from Davidson indicating that he planned to throw a bridge across the White River at Clarendon. Gunboat protection during the construction and subsequent crossing was needed. The sailor had spoken with Maj. Gen. Steele a few days before and was up to speed on the goals of the military movement.

The Bache task group weighed for Clarendon on the morning of August 8. When they reached that town, the tinclads would patrol the river. Embedded aboard the temporary flag boat *Cricket* was an unnamed correspondent from the *St. Louis Daily Missouri Democrat*.

The light-draughts continued on, meeting neither natural or human obstruction. St. Charles was found deserted and "but little signs of life" were seen on the river.[54]

Less than 24 hours after departure, Lt. Bache's four tinclads came to at Clarendon, 130 miles up the White River from Helena. There the naval officer shook hands with Brig. Gen. Davidson, who was tremendously frustrated. Although the entire area was clear of guerrillas, it was impossible to bridge the river anywhere near the village, "the country being overflowed on the opposite bank." As Davidson reported, the water was "higher than it has been at this season of the year since '44."

Considering the alternatives, the naval officer offered a nautical idea. If Davidson would send down for a pair of coal barges that could be employed as ferries, he would send two of his light-draughts back to Helena. One would convoy up Steele's VII Corps troops while the other towed up the barges to be employed in crossing the legions. The *Marmora* and *Linden* were dispatched before dusk. Next day, Steele's 6,000-man Army of Arkansas, with 39 cannon, quit Helena and headed for Clarendon. Its transports were convoyed by the *Linden* while the *Marmora* towed barges.

Also on August 10, the tinclad *Cricket* pushed on up the river on reconnaissance, hoping to catch the Confederate mail at Devall's Bluff. A detachment of Brig. Gen. Davidson's cavalry went along. Although a mail was taken, the bigger news was that the Little Rock train had ceased running.

Back at Clarendon next day, Lt. Bache found the requested big gun *Lexington*. In a report to Porter on August 12, the task group leader indicated that he would be pushing on up toward Jacksonport on the morrow, together with the *Cricket* and *Marmora*, each with two companies embarked from Lt. Col. G.A. Eberhart's 32nd Iowa Infantry. The *Linden* would be left behind to guard Steele and Davidson's crossing.

The scout boats would seek information on the location of the Confederate army and hopefully capture the fugitive Rebel side-wheel steamers *Kaskaskia*[55] and *Tom Sugg*.[56] The soldiers were to land at Des Arc and destroy the telegraph.

The *Lexington* task group departed at 3 A.M. on the morning of August 13 and, with great clouds of black smoke escaping their chimneys, thrashed their way upriver toward Des Arc. The timberclad was preceded by the *Cricket* and followed by the *Marmora*. As the trio approached Devall's Bluff, enemy pickets were seen in the woods about 100 yards from the river. They allowed the *Cricket* to steam by until, passing the bend of the river, her stern was presented toward them. At that point, they loosed a volley into her. At that very moment, the *Lexington* appeared and flaming messages from her broadside forced the horsemen to rapidly disappear.

Following the fleet's passage of Devall's, one of the *Cricket*'s chimneys, riddled by rifle balls, carried away. Following brief repairs, the push upstream was continued. The remainder of the morning was spent aboard all three vessels in the productive work of covering boilers with crewmens' hammocks and placing cotton bales alongside pilot-houses. The Federal gunboats landed at Des Arc at 2:30 in the afternoon. Eberhart and his soldiers went ashore from the tinclads, where they were joined by some 40 marines from the timberclad. Over the next several hours, the bluecoats and bluejackets destroyed the telegraph and its wires out of town for half a mile.

It was relatively cool next morning when the three vessels reached the mouth of the Little Red River, the same narrow, twisting waterway transversed by Lt. Cmdr. Selfridge the month before. Believing the two fugitive steamers Bache sought were up this stream, Acting Volunteer Lt. Amos Langthorne was sent to fetch them with the *Cricket*.

As the tinclad disappeared up the tree-lined Black River tributary, the *Lexington* and *Marmora* continued on toward Augusta, 30 miles further up the White and 75 miles below Jacksonport. Following the disembarkation of the bluecoat pickets, the St. Louis newspaperman stepped ashore, where he found that the surprised citizens were "much alarmed." Happily for all, within a half an hour, Lt. Commander Bache accomplished one of his principal objectives when he learned the location of the Brig. Gen. John S. Marmaduke's Confederate command northeast of Little Rock.

Returning back downstream, the *Lexington* and *Marmora* came to the mouth of the Little Red about 3 P.M. There was no sign of the *Cricket*. Leaving the *Marmora* to guard the entrance after waiting for her consort an hour and a half, Lt. Bache took the big black timberclad into the crooked little river to conduct a search. "There was plenty of water," the reporter noted, "but the channel is narrow and very crooked, making it very difficult for a boat the size of the *Lexington.*" Pushing up about 25 miles "nearly as high as we could go," Bache met the *Cricket* about three hours later. Behind her, wearing Union flags, were the *Kaskaskia* and *Thomas Sugg* that she had taken at Searcy, 15 miles farther on.

While en route back down the Little Red, the *Cricket* and her prizes were attacked by several companies of Brig. Gen. Marmaduke's Rebel soldiers. The encounter was quite ferocious, and two of the seven sailors wounded eventually died. Following the rendezvous, the *Cricket* passed with her charges, leaving the *Lexington* to bring up the rear.

As the procession meandered back down the river, the newsman aboard the timber-clad heard a volley of musketry up ahead. No more than five miles downstream after the naval rendezvous, all four boats were attacked once more, beginning with the tinclad. The ambush, executed from a distance of between 70 and 100 yards, was mounted by over 60 Southerners hidden in weeds along the bank and behind a levee.

Lt. Col. Eberhart remembered what happened next: "The *Cricket* opened with her howitzers; the old *Lexington* with her 8-inch guns." The latter, he continued, "must have given them such a scare as they never had before, for they left very suddenly." The soldier's testimony was later contradicted in print by the St. Louis special. As he recalled, the fire was returned by the "infantry, marines and guns of both boats, but they [the Confederates] held their position and fired on us until we were out of their range."

Throughout the remainder of the group's voyage to and down the White, the vessels were "fired on with small arms at almost every available spot, though by no very large number of men." Wherever enemy pickets could be spotted, they were subjected to howitzer fire. At Taylor's Bluff, a Rebel party of 40 to 50 men appeared, but were chased off "in haste" by several shells. Later, at Arkapola, a few stray shots were fired at the vessels, but these did no damage.

When the Bache task group returned to Clarendon on the evening of August 15, it recorded that the White was falling at the rate of 12 inches per day. At the same time, under protection from the *Linden*, Brig. Gen. Davidson started the transfer of his men. Climbing the bank, Bache and Eberhart waited upon Davidson to give him a first-hand account of their voyage and the intelligence gathered at Augusta. When the cavalry general heard the details of the cruise, he was, in the words of his Iowa military subordinate, "tickled wonderfully at the unexpected success of the expedition."

By August 19, all of Davidson's cavalry division was across the river on the coal barge ferries. Writing to Porter from Clarendon during the day, Lt. Bache predicted that Steele's men would be over three days hence.

Little Rock was evacuated by the Confederacy on September 9 and occupied by the U.S. VII Corps within a day or so. Writing from newly liberated Little Rock on September 22, Maj. Gen. Steele praised his naval support, indicating to Maj. Gen. Grant that Phelps and Bache did "everything in their power to further the object of the expedition."[57]

Founded by the French in the mid–18th century and enjoying its greatest prosperity a century later, the town of Rodney, Mississippi (abolished in 1930), was the site of an unusual episode in September 1863 — the first capture by a small cavalry unit of much of the crew of a Federal gunboat.

During August, Acting Master Walter E.H. Fentress's tinclad *Rattler* was stationed off the town wharf to ensure Rodney's loyalty and compliance with Union commercial regulations. While by General Order from Rear Adm. Porter none of its crew was to set foot ashore, the vessel was to make certain that no illegal trade or Confederate trans-river traffic occurred at the 1,000-citizen community, located about 32 miles northeast of Natchez.

The summer was peaceful and the light-draught's blockade duty was boring. Porter's order prohibiting shore visits was often ignored. Off-duty officers and men from the squadron blockaders often went ashore at various locations on the rivers to gather fruit and produce, hunt, or visit with acquaintances. Watching the ladies and interacting with them when possible was a coveted pastime. These visits increased during the month after the capture of Vicksburg and participants often neglected their own protection to the extent of not even wearing sidearms.

Acting Master Fentress, rightly or wrongly, had the reputation of being a ladies' man. According to the captain of the dispatch boat *New National*, as quoted in the *Chicago Daily Tribune* some time later, he often invited his friends to stop over and visit

Rodney with him. The *New National*'s skipper was told that he could be introduced to "some splendid women" and they could "have a fine time." The newspaper related that Fentress was told by his colleague to "leave the women alone" else he would "get gobbled up."

A highlight for the *Rattler*'s sailors, according to the modern *Southpoint Travel Guide*, was for her men "to line the decks on Sunday mornings and watch the southern belles as they paraded into church." Although visits to homes or other locations known to be actively under Southern control occurred every day, Sunday, with its lure of divine services, was the most popular time. This pattern was noticed by Confederate irregulars at every point where gunboatmen stepped ashore, but it was Fentress's misfortune to be the man whom they planned to trap first.

While awaiting transport north on September 13, a recently resigned Presbyterian minister was aboard the *Rattler* meeting with Acting Master Fentress. During the conversation, the preacher indicated that he had been offered the chance to offer one last ser-

While stationed off the town of Rodney, Mississippi, in September 1863, Acting Master Walter E.H. Fentress led a large percentage of the unarmed crew (only one revolver was carried) from his light-draught ("tinclad") *Rattler* ashore to church one Sunday morning—and all were taken prisoner. The first capture by a small cavalry unit of most of the sailors from a single Federal gunboat caused great consternation throughout the Mississippi Squadron (Naval Historical Center).

mon at the local church and invited the sailor and his men to the service. Contrary to Porter's orders but in tune with his own practice, Fentress accepted.

Dressed in their best uniforms, somewhere between two-thirds and three-fourths of the gunboat crew (23 men led by Acting Master Fentress) were rowed to the wharf, walked to the Rodney Presbyterian Church, and seated themselves with the congregation. The complacent men did not expect any problems; only one man was armed and that with a revolver.

Hidden in the hills behind the town was a cavalry detachment from what would become the 4th Mississippi Cavalry Regiment under a Lt. Allen (the unit had two Allens, 2nd Lt. S.R. and 3rd Lt. Robert A.). Seeing the Federals enter the church, it struck. As a hymn was being sung, Lt. Allen boldly opened the door, walked to the pulpit, apologized to the minister, and then demanded the surrender of the Union sailors. A scramble ensued and when the dust settled, 17 Yankees were POWs, including Acting Master Fentress.

Alerted by the noise and informed of its cause by a friendly African-American on shore, the *Rattler*'s executive officer, Acting Ensign William Ferguson, had fewer than a dozen men with which to offer a response. Several of these rowed ashore to secure the wharf and rescue escapees (there were six). The seriously depleted gun crews began dropping howitzer shells into the town. Fourteen explosive shells hit, setting fires and damaging four houses and the church.

When Acting Ensign Ferguson dispatched an armed detail to set fires, Lt. Allen sent back word that such an action would cause him to hang his prisoners. Ferguson relented. Later that night, the town solons sent a petition claiming lack of prior knowledge and begging that their community be spared. A similar petition was forwarded to Rear Adm. Porter three days later and he agreed not to destroy the town.[58]

Attacks on Union shipping continued throughout the late summer. A tactic that sometimes brought Southern success with unescorted transient steamers was the hail from shore by people (including the occasional woman) appearing to be in distress. Once the boat put into the river bank, guerrillas hidden further back could rush aboard, making an easy capture. Wherever steamers were forced to ease through a bend or otherwise approach the shore, regardless of which Southern river, the presence of Confederate riflemen, regular or irregular, could be anticipated. One such encounter involved the side-wheeler *Gladiator*, en route from Helena to Memphis on the afternoon of Sunday, September 21.

With his passenger cabins bulging, Capt. John Simpson Klinefelter, part-owner and master since 1858 and a legend on the St. Louis-to-New Orleans run, approached Harrison's Landing. As his craft neared Burdeau's chute on the Mississippi shore, a volley of musketry crashed out from unseen Southerners hidden in deep brush along the bank. As the *Gladiator* steamed out of range, a review found over 20 balls lodged in different parts of the boat. One had passed entirely through the clerk's office just as that worthy was stepping outside of it.[59]

On October 10, Navy Secretary Welles transmitted to Rear Adm. Porter at Mound City a War Department request for gunboat assistance for the operations of Maj. Gen. William T. Sherman on the Tennessee River. Sherman was marching to the relief of Chattanooga and naval craft were required not only to help transfer troops across the river but to convoy the additional supplies required. The precedent set by Rear Adm. Porter on the Mississippi below Vicksburg in April when his fleet crossed Grant's army was well remembered.

Porter replied that the shallowness of the water prevented his immediate action but promised: "The gunboats will be ready to go up the moment a rise takes place...." Ten days later, General Grant urged: "The sooner a gunboat can be got to him [Sherman] the better." Porter answered that gunboats were on their way up the Tennessee and Cumberland Rivers. "My intention," he wrote, "is to send every gunboat I can spare up the Tennessee. I have also sent below for light-drafts to come up. Am sorry to say the river is at a stand."

The Union XV Corps reached the Tennessee and camps sprang up along the 30-miles railroad stretch from Iuka, MS, to Tuscumbia, AL. There it stalled as Sherman, Grant, and Porter waited for a Tennessee River freshet sufficiently high to permit steamers to take the men across. Acting Master Edward M. King dispatched daily reports on water depth in that stream from Paducah while Lt. Cmdr. Fitch communicated the same for the Ohio River from Cincinnati.

While Union forces raced toward southern Tennessee, the tinclad war on guerrillas and irregulars on the Mississippi continued. On October 15, several boat crews from the *Forest Rose* searched St. Joseph, LA, seeking evidence of Confederate activity. Finding none, the vessel dropped down to a point about eight miles above Bruinsburg, MS. After anchoring, a boat was sent to the eastern shore to destroy skiffs seen at the edge of a plantation. As it approached the bank, a lookout aboard the tinclad saw a man ride up to the river's edge and fire thrice toward the rowing sailors. About the same time that guerrilla raced away, the *Forest Rose*'s gunners "sent half a dozen shell after him."

The cost exacted for this affront was severe. After shelling the plantation, Acting Ensigns Symmes Brown and Conrad Erickson led 20 men ashore "and burnt every sign of a house on the place." Patrols featuring landings continued in the area over the next several days.

As the month's second week passed into the third, it appeared as though there might be water enough upriver on the Tennessee and Cumberland to allow army cooperation. Taking that bet, Porter detailed Lt. Cmdr. Phelps to make an effort to reach Sherman.

On October 20, Maj. Gen. Burnside, now the Knoxville commander, sent a lengthy telegram to Maj. Gen. Grant at Tennessee's capital setting forth the disposition of forces in his Department of the Ohio. A review of his supply situation concluded with a sentence that would come to have a significant impact on the Navy's mission: "I have already taken steps to repair the road from Clinton to the mouth of the Big South Fork on the Cumberland to which point stores can be transported by water as soon as that river becomes navigable which may not be 'till January."

From Cairo later in the morning, Rear Adm. Porter wired Washington that the water was rising significantly in all theater rivers because, he was told, it was raining heavily in Virginia. As he expected the rise would be permanent, Porter took the action of ordering as many gunboats as possible into the upper streams.

Also that day, Quartermaster General BG Montgomery C. Meigs, then in Louisville, wired War Secretary Stanton with news that steamers had started from the Kentucky city for Nashville with forage and supplies. "The Navy Department should order gunboats at once into the Cumberland," he added, "to convoy and protect our steamboats."

The army's quartermasters were now sending an ever-increasing amount of goods, which were stockpiled both in Nashville's warehouses and at Carthage. Some percentage was sent by rail to Chattanooga and some would eventually be forwarded to the mouth of Big South Fork and then hauled overland to Burnside in Knoxville. To guard the increased influx of supply steamers, the strict and regular naval convoy system last seen on the Cumberland in the spring was reintroduced.

On the evening of October 21, the *Hastings* and *Key West*[60] departed for up the Tennessee, the latter towing a coal barge. They did not get far; darkness and storms, coupled with dangerous low depths, forced the pair to anchor after the moon set.

Grant reached Chattanooga on October 23. Next day, Porter promised his close friend, Maj. Gen. Sherman, at Iuka, MS, to line the Tennessee "with gunboats" and keep his communications from being interrupted "if there is water in the river." Phelps's tinclads, meanwhile, continued their trip and arrived at Eastport, MS, shortly after daylight on October 24.

The two gunboats were immediately contacted by officers from a Federal cavalry regiment stationed near the wharf to await their arrival. Riders quickly took the news over the eight miles to Sherman's headquarters at Iuka. The XV Corps commanding general, sick on his cot, was roused by the arrival of the horsemen, waving their hats and yelling that the gunboats had arrived. Sherman immediately dispatched an officer with an extra horse, an escort, and an invitation for Phelps to come to camp.

Sherman was so pleased to receive the *Hastings'* commander that he "almost shook his arm off." The sailor was

Depicted in an 1873 lithograph, Lt. Cmdr. Seth Ledyard Phelps (1824–1885), a veteran of the Western Flotilla and the Mississippi Squadron, played a pivotal role in the river war from 1861 through his 1864 resignation. Not only did he command one of the early timberclads, he also captured and commanded the great ironclad *Eastport*, which he lovingly restored and captained until she was sunk up the Red River in 1864. Phelps was also intimately involved with the tinclads, choosing several for conversion, including the *Fort Hindman*. Phelps captained the *Hastings* in 1863 and 1864 during his time as a district commander, when he battled irregulars up the White River and made it possible for Maj. Gen. Sherman to cross the Tennessee River and reinforce Chattanooga (Naval Historical Center).

invited to spend the night and the two men spoke of many issues, most importantly the matter of getting the thousands of XV Corps men across the Tennessee. Both understood that the two gunboats could easily transport the soldiers, but getting the horses, guns, and wagons over was another matter.

Phelps suggested that his nearly-empty coal barge be planked over and that it could serve to take the "grub and mules." Seizing upon the idea, Sherman immediately dispatched carpenters with tools to Eastport to do the job. The modifications were made within hours and the trans-river lift was started late on October 26. The process was slow and it was the night of October 28 before the premier division was taken over.[61]

Over the next few days, a sizable naval force, assisted by a "fortunate rise of water," arrived in the Eastport vicinity to support Army operations along the Tennessee River. Rear Adm. Porter on October 29 encouraged the officers of his Mississippi Squadron "to give all the aid and assistance in their power" to the Chattanooga relief force. The same day, Sherman was appointed commander of the Federal Department of the Tennessee as Grant, elevated to Lt. Gen., was transferred to the East.

Next day, Porter advised Secretary Welles: "The *Lexington, Hastings, Key West, Cricket, Robb, Romeo,* and *Peosta*[62] are detached for duty in the Tennessee River; and the *Paw Paw,*[63] *Tawah,*[64] *Tyler,* and one or two others will soon join them, which will give a good force for that river."

The effort to support the army was not always easy. When the *Tawah* reached Saltillo after dark on November 18 to take on wood for her boilers, she was greeted with distress signals. Inching ahead, Acting Master Jason Goudy found the tinclad *Hastings* hard aground on a sandbar. A line was cast over and the newcomer pulled off the district flag boat. Lashed together, the *Tawah* and *Hastings* steamed up to Savannah, arriving at dawn to find that the west side of the town had been burned the day before, ostensively by "guerrillas." The two continued on to Eastport, arriving the next morning.

The following day, the *Hastings* left the *Tawah* at Eastport and returned upstream to meet a troop convoy. She returned on the morning of November 22, accompanied by the *Paw Paw* and steamers transporting 5,000 troops, including two Zouave regiments. As the transports arrived and put into the bank to wood, they were taken under fire by Confederates on the eastern side of the Tennessee. Two woodcutters from one steamboat were killed. The gunboats all returned fire, tearing up the brush and woods inland of the beaches.

The military ashore put on a full-scale review on the morning of November 23. It looked "nice from the boats," remembered Seaman James Dickinson aboard the *Tawah.* All during the night, however, Confederate forces fired on the landing. Three times the tinclads were called to quarters. The *Tawah* "threw 20 shell back over the hills."

On the morning of November 25, a long line of wagons and 9,000 soldiers departed for Eastport. They were accompanied by four artillery batteries. More Federal troops departed the next day and the remainder on November 27, "all for Chattanooga." Sherman's corps was across the Tennessee in time to make a difference in the outcome of the Chattanooga campaign. The tinclad ferry and associated convoy work, though not strictly a combat operation, was a vital element in that success.

Meanwhile, over on the gradually-rising Cumberland River, a large number of unprotected transports paddled to Nashville from Louisville in a logistical effort ratcheted up in response to the army's increased need of supplies. Confederate riflemen, waiting along the banks, made the steamboatmen pay in the weeks before November 4, when the tinclads of Lt. Cmdr. Le Roy Fitch arrived at Smithland, KY, from the low waters of the Ohio to offer convoy.

Of the eight steamers that reached the landings of the Tennessee capital on November 1–2, three had been badly shot up while passing the village of Davis' Ripple. Although bullet holes on the boats were everywhere, none of the crew were wounded. Even after convoys were introduced a week later, some captains preferred to travel alone, presuming that their speed would offer protection.

As that inaugural convoy had passed down on November 7, word was received from friendly locals that a party of 15 to 20 irregulars had fired into the 122-ton stern-wheeler *John A. Fisher* only a mile and a half or two miles below Dover. William Strong, captain of the four-year-old steamer, was wounded and now faced a long convalescence at his home in Nashville.

In reviewing the contribution of Lt. Cmdr. Phelps and the vessels of the Mississippi Squadron, Rear Adm. Porter informed Secretary Welles on December 2: "In the operations lately carried on up the Tennessee and Cumberland rivers, the gunboats have been extremely active and have achieved with perfect success all that was desired or required of them."[65]

The removal of several gunboats from districts further down the Mississippi now created opportunities — at least so the Confederates believed — for mischief and for enhanced, if not coordinated, movement against far-flung Federal targets of opportunity on all of the rivers. Writing from the mouth of the White River on November 4, "Pontiac," a correspondent for the *Chicago Daily Tribune*, informed his readers that the "guerrillas" were launching an antishipping campaign designed "to put a stop to the navigation of the Mississippi, if such a thing is in the range of possibility."

According to the newsman, captured Southerners were quite forthcoming in revealing their goal of river denial to all Federal steamers "except armed convoys." Their tactics of accomplishment were simple: "open fire from the points where the boats pass nearest the shore, on occasions when they are least expected." Chances of causing damage were high, though it was problematic as to whether mobile flying artillery could actually establish an effective blockade. Still, river bank foliage offered the assailants "perfect concealment and nothing but grapeshot and shells can drive them out."

During the week between October 27 and November 3, eight to ten Northern steamers were attacked steaming independently on the Mississippi, mostly without casualties. Aboard Capt. James H. Maratta's new stern-wheeler *Emma No. 2*,[66] a man had two bullets pass through the sleeve of his coat without grazing his skin. A lady had her comb shattered by a Minie ball as she stood with her side toward the bank from which the Rebels opened fire. A small cannonball entered the side of the main cabin and passed through the entire length of one of the staterooms, just over the berth where a sick man was resting. Eight people were wounded aboard the world's largest stern-wheeler, the *Adriatic*,[67] but no one was killed.

Tinclad escort was available on the main river, but, as was occasionally still the case on the Cumberland, numerous civilian captains believed they could successfully elude Confederate riflemen and so chose not to delay their voyages as thrice-weekly convoys were assembled. The value of convoys was seldom disputed on the narrower streams, such as the White River, particularly when the water level was low.

Hoping to ascend the White to Little Rock on November 3, newspaperman "Pontiac's" steamer was one of several that just missed convoy departure time from the mouth of the river and was forced to wait 24 hours. He and his fellow travelers were "obligated to pass the time as best we can on a small boat with 150 passengers, when there are accommodations for but 20." Even after the convoy sailed on November 5, the trip to the Arkansas capital would require three days on the torturous stream. The escorted group could "run but eight or ten hours each day and while in motion make but slow progress."

On November 7, Acting Master Lyman Bartholomew went aboard the stern-wheeler *Allen Collier*[68] from the gunboat *Essex* and granted her captain permission to put in to the Arkansas shore just below Laconia Landing, itself four miles below Island No. 69. As the spot was not garrisoned by U.S. troops, the steamer was vulnerable to attack, and that is just what happened when a detachment of Confederate cavalry attacked and boarded. In addition to significant funds found in the *Collier*'s safe, the Rebels also cap-

While stationed off the mouth of the Red River on November 18, 1863, the giant Federal ironclad *Choctaw* came to the assistance of the badly-damaged light-draught ("tinclad") *Signal* as she attempted to fight masked Confederate batteries. Maintaining the station alone after the *Signal* was detached for repair, the monster (whose mass can be seen when compared to the tugboat behind her in the photo above) offered protection three days later to the steamer *Black Hawk* as she tried to pass those same Rebel guns (Naval Historical Center).

tured Acting Master Bartholomew, who hadn't been able to get off before the raid, plus several Union soldiers. Once the vessel was properly looted, it was burned.[69]

On November 18, the *Signal* was assigned one of those towing jobs common to the tinclads during the conflict. Sailors aboard the monitor *Neosho*[70] had transferred a 9-inch gun aboard a flatboat and Acting Volunteer Lt. Cyrenius Dominy[71] was ordered to take it to the main Third District anchorage at the mouth of the Red River. There he would turn it over to squadron unit leader Lt. Cmdr. Frank M. Ramsay[72] aboard the giant *Choctaw*.[73]

No difficulties were anticipated, though a watchful eye was kept by lookouts aboard the light-draught. As the *Signal* paddled into a bend abreast of the woods on the Red River side of Hog Point, LA (a mile from the mouth of that stream), she was taken under fire by a masked Rebel battery of five guns on the bank. The Confederates, as Lt. Cmdr. Ramsay later reported, employed antishipping tactics becoming almost standardized.

As was becoming common practice, horse artillery was unlimbered in a hidden position and, in this case, one was mounted in the bight of the bend, plus two to the left and two to the right. Then, when an unsuspecting victim moved into the trap, they were allowed to pass (depending upon direction) the guns on either the right or left. Once past, all the guns would open fire, often aiming for wheelhouses and boilers. This tactic reached perfection in the hands of Lt. Gen. Nathan B. Forrest and his lieutenants on the Tennessee and Cumberland in late 1864.

As Dominy took his tow toward the mouth of the Red River, he unknowingly passed two guns that remained silent. When he was past, he was opened upon by all five, "bow, stern, and amidships." The *Signal* returned fire with her howitzers and continued on. As she steamed on, her plight was seen by Lt. Cmdr. Ramsay aboard the *Choctaw*, which giant vessel immediately opened fire on the Confederates with her 100-pounder rifle.

The decks of the *Signal* were badly cut up in the exchange and her upper works were shattered. Nine shots were taken, one of which narrowly missed (by a reported two inches) her steam drums. Five men were wounded when a shell came in on the port beam, exploding when it hit a mess chest. Several flew through the wardroom over the boilers. Plating around the boilers provided "little or no protection" and a hit would have been catastrophic.

Once the tinclad was out of danger and her flatboat was cast off, the *Choctaw* weighed anchor and steamed past the battery and, after rounding to, passed back dropping huge shells into the trees in both directions. Naturally, by this time, the guns had been removed.

Temporary repairs were made aboard the *Signal* overnight. Early the next morning, she weighed anchor and in column behind the *Choctaw* led a pair of merchantmen down past the site of the batteries. Once past, the big ironclad returned to her anchorage and the tinclad shepherded her small flock on down the river.[74]

On the afternoon of November 21, the steamer *Black Hawk*,[75] en route from Memphis to New Orleans, briefly came to off the mouth of the river where her captain and a U.S. Treasury agent went aboard the *Choctaw* to confer with Lt. Cmdr. Ramsay. Both

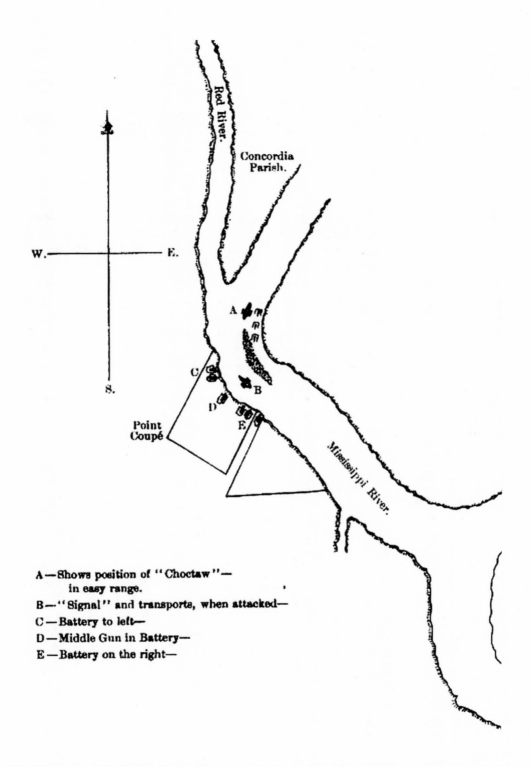

A—Shows position of "Choctaw"—
    in easy range.

B—"Signal" and transports, when attacked—

C—Battery to left—

D—Middle Gun in Battery—

E—Battery on the right—

The November 1863 fight between the Confederate batteries and the Union gunboats *Signal* and *Choctaw* is dramatically demonstrated in this contemporary map (*Official Records of the Union and Confederate Navies* 25).

were told of the danger ahead and were offered convoy if they could wait until the following morning; the merchantman's captain declined.

The *Black Hawk* had only proceeded about half a mile down the river when the same batteries that plagued the *Signal*—and had since returned—opened fire. Approximately 20 Rebel shells hit the boat, with one starting a fire on her Texas deck while others disabled her steering apparatus, forcing her to put into shore opposite Hog Point. The bombardment claimed one life and four other crewmen were wounded.

Seeing the assault, Ramsay ordered the *Choctaw*'s gunners to fire their heavy pieces into the woods from which the horse artillery was firing and got his boat underway to go to the rescue. By the time she arrived, the Southerners were gone. A towline was passed to the *Black Hawk* and she was hauled back to the mouth of the Red for repairs.[76]

Steaming north at a point near Waterproof, LA, about 10 miles below Rodney, MS, on the evening of November 24, Capt. Thomas Townsend's brand-new unescorted 449-ton side-wheeler *Welcome*[77] was fired into from the bank by a concealed group of Southerners employing a six-pounder field gun. Townsend faced the usual challenge cannon gave to the unprotected trader: run into the bank and surrender or steam on. He chose the latter action and escaped in a hail of shot and shell.

The tinclad *Curlew*[78] steamed to provide assistance, but, as was often the case, the Rebels were gone by the time she arrived. In a letter home, Acting Ensign Symmes Browne of the *Forest Rose* said of the *Welcome* that "she was struck near a hundred times, exploding two shells in her cabin." He was amazed that the vessel was not captured, no one aboard was injured, and "her boilers were not struck."[79]

Irregular attacks upon river traffic in the lower Mississippi River area continued apace in December. In a letter to Maj. Gen. Grant congratulating him upon his Chattanooga victory, Rear Adm. Porter admitted that "the guerrillas are kicking up the mischief on the river, especially about Natchez and down about Red River." It was believed that upwards of 4,000 men and 22 cannon had been committed to a river blockade. The Confederates did not, he noted, "trouble the gunboats," but sought out the transports, cutting them up badly "even when they are convoyed."

While en route from New Orleans to St. Louis on the morning of December 8, Capt. Patrick Gorman's 709-ton packet *Henry Von Phul*[80] was bombarded by Confederate cannon at a point three to five miles below the bend at Morganza, LA. Capt. Gorman was killed by a ball that passed through the forward cabin, while the barkeeper and a deckhand were fatally wounded. The *Von Phul* pushed on a few miles to the Federal anchorage off Morganza, where the assault particulars were reported to the commander of the *Neosho*.

In late afternoon, the cut-up transport, led by the monitor, steamed up the river. The two boats had only ascended about three miles when some four pieces of Confederate horse artillery, having let the escort pass, opened fire on the *Von Phul* from the levee. The Rebel gunners hit the U.S. transport at least 20 times. Three of their shot passed through the steamer's hull below the waterline, one cut off her supply pipe, and another penetrated one of her portside boilers. The side-wheeler was disabled and lost way. Two deckhands and seven passengers were wounded.

While the *Neosho* engaged the battery, driving it off, Capt. Harry McDougal's

Atlantic,[81] en route to New Orleans from St. Louis, came down the river and moved alongside the *Von Phul*. The big side-wheeler then made fast and, at considerable risk, towed the late Capt. Gorman's vessel to the mouth of Red River.

During the evening, the tinclad *Signal* arrived off Morganza convoying three steamers. The following morning she, together with the *Neosho*, escorted the merchantmen down the river. When off the points where the Confederate batteries had appeared, the two Union warships shelled the shores until all were past.

On the Mississippi side of the Rodney bend on December 11, horsemen from Col. Wirt Adams's regiment attacked the 211-ton stern-wheeler *Brazil*[82] with four field cannon and muskets. The nine-year-old McKeesport, PA-built transport was badly cut up, two women passengers were killed and four men were wounded. The *Rattler* responded rapidly, arriving in time to fire upon the cavalrymen as they limbered their guns and made away into the woods. Neither troopers or sailors were hurt and the steamer continued upriver.

As the tinclads danced on the Mississippi, the boats on the Tennessee and Cumberland found the ball rather dull in comparison. True, the *Exchange* was assaulted at Florence, AL, at the beginning of the month. She made it to Cairo for repairs, sporting "four shot-holes in her and her woodwork and chicken fixing pretty well marked by musket balls."

Convoy work was maintained on the twin upper rivers without fanfare through the remainder of December. Two dozen steamers were tied up at the Nashville docks on December 11, a number which swelled, in two days, to 35. All in the depot city were treated to a loud cannon salute on December 14, made, according to the next day's *Nashville Daily Union*, in honor of "recent victories of the national arms."

The weather was now turning cold and severe. Large-scale military operations in the Tennessee theater ceased, with all others limited to patrols and reconnaissance or support missions.[83]

On December 22, the Eighth District's CO, Lt. Cmdr. Fitch, received a request from Maj. Gen. Grant, via Nashville's chief quartermaster Col. James L. Donaldson, for a gunboat to conduct a reconnaissance up the Cumberland to Big South Fork. Acting Volunteer Lt. Henry A. Glassford was detailed to take the *Reindeer*, prepared earlier in the month to conduct the long-desired escort of Upper Cumberland supply boats, to Nashville to learn the mission parameters from the commanding general himself. The press of convoy work allowed only one tinclad to be spared, though the army could use its oak-covered gunboats in support of the *Reindeer* if it so chose.

Fitch offered his subordinate only general instructions, choosing to leave most operational details to the enterprising volunteer. The *Reindeer*'s commander was warned to be very cautious, not to venture where there was insufficient water depth, and above all, not to be caught above shoals. The tinclad was needed back in good shape as soon as possible.

The *Reindeer* anchored at Nashville on December 23 and Glassford immediately conferred with Grant. The cigar-chomping general told the Canadian-born naval officer that his mission had three objectives: the convoy of supply steamers to Carthage, determination of the existence of any supplies of coal which might be barged down to Nashville, and a general reconnaissance as far upstream as possible — hopefully the whole 400 miles to the head of steamboat navigation at Big South Fork.

While Glassford and Grant talked over the mission ahead, a number of old rivermen, who like everyone else seemed to know what was afoot, ambled up the landing and engaged the *Reindeer's* new acting assistant paymaster in conversation. New Englander William Wesley Barry, as yet unfamiliar with the Western rivers, especially the Cumberland, remembered for the editor of the *New Bedford* (MA) *Evening Standard* how he was warned as he prepared to board the tinclad:

> You will never come back. The river is so narrow in places the limbs of trees will hit your boat and perhaps your smoke stacks, and when you get above these narrow places, the rebels can easily fell large trees into the channel.[84]

The reconnaissance of the Upper Cumberland requested by Maj. Gen. Grant got underway on December 26 when the tinclad *Reindeer*, with Army Lt. John S. Roberts's military steamer *Silver Lake No. 2*,[85] departed Nashville for Carthage. In addition to the two warships, three transports went along with 140 sharpshooters and three officers from the 129th Illinois Volunteer Infantry embarked. Also along, though not mentioned in official reports, was Capt. John W. Donn of the U.S. Coast Survey. The little task group chugged and puffed the 150 miles from Nashville to Carthage without incident, arriving off that town just after noon on December 28.

Expedition commander Glassford interviewed a number of local citizens and soldiers and then wired Nashville to report that a large quantity of excellent and already-mined coal, maybe half a million bushels, lay on the bank in the vicinity of Olympus, in Overton County, about 50 miles from the mouth of Obey's River. His informants believed barges could take it out if the army first cleared the area of local irregulars. During the night, Glassford discerned the possibility of a considerable rise in the river's depth which boded well for their endeavor.

After conferring with Lt. Col. A.J. Cropsey of the 129th, Glassford ordered 100 soldiers to remain behind to guard the transports while they were unloaded at Carthage. Cropsey and 40 of his best men transferred aboard the *Reindeer* and *Silver Lake No. 2* at daylight on December 29. Before their departure, Glassford and Cropsey were warned that a part of Jackson County, south of the Cumberland and Overton as far east as the Obey's River, was a hotbed of guerrilla activity. This well-merited reputation would be fully appreciated as by the two officers as they passed through.

The Cumberland River above Carthage winds northeast with a shape something roughly akin to a pair of Ws end to end. The progress of the noisy, smoky gunboats was easily observed by residents and as easily communicated. As the craft approached the Jackson County line, irregulars turned out in significant numbers, perhaps as high as 200, to contest their intrusion. Their leaders were believed to include Oliver P. Hamilton, John M. Hughs, Champ Ferguson, and Robert V. Richardson. As gunboatman Glassford later put it, the "whole region seemed roused." Choosing the tops of precipitous bluffs or cliffs, bands numbering from 10 to 15 men up to 75 to 100 concealed themselves in the thick timber or behind rocks and boulders waiting to loose volleys of small arms fire on the steamers.

The *Reindeer* and *Silver Lake No. 2* were taken under fire five times on the 29th. At Ray's Ferry, a party of 15 or 20 men shot into the gunboats; the ambushes were repeated by 15 or 20 men at Flynn's Lick, 40 or 50 at Gainesboro, 15 or 20 at Ferris wood yard, and at Bennett's Ferry, two miles below Celina, by 80 to 100.

The Confederates' positions, Glassford later reported, "availed them nothing, however, against the guns of this vessel and those of the *Silver Lake No. 2*; they were completely shelled out of them whenever they let us see them after a few volleys." Lt Col. Cropsey allowed as how the Rebels "manifested much zeal and skill," but were no match for the gunboats, which quickly dislodged them with shot and shell "in fine style under the supervision of Captain Glassford." So well positioned was the enemy that his flight after each attack was easy. Cropsey did not land his sharpshooters or attempt any kind of foot pursuit.

This is not to say that the Rebel assaults accomplished nothing. The stacks and upper works of the *Reindeer*, which were already damaged by all of the trees and low-hanging brush through which she was passing, were perforated with bullet holes. Additionally, the boiler deck bulkheads, always weak and defective, were almost destroyed by the firing of the howitzers. Considerable repair, if not replacement, would be required before the officers could again occupy their quarters. Damage to the *Silver Lake No. 2* is not recorded, though it is probable that she was also riddled. Although the Army sharpshooters apparently had no luck against the bushwhackers, no Yankee soldiers or bluejackets were killed, but two were wounded.

While passing Gainesboro, Acting Volunteer Lt. Glassford toyed with the idea of stopping to destroy the place much as his superior, Lt. Cmdr. Fitch, had torched Palmyra earlier in the year. The town was supposedly a notorious rendezvous for irregulars and Rear Adm. Porter was on record as having ordered it destroyed. Still, Glassford had learned, quite possibly from Maj. Gen. Grant, that Tennessee Governor Andrew Johnson wanted to build a military post in the community and would need the town's buildings. For that reason alone, Gainesboro survived. The residents of other small hamlets en route were intimidated by the gunboats, which threw shells at them, according to historian Byrd Douglas, "on the theory that 'guerrillas' [among them] were sniping at the boats."

After what Capt. Donn later called a hundred-mile or more "running fight with guerrillas," the two gunboats reached the mouth of Obey's River. There a quantity of loose coal was found, a small portion of a partially-burned cache of 500,000 bushels that had been dumped in 1861. The fuel had originated 50 miles inland at a coal mine near the town of Olympus. Lt. Roberts's boat, now almost out of fuel, was ordered to stop and coal from the piles while the *Reindeer* provided cover and gave Capt. Donn a chance to examine the navigational features of the stream.

At this point, Glassford noticed a certain uneasiness among the people on shore and decided to back off into mid-stream to investigate. A half mile downstream, he came upon the head of a mounted guerrilla band approaching toward the coal dump. Apparently the Rebels believed both boats were in Obey's River, jammed among the branches of the trees that overhung the banks and scooping up the precious fuel. Any idea of an attack on the part of the horsemen was "dispersed with a few rounds of shrapnel and canister."

Moving into Union County, the gunboats found the populace well disposed towards the United States, with many on the bank cheering them instead of shooting. The gunboats crossed over the Tennessee-Kentucky state line and reached Creelsboro, KY, about 12:30 P.M. on December 30. There Acting Volunteer Lt. Glassford took stock of his magazine and recorded his expenditure thus far: 57 rounds of shell, 62 rounds of shrapnel, three rounds of canister. If need be, he could continue fighting, ahead or on the way back, with the 81 rounds of shell, 75 rounds of shrapnel, and 48 rounds of canister which remained. There was just 65 miles to go before the expedition reached the mouth of the Big South Fork.

Then forward progress ceased. The weather changed significantly late on December 30, becoming extremely cold. Overnight, the level in the Cumberland declined by four feet, giving unmistakable signs of a fall. Having determined that there were would be no coal barges available for towing to Nashville before the February rise, the mission commander elected to return downstream. Leaving the *Silver Lake No. 2* as guard boat at Carthage, Glassford, with Cropsey as passenger, returned to Nashville on January 3, 1864.

Meanwhile, the *Tawah* and *Paw Paw* stood cold guard duty off Clifton, TN, on the last day of the year, trying to keep Confederate irregulars from attacking the coal barges anchored there. Seaman James Dickinson of the former was able to get ashore and purchase "a chicken for 25 cents all in greenbacks. Dressed and cleaned it." For a share, a fellow crewmember offered to "stuff and roast it for me."[86]

7

Troubled Rivers, January–March 1864

As 1863 turned into 1864, the Civil War in the west was at a standstill due to a severe winter, the worst prolonged spate of bad weather experienced during the entire conflict. On New Year's Eve, as his friend prepared their holiday chicken, Seaman James Dickinson stood night guard on the forecastle of the *Tawah*. "Froze nearly to death, could hardly hobble in after being relieved," he confided to his diary. Although the bird was cooked and the two shared a "bully meal," the Tennessee River sailor had to go on the sick list. He would spend several days on crutches and lose several toenails.

While Acting Volunteer Lt. Henry Glassford's previously-noted reconnaissance expedition to Big South Fork was underway, Maj. Gen. Ulysses S. Grant, beginning on December 26, made his own inspection trip. "The Army of the Ohio had been getting supplies over Cumberland Gap until their animals had nearly all starved," and the Union theater commander wanted to find out for himself "if there was any possible chance of using that route in the spring, and if not to abandon it."

Patrols on the Tennessee River by the *Tawah*, *Paw Paw*, and *Peosta* continued, with the latter operating out of Clifton, TN. While on patrol between that community and Perryville on Sunday, January 10, the *Peosta* came upon the *Paw Paw*, which was stopped to bail out a leak. The newcomer went alongside the stranded vessel and tied on so that several from her crew could be sent over to help pump her out. During the process, two *Peosta* bluejackets fell into the river and one, a quartermaster, drowned.

The need for enhanced riverine logistics on the Upper Cumberland was confirmed by the Ohio-born general in a January 15 message to Washington in which he informed Maj. Gen. Henry Halleck: "I am satisfied that no portion of our supplies can be hauled by teams from Camp Nelson." The chief U.S. general was informed that "on the first rise of the Cumberland, 1,200,000 rations will be sent to the mouth of the Big South Fork" by gunboat-escorted steamers. The road from that point to Knoxville was better than that over the Cumberland Gap. Until that goal could be accomplished, the troops in the East Tennessee citadel would have to live off the land and on what little could be sent by rail and up the Tennessee by improvised steamboats from Chattanooga.[1]

An early effort was made to get supplies by river to Carthage. However, the same irregulars that menaced Glassford's reconnaissance continued to contest the U.S. Army's logistical passage. Word was received at the headquarters of the Eighth District of the U.S. Navy's Mississippi Squadron at Smithland, KY, that the transports at Carthage were in danger from guerrillas and the "Army gunboats not sufficient to protect them."

Mosquito flotilla leader Lt. Cmdr. Le Roy Fitch arrived at Nashville on January 26, whereupon he conferred with Brig. Gen. Eleazer Paine, and then confirmed to Rear Adm. David D. Porter that "the exigency of the service at the present moment requires that we should take some little risk, as the army above need supplies very much." From information coming into the Tennessee capital, it seemed "that the entire population of Jackson County" was rising to prevent the transports' getting through.

As the Union Navy's top Western convoy commodore prepared to dispatch a relief expedition, the ersatz Army gunboat *Newsboy*[2] returned to Carthage carrying a few soldiers and, more importantly, information that a thousand others would follow. Uncertain of what he faced in Jackson County, Fitch believed his old foe, John Hunt Morgan, was behind the resistance; "I believe it is thought that this will be Morgan's first endeavor to cut off supplies." Fitch secretly relished a rematch. "I trust that for our benefit," he wrote Porter, "the enemy may stick to his purpose."

Next morning, the *Moose*, *Reindeer*, and *Victory*, the tinclads especially acquired prior to Morgan's 1863 Ohio Raid as "super light-draughts" to handle shallow streams, departed for Carthage, The river was falling very slowly, but it was hoped that there would be no danger as it was expected to rise again in a day or so. It was possible, if a rise did not occur, that the enterprise might be detained above a week or two, but that was not considered a likelihood given the expected wetness of the season.

Upon their Carthage arrival next day, the three tinclads found eight steam-

After leading Federal armies in the West for over two years, Maj. Gen. U.S. Grant (1822–1885), in the winter of 1863–1864, was concerned with the resupply of the beleaguered city of Knoxville, Tennessee. In December, he arranged for light-draught ("tinclad") gunboats of the Mississippi Squadron to join his own quartermaster gunboats in reconnoitering the upper waters of the Lower Cumberland River, whence supplies could be sent overland by wagon. After undertaking a perilous mounted inspection of his own, the general concluded that waterborne logistics to the threatened city remained essential. Consequently, the effort to get escorted steamboats through continued into the spring, even after Grant had departed east to fight Robert E. Lee (National Archives).

ers loaded for Point Pleasant and the Big South Fork, along with the army gunboats *Newsboy* and the *Silver Lake 2*. After a brief conference in which he stressed how important it was to get provisions through to the forces at Big South Fork, Lt. Cmdr. Fitch turned the enterprise over to his highly-regarded deputy, Acting Volunteer Lt. Glassford, giving him also the *Victory*. The *Reindeer*, though still hurting from her previous mission, would be ample with the *Victory* and the two army boats for the convoy. Any more, the Indiana sailor judged, would, owing to the narrowness of the river, "be in the way." On the scene, it was found that it would be at least a week before there was sufficient water to let the convoy over the shoals.[3]

Far to the south, the weather had little impact upon the river war, though the water levels in most of the tributaries of the Mississippi were as yet too low to permit aggressive full-scale Federal military operations. Still, defenses were maintained against the incessant Confederate attacks on transport steamers and graycoat efforts to further disrupt trans-river trade and supply.

During the first week of January, Brig. Gen. Lawrence "Sul" Ross, commander of the Texas Cavalry brigade, appeared above Greenville, MS, for the purpose of ferrying goods across the Mississippi and harassing Union shipping. While the crossings were made, horse artillery was unlimbered not far from Island No. 82.

About this time, two steamers, the *Delta* and *Belle Creole*,[4] appeared and were fired upon. Although they were damaged to one degree or another, neither was taken. By the time news of the assault reached the tinclad *Petrel* on patrol near Sunnyside, AR, and she was able to come down, the enemy had disappeared. The abandoned ferry flatboats were, however, captured and destroyed.

As she passed the foot of Rodney Bend with a tow of coal for the Army on January 25, the steamer *Champion No. 3*, sometimes known as the *New Champion*, was volleyed from the west bank of the Mississippi by riflemen who did little damage. When apprised of the incident, the tinclad *Forest Rose* steamed in fruitless search of the perpetrators. Near the town of Rodney, an "armed Rebel" was seen fleeing from the ruins of an abandoned sawmill, which was promptly burnt by a landing party from the gunboat.

During the same week, according to a Philadelphia newspaper, the steamer *Gilburn*[5] was seized by irregulars near Island No. 75 and employed to transport their horses, mules, and wagons from the Louisiana to the Mississippi side of the river. They also carried away cargo from Bolivar Landing and set fire to several houses in the town. For some unknown reason, "no harm was done to the boat or cargo."

At the end of the month, the stern-wheeler *Freestone*[6] hove to off Carson's Landing, about 15 miles above the mouth of the White River. There she found the gunboat *Queen City*, together with another transport, waiting to depart downriver next day. The captain of the *Freestone* was advised that irregulars had recently been committing outrages along the river bank, including the robbing of civilian stores and homes at Friar's Point.

The captain elected to remain overnight and, with some of his men, went ashore. The skipper and his crewmen returned to their vessel in a locally-owned rowboat oared by local citizens, resident near the landing. As they were returning to shore, the locals suddenly whipped out revolvers at began firing at the stern-wheeler. This was apparently a signal, as suddenly a host of men rose up from the shoreline and offered a general volley.

The attack upon the *Freestone* resulted in the *Queen City*'s shifting her anchorage to engage. The contest between the gunboat and the hidden Rebels lasted about 15 minutes and ended as quickly as it began. Although the merchantman wore a number of new bullet holes in her superstructure and there were craters from howitzer shells in and around the levee, no one was hurt.

Subsequently, the raiders were said to have crossed the point to Beulah Landing. There they fired into and captured the little cotton steamer *Lillie Martin*.[7] She was taken up the Arkansas River, her immediate fate being unknown. Eventually, she was released there and loaded a cargo of 500 captured cotton bales.

Before the month ended, the steamer *Shreveport*[8] was fired into at Budo Island and a soldier aboard was killed before unnamed gunboats could drive off the rebels.[9]

At the end of January, Army of the Tennessee commander Maj. Gen. William Tecumseh Sherman elected to further safeguard the hard-won citadel at Vicksburg by destroying the rail system that supported Confederate forces remaining in central Mississippi. The junction town of Meridian was the principal target. The venture would be conducted by main units operating out of Vicksburg and south from Tennessee, with a diversion up the Yazoo River designed to further confuse the inland Rebels. It is the latter which concerns us here.

This Yazoo expedition, the latest in a series of Federal ascents of that stream that had begun in December 1862, would be a joint Army-Navy force tasked with the execution of miscellaneous mischievous amphibious landings and the liberation of cotton. One thousand soldiers from a cavalry unit and two infantry regiments (one African-American), acting as a provisional brigade under the command of Col. James H. Coates, departed Vicksburg for a rendezvous up the Yazoo at Haynes Bluff—a fortified hill on the eastern bank—with a tinclad task group led by the Mississippi Squadron's Fifth District commander, Lt. Cmdr. Elias K. Owen. The light-draughts *Romeo*, *Exchange*, *Prairie Bird*,[10] *Petrel*, and *Marmora* preceded the transports when the mission paddled into the mysterious Yazoo delta early on February 2.

The western bank of the winding Yazoo north of Haynes Bluff was a relatively level marshy maze of timber and underbrush. The eastern bank was more dangerous for the Federals, with additional tall bluffs covered by trees and impenetrable growth. In anticipation of Southern attacks, Col. Coates ordered his men to throw up makeshift barricades on the starboard (eastern) sides of the transports.

The Coates-Owen strike force made slow but peaceful progress until abreast of the village of Satartia, where it was fired upon from the east bank. The army steamers immediately put into shore and landed a pursuit force. Skirmishing continued ashore until dark, when both sides withdrew.[11]

The tinclads and Coates's brigade faced their first serious resistance the following morning. Not long after sunup, the convoy headed into the bend below the heights at Liverpool. Confederates from two Texas cavalry regiments, dismounted, hiding, and looking down from the east bank hills, allowed Owen's light draughts free passage. When the transports came within their range, however, they were fired into with artillery and small arms. None of the four were badly damaged, and they furiously backpaddled downstream. As they withdrew, the gunboats returned and raked the river bank with their howitzers.

While the five tinclads dropped shells on the Rebels (aiming many at the shooters on Liverpool Heights), the army transports put into shore at the foot of the bend and troops were disembarked. With Owen's craft providing support where possible, Union soldiers advanced against the entrenched Confederates. The fighting lasted most of the day with the defense having the best of it. The *Petrel* was struck four times by cannon shells that did no damage; the *Exchange* and *Romeo* were hit by rifle fire with the same effect. Just before sunset, Coates withdrew to the transports, which moved across the Yazoo to tie up out of range.

Missing a few minutes of 4:30 A.M. on February 4, the Federal force got underway and began a run past the Confederates at Liverpool Heights. Once more, the gunboats were allowed to pass unchallenged. When the transports came within range, they were again greeted with intense Rebel fire. This time the steamers pressed on, making it past with minimum damage and but one man mortally wounded. The convoy put into the bank at Goosey's Mill, some four miles below Yazoo City. There the soldiers were put to work gathering cotton.

While the bluecoats labored ashore, Lt. Cmdr. Owen aboard the *Marmora* led the *Exchange* on a reconnaissance to Yazoo City. When within 250 yards of the shore, the pair were taken under fire by a Confederate battery. Four shells whizzed by the boats, with two others striking the *Exchange*. One hit within two feet of the tinclad's boilers, but no damage was done. Having determined that the town was protected, Owen withdrew back to Goosey's Mill.

Coates and Owen withdrew their boats downriver on February 5; no one shot at them from Liverpool Heights and they reached Satartia without incident. There a small Confederate force was seen and pursued on land. Over the next day or so, Coates waited, hoping that a requested ironclad, the *Louisville*, would arrive. When it did not, he ordered his boats back upriver.

Regional Confederate leadership had, several days earlier, learned that the Coates-Owen Yazoo expedition was a feint and ordered butternut defenders guarding Yazoo City and its environs to temporarily abandon their fortifications and move north to assist in repulsing Sherman's main thrusts. This was the reason that the four transports and their tinclad escort were able to pass Liverpool without taking fire and to reach a point about six miles below Yazoo City on February 7 without incident.

The following morning, Lt. Cmdr. Owen and two light-draughts again approached the Confederate town, while a cavalry detachment rode toward it from the western shore. These visits confirmed that Yazoo City was undefended and it was duly occupied without opposition on the morning of February 9. There the Federals rested and awaited reinforcement by additional cavalry.[12]

While Coates and Owen waited at Yazoo City, Federal logisticians in the upper portion of the Mississippi Valley were straining to maintain avenues of supply to beleaguered Knoxville. At this point, that post was hanging on with minimal succor. Acting Volunteer Lt. Henry Glassford's Upper Cumberland convoy began making its way, with difficulty, above Carthage toward Burnside Point, KY, on February 1.

The mission was difficult, but the captain of the *Reindeer* made good progress, seeing eight steamers hauled through the shoals, discharged, coaled and prepared for their

First in action in December 1862 during the Chickasaw Bayou campaign, the light-draught ("tinclad") *Marmora* was a veteran of army support and anti-partisan operations by the winter of 1863–1864. In February 1864, she participated in a joint U.S. Army-Navy task force assigned to create a diversion up the Yazoo River while troops under Maj. Gen. W.T. Sherman attacked the Confederate railroad center at Meridian, Mississippi. Five light-draught ("tinclad") gunboats guarded troop transports and conducted reconnaissance as far as Yazoo City, where the *Marmora* and *Exchange* engaged Confederate batteries early in the mission (Naval Historical Center).

return. The escorts and their charges reached Big South Fork on February 9, where the freight was unloaded. It was anticipated that the army at South Gap would have rations for some time and that the fleet would return downriver within a week on an expected rise.

At the same time, convoys and counterinsurgency and anti-guerrilla operations continued on both the Lower Cumberland and the Tennessee. Anchored near Reynoldsburg Island, in the latter stream, the tinclad *Tawah* was fired into at dawn on February 4, just as her men were, as they did every morning at sunrise, manning their stations. The craft "returned compliment setting fire to a house." The *Tawah* was shot into again at dusk and once more the following morning. This time, one of the light-draught's men was wounded. On the morning of February 6, a landing party was sent ashore on a reconnaissance, but it was driven back to the river and under the bank. The gunboat opened fire and swept the area above them with shells until she could get up sufficient steam to rescue her men.[13]

Reinforced with additional horse soldiers, Col. Coates ordered the boats of his expedition to proceed above Yazoo City on the morning of February 11. Federal cavalry rode on various diversionary duties ashore while the task group made its way uneventfully to the little town of Greenwood, arriving on the evening of February 14. There, near the confluence of the Yazoo into the Tallahatchie and Yalabolusha Rivers, Lt. Cmdr. Owen found the water would probably be too low to permit a further waterborne advance.

While elements from Coates's provisional battalion spread out over the countryside seeking contact with the enemy, sailors from the tinclads busied themselves "harvesting" cotton. Within a day or so, some 450 bales were gathered, 80 bales of which were stored aboard the gunboats and the remainder on the transports. Meanwhile, the *Marmora* conducted a watery scout up the Tallahatchie, finding several sunken ships in the stream. Great difficulty was experienced in rounding to, and the tinclad's light upper works suffered "to some extent."

Col. Coates ordered a return downstream on February 19. The Yankee force, as Jim Huffstodt put it years later, "lazily descended the Yazoo with numerous stops at previously unvisited plantations where the troops quickly expropriated any items of value." Having gathered many spoils and been largely unopposed since early in the month, the boats came to off Yazoo City on Sunday morning, February 28.[14]

Although the tinclads on the Upper Rivers and the Yazoo seldom fired their guns in anger during the last two weeks of February, the same could not be said for at least one boat on the Mississippi. While on patrol in the Fourth District, the *Forest Rose* offered assistance sufficient to prevent a Confederate triumph.

Having been appointed to command of the veteran tinclad at the first of the year, Acting Volunteer Lt. John V. Johnston was patrolling the river off Waterproof, LA, 20 miles above Natchez, on February 8. The *Forest Rose* was there to serve as a mobile guardian while the army established a military post to serve as a depot for cattle and captured cotton, horses, mules, and so forth. It was manned by about 280 new African-American soldiers who, together with their white officers, expected reinforcements from Vicksburg momentarily. That evening leading citizens of the town, together with the garrison commander, Capt. Joseph M. Anderson of the 80th Ohio Volunteer Infantry, were entertained at dinner aboard.

The army, as it foraged on nearby plantations, was also relied upon to provide daily pickets for its new depot, supported with passing visits from the gunboat. The *Forest Rose* spent most of the following week in the vicinity, protecting the 220-ton USQMD stern-wheeler *Ida May*[15] as she gathered cotton left for her along the bank by U.S. treasury agents and cotton speculators. No new reinforcements had come to the post during the week.

Unlike earlier cotton expeditions, *Ida May*'s was one of the newly sanctioned missions of the type recently reported in the press. For example, on February 11, the *North American and United States Gazette* reported that "small boats are running short trips below Memphis and continue to pick up loads along the river." Readers of that Philadelphia paper were not told that the "loads" usually comprised cotton.

On the morning of February 13, Capt. Anderson heard rumors that Col. Isaac F. Harrison's 3rd Louisiana Cavalry Regiment (C.S.A.) had crossed the Tensas River and was advancing toward Waterproof. It was reported that a portion of the Rebel force would drive cattle across the Mississippi at that point, while several companies engaged the Federal outpost. To test the validity of his information, Anderson sent a small reconnaissance team out to see if it could make contact. Apprised of these rumors, the two Northern steamers dropped down to Waterproof and tied up to the bank. While laborers from the quartermaster boat loaded cotton left at the Waterproof levee, seamen aboard the tinclad made preparations to defend the post.

By mid-afternoon, Anderson's scouts were about 8 miles out when they were fired into by Rebel pickets. The Federals advanced and even managed to capture a few Southerners before some 300 cavalry suddenly dashed toward them from the underbrush.

The men aboard the *Forest Rose* soon heard both their own lookouts and soldiers ashore shouting, "Here they come, here they come!" Horsemen from the 3rd Louisiana, backed by a pair of artillery pieces, were driving the Federal pickets and all of the civilians, black and white, into the North's small earthen fort. All was pandemonium and noise ashore as the lines securing the tinclad to the bank were cut and her drummer beat to quarters.

As the *Forest Rose* backed out into the Mississippi, her men quickly manned their stations. Even before her great stern wheel was reversed, the forward Parrott rifles were fired into the Rebel-suspect woods and down the roads in the rear of the town. As soon as they could be brought to bear, the broadside howitzers also opened up.

Neither the tinclad's gunners or lookouts could actually see the Rebel troops pressing the African-American defenders "very hard" to within two miles of their post. Learning of the boat's blindness, Capt. Anderson signaled the direction and approximate range of the enemy. For almost two and a half hours, as Union and Confederate soldiers fought ashore, the *Rose* steamed up and down the river blasting away, expending, Acting Ensign Browne said later, some 179 shells. Eventually, Harrison's men fell back and the light-draught anchored abreast the town.

Col. Harrison was not finished with Waterproof that day and about 8 P.M. some of his men again rushed the town. This time they were visible and as the *Forest Rose* "was well posted as regards the approaches," drove them back "with a few shell."

On the day, the Union lost five dead and six wounded while the Rebels suffered seven or eight deaths. The Confederates made camp at a place owned by one Holmes and from there a captured Union soldier escaped, returning to Waterproof with word that the attacks would be renewed in the morning.

Fourth District boss Lt. Cmdr. James A. Greer arrived off Waterproof after dark aboard the tinclad *Rattler* and conferred with both Johnston and Anderson. The latter asked that the navy leader please seek ammunition and reinforcements. When Greer arrived at Natchez later that night, he met the town commander, who agreed to send 200 soldiers and ammunition at first light.

The Confederates' Waterproof attack force was bolstered during the night to include two infantry and one cavalry regiments, plus four fieldpieces. As light started to remove the night about 4 A.M., Harrison sent his men forward again. Once more, the *Forest Rose* cleared for action. Within five minutes of the first drum beat, her anchor up and she was under way, with the forward Parrotts firing in the supposed direction of the enemy.

The tinclad now ran up to the town wharf, where she was boarded by Capt. Anderson, who wanted to consult with Acting Volunteer Lt. Johnston. According to eyewitness Acting Ensign Browne, Anderson was badly rattled. Having heard many of the atrocity stories circulating concerning Confederate treatment of captured African-Americans and their white officers, the young infantryman wanted the naval vessel to evacuate his men to an island on the other side of the river.

Johnston refused. Anderson was told to fight and "if they got whipped, we would cover them with our guns and take them aboard in the cutter." After Anderson returned ashore, the gunboat dropped down to the levee off the fort, where several officers hailed, asking the gunboat to send a boat to take them off and across the river. They, too, were refused.

Within a half hour of these requests, U.S. soldiers were engaged with Confederates about a mile away. Lookouts shouted out the location of the butternuts, and gunners on the main deck of the *Forest Rose* sent shells after them. The resulting explosions caused the Southerners to fall back into heavy timber and pass around toward the north side of the town.

Meanwhile, Rebel horse artillerymen attempted to unlimber a battery on a plank road leading to the town. This action too was seen from the tinclad's pilothouse. "A few well-directed shell from the Parrott guns," Lt. Cmdr. Greer was later told, "sent them in confusion out of range."

With the example of the gunboat as guidance, bluecoat soldiers ashore maintained their resistance. A week later Capt. Anderson testified that he had never seen "more accurate artillery firing" than that from the *Forest Rose* in this engagement. Everyone in the post came to "feel perfectly secure against a large force, so long as we have the assistance of Captain Johnston and his most excellently drilled crew on board the No. 9." About 1 P.M. the Natchez reinforcements arrived together with the Federal ram *Switzerland.* Col. Harrison and his men faded away once more.

Late that afternoon, the *Rattler* once more stopped off Waterproof. Ammunition was passed to the *Forest Rose* to replace the 270 shell she had expended during the two-day action, while Acting Volunteer Lt. Johnston provided a verbal after-action report to Lt. Cmdr. Greer, one which did not omit the evacuation requests of the fort's white officers.

About 4 A.M. on February 15, Col. Harrison made one more attack on Waterproof, this one in a howling windstorm. This assault was also beaten off by the *Forest Rose* and the soldiers, after which the Confederates retreated toward Harrisonburg, LA, burning the bridges behind them. When Lt. Cmdr. Greer heard of this final effort, he boasted in a letter to Rear Adm. Porter: "The rebels can not stand the fire of gunboats and in the last 10 days received some severe lessons from the vessels of this district."

Anderson and Johnston had approximately one week of peace before Col. Harrison reappeared. On Monday, February 22, the Rebels recrossed the Tensas River and headed toward Waterproof with two regiments of cavalry, two of infantry, and six fieldpieces. This time the gunners would concentrate on the gunboat while all of the troops charged the outpost.

A spy within the Confederate force alerted the Union captain, who once more discussed the possibility of withdrawal with the captain of the *Forest Rose.* This time the two agreed that the danger was overwhelming and, at midnight of February 22–23, the gunboat withdrew Anderson and his men, together with such booty as could be transported.[16]

These February events on the Mississippi's tributaries paled in comparison to a new Federal advance just over the horizon, the last major Union riverine offensive of the conflict—the Red River campaign. Estimating the situation west of the Mississippi back on January 4, Confederate Lt. Gen. E. Kirby Smith, CSA, had written to Maj. Gen. Richard ("Dick") Taylor: "I still think the Red and Washita [Ouachita] Rivers, especially the former, are the true lines of operation for an invading column, and that we may expect an attempt to be made by the enemy in force before the rivers fall." Little did he know at that time that, within eight weeks, Rear Adm. Porter would be leading just such a joint expedition.

For some months now, Federal forces from Washington to the West had been involved in planning an incursion into the Trans-Mississippi theater. By the beginning of the new year, generals as diverse as Grant, Sherman, and Nathaniel Banks, the eventual expedition ground leader, were on board with a plan to move up the Red River through Louisiana, via Alexandria and Shreveport, toward Texas.

The forthcoming operation would, in actuality, be a "rather grand undertaking," in the words of historian William Riley Brookshire. Although championed by, among others, President Lincoln and Maj. Gen. Halleck, the undertaking was initially opposed by Grant and Banks. Although, in the end, it would really consist of a "loosely connected joint land and naval exercise," it did have as its ultimate military objective "completion of the subjugation of Louisiana and Arkansas." If this thrust was successful, it "would effectively remove the Confederate Trans-Mississippi Department from an active role in the conflict."

In addition to the purely military benefits of such a gambit, a big Red River offensive could disrupt Confederate commerce and have some hope of dissuading a northward view by French forces then trying to subdue Mexico. Naturally, the Mississippi Squadron was invited along to provide support and guard the many necessary transports.

While the political, military, and logistical difficulties of a Red River campaign were reviewed and resolved (details far outside the scope of our story), the work of the gunboats on the Lower Mississippi continued apace. Guerrilla and irregular force suppression remained a constant concern, as was the maintenance of an effective blockade against contraband goods and produce. These activities afloat were undertaken during a time of terrible winter weather that extended much further south than might ordinarily be imagined. At times, it was so bad ashore that horses were covered with snow and tents were frozen solid and could not be struck.

Without a steady supply of coal, the gunboats maintaining station off the entrances to rivers like the White and Red were often forced to stop and gather wood. This was not often easy or safe along the shores. In some places, woodpiles were available, but mostly they were not. As a result and even though they had to be cut shorter to fit the boilers, a favorite fuel for the boats was fence rails.[17]

The water level in the Red River was quite low during the first weeks of 1864, contributing to a delay in the start of the planned Federal campaign. Still, once he had signed on, Rear Adm. Porter promised to obtain all of the hulls and guns needed. Indeed, he boasted to Sherman that he would ascend the Red "with every ironclad vessel in the fleet."

Gary D. Joiner reports that a crucial piece of evidence received by Rear Adm. Porter on February 14 was a chart of Shreveport and vicinity drawn on the back of the death certificate of a Federal seaman, James O'Leary. The detail on this map was "perhaps the greatest influence of Admiral Porter's decision of which vessels should be included in the expedition." The USN ironclads, a ram, several support vessels, plus two large and nine standard tinclads chosen on the basis of the O'Leary document, were assembled for the upcoming Trans-Mississippi campaign over the next two weeks. Porter himself arrived off the mouth of the Red River during the last week of February.

Calling Third District chief Lt. Cmdr. Frank Ramsay aboard the flagboat *Black Hawk*, the squadron commander ordered that a naval reconnaissance expedition ascend Louisiana's Black and Ouachita (pronounced Washitaw) Rivers. Consulting their maps, the two officers noted that the Ouachita rose in Arkansas and emptied into the Red, about 45 miles from the mouth of the latter. The last 60 miles or so of the course of the Ouachita was sometimes called the Black River. Porter wished to test Confederate defenses in this river system, geographically located next in line above the Red. Specifically, he was to destroy bridges and break up Confederate posts being formed along those rivers, destroying their provisions in the process.

Ramsay led the scouting mission in the river monitor *Osage*. Together with the *Neosho*, one of two stern-wheel light-draught river monitors completed by James B. Eads the year before, the 523-ton craft featured a single turret forward. Like that aboard the famous type namesake *Monitor*, it protected a pair of 11-inch Dahlgren smoothbores. Unlike the Ericcson vessel, the profile of Ramsay's boat was broken aft by her covered wheel-box. The task group commander was also permitted to take the giant *Ouachita*, plus the tinclads *Fort Hindman* and *Cricket*. Also along would be the timberclads *Lexington* and *Conestoga*, the latter (not known at the time) on her final campaign.

Ramsay's gunboats were away for about a week, during which time they battled both regular and irregular troops, recovered several cannon, and gained information of less than immediate value. When they returned on March 5, few were surprised to also see that their decks were loaded with captured cotton.[18]

A week earlier, Mississippi Squadron Fifth District chief Lt. Cmdr. Owen, slated to participate in the Red River campaign, had turned over command of the tinclads in the Yazoo to Acting Master Thomas McElroy of the light-draught *Petrel*. The latter was to remain at Yazoo City to protect Col. Coates's regiments. These troops were, for the most part, stationed in a small hilltop fort outside the town and in a redoubt to the southeast. The few remaining in the town were supported, in part, by a wheeled 12-pounder boat howitzer borrowed from the tinclad *Exchange* and manned by *Petrel* sailors under Acting Ensign Shepley R. Holmes.

McElroy had two other units in the river. The *Prairie Bird* was stationed off Liverpool, some 24 miles downstream, and the *Marmora* undertook patrols. No risks were to be run by the trio. All three boats were to make certain that nothing was captured by the Confederates while, at the same time, they were "to seize all the cotton" they could and were not to turn it over to any outside parties, government or civilian.

While Coates and McElroy settled into something of a routine, the local Confederate cavalry brigade returned to the area after helping to resist Sherman's Meridian campaign. It was now reinforced with another brigade. It was believed these could wrest back control of Yazoo City from the Federals, especially given that Rear Adm. Porter was away preparing to enter the Red River.

About 9:30 A.M. on March 5, the same day on which Lt. Cmdr. Ramsay returned from his reconnaissance, the Confederates moved on Coates. The Rebel push was furious; fighting became hand-to-hand. Several assaults on Fort McKee (named for Maj.

A large fleet of Federal transports and gunboats assembled off the mouth of the Red River in late February–early March 1864. Nine light-draught ("tinclad") gunboats were among the vessels assigned by Rear Adm. David D. Porter to the enterprise. The expedition actually started out before its land commander, Maj. Gen. Nathaniel Banks, arrived and made its way up to Alexandria, Louisiana, where he joined it (*Battles and Leaders*, 4).

George McKee, its 11th Illinois commander) were beaten back. Within hours, the 14th and 15th Tennessee Cavalry (C.S.A.) were able to attack into the town from the north. The troopers, however, were quickly engaged in street fighting with the Union defenders concealed in houses, doorways, and other hidden locations.

Coates sent Holmes and his howitzer to reinforce these urban defenders at a crossroad of the city's main streets. There the ensign mounted his piece behind a hastily constructed cotton breastwork. Finding their path blocked, Confederate soldiers charged the sailors, who rapidly discharged canister. After just a few shots, a round jammed in the howitzer barrel and could not be removed. By now, graycoats were upon them. Panicked, Acting Ensign Holmes fled, or, as Col. Coates later wrote, "shamefully deserted" his men. The gun crew fought back with cutlasses to the last, with three men distinguishing themselves by their bravery. Coates was furious at these developments, believing that Holmes and his men had simply abandoned the piece. When the ensign returned to the *Petrel*, McElroy refused him permission to come on board.

The Federals charged the now-Confederate-held breastwork and retook the howitzer. Coates was able to move the gun to another location and put it back in operation employing a military crew. The fighting continued all around and in the town throughout the morning and into the afternoon, while, from Liverpool, a steamer paddled furiously upstream with Union reinforcements.

During and after the Holmes incident, the *Petrel*, together with the *Marmora* also off the levee, poured cannon fire toward Confederate locations. Ashore, the Union resistance was steadily pushed back toward the Yazoo.

Acting Master McElroy ordered a broadside howitzer from the *Marmora* mounted on a carriage and sent ashore to replace the gun believed lost. Acting Master Thomas Gibson and his men landed their piece and began rapidly firing on Rebel positions, watching as some butternut soldiers were forced to flee from streets and houses back toward the hills. This success did not come without extreme danger for the gunners. Confederates several times unsuccessfully charged and rifle bullets chewed up the gun carriage and nearly cut the rammer in two.

The afternoon went to the Federals. Depending upon which report one reads, Col. Coates at 2 P.M. made a frantic charge, backed by Gibson's howitzer, and began clearing the Confederates from the town. This move was seen by Rebels besieging Fort McKee, who then also elected to withdraw, pursued by the men in the hilltop bastion. The Confederates later reported that they decided, some two hours later, to quit the fight because they were low on ammunition and the loud whistle of the steamer bringing the Liverpool soldiers was heard.

At approximately 4 P.M., Col. Coates signaled that the enemy was in retreat and requested that the *Petrel* and *Marmora* cease firing. By this time, the former had expended 250 shells. As the fighting died down, McElroy went ashore with a fresh gun's crew and relieved Gibson. The second naval howitzer would be manned ashore until the Rebel threat had fully subsided. Coates's troops reembarked aboard their transports the next morning, Sunday, and returned to Vicksburg, their month-long mission accomplished.

After the Yazoo City fight, four men from the howitzer crews were recommended for Medals of Honor. On the other hand, Acting Ensign Holmes was dismissed in disgrace.[19]

As these events unfolded, the antishipping war by Confederate irregulars continued apace. On March 8, while en route from Cairo to Memphis transporting 50 Rebel prisoners under guard, the *C.E. Hillman*[20] put into Island No. 18 to wood. There citizens informed the boat's master that better fuel could be had for less cost at a landing across the island's chute on the Missouri shore. The steamer duly ran across and made fast.

At this point, a large armed party descended upon the *Hillman*. Three men jumped aboard and attempted to torch the bales of hay stacked on deck, but were subdued by crewmen before they could light their matches. Meanwhile, three 54th Illinois Infantry soldiers were captured, having gone ashore, and were held hostage while the Missouri irregulars opened a hot fire on the steamer.

The armed Union troops guarding the prisoners, who were confined in the rear of the boat, rushed forward onto the boiler deck and returned fire, reportedly killing three of the attackers. Meanwhile, a deckhand seized an ax and cut the line securing the steamer to the bank and her pilot worked to back the *Hillman* into the stream. As she gained deeper water, the three captured men made their escape and swam out to her.

After the skirmish, one of the colonels taking passage aboard the *Hillman* was found hiding in a closet. Once the danger passed, in the words of the *Chicago Daily Tribune* correspondent, "he was as brave as a lion."

YAZOO EXPEDITION.

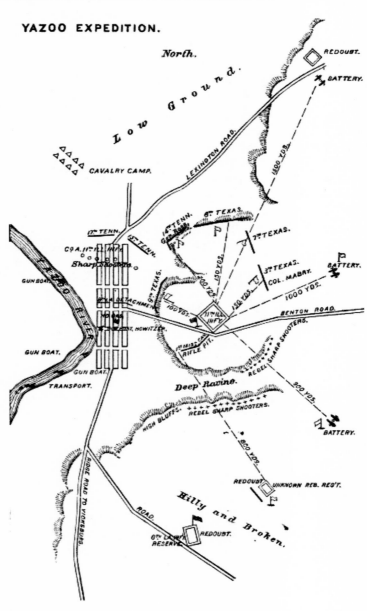

By the beginning of March, Confederate Maj. Gen. Taylor also knew that a large Federal force would soon be headed his way. To meet it, he had just 25,000 men. Maj. Gen. Nathaniel Banks and Rear Adm. Porter, co-equal commanders of the Union expedition, enjoyed a force superiority of 42,000 men, including 10,000 on loan from Maj. Gen. Sherman and 15,000 more from Arkansas area commander Maj. Gen. Frederick Steele, though his VII Corps would, in the end, not fully participate, leaving the land force total at 32,500.

Maj. Gen. A.J. "Whiskey" Smith and his men arrived at the mouth of the Red River on March 11 aboard 21 transports. They were borrowed; Sherman, who had agreed to allow them to participate, wanted his men back by April 15. These soldiers, their munitions and supplies, would be guarded up the Louisiana river by the Mississippi Squadron of the U.S. Navy.

In addition to the civil steamers chartered by the U.S. Quartermaster Department to transport the Union Army, Rear Adm. Porter, over the previous few days, had completed gathering what Lt. Cmdr. Thomas Selfridge later called "the most formidable force that had ever been collected in the western waters." As noted earlier, it drew from every flotilla in the squadron. The admiral was "determined there should be no want of floating batteries for the troops to fall back on in case of disaster." The naval and quartermaster transport force assigned to the operation was thus 104 vessels, mounting 300 guns (210 naval).

In reviewing this naval strength, the embedded *Philadelphia Inquirer* reporter was moved to observe that "a more formidable fleet was never under single command than that now on the Western rivers under Admiral Porter." On the other hand, he continued, "it might be said, also, never to less purpose. At the time of departure, the strength of the Rebellion in the inland waters had been crushed."

As this mighty armada assembled at the mouth of the Red, the convoy and counterinsurgency war on the Upper Rivers continued apace. Chugging up and down the Tennessee, the tinclad *Tawah* and her consorts, *Key West, Paw Paw, Alfred Robb,* and *Peosta* were often subjected to Rebel assault. A particularly vicious attack occurred on St. Patrick's Day.

For some time, the little towboat *S.C. Baker* had, with cover from the light-draughts, been carrying goods and pushing barges up and down the Tennessee between the various towns and points occupied by Federal troops. For the past week, Lt. Cmdr. James Shirk, Seventh District commander, was aboard the *Tawah* on an inspection tour. Both craft arrived at Clifton a day earlier.

Opposite: **During the Civil War years, many U.S. Navy warships were able to field howitzer crews, sometimes combining them, as in this photo, with those from other vessels. In March 1864, a howitzer crew from the light-draught ("tinclad") *Exchange* was sent ashore with its gun to help protect Federal soldiers garrisoning Yazoo City. This crew failed during a March 5 Confederate attack upon the city's defenses and was replaced with another from the *Marmora*. After the battle, four sailors from the howitzer crews were recommended for Medals of Honor while the Acting Ensign commanding the *Exchange* crew was cashiered. (Miller's *Photographic History of the Civil War.* This chart of the March Yazoo Expedition was taken from the Army *Official Records*, v. 32.)**

Just after dawn on March 17, the *Tawah* and *S.C. Baker* departed for Saltillo, five miles below Craven's Landing, where they arrived about 7 A.M. After the little transport landed her supply of flour, salt and bacon and was pushing off, a large band of Southerners approached the bank and began making off with the poorly-protected supplies. When local home guards attempted to stop them, a firefight broke out in which the Federals fared poorly, losing three dead and several wounded.

The tinclad opened fire on the acquisitions party and soon drove it back. However, "they rallied and we had it pretty hot for awhile," as *Tawah* Seaman James Dickinson remembered. Eventually, the Confederates broke off "just as the *Peosta* came down around the bend and chimed in on the last verse." Or, as her carpenter's mate, Herbert Saunders, put it, the tinclad "fired a few shells at the retreating rebels."

Once the shooting had stopped, a landing party from the *Peosta* went ashore and destroyed part of the goods left by the *S.C. Baker* and also buried several Rebels killed in the skirmish. A portion of the "groceries," primarily items in unbroken boxes and dry goods, were set aside for delivery back to their original owners at Clifton. As the *Peosta*'s men labored ashore, the *Tawah* and *S.C. Baker* departed for "up the river."

All that was loaded aboard the *Peosta*, as mate Saunders wrote in a letter home, "did not get off again." The seamen, thinking they deserved a share, stole liberally and did such a good job of hiding their loot that the officers, upon inspection, could not find it. "But what puzzles the officers most," Saunders continued, "was how the men got their whiskey." If there was any spirits around, it was certain "the men would find it." That night "half the crew were drunk boys." The following day was marked by a few quarrels as, with nothing new to pilfer, "they are stealing from one another."

En route downstream, the *Peosta* did not make it much further the next day than Pittsburg Landing. The woods for two or three miles above the place were shelled, "for there are plenty of guerrillas here." The roar of the cannon might also have had an intended impact upon the more pie-eyed among the crew.

As March continued to advance, the river stage of the Red, further south, did not. The gung-ho Rear Adm. Porter knew from recent surveys that this was "the most treacherous of all rivers; there is no counting on it, according to the rules which govern other streams...." Writing for *Battles and Leaders* after the war, Lt. Cmdr. Selfridge explained that the whole expedition hinged upon "the usual spring rise; but this year, the rise did not come." Indeed, in looking back, it was his opinion that: "Had the river been bank full, no force that the Confederates could have controlled could have stood for a moment against the fleet."

Just before Smith's arrival, Porter received the news that heavy rains were delaying Banks. He could not possibly reach Alexandria, one of the principal targets, before March 21. Additionally, the sailor found that work on the completion of the unfinished Fort De Russy, 30 miles south of Alexandria, was being pushed hard by the Rebels.

While the naval and military men bobbed on their vessels observing the overgrown marshlands ashore, Rear Adm. Porter and Maj. Gen. Smith held a meeting to decide what to do next in light of Banks's delay. The two men decided to capture Alexandria, taking Fort De Russy while en route. Their invasion armada started up the Red River at 8:30 A.M. on March 12.

Stripping so many gunboats away from their normal beats or anchorages to partic-ipate in the Red River expedition mean that numerous towns, crossings, and other points normally protected or regularly visited by one or more of the Mississippi Squadron units would be either defenseless or vulnerable. In the weeks ahead, there would be several effec-tive Confederate attacks further north, led by many Confederate partisans and cavalry-men, including the indomitable Maj. Gen. Nathan Bedford Forrest. Years later in his naval history, Adm. Porter was frank that "all of these successes gained by the Confederates were owing to the unfortunate Red River expedition, which had withdrawn the gunboats from their posts."

On the same Saturday morning, March 12, that Porter's armada started up the Red River, far up the Cumberland River, just 16 miles below Burkesville, KY, three Army trans-ports, the *Ella Faber, World,* and *Nettie Hartupee,*[21] were attacked by 50 to 100 insurgents believed to be led by Charles "Champ" Ferguson, a guerrilla leader notorious in Union circles. Word of a pending attack had been received in the Tennessee capital and the ersatz U.S. Army gunboat *Newsboy* was sent to rescue the trio from the worst Confederate assault on the Knoxville relief boats since the beginning of the year.

The three stern-wheelers, returning to Nashville after having delivered supplies to the head of navigation at Burnside Pont, were caught by Ferguson before the *Newsboy* could arrive. There was a squad of convalescent soldiers aboard the *Ella Faber,* who returned fire and thus protected their boat, plus the *World,* as they passed. Despite the upper works of the steamers being riddled by bullets, there were no fatalities, though two bluecoats were wounded.

The *Nettie Hartupee* was unable to pass by the fire and so hugged the other side of the river. At this point, a troop of 11th Kentucky Cavalry (U.S.A.) appeared and hailed the steamer, asking her pilot to take them aboard and cross them over. Believing the horse-men to be Rebels, the transport master ordered his boat to pass on, but could not get by the Southern chokepoint. Unable to proceed, she simply hove to. At this point, the Ken-tucky horsemen came up with the boat and their officers were able to convince the steam-boatmen of their true Union affiliation. As the soldiers and their horses were being taken aboard, the *Newsboy* arrived from below and shelled the Rebels, who faded away. The *Nettie Hartupee,* together with the *Ella Faber, World,* and *Newsboy,* passed on without further incident.[22]

Before sundown on March 14, the advancing Federal naval and military forces con-verged upon Fort De Russy and compelled its surrender. Upon taking possession, they learned that most of the defenders had already withdrawn, leaving but a gallant 300 to offer what turned out to be token resistance.

An order from Porter for pursuit of a known Confederate steamboat fleet toward Alexandria was delayed five hours in transmission. Upon its receipt, Lt. Cmdr. S. Led-yard Phelps, leading one of the naval task groups, dispatched his two fastest vessels, the timberclad *Lexington* and the oversize tinclad *Ouachita,* on the chase. Chugging off in the dark at 1 A.M. on March 15, they were soon followed by the sluggish giant ironclad *Eastport.*

The *Lexington* and *Ouachita* passed Fort de Russy at 8:30 A.M. As they sped by, Lt. George Bache, captain of the old wooden gunboat, hailed Acting Master Henry Gor-

The U.S. Army Quartermaster Department operated a fleet of ersatz gunboats on the Western rivers, mostly the upper tributaries of the Mississippi. The majority of these were very small, were manned by civilian crews with military gun crews for the usual two or three cannon, and were protected by cotton bales or planking. The most famous of these were the *Silver Lake No. 2* and *Newsboy*, which operated on the Cumberland River, and the *Stone River*, which steamed on the Tennessee. In March 1864, the *Newsboy* rescued three transports under attack on the upper Cumberland, while in October, the *Stone River* participated in the defense of Decatur, Alabama, from the army of Gen. John Bell Hood (*Harper's Weekly*, October 11, 1862).

ringe of the *Cricket* and Acting Volunteer Lt. John Pearce of the *Fort Hindman*, ordering them to follow upstream. The quartet came in sight of Alexandria about 5 P.M.

The initial Porter-Phelps communications failure caused the Federal vessels to miss coming up with the Rebel steamers before they succeeded in getting over the Alexandria falls. One tail-end vessel, the *Countess*,[23] grounded in her panic and, together with a barge left behind, was burned to prevent capture. The hulk of the blazing *Countess* was passed by the U.S. gunboats about 6:30 P.M. A half hour later, the four anchored off the town. Maj. Gen. Taylor, who had decided not to contest the Federal occupation, passed orders for his units to rendezvous at Natchitoches.

Several volleys of musketry were fired at the gunboats in the semi-darkness two hours later. Lt. Bache sent a boat ashore and removed the town mayor, sending him aboard the

Ouachita. He was undoubtedly lectured on the fiery fate awaiting Alexandria if the sniping continued. Late that night, the *Fort Hindman* returned downstream.

Nine Union vessels arrived at Alexandria by the morning of March 16 and a pair of landing parties occupied the town. Happily for the gunboatmen, the troop transports arrived at 1:30 P.M. and Maj. Gen. Smith's men took over the occupation duties. So far, the arriving soldiers, many of them from places like Wisconsin, New York, and Rhode Island, were not impressed with the Red River. "It is a dirty, sluggish stream, about an eighth of a mile wide," wrote Harris Beecher of the 114th New York, "flowing in an extremely crooked channel." Continuing, he added, "Its ends and curves are so exaggerated that they seem almost unnatural...."

Rear Adm. Porter was not at all pleased that Maj. Gen. Banks, plagued as he was by heavy rains, remained absent. The campaign seemed to be at a standstill. Shreveport, the principal objective, was still 350 miles up the Red. Until Banks arrived, Porter elected to use his men to make a little money. The law which gave sailors a third of the value of captured items applied, in his opinion as noted above, to cotton as well as ships. Even though the Confederates had an active policy of burning cotton to prevent its capture by the Northerners, there was just too much for all of it to be fired.

The bluejackets on this big outing were naturally excited to be turned loose to gather as much undestroyed cotton as possible. In the three days before Banks finally turned up, Federal sailors seized in excess of 3,000 bales. It goes without saying that Union soldiers, who could not participate in the rewards of these spoils, were displeased. Maj. David C. Houston later told the War Conduct Committee that it "was rather demoralizing to the soldiers to see the navy seizing the cotton for prize on land, while they did not get any."[24]

As the Federal expedition advanced past Simmsport, LA, toward Fort De Russy, efforts were made to not only provide it with nautical reinforcements, but to spread out the nonassigned naval assets to cover as much of the unprotected Mississippi as possible. As a result, the tinclads *Covington* and *Queen City* were passing through Memphis en route south when both were called to render quick coast guard action on the morning of March 22.

Just after 9 A.M., with a strong wind blowing toward shore, someone on the long line of steamboats anchored at the landing noticed flames shooting up from the stern of the White River packet *Des Arc*,[25] which was loading cotton just above the grounded steamer *Arago*.[26] As none of the civilian boats except the *Arago* had steam up, there was a significant chance of the conflagration spreading. Fortunately, lookouts aboard the tinclads, anchored a short distance below the landing, also saw the smoke and their captains quickly ordered action. The *Covington* slipped her anchor and ran up to the *Arago*. After several attempts, she was able to free the stranded vessel and tow her out into the stream.

The light-draught then made fast to the *Des Arc* and towed her across the river, forcing her into the bank on the Missouri shore. By the time the *Covington* had her moved, the *Des Arc* had lost most of her upper deck and shortly after she hit the bank, the fire broke through her deck from the hold. At this point, the *Queen City* fired a few rounds into the blazing wreck and, within 15 minutes, she was burned to the water's edge.[27]

While Porter and Smith moved into the Red River, Maj. Gen. William T. Sherman traveled to Nashville on March 18 to relieve his fellow Buckeye, U.S. Grant, as commander of the Military Division of the Mississippi. With suggestions from his colleague, now a Lt. Gen. transferred east, Sherman began to plan the spring campaign that would begin on May 1 and hopefully take him to Atlanta.

A friend of the Mississippi Squadron, Sherman always had a keen eye for the logistical necessities of war. His new Georgia advance would be no different in that regard. Years later, he wrote in his *Memoirs*: "The great question of the campaign was one of supplies. Nashville, our chief depot, was itself partially in a hostile country, and even the routes of supply from Louisville to Nashville, by rail and by way of the Cumberland River, had to be guarded." Only a month before, on February 22, Maj. Gen. Forrest, the greatest human threat to Sherman's supply apparatus, had defeated a Federal force at Okolona, MS, during the Meridian campaign and was now "on the loose" in West Tennessee. Ominously, and also on March 18, Memphis District commander Maj. Gen. Stephen A. Hurlbut passed the word: "It is reported that Forrest, with about 7,000 men, was at Tupelo last night, bound for West Tennessee. I think he means Columbus and Paducah."

Union concern over the whereabouts of the elusive Forrest, who reached Jackson on March 20, now intensified. On March 23, Brig. Gen. Mason Brayman, the army commander of the District of Cairo, sent a note over to USN Capt. Alexander Pennock announcing that he, too, had fresh intelligence. The Rebel raider was en route toward Union City, a crossroads town in northwestern Tennessee. If the news was accurate, the navy would be advised that gunboats might have to be sent to guard Columbus, Hickman, and Paducah. Indeed, it was reported that Confederates in force had volleyed the steamer *John D. Perry*[28] as she passed Hickman that day. A large number of shots were fired, but no one was hurt.

Early the next day, Pennock received army advice that Forrest was, indeed, marching in force upon Columbus and that communication with Union City had ceased. The fleet captain was asked to send a gunboat to Columbus posthaste and promised to have one under way by evening. Brayman, already at Columbus with 2,000 men, requested that the vessel report to him at that point as he was readying an expedition toward Union City, even though he suspected the enemy was off toward Paducah. The Cairo-based general came within six miles of Union City on the 26th before he learned of its surrender to one of Forrest's colonels the day before.

Also in mid-afternoon on March 25, Forrest himself led an attack on Paducah, driving its defenders (numbering about 650) into Fort Anderson on the Ohio River west of the city. Grayclad soldiers then occupied the nearby houses and fired into the fort.

The Rebels having rapidly reached the town and cornered its uniformed defenders, civilians were largely left to escape on their own or hide. Some fled aboard a ferryboat at the river bank to the left of the fort. These were able to get to the Illinois shore, but when the ferry returned for others, Confederate rifle fire prevented it from landing. Other citizens, it was later charged, were employed as human shields from behind which the raiders shot into Hicks's enclosure. During this time, several women and children were reportedly killed.

Largely unmolested in the streets of Paducah, Forrest's men plundered the town, capturing horses and supplies. When the general caused a flag of truce to be raised, fighting

On March 25, 1864, Maj. Gen. Nathan B. Forrest led an attack on Fort Anderson and the town of Paducah, Kentucky. The Confederates occupied much of the town, taking needed supplies and horses while torching many Federal depots and buildings (Library of Congress).

stopped for a half hour, during which the post commander, Col. Stephen G. Hicks, refused the surrender opportunity offered. He did not know that this was a familiar Forrest tactic designed to elicit victory without bloodshed.

In the hours following, two Kentucky regiments under Paducian native Col. Albert P. "Sam" Thompson repeatedly charged Fort Anderson. Sharpshooters and local insurgents sniped at targets of opportunity from the upper stories of residences and from the windows and roofs of the warehouses lining the river bank. The gunboatmen later believed that the Confederates might have captured Fort Anderson, "if it had not been for us." Low as they might have been on ammunition (27,000 of 30,000 available rounds expended), the mostly African-American defenders of the little bastion "fought bully," winning the admiration of the Federal sailors and many others.

In addition to Federal soldiers, Forrest's riflemen also made targets of the light-draught gunboats *Peosta* and *Paw Paw* lying in the river near Fort Anderson. The latter was stationship, while the former had arrived from up the Tennessee just after dawn. Mississippi Squadron Seventh District boss Lt. Cmdr. James W. Shirk, a veteran of USN action at the 1862 Battle of Shiloh, had departed the *Peosta* for Cairo later in the morning for consultations with Capt. Pennock and missed the fight. Ever afterwards he cursed his bad timing.

About 3 P.M., both Acting Volunteer Lieutenants Thomas E. Smith and A.F. O'Neill, commanders of the *Peosta* and *Paw Paw* respectively, learned that Federal pickets had been driven in by approaching Confederate skirmishers. Both of the tinclads weighed anchor and beat to quarters. When the enemy appeared, the former steamed to the upper end of the town and opened fire with her bow guns. The latter dropped down to defend Fort Anderson and also commenced firing.

The starboard battery aboard the *Peosta* was served as rapidly as possible. After some minutes, the gunboat dropped down to the foot of Broadway and fired directly up that street at targets of opportunity. When Col. Thompson's men executed their first charge, she steamed down to a point opposite Fort Anderson and joined the *Paw Paw* in resisting the attack. Two fruitless charges later, Thompson was dead. The *Peosta's* carpenter mate, Herbert Saunders, later told his mother in a letter: "He was shot with a rifle ball in the head and had a shell in him from the gunboat."

While Forrest and Hicks negotiated over a possible surrender and fighting was briefly suspended, the *Peosta* returned to her previous position off Broadway. From that point, her lookouts witnessed Confederate soldiers plundering the stores on that street. Soon thereafter the boat headed back toward Fort Anderson. Once more, the starboard battery opened. Meanwhile, the *Paw Paw* remained near the Federal citadel. Low on ammunition, Lt. O'Neill ordered that his gunners fire slowly taking care to aim as best they could.

Whenever they had the opportunity, Confederate troops peppered the two gunboats with musket fire. Lt. O'Neill thought that this action was a deliberate objective to "divert

The light-draught ("tinclad") gunboats *Peosta* (shown) and *Paw Paw* provided a spirited defense of Paducah during the March 1864 attack by troops under Confederate Nathan Bedford Forrest. Attacked by Rebel riflemen from buildings overlooking the river, the two gunboats replied with concentrated cannon fire. Their shots did as much or more damage to the town as the guns of both the Union and Southern land forces combined (U.S. Army Military History Institute).

the attention of the gunboats from the fort by harassing them with sharpshooters." The *Peosta*'s tall chimneys and wide wheelboxes were a particular favorite of riflemen firing from the buildings on Front Street. Carpenter's mate Saunders admitted that "while it lasted, their balls came pretty thick as some of them came in our portholes and some clean through the casemates...."

Lt. Smith later reported that he "reluctantly opened upon them, demolishing the Continental (or City) Hotel and brewery and setting several other buildings on fire." "One building in particular," a Confederate soldier remembered, "seemed to have attracted a well directed and concentrated fire." Officers from the 2nd Tennessee Cavalry (C.S.A.) later told a correspondent from the *Charleston Mercury* that the tinclad's bombardment sent "shingles, brick chimneys and window glass in wild profusion upon our heads."

The *Peosta* continued to assail the river-bank warehouse hideout of the dismounted Volunteer horse soldiers. "We directed our whole fire on them at short range with shell, grape, and canister," Mate Saunders noted.

The large Front Street brewery was a particular annoyance to the *Peosta*. Confederates shot down into the gunboat from the windows of its upper story, "riddling it considerably." Lt. Smith ordered his gunners to halt this insult. One *Peosta* shell collapsed the brewery's roof while another hit an adjoining shed from which a rifleman was seen firing. Several more smashed into the building itself, tearing it "asunder." Several men were wounded, a captain was killed, and a "blue wreath of smoke" quickly hung over the scene. Out of a gunport, Carpenter's Mate Saunders took satisfaction in seeing that the tinclad's cannon "soon fetched the bricks around their eyes."

The gunboats continued to fire into the town in support of the Union troops in Fort Anderson, who were themselves actively maintaining their position. Another Rebel in the warehouse district near the river and on the receiving end of the bombardment recalled the "bursting shells and the crashing of the solid shot from the gunboats thunder[ed] through the buildings above and around us."

Observers in the nearby town of Metropolis could now see Paducah in flames. It was reported that a number of women and children were able to escape across the river to Illinois in a large wharf boat. A number of families and other survivors reaching Metropolis reported street fighting. Later, it was reported that all of Front Street was in ashes.

When firing from the fort ceased about 8:30 P.M., the *Peosta* arrived and came to anchor abreast of it. A half hour later, the *Paw Paw* "fired half a dozen rifle shell, but neither saw nor heard anything more of the enemy."

Lt. Smith received word about 10:30 P.M. that the Rebels were destroying property and burning the quartermaster warehouses and commissaries' buildings as they prepared to fall back. The *Peosta* once again got underway, steamed up to the town, and opened fire, her shells landing, hopefully, in the general vicinity of the raiders. Her deliberate shoot was completed just before midnight.

During the Paducah engagement, the *Peosta* fired 530 rounds and was hit 200 times by rifle shot. Despite many perforations, she was not seriously damaged, though two men were wounded. The *Paw Paw* loosed 177 rounds. She was not hit and no one was wounded. Lt. O'Neill did, however, receive a scratch from a Minie ball on his right cheek and "a ball went through his pantaloons."

Neither boat fired again during the remainder of the night. At dawn, Lt. Cmdr. Shirk arrived from Cairo. As he approached the levee, he saw that the "shells from the gunboats and the fort did a great deal of damage to the town. Several buildings were burned, and a number have holes in them." Northern newspapers later reported that some 50–125 buildings, mostly privately owned, were destroyed or badly damaged, including "the hospital, gas works, some of the French residences of the city, the custom house, and post office," plus the railroad depot, freight forwarding facilities, and tobacco warehouses.

Although more action was anticipated by the Federals, the battle was not renewed the next morning. Unfortunately, Col. Hicks could not know this and, as a precaution, just after sunup ordered all of the houses within musket range of Fort Anderson burnt. Still, neither Shirk nor Brig. Gen. Brayman were very disturbed over the damage done. Paducah had long been considered a town made up of Rebel sympathizers profiting from Federal largess and, in the words of the naval officer, these had now "received a lesson which they will not forget in a hurry." In its report of the raid, the *Indianapolis Journal* made a blunt assessment: "Paducah is naturally destroyed."

Having held Paducah for 10 hours, Maj. Gen. Forrest, despite the spirited shelling of the gunboats, helped himself to Yankee horses and quartermaster stores while burning 60 bales of cotton, a steamboat, and a dry dock. Some merchants, the newspapers reported, "lost $25,000 to $50,000 worth of property."

The Confederate leader and his men then retired to plan their next adventure. As they left, Forrest supposedly observed, according to an April 3 letter from Carpenter's Mate Saunders to his mother, that "he did not care for that brown paper thing [the gunboat *Paw Paw*], but did like the looks of the *Peosta*." Puffed up by this, the young repairman boasted: "We are the strongest gunboat in the upper fleet."

On Sunday morning, the refugees who had crossed the river were allowed to return. Also during the day, seamen from the gunboats, by watches, were permitted liberty ashore to see "some of our work." One part of the city was "riddled with our shot for a mile back and about a fourth of the city is burnt down," Saunders and the men of the *Peosta* marveled.

At the end of March, Eighth District leader Lt. Cmdr. Fitch and Nashville garrison commander Maj. Gen. Lovell Rousseau learned of an expedition from Fort Donelson carried out by the tinclad *Silver Lake*. Col. O.L. Baldwin, 5th Kentucky Cavalry (U.S.A.), commanding that post, sent 50 soldiers aboard the light-draught on March 30 to scout the countryside below Eddyville. It was feared that Forrest might be in the vicinity, perhaps even on the eastern side of the Tennessee River. A group of soldiers from Hopkinsville were met by Baldwin, bringing in eight suspected guerrillas, and they reported the feared cavalry commander was not in the area. In his report to Rousseau, the colonel indicated that all was quiet at Smithland and no force was threatening any position on the Cumberland. He had heard from Fitch that Forrest was, in fact, near Columbus, on the Mississippi River.

Although Forrest was momentarily away from the rivers, Confederate irregulars continued their work on the Mississippi. On March 30, a dozen ruffians overwhelmed the captain's gig from the small side-wheeler *Columbia*,[29] which was anchored near the town of Austin, in the rear of Ship Island, 70 miles below Memphis. Gaining access to the steamer, they plundered it, "seizing all they could find of value."

As the *Columbia* was ransacked, the government agent who happened to be aboard, together with the engineer, escaped in a rowboat, taking the cash box with them. The five remaining crewmen were forced to move the *Columbia* to shore, where the raiders set it, and a few bales of cotton aboard, alight. Within minutes, it was consumed. Without insurance, the owner, Capt. John McDonald, suffered a total loss.[30]

8

Fort Pillow, the Petrel, *and Red River, April 1864*

As certain as is the spring blooming of dogwood along the rivers of the South, so too was the renewal of Confederate assaults upon Union outposts and logistical communications. As the weather improved in 1864, this insurgent activity became less a matter of *ad hoc* partisans pot-shooting at passing steamers. Rather, it assumed the caliber of a full-fledged and organized interdiction strategy more often implemented by regular military units.

On the Tennessee River, word spread concerning the attack on Paducah, KY, executed by Maj. Gen. Nathan Bedford Forrest. The tinclad *Alfred Robb* arrived at Clifton, TN, on April 2 with a report and, by then, the defensive role of the *Paw Paw* and *Peosta* was magnified. Seaman James A. Dickinson of the station boat *Tawah* wrote what he heard in his diary: "Forrest with 10,000 men attacked Paducah, but was driven off by the *Peosta* and the *Paw Paw* after losing 2,000 men."

On April 4, Forrest, writing from Richmond, TN, advised his superiors that, among other things: "There is a Federal force of five or six hundred at Fort Pillow, which I shall attend to in a day or two, as they have horses and supplies which we need." Before the month's first week was over, Forrest launched diversionary feints towards Memphis, Columbus, and Paducah. It was hoped that these moves would not only cover his descent upon Pillow, but might also net additional stores and horses.

Word came to Fleet Captain Alexander Pennock at Cairo from Lt. Cmdr. James Shirk, Seventh District commander, on April 11 that Paducah was again under Rebel threat. It was hoped that Col. Stephen G. Hicks might be reinforced. While District of Cairo commander Brig. Gen. Mason Brayman sent two regiments, Pennock sent Eighth District flotilla leader Lt. Cmdr. Le Roy Fitch. Several Cumberland River gunboats crossed district boundaries and began to reinforce Paducah on the morning of April 12. An attack was expected all day. Although the Rebels had not shown by evening, most of the Eighth District flotilla did. Forrest's ruse was working.

Much further down the Mississippi that morning, Fort Pillow, located some 35 miles north of Memphis and a target for the Western Flotilla in 1862, had lately resumed its previously abandoned function as a guard post protecting Federal navigation of the river. The former Confederate outpost was located atop a high bluff and nearly surrounded by two ravines extending back from the river. The one below it was home to several stores and homes, while right along the river bank were quartermaster and commissary facilities. Coal Creek ravine was above the fort, which was now encircled by the main body of Forrest's command.

The Yankee garrison, made up of approximately 262 African-American and 295 Caucasian soldiers from the 11th U.S. Col. Troop and a battalion of the 14th Tennessee Cavalry (U.S.A.), had a number of cannon, and was reinforced by the tinclad *New Era* under Acting Master James Marshall. Neither the defenders afloat or ashore knew that the feared Rebel commander was about to pounce.

Still, these Union army and navy elements had made some rudimentary preparations for mutual defense in the event of attack, including plans for evacuation. It was agreed that should the fort commander signal that he was under attack and about to be overwhelmed, his last men would "drop down under the bank" and the gunboat would "give the rebels canister."

First contact between Forrest's Confederates and Union pickets at Fort Pillow occurred at 6 A.M., quickly sending a few survivors among the latter scurrying back inside to sound the alarm. Within minutes, the Rebel charge was sounded and grayclad soldiers swarmed up to the ravines outside the enclosure and then over the walls while sharpshooters made certain Federal defenders kept their heads — and muskets — below the parapets.

When the first alarms went off, the *New Era* backed out into the Mississippi and cleared for action. As the sound of musketry increased and fires were seen, Fort Pillow's commander signaled Marshall, asking that the gunboat fire

Nathan Bedford Forrest (1821–1877) was one of a handful of Western cavalry leaders who understood the importance of interdicting Federal waterborne commerce. In February 1863, he participated in an attempt to block the Cumberland River at Dover and now, in April 1864, his men assaulted both Paducah, Kentucky, and Fort Pillow. A self-taught military genius who regularly outwitted Northern army and navy commanders, he would destroy the Tennessee River depot at Johnsonville in November 1864 and greatly assist Gen. John Bell Hood in his Nashville offensive in the fall and winter (Library of Congress).

into the two nearby ravines where Confederates were assembling to assault. These requests were conveyed by an officer standing at the rear of the fort and waving a flag. The gunboat immediately dropped shells onto the ravine at the lower junction of Ripley and Fulton Roads and before long, she was a big target for Forrest's enfilading riflemen. She then shifted to the Coal Creek ravine to the north of the outpost.

Maj. Gen. Forrest later reported that the tinclad's continuous cannonade "was without effect." Historian Fuchs later amplified that opinion of her efforts. "For the most part," he wrote in 2002, they "were ineffectual in causing either dislodgment of the enemy or casualties." At best, he added, the *New Era* did cause a few Rebel soldiers to move from one ravine to another.

A veteran tincladman later wrote his own assessment of the *New Era*'s bombardment, laying its ineffectiveness to her howitzers and their ammunition. Recording his memoirs at Saratoga Springs, New York, in 1881, E.J. Huling opined that she "had very little ammunition, except for her howitzers, and most of her shells fell short or did little execution." The one-time assistant paymaster went on to opine: "Had she been armed with the same kind of guns that the boat I served upon carried (30 pound rifled Parrotts, sending shells three miles), she could have aided materially in defending that fort, and perhaps have prevented the capture."

In this time, numerous civilian women, children, both white and African-Americans, made their way to the river bank and hid behind the largest of three moored coal barges. Alerted to this development, Marshall eased his tinclad back toward shore. Gaining the attention of the refugees with a speaking trumpet, the *New Era*'s commander told them to climb into the barge. A line was passed and the barge was towed, under fire, to a position above the bar at Coal Creek.

The gunboat cut the barge loose and turned to reenter the fray. As she churned away, the frantic passengers were advised to go ashore and hide in the woods. All this time, the noncombatants were under fire from Confederate sharpshooters, who managed to hit and kill one woman. Marshall saw the refugees crouching down and afraid to move and slowed the *New Era* in order to point out to them, by trumpet, a nearby house to which they might flee.

The side-wheel gunboat churned back to Coal Creek ravine, around 8 A.M., and resumed firing on the enemy per requests from the fort's defenders. N.D. Wetmore, a reporter for the *Memphis Argus* who was among the first to tour the field after the battle, wrote that the gunboat "shelled the rebels and drove them from a position which they had gained on the south side of the fort." The thick timber made it difficult to dislodge the advancing enemy. U.S. Congressmen later took testimony that the affected butternuts shifted position when targeted: "As they were shelled out of one ravine, they would make their appearance in the other." The swift current and rain-swollen river made navigation difficult, and required that the *New Era* fire from her starboard battery only. This necessity soon caused the guns to overheat and foul.

According to the gunboat's log, Capt. John Booth's 373-ton side-wheeler, *Liberty No. 2*, came down the river about 9:30 A.M. She landed at the refugee coal barge where Booth offered to take aboard all who wished to pass with him to Memphis. After the vessel pulled out into the stream, she passed the fort and the *New Era*, receiving a musket volley from shore in passing.

All morning the fighting ashore grew more fierce. Sharpshooters kept up a constant rain of fire onto the *New Era* from every direction. Shortly after noon, Acting Master Marshall later recalled, a two-gun masked battery opened on his boat under cover of Wolf's Hill, but did no damage.

A lull occurred about 1:45 P.M. when Maj. Gen. Forrest sent a surrender demand to the Union commanders under a flag of truce. The tinclad retired to midstream, a short distance from the fort, and maintained a "slow wheel" against the current. No effort was made to drift downstream or otherwise seek better firing positions. The discussions progressed for an hour and a half, after which smoke was seen down the river from approaching boats.

About two and a half miles below Fort Pillow, Capt. B. Rushmore Pegram's giant six-boiler side-wheeler *Olive Branch* was hailed from shore by several women. Easing in, the captain of the 697-ton Jeffersonville, IN-built steamer, completed earlier in the year, was told that Forrest had attacked the garrison. He had supposedly already captured two steamboats and would take Pegram's craft as well if she continued on.

Also aboard the 283-foot-long *Olive Branch*, en route to Cairo from New Orleans via Memphis, were 150 passengers, the reassigned Brig. Gen. George F. Shepley, and two whole field batteries complete with 120 men, caissons, and horses. Pegram decided to run past the fort, but was countermanded when he informed Shepley. The general, recently sacked as military governor of Louisiana, saw a chance to rush to victory and redeem his reputation.

About this time, the 598-ton side-wheeler *Hope*, built at New Albany, IN, the year before and usually engaged in the Ohio River trade, approached without passengers and towing coal barges. She was hailed by Shepley, who ordered her to discard her tow and take him and a section of battery aboard so they could steam to the rescue of Fort Pillow. Before this could be accomplished, yet another boat hove in sight from upstream. This was the *M.R. Cheek*, unrecorded in Way's directory, and she, too, was hailed by Shepley. Coming alongside the *Olive Branch*, this latest visitor received Shepley and two subordinate officers. Work began on transferring part of a battery.

As this business was progressing, the *Liberty No. 2* came in sight up the river. The decks of the 225-foot-long, three-year-old steamer were lined with soldiers and a few rescued civilians from the fort earlier towed to safety in a coal barge. There was initial suspicion aboard the *Olive Branch* that this might be a Confederate capture preparing to attack. That notion was quickly disabused when, drawing into voice range, Capt. Booth shouted that he had rapidly passed Fort Pillow and that all was quiet. A gunboat lay off the outpost, a flag of truce was flying, and it was safe to pass. The civilian captain, though possibly aware of a battle from refugee tales, had not experienced much shooting beyond what he probably took for a guerrilla volley as he sped by the fort on a strong current and passed down.

Shepley was not convinced of Pillow's pacificity and elected to mount a reconnaissance. Thus the *Olive Branch*, followed by the *Hope* and *Cheek*, steamed up toward the reported battle site. As they approached, Maj. Gen. Forrest ordered defensive preparations.

When the Federal boats came within range, Confederate sharpshooters, stationed on a bluff overlooking the close-in channel of the river, took them under fire. Several shots hit close to the *Olive Branch*'s pilothouse, and Capt. Pegram ordered his boat to steam across the Mississippi to a bar near the opposite bank. The *Hope* and *Cheek* followed.

Straining against the rapid current, the *New Era* came up with the *Olive Branch* group in midstream. A boat was lowered away and rowed over to the civilian streamer. A naval officer informed Shepley of the reason for the flag of truce and urged the general to proceed to Cairo at once for reinforcements. As the great wheels of Pegram's boat thrashed ahead, the *Hope* and *Cheek* were ordered tied up in the chute on the right side of the foot of Island No. 30.

Communications being what they were during this time, Union naval officers north of Fort Pillow simply did not know that the desperate fight was going on and believed Forrest was after them. For example, during the afternoon, Lt. Cmdr. Shirk wired Capt. Pennock informing him that Confederates had surrounded Paducah.

By 2 P.M., men from three Rebel Kentucky regiments appeared on line "on the borders of a timber," but made no assault. The town fort opened long-range fire, while "the gunboats, cruising up and down in front of the town, threw shells over the town in the direction of the enemy's position." Seaman Dickinson aboard the *Tawah* confided to his diary: "Rebels entered Paducah this afternoon but were driven out by the gunboats." When nothing further happened, it was speculated that the Southern horsemen might also have their sights set on either Columbus or Cairo and maybe even to crossing the Ohio River à la Morgan.

As the afternoon waned peacefully at Paducah, the opposite was true at Fort Pillow. Choosing to interpret the *Olive Branch* nautical maneuverings as a major reason to end the parlay, the Confederates resumed the battle at nearly 3:15 P.M. and charged the fort.

Although the two howitzers on Wolf's Hill did not damage the *New Era*, the gunboat could not silence them or otherwise help the Union defenders. The river channel ran directly under the bluff some 80 feet below and there was a broad bar causing shallow water opposite the fort. Neither permitted the tinclad to gain the space necessary to elevate her guns high enough to hit the masked battery.

With the fort about to be overrun, the last Union defenders ran below the bluff, hoping to take up new last-ditch positions while the *New Era* covered them with her guns. The tinclad did not "give the rebels canister." Nearly out of ammunition and acting out of prudence, if not confusion, Acting Master Marshall ordered his gunports closed and his craft to steam out of range. The fleeing bluecoat soldiers panicked when they found no naval support awaiting their flight through the bushes. Some tried to resist; most were killed by Southern troops closing in from every angle.

As the tinclad captain later testified to visiting U.S. congressmen, there was a real concern that, if he moved downstream closer in toward shore, his fire might hit the last-ditch defenders. Furthermore, he believed that the advancing Rebels might also find a way to board or sink the *New Era*. "Suffice it to say, at a critical moment," wrote historian Fuchs years later, "the gunboat was out of position and the captain exhibited a recreance that some would describe as 'criminal prudence.'"

Fort Pillow fell to Forrest late in the afternoon with U.S. losses of approximately 231 to 261 killed and 87 to 100 badly wounded. A total of approximately 168 Caucasian and just 58 African-American soldiers were POW. The large proportion of African-American deaths led to charges of a Southern massacre and a debate which rages to this day.

After Pillow's capture, according to Forrest's biographer Dr. Wyeth, the *New Era*, churning slowly offshore, was signaled by a Rebel officer on the bank waving a white flag.

The Confederates wanted to discuss arrangements that could be made for the removal of Federal wounded. The flag was either missed or ignored as the gunboat moved upstream around a bend.

When the boat was above, Acting Master Marshall ordered her to take aboard the women and children refugees. Just after midnight the tinclad dropped anchor off Barfield's Point. During the engagement, the *New Era*'s great guns had expended 191 rounds of shell, 85 of shrapnel, six of canister; her sailors and marines also used up 375 rounds of rifle cartridges.

About 5 P.M., as the battle climaxed, two messengers dispatched to Memphis by Marshall earlier in the day were received in the office of naval station commander Lt. Cmdr. Thomas Pattison. After hearing the facts of the fight as then known and taking a request for ammunition, the city's top naval officer summoned Acting Master William Ferguson, previously executive officer of the tinclad *Rattler*, and ordered him to take his gunboat, the *Silver Cloud*, to Fort Pillow posthaste. There he was to offer the defenders whatever assistance might be required.

The *Silver Cloud* lay off the Tennessee city without steam up as workmen completed repairing her furnace fire walls. Unable to move on her own, the tinclad was tied to Capt. Robert K. Riley's mail steamer *Platte Valley*. As Ferguson's boat pushed north against the stiff current lashed to the 220-foot-long, much larger side-wheeler, it was hoped that Fort Pillow was safe. About 20 miles above Memphis, the gunboatman learned that such was not the case. A passing transport "spoken" about 10 P.M. confirmed that the little bastion had been taken.

The fire wall repairs were completed shortly after this midstream rendezvous and the light-draught's engineers were able to raise steam. Even though she had "steam enough to make 6 knots against the current," the *Silver Cloud* did not immediately cast off from her tow. Two sets of paddle wheels thrashing north would provide more speed than one stern-wheel alone.

The two Federal steamers reached Fulton, MO, about three miles below Fort Pillow, at 6 A.M. on April 13. There Ferguson learned that Rebel pickets were on the river banks about a half mile further on. The two craft separated and continued cautiously upstream, the civilian craft carefully following in the wake of the gunboat.

Upriver at this time, the *New Era* was just getting underway, having transferred her refugees to the newly-arrived Madison Packet Company stern-wheeler *Lady Pike*. With the 207-ton civilian boat following behind, Acting Master Marshall's gunboat headed back toward Fort Pillow, intent upon seeking a truce under which to rescue the wounded and bury the Northern dead.

Meanwhile, as warned, the *Silver Cloud* came upon the Southern vidette outpost. Small groups of cavalry were seen in the area, including the nearby hills, but they did not resist. Ferguson ordered his gunners to bombard the nearby woods and all suspicious-looking landmarks as the gunboat and transport slowly made their way to a point opposite the fort.

About 8 A.M., the gunboat crept on a short distance further, rounded to, and stood down the river near the bank. As the imbedded *Argus* reporter Wetmore wrote, everywhere in the fort, public and private buildings were afire. Small Confederate groups were seen moving about applying the torch to barracks, huts, and stables.

From their hiding spots, Union survivors and wounded came out and waved to the black savior. The *Silver Cloud* landed and began taking them aboard; as she did so, she was fired upon, without effect, by Rebel sharpshooters. The gunboat stood out into the river and began shelling the hills and bluffs adjacent to the fort. Within a few minutes, riders appeared waving a flag of truce. Firing ceased on both sides and a cutter was sent ashore to inquire.

Maj. Gen. Forrest offered, via his aide-de-camp, to allow the Federal boats to send landing parties ashore until 5 P.M. to bury dead Union soldiers and take aboard, under parole, the wounded. This gesture was quickly accepted. As the gunboat moved to shore, the *Platte Valley* was signaled to move up and come alongside.

Burial parties were active from both sides, with the Confederates interring far more than the Union sailors. As the bluejackets continued their grisly work and the injured were taken aboard the *Platte Valley*, smoke from the *New Era* and *Lady Pike* was seen upstream. The pair signaled and came in, with the former sending a party ashore under an officer to assist with the burials.

Having taken aboard all the known wounded, the *Platte Valley* departed for the naval hospital at New Madrid, MO. Just after her departure, something on the order of 20 additional wounded soldiers appeared from beyond the Confederate lines. As fortune would have it, the *Red Rover*, the first USN hospital ship, was en route downriver at this time and put into shore to provide assistance.

The total number of injured rescued totaled 89; sailors from the *New Era* and *Silver Cloud* buried 205 Federal comrades. When the truce flag was withdrawn, the *Silver Cloud* immediately stood down the river to report to Lt. Cmdr. Pattison at Memphis. The *New Era* took station about three miles below the fort, reclaiming a coal barge that was cut loose during the battle and subsequently grounded on the bar at Island No. 34.

Early that afternoon, Brig. Gen. Brayman was informed that the Rebels had demanded the surrender of Columbus, but were refused. Sending the women and children to Cairo, the garrison commander posted a message with them calling for help. Brayman wired Capt. Pennock, and, about 3 P.M., the fleet captain sent Lt. Cmdr. Fitch to the rescue.

The *Moose*, in company with the *Hastings*, churned down the 19 miles from Cairo to Columbus later on the 13th and found the tinclad *Fairy*[1] already on station. Ashore, Fitch learned that the threatening Confederates had retired. The Union officers did not know that his enemy consisted of 150 picked Confederates sent to create a diversion.

About this time, Navy Secretary Gideon Welles received a telegram from Pennock reporting that Fort Pillow had, indeed, been attacked. This atop a Confederate demand for the surrenders of both Columbus and Paducah. The fleet captain reported his order that, if Fitch could be spared from Columbus, he would proceed to Fort Pillow. There he would endeavor to shell the Rebels from the fort and to keep the river open.[2]

When Lt. Cmdr. Fitch learned that Pillow had fallen, he ordered his two boats to cast off and speed downstream. The tinclads had to arrive as quickly as possible, he believed, in order to prevent Forrest from throwing up batteries and cutting off communication with the squadron below.

The *Moose* and *Hastings*, in company with two steamers met along the way, arrived off Fort Pillow on the afternoon of April 14. There they saw the *New Era* shelling a group of Rebels who were setting fire to coal barges at a point just above Coal Creek. One of the barges had been towed to that location by the *New Era* the previous evening. The grayclads "displayed considerable bravery," admitted Fitch, as they fired one barge and pushed it adrift. As she came on, the *Moose* also opened fire in the same general direction as the *New Era* and also moved to communicate with that vessel. The new senior officer on scene learned something of the events of the past two days from Acting Master Marshall.

The *Hastings* rounded to and shelled the woods along the shore up to Plum Point Bend, where Rebel soldiers were "showing their honesty and bravery" by firing the wood-piles along the river meant for steamboat replenishment. The *Moose*, meanwhile, ran downstream and picked up the empty coal barge which was sent adrift from Coal Creek. Men from the tinclad's crew jumped aboard and put out the fire before it could do much damage, and it was taken in tow and landed opposite Fort Pillow. The warship then steamed up to Plum Point, saw the *Hastings* pounding men hiding behind several wood-piles, and emptied five rounds of shrapnel from her own howitzers toward horsemen along the shore.

The two civilian steamers tied up at the foot of Island No. 30 were still there await-ing release from the orders issued by Acting Master Marshall. They were joined by one of the newcomers escorted down by Fitch. A force of Rebel cavalry was seen, congregat-ing in the area above, preparing to make an attack on these transports. The *Moose*, *New Era* and *Hastings* steamed after the riders, and as the butternut troopers galloped off down the wooded shore toward Ashport, the tinclads paddled after them in line ahead forma-tion, right through the chute to the right of the island, loosing random shots toward the men. The pursuit lasted from about 4 P.M. until dark, at which point the Confederate horsemen faded down the Ripley road.

Having determined that the enemy had not crossed Hatchee River, the USN task group commander knew that Fort Pillow was safe—if still smoking. His tinclads now met the *Hope* and *Cheek* and convoyed them below the fort. Once they were off down the river, the gunboatman's vessels returned to Pillow and landed. The remaining women and children in the fort went aboard one of the civilian craft while 10 additional wounded soldiers were brought aboard the *Moose*. The vessels all tied up about noon to the tow-head opposite, where they lay until dawn on April 15.

Fitch did not know that the Confederate diversionary force made a move on Padu-cah that day, driving in the Union pickets and once more offering the city a flag of truce to remove women and children before attacking. When the hour was up, no assault mate-rialized. During the day's action, Southern riders managed to steal into the city and cap-ture all of the U.S. government horses remaining in town—their major goal—and some belonging to civilians as well.

Lt. Cmdr. Shirk was ready to do his part during this return visit, with the *Peosta*, *Key West*, *Fairplay*, and *Victory* offering protection. With Confederate troops reported in the upper part of the town and nearby Jersey, the four tinclads pounded the areas, reported-ly driving the enemy back to the local fairgrounds out of range.

Just after dawn on Friday, the *Moose* and *New Era* moved across to Fort Pillow and landed. Pickets were sent out a sufficient distance to prevent surprise and to permit a detail to finish burying the dead. Many bodies had been left untouched and the job of interring those already buried was done poorly. Once the Fort Pillow interments were completed and the *New Era*'s magazines were replenished, Acting Master Marshall was ordered to remain behind and guard the fort. The *Moose* and *Hastings* departed for up the river. Minutes after starting, the Yankee vessels came upon a squad of Rebel cavalry that had camped in the woods near the river bank at Ashport the night before. The horsemen were shelled as they rode off, but none were seen to fall.

Upstream at Cairo that evening, Capt. Pennock wrote to Rear Adm. David Dixon Porter providing him with the latest available information concerning events at Columbus, Paducah, and Fort Pillow. "With the able assistance of Shirk and Fitch, I have no doubt of being able to take care of the river and keep it open."

Even further upstream on the night of April 15–16, a party of about 100 Confederates, hidden out along the shore about a mile above Metropolis, opened fire on the patrolling tinclad *Victory*. The super light-draught was not damaged and no one aboard was injured, even as she returned fire.

Upon his arrival in Illinois waters on the evening of April 16, Lt. Cmdr. Fitch reported to Pennock that it was safe for river traffic to pass Fort Pillow. The fleet captain then relayed the essentials of his subordinate's Fort Pillow review in a report to Porter and a telegram to Secretary Welles. When the squadron commander, then up the Red River, learned of the loss, he passed orders for the *Essex*, *Benton*, *Choctaw*, and *Lafayette*, the four heavy gunboats not on the expedition, to steam north and secure Pillow against further assault.[3]

While the tinclads attempted to hold the line against the Confederacy on the Yazoo and on the upper rivers during the first half of the month, the grand Federal advance toward Shreveport was stopped and reversed. Having taken the lightest gunboats available to him at Alexandria above the falls and to the north guarding troops and supply transports, Rear Adm. Porter succeeded in reaching Grand Ecore, LA. One ironclad, two light-draught monitors, the timberclad *Lexington*, and the tinclads *Cricket* (flag) and *Fort Hindman* proceeded ahead from there, escorting a number of troop transports. The latter tinclad, like the *Lexington*, mounted 8-inch cannon and was, therefore, a welcome addition.

While the expedition's Union land commander, Maj. Gen. Nathaniel Banks, maneuvered inland of the task group, Porter slowly advanced northwest through the so-called Narrows for three days. All along the way Rebel riflemen pursued the boats "like a pack of wolves," targeting them from the bluffs along the shore. It was a very tough trip, with boats frequently grounding. Acting Master Gorringe of the *Cricket* often found his tinclad acting as the admiral's sheepdog in prodding the task group forward. Arriving at Loggy Bayou on the afternoon of the April 10, the Union force, 110 miles above Alexandria and just 40 miles from Shreveport, found the way blocked by a sunken steamer.

Before the wreck could be cleared, Union horsemen arrived with news that Banks was defeated in battles at Mansfield and Pleasant Hill and was withdrawing. Porter ordered a retreat that turned out to be very unpleasant. The defeated army corps reached Grand Ecore on April 11 and went into camp behind rapidly-constructed entrenchments. It would remain at this location for the next 10 days.

During the day, Porter's fleet worked its way down the frustrating Red River. The men aboard did not know that, at dawn, the Confederate theater commander Maj. Gen. Richard Taylor had dispatched a brigade of cavalry and a battery from Mansfield to cut off the boats at the docks of Bayou Pierre. Luckily for the Federals, they passed Grand Bayou Landing several hours before the Rebel horsemen arrived.

On several occasions, Confederate riflemen atop the river-bank bluffs peppered the vessels with musketry, just as they had on the way up. Such bee strings continued to elicit massive cannon fire in response. "In the first years of the war," Taylor wrote later, it "was popularly believed that the destructive power of these monsters ... could not be resisted." Many of the Confederate soldiers pursuing Porter's task group still believed this, though, notably, at least one did not.

Advised of the movements of the Federal boats, Confederate Brig. Gen. Thomas Green determined to catch them at Blair's Landing. About 45 miles north of Grand Ecore and due west of Pleasant Hill, that point would most likely be passed by Porter next day. Green was specifically instructed to find an attack point before Porter passed it.

As planned, heavy fighting flared at Blair's Landing. At one point, the *Lexington* and *Osage* beat off determined Confederate attacks by unmounted Texas cavalry. Green himself was killed by a shell from the latter gunboat.

Upstream by about two miles, the transport *William H. Brown*, the *Fort Hindman*, and the grounded monitor *Neosho* were also attacked by Green's troopers. The warships responded, smashing the woods along the shore. Eventually, the *Neosho* freed herself and the three moved to safety.

Other vessels were also assaulted. In the end, no one was certain exactly how many were killed in what the Federal admiral called a "curious affair of a fight between infantry and gunboats." Fatalities may have been as low as a dozen.[4]

There was great uncertainty about whether or not the Confederates would resume their attack that evening. Taking no chances, either with his crews or the supplies aboard his transports, Porter ordered the fleet to make the best speed away from Blair's Landing as river conditions permitted. Actually, the progress of the Union task group was not very slow, considering the many sandbars encountered. In pitch dark, the boats had only torches by which to navigate the risky stream. Several struck rocks or were temporarily grounded. About 1 A.M. on April 13 the fleet finally tied up for the night.

The withdrawal to Grand Ecore resumed about 6 A.M. when it was light enough to check for obstructions ahead. Not long after this the 391-ton side-wheel quartermaster steamer *John Warner*, while moving through a dense patch of fog, hit a snag and grounded so firmly that she could not be immediately worked off. Confederate forces, continuing to follow the fleet on the east side of the river, now determined to take advantage of the *Warner* situation to again harass the Federals. Two sections of field artillery (two 6-pounders and two 12-pounder howitzers) were unlimbered atop the hill overlooking Bouledeau's Point, where the grounded 220-foot-long side-wheel steamboat lay. Between noon and 4 P.M., Rebel gunners attempted to hit her or any of the vessels strung out across the river under the bluff, realizing that a lucky shot might blow up an ammunition steamer or penetrate a boiler. Their efforts were supported by riflemen whose balls were dangerous from that distance to Union crewmen but not, if they came no closer, to their vessels.

To make certain that a lucky hit was not scored, those few steamers not required to assist the *Warner* were ordered to continue on downstream. The inexact blockade by the Rebel cannoneers, firing from so far away, was deemed passable. Three made their way around the point, all of them taking small arms hits that caused neither damage or casualties. Once the merchantmen were away, the *Osage* and *Lexington* steamed up to take on the batteries, while the *Fort Hindman* and two other steamers unsuccessfully hauled away on big hawsers run over from the *Warner*. After the transport trio was past Bouledeau Point, the *Lexington* followed, providing convoy. The *Hindman* remained behind with the *Warner* for the next couple of hours until she was freed.

Toward 4 P.M., the impressed quartermaster steamers reached the village of Campti, tying up about the same time that an army relief force marched in. The *Lexington, Fort Hindman,* and *John Warner* arrived around 7 A.M. on April 14. Soon they cast off for "down the river," finally reaching Grand Ecore two days later. Although many of the vessels that escaped from Loggy Bayou bore the marks of Rebel sharpshooters, those reassembling at Grand Ecore were, in fact, little the worse for their ordeal. Still, the *St. Louis Daily Missouri Democrat* newsman embedded aboard one of the transports called the fleet's escape to Grand Ecore "one of the most daring, as well as one of the most successful ... feats of the whole war."

The reader will recall that while he was away upstream, Porter left his largest vessels behind under Lt. Cmdr. Seth Ledyard Phelps, skipper of the *Eastport*. Determined that these units should now retire from the river regardless of whether or not the Army of the Gulf returned to the offensive, the squadron commander ordered them to cross the bar below the town and steam for Alexandria. Following the *Ozark*, the giant *Eastport* was about eight miles below Grand Ecore on April 15 when her bow struck a torpedo. It was one of six prepositioned by the Confederates below the Grand Ecore ferry in mid–March. The explosion of the subsurface mine caused the ironclad to tremble, not unlike the times already when, while steaming ahead, she had hit sandbars or snags. Rushing on deck, her captain quickly ordered her steered toward the river bank.

The damage to the *Eastport* was more serious than a mere glancing blow. Water rushed into her forward holds even as damage control parties were told away to man a steam siphon pump and the ship's three hand pumps. Idle sailors were set to work bailing by hand. A half hour into this melee, Phelps ordered the whistle blown five times in the prearranged distress signal. The sound was heard at Grand Ecore. The ironclad captain also dispatched an accompanying tug down to Alexandria to get word to Porter and to return with the two pump boats stationed there with other fleet auxiliaries. Although aided by the *Lexington*, first on the scene from Grand Ecore, efforts to help save the *Eastport* failed. At 11 P.M., the giant's bow struck bottom and water covered the forward end of her gun deck.

As soon as Rear Adm. Porter arrived aboard the *Cricket*, he met with Phelps and the timberclad's commander, Lt. George M. Bache, and ordered that the *Eastport*'s battery and ammunition be removed next morning while additional aid was sought at Alexandria. Damage control parties worked through the night to try to find and isolate the damage; the vessel's heavy wooden bulkheads frustrated their efforts. As the sun rose on April 16, the *Lexington*'s steam pump was fired up again, along with that of the *Eastport*. Those two were joined by another provided by the newly-arrived stern-wheel tinclad *Juliet*.[5] The two undamaged vessels alternated this bailing service as the day wore on.

Crews from the *Eastport* and the *Lexington* were also set to work passing ammunition to the nearby monitor *Ozark*. When that task was completed, parties from the timberclad dismounted the aft 9-inch guns, which were manhandled through the gunports to the waiting *Ozark*. Although all of the big guns were transferred by dark, the men of the *Lexington* and the *Juliet* stood to their pumps off and on throughout the night and into the morning of April 17. Just after 9 A.M., the specialized steam pump boat *Champion No. 5* arrived and tied up alongside the sunken ironclad. Once the salvage boat had her giant 10-inch and 20-inch steam pumps in action, the *Lexington* disengaged and returned to Grand Ecore.

On April 19, Maj. Gen. Banks ordered his army moved to Natchitoches, a town "as old as Philadelphia." Back from below, Rear Adm. Porter found it impossible to remain upstream any longer and ordered his transports and lighter gunboats to initiate their withdrawal from Grand Ecore the same day. Having thrown in the towel on any further Red River exploits, Banks would begin his final overland withdrawal two days later.[6]

While elements of the Mississippi Squadron struggled up the Red, others left below had to contend with Confederate resistance to Federal resupply efforts. These Rebel assaults took place not only against vessels on the Red, but those approaching it on the Mississippi.

Escorted by the gunboat *General Price*,[7] the steamer *Superior*,[8] with the 3rd Rhode Island Cavalry embarked, departed New Orleans for Alexandria on April 18. For safety's sake, cotton bales were piled about the boiler and stacked on the hurricane deck, forming barricades. About 3 A.M. the following morning as the pair entered Tunica Bend, some 12 miles below the mouth of the Red River, they were fired upon by a two 12-pounders from shore.

The Rebel gunners sent eleven bolts toward the Union vessels, but only two hit, one aboard each craft. The present for the *Superior* passed through the ladies' cabin, set a stateroom on fire, and exploded in a pantry. The *General Price* simultaneously engaged the horse artillery, which quickly limbered up and moved down the shoreline some 200 yards past a house and stables employed earlier. Knowing the guns could not be caught, the gunboat sent a landing party ashore to destroy the structures.

The ordeal of Capt. Dexter's *Superior* and her guests did not end, even after they entered the mouth of the Red River and their protection was turned over to the tinclad *St. Clair*. Heading into a bend in the river below Alexandria on April 21, the craft were taken under fire by two Confederate fieldpieces, backed up by swarms of infantry and dismounted cavalry. The first incoming shell exploded on the steamer's hurricane deck, near one of her chimneys, killing two men and wounding 17 others. Another sliced through the iron plating and screamed into the pilothouse. Topside, Rhode Island horse soldiers returned fire with their carbines from behind the makeshift cotton barricades.

At this point, the Red River pilot, employed to guarantee the passage, panicked and began ringing the engine room bell to stop the vessel so she could surrender. Sitting nearby, the regular Evansville pilot jumped up, grabbed the giant steering wheel, and proceeded upstream.

While the *St. Clair* returned fire, she too was targeted, but suffered nowhere near the damage of the *Superior*. Riflemen shot up both craft. Minie balls rained down on Dexter's boat, with over 50 striking the armored pilothouse. Pilot George See was nearly killed twice, the first time when a rifle ball splintered a spoke of the great wheel and again when another buried itself into the wood of the wheel itself.

As the two Federal steamers continued along, so too did the enemy. The troops aboard the civilian craft fired at every white man seen, as well as every dwelling within range. The *St. Clair* and *Superior* were under fire over a distance of two miles before they were finally able to outrun their attackers. After the gauntlet was run, Capt. Dexter, Pilot See, and the other survivors counted bullet holes; there were over 200.

After this charter, the *Superior* returned to New Orleans for temporary repairs before heading north to Evansville. During a stop at Cairo, IL, a local newspaperman came aboard to examine her condition and found that "her cabins and staterooms are most beautifully ornamented with bullet holes, and her chimneys present a splendid specimen of network having about 40 shotholes to a square foot."[9]

Also during this week, a little over 200 miles to the northeast, Federal forces on the Yazoo River launched a small-scale expedition into central Mississippi destined to have a very unhappy ending for the U.S. Navy. Ostensibly begun with the intention of finding a way to disrupt Confederate attacks on Mississippi steamers and their escorts, it would result in the loss of a tinclad.

In response to a high command request, Vicksburg commandant Brig. Gen. John McArthur called in Col. Hiram Scofield on April 17 and charged him with capturing Yazoo City. To do the job, he was given a section of artillery, cavalry, and three infantry regiments. Scofield was also ordered to obtain the cooperation of Acting Master Thomas McElroy, the senior local naval officer.

While marching to the Haynes Bluff assembly point next day, Col. Scofield wrote to the Yazoo flotilla chief asking that the two men coordinate their movements and simultaneously descent upon their objective in the early evening of April 21. After Yazoo City was secured, McElroy would maintain communications between that point and Vicksburg.

The tinclad *Petrel*, flag boat of Acting Master McElroy, had gone up the Big Sunflower River several days earlier and was not available at the squadron's Snyder's Bluff anchorage next day to receive the army petition. Instead, it was delivered to Acting Master John W. Chambers's *Prairie Bird*. Believing the message important, Chambers immediately cast off and steamed up the Yazoo and then into the Big Sunflower. After the *Prairie Bird* made rendezvous with the *Petrel* and Scofield's communication was delivered, both craft returned downstream.

Behind schedule on the joint mission, the tinclads pushed on toward Yazoo City as rapidly as possible. As the duo approached Liverpool Heights, Federal soldiers, who had marched overland independently from the flotilla, were spied ashore. McElroy ordered his command to pull into the bank while contact was made.

By this spring, much of the Confederate defense in this area, now under Brig. Gen. W. Wirt Adams, was gone. About the only force of any importance left was Col. Hinchie P. Mabry's 700-man cavalry brigade and its four-cannon Arkansas battery at Canton.

When Adams learned of the Federal incursion, these men, including many from Arkansas, were ordered to block it. Over two days, spirited actions occurred, blunting the Scofield advance and causing a halt at Liverpool Heights while the gunboats were awaited. Adams and his butternut troops withdrew to Yazoo City uncertain about whether the National soldiers would attack them or turn and cut the railroad line at Way's Bluff.

During their meeting on April 21, the same day Maj. Gen. Banks quit Grand Ecore, Col. Scofield asked Acting Master McElroy to reconnoiter Yazoo City. If the town defenses and Confederate strength were weak, his regiments would continue forward. Agreeable to Scofield's request, the *Petrel* and *Prairie Bird* were soon underway up the Yazoo, in company with the stern-wheel steamer *Freestone*. Landing parties were sent ashore at news-possible points and were told that fewer than a thousand enemy were west of the Big Black River, but no intelligence could be gleaned on whether or not any were in Yazoo City.

The two tinclads continued to cautiously move up the river and tied up just below the burnt-out ruins of the former Confederate navy yard. Warning the *Prairie Bird* not to proceed above a given shipwreck, the *Petrel* eased ahead. Soon her lookouts spotted a crowd of women and children gathered at the town levee. Seeing the apparently friendly ladies and youngsters, Acting Master McElroy and his bluejackets doubtless breathed a sigh of relief. As their craft chugged on, they hoped that Yazoo City was unoccupied. They were wrong. Waiting for them on the nearby hills were the 10-pounder Parrotts of the four-gun Arkansas battery.

As the *Petrel* headed into the river bend in front of Yazoo City, the Razorback gunners, located on a hill overlooking the river, opened fire, pouring a hail of shot and small arms fire at the light-draught. McElroy signaled Acting Master Chambers, who was following, to "commence action." The howitzers on the starboard side of the flag boat replied as rapidly as they could be brought to bear. Up in the *Petrel*'s pilothouse, one of the two pilots informed the captain that there was not enough space to round to, particularly under the hot fire falling all around them. Acting Master McElroy, seeing the danger, ordered the engine room bell rung for flank speed and quickly the *Petrel* shot ahead out of danger. Although 15 shells had thrown up water on both sides of the boat, miraculously, none had struck home.

Once Adams's gunners were finished with the *Petrel*, they turned their guns on the *Prairie Bird* and, together with infantry riflemen, blazed away at her. She was hit thrice and quickly. Two shells slammed through the hurricane deck and passed harmlessly out the cabin. The third bore through the casemate and struck the starboard engine cylinder, causing a nasty steam leak and wounding two engineers. Even though she had managed to fire 33 rounds at the enemy, the boat had to escape this murderous hail. Consequently, the *Prairie Bird* disengaged and retired some two miles downstream to tie up at the west bank.

Out of range above the town, the *Petrel* came about and prepared to run back down and join the *Prairie Bird*. At that point, Acting Master Chambers's tinclad was seen dropping back out of range and, coincidentally, withdrawing herself from the possibility of covering the *Petrel*'s return run. Electing not to move until he knew why the *Prairie Bird* had backed off, the flotilla commander ordered his craft tied to the bank. There he wrote out two messages, one seeking information and ground assistance from Col. Scofield and the other for that officer to give Chambers demanding that the *Prairie Bird* provide naval support.

Acting Master McElroy's overland communication reached the captain of the *Prairie Bird* before it reached the army. Chambers explained his own misfortune, but promised to cover the *Petrel* when she was ready to move. Noting that overland or steamboat message delivery was very risky, he suggested they work out a system of coded boat whistle blasts. He then forwarded McElroy's Scofield message down to Liverpool Heights with the captain of the *Freestone*.

During the day, the army expeditionary force did not advance on Yazoo City as McElroy expected it might. Instead, its leadership, spooked by rumors that Brig. Gen. Adams had more men and stronger defenses there than they had at first believed, remained in camp.

Early on April 22, the colonel penned a message to the commander of the *Petrel* informing him that his bluecoats could be of no assistance to the tinclads. Indeed, it would be better if both returned to Liverpool Heights to "cooperate with us here in any movement it may be thought best to make." The note was safely sent to McElroy by steamer, but did nothing to allay safety concerns aboard the isolated tinclad.

An hour before noon, lookouts reported that the Confederates were deserting the hills south of Yazoo City. Hopes rose that Col. Scofield was advancing on the town and had driven them off, but then, no bluecoats were seen either. Until the situation ashore became clearer, the *Petrel* steamed up and down, to confuse possible enemy intentions and make of herself a more difficult target.

The Rebels had not been engaged by the Federal corps from Liverpool Heights. Instead, the commander of two forward Arkansas regiments, Col. John Griffith, after conducting a scout, obtained permission from Brig. Gen. Adams to make an attempt to capture the *Petrel*. The men seen disappearing from the bluffs by the gunboat's sailors were 130 of his.

Led by locally born troopers, Griffith and his combat team, accompanied by a pair of 10-pounder rifles, rode "through the valleys of the Petite Gulf hills out of sight of the spy glasses of the boats" toward the river. The guns were emplaced in a clearing in the thickly-timbered bottom land, 400 yards below the gunboat. About 40 dismounted Arkansas cavalry, under Maj. Benjamin P. Jett, were posted in the underbrush directly opposite the *Petrel*. The remainder dismounted, ready to advance.

After moving to and fro for an hour, the *Petrel* tied up to the west bank of the Yazoo, approximately two and a half miles above the town, near the mouth of Tokeba Bayou. Here McElroy sent his executive officer, Acting Ensign Michael E. Flanigan, and a deck-hand party ashore to retrieve fence rails for fuel. Those remaining aboard manned the starboard battery while others, under 17-year-old Quartermaster John Nibbe topside, kept a close eye out for the enemy.

Having concealed themselves in the vines and brush of the river bank, Col. Griffith's gunners opened upon on the *Petrel* a little after 2 P.M. The Federal sailors immediately returned fire, but missed as their guns could not be brought to bear. Simultaneously, the tinclad backed out from the bank as Acting Master McElroy frantically rang the engine room bell.

The light-draught was only able to rush ahead about 200 yards before she ran on a sandbar. As she attempted to back off, the Confederate Parrotts fired again — and with precision. The first of their shells ploughed into the *Petrel*'s stern, cutting off her steam pipe (thereby disabling the engine) and dismounting the after gun. The second crashed into the magazine. Although there was no explosion, the gunner's mate and quarter gunner were mortally wounded and the flow of munitions to the remaining howitzers was disrupted, causing a temporary cessation of firing.

Ashore, the Parrotts were moved forward by hand over 200 yards. Butternut riflemen aimed at the gunboat's portholes in an effort to keep her gunners from reloading. Panic set in aboard the tinclad and not only enlisted personnel were affected. Several of the volunteer officers were, putting it generously, erratic in the performance of their duties and contributed to the difficulties Acting Master McElroy faced as he tried to defend his command. While Confederate sharpshooters pinked every inch of the hull, concentrating on men seen through the gunports, and others moved still closer, the *Petrel*'s commander came to the realization that he could soon lose his boat.

Small arms were now issued to the *Petrel* crew and preparations were made to fire the vessel if she could no longer be defended. At the same time, another 10-pounder shot thundered into the boat's stern and exploded the boiler. The escaping steam was not immediately deadly, though it did fill several spaces. Extremely dispirited, all but two of the officers and all of the unhurt crew chose to flee ashore before a cloud could appear.

Acting Master McElroy, along with Pilot Kimble Ware and Quartermaster Nibbe, remained aboard as the steam cloud dissipated. The trio helped the wounded men off to the bank over the wheelguards and then returned aboard, still under incessant fire, to torch the wounded gunboat. Descending to the engine space, McElroy gathered up some hot coals which he placed on the newly-gathered fence rails, setting them ablaze.

As the Union sailors abandoned ship, Confederate soldiers crossed the river to the west bank and began to surround the doomed *Petrel*. McElroy was forced to surrender while Quartermaster Nibbe was caught just before he had a chance to completely refire the gunboat's fuel. While they sat on the bank under pointed muskets, a number of butternut soldiers ran aboard and successfully extinguished the still-sputtering scuttling blaze. When they boarded the *Petrel*, the Confederate troopers found "dinner on the table, and such a dinner as they hadn't seen in three years." As Maj. Jett remembered years later, "the Yankees hadn't had time to eat just then — they had other business."

Although pursued by a number of Gibson's troops, 13 officers and 40 crewmen who had earlier abandoned the *Petrel* made it overland through the swamps to the safety of the *Prairie Bird*. The 13 captured men were dead or held as POWs. The gunboat was stripped of her stores, victuals, usable furniture and furnishings, ordnance stores, and cannon, and was then burned to the water's edge. Union newsmen later learned that the howitzers were sent via Canton down to Mobile, AL.

Seeing smoke but unaware of the flag boat's fate, Acting Master Chambers of the *Prairie Bird* started to send a small party to reconnoiter. About this time, the scared and fatigued *Petrel* survivors began to arrive from above Yazoo City and tell their stories, causing the landing party scout to be canceled. Certain that McElroy was gone, the *Prairie Bird* withdrew to Liverpool Heights, from which Col. Scofield retreated next day.

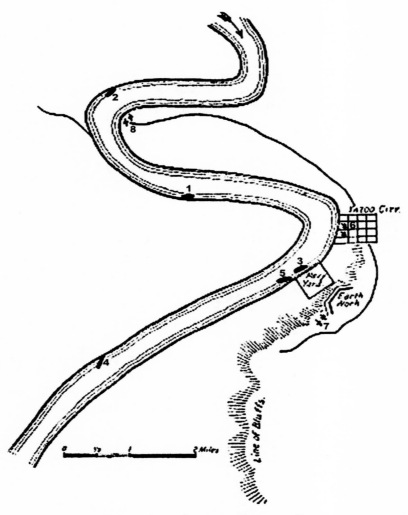

CAPTURE OF THE "PETREL" ABOUT 31 MILES ABOVE YAZOO
CITY APRIL 22, 1864.

1. Position of *Petrel* at bank after passing beyond range of fieldpieces
   (at 6) in Yazoo City, afternoon of April 21.
2. Position of *Petrel* when opened upon and afterwards captured by
   the enemy, 3 p.m., April 22.
3. Position of *Prarie Bird* at navy yard when opened upon by fieldpieces,
   afternoon.
4. Second positon of *Prarie Bird*.
5. Transport *Freestone*, probably after cotton, on some shallow pretext
   of service.
6. First position of battery of two fieldpieces, thought to have been
   Parrott 10-pounders.
7. Second position of battery to drive off *Prarie Bird* and *Freestone*.
8. Third position of battery, causing the abandonment of the *Petrel*.
   Respectfully submitted.

Robert Townsend.
Commander, U.S. Navy, Senior Officer

VICKSBURG. *April 24, 1864.*

Sketched from report of those engaged, made to me verbally,
April 21, 1864.
R. T.

The *Petrel* was one of the inland fleet's "favorite tinclads" and her capture galled not only Rear Adm. Porter, but the entire Western naval officer corps. With all but two of the boat's officers indicted for cowardice, it was, the flotilla commander later wrote in his naval history, "one of the few cases where officers behaved badly on board a vessel of the Mississippi Squadron."

There were other unpleasant features "connected with this affair." With the boat gone and her captain a POW, it was wondered why she had run the batteries for no apparent reason. Reviews conducted later by senior naval officers concluded that Acting Master McElroy was too anxious to accommodate top Vicksburg army officers, several of whom were believed corruptly involved with cotton speculators. Cmdr. Robert Townsend informed Porter that the loss was due entirely to a "desire to procure cotton, rather than the noble ambition of advancing the public service." Some of this pale drifted over onto the *Petrel*'s captain, but he was able to redeem "his own mistakes by his gallantry." On the other hand, Quartermaster Nibbe became one of the youngest to receive the Medal of Honor.

Above: The tinclad *Prairie Bird*, shown off Vicksburg, accompanied the *Petrel* on the Army support mission to Yazoo City in late April 1864. The two were separated under fire there. Although damaged, the *Prairie Bird* was not taken or destroyed, escaping to face the Texas gunners of Col. Colton Greene on the Mississippi a month later (Naval Historical Center). *Opposite:* Chart describing the April 22, 1864, capture of the tinclad *Petrel*, a great embarrassment to the Mississippi Squadron. Many in and outside of the Navy believed it happened because of greed on the part of certain officers who sought to pick up easily-available cotton (*Official Records of the Union and Confederate Navies* 26).

Some, like Acting Ensign Flanigan, supported in his opinion by Rear Adm. Porter himself, attempted to blame the loss, at least in part, on the large number of African-Americans comprising the *Petrel*'s crew. Writing after his escape, the boat's executive officer claimed that "during the engagement the officers and men acted most gallantly with the exception of a few contrabands who were lately shipped."

This view was not supported by McElroy in his post-imprisonment report, but was reprinted in Porter's history where the former squadron boss wrote: "As an excuse for the conduct of the crew, it must be remarked that there were only ten white men and boys on board the vessel; the rest were all contrabands and some of these were sick."[10]

Late in the afternoon of April 25, the timberclad *Lexington* landed about a mile below Rocky Point, in the shadow of Deloach's Bluff on the opposite shore, at the mouth of the Cane River. There, across from the craggy Red River shoreline known as Deloach's Rocks, her sailors were put to work sounding and buoying the channel in anticipation of the arrival of the *Eastport*. None of them knew that the hill across the river was actually named for the Deloges family, whose cemetery lay just inland from the top of the hill. The family name for the spot would be recognized by geographers on maps in the next century and so we use it here.

Elsewhere on the big Louisiana river during this time, Union gunboats and transports, especially those working to save the *Eastport*, were about to be subjected to merciless Confederate attacks. To intercept these craft as they worked their way downstream as well as to blockade the river against further Northern passage, Maj. Gen. Taylor deployed one of the largest forces to yet assail Porter's retreating Yankee bluejackets.

Dispatched early in the morning were at least 200 additional soldiers from the division of Maj. Gen. Camille de Polignac and a number of cannon. Historian Chuck Viet, in his internet article, admits that the number of guns rushed to the scene to fight the Federals could have ranged between four and 11 cannon. Confederate artillery units represented in the fray included Capt. Florian O. Cornay's St. Mary's Cannoneers (1st Louisiana Battery) with two 12-pounders and two 24-pounder howitzers, the 3rd Louisiana Light Artillery ("Bell's Battery"), with two rifled cannon, and the Val Verde Battery under Capt. Thomas O. Benton, armed with three 6-pounder Napoleons and two recently-prized 12-pound rifled cannon. It is the latter unit that initially elicits our attention here.

When Capt. Benton arrived at Deloges Bluff he could clearly see the *Lexington* lying in the Red River about 450 yards away. The *Osage* lay even closer to him, but was shielded by her position under the bank. After the butternut artillerymen struggled their six guns into a protected position by hand, the pieces opened fire.

About 20 miles above Deloges Bluff, it was proving to be impossible to save the stricken *Eastport*, despite the best efforts of the *Cricket*, *Juliet*, *Fort Hindman*, and two pump boats. These civilian charters, the *Champion No. 3* (also known as the *New Champion)* and the *Champion No. 5*, were primarily responsible keeping the ironclad afloat so she could come this far. During the morning, after her guns and stores were removed, the decision was taken to destroy the *Eastport*. While Lt. Cmdr. Phelps packed the ironclad with 40 barrels of powder, her officers transferred to the *Fort Hindman* and her crew to the *Juliet*. The *Cricket*, meanwhile, was tied to the bank where her men were ashore "railing," or gathering fence rails for use as fuel.

About 10:30 A.M., a large force of butternut soldiers opened fire on the stopped vessels, with many rushing on in an effort to board the flag boat. Still, those men left aboard the *Cricket* were alert and instantly responded to the threat with grape and canister. The men ashore were recovered as a brave unknown soul cut the mooring line, allowing the boat to drift offshore. Her guns, joined by those of the *Juliet* and *Fort Hindman*, were able to drive off the attackers before an hour passed.

Phelps was able to successfully and very noisily blow up the *Eastport* by midafternoon. At this point, he transferred to the *Fort Hindman*, where he was met by Rear Adm. Porter and the boat's captain, Acting Volunteer Lt. John Pearce. The admiral had earlier called in Lt. Frank Church's 27 Marines from picket duty ashore, but instead of returning them to the flag boat *Cricket* sent them instead to the larger *Hindman*. Porter and Phelps concurred on the necessity of heading downstream straightaway. Porter would soon find himself personally in combat and the possible death of the squadron commander in action is the reason why we have chosen to review this campaign so far outside the realm of guerrilla actions.

With the *Champion No. 3* just astern and the *Champion No. 5* lashed to the *Juliet*, the *Cricket* started down the Red in late afternoon. Phelps, now in command of the *Fort Hindman*, brought up the rear. In addition to her crew, the *Champion No. 3* was packed with about 175 African-American contraband refugees from upriver Red River plantations taken aboard just as the boats departed Grand Ecore.

Confederate scouts saw the little task group pull away from the wreck of the ironclad and rushed to inform Confederate leaders. Orders soon came down for a big gun ambush at the confluence of the Red and Cane Rivers at Deloges Bluff. With lookouts posted everywhere, the five Union craft were able to make good speed down the river. Porter, so the story goes, found a comfortable chair on the *Cricket's* upper deck and read a book, though probably with some interruptions.

Not far beyond the mouth of the Cane River, sometime after 6 P.M., the admiral saw a number of men shadowing his command in the brush over on the right bank and ordered the gunners manning the upper deck boat howitzer to disperse them with a two-second shell. After firing, the gunboat drifted toward shore, coming within about 20 feet as she prepared to send away another round of shrapnel.

The men in the bushes ashore were actually part of a much larger group. Before the *Cricket* could get away another shot, a wall of flame burst out of the woods as massed cannon and musket fire was poured into her. Within seconds, the tinclad was hit 19 times by cannon fire and countless musket balls. The "pelting shower" went "through and through" the *Cricket*. Her decks were cleared "in a moment" and she was shattered "in all her parts."

Among the incoming munitions, one shell destroyed the upper deck howitzer and killed its gun crew. Porter was stunned and slightly wounded as another round hit just as he was opening the pilothouse door. Climbing inside, he found the pilot wounded, but able to perform his duty.

Wounded himself, Acting Master Henry H. Gorringe quickly informed the admiral that he was trying to bring the tinclad about so that her starboard battery could stop the boat and answer the Rebel barrage. There was no response as he rang the engine room bell and neither man could hear either exhaust or gunfire from their own vessel. Porter believed that most of the gun crews below had to have been killed by incoming shells and told the boat's commander to belay his fighting instinct and instead to run by the batteries. While Gorringe and his pilot worked to steer the *Cricket* downstream in a four-knot current, Porter started below to find out why she was not firing and why her engines were stopped.

Porter and the flag boat were saved by panic and tragedy aboard the *Champion No. 3*. The civilian captain was so unnerved by the heavy Rebel attack that he suddenly and without warning backed his boat as rapidly as possible to get out of range. In so doing, he ran her right into the bow of the oncoming *Juliet*, which, because she was lashed to the *Champion No. 5*, could not get out of the way. Seeing the confusion in the river below, Confederate gunners opened on the big fat target of the two *Champions* and the gunboat. As the sailors aboard the *Champion No. 3* and the *Juliet* rushed to separate the two vessels, shells smashed into them both.

A 12-pounder shell punctured the boiler of the *Champion No. 3*, which was enveloped in a cloud of steam. Over a hundred crew and contrabands were instantly scalded to death. Another 87 were so badly burned that they died within a short time. Survivors jumped into the Red and swam for shore or clung to the wreckage as it drifted away. Only three aboard were actually believed to have lived to see another day.

The cloud of steam that hid the stricken pump boat also helped the *Cricket* to survive. Badly damaged, she floated under the bluff and was momentarily safe from the Confederate gunners above. Musket fire was another matter, and small arms bullets continuously plinked into her. As the tinclad rounded the point and reentered the artillery killing zone, she was immediately hit by another 19 rounds, most of these into her stern and into the boat's interior.

Exhibiting considerable personal courage, Porter ran down the exposed starboard side of the *Cricket* toward the engine room spaces. En route, he passed through the gun deck and saw the carnage. Guns were overturned and at least 24 dead and wounded lay about with "everything torn to pieces." Among the dead was Ann Stewart, a laundress and wife of the ship's steward. Only one gun remained and the admiral rallied sufficient

Acting Master Henry Hornchurch Gorringe was named an Acting Volunteer Lt. by Porter personally on April 27, 1864, for his gallantry aboard the tinclad *Cricket* (*Harper's Weekly*, July 18, 1885).

able-bodied men — mostly contrabands-now-sailors — to service it. He told them to load their "bulldog" and fire it and not to worry about aiming. The fact that it fired at all would tell the Rebels the boat was still fighting and would also encourage those craft coming behind.

When the squadron commander reached the engine room, he found it devastated as well. All but one of the firemen was wounded and Engineer Charles Parks, while trying to respond to Gorringe's bell, had died at his post. As he collapsed, his hand on the throttle, he turned the steam off rather than on. Porter reversed the throttle, allowing the *Cricket's* engines to sputter back to life. The *Cricket* was under fire for a total of about 5 minutes. In that time, she was hit 38 times and lost nearly half her crew (12 men killed and 19 wounded, almost all of the latter badly). Once again under power, the flag boat sputtered ahead — and ran aground. Fortunately, she was out of sight of the Confederate gunners — though not out of range. She would remain hung up for the next hour.

Following the April 26, 1864, loss of the Federal ironclad *Eastport* up the Red River, the vessels attempting to prevent her destruction ran through a gauntlet of Confederate artillery to safety. Skippered by Acting Master Henry Gorringe and, while he was temporarily disabled, by Rear Adm. Porter himself, the tinclad *Cricket*, flag boat for much of the Red River expedition, was severely pounded. Under fire for five minutes, she was hit 38 times and nearly half of her crew (12 killed, 19 wounded) was incapacitated (Naval Historical Center).

Although Porter and the *Cricket* were safe, the four vessels following him remained in extreme danger. The shells that had doomed the *Champion No. 3* also slammed into the *Juliet* and *Champion No. 5*. The former's tiller ropes were cut, the steam line that provided engine power was sliced, and the wheel was shot out of the pilot's hands. Nonlethal vapors enveloped the ship, making vision difficult.

The Confederate attack also damaged the rudder of the second pump boat and unnerved her civilian crew. Her captain tried to round to and retreat upstream, while his deckhands began furiously chopping at the hawsers that bound her to the *Juliet*. As the steam cloud on the *Juliet* cleared, Acting Master John S. Watson and pilot William Maitland looked out of the pilothouse to see that the master and pilot of the *Champion No. 5* had now abandoned their posts. Simultaneously, that craft — and the tinclad — had turned perpendicular in the channel. Across the way, the wreck of the *Champion No. 3* could also be seen, lodged sideways into the right bank not far from the Rebel battery.

With the safety of the bound Federal craft of paramount concern, Watson and Maitland ran down to the main deck of the *Juliet* as fast as they could, drawing their pistols as they descended. Confronting the men with axes directly across from them on the *Champion No. 5*, they threatened to shoot anyone attempting to sever the single line that yet held the two boats together.

The Confederates also aimed their guns on the *Fort Hindman*, last in the line. A shot holed her "between wind and water" while others wounded several men and killed one sailor and the former executive officer of the *Eastport*. At this point, panic began to spread among the big tinclad's gun crew, the members of which had seen the terrible toll taken on the boats steaming ahead of them. Phelps was able to settle his petrified sailors, though not without reference to possibly shooting "the first man who should flinch from his gun." The *Fort Hindman* increased speed to close the bluff in an effort to help the others.

The terrified civilian sailors and several others on board the *Champion No. 5* meanwhile attempted to desert. By this time, the *Fort Hindman* was drawing closer and Lt. Cmdr. Phelps, through a speaking trumpet, warned that anyone moving to abandon the pump boat would be shot. His decisiveness was backed up by Lt. Church's Marines, who fired their muskets in warning. While the leathernecks cowed the despairing hands, Pilot Maitland voluntarily jumped aboard, climbed to the pilothouse through Confederate small arms fire, and took control of the *Champion No. 5*. Fortunately, the lashed boats had now drifted under the bluff out of range, giving him time to gain control.

During these minutes, the lashed-together pump boat and tinclad were able to turn about and steam back upstream. As they passed her, the *Fort Hindman* covered their withdrawal. Downstream, the *Cricket* worked to free herself. It would take three hours for Porter to get his command tinclad afloat and during this time a rather constant noise of cannon fire could be heard from above. At the same time below, the African-American gunners aboard the *Cricket* were also firing away toward the Confederate batteries with their "bulldog." The shells from the two tinclads had some effect. One of them killed Florian O. Cornay of the St. Mary's Cannoneers in late afternoon.

The three battered survivors proceeded about a mile above the Deloges Bluff battery and ran into the bank, tying up for the night. Rather than attempt to pass by the guns at night and more than likely run aground in the shallows during the process, Lt. Commander Phelps ordered that repairs be made pending action next day. While carpenters addressed her waterline damage, the *Hindman*'s gunners fired her stern guns toward the wreck of the *Champion No. 3* in an effort to prevent the Confederates from pushing her back into the river and blocking the channel. Meanwhile, the *Juliet* and *Champion No. 5* were separated.

Unable to offer further help to Phelps's isolated unit, Porter, the feisty Mississippi Squadron commander, decided to head downstream toward a pair of pre-positioned support ships. It was well after dark when the admiral reached the place appointed for rendezvous with the heavy reinforcements. There he found the *Osage* lying opposite Benton's battery, which had returned at 2 P.M. to block the river. He also observed that the *Lexington*, which "had been hard at work on them," was badly splintered.

Lt. Cmdr. Selfridge, who was ill during most of the day's contest, and Bache met with Porter to determine if anything more could be done yet that night. The noise of gunfire from above had ceased. Unbeknownst to the three Federals, Capt. Benton would be recalled two hours before midnight.

There really was not much Porter could do. The *Lexington* was for all intents and purposes out of action. Darkness and the tricky channel prevented the dispatch of the *Osage;* had she attempted, she might very well have run aground and become another victim. On the morning of April 27, the *Lexington* and *Cricket* steamed toward Alexandria, where their most serious damage could be repaired, while the *Osage* steamed back upstream.

At daybreak, Confederate soldiers made their way up toward the Federal boats and took them under small arms fire. The *Fort Hindman* returned the compliment, dropping 8-inch shells into the woods back toward the battery.

Frightened anew, the surly officers and men of the *Champion No. 5* petitioned Lt. Cmdr. Phelps to abandon the pump boat. They wanted to make their escape on board the tinclads. The veteran gunboatman adamantly refused, pointing out that the *No. 5*, protected by dozens of cotton bales, was as safe as the either the *Juliet* or *Fort Hindman*, where just a few bales had been placed to buttress their wafer-thin tin sides. The scared men were refused permission to leave their ship, and to make certain that they stayed aboard and performed their duty, the civilian captain was relieved and replaced by Pilot Maitland.

Although some repairs were finished aboard the three craft, the steering gear of the *Juliet* was still not operable. She was helpless and could not depart downstream without a tow. Just after 9 A.M., she backed out and with much help, was lashed to the port side of the *Fort Hindman*. Phelps would not take a chance on tying her up again to the pump boat, which would now follow along behind.

The trio slowly departed back down the river toward the battery of death, but only steamed a few hundred yards before the *Juliet* struck a snag. Water came in through a hole in the bow below the waterline and Acting Master Watson ordered "abandon ship" preparations. Phelps believed the tinclad could be saved and ordered the shackled pair back to their previous night's anchorage. The *Juliet*'s leak was rapidly controlled with boards and mattresses, permitting the task unit to try the downstream course again. Gun crews stood ready and, as soon as they were underway, began to pepper the woods on the shoreline as they passed.

It was about 9:40 A.M. when the three Union boats approached Deloges Bluff. At a range of 500 yards, Confederate cannon joined in the hours-old musket salute. From the pilothouse of the *Fort Hindman*, Lt. Cmdr. Phelps could see the wreck of the *Champion No. 3*, lying near the bank partially blocking the channel. It would be a tight squeeze getting by it in the shallow water.

Despite shell splashes in the water, the boats moved ahead. Suddenly, a pair of 12-pounder rounds whirled into the *Hindman*'s pilothouse. Skipper Pearce was wounded, the tiller ropes were cut, and the big steering wheel was partially disabled. Out of control, the two boats spun in circles in the current, alternately striking their bows and sterns on the banks.

There had been plans to concentrate cannon fire on the wreck of the *Champion No. 3* as the tinclads passed. These now evaporated. Still, the gunboats did fire their guns, aiming at anything that came into view on the Deloges Bluff side of the river.

Rebel shells struck the *Juliet* again, destroying her rudder and continuing the destruction of her upper works. Confederate cannon also scored anew on the *Fort Hindman*, rewarding her with new holes below the waterline. One ball hit her port crankshaft, disabling both the engine cylinder heads. Another actually passed through the magazine, breaking several powder barrels; miraculously, there was no explosion.

The spinning gunboats were of no help to the also-targeted *Champion No. 5*. Pilot Maitland was wounded eight times as the pump boat neared the battery. Battered, he nevertheless was able to steer the boat to the bank not far from the wreckage of the *Champion No. 3*. With a fire in her hold, the steamer was beached and her crew was finally able to flee — right into the waiting arms of Southern soldiers.

The two survivors of the *Eastport* rescue group drifted out of range ("waltzing as I may say," Phelps later wrote). They were pursued along the banks by Confederate riflemen who continued to annoy both boats with musket fire. Twelve miles below, the *Juliet* and *Fort Hindman* finally reached the safety of the anchored *Osage* shortly after 1 P.M. Early next morning, all anchored above Alexandria's upper falls.

In two days of heavy fighting, the *Cricket*, *Juliet*, and *Fort Hindman* lost 42 men dead and wounded, with all three boats physically shattered, though repairable. The two lost civilian pump boats suffered horribly, with over 200 killed. All of their survivors were captured. Rear Adm. Porter survived "the heaviest fire I ever witnessed," but had to admit that "the passage from Grand Ecore down could not be called a success."

The Deloges Bluff encounter was one of the stiffest naval fights of the Civil War. Only one or two other tinclad engagements rivaled it in ferocity and the outcome for the Federals on those occasions was far less successful. By 7:45 A.M. the next morning, these vessels had joined the *Cricket* and were anchored above Alexandria's upper falls. There Porter learned of the *Petrel*'s loss in the Yazoo days earlier.

Alexandria, despite fortification efforts by Maj. Gen. Banks, was now encircled by Dick Taylor's forces. In addition to stationing troops north and east of the town, the Confederate theater commander dispatched a cavalry brigade and J.A.A. West's battery of horse artillery to David's Ferry, on the Red 30 miles southeast of the city near Marksville. Other

Rebel groups also placed their guns downstream, with Pierce's Landing some 20 miles below (also not far from Fort De Russy) a favorite spot. This encirclement would hopefully prevent the Federals from communicating with their fellows on the Mississippi River.

On April 28, Rear Adm. Porter, stranded above the rapids at Alexandria, advised Navy Secretary Welles of his precarious position, due to the falling water level of the Red River as well as Banks's withdrawal. "I find myself blockaded," he wrote, "by a fall of 3 feet of water, 3 feet 4 inches being the amount now on the falls; 7 feet being required to get over...." Facing the distinct possibility that he would need to destroy his entire $3 million squadron, as he had the *Eastport*, to keep it out of Confederate hands, he lamented to his superior: "...you may judge of my feelings at having to perform so painful a duty."

Porter enjoyed some initial success in getting at least a portion of the transports and his flotilla through the available little 20-foot-wide channel. Led by the admiral aboard the *Cricket*, a number of quartermaster boats and tinclads, including the *Juliet*, thumped their bottoms along to safety in the deeper waters south of Alexandria caused by a growing back swell from the Mississippi. Still, the heaviest vessels, including the ironclads and the *Fort Hindman*, remained stranded above behind the falls.

Working with Maj. Gen. Banks and his officers, the Mississippi Squadron chief fortunately came up with the correct solution and the right man to carry it out, XIX Corps staff engineer Lt. Col. Joseph Bailey, whom Nicholas Smith years later called "the Moses

The *Glide II*, caught at Brasher City, Louisiana, in 1864, was one of the ocean-going tinclads assigned to the West Gulf Coast Blockading Squadron. Her entire war was spent guarding Berwick Bay and conducting patrols and anti-guerrilla sweeps up surrounding bayous. The only news her crew had of naval events on the upper rivers was spotty and mostly came from reading the New Orleans newspapers. Much the same case existed in reverse for the bluejackets stationed further upstream (Naval Historical Center).

of Porter's fleet." For years, the story of Bailey's dam was the most celebrated single event of the entire Federal Red River fiasco. The presence of the one-time 4th Wisconsin Cavalry officer with Banks's expedition was, wrote Smith and Castille in 1986, "one of those coincidences of history that sometimes result in turning the course of events." So it was that, on April 29, Bailey was tasked by Banks and Porter with constructing a dam that would raise the water sufficiently to allow the fleet to escape.

Straightaway, Maj. Gen. Banks set over 3,000 men to work chopping down trees or dismantling whole buildings, finding stone and rock, and hauling the materials to the sites on either bank where the dam would be constructed. Interestingly, black troops worked the Alexandria side, while soldiers from Wisconsin, Maine, and New York labored on the Pineville shore. None of these details were, of course, known to the gunboatmen active — and inactive — on the upper rivers hundreds of miles to the north. This was particularly true for the tinclad *Peosta*, which seldom got away from Paducah except for an occasional trip up the Tennessee River. There was, however, a general understanding that "they have had a licking up the Red River."

On the last day of April, a number of her crewmen were permitted liberty ashore, a custom honored whenever the craft was at the port tied up to the shore. For some, the exercise was costly. "When any of the gunboat men go up in the town," Carpenter's Mate Herbert Saunders wrote to his mother a week later, they were followed by army provost marshals. When any of the bluejackets got drunk, "they put them in the guard house and then fetch them on board." The military police received a reward of $5 per man for every returned sailor, deducted from "their monthly pay." Half a dozen *Peosta* tars were returned on this date "after they had been drinking."[11]

9

The Big Guns of Brig. Gen. Major, Col. Greene, and Capt. Creuzbauer, May 1864

As the Herculean dam-building labors of Lt. Col. Joseph Bailey began at the end of April 1864, the Mississippi Squadron elements below the city of Alexandria, LA, attempted to continue, as they had since the campaign began, the provision of convoy escort and communications services to and from the mouth of the Red River. Now they faced the enthusiastic Confederate horsemen and gunners.

Brig. Gen. James P. Major's First Division of the Confederate Cavalry Corps was sent southeast of town on blockade duty by Trans-Mississippi theater commander Maj. Gen. Richard Taylor. The Horse Artillery unit with him, under Maj. Oliver J. Semmes, were mostly from Texas, but included Capt. John A.A. West's Grosse Tete (LA) Flying Artillery Battery.

The first boat ensnared in Taylor's Rebel net was the unescorted transport *Emma*.[1] homeported at St. Louis. After a two-mile May 1 chase, she was disabled and ran into the bank at David's Ferry where, without a guard, she was easily captured. Immediately boarded, she was looted and burned.

The same day, the 400 men of the 120th Ohio Infantry Regiment at Baton Rouge boarded the *City Belle*[2] with orders to reinforce Maj. Gen. Banks at Baton Rouge. They were joined by officers from several other regiments, including the 92nd U.S. Colored Infantry. Cargo, including ammunition and sutlers' stores, were also loaded. None of the bluecoats had any idea that they would soon be facing Southern gunners or of the horrible fate that would smash their regiment.

The following afternoon the steamboat *Laurel Hill*[3] from New Orleans came to at Fort De Russy, where she found the stern-wheeler *Rob Roy*[4] with 400 men aboard awaiting the arrival of the tinclad *Argosy*. At sunrise on May 2, the three departed for Alexandria. Steaming upstream, they soon encountered charred floating debris indicating a wreck above. As the *Laurel Hill* moved slowly ahead, followed by the *Rob Roy* and the *Argosy*, she was hailed from the left bank by several elderly women. The tinclad moved close ashore where her captain was told that about 200 Rebels had burned a boat up ahead the previous night and continued to lurk on the shore with some artillery.

In early May 1864, the tinclad *Argosy* was involved in providing round-trip convoy escort on the lower Mississippi as well as from the Red River's Fort DeRussy to Alexandria. On May 3, she successfully protected the steamers *Laurel Hill* and *Rob Roy* as they steamed past waiting Confederate batteries. A few days later, she rescued a number of survivors from the steamer *John Warner*, sunk by Rebel batteries (Naval Historical Center).

The Federal trio continued on. Preparations were made aboard the merchantmen to offer resistance to any attack. Cargo such as sanitary stores and boxes of hardtack (hard bread) were turned into impromptu barricades. The leading *Laurel Hill* carried two wheeled 12-pounder howitzers on her boiler deck as regular armament. To this at New Orleans was added a 3-inch Parrott rifle under the command of Lt. E.B. Matts of the 92nd USCI.

At approximately 8:30 A.M., lookouts aboard the leading steamer alerted its pilot, James Robinson, of enemy troops ahead at Pierce's Landing. Crewmen and soldiers aboard immediately jumped to their assigned defensive posts and as the *Laurel Hill* came in range, musket volleys and canister were expended against the butternuts. As the other two craft came up, they, too, opened fire.

The Confederates returned the Federal tribute in kind, sending clouds of musket balls against the wheels and works of the three steamers. A running two-hour fight ensued over a distance of some four miles. As soon as the *Argosy* or one of the others drove attackers away or passed beyond them from one point, they would cut across country and intercept them at another. Eventually, the tiny convoy escaped to reach Alexandria. In the exchange, one man was killed aboard the *Rob Roy*. Southern casualties are unknown.

Coming on from Fort De Russy on the afternoon of May 3, the steamer *City Belle* was not as fortunate as the *Laurel Hill* and *Rob Roy*. Loaded with Buckeye troops and stores (to say nothing of written dispatches and orders, including some from Lt. Gen. Ulysses S. Grant), she was accosted at a bend of the river near Snaggy Point, opposite Dunn's Bayou on the right bank, not far from David's Landing, by Rebel artillerymen and dismounted riflemen.

The first Parrott shot, according to contemporaries, either killed or disabled the *Belle*'s pilot, at which point the steamer spun around into a position that allowed the second Confederate round to penetrate her boiler and envelop the transport with hot steam. Several men were scalded and the craft became unmanageable. With the ranking officers of the Federal army troops dead, a lieutenant hoisted a white flag as the *Belle* floated over toward the opposite shore.

Seeing the boat supposedly surrender, the Confederates ceased firing and a boarding party of graycoats set out across the river in skiffs to take possession. Unhappily for all concerned, a number of men on the lower deck did not see the flag and continued firing. This brought another brief resumption of cannon fire by the Rebels and a more emphatic and better-communicated truce flag.

Approximately 160 escaped the ordeal and made Alexandria on foot the next day. The others were prisoners, dead, wounded, or drowned. The *City Belle* was taken over to the Rebel bank, where her stores were removed, and she was scuttled across the channel to block it.

About the same time as the *City Belle* suffered her ordeal, the tinclad *St. Clair* was en route to Alexandria from Fort De Russy towing a barge. At Dunn's Bayou, she was attacked by about 100 Confederates, with about 30 more firing at her after she had gotten by and was nearing Wilson's Bend. Although the light-draught was hit over 200 times, all of the damage was done by musketry. One man was wounded and, as the captain put it in his report, there was no other damage "save the spoiling of some of our furniture."

Following her ordeal during the passage down from the upper Red River earlier in the month, the big side-wheeler *John Warner*[5] escaped over the falls to deep water south of Alexandria. There her 220-foot long hull was packed with many hundreds of confiscated cotton bales for delivery to the prize court at Cairo. A number of these valuable trophies were stacked against the pilothouse and at key superstructure points as added protection.

On May 4, the tinclad *Covington* was designated escort and departed astern of the *Warner* for the Mississippi, via Fort De Russy, at 9:30 A.M. Aboard the *Warner*, in addition to her valuable cargo of produce, were 250 soldiers from the 56th Ohio Infantry en route home on veterans' furloughs, along with a few men from other regiments, including the 128th New York Volunteers. The pair paddled downstream for some 20 to 25 miles and, while passing in the bend at Wilson's plantation, the transport was attacked.

Above and opposite: The side-wheel *Covington* (above) and veteran stern-wheel tinclad *Signal* (opposite) departed Alexandria, Louisiana, on May 4 for the mouth of the Red River, guarding the transport *John Warner*, which was carrying soldiers home on furlough and hundreds of bales of confiscated cotton. Before long, the trio ran into a hornet's nest of Confederate riflemen and artillery and a running battle ensued (Naval Historical Center).

Approximately 100 butternut cavalry firing carbines from the right bank succeeded in killing one man on the *Warner*. Coming on, the *Covington* fired her stern guns at them for several minutes and, like her charge, passed on.

Several hours later, the tinclad *Signal* was ordered to take dispatches for Maj. Gen. Banks from Alexandria to the mouth of the Black River. En route, she was to join the *Warner* group and enhance the escort. About 10 miles below, lookouts aboard spotted a group of men hailing them from the shore. Acting Volunteer Lt. Edward Morgan ordered a cautious landing and took aboard a number of 120th Ohio Volunteer soldiers who had escaped from the *City Belle.* Continuing on an equal number of miles, the *Signal* came to Wilson's Bend, where she, too, was fired upon by Rebel horsemen. The gunboat returned fire with her starboard battery and kept on. Soon after rounding the next point, she was fired upon again, probably by the same bushwhackers.

In the time following their own Wilson plantation encounter, the *Covington* and *Warner* were only able to make four miles' additional progress. After escaping from the cavalrymen, the tinclad struck her stern against a bar, breaking the port rudder (side-wheelers usually had two) and badly shivering the tiller. Realizing that his craft needed urgent repairs and that they could not make their destination before nightfall, Acting Volunteer Lt. George P. Lord ordered the boats to tie up about a mile from a point noted on charts by its Red House. The *Signal* joined them about 5 P.M., rounding to and making fast astern of the *Covington*.

Information regarding the upriver engagement was not immediately known in Union circles, though by this time news had arrived at Fort De Russy concerning the loss of the *Emma* and the *City Belle*. When rumors began to come in concerning a loud battle above, the *Argosy*, back from her trip with the *Laurel Hill*, was sent to investigate.

Later that afternoon, convoyed by the *Forest Rose*, the side-wheeler *Shreveport* arrived at the former Rebel bastion with 250 replacement troops from several regiments. Officers aboard both the Louisville-built transport and her escort were surprised not to find a gun-boat, given that Fort De Russy was now a regular forward station. It was here they learned of the loss of the two steamers earlier in the week.

Workmen labored all night to make repairs on the *Covington*'s rudder and steering apparatus. During this time, congregating Confederate riflemen on the right bank annoyed them. Almost every fusillade was answered by howitzer fire from the tinclads. By dawn, Confederate Col. George Wythe Baylor, commanding the men of Lane's Brigade, was ready to hunt rivercraft.

Just after first light, the cotton convoy weighed for downriver. The *Warner* took the lead, followed by the *Covington* and the *Signal*. Not long before 5 A.M. as they rounded through the bend near Snaggy Point, the *Warner* sounded a whistle signal: "Enemy in sight."

The *John Warner*, targeted from the high overlooking banks by reinforced masked batteries, suffered the first assault. Cannonballs and hundreds of Minie balls swept the craft. A survivor, Capt. M. Manring of the 56th Ohio, later wrote that 15 artillery rounds went through the main cabin and four through the pilot house, initially killing 34 men. Soldiers aboard the side-wheeler returned fire, hiding behind crates and cotton bales. "They kept the fire hot on us," remembered Private J.O. Bingham in 1888.

The big steamer's pilothouse was, indeed, hit, several pipes were severed, the rudder was smashed, and the paddle wheels were riddled. Still she ploughed ahead downstream until she reached a short point in the river where she went into the left bank, with flames escaping from several burning parts of the upper deck. As she grounded, Confederate gunners, about 100 yards away, continued to pour it on and soon the transport's decks were covered with additional dead and many wounded bluecoats. Officers ordered off surviving infantrymen and many were able to escape ashore and run into the woods.

As she rounded Snaggy Point and the plight of the *Warner* was revealed, the *Covington* stopped and backed into the shore opposite the Rebels. The *Signal*, following, also halted and came to astern and above her consort, both boats heading downstream. Both now opened a rapid and continuous fire.

Acting Volunteer Lt. Lord sent a boarding party over from the *Covington* to torch the *Warner* after the boat's master, a Mr. Dean, raised the white flag. The colonel of the Buckeye regiment, pointing to over 125 Ohio soldiers lying wounded and exposed, pleaded for their lives. Lord was contacted by Lt. Col. James P. Foster of the 128th New York Volunteers and withdrew his orders; the gunboatmen left the transport and allowed her to surrender.

Despite the pending loss of the cotton steamer, the *Covington* and *Signal* fought on. At this time, the Confederates were moving a Parrott or two above with which to rake the stern of the *Signal*. With no stern guns, the tinclad would have been unable to reply. This development was communicated to the *Covington*, just as the Rebels opened fire from their new location.

At this point, the *Covington* cast loose from shore and started to round back up the river, alerting the *Signal* to do likewise. As the latter hauled in her lines, a shot passed through her pitman, thus disabling her port engine. Simultaneously, two shells passed through the pilothouse, damaging the boat's big steering wheel and carrying away the sheaves. This incoming fire put her steering gear out of action. Acting Volunteer Lt. Morgan grabbed a speaking trumpet and hailed his counterpart, Lord, to tell him the sternwheel *Signal* was disabled.

In advance of the escorting tinclad *Covington*, the transport *John Warner* was attacked, as depicted in this drawing by C.E.M. Bonwill, in the Red River below Alexandria on May 4. Although they would escape this encounter, the pair, even after being joined by the tinclad *Signal*, would be destroyed the next day (*Frank Leslie's Illustrated Newspaper*, June 18, 1864).

Still mobile, the big side-wheel gunboat came alongside the *Signal* and made fast. At this point, Acting Volunteer Lt. Lord and several of his crewmen, plus a number of volunteers from the 56th Ohio, started across to provide assistance and Acting Volunteer Lt. Morgan headed aft to confer. Before he could reach the visitors, a shell cut the branch steam pipe on the port side and steam began to rapidly escape from an open throttle valve. At the same time, the escape pipe on the *Covington* was cut by an enemy round, also releasing steam in a quantity so significant as to "make the impression that the boilers had been struck."

The prospect of becoming victims of the deadly vapors caused great concern and even panicked a number of crewmen. Pilot Perry Wilkes, who had fortunately survived the destruction of the pilothouse, and several men from the *Signal* were out on the port guards next to the *Covington*, where he first apprised Acting Volunteer Lt. Morgan and then Acting Volunteer Lt. Lord of the stern-wheeler's condition. In need of additional help in the pilothouse, Lord ordered Wilkes to withdraw aboard the *Covington* along with several men.

Back aboard the *Covington*, her skipper made a brief effort to continue the tow, but this only resulted in further damage to the side-wheeler's already injured rudder. "The *Signal* getting adrift from us," Lord later confessed, "they were not able to return to my vessel." Unable to further assist the *Signal*, Acting Volunteer Lt. Lord knew that the disabled vessel would drift down upon the *John Warner* and both the boats would be captured, not just the transport. A signal was made to her commander to anchor. At the same time, his own pilot informed him that there was insufficient space in the river below to get past the now-surrendered *Warner*.

With her rudder disabled, the *Covington* could not go on. Fearing that he would also find himself on the Dunn's Bayou side, Lord caused her to cross the Red and tie up to the opposite bank, headed upstream. There her gunners returned fire across the river for another hour.

The *Covington* was doomed. Sixty minutes after landing, shells cut her steam drum and struck under the boilers, letting out their water. By now, the ammunition supply was exhausted and all of the howitzers were disabled, mainly because their bracket bolts had popped out. The tinclad was hulled five times during the five-hour action and hit 40 to 50 times in her upper works. At this point, the captain ordered the ship abandoned and, together with his executive officer, Acting Ensign Edward Alford, personally set her alight.

The surviving *Covington* men scrambled ashore from the gun deck and up the bank. Several were killed by intense enemy musketry. Gathering in a small open space just outside the woods, Acting Volunteer Lt. Lord mustered his men and found that, from a crew of 14 officers and 62 men, only nine officers and 23 bluejackets had made his rendezvous, including Col. Foster and Pilots Wilkes and Frank McCloskey. At least one man was killed when a shot went through the shell room. These people set off through the underbrush to Alexandria.

As Lord and his men made their escape and flames shot up from the *Covington*, the Confederate cannoneers turned their guns on the *Signal*. A "perfect storm of Minie balls" flew in through the gunports, wounding 12 sailors, but none were killed. By now the gunboatmen had expended some 330 shells, but were no safer. Still, the effort was heroic; two gunners, George Butts and Charles Asten, quit the sick bay to do their duty during the entire fight.

After anchoring, Acting Volunteer Lt. Morgan decided to slip his boat's chain and drift ashore where, if necessary, it would be easier to escape. This action resulted in the *Signal*'s sliding into the bank, but higher up than expected. Executive officer Acting Ensign C.P. Bragg and Acting Ensign William F. Loan, assisted by Seamen John Highlan and George McCauly, gallantly performed — and survived — these duties under galling fire.

As the vessel neared the shore, Morgan called for volunteers to get a line to shore in an effort to haul the *Signal* into an easier position from which to escape. Seaman George McClurg and several others readily made the effort, though only he made it up an almost perpendicular bank to tie it off. Unhappily, this did not help, and with the tinclad's wheel stuck in the mud, she could not be shifted.

At this point, the abandon-ship call was made and preparations made to burn the *Signal*. In addition to the damage to the power plant and steering gear during the six-hour engagement, the gun deck casemate was penetrated 11 or 12 times by shot and shell, several of which exploded on the gun deck. One cut the steam pipe, another the steam drum, and one hit the port boiler. Many of the guns were out of action and the decks were covered in wreckage.

Before she could be destroyed and the crew escape, the stern-wheeler was surrounded and Morgan reluctantly raised a white flag. A total of six officers and 48 crewmen were mustered on shore to surrender, including three stranded aboard when the *Covington* released her tow line. As the prisoners were led off, Rebel soldiers salvaged every usable item, especially her guns. When this requisition was completed, the light-draught was floated out into the channel and sunk as an obstruction. Confederate reports indicated that a third Union gunboat approached the scene, but was driven off. This may well have been the *Argosy*.

Nicholas Smith, a soldier with the 33rd Wisconsin who had survived aboard the *John Warner* above Grand Ecore, came to know the boat's pilot, a man named Green. Years later, the old campaigner, who was not along on this trip, recalled a conversation with the river sage that fills in a gap. It seems, according to Smith, that Green, along with the ship's captain, was taken captive after the transport went into the bank and was among those started off by Rebel troopers to a POW holding camp. After marching some 15 to 20 rods along the shore through heavy underbrush, Green "leaped from the ranks with the quickness and alertness of a deer and started up the river bank." The startled guards "sent a dozen balls after him," all of which missed. They gave pursuit, but were eluded. Green met a gunboat after fleeing about two miles, hailed, and was taken aboard, where he reported the loss of his craft and the *Covington*.

As the *John Warner*, *Covington*, and *Signal* steamed into disaster, the *Shreveport* and *Forest Rose* weighed for Alexandria early on May 5. About 12 miles above, they spoke the returning *Argosy*, learning that the *John Warner* had surrendered and the *Covington* had gone into the bank. It was not known if the *Signal* was taken or not.

The decision was taken that the trio would proceed cautiously onward, in order to learn whether the battery was a temporary matter of horse artillery or something more permanent involving artillery placed in embrasures behind the levee. To do this, they would "draw their fire," as Acting Ensign Symmes Browne wrote in a letter home.

Paddling along with all stations manned and the guns run out, the *Forest Rose*, trailing the *Shreveport*, soon stopped to pick up a few survivors from the *John Warner*. As they turned into a bend a little further on, the Union craft came across the wreck of the *City Belle*. At about the same time, the magazines of the nearly-consumed *Covington* exploded.

Simultaneously, an enemy shell crashed into port side of the *Forest Rose* just below the waterline amidships, starting a leak. As repair parties hustled, the forward Parrott gun returned fire. At this point, a shell blasted into the casemate just over the howitzer mounted aft the boilers. Fortunately, it failed to penetrate, but when it burst, splinters were sent flying everywhere.

At this point, lookouts aboard the troop boat also spied the Confederate guns on the right bank. The *Shreveport* immediately rounded to before they could shift fire to her from the tinclad and ran back down under the protection of the *Argosy*. Having drawn fire and determined that the Confederate battery, comprising several pieces, was formidable, the decision was taken to retreat back down to Fort De Russy in order to avoid sharing the fate of the three boats dispatched earlier in the day.

As the vessels returned, about 200 survivors from the 56th Ohio were rescued, along

Occasionally misidentified in this photo as the *Signal,* the light draught *Forest Rose* was among the first of the purpose-altered tinclads commissioned. Shown here assisting in the construction of the Red River dam in 1864, the stern-wheeler led a particularly exciting career, participating in numerous campaigns and adventures on the Mississippi, Red, and Yazoo Rivers, including the February 1864 defense of Waterproof, Louisiana (Naval Historical Center).

with about 10 civilians also from the *Warner,* and 100 or so others who had escaped from the gunboats. When the boats reached Fort De Russy, the *Argosy* and *Shreveport* continued back to the mouth of the Red, leaving the *Forest Rose* to hold the station and patch her hull.

Casualties incurred during the destruction of the *Emma, City Belle, John Warner, Signal,* and *Covington* exceeded over 600 men. These losses, in just five days, represent one of the largest setbacks suffered by Federal forces on the Western waters during the entire course of the war — and these setbacks were not over yet.

On the other hand, there was no shortage of gallantry by U.S. Navy sailors during the engagements below Alexandria. In one of the largest awards made to men fighting aboard a single vessel during the Civil War, six men of the *Signal* received the Medal of Honor in a mass notification on December 31: Brooklyn-born Pilot Perry Wilkes (1830–1889), who entered service at Jeffersonville, IN, and died at Louisville, KY; Quarter Gunner Michael Charles Asten (1834–1885), born and died in Nova Scotia; Rome, NY-born Gunner's Mate George Butts (1838–1902), who entered service from and is buried at Lorain, Ohio; Irish-born Seaman John Hyland (1819–1867), who died shortly after the conflict and is buried at Manistee, MI; Irish-born Boatswain's Mate Michael McCormick (1833–1865), who never recovered from wounds received during the action and is buried at Milwaukee, WI; and Rochester, NY-born Seaman Timothy O'Donoghue (1841–?).

There was a third tinclad casualty on May 6 in a little-known engagement hundreds of miles away across Louisiana on the border with Texas not far from Sabine Pass. Having moved up the Calcasieu River near present-day Cameron, LA, the *Wave*, formerly the Mississippi River steamer *Argosy No. 2*,[7] became the first of the newly-delivered West Gulf Coast Blocking Squadron (WGCBS) light-draughts lost to the enemy.

The Navy Congressional Medal of Honor was presented, on December 31, 1864, to six heroes from the crew of the tinclad *Signal* for their actions during the Red River battle of May 5. This was the same medal given to Quartermaster John Nibbe for his gallantry during the loss of the tinclad *Petrel* a few days earlier (Naval Historical Center).

Since the Federal defeat at Sabine Pass 30 miles west the previous year, both sides in the Civil War gave the Calcasieu Pass inlet on the lower Texas-Louisiana border area off the Gulf of Mexico scant attention. Bisected by the northwestern-flowing Calcasieu River, the stream was bordered on both sides by low flat coastal plains. Here blockade runners had offloaded cargoes, Union foraging parties from blockaders had sought intelligence on these "outlaws," and Union sympathizers had herded cattle. A small mud fort, for protection against "Jayhawkers" and others hostile to Confederate interests, was abandoned by the spring of 1864.

Among the most inflexible Unionists living in the Calcasieu Pass was one Duncan Smith, who, together with his sons and several neighbors, traveled to New Orleans at the beginning of April to convince Federal authorities that it was safe to come to their assistance. In return for their help, these refugees promised to picket the area against Rebel attacks, to assist in naval recruitment, and to help acquire upwards of 450 horses, sheep and cattle.

On April 15, Commodore James S. Palmer, WGCBS commander, called in Acting Volunteer Lt. Benjamin W. Loring and ordered him to lead a two-ship expedition to the Calcasieu River in support of Smith's proposal. Loring's consort would be the 450-ton schooner-rigged side-wheeler *Granite City*,[8] a veteran blockader and participant in the previous fall's Sabine Pass operations. The tinclad, with the "refugees" embarked, weighed for the Pass immediately, but was forced by a storm to put into Atchafalaya Bay to make repairs, and so did not arrive at Calcasieu until the morning of April 24.

Once she arrived and crossed the bar, the copper-bottomed *Wave* immediately spied the Confederate fort, which was shelled. When there was no return fire, Loring sent parties ashore to reconnoiter. Finding the facility abandoned, they burned the barracks and scouted the river bank. Believing the shore clear of the enemy as Smith had promised, the craft steamed two miles upstream and dropped anchor right below the Unionist's home. From here, the gunboatmen would accomplish the mission goals.

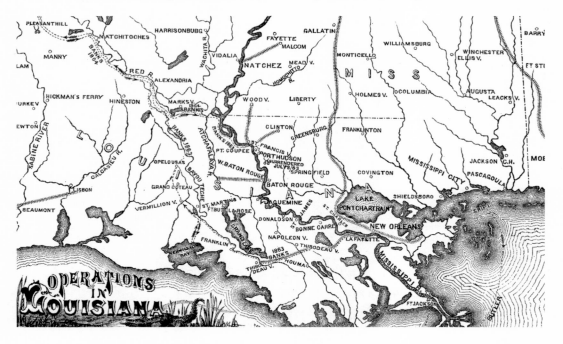

This 19th century Civil War map of Louisiana clearly depicts not only the Red River, but the Calcasieu River to its southwest as well. When the ocean-equipped tinclad *Wave* steamed from New Orleans to Calcasieu Pass in May 1864, she hugged the coast to the west of the city. Those light-draughts sent to Mobile Bay later in the summer would likewise steam close to shore, moving east through the Mississippi Sound (Lossing, *Pictorial Field Book of the Civil War*, v. 3).

A number of willing Federal sympathizers soon appeared, allowing additional pickets to be set out. The bridges over two bayous were destroyed, cutting communications over the Sabine Pass road to Texas. Smith assured Loring that the Confederates would not now be able to get at his tinclad. The *Granite City* arrived on April 27. After anchoring further down the pass on the opposite side of a bend from the light-draught, she sent a lieutenant and 27 Illinois soldiers ashore to picket the east bank. The work of recruitment, livestock acquisition, and refugee relief began in earnest.

The *Wave* had barely anchored when local dispatch riders rode to Sabine and Niblett's Bluff to inform Southern commanders of her arrival. In light of the previous Union attacks on the area and the present expedition across the state on the Red River, Lt. Col. William Griffith and Lt. Col. Ashley W. Spaight immediately believed that her presence foretold of another Texas invasion.

Both men passed their information up the chain of command to Houston and received orders back from the District of Texas, New Mexico, and Arizona to attack, disperse, or destroy the gunboat incursion. Efforts between the two officers were coordinated and put into effect starting on May 4. Soldiers and a few cavalry from the two commands were assembled, along with two 6-pounder and two 12-pounder field guns from a battery under Capt. Edmund Creuzbauer. The same day, Commodore Palmer sent orders for Loring to return as soon as his duty was discharged.

The Federal navy crewmen, together with the refugee Unionists, made great progress on gathering men and livestock during the nearly two weeks they were so engaged. Had Palmer's instructions arrived on May 5, the two boats could have left, having successfully emptied the area of available recruits and beeves. Instead, the retrieval and signing business continued into the evening, when pickets were, as usual, stationed at key locations to guard the roads and boats. Sentries were posted aboard the warships and, as he did every night, Loring paced his deck checking precautions.

While the sailors afloat and the Federal pickets ashore passed the night in peace, the soldiers of Lt. Col. Griffith maneuvered silently for an early attack. By 4:30 A.M., the Rebels had rebuilt the bridge and were across one of the bayous. Lt. Charles Welhausen's two 12-pounders were unlimbered 1,000 yards from the *Granite City*, while the pair of 6-pounders from the section of Lt. J.D. Micksch were parked a similar distance from the *Wave*. The butternut riflemen hunkered down in preparation, praying that the forthcoming charge would be a complete surprise because they could anticipate almost no protection except for a low wooden fence and some scrub bushes.

When the first sun rays pierced the horizon on May 6, the guns of the Creuzbauer Battery opened on the Union warships, getting away upwards of eight bolts before there was any response. The bluejackets on both the *Wave* and *Granite City* were caught unawares, but were quickly beat to quarters and started to return fire. Their anchorages on either side of the bend allowed their counterbattery action to provide a crossfire against the Confederate cannoneers.

During the initial cannon exchange, four Confederate gunners were killed, even as graycoat infantry scrambled forward at double pace. When they reached the river levees, the riflemen hunkered down in the tall grass and began to volley the gunboats 50 to 100 yards away. Musket balls splattered against the metal-covered casemate of the *Wave* while many cut splinters. The men leaning out the gunports to reload the howitzers or attempting to get up the anchors were inviting targets.

At this point, Lt. Micksch found that his horses had been taken to the rear and he could not follow the soldiers toward the *Wave*. On the other hand, Welhausen's 12-pounders were advanced and together with the sharpshooters, were able to compel Lamson to surrender his paddlewheeler about 45 minutes into the fight. The *Granite City* had fired only 30 times, while losing four dead and 11 wounded.

After losing a gun to an accident during the fight, Lt. Welhausen was able to recruit a number of soldiers to help Corporal Walter von Rosenburg, gun captain of his No. 2 gun, transfer the remaining 12-pounder over to the levee facing the *Wave*. There, with shell and canister also carried over from the previous engagement site, the big fieldpiece joined in the musket assault on the tinclad. Corporal Joseph Brickhouse's No. 1 gun was eventually returned to duty, doubling the murderous rate of fire directed against the tinclad.

On board the light-draught below, Acting Volunteer Lt. Loring valiantly attempted to get up steam, but was several times chased from the pilothouse by canister from Welhausen's cannon. The *Wave* was unable to get her anchor up and could only gain the indifferent assistance of the river current in altering the aim of her broadside howitzers. The rifle and cannon fire on this light-draught was not dissimilar from that being experienced by Acting Volunteer Lts. Lord and Morgan and the men of the *Signal* and *Covington* at almost this exact same time over on the other side of the state.

Lt. Welhausen now shifted his aim lower on the gunboat's superstructure. One of his 12-pounder shells ploughed into the engine room and punctured the steam drum, ending the service of the boilers and starboard engine. As related by Corporal Brickhouse in a May 1909 newspaper memoir, a round from his cannon scored a direct hit on the muzzle of the 32-pounder, splitting the barrel four feet and completely disabling it.

Loring's command was caught in a deadly crossfire between riflemen and artillerymen, and though he was able to fight on for an additional 45 minutes or so, the outcome was not in doubt. Powerless to escape and with 10 men already wounded, the *Wave*'s captain raised a white flag.

Maj. Felix C. McReynolds of Griffin's Texan battalion hailed the gunboat, ordering that a cutter be sent to shore to pick him up. There was no immediate reply, but Lt. Col. Griffin could clearly see sailors throwing small arms and an iron safe (learned to contain $9,000) overboard. When they tired to jettison two howitzers, a 12-pounder shot was sent across the defeated boat's bow, but brought no response. Finally, a second bolt was sent into her bow; the white flag reappeared and the required boat was sent ashore.

The victory over the *Wave* and *Granite City* was savored in local Confederate circles and added to the joy already being made manifest throughout the Trans-Mississippi theater by the continuing inconvenience of the Red River campaign to Rear Adm. Porter and Maj. Gen. Banks. During the sharp skirmishing, 22 Rebels were killed, including 16 with Creuzbaur's Battery.

On the other hand, Acting Vol. Lt. Loring in particular was excoriated in Federal naval circles and came to be "remembered only as disgraced." After reading several letters and hearing a number of accounts, no less a figure than Rear Adm. David G. Farragut wrote to Commodore Palmer in early June. Believing Loring and Lamson cowards, the hero of New Orleans cared "but little for the commanders of the *Granite City* and *Wave.* They ought to have whipped off four times the force and they surrendered [16 guns and 166 men] before they had anyone killed on the *Wave* ... besides they took no precautions."

When he had a chance to pen his official report in early 1865, Loring, who twice escaped from his POW confinement only to be recaptured, let it be known that he was hurt to believe his reputation besmirched, partially because his action had actually saved lives. The *Wave* was hit 65 times in 90 minutes and literally splintered. It is surprising that, although she "had sustained four-fifths of the shell hits and had fought twice as long," she suffered the fewest casualties. If disgraced, at least Loring and his crew had their lives.[9]

The men working for Lt. Col. Bailey, meanwhile, strained around the clock for eight days without cessation, beginning the initial Alexandria dam not far above the lower, downstream rapids where the river was about 758 feet wide. It was hoped that, when the project was finished, the water behind the structure would have risen enough to float the gunboats over the upper rapids. Then, when the time was just right, the dam could be broken and the gunboats could rush free over the lower rapids, carried by the force of the released water.

Despite a 9 mph current, the work continued and gradually the water level began to rise. On May 8, the stage on the upper falls was up sufficiently to allow the *Lexington* and *Fort Hindman* and the light-draught monitors *Osage* and *Neosho* to move down and make ready to pass the main dam the instant it was ready.

Early the next morning, great crashing sounds were heard in the vicinity of the dam. The tremendous water pressure against the dam forced two of the barges employed in its construction to burst loose, swinging in below the dam on one side. The admiral quickly saw the situation and, skilled equestrian that he was, jumped on a steed and galloped up to the upper falls where his craft were anchored. Screaming from horseback at 6 A.M., Porter ordered Lt. Commander George Bache, the only one of the captains with steam up fully ready to go, to immediately pass the upper falls, run down over the rocky stretch before the level fell, and exit to safety through the dam. It only took 20 minutes for the *Lexington* to speed from the upper falls through the dam to the safety of the waters below the town. There she anchored and observed the monitors and *Fort Hindman* come down a short time later. This emergency exodus proved Lt. Col. Bailey's dam would work and he resumed its construction with spirit.

Patrol and convoy work continued on the Red River below Alexandria during this time and was often met by Confederate resistance. A *Forest Rose* episode illustrates the level of resistance and response.

Having been engaged below, the light-draught came up the river to Fort De Russy on May 11 and anchored behind Lt. Commander Frank Ramsay's giant ironclad *Choctaw.* During the day, Rebel sharpshooters entered the rifle pits below the fort and endeavored to pick off the officers and men when they appeared on deck. Some grayclad riflemen fired directly into the cabin and wardroom of the *Forest Rose*, narrowly missing her captain. For awhile, the gundeck howitzers returned fire, but with little effect. After awhile, the best shots among the crew were sent to the pilothouse and shot at their enemy with their own rifles. Their marksmanship was good, causing the perpetrators to move back and keep their distance.

The following morning, the *Rose* was ordered to follow the *Choctaw* upstream. About a mile up, the crews of the two boats were beat to quarters. As the gunners stood by their pieces (often relieved), the two steamed slowly ahead, stopping at every place people were gathered to make inquiry concerning the strength and location of nearby Confederate units.

After destroying a flat used by the Rebels to cross the Red, the two boats rounded to stand downstream, the *Forest Rose* leading. The *Choctaw* was not quite turned about when a masked battery, estimated as five rifled 10-pounders, opened upon the smaller craft from below and nearly straight ahead. Sharpshooters simultaneously hailed musketry into the side of the boat from the river bank.

The first Confederate artillery shell aimed at the light-draught zoomed high, but the second had the range. Almost instantaneously thereafter, five rounds hit the *Rose* simultaneously, three penetrating her port side. Two spent rounds came in on deck, but did no damage, while the third broke the stanchion. One shot smacked into the forward casemate just above the starboard bow Parrott, while another hit the gunboat's stern, about a foot below the deck. Except for dents, no material damage was done.

As soon as the guns of the tinclad could be brought to bear, they spoke back rapidly as fast as they could be loaded and fired. Soon, the entire starboard broadside was loosed, dropping grape, canister, and shrapnel among the insurgents. Despite this noisy exchange, no one aboard the *Forest Rose* was hurt and the tinclad suffered no significant damage. By the time the *Choctaw* was able to come up and bring her guns on target, there was no target. The Southerners had skedaddled.

By May 13, all of the gunboats were safely below the Alexandria rapids and Union forces were now able to exit that town, reaching the mouth of the river eight days later. "And thus ended the 69-day Red River expedition," Lt. Commander Selfridge wrote in his *B&L* contribution, "one of the most humiliating and disastrous that had been recorded during the war." The Federal Red River expedition of 1864 has been the subject of debate from the day it first entered that stream. It is far outside the scope of this work to enter into such a review. We can report that, during the adventure, the U.S. Navy lost about 320 men, two tinclads, one ironclad, two pump boats, and four transports.

"After the Red River campaign," wrote Lt. Col. Richard Irwin, "no important operation was undertaken by either side in Louisiana." It is true that the few tinclads of the WGCBS were active on some of the state's streams and bayous near New Orleans, patrolling and enforcing the Union blockade. For the Mississippi Squadron and its tinclads, however, the scene of action now reverted to the familiar territory along the banks of the Mississippi, Ohio, Cumberland, Tennessee, White, and Arkansas Rivers. The Red River was blockaded, while the interior lands up the Yazoo were largely abandoned.[10]

As the main field armies of both sides moved further east, the partisan and antiship-ping war continued in the West. To meet it with the resources available to him, Rear Adm. Porter now revised the district structure of the Mississippi Squadron, adding two more divisions. New General Orders promulgating the scheme were published on May 20 and 27 and provided, once again, that heavy units anchor at key geographical loca-tions from which they could provide support-on-demand, leaving the light-draughts to undertake patrol and convoy duties. This chart represents the district breakdown which, with the fall addition of an Eleventh District to cover the Upper Tennessee, would remain largely the same for the rest of the war:[11]

District #	Location
1	New Orleans to Donaldsonville, LA
2	Donaldsonville to Red River
3	Red River to Natchez, MS
4	Natchez, MS, to Vicksburg, MS
5	Vicksburg, MS, to White River
6	White River to Cairo, IL
7	Cairo, IL, to head of Tennessee River
8	Cumberland River to its source + Upper Ohio River

Union Maj. Gen. Frederick Steele's VII Corps participation in the Red River cam-paign is often called the Camden expedition because that is as far as his Federal army was able to get from Little Rock before turning about and returning to the state capital on May 3. The details of the various actions and operations involved in the Camden enter-prise are not important to this story except to say that the general's failure emboldened Confederates within Arkansas and elsewhere in the Trans-Mississippi theater to resume the offensive.

In mid–May, Confederate Lt. Gen. Edmund Kirby Smith ordered preparations begun for a late summer invasion of Missouri. As the month closed, a deputy, Maj. Gen. Sterling Price, commander of the District of Arkansas, turned the cavalry division of Brig. Gen. John S. Marmaduke loose to recruit new troops and to disrupt Federal logis-tics.

In the wake of the VII Corps's retreat to Little Rock after the Camden adventure, Rebel horsemen rode roughshod over Arkansas, "plundering and overawing the Union-ists," as Benson J. Lossing put it right after the war. The gunboatmen on the Mississippi, Arkansas, and White Rivers now faced the same dilemma as their colleagues on the Cum-berland and Tennessee Rivers: a concentrated strategy of blockade initiated by regular troops.

Partisans and guerrillas remained a significant danger on the White River. In a let-ter home on June 6, Paymaster's Steward John Swift of the tinclad *Silver Cloud* remem-bered that, on a recent trip up that stream, Rebels were "as thick as peas everywhere." Southerners dreamed, he believed, of capturing a tinclad and had planned just how to take one. Concealing themselves along the river banks where a gunboat was expected to land for forage, the butternuts held themselves silent, hoping one would land and tie up. If it did, Rebels would run down and try to board and overwhelm the crew. Swift's thoughts were probably based on actual events when irregulars had overwhelmed the crews of steamboats putting into shore.

Inland of the Mississippi, one of the Confederate riders deputized to interdict Union transport was not Nathan Bedford Forrest, but another legendary butternut cavalryman, Brig. Gen. Joseph O. ("Jo") Shelby,[12] the most famous horse soldier in the Trans-Mississippi theater and commander of one of Marmaduke's two brigades. Along the banks of the Mississippi, the less-famous but equally-determined Col. Colton Greene[13] also harassed Union shipping.

During May and June, Shelby and his mounted force of between 2,000 and 3,000 men with the Missouri battery of Capt. Richard Collins moved across the Arkansas River east of Little Rock and headed toward the White River country, marching down the east bank of that stream toward Devall's Bluff. His purpose was threefold: to recruit soldiers to the Southern cause, to end the depredations of guerrillas turned terrorists, and to block Steele's logistical flow by attacking his supply lines between Little Rock and the Bluff.

While Shelby undertook a difficult march toward Clarendon that led him through the overflowing bottoms of Cache River and Bayou DeVue, Col. Colton Greene of the Third Missouri Cavalry (CSA), leading Marmaduke's other brigade while his superior was on leave, took his horsemen via Monticello eastward across Bayous Bartholomew and Macon to the flat, featureless bottom lands along the west bank of the Mississippi. There he was to put "an immediate quietus" on local cotton trading with the Federals and to harass river traffic.

Accompanying Greene were 800 to 900 men drawn from Greene's own regiment, temporarily led by Capt. Benjamin Crabtree, along with the Confederate 4th Missouri Cavalry (Col. John Q. Burbridge), 7th Missouri Cavalry (Col. Solomon G. Kitchen), and 8th Missouri Cavalry (Col. William L. Jeffers), plus six fieldpieces of Capt. J.H. Pratt's Texas Battery. These men would engage Northern gunboats and amphibious forces in a spirited, but largely unremembered, campaign from Chicot County, the southeasternmost county in Arkansas. Greene would blockade the great river for over a week and leave several tinclad captains reeling.[14]

As ordained, the commanders of the various Mississippi Squadron sectors made regular reports to Rear Adm. Porter concerning the activities of their vessels and their dispositions. From his flag boat, the Pook turtle *Louisville*, Lt. Commander Elias K. Owen, chief of the Sixth District, wrote regarding his tinclads on May 17. "The *Prairie Bird* was in the Yazoo, the *Exchange* was at Skipwith's Landing, and the *Romeo* was stationed off Gaines Landing [five miles above No. 82] as a center," he confided, while the *Marmora* patrolled "from Island [No.] 76 to Napoleon."

Of course, other vessels passed through Owen's district every day. On May 22, the tinclad *Curlew*, for example, with orders to transport a party from the U.S. Coast Survey to Cairo, had stopped briefly at Vicksburg to coal.

Before departing the former Rebel bastion, the light-draught's officers, including Acting Master's Mate De Witt C. Morse, learned "that Marmaduke, with 6,000 men and a battery of ten or fifteen guns, was at Island No. 82 preparing to blockade the river." Rebel irregulars also attacked at the heads of Islands No. 80 and 81. Earlier, a "reliable woman" had suggested to Baldwin that the Southern general would "have 30 pieces of artillery on the river in a few days."

Three days later, as she passed Columbia, AR, lookouts aboard the *Romeo* watched the shoreline for signs of Confederate cavalry said to be in the area. Acting Master Thomas Baldwin, like Morse and his colleagues, had heard that butternut scouts had several times foraged to the edge of the river and had fired into transports at the foot of Island No. 82, where the more heavily loaded boats going down were forced to hug the shore as they turned in through the river bend.

On the evening of May 23, a few days after the Federal expedition quit the Red River, Col. Greene's regiment, with Pratt's attached artillery, arrived at Campbell's Landing, on the Arkansas side of the Mississippi River near Gaines Landing. Greene, like Col. the Rev. David C. "Parson" Kelley on the Tennessee and Cumberland Rivers in the fall, had very definite ideas about assaulting riverboats.

Col. Greene would employ the navigational dangers of the winding river stretch between Chicot Lake and Gaines Landing to his advantage. Here in these Greenville Bends (named for the town on the eastern bank in the state of Mississippi), steamboats, with a top speed of about 9–10 mph, had to navigate through long river curves separated by narrow peninsulas of land. Depending upon their north-south direction, the boats would always come closer to shore on one side than another. Given this topography, batteries could be placed in two or more locations, allowing vessels to sail past one into the teeth of another without the possibility of backward escape. Or these horse artillery units could be quickly limbered and speed across a neck of land from one bend to another, catching surviving steamers more than once.

One of the bends, Cypress Bend, was a particular favorite of the Confederate leader. Columbia, AR, was at the upper side and Leland Landing on the lower. A steamer negotiating this bend traveled 18 miles around by water, but horse artillery and

Seldom recognized in modern Civil War histories, Col. Colton Greene (1832–1900) was one of the most effective Confederate antishipping commanders to operate in the Western theater. Employing his own 10th Missouri Cavalry, parts of several other Missouri cavalry regiments, and Capt. Joseph Pratt's Texas Battery, Greene halted Union shipping on the Mississippi River in the Greenville Bends for several weeks at the end of May and into June 1864. During his mobile foray from positions in Chicot County, Arkansas, he punished a number of Federal gunboats, including the tinclads *Curlew*, *Romeo* and *Exchange*; played havoc with the Mississippi Marine Brigade; and escaped an expedition by Red River veterans of the U.S. XVI Corps (U.S. Army Military History Institute).

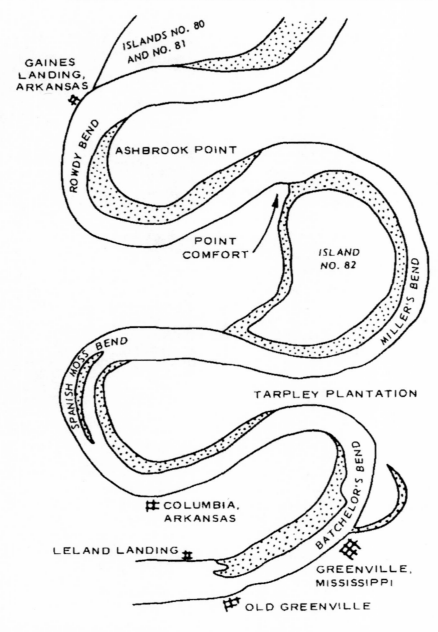

Federal shipping, escorted or not, passing through the Greenville Bends was often subjected to attack from Confederate rifle and/or artillery-armed partisans or regular troops waiting along the Arkansas shore. The Mississippi River at this point was entirely blockaded by Southern Col. Colton Greene during late May–early June 1864. Nothing remains of Gaines Landing, Columbia, or Old Greenville as depicted in this chart adapted from Col. Charles Suter's 1874 reconnaissance map of the Lower Mississippi. Present-day Greenville sits on an oxbow-shaped lake (Marion Bragg, *Historic Names and Places on the Lower Mississippi River*, Mississippi River Commission, Department of the Army, 1971).

cavalry, operating at the base of the neck, had only to race 3.5 miles over a good road to get from one side to another.

At daybreak the next morning, a 40-man detachment from Company F of the 4th Missouri Cavalry was sent to capture the stern-wheel cotton boat *Lebanon*,[15] discovered lying at Ford's Landing, 10 miles below Greenville. Stealthily seizing a yawl at the bank, a number of the men managed to get aboard, capture the boat, and remove her goods, including $20,000 worth of dry goods and $20,000 in cash, to say nothing of cotton. Once that task was accomplished, the vessel was burned. The freed crewmen were told to pass the word that any additional cotton traders or speculators captured would be executed.

While the 4th Missouri detachment was taking the *Lebanon*, the six guns of Capt. J.H. Pratt's battery were placed on top of the river-bank levee at Gaines Landing, with their support stationed under cover 50 yards in the rear. The wait for action was not long.

It was just past 4 A.M. when the *Curlew* paddled past Island No. 82, following the timberclad *Tyler* by about two miles. During the next hour as daylight appeared and the men, as they did every morning at that time, stood to their guns, nothing was seen along the western shore. From his location on the quarterdeck, Acting Master's Mate Morse ordered the piping up of hammocks while, simultaneously, peering into his spyglass at the river bank ahead.

As the *Curlew* passed Gaines Landing, Morse and the other lookouts could see men arriving at the bank and starting to unload what appeared to be wood or cotton. As the gunboat splashed closer, it was determined, with some horror, that the fellows were, in fact, hurriedly "preparing a battery for our benefit." Still there was some hope; as the boat was steaming up the river, she was able to lay close to the opposite side of the Mississippi across the point in shoal water.

When the light-draught reached a point about ¾ of a mile away from the enemy, the disposition of the Confederate mobile battery, which Greene would repeat in the days ahead, could be clearly distinguished. Three or four guns were mounted on the edge of the bank in clear sight while the remainder were hidden behind the levee. The Rebel gunners, perhaps familiar with the big guns of the timberclad, chose to let the *Tyler* pass.

All of a sudden, as the men aboard the *Curlew* cleared for action, the Confederate battery on shore opened fire. The prompt response aboard the gunboat ("every officer was at his station as soon as the ball opened," wrote Morse later) allowed the four port-side howitzers to "give them one broadside before the thieves had given us their second round."

Perhaps expecting to easily sink the tinclad with their opening salvo, Greene's gunners, like the men of the *Curlew*, found themselves engaged in a very spirited 20 to 35 minute (depending upon your source) gun fight. The Rebel cannoneers fired quickly; bluejackets aboard the light-draught thought themselves under a hail of cannonballs, shells, and shrapnel, to say nothing of small arms fire.

"Pieces of casemate and splinters were flying all around the decks," Morse remembered, and bullets and shrapnel riddled the cabins and staterooms. Many of the Confed-

The Model 57 12-pounder Field Howitzer, better known as the Napoleon, was one of the most popular of all Civil War cannon and was found in most Confederate horse artillery batteries, including the 10th Texas, led along the banks of the Mississippi River in May–June 1864 by Capt. Joseph H. Pratt. The guns shown were captured by Federal forces at Chattanooga (Miller's *Photographic History of the Civil War,* v. 5).

erate shots were aimed, as they always were in these fights, at the gunboat's pilothouse and paddle wheel. Many of these rounds flew over and landed in the river beyond. The *Curlew* was hit multiple times by the Confederate cannon in what many would remember as the "hottest engagement" in which the boat was ever engaged.

A 12-pounder shell was seen to skip over the water, losing most of its energy but retaining enough to fly up, strike the tinclad's casemate, and fall, unexploded, onto the wheelguard. A 6-pounder ball lodged itself halfway through the rudder without breaking it. Another came through the casemate very near the No. 2 gun without exploding, while two other 6-pounder balls went completely through on the port side, sailing just above the deck without doing much damage.

In response to the Rebel gift, the *Curlew*'s howitzers returned the Southern compliment, firing 28 shots of their own toward shore, some of which were believed to have struck "in their midst." At the same time, the tinclad's executive officer, Acting Ensign

H.B. O'Neil, repeatedly pulled on the whistle cord to warn the timberclad *Tyler*, two miles ahead, that the *Curlew* was under attack. Before the *Tyler* could round to and come to the *Curlew's* assistance, Col. Greene's horse artillery limbered up and moved down the river bank, taking a position at Daniel Sessions's plantation. As the Confederates were moving, the *Tyler* arrived and its commander offered his congratulations on the light-draught's gunnery.

The *Tyler* had to continue on to White River. Before she departed, her captain, the ranking on-scene USN officer, ordered the *Curlew* to proceed up and meet the tinclad *Romeo* (lying a few miles above). From there they would convoy Capt. Joseph H. Williams's big side-wheel steamer *Nicholas Longworth*,[16] which had just come down with troops and horses, below Gaines Landing.

The three Union vessels proceeded downstream without interference. Coming abreast of Island No. 82, the machinery of the *Curlew* broke down, compelling her to anchor and effect repairs. Rather than heave to and wait for her, the *Romeo* and *Longworth* continued on.[17]

Proceeding down about 10 miles to a point about a mile above Columbia, AR, the tinclad and the transport were attacked by musketry. Sharpshooters firing from behind the levee riddled both craft. While the *Romeo* engaged the enemy, Capt. Williams, whose crew and volunteers had initially joined in the resistance with their 6-pounder, a howitzer, and rifles, was signaled to run on.

The *Nicholas Longworth* paddled on into Cypress Bend, but, as she passed Columbia, she was fired upon by Greene's battery, which dropped shot and shell all around her. This firing was heard at Greeneville, where three boats of the Union's Mississippi Marine Brigade (MMB), under Col. George E. Currie, were stationed to protect river traffic. This amphibious brigade, descended from the outfit established by Col. Charles Ellet before the June 1862 Battle of Memphis, had something of a controversial reputation with all sides, Union and Confederate, U.S. Army and U.S. Navy.

When she was attacked in Columbia Bend, the *Longworth* was hit by eight Rebel shells. One went through Williams's room, two through the cabin, and a fourth through the pilothouse. As the *Longworth* pressed on, the little cotton boat *Delta*, the same one fired into near Greenville in January by Confederate Brig. Gen. Lawrence "Sul" Ross, came upriver upon the batteries and was likewise taken under fire.

While the two civilian steamers were under attack, the *Romeo*, out of ammunition, raced up to the location of the disabled *Curlew* and borrowed several boxes of shells, before returning down to seek the *Longworth*. Reunited, the two boats continued down together, both taking hits in their hulls and upper works.

During this time, Col. Robert Lawther's 10th Missouri Cavalry joined Greene. Thinking the *Longworth* and *Romeo* would soon be out of immediate danger and would continue past Greenville rather than stopping, Col. Greene limbered four of his cannon and sped across the peninsula to deploy them on its lower side at Leland's Landing, ready to catch them as they puffed past. One section of artillery, then pounding the *Delta*, was detached to remain with Lawther.

Looking like so much Swiss cheese, the *Nicholas Longworth*, together with the *Romeo*, was able to make it back to Greenville. The *Delta*, in flames, had in the time since careened over and made for the opposite bank as she approached the town. A towboat was sent to save her from beaching and to bring her in.[18]

At Greenville, Capt. Williams called upon Col. Currie, provided details on the Confederate assault, and asked for assistance in passing below. The MMB officer readily agreed and ordered that the *Nicholas Longworth* be lashed to one of his own vessels. Another MMB boat would lead and provide cover with its Parrott rifles.

While the Yankees made their preparations, Col. Greene, below the town, made his. There was no natural cover along the river bank below Greenville so the Confederate officer spaced his artillery out along the shore. Separation was also a form of protection.

The three Federal boats, with Currie in the lead unit, came within range of Greene's gunners at Miles' Plantation during the afternoon. The Southerners wanted to destroy the troop boat and so paid no attention to Currie's lead vessel, allowing it to pass as they had the *Tyler* earlier that morning.

It turned out that the *Nicholas Longworth* was effectively shielded by the second MMB boat, and even though the Rebels poured a hail of shot and shell at the two, it was the military vessel that suffered the brunt of the attack, taking 14 hits. Once the *Longworth* was out of artillery range, the shooting stopped. Greene retired from the river bank and Currie's two vessels limped back to Greenville, having lost one man killed and two wounded.

Records are sparse as to whether or not one of the USN tinclads accompanied Currie's escort mission. There is no mention of it in the Navy *Official Records* if she did. On the other hand, contemporary Federal newspapers and Greene both agree that there was a gunboat engaged. In his description of the May 24 encounter near Leland's Landing, the colonel was quite specific:

> We went into battery and waited the enemy's approach. He came down in line of battle, crescent-shaped, with two marine boats, one gunboat, and a transport. I engaged the fleet, which held its position, maneuvering for near two hours, when it passed on. The gunboat was disabled, the marine boat *Diana* roughly handled, with many killed and wounded, and the transport penetrated in many places.

If there was a tinclad engaged, it was most likely the *Exchange*, the only boat then positioned to participate. More than likely, however, the contemporaries mistook one of Currie's MMB boats.

Following the Leland's Landing fight, Col. Greene limbered up and galloped back to Columbia, where the *Romeo* was found completing repairs. The Confederates went back into battery and once again engaged the Union light-draught. The Rebel leader later boasted that she was quickly disposed of: "struck 17 times; greatly damaged; got out of the way and has not since made its appearance before my batteries." Among those wounded on the gunboat was Acting Ensign John B. Dwyer, hit in the thigh by a musket ball.

After resting, Col. Greene moved his command back to Gaines Landing in the middle of the night, May 24–25. As the sun rose, he saw three gunboats out in the stream; these he ordered subjected to musket volleys. Being low on ammunition, he refrained from an artillery attack, electing instead to move to a point on the river 10 miles above Gaines.

On the 26th, Greene's gunners attacked the Ellet ram *Monarch*[19] in sight of an unnamed gunboat. Although the amphibious warfare craft was hit several times, it escaped. The same day, Mississippi Squadron Sixth District commander Lt. Cmdr. Owen, cruising off Lake Providence, LA, received dispatches advising him of affairs in the Cypress Bend area. Hearing that Greene's pieces were superior to those of the light-draughts, he immediately got underway to provide help with his *Louisville*.

The next two days were taken up by Col. Greene's command with marches to Parkers's on Bayou Macon and the Old River Lake, near Ditch Bayou. On May 28, the *Louisville* hove to off Gaines Landing. With the Confederates gone, Lt. Cmdr. Owen could, naturally, "see or hear nothing of the Rebel forces." When several Southern scouts peeked out upon the ironclad, they were greeted with a few Navy shrapnel shells. In a report to Rear Adm. Porter, Owen guessed that the insurgents might have moved down the river to attack Lake Providence and Goodrich's Landing, where troops were protecting stores and no gunboats were stationed.

The *Louisville* reached a peaceful Skipwith's Landing on May 29. The district had been so quiet during the previous three days that Lt. Cmdr. Owen was convinced that the enemy had left the river. It was true, he believed, that there were a few guerrillas left on both banks, but they were "chiefly employed in conscription and getting animals."

Having been joined by the 7th and 8th Missouri Cavalry Regiments, Colton Greene's command rode on the same day to Smith's Plantation, 4 miles from the Mississippi River town of Sunnyside. There it would endeavor to disabuse Owen of his faith in its absence.

Toward dusk, Capt. John Wolf Jr.'s 176-ton stern-wheeler *Rocket*,[20] a veteran of the Shiloh campaign in 1862, hove in sight at Batchelor's Bend. Among her many passengers was the U.S. Army Adjutant General Lorenzo Thomas and his staff. Greene's gunners and sharpshooters riddled the boat's upper decks before she could get away. The *Chicago Daily Tribune* later reported that "some nine shots passed through her; yet, strange to say, no one on board was injured."

As the *Rocket* moved deeper into the bend, the Confederate horse artillery limbered up and raced above Columbia to continue the assault. At the same time, Col. Currie heard the gunfire and three of his MMB boats quickly steamed out of Greenville to effect a rescue. When the military craft reached the *Rocket*, a convoy past Columbia was organized. It didn't work. When the quartet came within range of Greene's guns, they were met with such a rain of fire that they had no choice but to round to and return to Greenville.

Employing an enhanced version of the combination he had used to convoy the *Longworth*, though with three protective craft instead of two, Currie undertook to get the *Rocket* up the river on the last day of the month. The Federal craft navigated safely past Columbia as, once again, Col. Greene had moved, this time to Smith's Plantation, just above Sunnyside.[21]

Leaving only a few men to harass Currie and Thomas, Col. Greene now laid into the 200-ton Wheeling, WV-built stern-wheeler *Clara Eames*.[22] His cannoneers quickly cut the cotton boat's escape pipe and penetrated her boiler, sending up hot steam. Signaling her distress, the *Eames* put into the bank and surrendered. "She was loaded with cotton," the colonel later wrote, and she was stripped of everything valuable. Three men were killed and one wounded on the boat; the 15 surviving Caucasian and seven African-American crew members were taken prisoner.

From the *Eames'* captain, the Confederate leader learned that Union Maj. Gen. A.J. Smith was assembling a force at Vicksburg to come after him. It was uncertain when his fleet of transports would weigh anchor. Believing the local MMB enemy en route to attack, Greene ordered his prize burnt to the water's edge.[23]

That night the steamer *Pauline Carroll*[24] was attacked. Although one wheel was disabled, she escaped, largely because of a Confederate shell shortage. After several days of assaults, the Confederates had only 12 rifle shells, 6 roundshot, and 30 howitzers shells left. Simultaneously, the Southerners found themselves facing an "ironclad" that came up and shelled their positions for some time. The Rebel batteries did not reply; however, sharpshooters plinked at her from long range.

At this time, Greene was reinforced with four more cannon from Hughey's Missouri Battery. Col. Lawther was left at Smith's Plantation with instructions to fire on anything coming his way, while the commander, together with Pratt's Battery, transferred back to Columbia.[25]

Leaving Col. Lawther above, Col. Greene and his men reached Columbia by dawn, June 1. As previously, the battery was divided into two sections, dug in about 200 yards apart on and behind the levee. The upper section contained one-each 18-pound rifle, 12-pound rifle, and 6-pounder fieldpiece, while the lower section held six guns: three 12-pound smoothbores, two 12-pounder rifles, and a 10-pounder rifle. All was in readiness when another of Lt. Cmdr. Owen's light-draughts, the *Exchange*, steamed into the trap.

The gunboat, on the lookout but completely unaware of the enemy disposition, was allowed to pass the lower battery unmolested. As the Southern gunners silently watched, the *Exchange* steamed slowly around the point of a sand bar abreast the village. Once she was past (and therefore unable to back down), Hughey and Pratt opened a destructive cross fire. With shells splashing all around, the tinclad's captain, Acting Master James C. Gipson,[26] seeing that he had no alternative but to press on, ordered his pilot to proceed upriver past the upper battery at flank speed. As the paddle wheel increased revolutions at the rear of the boat, the port broadside guns returned fire.

The *Exchange* did not make it very far upstream before one of the Confederate shells disabled the port engine. With only one engine available, the speed of the light-draught was reduced to a crawl and she suffered badly during the 45 minutes it took her to work her way out of range. During the fight, Gipson's command was pierced by 35 shots. Of that number, eight smashed into the hull above the waterline and five pierced the casemate, exploding in the coal bunkers abreast the boilers. Another entered the port shell locker; it did not find a percussion shell and there was no burst. Yet another round sailed through the pilothouse, knocking Gipson cold for 10 to 15 minutes and leaving him wounded in his head, leg, and shoulder. One bluejacket was killed and two wounded.

Once the *Exchange* was out of range, her port hogchain, hit during the passage, gave way, causing the remaining engine to stop cold with a ruined pitman. The gunboat was immovable and an easy target for Confederate gunners if they followed her upstream. The tinclad anchored and emergency repairs were made, while every man aboard anxiously prayed that the Rebels would not move their battery above and resume the contest. Within a short time, one engine sputtered back to life and the *Exchange* was able to limp off, making it to the east bank where she remained until she could be towed off.

Satisfied that the *Exchange* was "badly disabled in her hull and boilers," Greene made no effort to pursue her, being content to remain where he was in wait for additional targets. No other boats appeared, however, in the river under his guns that Wednesday.

Rear Adm. Porter later paid tribute to the thrice-wounded Gipson. His gallant action was seen as redemption for the *Petrel*'s loss, a stain on the reputation of the Mississippi Squadron. The action of the *Exchange*'s skipper was held up as an example of "how a cool and brave commander can get out of difficulty if he is determined to do so."

The success of Greene's gunners in combating the lightly armored tinclads was remarked upon by Shelby's adjutant, John Edwards, in his postwar history. There he claimed that the attacks on the *Curlew*, *Romeo*, and *Exchange*:

> ...utterly destroyed the prestige and name of terror of these boats with the soldiery; indeed, so little did they come to care for them, that while the batteries were engaged, the soldiers not on duty did not interrupt their games of cards, or other amusement of the moment, though sharply exposed to their fire.

It is quite probable that news of the Louisiana-Arkansas anti-tinclad triumphs enjoyed by the Confederates in May and June was picked up by other Southern military leaders in the West, most especially Nathan Bedford Forrest. The destruction of the *Covington* and *Signal* in the Red River was widely known and it was acknowledged, even in Northern newspapers, that, as a result of these successes, the Confederates of the region "have become emboldened and have less fear of the navy than formerly."[27]

Col. Greene, though low on ammunition, maintained his blockade. With 10 to 14 guns now available, he was able to split and rest his forces, alternating one battery and a covering regiment to the river each day. Additional exchanges occurred between the butternut cannoneers and the MMB, but by June 3, river traffic through the Greenville Bends had ceased. In a report to his superiors, the gallant horseman proudly announced that, for the loss of six men wounded, his little command had fought 21 Federal vessels, "of which 5 gunboats and marine boats were disabled, 5 transports badly damaged, 1 sunk, 2 burned, and 2 captured."

As might be expected, those on the receiving end of Col. Greene's largess greatly overestimated the forces they faced. MMB, U.S. Army, and Mississippi Squadron officers all believed themselves engaged against 5,000 to 10,000 men with upwards of 40 guns. It would take a large force, they reasoned, to break the stranglehold. So it was that two divisions of Red River veterans from Maj. Gen. A.J. Smith's XVI Corps, then at Vicksburg preparing to voyage to Memphis for reintegration into the Army of the Tennessee, were ordered to make a detour. Working with the MMB, it became their job to "clean out the rebels" in Chicot County or otherwise halt their antishipping war by giving them "such a lesson as will deter them from a renewal of similar attempts."

Smith's people and the MMB arrived at Sunnyside Landing on the evening of June 5. When the men were ashore, they marched in the rain next day in overwhelming numbers against Col. Greene's few, but prepared men. The Battle of Ditch Bayou resulted in a Confederate withdrawal.

As soon as the little campaign was completed, the bluecoats reboarded their transports and departed up the river. The Southerners also rode out of Chicot County, headed for the Arkansas and White River regions. As the emphasis of our story shifts elsewhere, we note that the commerce of the Mississippi was resumed and, with a few exceptions, it was not troubled by further organized regular army antishipping campaigns.[28]

10

Long, Hot Summer, 1864

The activities of the various Confederate cavalrymen riding through Arkansas in the summer of 1864 did not occur without some rumor or intelligence concerning them reaching Federal ears. As was the case with Brig. Gen. John S. Marmaduke and Col. Colton Greene, this was true of those mounted by the well-known Brig. Gen. Joseph O. ("Jo") Shelby. While on a reconnaissance up the White River to DeVall's Bluff, Federal naval forces learned that the last-named Rebel horseman was nearby, but so far all was quiet as Shelby was engaged in a recruitment campaign.

Despite a modicum of momentary confidence, Lt. Cmdr. S. Ledyard Phelps, commander of the Mississippi Squadron's Fifth District, still took precautions to protect river shipping and local bases or communities. The *Queen City, Naumkeag,* and *Fawn*[1] were spaced out between Clarendon and St. Charles, while the old timberclad *Tyler* was tasked to directly protect the former town. And then these preparations were knocked into a cocked hat.

Supplies for Maj. Gen. Frederic Steele's Little Rock garrison were usually taken up the White River to DeVall's Bluff, 30 miles below the state capital, and then transferred for shipment by the Little Rock and DeVall's Bluff Railroad. Soldiers often came in overland, but occasionally by steamboat. The U.S. Quartermaster Department was always quite insistent about running supply convoys up the chalk-colored White or its sister stream, the Arkansas, and required naval protection. Sometimes local area commanders suddenly demanded escort for waterborne troop movements.

When the sectional Federal naval leaders protested the danger, there was usually a gnashing of teeth and barrages of complaint from the logisticians or thoughtless generals. Added to the difficulty was the fact that the local Mississippi Squadron district commanders, whether on the White, or Arkansas, or Tennessee, or Cumberland, were not always informed of steamer movements. Just such an occurrence took place at the mouth of the White on the evening of June 18. Both Lt. Cmdr. Phelps and his White River deputy, Lt. George Bache,[2] were dumbfounded when, toward dusk, a convoy of nine troop transports emerged from the White River to go up the rising Arkansas. Maj. Gen. Steele wished to move some of his men around to Little Rock from DeVall's Bluff and believed the trips would not be overly difficult to make.

Welcomed aboard the Fifth District flag boat *Hastings,* Col. William P. Fenn informed the two naval officers that he was charged with getting his men and supplies upstream to Little Rock and beyond to Fort Smith while the river was in good stage and rising. He then handed over dispatches from Steele and Maj. Gen. William Rosecrans, the St. Louis commander, indicating that large risks should be mounted to get the personnel through. On top of these, he produced an order from Rear Adm. Porter authorizing the provision of convoy if the water stage made it prudent.

Lt. Cmdr. Phelps found himself in a box. Wanting to make certain that the rivers were covered against Confederate brigadiers Shelby and Marmaduke, plus Col. Greene, he had nevertheless to provide escort. After conferring with Bache, Phelps informed Fenn that he would send along an escort from the mouth of the Arkansas up the most dangerous 25 miles to South Bend, but that only one small gunboat would ascend beyond that point. And, of course, if Bache learned that the enemy was blockading the river, he was authorized to turn the combined fleet back immediately.[3]

After ferrying the Cache River and wading the mires of Bayou de Vue, Brig. Gen. Shelby paused on June 20 to review his options. DeVall's Bluff, he knew, was the closest point to Little Rock on the White River and its railroad to the capital was the only train system then working in Arkansas. The Federal logistical hub at the Bluff was fortified, contained a good-sized garrison, and was constantly watched by gunboats. Attacking it directly would be difficult.

On the other hand, this heart in the Union supply chain could be killed if the vital watery artery to it could be cut below. It was obvious from the map that the *point d'ap-pui* should be the town of Clarendon, 14 miles downstream. Easy to reach or escape from, the largely deserted community offered a good position at which to plant cannon and blockade movement up or down the river.

Shelby led his regiments toward Clarendon next day. The trek was hard. It rained incessantly, resulting in swift streams without bridges, roads without bottoms, and endless swamps and muck.

Also on the afternoon of June 21, Col. Robert R. Lawther's 10th Missouri Cavalry (CSA) launched a visit to White River Station, where the just-completed stockade was manned by a small 50-man garrison from the 12th Iowa Infantry. Leaving their horses on the opposite side of the Arkansas River, 300 Rebels crossed the stream in small boats or skiffs and marched all night to the outskirts of the National camp, which they charged just after sunup. Musket volleys from the bluecoats and shrapnel from the *Lexington* caused Lawther to retire.

After service aboard the ironclad *Cincinnati* at Vicksburg and in the Red River expedition of 1864, Washingtonian George Bache (1840–1896), son of a naval hero, implemented the Federal convoy system on the White River. It was Bache's task group that attempted to rescue the tinclad *Queen City* and battled the forces of Brig. Gen. Joseph O. "Jo" Shelby at Clarendon in June (Porter, *The Naval History of the Civil War*).

A few days later, the Memphis newspapers, in a report republished by the *New York Times*, briefly noted that 600 of Marmaduke's marauders attacked the two Iowa companies and were repulsed after severe fighting. Not knowing that the assault was part of a larger Confederate antilogistics operation, the newspapers opined that "the removal of the gunboat *Tyler* from that station probably emboldened the rebels." Continuing, they noted that, "but for the fortunate arrival of the gunboat *Lexington*, the result might have been unfavorable to us."[4]

While Brig. Gen. Shelby was en route toward Clarendon and the *Lexington* was safeguarding White River Station, Lt. Bache ascended the Arkansas with his convoy. At Red Fork Landing, he found Col. Greene's batteries blocking the river. He and his superior, Maj. Gen. Marmaduke, were preparing to cross the stream and threaten St. Charles. In accordance with his orders, Bache turned back. The nine troop steamers were then escorted to DeVall's Bluff, where the men could be unloaded and sent to Little Rock by train.

Maj. Gen. Steele happened to be at the Bluff when Bache's vessels arrived on June 23 and angrily confronted the sailor as to why they had not gone up the Arkansas River as he wanted. When the *Tyler*'s commander explained that it was blocked by Rebel cannon, Steele refused to believe him and indicated his desire that the boats be turned around and sent back down the White and up the Arkansas to Lit-

While Col. Colton Greene entertained Federal tinclads on the Mississippi during May–June 1864, Brig. Gen. Joseph O. "Jo" Shelby concentrated inland. Like Maj. Gen. Nathan Bedford Forrest, Shelby believed that Federal control of Arkansas could be significantly hampered if he could interdict Union convoys on the White River. In late June, he personally led a force to Clarendon and sank the tinclad *Queen City*. Within hours, he fought and withdrew from a tinclad counterattack led by Lt. George M. Bache (U.S. Army Military History Institute).

tle Rock. Of course, Steele added the matter at that point was left to Bache's judgment.

In reporting this interview, Lt. Bache, perhaps having heard of similar charges of non-support leveled earlier by the Army against Lt. Cmdr. Le Roy Fitch over on the Cumberland, noted he would fulfill the general's wish and return as suggested. "Not wishing that the army should think us backward in cooperation," he indicated, "I determined to shove them there as far as the gunboats could go and let them trust to luck afterwards!"

While Shelby's cavalry and horse artillery rested near Clarendon on that sultry Thursday afternoon, an advance party of scouts went forward to reconnoiter. Carefully, the men examined the town and the nearby woods, finding them nearly devoid of activity. The river was a different matter; about 170 feet (10 rods) from the wharf lay the wooden paddle-wheeler *Queen City*, "dark sentinel of the place."

Advised of the situation ahead, Brig. Gen. Shelby ordered his advance riders to throw a cordon around the town. To maintain secrecy, anyone entering or attempting to leave was to be arrested. By dark, the remainder of the command was quietly stationed within the community and in the trees along the river bank within 100 yards of the gunboat. Just before his craft buttoned up for the night, the gunboat's captain, Acting Volunteer Lt. Michael Hickey,[5] sent a reconnaissance through the streets of Clarendon. The check was thorough and just missed Shelby's advanced shirmishers. who were able to duck out of the way while maintaining their vigil.

Plans made earlier to surprise the *Queen City* at dawn and capture or destroy her progressed to the next stage. Just after midnight, while the unmounted horsemen rested beneath the gigantic cottonwoods, the four-gun Missouri Battery of Capt. Dick Collins drew up to Clarendon's outskirts on its main road. At a point out of earshot of the water, the guns were unlimbered and their horses led away. Then, aided by the sweat of a hundred soldiers, the cannon were stealthily and noiselessly dragged by hand to within 50 feet of the river's edge. Once the guns were in position, "crouching and clinging to the shadows of the houses," the troopers also advanced to the shore of the White. "Silence, like a tired queen, brooded in the whisperings of the leaves." The "thug-like" warriors watched ahead, some with "suppressed breathings."

Personally curious, Shelby himself went up close to the tinclad to check its state of preparedness. It seemed ready, with steam up and its guns loaded. Right after the war, Shelby's friend and adjutant John Edwards painted the picture:

> A low, large moon, lifting a realm of romance out of the waves, lit up the scene with a weird light, and crested the "stars and stripes" that flapped in melancholy motion against the painted gaff.... The drowsy sentinel paced his narrow beat.... Somber as an iron island, with all her red lights in gloom, and the deep peal of her time-bell sounding solumn and chill, the doomed craft sat upon the water unconscious of the coming daylight.

The nights were shorter now as the earth approached its summer solstice, but still the hours after midnight passed slowly for the sleep-deprived Southerners. There were no clouds and the only sounds that could be heard were the waves in the river as they "sobbed on the beach, and curled and sparkled in sheer wantonness around the iron beak of the river falcon."

At approximately 4 A.M., "little shreds of daylight" poking up in the east, Brig. Gen. Shelby ordered his men to open fire on the *Queen City*, while at the same time, in his words, he "notified her commander of my approach and intentions." Caught in as complete a surprise as any in U.S. naval history, the tinclad was immediately subjected to a heavy barrage of musketry from two regiments and shells from 10-pounder Parrott rifles and 12-pounder smoothbores. The first or second round from Collins's guns smashed into the *Queen City*'s starboard engine. A piece of it flew on into the steam pipe of the starboard power plant, which fortunately did not burst. The one-sided contest continued for about 15 minutes during which, a Memphis newspaper later stated, the gunboat was struck 45 times by artillery shots "and her pilot house was completely torn away."

Originally a ferry, the tinclad *Queen City* was disabled during a night attack by troops of Brig. Gen. Joseph O. "Jo" Shelby at Clarkendon, Arkansas on June 24, 1864, and captured. She would be blown up before a U.S. Navy rescue force could reach and save her. This remarkable photograph is better than most in providing the reader with a sense of size perspective; note the men on the decks and the cannon protruding from the casemate (Naval Historical Center).

As the ship was riddled with cannon shell and rifle bullets, the able men in his crew (Shelby's count was 65, but it was far fewer) were advised by their captain that they could also give up or dive overboard and swim to the freedom of the opposite bank. The ethnic makeup of the crew is not certain, but it was not the band of "devil-may-care Irishmen" John Edwards later reported. There were many African-Americans and the fate of any of those tars who gave up was very uncertain. Rumor had it that Shelby routinely ordered such prisoners shot.

The *St. Louis Daily Missouri Democrat's* July 2 coverage indicates that the *Queen City* attempted to drop down with the current to get a range for his cannon. This was a goal she was unable to accomplish. It was not long into the fight before Acting Volunteer Lt. Hickey knew that he would have to surrender. Writing about the white flag years later, Rear Adm. Porter was contemptuous of Hickey for "not having the bravery to fight it out as many of his contemporaries would have done."

With one seaman dead in the fight and nine wounded, Hickey signaled his surrender and Shelby's men stopped shooting. The wreck of the heavily perforated tinclad was pulled to shore, where Hickey was taken prisoner, along with four officers, 20 seamen (four wounded), and eight African-American contrabands. The latter, reported the *Chicago Daily Tribune* on Independence Day, "were immediately put to death." The remainder of the crew had escaped to the opposite shore, though one white crewman and one African-

American were drowned. As late as July 12, the *Memphis Argus* would report that 23 men got away and 11 were killed or remained missing.

While the crewmen were interrogated and the officers paroled preparatory to their release to Helena authorities, Confederate horsemen ran aboard and ransacked the gunboat. Immediate prizes included in excess of $10,000 just drawn by the paymaster a few days earlier, the paymaster's stores, wearing apparel, small arms, most of the ammunition, and a brass 12-pounder wheeled boat howitzer. Fearing that there were other gunboats in the vicinity that could arrive before he was finished, Shelby canceled plans to unship the 24-pounders and a 32-pounder and use them in a formidable blockading battery ashore.

Within a half an hour of the time Shelby's gunners opened fire on the *Queen City*, the nine-boat troop convoy of Federal supply steamers departed DeVall's Bluff for Clarendon under escort of Lt. Bache's gunboats. Puffing slowly ahead in standard escort formation with the *Fawn* in the lead, the *Naumkeag* in the center, and the *Tyler* at the rear, the fleet paddled along peacefully for almost 30 miles.

As daylight intensified, the leading steamer was hailed from the western shore by two officers, a powder monkey, and five African-American "contrabands" who had escaped the *Queen City*. Putting in, the transport picked up the men and took them out to the *Fawn*, where they told their story to Acting Master John R. Grace. Signaling the following vessels to pause, Grace came to and awaited the arrival of *Naumkeag* and *Tyler*, which sped ahead to learn what was holding up the procession. Following the 9 A.M. rendezvous of the three guardians, now less than 10 miles from Clarendon, Grace gave Bache and Acting Master John Rogers[6] the news that the *Queen City* was captured and that Shelby occupied the town with 2,700 men.

Decisive ever since his days aboard the *Cincinnati*, the intrepid Bache immediately ordered the merchantmen back to DeVall's Bluff to escape possible entrapment and to let the U.S. Army know what was happening. Realizing that it was only five hours since the *Queen City* was seized, the officer knew that Shelby could not have already gotten much out of her, particularly her cannon. On the other hand, it was possible that she could be manned by butternut artillerymen and employed, in conjunction with the Rebel guns on the bank, against him or any force Lt. Cmdr. Phelps might send from the mouth of the river.

Bache, fresh from combat against shore-based cannon on the Red River just over a month earlier, was determined that Shelby and his cavalrymen would face the wrath of his big guns just as butternut riders had earlier. Thus it was that he ordered his fellow officers to form their gunboats into line of battle, *Tyler*, *Naumkeag*, and *Fawn*. There would be action this day as Confederate horsemen, like those at Blair's Landing, were engaged by the aggressive gunboatman.

While the Federals assessed the situation upstream, Brig. Gen. Shelby made his own preparations for the fight all in his command knew to be coming. The pieces of Collins's battery were dispersed to prevent them from taking massed naval fire, while the remainder of the brigade deployed as skirmishers, lining the bank in front of the town and down around a bend and on both sides of its wharf. Knowing that he could get no more out of the captured tinclad before the Yankee rivercraft arrived, Shelby ordered her destroyed.

Captured on the White River in December 1863 and converted, the tinclad *Fawn* was a stalwart defender of Federal convoys attempting to make use of that Arkansas stream in 1864. In June, she formed, with *Naumkeag* and *Tyler*, a relief force sent to retrieve the tinclad *Queen City*, captured by Confederate Brig. Gen. Joseph O. "Jo" Shelby at Clarendon. Although the mission was unsuccessful, the *Fawn* and her consorts battled Shelby's troops over the next several days, preventing them from establishing a blockade that could have strangled Little Rock (Naval Historical Center).

When within a few miles of Clarendon, Lt. Bache and his crews heard two successive reports, which they later learned were the sounds of the *Queen City* blowing up.

John Edwards, in his colorful account of the Clarendon skirmish, makes it perfectly clear that the Confederates knew that Bache was coming long before he arrived. For over an hour, they could hear the whistles of the leading vessel. As the morning grew warmer, "louder and louder sounded the dull puffing of the advancing boats." It was understood, from their whistles, that the Union boats were being kept close up and in good order. How many there were was unknown. Was there a transport fleet or just warships? In addition, Shelby did not know if his enemy would attempt to run by or whether they would actually engage.

Great clouds of smoke, heavy and dark in the light blue of the morning sky, could be seen up the river by the Confederates just before and certainly after their enemy advanced to a spot a little over a mile away. Soon, the first pitch-black object, not quite distinguishable to those without field glasses, loomed into sight, followed by several more. Banners streamed out in the wind from their tall vertical staffs that looked for all the world like flagpoles. "The leading boat, gigantic and desperate, forged slowly ahead," wrote Edwards, "every port closed, and a stern defiance on her iron crest." This was the *Tyler,* "scarred and rent in previous fights, but wary and defiant still."

As the timberclad and her tinclad consorts ("a noble trio," according to the *Daily Missouri Democrat*) came abreast of the Cache River at 9:45 A.M., Brig. Gen. Shelby gave the order to his artillery chief to open fire on the leading gunboat. Collins's men were good; Bache later reported that one of their "first shots went through the pilot house."

"A white puff of smoke burst suddenly from the bow of the *Tyler*," Edwards relates, "and curled gracefully in thin wreaths far astern." A large shell then "passed overhead with a noise like an express train and burst in the river half a mile away." Even though the approaching timberclad could initially reply to Shelby's overtures only with a bow Parrott, the ball was truly opened as the *Fawn* and *Naumkeag* also joined in with their forward guns.

The three Federal gunboats paddled defiantly toward the Confederate guns, coming within an easier range. "With a bravery worthy of a better cause," said a St. Louis scribe, "the rebel general with his men worked their batteries."

Early in the engagement, shrapnel from a 12-pounder flew through the port shutter of the *Fawn*'s pilothouse, mortally wounding her pilot and carrying away the bell system. This rang the bells and the engineers thought they were to stop the boat, which they did — directly under the Rebel guns. At least 10 shells or heavy pieces of shrapnel found the little tinclad, to say nothing of musket balls. She was fortunate to escape, but could offer little more immediate aid to her consorts.

In the meantime, the *Tyler*, followed by the *Naumkeag*, steamed slowly past the batteries, pumping out broadside after broadside of one-half second shrapnel and canister. When she came abreast of the town wharf, Shelby, who was riding between pieces encouraging his gunners, was heard to shout: "Concentrate fire of every gun on the *Tyler*."

To some it appeared that the big dark craft now "staggered over the water like a drunken man." The defiant old timberclad and the *Naumkeag* continued through the fiery gauntlet and after they passed by it, a number of Confederates thought that the two would continue on down the river toward its mouth. Thus it was they were amazed when both craft rounded to and steamed up at them again. Bache was later told that "the rebels now exclaimed in despair, 'There comes that black devil again!'"

The ship vs. shore contest had now eaten a half hour, with, according to Brig. Gen. Shelby, his men on open ground "and not 60 yards from the boats." The masked batteries ashore dished out considerable punishment, but the gunboats scored as well. The *Queen City*'s captured howitzer, for example, manned by Rebel crew near the bank, was only able to get off a couple of shots before gunboat shooting drove everyone from it.

Moving ahead, the *Naumkeag* and *Tyler* were joined by the *Fawn*, now restored and steaming above the wharf. Together, the three boats captured Shelby in a cross fire. The *Tyler*, of course, being the largest vessel with the biggest guns, remained the center of butternut concern, even as the tinclads poured in their own enfilading fire of grape and canister.

"Full broadside to the wharf she [*Tyler*] stood sullenly at bay, giving shot for shot and taking her punishment like a glutton." Edwards suggests that one two-gun battery was destroyed in a cloud of dust and smoke by one of her broadsides that sounded "like the rush of 500 steeds in motion."

As 10:30 A.M. approached, Lt. Bache, from his position aboard the *Tyler*, her head pointed upstream and her guns continuing to blaze, thought he discerned some of the briskness pass out of the Rebel fire. "The result was the usual one between field batteries and gunboats," opined Duane Huddleston and his colleagues over a century later. Bache was probably not surprised at this. The Red River veteran found that the pace of shooting by his own command had thus far been "terrific; the trees on shore for the space of a mile" were marked by its projectiles, "and that low down."

Caught in a gunboat trap, Jo Shelby threw in the towel and ordered his men to withdraw to their "former camp, some two miles from town." Watching from his pilothouse, Lt. Bache "had the pleasure of seeing them skedaddling from the field." Clarendon was back in Union hands. Under protection of the *Tyer*'s big guns, a landing party from the *Naumkeag*, led by Acting Master Rogers, went ashore to assess.

During their exit from the scene, the butternut troopers abandoned nearly everything they took within 300 yards of the river bank. The *Queen City*'s wheeled boat howitzer, somewhat the worse for battle, was recovered, along with a significant quantity of ammunition, her cutter and four oars, and an anchor. Five crewmen (two badly wounded) from the sunken tinclad were rescued, while several wounded Confederates, left behind, were also saved.

Parts of the wreck of the *Queen City* herself could be seen in the water about a mile below the town. She was completely burned out and her casemates had tumbled in. A portion of the afternoon was spent by men from the Union vessels in attempting to salvage her some of her guns.

During the afternoon, the *Fawn* and the *Naumkeag* patrolled up and down the river for a mile or two, occasionally being subjected to musketry. Every time they were shot at, they replied "with one-half second shrapnel." Meanwhile, aboard the *Tyler*, the task group commander wrote out a report on damage and casualties. The Confederates liked to believe that the *Tyler* was hard hit and "bled fearfully with half her crew dead." In fact, even though she was hit 11 times, the old gunboat stood up fairly well. It was later pointed out that an extra 24 inches of protective iron recently installed around her boilers were instrumental in her protection.

The tinclads, on the other hand, lived up to their own reputations as death traps, an unenviable status earned by their class over a few weeks. Not meant to stand against land batteries, they were hurt. It was fortunate for them, as well as the *Tyler*, that Brig. Gen. Shelby had located his guns on nearly level banks. The three vessels had not been faced with the effects of plunging shot, as, for example, the *Cricket* was on Red River. Still, the *Naumkeag* was hit at least twice, but suffered more serious damage from the concussion of her guns, which caused her to leak and the eyebolts of the casemates to break. Acting Master's Mate John Dunlap, who took himself off the sick list to lead his division, was mortally wounded. The engine room of this vessel was also protected by 24 inches of extra iron, a defensive move later praised. The *Fawn* suffered 10 hits during the battle. In addition to the loss of Pilot Thomas Barnett, 10 other crewmen were casualties, including her acting surgeon.

Bivouacked on the other side of the community, Brig. Gen. Shelby, anticipating that the gunboats would be gone, plotted his Clarendon return next day. If he could throw up somewhat better temporary earthworks and hold the spot for 10 days, he would duplicate Greene's achievement out on the Mississippi and seriously disrupt the Union's White River navigation.

Unfortunately for the Rebel brigadier, the gunboats did not all leave. The *Naumkeag* and *Fawn*, under command of Acting Master Rogers, remained off the town to prevent any further mischief while the *Tyler*, with the wounded and shipless aboard, steamed back up to DeVall's Bluff. Bache hoped to personally persuade Maj. Gen. Steele to send a force to "capture the guerrillas." It did not take much effort for the *Tyler*'s commander to convince Steele that an expedition should return to Clarendon right away. The next morning, June 25, a troop of cavalry boarded two transports and prepared to depart downstream under escort of the timberclad.

While the Federal horsemen were being shipped at the Bluff, Brig. Gen. Shelby went ahead and made his effort to return to Clarendon and throw up some earthworks or rifle pits. Patrolling the river, the *Naumkeag* and *Fawn* rounded a point and discovered the Confederates at work digging. Puffing into easy range, they fired over 50 shells at the butternuts, who retired into some woods.

The little Northern cavalry armada pushed off at 2 P.M., but was unable to proceed more than 10 or 15 miles before an accident halted progress. The three boats lay to as repairs were made and finally reached Clarendon on Sunday morning. With the Southern cavalryman gone for the moment, all returned to DeVall's Bluff on the evening of June 28.

Rebel attacks on transport steamers passing up and down the White and Arkansas continued as Marmaduke and Greene joined Shelby in haunting their banks. On June 30, Rear Adm. Porter ordered Lt. Cmdr. Phelps to remove his gunboats from the latter; otherwise, "we will lose them all." Efforts would be concentrated on the White; several ironclads and the tinclad *Silver Cloud* were dispatched as reinforcements, though the use of the former was hampered by falling water.[7]

While the several gunboats of the Union Navy were occupied in the White and Arkansas River areas, horsemen of the Western Confederacy also paid attention to their colleagues on the Mississippi. Employing what was believed to be artillery captured from Northern forces on the Red River and elsewhere, these troops harassed shipping in that stretch of the river between Natchez and Port Hudson.

On Thursday morning, June 13, Col. John S. Scott of the 1st Louisiana Cavalry, commander of the District of Southwest Mississippi and Eastern Louisiana, led two regiments and five field guns to Tunica on the Mississippi at the request of the accompanying Maj. Gen. Simon Bolivar Buckner. The following day, as Buckner reviewed the area as a potential crossing point for Trans-Mississippi theater troops ordered east, Scott placed two 12-pounder howitzers and a 3-inch rifle at Ratliff's Landing. The battery was separated as two 3.67-inch rifled Sawyer guns were unlimbered at Como Landing, 3 miles above at the northern end of the bend. On the evening of June 15, the patrolling Federal gunboat *General Bragg* anchored off the upper landing.

At about 1:45 A.M. on Sunday morning, Scott's Sawyers took the *General Bragg* under fire. Aboard the gunboat, the crew was beat to quarters and the boat quickly slipped her cable, backing out slowly. The gunboat had been lying close enough to the bank for Scott's sharpshooters to have a significant impact. Musket and rifle volleys swept her decks and initially kept gunners away from their ordnance.

When the engagement was some five minutes old, a Rebel shot smashed into the walking beam, completely disabling the *Bragg*'s engine. The gunboat began to drift downstream, with her guns continuing in action. Before this, Confederate cannoneers hit her 22 times, riddling the officers' quarters and cabin and the berth deck. Although the boat was badly cut up, only one sailor was wounded. In his after-action report, Col. Scott claimed 32 of his 42 rounds struck the gunboat and that she "succeeded in firing but 3 shots."

As cannon muzzles flashed and thundered in the dark, the steamer *Joseph Pierce*,[8] whom Col. Scott identified as the *Landis*, approached from the north. Unable to round to in the dark, the captain of the civilian steamer elected to continue on. When nearly upon the battle, the officers of the *Pierce* actually saw six bolts strike the *General Bragg*; later, they remembered hearing the report of 18 shots fired. The *Pierce*, uncertain of what action to take, steered close to the now-drifting gunboat before continuing down the river.

As the *Joseph Pierce* exited the scene, a Confederate shell screamed overhead and splashed into the dark waters off her port bow. A number of terrified women passengers on board now panicked completely and began running and shrieking up and down the decks. Male passengers, including A. A. Stone, the principal witness interviewed in the *New York Times* story we quote, soon "succeeded in restoring confidence and order," as that newspaper put it. All praised pilot Thomas Montague for his coolness in getting the steamer out of danger.

Coming up the river about 3:45 A.M., the tinclad *Naiad*[9] saw the stricken *General Bragg* near Ratliff's Landing where, simultaneously, Col. Scott was now shifting his Sawyer guns. As the first streaks of daylight pierced the eastern sky, the Confederate bombardment, from masked guns somewhere on and behind the left bank levee, was resumed. Musket balls also rained down.

Shortly into the renewed fight, bells rang in the engine room of the light-draught and steam was increased, allowing her to run up to the *Bragg*'s assistance. When the *Naiad* reached a point about a half mile from where the damaged Union gunboat lay, Scott's gunners shifted their fire to her. Immediately the *Naiad*'s starboard chimney was crumpled by a shot and two rounds went through the pilothouse, destroying the barrel of the steering wheel and hence the steering gear. A fourth ball passed abaft the pilothouse, damaging the steerage and skylights. When the wheel was shot away, First Class Pilot James M. Harrington was badly wounded.

The little warboat, steering by relieving tackle, was able to get bows on to the Rebel battery and commence a brisk fire, even while being pounded. The fifth time the graycoats found the range, their bolt passed through her cabin. Four more rounds ploughed through the casemate, killing one man and wounding three others. Among these were shots that ruined the armory and dispensary on the gun deck.

While Col. Scott concentrated his fire on the *Naiad*, the *General Bragg* struggled to aid her consort and was once again subjected to intense Confederate bombardment. This time, her gunners were able to expend a significant number of shells from their Parrotts. Also, and very fortunately, the brand-new double-turreted monitor *Winnebago*,[10] soon to join the West Gulf Coast Blockading Squadron (WGCBS) and participate in the Battle of Mobile Bay, also hove into sight and brought her giant 11-inch guns into action.

The morning engagement lasted about three hours, during which time the *Winnebago* towed the *Bragg* to safety. Nearly out of ammunition, Col. Scott threw in the towel and moved his guns down to Magnolia Landing, about seven miles above Port Hudson. The stricken *Naiad*, which had, nevertheless, managed to get off 37 shots, was beached on Cat Island Bar, near the head of Tunica Island, until she could be towed to New Orleans for repairs.

Soon after Col. Scott's horsemen reached Magnolia Landing, the *Joseph Pierce* was seen chugging down the river. Navigational requirements forced her to pass within 100 yards of shore, at which point the Southerners started shooting at her. Once more, the vessel was lucky. Because the friction primers of his guns chose this time to fail, Scott could only get off seven shots, all of which missed. The steamer's loud whistle shouted her distress. Within a short time, two gunboats from Bayou Sara, 3 miles above, arrived on the scene and escorted her out of danger.[11]

In the Confederate Trans-Mississippi department, much of July and August was taken up with preparations for an invasion of, or at the very least, a large cavalry raid into, Missouri. There, as in the North on the Ohio, Cumberland, and Tennessee, low water again impeded or made more dangerous river use by the Federals as logistical arteries. Still, the Confederate antishipping war continued whenever the opportunity presented itself.

On July 4, the *Fawn* and *Hastings* escorted eight steamers south from Devall's Bluff toward White River Station. At a point a little above St. Charles, the convoy was attacked by Confederate riflemen hiding in the woods along the bank no more than 25 yards from where the boats passed. These Southerners were very bad shots. Although a number of persons were exposed on the decks of the boats, not one was hit and the only damage was that done "to woodwork and furniture." Return fire from the tinclad howitzers dispersed the assault. "I had been at a loss to know how we should celebrate the Fourth," Lt. Cmdr. Phelps told Rear Adm. Porter. "But this attack occurring about noon," he continued, "furnished the opportunity of at once punishing the enemy and celebrating the day by firing cannon."

Also on Independence Day, the 193-ton *Mariner*, aground on the foot of St. Francis Island, on the Mississippi about 12 miles above Helena, AR, for several weeks and only lightly guarded, was attacked by a Rebel raiding party. The stern-wheeler was burned to the water's edge and declared a $19,500 loss.

Convoys protected by tinclads continued to operate up the White, even as irregulars persisted in gathering along the river to shoot at them. Passengers and crewmen interviewed by newspaper correspondents reported "the guerrillas in force and troublesome around St. Charles." The water was falling so rapidly that gunboats and transports were frequently aground.

Opposite: **On June 16, 1864, the tinclad *Naiad* (bottom) steamed to the rescue of the Federal gunboat *General Bragg* (top), then under fire from Confederate artillery at Como Landing, at the northern end of Tunica Bend on the Mississippi. Although badly pounded by the Rebel gunners, the light-draught returned effective fire and was herself rescued by both the *Bragg* and the passing monitor *Winnebago* (Naval Historical Center).**

On July 6, the unescorted steamer *Commercial*[13] weighed from White River Station for DeVall's Bluff. As she steamed slowly past Lambert's Landing, the side-wheeler was attacked by butternuts. Several volleys slammed into the vessel's upper works, wounding the second mate.

Near Indian Bay the next day, the steamer *Golden Era*,[14] convoyed by the *Hastings*, was assaulted. No major damages were incurred and the gunboat scattered the riflemen.

By this time, Maj. Gen. Steele was largely bottled up by Confederate riders, even as the river fell. These developments, highlighted by the Rebel reoccupation of Arkansas Post, required Lt. Cmdr. Phelps to make new dispositions between the mouth of the White and Clarendon. "We will patrol the river ... with tinclads," he informed Maj. Gen. Steele, "and let the transports pass back and forth without convoy."

On July 12, Col. G.W. Anderson at DeVall's Bluff inquired whether or not the Little Rock commander objected if he inaugurated the Phelps policy by sending the steamer *Commercial* out of the river without escort. Steele deferred to Acting Master Rogers of the *Fawn*, who granted permission, even though he shared the general's concern that "100 riflemen at St. Charles could do great damage to a transport without convoy."

Taking the Eads monitor *Neosho* as heavy cover, Lt. Commander Phelps undertook a significant convoy from White River Station to Clarendon and hence to Duvall's Bluff beginning on July 15. Light escort for the mission, concluded on July 22, was provided by the *Hastings* and Tinclad No. 57, the *Peri*,[15] newly arrived from the Fourth District.

Far to the north in the Tenth District of Porter's squadron, irregulars had, as in each of the war years so far, intensified their attacks upon river traffic and communities along the Ohio River. On July 21, Rebel insurgents attacked the town of Henderson, KY. That night, according to passengers reaching Louisville, the tinclad *Brilliant* shelled the woods at the lower end of the town, though no one knew for sure whether "the guerrillas are there or not."[16]

With Col. Greene off to the Arkansas River, U.S. Navy Lt. Cmdr. Robert Owen was able to report "everything quiet at this [Sixth] district; only a few guerrillas on both banks...." Those continued to annoy passing steamers, but did not great damage.

En route from Natchez on July 21 with nearly 600 souls aboard, including 440 from the 10th Missouri Cavalry (U.S.), the 1,300-ton side-wheeler *B. M. Runyon*[17] struck a snag in Walker Bend at the foot of Island No. 84, off Gaines Landing, 15 miles below Greenville. She had just reentered service that spring after having been sunk at Alton, IL, the previous December, raised and refurbished. The enlistments of many of the soldiers had expired and they were looking forward to mustering out at Cairo. The steamer sank rapidly to the hurricane roof in about five minutes and the estimates of life lost among the deck passengers (primarily soldiers and a few Union sympathizers) ran from about 50 to over 150. Some survivors swam to shore, while others struggled in the water. Some $200,000 worth of government property was also lost, including more than 100 horses and mules, 28 wagons, and all of the regiment's camp and garrison equipment.

The tinclad *Prairie Bird* happened to be on patrol in the vicinity and arrived on the scene about 20 minutes after the disaster. Her bluejackets were able to recover about 40 cabin passengers. The cabin of the sunken *Runyon* had meanwhile separated from the hull and drifted down the river, lodging on a sandbar in American Cutoff. A boat party from the *Prairie Bird* was sent to burn it so that it could be of no use to the Rebels. All of the survivors were taken to Greenville, where arrangements were made to send the civilians to Memphis aboard a commercial boat and the cavalrymen via a Mississippi Marine Brigade (MMB) transport.[18]

On July 23, the 139-foot-long side-wheeler *Clarabell*[19] departed Vicksburg for the White River transporting four companies of the Sixth Michigan Infantry. As she passed Ashton Landing, in Louisiana Bend, the next morning, the 350-ton transport was attacked by a masked Confederate battery, supported by upwards of 500 infantry. After a brief but sustained shoot by four fieldpieces, the Rebels believed they had captured another fine Federal vessel as she blew her whistle and sounded her bell as a token of surrender. The steamboat's crew discovered, however, that the assault was not as damaging as initially suspected. And so, even as grayclad soldiers prepared to shove off from shore in skiffs to board her, she started ahead once more.

As her wheels thrashed the muddy water and great clouds of smoke escaped from her chimneys, the dishonorable *Clarabell* was targeted by angry gunners and sharpshooters. Confusion reigned aboard the *Clarabell* as round shot and musket balls slammed into her sides. Soon she had taken three shots below the waterline and the river began to stream into her hold. Everyone aboard and not in command rushed to the starboard side and, consequently, the vessel started to careen and became increasingly unmanageable. Another round plus hundreds of Minieballs hit topside, wounding seven passengers.

Escaping out of range, the Federal boat came to on the bar off Caroline Landing to make repairs. As damage control parties descended into her hull, a message was sent across the six miles to Skipwith's Landing. Since it was clear that the enemy would limber up and cross the point to resume the attack either in the bend above or at Grand Lake, a gunboat was urgently requested. Having earlier heard the firing, the tinclad *Prairie Bird*, fresh from the *B.M. Runyon* disaster, now hove into sight. Unhappily, her howitzers were unable to influence the Southerners and she elected to return to base and send the more powerful ironclad *Louisville* in her place. Feverishly, the stranded *Clarabell's* crew worked to repair her damage.

Before Lt. Cmdr. Owen's flag boat could reach the scene, the Confederates, having moved guns to the bank opposite from where she was lying, struck again. Prior to resuming their shoot, butternut soldiers thrice came to the water's edge seeking to communicate. Three times the colonel commanding the Michigan troops refused to allow an exchange, sealing the boat's fate. Rebuffed, the Southerners once more opened fire, at about 4 P.M. This time the shells ploughed into every deck of the stationary vessel. One round burst in the texas, setting the boat afire. It was said the steamer was hit 30 times this day. Soon, the *Clarabell* was enveloped in flames. Although none of the crew was injured, thirteen Michigan soldiers were wounded, two fatally.

The *Louisville* came on the scene just after dark. By this time, the uninjured survivors had successfully abandoned ship and the *Clarabell* had burned to the water's edge. All of the regiment's military equipment was destroyed in the blaze. Together with the crew, the largely unarmed soldiers marched overland to Skipwith's. The wounded, left behind to await the gunboat, were taken aboard and also returned.

On Monday morning, the captain and mate of the *Clarabell*, together with a newspaper correspondent who happened to be aboard the steamer, were entertained at break-fast aboard the *Prairie Bird*. In mid-morning, they, together with the other crew members and soldiers, departed for Vicksburg aboard a southbound transport.[20]

Attention North and South was riveted on the Alabama Gulf coastal city of Mobile at the beginning of August 1864. Although the Union had decided months earlier that it posed a threat to the Georgia campaign of Maj. Gen. Sherman as well as providing a continuing haven for blockade runners, the intervening Red River campaign had forced a postponement in plans to act against it.

During this interim, a number of tinclads were, according to earlier plans reviewed in Chapter 3, transferred down the Mississippi from Cairo to New Orleans. There they were, as necessary, enhanced for salt water and assigned to patrol and escort duties as part of the WGCBS. The area around New Orleans, including Lake Pontchartrain and the Tchefuncta River, as well as other locations, were their usual beats. In addition to the *Wave* already mentioned, the *Stockdale*[21] and *Rodolph*[22] were active and deserve coverage.

In addition to a strong Confederate naval defense, built around the ram *Tennessee* and outside the scope of this account,[23] three forts guarded the entrance to Mobile Bay: Fort Gaines, on Dauphin Island; Fort Morgan, on Mobile Point; and Fort Powell, on Tower Island guarding the western approach to the Mississippi Sound. It is this latter bastion, located between Cedar Point and Dauphin Island, that attracts our attention.

In preparing for the offensive against Mobile and her defenses that they knew must be coming, the Confederates spent more time and resources on Forts Morgan and Gaines than upon Fort Powell. The big guns of the latter did, however, cover the Mississippi Sound entrance and channels. Even if its rear, facing Mobile Bay, was unfinished and unprotected, it still served to guard Grant's Pass, the deepest passage through the shoal water.

On July 23, the *Stockdale* found herself one of many vessels ordered to the Mississippi Sound to participate, directly or indirectly, in the impending Union attack on Mobile Bay. Upon her arrival, she was assigned to the Mississippi Sound Flotilla, which consisted of five gunboats under Lt. Cmdr. J.C.P. De Krafft, and herself, the only tinclad. According to plans drawn up by Rear Adm. David G. Farragut, when the fighting started, these vessels would assault Fort Powell.

Dropping anchor off Petit Bois Island on August 2, the *Stockdale* steamed up to Dauphin Island the following day. There she contributed all of her small boats to a combined pool employed in landing troops from Army transports. These soldiers were to invest Fort Gaines The small boat enterprise was continued on August 4.

The *Stockdale* was the only tinclad to participate in a large-scale fleet engagement during the Civil War. Neither she nor any of her sisters were around for the April 1862 Battle of New Orleans, the May Battle of Memphis, or the July encounter with the *Arkansas* off Vicksburg. All of the other ship-to-ship actions, save Mobile Bay and the attempt to sink the *Undine*, were in the East. Although her role was not large, it was sufficient to put her into the tinclad record book.

The grand naval advance was signaled at just after 5 A.M. on August 5. While the monitors and larger wooden warships in the battle line pushed their way past Fort Morgan and the small Confederate fleet, the six vessels of the Mississippi Sound Flotilla were

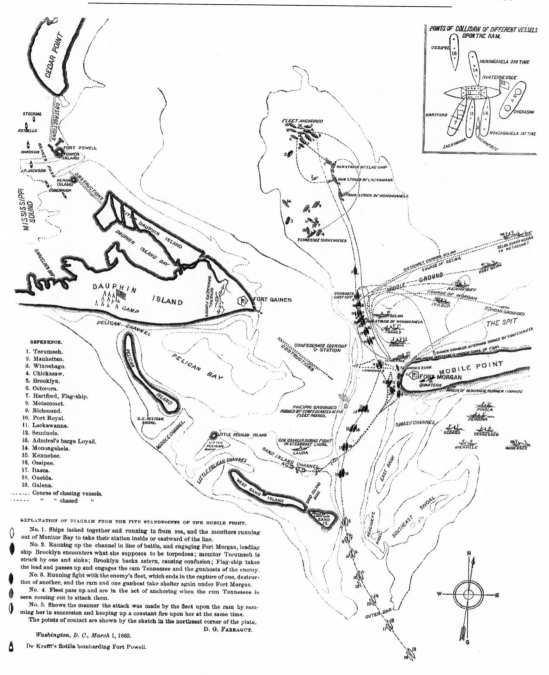

The tinclad *Stockdale* was the only vessel of her class to participate in the August 5, 1864, Battle of Mobile Bay. Together with the other gunboats from Lt. Cmdr. J.C.P. De Krafft's Mississippi Sound Flotilla, the light-draught assaulted Fort Powell in an effort to distract Confederate defenders while the main fleet under Rear Adm. David G. Farragut entered the bay (Naval Historical Center).

to provide assistance. The job of De Krafft's vessels was to offer fire support and distract the Confederate defenders by shelling the east face of Fort Powell while Farragut entered Mobile Bay. Elsewhere, another small flotilla would also harass the unfinished citadel, but from long range. Additionally, they were to challenge any unidentified ships coming near Fort Gaines and to help cover the army investment.

The *Stockdale* followed the other gunboats of her unit toward Fort Powell and cleared for action when they reached Grant's Pass. According to her logbook, the main fleet started to pound Forts Morgan and Gaines at precisely 7 A.M. Within the hour, De Krafft's task group was underway toward Fort Powell, with all boats beat to quarters.

The bombardment of Fort Powell by the *Stockdale* and her companions began about 7:40 A.M. and continued until 9:30. The vessels ceased firing about 10 A.M. while their effort was assessed, but by 11 A.M., all were once again emptying their cannon barrels at the small citadel. The second shoot also lasted about 1½ hours. Both attacks were, in the end, slightly effective as diversions, but ineffective in inducing the defenders to quit.

Anxious that troops and supplies be fed into Mobile Bay without their passing Fort Morgan, Rear Adm. Farragut now determined to employ greater firepower to destroy Fort Powell's resistance. That afternoon, the monitor *Chickasaw* moved to within point-blank range of the fort's weak rear face and began sending 11-inch bolts against it. After two visits by the ironclad, the place surrendered.

During the remainder of the month, *Stockdale*, joined on August 14 by the *Rodolph*, participated in the Union Navy's mopping up of the Mobile Bay forts. Both vessels landed at Fort Morgan on August 23 with troops. Acting Master's Mate Nathaniel B. Hinckley, serving on board *Rodolph*, told his son many years after the war that he had carried the Confederate flag from the captured bastion and turned it over to a patrol boat.

In the months ahead, work remained for these two Gulf tinclads, including September expeditions to Bon Secours and Fish River. In the end, only one of the pair would survive. When the fighting intensified in Georgia and Tennessee during the fall and winter, capture of Mobile itself was left for spring.[24]

As Federal forces moved southeast away from the Mississippi toward Atlanta, many more supplies were forwarded to them from the huge Union logistical hub at Nashville. Here goods arrived by water and rail in an increasing stream from Louisville and the north, despite the summer hazards imposed by low water on the Cumberland. In May, the Nashville and Northwest Railroad was completed between the state capital and the growing intermediate supply depot and arsenal at Johnsonville, enhancing the flow considerably.

The man-made port on the deeper Tennessee River, named for the Volunteer State's wartime governor, Andrew Johnson, was also the site of a forward anchorage of the Mississippi Squadron's Ninth District. From his headquarters in Paducah, Lt. Cmdr. James Shirk stationed three tinclads at the advanced base under the command of Acting Volunteer Lt. Edward M. King.[25] These provided convoy to the many steamers arriving at and departing from the transfer point on an almost daily basis.

Although Southern leaders were aware of the Johnsonville logistical facility, it remained safe from direct attack for many months after its opening. Indeed, the Confederate leadership seemed more concerned with safeguarding inland territory against large-scale Union cavalry incursions than sending Maj. Gen. Forrest or other regular forces against Northern communications objectives, including the many steamers headed south from Paducah.

During the summer, particular attention was paid by both sides to railroad communications, which were steadily becoming at least an equal to that available by steamboat up the rivers. To counter Confederate raids and keep Forrest and his colleagues on the alert, Maj. Gen. Sherman not only took extraordinary efforts to protect and repair his trains but sent his own cavalry out to distract the enemy. Consequently, as historian Christopher Dwyer wrote a decade ago, the red-haired Federal leader "won the rear battle with an amazing logistical system that secured his lifeline...."

Prior to the November cataclysm, Rebel interdiction of river traffic on the upper rivers was left largely to bands of "guerrillas" roving along the banks "ready to pounce upon unsuspicious passing transports." A few of the attacks against these steamers were sizeable enough to be reported in the Northern press.

On August 9, a small fleet of transports, guarded by USN tinclads, arrived at Paducah from Johnsonville. There at the confluence of the Tennessee and Ohio, officers from Capt. William G. Vohris's 223-ton stern-wheeler *Eclipse*[26] told reporters that the convoy was twice attacked as it passed near Fort Heiman. On the way up to Johnsonville, Minie balls from at least 30 muskets slammed into the passing vessels, including the *Eclipse*. No human was hurt, though a bullock was killed when hit in the head. On the way back to the Ohio, Vohris's boat was in the rear and was again fired upon; seven shots struck the boat doing no harm. In both instances, the light-draught escorts shelled the suspected ambush points.[27]

En route from New Orleans, Capt. John Molloy's 854-ton *Empress*,[28] the largest packet plying the Mississippi, halted in the Greeneville Bends just before noon on August 10, anchoring alongside the light-draught *Prairie Bird*. Two more passengers were taken aboard from the gunboat, raising the number of souls on board this trip to 455 passengers and 45 crew. After receiving the latest intelligence on the dangerous curves ahead, the giant side-wheeler proceeded on up the river.

The Sixth District USN leadership, still believing that Col. Greene and Capt. J.H. Pratt were off in the Arkansas interior, did not know that a unit, believed to be Adams's battery from Marmaduke's division, had been sent back to once more pester traffic off Chicot County. Even as the captains of the *Empress* and the *Prairie Bird* conferred, a six-gun Rebel battery was unlimbered and planted on the levee about two miles below Gaines Landing. Two 10-pounder Parrotts were stationed at one point, with two 12-pounder howitzers and two 6-pounder Napoleons deeper in Rowdy Bend. The tinclad *Romeo*, anchored off the landing, was equally unaware of this grayclad arrival. Meanwhile, the *Prairie Bird*, moving upriver on patrol, approached the foot of Island No. 82.

Lookouts aboard Acting Master Baldwin's *Romeo*, as well as the Confederates hidden ashore, were able to see and hear the *Empress* as her giant paddle wheels thrashed the water, driving her north. With great clouds of smoke climbing away from her chimneys, the boat came within about 450 yards of the two Parrotts at about 5: 30 P.M. When the pair opened, there was no way they could miss, and their missiles ploughed into the steamboat at an angle of almost 30 degrees. One of the first bolts disabled the lateral engine, but the boat's engineers were able to quickly replace it.

The largest Rebel guns were followed into action by the four smaller ones. Riflemen also unleashed volley after volley of musketry. As she steamed slowly on over a distance of approximately 300 yards, the *Empress* was frequently hit. Shells and musket balls plagued every deck and smashed through the packet's bulwarks as if they were made of paper. A well-placed shot broke the doctor engine while others disabled her supply pipes, stopping off the water from her boilers and allowing steam to escape.

Capt. Molloy, standing at his post forward of the texas, was killed instantly when a cannonball took off his head. Fifteen aboard were wounded; four subsequently died, bringing the total deaths, including Capt. Molloy, to five.

The beginning of the attack on the civilian steamer brought a prompt reaction from Capt. Baldwin, who immediately ordered his vessel to raise anchor, clear for action, and steam to her assistance. As the engineers aboard the *Romeo* rapidly boosted speed, the *Empress* found herself in imminent danger of being sunk or taken, with the souls aboard killed, wounded, or made POW.

Throughout the fight, bravery and cowardice were exhibited aboard the *Empress*, the former in greater quotient. Clerk William C. Fall organized bedding and linens for the wounded while female passengers volunteered as nurses. A few men and women called out for surrender as Rebel horsemen ashore demanded that the transport put into the river bank.

As the boat staggered on, she was hit by at least 20 cannon rounds, including 11 that entered the hull and others that burst in the hold or perforated her chimneys. The number of rifle shots taking effect were too numerous to count. The *Empress* was beginning to take on the appearance of a colander. Indeed, by the time word of the attack reached Little Rock a week later, Maj. Gen. Steele was telling colleagues, "The steamer *Empress* had 63 shots put through her at Gaines Landing...."

When directly opposite the Southern Parrotts, indeed only about 50 yards distant from them, the *Empress* almost ceased moving, sliding toward the west bank. The boat's supply pipe water had entirely given out and none could make it into the boilers until minimal additional repairs could be made. At this point, Confederate soldiers moving down the bank, perhaps imagining themselves soon possessed of a rich prize, were probably startled to look up and see the hard-charging *Romeo* headed toward them.

Meanwhile, the officers and engineers aboard the *Empress* were heartened and, through their extreme energy, made repairs sufficient to allow the steamer to move slowly away from the fierce pounding. Although she was able get out of range of the artillery, mounted horsemen chased her up the river banks for another three-quarters of a mile. At this point, the *Romeo* arrived and her gunners dispersed the Confederate cavalrymen, ending their pursuit with five shrapnel shells from her starboard howitzers. In this case, as was often the case during such shootouts, "dispersed" only meant that the Rebel battery had stopped firing and pulled back.

The disabled *Empress*, 30 minutes into her ordeal, was then taken in tow by the tinclad and drawn five miles upstream to a landing on the Mississippi side of the river. The *Romeo* anchored offshore to provide a guard while the steamer's machinery was repaired.

That night, as the power plant of the *Empress* was renewed, a burial party interred the four lost passengers just ashore. Final respects were paid by off-duty officers and crewmen from the steamboat, colleagues of the passengers, and Acting Master Baldwin. Words were said over the graves by a civilian minister taking passage.

The *Empress* was able to resume her voyage north at 2 A.M. on August 11. Just to make certain that the big civilian boat had no further problems, the *Romeo* accompanied her 25 miles upstream, finally parting company off Catfish Point. As the side-wheeler paddled off and the sun rose higher, the gunboat rounded to and returned downstream.

In an interview with the *Chicago Daily Tribune* at Cairo on August 15, Clerk Fall paid high tribute to the *Romeo* and her captain. Indicating quite simply that his boat "would have made a valuable prize ... had not the gunboat come up," the *Empress* officer continued, "Captain Baldwin and his officers ... are entitled to every praise for their conduct."

The packet completed her trip to St. Louis on August 16, "bearing about her ample evidence of hard usage, but not permanently disabled." There Maj. Gen. William S. Rosecrans, the U.S. Army commander of the Department of the Missouri, issued a public commendation to the steamer's officers and crew, reminding all that these civilians had been every bit as brave as the "veterans of the naval service." When Sixth District chief Lt. Cmdr. Owen heard about the attack, he also agreed, "The *Romeo* undoubtedly saved the *Empress*."[29]

Continuing her patrol above Island No. 82 on August 11, the *Prairie Bird* reached Rowdy Bend a little after 3 P.M. There she went to quarters and began shelling the woods where intelligence indicated Confederates might be lurking. Like the *Romeo*, she too had no definite information that a large masked battery awaited. As the hour ticked on, the gunboat unwittingly advanced into the same trap that befell the *Empress*. The Rebel howitzers and Napoleons opened a rapid and accurate fire upon her, accompanied by intense musketry. As she staggered on, returning fire from her starboard battery, the *Prairie Bird* was attacked by the two upper 10-pounder Parrotts.

The *Prairie Bird* was punished by the enemy. Three shells hit her side while five smashed into her hull, including two at the waterline. As shrapnel burst all around and over her, six bolts hit her upper works and four tore holes in the paddle wheel. Large pieces of burst shell fell like big hail as, altogether, the light-draught was struck 34 times. Five men were wounded, one fatally. With big splashes mushrooming out of the river all around her, the little gunboat moved ahead as rapidly as she could. This extra effort permitted the tinclad to get beyond the bar, separating her from the enemy.

The *Romeo*, which by this time was approaching Gaines Landing from above, heard the firing below. Once more she was beat to quarters and laid on full speed. Continuing down, she was able to observe her consort passing the battery and returning fire. As the *Prairie Bird* surged ahead, the *Romeo* arrived on the scene and aimed her howitzers at grayclad horsemen and soldiers advancing along the shore. When the *Romeo* reached the *Prairie Bird*, she rounded to and accompanied her up the river to a landing at Anderson Plantation, on the Mississippi side of the river not far from where the *Empress* had put in the previous evening.

Once more, bluejackets aboard the *Romeo* watched as crewmen aboard another boat

Commissioned in April 1864, the tinclad *Nymph* spent the next year patrolling the lower Mississippi River, largely without fanfare. On August 28, she steamed to the rescue of the steamer *Henry Chouteau*, which was under attack from Confederate shore batteries below Bayou Sara (Naval Historical Center).

made repairs and a burial party interred a colleague. About 8 P.M., the two tinclads got underway for below and passed the site of the battery in line, shelling the area and the woods further back. Having moved on, the Confederates made no reply.[30]

Although the attacks in the Greenville Bends now seemed to dry up, there was action further south in the Morganza to Donaldsonville Second District of the Mississippi Squadron. Rebel batteries now appeared on the Louisiana banks of the great river and launched fresh attacks.

While en route north from New Orleans on the morning of August 28, the side-wheeler *White Cloud* was attacked from the left (Louisiana) side of the Mississippi near one of the islands below Bayou Sara. Confederate cannoneers were said to have gotten off 13 shots, of which five took effect in the hull and cabin. One hit her steam pipe, causing her to be disabled. Her upper works were peppered by volleys of musketry, but no one was injured.

The episode seemed to be almost a repeat of the *Empress-Romeo* incident earlier in the month. As the *White Cloud* drifted toward her enemy, the tinclad *Kenwood* came to her rescue. After firing her guns at the grayclad attackers, the light-draught passed and line and towed the transport out of danger, remaining with her until her engineers could make repairs.

Further up the river, a battery, said to contain eight cannon, including two 12-pounder howitzers, fired into the 633-ton packet *Henry Chouteau*[31] as she, too, was making her way north from the Crescent City to St. Louis. In addition to Minieballs, five cannon shells ploughed into the craft, but she was not damaged and none of her passengers or crew was hurt. The patrolling tinclad *Nymph*[32] heard the gunfire and went to the giant steamer's assistance. In this case, she arrived in time to provide escort out of the danger area.[33]

By the middle of August, the river stages of the Ohio and Cumberland had fallen almost to their lowest points. On August 13, Brig. Gen. Adam "Stovepipe" Johnson took advantage of this annual occurrence to capture three small steamers, cross the Ohio, and go ashore at Saline Creek, approximately 100 miles north of Cairo, IL. Unhappily, but not unexpectedly, the Tenth District tinclads were unable to interdict the raiders and the pursuit over the next week had to be undertaken by Indiana troops assisted by ersatz army gunboats. The inability to react to pinpoint attacks on the upper rivers occasioned by water depth — and there were several — was a source of frustration to the Federal naval officers whose patrolling tinclads otherwise provided active protection.[34]

The remainder of the summer was, for the officers and men of the Ninth, Tenth, and new 11th (created September 29) Districts, Mississippi Squadron, largely a repeat of the previous year. Efforts were made to ensure efficient traffic flow at a time of low water. While Federal forces moved on Atlanta in September and October, U.S. Navy escort and counterinsurgency efforts once again shifted from the Ohio River to the Cumberland, and her sister, the Tennessee. The merchant fleets guarded up the Cumberland were now often smaller than in months past, due largely to increased reliance on the Nashville and Northwestern Railroad. The well-protected NNR steel route permitted easy transport of essential goods the 75 miles from the Tennessee River port of Johnsonville to the state capital.

Despite the completion of the 60-mile-long Edgefield and Kentucky link between

Nashville and Clarksville around Harpeth Shoals, much traffic was forwarded to the new Johnsonville location, thereby permitting the avoidance of the low-water 185-mile trip down a long and slender route through the heart of a disaffected, if not disloyal, region.

An example of the reduced Cumberland service was seen on August 26, when the *Silver Lake* convoyed just six steamers from Smithland to Nashville. Once in the capital city, the gunboatmen were, as in the past, granted liberty; the city editor of the *Nashville Daily Press* defined USN bluejacket shore activities as "grogging around."[35]

Although water levels may have affected tinclad operations on the upper rivers, the little boats remained vulnerable to Confederate masked batteries along the entire course of the Mississippi. To add to Federal available protection, the new tinclad *Siren*[36] was commissioned on August 30 and ordered to patrol the Father of Waters between Columbus, KY, and Memphis.

September began with yet another attack as five horse-drawn Rebel guns appeared at Rowe's Landing, in Tunica Bend, LA. The pieces were unlimbered on the levee, three 12-pounder howitzers in one position and two Napoleon 6-pounders in another, separated by some 400 yards. The next morning as she passed downstream, the tinclad *Naiad* was allowed to pass the upper location and when she was midway between the two Southern gun emplacements, a brisk cross fire was opened upon her. The light-draught rounded to under fire and attacked.

The little Union warboat attempted to give as good as she took, expending 52 rounds of shell and shrapnel. In the exchange, she was hit 22 times. No great damage was done, save the cutting of the *Naiad*'s escape pipe and port hog chains. Her upper works were perforated by musket balls and round shot. Fortunately, none of her bluejackets were hurt.

Tinclads were not designed to stand against land batteries and the *Naiad*'s good fortune would probably have changed had not the monitor *Ozark* come into view, steaming to her assistance. Seeing the ironclad, the Confederate gunners pulled their pieces back before she could come in range. The tinclad withdrew to the bank on the opposite river, while the *Ozark* steamed back down the river a short distance and anchored. The battery remained, awaiting fresh victims.

Puffing her way south about 2 A.M. on the morning of September 4, an unnamed steamer was attacked. The assault was witnessed from the upper deck of the *Naiad*, where repairs were nearly finished. Ordering steam shortly before dawn, she backed out into the stream, whistling to the *Ozark*. When the ironclad arrived, the two vessels bombarded the woods where the battery was believed hiding. When no response was obtained, the shoot ended and the two returned to station or patrol.[37]

Perhaps the strangest tale in the annals of the tinclad began on September 4. Although it played out over a period of five months, we place it here for the convenience of the reader.

Following the end of the Red River campaign, Rear Adm. Porter's district system established a chain (admittedly with holes) of gunboats up and down the Mississippi. In addition to convoy protection, these vessels made constant patrols designed to intercept contraband cargo and, more importantly, keep Confederate forces away from the river. The effectiveness of this defense was known to the Western Confederate leadership.

Having earlier advice that any west-east transfer of troops was rendered impossible in the face of the Federal gunboats, Confederate Trans-Mississippi Department commander Lt. Gen. Edmund Kirby Smith was surprised to receive orders in early July from Richmond for just such a movement. After two weeks of stalling, Smith called upon Lt. Gen. Richard Taylor to push two divisions over "with as little delay as possible." Taylor also believed there was little chance to get any significant number of men through the Union blockade. Perhaps the prospect might improve if a Union gunboat could be captured. Such an opportunity presented itself on August 4.

Writing from the Mississippi near St. Joseph, a planter by the name of Briscoe sent an amazing letter to the local Confederate commander, Col. Isaac F. Harrison. The contents of the communication spelled out how the captain of a tinclad would lessen the security of his boat so she could be captured and then turn over his copy of the Mississippi Squadron signals, both in return for a consideration. The letter was immediately forwarded to theater headquarters in Shreveport, along with the farmer's assurance that the offer was genuine.

After reviewing the missive, Lt. Gen. Smith advised Col. Harrison to communicate with the gunboat commander and reach an understanding. Officers and men from the Shreveport-based Confederate ram *Missouri* would be sent to help accomplish the task. Meanwhile, the gunboat was to be moved to a position off the plantation of Southern sympathizer and activist Joshua James at Carthage Bayou, LA, not far from Hurricane Island. The owner's sons were active officers in the Confederate army.

The negotiations, no record of which naturally exists, were successfully completed and a takeover strategy was developed, complete with a cover story should it fail, The gunboat was moved and the entire crew of the *Missouri* was conveyed to the river in order to man the boat after her capture.

The vessel in question was the veteran tinclad *Rattler*. Ever since her commander, Acting Master Walter Fentress, and part of her crew were captured at Rodney a year earlier, the gunboat had continued as one of the guard boats in this district. Two more captains had served aboard since Fentress. The latest was Acting Master Daniel W. Glenney,[38] a one-time mate on a civilian vessel trading out of New York, who joined the Navy from Connecticut in December 1861 and became the tinclad's skipper in July. Glenney's orders were to patrol the area between Rodney and Bruinsburg, via St. Joseph. He was authorized to occasionally put into Grand Gulf for coal. In July, when the *Prairie Bird* steamed to Memphis for overhaul, the Hurricane Island vicinity was added to his beat.

The vessel usually anchored in midstream at night, and life aboard over the months had become rather routine, with few expecting much trouble. One sailor, William N. Bock, even told his mother in a letter home: "We do not stand a chance of being hit by bullets."

The night of September 4 was the arranged time for the *Rattler* plot to unfold. Supposedly having received information that Joshua James's two sons were at home, Glenney dispatched 22 bluejackets ashore in the gunboat's cutter to capture them. When the boat touched shore, two miles from the plantation house, their officer left them in charge of two African-American tars and took the others inland.

At a point about halfway to their goal, the stealthy sailors heard gunshots coming from the location of their boat. At about the same time, the *Rattler*, out in the river, blew

Her reputation already besmirched by the Rodney Church incident of September 1863, the tinclad *Rattler* suffered further embarrassment in September 1864 when her commander, in league with Confederate Trans-Mississippi Department commander Lt. Gen. Edmund Kirby Smith and elements of the Confederate States Navy up the Red River, conspired to sell his boat for cash and cotton. Although the attempt was made, it was foiled by an alert junior officer aboard the light-draught (Naval Historical Center).

her whistle as a signal to the gig to return from her defensive patrol. Electing to abandon their goal, the 22 sailors started back toward their cutter. Marching single file in the dark over uncertain ground, they were surrounded by a large Confederate party and ordered to surrender. The men refused and opened fire. The Rebels immediately shot back and the U.S. bluejackets quit. The expedition officer and two men managed to escape capture.

The grayclads making the capture of the Federal landing party were from the crew of the *Missouri*. Back at the cutter, the Confederate gunboat's builder and commander, CSN Lt. Jonathan H. Carter,[39] and the party of sailors who had killed the two black boat attendants, pushed the craft out into the stream and rowed for the *Rattler*. So far, the scheme was unfolding according to plan.

Aboard the *Rattler*, executive officer Acting Ensign Henry N. Wells[40] heard the commotion ashore and immediately told away a party in the boat's dinghy to investigate. Wells and his men spied the cutter coming toward them and hailed it with the night's password. When an unsatisfactory reply was shouted, the Federals fired on Carter's stolen boat. Wells sounded the alarm, advising Acting Master Glenney that the boat's cutter was captured and attempting to board, and pointing out her mid-stream location.

Foiled, Lt. Carter canceled his attack on the *Rattler* and, instead, quickly made for the Louisiana shore, where he and his sailors faded into the dark woods. In the interim, Glenney ordered the gunboat to hoist anchor and head toward the point where the cutter was sighted. When the *Rattler* arrived, the small boat was gone.

The tinclad was rounding to off the head of Hurricane Island when Joshua James was sighted on the river bank. Glenney hailed him, asking if any of his crewmen had visited his home that night; the reply was "no." About this time, the escaped Union officer and two seamen hailed the *Rattler* from shore and were taken aboard. As she anchored in the stream abreast of the point where the cutter had initially landed, they told the captain their story.

Just after sunup on September 5, the *Rattler* moved up abreast of the James plantation house and anchored on the Louisiana bank. Acting Master Glenney took several crewmen ashore and, with the help of a quickly-procured local African-American guide, made their way to the camp of Col. Harrison under a flag of truce. There they arranged the release of the other sailors captured by Lt. Carter's men.

That afternoon, contrary to Mississippi Squadron standing orders, Acting Master Glenney hailed a passing steamer and took passage down to the District flag boat, lying between Waterproof and Natchez Island. There he reported on events to Lt. Cmdr. Selfridge. After giving his testimony, the *Rattler*'s captain was ordered to immediately return to his vessel. Instead, he went to Vicksburg, where he idled about for five days and was seen in conversation with various known Confederate sympathizers.

When the major general commanding at Vicksburg alerted Selfridge to Glenney's activities in his town, away from his boat, the Fifth District commander acted immediately. The *Rattler*'s skipper, now back aboard his boat, was ordered confined to close arrest in irons and replaced with an officer sent over from another ship. Acting Ensign Wells was also relieved. Later, Glenney was placed in close confinement, officially unable to depart his vessel.

There the situation remained for several weeks until early October, when a Confederate Navy deserter by the name of J.P. Green found himself aboard the big gunboat *Benton*. Subjected to the usual interrogation of prisoners, Green let it be known that he was present in Shreveport when the plans were made by the *Missouri*'s officers for the capture of the *Rattler*. Further, he indicated that it was common knowledge that Glenney was selling his ship.

This information was passed to Rear Adm. Porter, who ordered the *Rattler*'s former commander re-arrested and sent to the brig, subject to a courts-martial. The naval trial would not occur. Acting in collusion with the boat's new executive officer (who joined him), Glenney deserted early in the morning of November 4. The escaped prisoner was never captured and remained the only Civil War naval officer to engage with the Confederacy in a plot to sell his own command.[41]

As August fell into September, Union forces in Arkansas remained puzzled over the mission of their famed cavalry opponent, Jo Shelby. Many believed his force was continuing to lurk near the rivers, while others believed he was departing for a larger raid into Missouri. Whatever his plans, Maj. Gen. Steele wanted him found and destroyed. Local insurgent forces, backed by regulars, continued to resist, particularly along the White River, the water stages of which were then very low.

Several expeditions were sent out by the 2nd Division of the U.S. VII Army Corps from Devall's Bluff in an effort to come up with the elusive Shelby or to assist other Union forces known to be after him. Immediately on the heels of the September 2 conclusion of an unsuccessful first advance up the river from DeVall's, orders were received for a second.

At daybreak on September 3, the transports *Commercial, Celeste*,[42] and *Nevada*,[43] carrying 1,000 officers and men from Michigan, Wisconsin, and Illinois regiments and escorted by the tinclad *Fawn*, shoved off. Progress was steady and the first Confederate pickets were not seen until the convoy passed Peach Orchard Bluffs the following morning.

The Rebel outriders continued ahead on the left bank, keeping an eye on the Federal boats. Finally, at about 4 P.M., the leading steamer *Commercial* received at least 50 musket balls as it passed Gregory's Landing from an estimated 300 to 400 men concealed in bushes. Hundreds of balls hit the steamer, killing one man and wounding eight others, including the Union commander, Col. William H. Graves. Some 40 to 50 butternut soldiers opened fire from the right bank immediately afterwards.

The Confederate attack on the *Commercial* prompted a quick response from the *Fawn*, which, with black smoke pouring out of her chimneys, ran up and began pouring howitzer fire into the woods and shrubbery on both sides of the White. It was subsequently learned that the enemy force was smaller than the numbers here given. Aboard the *Commercial* and the other two steamers, troops, after the initial shock, barricaded themselves behind boxes and other fixtures and briskly returned fire. During the exchange, one man was wounded aboard the *Nevada*.

Soldiers from the three Union transports went ashore the next morning and captured the town of Augusta, about a mile and a half from the landing beach. There it was learned that the Confederates that had fired into the task group had gone toward Jacksonport. As the water continued low and the enemy elusive, no one aboard the Federal boats was disappointed when orders arrived for a curtailment of the adventure. The three troop boats and the *Fawn* returned to DeVall's Bluff on September 6.[44]

By this time, the Confederate force of Maj. Gen. Sterling Price, accompanied by Shelby's cavalry, was well on its way toward Missouri. Despite this development, attacks on White River and Mississippi River traffic continued.

Federal concern over the real and supposed sightings of Confederate forces under Generals Price and Shelby continued throughout September, even as actual Rebel attacks on river transport continued. It being reported that Shelby was about to mount an attack upon Cape Girardeau, the new tinclad *Siren* was sent to bolster the defenses of that Missouri post on September 23. Before long, it would be determined that the alarm was groundless and the new gunboat was released to take station in the Fourth District.[45]

On Sunday, September 25, the stern-wheeler *Melnotte*[46] departed DeVall's Bluff for Cairo. As she headed for the mouth of White River, she was fired upon by Southern irregulars at Prairie Landing, 23 miles up. An unknown number of shots from the Rebels in the woods hit her pilothouse and the second mate narrowly avoided being hit. Once past, the vessel successfully completed her voyage.[47]

Hidden on the Tennessee shore near Tiptonville, 20 Rebel irregulars spotted the side-wheeler *Adam Jacobs*[48] as she puffed down from St. Louis toward Memphis on Thursday, September 29. Waiting until she was near to shore, they fired upwards of 30 shots toward the craft, hitting her upper works and wheel houses. No one aboard was injured and the *Jacobs* continued on without stopping.[49]

While en route from Memphis to Cairo on the morning of September 30, the big side-wheeler *C.E. Hillman* was warned of active irregular activity on the western bank via a hail from the steamer *Belle Memphis*. As she continued on past Tiptonville, the *Hillman*'s officers spied Rebels but veered to the other side of the river out of musket range and was not molested. As she passed Island No. 14, however, butternut partisans fired on her from the western shore. Her texas and pilothouse were perforated and the bell rope from the latter to the engine spaces was cut. A number of people were standing outside of the pilothouse, including the two pilots, but none were hurt.

When the *Hillman* reached New Madrid, MO, her captain immediately informed the commander of the tinclad *New Era*, the USN patrol vessel assigned to that area, of the attack, as well as the declining river stage below. He also notified the captain of the steamer *Darling*,[50] then preparing to depart down the river. When she did so, she avoided the western bank of the river as she came upon Islands No. 12 and 14, avoiding danger.[51]

The *Romeo* was on patrol off the foot of Little Island the same day when "guerrillas," first on one side of the river and then the other, blasted her with musketry. Several volleys were aimed in her direction, but fortunately for the bluejackets, no one aboard the light-draught was injured. Upon attack, the tinclad returned fire with shrapnel against the estimated 100 enemy and it was later claimed that "eight or ten" of the fellows were seen to fall and be carried off by the comrades.[52]

Later in the day, on a bend of the White River near Clarendon, a lurking irregular band attacked Capt. James Maratta's stern-wheeler *Emma No. 2*[53] as she made her way to the mouth of the river. Navigational requirements forced the boat to approach the shore, where she made an easy target. An estimated 200 musket shots rang out, with more than 60 balls striking the cabin. Many passengers and crewmen had narrow escapes from them, but the vessel safely emerged from her ordeal.[54]

While en route from St. Louis for the White River with a cargo of goods and horses on the evening of October 5, Capt. William G. Vohris's *Eclipse* moved past Thweet's Landing on the Mississippi River bend at the foot of Island No. 17. At this point, a volley of musketry from 10 or 12 partisans rang out from the Tennessee shore, followed by quick but irregular firing.

Four balls passed through the stern-wheeler's pilothouse, narrowly missing the pilot. Three others hit the texas and saloon while an indefinite number smacked into points below. As they fired, the Confederates shouted out for the boat to surrender and come into the western bank. Two men were wounded and two horses were killed. Vohris remained on course and called for more steam, moving out of range of the enemy muskets. A number of enemy soldiers chased the *Eclipse* along the bank, but she soon moved beyond their pursuit. A little beyond, a refugee family shouted a hail and was picked up.[55]

11

Decatur and Johnsonville,
October–November 1864

Following Maj. Gen. William Tecumseh Sherman's triumph at Atlanta at the beginning of September 1864, the Union high command had next to decide in which direction to send the scrappy redhead. Sherman himself favored a "scorched-earth" ride east, destroying Confederate logistics between the Georgia capital and the Carolina seacoast. It would be his intention to emulate his greatest communications foe, Maj. Gen. Nathan Bedford Forrest, by encouraging his Army of the Tennessee, made lean, to live off the countryside. "I can make this march and make Georgia howl!" he promised Lt. Gen. Ulysses S. Grant. Maj. Gen. George Thomas and 60,000 men could be sent north to guard the Tennessee rear.[1]

Confederate Gen. John Bell Hood now contemplated a visit north in a move historian Bruce Catton called a "strategy of despair, verging on the wholly fantastic, based on the belief that the way to counter Sherman's thrust into the deepest South was to march off in the opposite direction." The Confederate field commander believed that, if lucky, he could move "smartly" enough in western and middle Tennessee to defeat General Thomas and/or capture Nashville. Taking the Tennessee capital would not only destroy a major Northern supply depot, but could force Sherman to return to the Volunteer State.

During September and early October, Sherman and Hood took advantage of fine weather to reorganize their commands for what Benson J. Lossing later called the "vigorous work" ahead. As a precaution against any Southern gambit, Sherman sent Maj. Gen. Thomas to Nashville on October 3. Over the next two weeks, Hood marched to the west of the Chattahoochee, trying to lure his opponent out of Georgia while avoiding a decisive battle.

Hood, on October 7, called upon his cavalry to aid in the grand endeavor of removing Sherman by smashing up the Union supply line from the North. In particular, he needed Maj. Gen. Forrest, the man whom Sherman himself had named "the very devil." President Jefferson Davis, Confederate Department of the West commander Lt. Gen. Pierre G.T. Beauregard, Gen. Hood, and everyone else on the Southern side hoped that the famous cavalry leader could divert the Yankees while the Confederate Army of Tennessee strode into the Volunteer State.

Sherman was contemptuous of Hood's wild-goose-chase northern goal and remained supremely confident in his own mission and men. Consequently, he determined to quit the Hood chase, go the other way, and march toward the sea. Lt. Gen. Grant approved his subordinate's Savannah strategy on October 13. Seven days later, Sherman gave Thomas full authority to deal with any northern Confederate incursion and started reinforcements to Nashville.

Unable to gain any advantage in Northwest Georgia, Hood turned to cross the Tennessee River, first at Guntersville and then at Decatur, AL, where a key railroad terminus could deliver supplies from northern Mississippi. So it was that the Army of Tennessee headed for Decatur.[2]

By October 6, the "devil," also known as the "Wizard of the Saddle," had already made a sixteen-day circuit from Cherokee station in Alabama as high as Spring Hill outside Nashville, assaulting Sherman's supply lines. Confederate hopes that Forrest would, according to General Cox, "occupy Thomas' forces so as to create a diversion in his favor" were met. It was during this sojourn that, according to Jordan and Pryor, Forrest first became aware of the Yankee treasure trove at Johnsonville and put it on his target list:

> He also received information, through citizens, that a vast amount of army stores had been collected at Johnsonville on the Tennessee River, the terminus of the Nashville and North-Western Railroad, destined and essential for the Federal forces at Chattanooga and Atlanta. This depot and the bridges on the railroad leading to it, it was likewise his purpose to destroy, if the condition of his horses, on reaching Spring Hill, would warrant him in undertaking it.

During his Middle Tennessee raid, Maj. Gen. Forrest was pursued by numerous Federal units. While several of his subordinates made feints to draw off the bluecoats, the "devil" was able to get his command back to safety over the swollen Tennessee River via a cane-covered island which kept the men from view.

Among those detailed after Forrest's raiders was Col. George B. Hoge of the 113th Illinois Regiment, bivouacked at Clifton, TN. Hoge was to move his 1,300 men by water up to Eastport, MS, a community on the west bank of the Tennessee a few miles from Florence, AL, and near Chickasaw Landing. Here he would link up with a larger Union force that would then march over to the Iuka, MS, area and destroy its railroad connections. Unhappily for the colonel, the Confederate leader learned of the plan from scouts, and, on October 6, dispatched Lt. Col. David C. Kelley[3] of the 26th Tennessee Cavalry (C.S.A.), with 300 men and several artillery pieces to give the Northerners a welcome. The Parson's greeting party hid a masked battery at the base of a hill about 600 yards from the river and another of equal size at Chickasaw.

On the morning of October 10, the Federal troop boats *City of Pekin*,[4] *Kenton*,[5] and *Aurora*,[6] guarded by the tinclads *Key West* and *Undine*,[7] departed Clifton and steamed up the Tennessee, reaching Eastport without incident. The transports lay at the bank, opposite a pair of warehouses, and between the gunboats and the shore. Within a short time, the trio began to disembark their passengers and a battery of four guns. Because Col. Hoge failed to make a reconnaissance or post pickets, the Northerners did not suspect the presence of their enemy and soon began to march inland down a road that connected the landing with the hill beyond.

When the advancing Federals reached a point about halfway between the river and the hill, Kelley's gunners and riflemen opened up. There ensued a mad scramble by the bluecoats, who deserted their cannon, to get back to and aboard their boats. The ambush was complete as shells fell all around the Federals — and their vessels as well. The *Kenton* was struck numerous times. One shell exploded in the engine room, rupturing a steam line and killing a crewman. Still, Capt. Dunlap was able to get her away from the landing, while his crew extinguished a fire. The skipper said later that mental visions of Andersonville were a great inspiration.

The *Aurora* was not as lucky. Confederate bolts killed Capt. Patterson Marshall and 20 embarked soldiers. Many men fell into the stream and drowned as the boat cut her cable and fled. The counterfiring light-draughts were also hit while the *City of Pekin* tried to pick up survivors.

While the civilian steamers struggled to get clear in what Col. Hoge called a "scene of confusion," the *Key West* and *Undine* fired on what they thought were Rebel positions back of the landing. The correspondent "Old Kentuck" of the *Chicago Daily Tribune* later interviewed a number of expedition survivors for an October 21 report and concluded that "the worst feature of the whole inglorious defeat" was that the gunboat pair "killed more of our own troops and did more damage to our men than to the enemy."

Eventually, the little task group was reunited and fires were extinguished. It then retired to Clifton, assessing its losses while en route. Both the *Undine* and *Key West* would face Forrest's cannoneers again and next time they would not escape. But, as Forrest biographer Brian Steel Wells put it, Kelley's success against the gunboats gave the Confederates "the confidence to engage them again."

Nicknamed "The Parson" from his days as a Methodist minister, Col. David C. Kelley (1833–1909), a confidant of Maj. Gen. Nathan Bedford Forrest, led the 26th Tennessee Cavalry (C.S.A.) during the fall of 1864. After disposing of Col. Hodge in October, cannoneers under his command would deny Federals the use of the Cumberland River during the December Battle of Nashville. On two occasions during that blockade, the Southern gunners beat off attacks by Union Navy ironclads and tinclads, and when their army retreated, they escaped as well (courtesy Robert Henderson).

Years later, in reviewing the episode, Admiral Porter, though not directly naming him, insisted that Ninth District chief Lt. Cmdr. James Shirk shoulder some of the blame for King's setback. "Sometimes the naval commander of a district, from a feeling of over-security," the former Mississippi Squadron boss asserted in

1886, "sent an insufficient force of gunboats when trouble would ensue and the undertaking became a failure."

From the field near Centerville, GA, during the day, Maj. Gen. Sherman wrote to Acting Volunteer Lt. Henry Glassford, still believed to be in charge of the Eleventh District, regarding the threat posed from the Army of Tennessee. John Bell Hood and his divisions, now west of Rome, were headed toward the Volunteer State. Sherman was not quite certain, however, as to his opponent's exact and immediate intentions. Although it was suspected Hood was en route to the Tuscumbia vicinity, it was possible that he might aim for Whitesburg or Gunter's Landing. Just to be certain, Glassford was asked to keep his new boats "watching and patrolling the Tennessee." Hood had to be "prevented from crossing the Tennessee River anywhere above Mussel [sic] Shoals."

Forrest, as he told his immediate superior Lt. Gen. Richard Taylor on October 12, had to his way of thinking "done something toward accomplishing" the goal of destroying Maj. Gen. Sherman's logistical apparatus, but not nearly enough,

Captured off Memphis, the tinclad *Key West* provided most of her service on the Tennessee River. In October 1864, the gunboat, in company with the light-draught *Undine*, protected an amphibious force under Col. George B. Hodge dispatched to Clifton, Tennessee, to help trap Maj. Gen. Nathan Bedford Forrest. The gunboat, her consort, and the steamers they protected were instead attacked by artillery under Forrest's chief of staff, Col. David C. Kelley, and forced to retreat. Later, on November 4, Forrest attacked the Federal depot at Johnsonville, destroying not only the *Key West*, but two other tinclads and numerous transports and barges (Naval Historical Center).

and was "anxious to renew the effort." The question was where he and his horsemen could apply the greatest leverage and secure the greatest return. Like Morgan before the Ohio Raid, Forrest took out his maps and studied the possibilities closely.

The Yankee campaign in Georgia was supplied from Louisville, the North's central point for provisioning its western armies since the beginning of the conflict. There were three major corridors available to bring goods south to such big intermediate Union depots as Nashville and Chattanooga. The first two were old and known: the Cumberland River, the primary route for goods in bulk when it was high, but which was still at a low stage; and the well-guarded Louisville and Nashville Railroad.

The newest and most vulnerable route was one humming along with, to date, virtually no interference: the Tennessee River from Paducah down to the transfer point at Johnsonville and hence east along the Nashville and Northwestern Railroad. Laying down his charts, Forrest determined "to take possession of Fort Heiman on the west bank of the Tennessee River below Johnsonville, and thus prevent all communication with Johnsonville by transports."

Back in May, the Nashville and Northwest Railroad had been completed between the state capital and Johnsonville, 78 miles to the southwest near Reynoldsburg, in Humphreys County on the eastern or right bank of the Tennessee River. A range of hills came down at this point to within 100 yards of the stream and the railroad had to run several miles along the base of those hills before it reached the river. Previously known as Lucas Landing, Johnsonville was located about two or three miles above the old town of Reynoldsburg. The two communities were separated by the Trace Creek valley, while Reynoldsburg Island was a few miles south.

The area north of the railroad toward Reynoldsburg was flat; all of its timber had been cut off for over a mile from the river bank. The ground on the western or left bank of the Tennessee was heavily wooded and high. As the Tennessee River, 400 yards wide at Johnsonville with a straight course, was not subject to the annual low-water navigation difficulties of the Cumberland, its importance as a supplementary avenue of supply was enhanced. During late spring, summer, and into the fall, steamers from Louisville, after churning upstream to Johnsonville via Paducah, unloaded their cargoes of stores, clothes, guns, and ammunition almost directly to waiting trains. Heavily laden with supplies, sometimes five steamers a day reached the port.

The NNR tracks, which followed the south bank of Trace Creek, hosted upwards of a half dozen daily trains running in either direction between the base and Nashville, where their cargoes could be "shipped direct to Knoxville, Chattanooga, or Atlanta as desired." Some 800 employees of the U.S. Army Quartermaster Department provided the labor needed to handle the trains, as well as the dozen or more steamers and barges which came to the wharf every day.

Named for the Union's Tennessee governor Andrew Johnson, Fort Johnson, an earthen redoubt and blockhouse, overlooked the port's landscape from a prominent hill south of the railroad. From here Col. Charles R. Thompson's depot was guarded by 700 untested troops. A total of 14 cannon protruded from this citadel or from nearby entrenchments. Johnsonville was also a forward base for Lt. Cmdr. Shirk's Ninth District of the Mississippi Squadron. Four tinclads, *Undine*, *Key West*, *Elfin*,[8] and *Tawah*, often commanded by Lt. Edward M. King in two-boat task groups, made frequent stops at the levy while on convoy escort or patrol. Johnsonville's destruction might not halt Sherman's upcoming march to the sea, but it could, perhaps, slow it down.[9]

"The movement of the Confederate army through northern Alabama to Decatur and Florence, and thence across the Tennessee River towards Franklin and Nashville was now in full swing," wrote Maj. Gen. Forrest's biographer, Dr. Wyeth, years later. The "Wizard" was also beginning his mission against the Johnsonville supply depot.

On October 16, Forrest's advance elements set out from Corinth, MS, for various points in West Tennessee. Among the units available to the "devil" on his last independent raid of the war was the division of Brig. Gen. Abraham Buford, Col. E.W. Rucker's brigade, and two batteries of horse artillery. These, together with Forrest and the division of Brig. Gen. James R. Chalmers, came together and made their headquarters at Jackson on October 21. There they rested while the command's weary horses were reshod.

By next day, Hood's main force occupied Gadsden, AL. There, in conference with his nominal superior Lt. Gen. Beauregard, the veteran laid out his plans to cross the Tennessee River and employ Decatur's key rail facilities. Heavy shore batteries, submarine mines in passable channels, and a portable pontoon train would allow him to cross unimpeded by Federal gunboats.

Just as Hood's advance required Sherman to shift west of Rome, GA, to guard Chattanooga and Atlanta, Forrest's move toward Tennessee was noticed by other Federal authorities, who began making their own preparations. The telegraph wires buzzed with sightings, reports, movement orders and the like. Garrisons at Columbus, Memphis, and Paducah braced for return visits by the butternut horsemen who had come their way earlier.

Forrest himself wondered if Union troops might make the same response now as they had earlier, coming at him from several directions. While blacksmiths worked their forges and Rebel enlisted ranks were boosted through local recruitment, his scouts determined that no Federal operations were actively underway against them from any quarter. Yankee cavalry patrols in western Tennessee had recently been decreased in order to send riders to North Alabama to watch for Hood along the Upper Tennessee, while the sheer number of Forrest sighting reports coming into army posts and naval bases actually helped mask the Confederate's mission.

As early as October 12, Acting Master Gilbert Morton's Bridgeport–built tinclad *General Thomas*,[10] having been assigned by new Eleventh District commander Lt. Moreau Forrest to the area between Whitesburg and Decatur, was requested to steam up and beyond Whitesburg, gaining intelligence. She was joined by the ersatz army gunboat *Stone River*.[11]

On October 15, Acting Master Morton sent word to Brig. Gen. Robert S. Granger, the Union Army's commander of the District of North Alabama headquarters at Decatur, AL, that Hood's army was marching toward a projected crossing point at Caperton's Ferry. Army riders confirmed the gunboat report. The volunteer officer promised to depart his anchorage at Larkinsville and proceed up toward the danger spot, hoping to arrive before midnight. Orders were left for the *General Grant*[12] to follow as soon as she arrived.

Morton's message was passed from Granger to Maj. Gen. Sherman at Nashville, who asked several of his subordinates to scout the mentioned areas with cavalry. He also asked that, while his horsemen rode toward Rogersville and Florence, Ninth District gunboats patrol the river as far as Waterloo and Eastport. Having conducted his own scout, Brig. Gen. Granger did not initially believe Morton, who sent additional reports that the Confederates were on the move. If Hood had as large a force as was being reported, in the general's opinion, "the gunboats will do little toward stopping the crossing of the river." Thomas, for his part, assured Maj. Gen. Sherman two days later that the gunboats were patrolling between Bridgeport and Decatur and that the Eleventh District was cooperating with him "very cordially."

Granger, whose largely oversaw the operations of the ersatz army gunboat *Stone River*, was not impressed with those leased to the USN, including the *General Burnside*[13] and *General Sherman*,[14] sisters to the *Grant* and *Thomas*. "They have no protection for their boilers," he complained in a message to Thomas, "none indeed for any part of the boat." He added, "Any of them could be totally disabled by three batteries in 15 minutes."

Sighting reports continued to pour in and, on October 19, the District of North Alabama commander went up the Tennessee all the way to Bridgeport on his own reconnaissance aboard the *Stone River*. Meanwhile, Morton was forced to report to Lt. Forrest that low water was holding up his arrival at Claysville Landing.

Hood's main force departed Gadsden for Decatur on October 22. Granger knew that it was approaching and strengthened the defenses of his town. The *General Thomas* and *Stone River* stepped up their patrols. Two days later, the commander of the Whitesburg post reported 15,000 Rebels 20 miles inland and closing on the river.

Calling upon Maj. Gen. Thomas for reinforcements and concluding that Decatur was Hood's target, Granger nevertheless sent 250 soldiers to Whitesburg on the *Stone River* to conduct another, more precise reconnaissance. Fortification of Decatur intensified and 1,600 yards of rifle pits and defensive parapets were manned along with two forts, to say nothing of the gunboats.

Also on October 24, Maj. Gen. Forrest's horsemen saddled up and broke camp, headed northeast toward the Tennessee-Kentucky line. The tinclads of the Ninth and Tenth District, meanwhile, continued to patrol and convoy steamers on the Tennessee and Cumberland rivers, ignorant of the "devil's" movements.

Acting Master Morton on the *General Thomas* found the waters of the upper Tennessee so low on October 25 that he was unable to patrol beyond Beard's Bluff and could not go with safety below Whitesburg. The army gunboat *Stone River* was below that community, where it was hoped Brig. Gen. Granger would use her to scout the Tennessee as far as Decatur. The Navy craft, after stopping to "rail," or pick up fence rails for fuel, continued toward Hobson's Island, 3 miles below Whitesburg. During her reconnaissance Rebel cavalry were increasingly seen along the river bank. Water depth kept Lt. Forrest from sending other craft to the scene.

Demonstrating the time lag of Civil War communication, Maj. Gen. Thomas sent two telegrams to Lt. Forrest at Bridgeport on October 26 strongly requesting that the gunboats under his command be moved to Claysville and Fort Deposit. Once there, they were to assist Brig. Gen. Granger in defending the Tennessee River fords and crossings at those points.

In response to these wires, Forrest replied that both the *General Grant* and *General Thomas* were on the Tennessee at or near the points Thomas mentioned. The *Grant* was trying to steer her way over the bars to rendezvous with the *Thomas*, but the river level was frustrating the effort. Attempts to get a third craft, probably the *General Burnside*, away from Bridgeport were stymied by the bar in the low river off that town.

Hood arrived near the outskirts of Decatur that Wednesday, where he learned that Maj. Gen. Forrest was way up in the north-central part of the Volunteer State. Elements of the main force attacked the Alabama town during the afternoon, but were beaten back.

Late in the afternoon, Brig. Gen. Granger wired Maj. Gen. Thomas asking that he once more petition Lt. Forrest to send help from Bridgeport. Unwilling to concede that the river level was down, Decatur's defender argued that "a gunboat at Bridgeport [with] 500 men could be sent to Claysville in a few hours."

That night, the *Stone River* tied up at the Decatur wharf and disgorged 200 Ohio and Michigan reinforcements, bringing Granger's defense to about 3,000 men. The *General Thomas*, slowly steaming up the Tennessee, was able to hear "heavy trains moving along the mountain roads all night."[15]

Hood spent October 27 encircling Decatur. That morning, Acting Master Morton informed his Bridgeport superior that the *General Thomas* finally made it up the river near Fort Deposit and Beard's Bluff. Off Hobson's Island, a pair of Granger's scouts from Warrenton and Guntersville were taken aboard. The tired men reported that Hood's main force was moving down the river toward Decatur.

It had rained heavily all during the preceding night. The downpour had some effect on the river level, allowing the Upper Tennessee to rise almost an inch. Taking advantage of this welcome development, Morton handed a courier his message to Lt. Forrest and cast off, expecting to make it to Whitesburg by nightfall.

Meanwhile, out on the Mississippi, Rebel attacks on Federal shipping continued. Lt. Col. Jesse Forrest, with between 50 and 100 men from the 21st Tennessee Cavalry Regiment (C.S.A.), was hidden behind the levee at Randolph, TN, awaiting the first unfortunate steamer to put into shore. That victim was Capt. Alexander Ziegler's *Belle Saint Louis*,[16] en route from Memphis to St. Louis, with both civilian and military passengers and $40,000 in U.S. Army paymaster funds.

About midnight on October 27, the vessel reached Randolph, 60 miles above Memphis, where, by prior arrangement, she was to stop and take on eight bales of cotton. As soon as the staging was run out and the deckhands went ashore for the produce, Capt. Ziegler saw a number of men rushing toward the boat. Orders were immediately passed for the craft to back out into the stream, but before it could get completely off, eight to ten men jumped aboard. The others poured in small arms fire, making everyone dodge for cover. Several "guerrillas" descended below to force the engineers to return the craft to shore, while the others rushed the pilothouse and the cabin. At this point, the passengers panicked.

The four tinclads of the 11th District of the Mississippi Squadron were seldom in port at the same time as here at Bridgeport, Alabama, in March 1865. The craft, from left to right, are the *General Sherman*, *General Thomas* (with smoke rising from her chimneys), *General Grant*, and *General Burnside* (Miller's *Photographic History of the Civil War*, v. 6).

In the confusion, two Union officers aboard attempted to jump the Southerners guarding the main cabin doors. Stealthy they were not, and in the exchange of pistol fire that followed, two Rebels and a Federal were killed.

At this point, as the *Belle Saint Louis* once more neared the bank, the engineers seized the moment and backed her out again. The remaining Confederates on board jumped overboard and the big steamer gathered speed out of their musket range. The vessel soon encountered the tinclad *Curlew*, which convoyed her the rest of the way to Cairo.[17]

Later that day, with Brig. Gen. Buford's cavalry in the lead, two batteries of Maj. Gen. Forrest's Cavalry Corps, under the command of Capt. John W. Morton, arrived at the mouth of the Big Sandy River on the Lower Tennessee. After a reconnaissance by horsemen for several miles on either side of the Big Sandy's mouth, it was decided to post cannon at the abandoned Confederate Fort Heiman, two miles above Fort Henry, and at Paris Landing, five miles below. This spider trap was laid in such a way that unsuspecting Northern vessels might pass in, but would, in all likelihood, never exit. If the strategy worked, navigation of the Tennessee would be obstructed and communications would be cut off with Johnsonville, 40 miles away.

Under the personal command of Capt. E.S. Walton, Lt. W.O. Hunter's section ("Walton's Battery") of 20-pdr. Parrotts — the two heavy guns railroaded from Mobile — were placed in the upper fort at Fort Heiman while lighter guns from Lt. J.W. Brown's section ("Morton's Battery") of 3-inch Rodmans were placed 800 yards below Hunter on the river bank. A dismounted brigade of cavalry under Brig. Gen. Hylan B. Lyon was deployed as skirmishers. Down at Paris Landing, 10-pdr. Parrott rifle sections of both Walton's Battery and Morton's Battery were enplaced, the former at the landing and the second a thousand yards above near the mouth of the Big Sandy. Brig. Gen. Tyree H. Bell's brigade of dismounted cavalrymen were the skirmishers here.

The masked batteries were given the strictest command not to open fire until ordered. The plan was to await fully-laden boats and to leave alone those empty craft returning for new loads. A whole day — and four empty steamboats — would pass before such a target arrived. Meanwhile, on October 28, the *General Thomas* of the Eleventh District fired her first shots in anger.

During the night of October 27, Army of Tennessee units moved to the south edge of the Tennessee River to the right of Decatur and began to encircle the town while others established two batteries at different locations on the river bank about 1,500 yards from the principal Federal defenses. The Rebel emplacements, of four and six guns, were linked to each other and their main line by a chain of rifle pits.

Although fog made the darkness more ghostly, Brig. Gen. Granger, having learned of the enemy cannon, ordered a small earthwork set up on the north side of the river opposite the Confederates. Here he emplaced a section of his own guns (Co. A., 1st Tennessee Artillery, U.S.). When the fog lifted, these pieces opened up on the Confederates and were soon joined by gunners aboard the *Stone River*. Combat swayed back and forth on the right of Decatur all morning. Over on the left, the Tennessee battery, joined by the *Stone River*, engaged the Confederate guns, soon catching defending Rebel riflemen in a cross fire.

About noon, the *Stone River* was ordered to run by the enemy's battery, in much the same fashion Rear Adm. Porter's fleet had passed Vicksburg in April 1863. The converted transport made it by without damage and took a position above to fire against the rear of the enemy emplacements.

The *General Thomas* arrived in mid-afternoon from patrol and joined the *Stone River*. Brig. Gen. Granger now sent both boats orders to bombard the Confederate battery, in conjunction with the field pieces of the 1st Tennessee and several others now available from the right. The cross fire from the Union land-based artillery chased many Rebel gunners from their cannon, two of which were dismantled. During that shoot, the two gunboats dropped down the river until they were immediately opposite the Confederate emplacements, no more than 500 yards away. Both then opened with their broadside guns. "Their guns were most admirably served," Granger later reported, so that it was "impossible for men to withstand this attack." One shell from the *Stone River* reportedly exploded a caisson, killing 17 graycoats.

Over the next half hour, the two Federal vessels poured shot, shell, and canister onto the Confederate position. The range was gradually decreased to 300 yards. Abreast the battery, the *General Thomas* was hit four times, with one bolt passing through the hull, one through the wheelhouse, and two entering the cabin. As the naval fire intensified, Rebel cannoneers and crews deserted their pieces, with many fleeing to the river bank to seek the protection of large trees at the water's edge. "Many bodies," the District of Northern Alabama commander later wrote, "were afterward found in the river."

Though hit a number of times, the two gunboats suffered few casualties, losing two killed (one each) and 11 wounded. The captains of the two boats were praised in official dispatches for the skillful manner in which they handled their craft and even for "continuing to shell the crowd of fugitives as they fled back from the river."

The fighting at Decatur died down late on October 28, by which time it was decided to call the fight a demonstration and turn the Army of Tennessee toward Tuscumbia, on the south side of the Tennessee, where a safe crossing could be made below the shoals and beyond the reach of naval craft. The *General Thomas* passed the battery and landed at Decatur.

During the afternoon, the *General Thomas* briefly departed Decatur, continuing to shadow the movement of enemy cavalry along the river bank. As Acting Master Morton noted in a message to Maj. Gen. Thomas and Lt. Forrest, he "fired canister [6 shots] at them, and could see them running through the cornfield."

The Army of Tennessee removed the offending battery from the river bank near Decatur at 3 A.M. on October 29, covered by a dense fog. As it became increasingly evident that the Rebels were gone, the *General Thomas* and *Stone River* returned to their patrols.

Meanwhile, far up on the Lower Tennessee that day, the first prize snared in Maj. Gen. Forrest's trap was the stern-wheel transport *Mazeppa*,[18] towing two barges and en route from her Cincinnati homeport on her maiden voyage. She was disabled by the Paris Landing batteries and musketry during the morning after having been allowed to steam in ignorance past Fort Heiman. Laden with 700 tons of quartermaster's and subsistence stores, the big steamer, whose crew had fled permitting her easy capture, was quickly unloaded and burned. Some of the plunder was sent on to Gen. Hood.

October 30 was only five minutes old when Southern cavalry attacked the *General*

Thomas on the Upper Tennessee as the gunboat slowly cruised upstream. Howitzer fire was returned with unknown effect. By 7:30, the tinclad reached Whitesburg, where she ran aground on the bar.

Later that morning the surrender of the 110-ton side-wheeler *Anna*[19] was arranged after she had passed Paris Landing and been caught at Fort Heiman. However, before the Confederates could take possession of their prize, her captain ordered up full steam and the vessel turned downstream and headed toward Paducah. When almost out of range, several lucky shots riddled her masthead, pilothouse, texas, cabin, and chimneys. Her steam pipe was partially severed but, fortunately for her, she had sufficient headway to carry her out of range.

Forty miles from Paducah that Saturday the transports *Naugatuck*[20] and *Alice*[21] were both captured by local partisans at Widow Reynold's Bar. At the same time, several *Mazeppa* personnel reached the Federal post 10 miles downstream at Pine Bluff and informed its commander of the attack on their boat. Word was quickly sent to Nashville and Johnsonville, where investment of the depot was anticipated on Wednesday or Thursday, November 2 or 3.

Hardly was the *Anna* out of harm's way before combat at the Fort Heiman–Paris Landing trap was resumed. The *Undine*, which had escorted the *Anna* to Sandy Island, a point just above the spot where the transport was ambushed, was en route back to Johnsonville when the sound of big guns was heard. The tinclad came back to investigate, cleared for action. And action she found.

Bell's brigade and the guns at Paris Landing took the *Undine* under fire and a contest of wills and iron ensued for most of an hour. The light-draught, which was not designed to stand up against heavy cannon, was badly damaged and forced to retire downriver out of range of the guns at either Rebel position. At anchor on the river bend, her crew worked to repair her damage while her gunners fired at the Paris Landing battery as well as Confederate marksmen harassing them from the west bank.[22]

While the *Undine* was so occupied, Capt. John Allen's transport *Venus*,[23] with a barge in tow, came in sight from downriver. Blithely choosing to ignore warning signals from the tinclad, she paddled within range of the Confederate upper battery and was taken under fire. Although not damaged, Capt. Allen was wounded before she could run past the guns and anchor near the *Undine*.

Paris Landing was reinforced by troops from Brig. Gen. Chalmers's division and sections of Walton's Battery an hour before noon. It being a busy morning for all concerned here, not 20 minutes later, the barge-towing, 215-ton stern-wheel *J. W. Cheeseman*[24] came down the Tennessee. Her captain, Thad Wirthlihn, ignored a warning from the *Undine*, but, unlike the *Venus*, she did not escape. Rebel gunners shot off her steam pipe and otherwise so damaged her that she was forced to run into the west bank near White Oak Island and surrender, a useless wreck.

Capt. Morton now received orders from Brig. Gen. Buford to take a section of horse artillery down to the bend where the Yankee vessels were licking their wounds. Once in place, he was to destroy them or force them to steam back under the guns of Fort Heiman or Paris Landing. The day was chilly, with the sun obscured by hanging clouds; still, the sweating and exhausted graycoats manhandled their cannon into place and, just after 3

P.M., opened fire on both the *Venus* and her escort. Musketry from the Tennessee battalions of Cols. Kelley and T.C. Logwood was also telling, even though Bryant's howitzers spit canister at them from a distance of less than 100 yards.

The battle between the tinclad and the guns on the river bank continued loudly. Word that Forrest had batteries at Fort Heiman and Paris Landing and that the two Union boats were in trouble between them made it to Johnsonville, via Pine Bluff, later in the day. With this message in hand, Capt. Howland rushed down to the wharf, where he found the executive officer of the U.S.S. *Tawah*, Acting Master James B. Williams.[25] With the boat's commander, Acting Volunteer Lt. Jason Goudy, away at Paducah, Williams agreed to cast off and steam to the rescue.

The *Undine* and the Rebel batteries traded iron for nearly three hours. At 3:45 P.M., the steam pipe in the paddle wheeler's doctor room was cracked and filled the engineering spaces with hot gasses that forced the engineer and his men out. *Undine* was now unmanageable. With her ammunition nearly exhausted, Bryant ordered the tinclad headed into the east bank so that as many of her crew as possible might abandon ship. Before quitting ship, the captain, unable to resist further, ordered his guns spiked (two were) and unsuccessfully attempted to destroy his vessel.

At 4 P.M., the colors were struck. This surrender was not immediately observed by the Confederates, and firing continued for a period thereafter. *Undine* was the last U.S. warship surrendered in action prior to the U.S.S. *Pueblo* (AGER-2) in 1969. A Chicago correspondent later remarked that the boat was very slow, "one of the poorest of her class and, in a pecuniary view, the loss is trifling."

The *Venus* was simultaneously taken under fire, and suffered considerably. According to pilot Joseph A. Enghauser, who subsequently escaped back to Louisville and shared his recollections with the press, the loss of life was heavy, including 15 of 18 soldiers from Paducah, and "four men on deck were literally split in two." Also aboard but not hurt were the wives of the captain and mate, plus two families each with 10 children. The transport could not resist, but put into the west bank to surrender.

With the *Undine* taken intact, as well as the two transports, Forrest's command had possession of three boats that could potentially be put to good service in ferrying troops across the Tennessee River. Lt. Col. Kelley put two companies aboard the *Venus*, taking prisoner the surviving members of her 20-man armed guard. The "Parson" then crossed over to the other bank, where he took possession of the *Undine*. Kelley also, unknowingly, came into possession of the secret USN signal books. Loss of the codes set off something of a panic in Union Navy offices from the Mississippi to Washington, D.C., but there is no evidence that the Confederates who had them knew how to use the codes — or even that they had them.

As Lt. Col. Kelley was securing the Rebel prizes, another Yankee gunboat hove into sight from above. This was Lt. Williams's *Tawah* from Johnsonville. Despite the best of intentions, Williams quickly found that he was outgunned by Forrest's artillery. To be on the safe side, the *Tawah* anchored about a mile and a half above, but her long-range cannonade had no impact on the Confederates near Paris Landing. Brig. Gen. Chalmers ordered a section of his artillery shifted to handle the newcomer, and when those Parrotts opened fire, Williams found it necessary to withdraw.

Meanwhile, under Lt. Col. Kelley's direction, the *Venus* towed the *Undine* down to Paris Landing and a cheering welcome from Southern troopers. "The Parson," who had directed fire on the tinclad at Eastport, MS, earlier in the month, was pleased to find that, although she had four shell holes in her casemate, the warship was otherwise not seriously injured in hull, machinery, or armament. The barges were emptied and destroyed, as was the hulk of the *J. W. Cheeseman*.

Having missed the action of the previous days, Lt. Gen. Forrest arrived at Paris Landing on the morning of October 31 overjoyed to find that he now had a Confederate "Tennessee River Navy." As plans were made as what exactly to do with this windfall, Capt. Morton was asked to overhaul the *Undine*, make sure her guns were operable, and take charge of the "fleet." The artilleryman agreed to handle the upgrade, but asked that someone else with nautical experience skipper the gunboat.

The man chosen to take over the former Yankee warship was an experienced Cumberland River steamboat man, Capt. Frank P. Gracey of the 3rd Kentucky. His crew, recruited from his own unit, included several who had previously served aboard the C.S.S. *Arkansas*, the ironclad which had threatened the Union fleet at Vicksburg in 1862. Another steamboat man, turned horse soldier, Col. William A. Dawson of the 15th Tennessee, took over the *Venus* as "fleet commodore." With Forrest and Morton embarked upon the transport, the two boats made a trial run to Fort Heiman. There the *Venus* was armed with the two 20-pdr. Parrott rifles moved down from Walton's upper battery.

The capture of the *Undine* and *Venus* offered Forrest a golden opportunity to mount a coordinated attack on Johnsonville. The "Tennessee River Navy" would create a diversion to draw off Lt. King's tinclads — and any others which tried to interfere — while Rebel ground pounders and artillery assaulted the town, at the very least destroying its stores while perhaps even capturing the giant hoard of goods for transfer south.

Throughout the remainder of the day, volunteer Southern "horse marines" learned the ropes aboard the prize boats as preparations were made to move upstream. Fort Heiman, which had not previously played a very big role in the conflict, would be left behind after having proved to the world once and for all that, with a minimum of artillery, Confederate riders could "fight the Federal gunboats on even terms."[26]

Halloween on the Upper Tennessee started auspiciously for the *General Thomas* when the *Stone River* arrived off the Whitestown bar. Making fast to the stern of the tinclad, the ersatz army gunboat hauled her off into deeper water. Once Acting Master Morton's vessel was free, she rounded to and began a return trip to Decatur. En route, above Triana, she fired eight rounds of canister at a number of Confederate cavalry seen along the shore.

Acting Master Bryant and a number of surviving *Undine* crewmen made their way to Pine Bluff, arriving well before sunrise on October 31. Their reports on the loss of the *Undine*, *Venus*, and *J. W. Cheeseman* were wired by the post commander to Nashville and Johnsonville, from which they were telegraphed to others in authority. The Johnsonville post commander was quite emphatic: "I have not now, nor have had any idea of surrendering. Will fight to the last if attacked. I feel confident that I can hold the place...."

As the fall sun rose, guerrillas, over on the Cumberland River, captured and burned the chartered 250-ton stern-wheeler *David Hughes*[27] and her barge. This loss of U.S. government stores was recorded at a point 15 miles above Clarksville.

Alarm bells now began to sound all along the rivers; Paducah was once more thought to be a major Rebel target. When the tinclad *Curlew* came into Mound City from Louisiana, she was granted one hour in port to discharge the clerk and a passenger of the *Belle Saint Louis*. She was then hurried off to reinforce Lt. Cmdr. Shirk. Elsewhere, shipments out of Louisville and St. Louis up the Tennessee were halted.

Next morning, November 1, Lt. King, with the *Key West* and *Elfin*, arrived at Johnsonville from Paducah. Also in the hours after breakfast, Acting Rear Admiral Lee assumed command of the Mississippi Squadron in a brief ceremony aboard the flag boat *Black Hawk* at Mound City. The new squadron commander's joyful day quickly turned sour. As his predecessor put it, Lee "was not fortunate on his arrival in the West." In his first report to Secretary Welles, the cabinet official who had fired him earlier in order to give his slot to Porter, Lee had to acknowledge that the *Undine* and two transports were reported ("but not officially") captured on the Tennessee River.

With some of the goods from the *Mazeppa* and the two 20-pder. Parrotts transferred to the *Venus* and the *Undine* readied, Forrest's command struck out for Reynoldsburg and Johnsonville this same morning. The general had, unhappily, found it necessary, due to the poor roads and the worn-out condition of his artillery horses, to load the big guns and the *Mazeppa* plunder aboard the *Venus*. The weather was damp and miserable. A cold rain plagued the butternut troopers all day and into the night as they marched along the muddy bank working to keep up with the troop-laden boats in the river.

Brig. Gen. Chalmers men were in the lead with Buford's in the rear; the horse artillery attempted to remain close to the ex–Yankee steamers, which had orders not to get ahead. The underbrush was thick and thorny and the trails available did not always permit easy access to the river. The trek was particularly nasty for the cannoneers, who were, nevertheless, prepared to "drop the trails and begin shooting in defense of the vessels at a moment's notice." At dusk, the Confederates made camp near the wrecked Danville railroad bridge.[28]

All Soul's Day, November 2, was particularly busy in Union circles, as the Northern army and navy began to learn of or react to the crises on the Upper and Lower Tennessee. News of Forrest's victories on the latter speedily reached St. Louis, Nashville, Paducah, Smithland, and Columbus, KY, by telegraph. Maj. Gen. Thomas at Tennessee's capital wasted no time in calling upon regional USN commanders that day, asking that they lift Forrest's blockade of the Tennessee. When the *Curlew* arrived off Paducah that afternoon, her crew expected to perhaps find the town invested by "the devil's" Cavalry Corps. Instead, Acting Ensign H.B. O'Neill's boat was immediately sent up the Tennessee by Lt. Cmdr. Shirk in company with the *Fairy* and *Paw Paw*. The expedition was under the command of Acting Volunteer Lt. Goudy, whose *Tawah* had been in action against Morton's gunners two days earlier.

Lt. Cmdr. Shirk wired Mound City two hours later, reporting that he had dispatched three boats upstream already and was calling upon the Tenth District for reinforcement. Though Forrest may have bottled most of his fleet up at Johnsonville, it was entirely possible for Shirk to recombine against him through a judicious transfer of squadron elements from the Cumberland, via Smithland and Paducah. Shirk's message, similar to one sent to Maj. Gen. Thomas, was acknowledged at 8 P.M. by Acting Rear Admiral Lee.

About 10 P.M., a messenger from Smithland brought Shirk's call for help from the local telegraph office to Lt. Cmdr. Le Roy Fitch aboard his flag boat, the *Moose*. Although the Tenth District commander readily determined to reinforce his neighbor, it was too dark to get over the bars at the mouth of the Cumberland. The captains of the *Brilliant* and *Victory*, Acting Volunteer Lt. Charles G. Perkins and Acting Master Frederick Read, were ordered to get their boats ready to leave in the morning.

Early on November 3, just before departing, Lt. Cmdr. Fitch appeared at the Smithland telegraph office and sent a reassuring wire to Maj. Gen. Thomas indicating that he would reinforce Lt. Cmdr. Shirk. Fitch optimistically opined: "I think there is no doubt that we can reopen the Tennessee." Fitch's little task group arrived at Paducah later in the day.

There the Federal Cumberland convoy commodore conferred with his Tennessee River counterpart. Both Fitch and Shirk were convinced that Confederate forces might yet attack Paducah. Maybe, they wondered, the enemy really wanted to cripple the upper river gunboat flotillas in order to have free reign over the rivers. Whatever the "Wizard's" motives, he had to be halted and the two officers, attempting to "cover all the bases," settled on a plan. Fitch would take his boats up the Tennessee, assume tactical command of all naval craft in the Johnsonville area, and try to stop Forrest if he was there. Shirk would remain behind with the *Peosta*, then undergoing repair, to guard Paducah just in case that town was again the Rebel goal.[29]

Upstream this day, the Rebel columns moving along the west bank, together with the Tennessee River Navy, made steady and uneventful progress toward Johnsonville until about 3:30 P.M. The *Venus*, faster than her consort, had, contrary to orders, pulled ahead of the *Undine* and moved out of range of the supporting horse artillery. Moving into a sharp bend in the stream off Green Bottom Bar, some six miles below Johnsonville, her luck ran out. Almost like a train running head-on toward a broken trestle, the Parrott-equipped steamer came into gun range of the *Key West* and *Tawah*.

The Yankee tinclads had started a river reconnaissance from Johnsonville a half hour before this encounter and it is quite probable that the tars on the opposing craft, professional and amateur, were equally surprised to see one another. Recovering quickly from any astonishment, Lt. King's two boats "made short work of Forrest's sailors," wrote Dr. Wyeth years later. In a 20-minute engagement, the *Venus* was badly damaged and, in an effort to avoid her capture or destruction, she was run ashore. There her officers and crew abandoned her, "without setting it on fire." The *Undine* rounded to "and sought safety in flight," moving, "with shot through her," according to Lt. King, under the protection of the Rebel mobile field batteries. Heavy fog and mist and the unknown placement of the Southern guns prevented her pursuit. King, whose *Key West* had worked in tandem with the *Undine* earlier, sarcastically noted that "she went downriver faster than ever before!"

Lt. King's prize was significant and helped to raise Union morale. Not only was the transport taken intact, she had aboard Forrest's two largest cannon (the 20-pdr. Parrotts), plus two hundred rounds of ammunition and the freight from the *Mazeppa*. After running a gauntlet of musket fire at the head of Reynoldsburg Island, King's two boats returned to Johnsonville with the *Venus* about 6:30 P.M. Running to the telegraph office, he wired Lt. Cmdr. Shirk to report the capture of the steamer and the escape of the gunboat. With the Confederates known to be just over five miles away, a more ominous note was also sounded: "All anxious about this place. Please send up more gunboats at once.... We won't allow this place to fall into enemy's hands, if our forces can prevent, but please send up more gunboats."

While King's message was humming toward Paducah, the task group under Acting Volunteer Lt. Goudy finally reached the vicinity below Forts Henry and Heiman. Progress up the river had been slowed by the *Paw Paw*. The center-wheeler "was so slow that we were over two days getting up to that place," remembered Acting Master's Mate De Witt C. Morse, alias "Gunboat," aboard the *Curlew*.

Next morning, the *Paw Paw*, *Fairy*, and *Curlew* undertook a reconnaissance by fire into the areas surrounding Fort Henry and Fort Heiman, pumping shells at suspicious wooded areas and neighboring hills as they steamed past. "Our shell would not bring a man in sight at either place," noted Mate Morse. As the three were so engaged, the task group under Lt. Cmdr. Fitch came up, allowing the veteran Hoosier officer to assume overall command. After "speaking" Goudy, Fitch directed that the six boats all drop back and form into a line-ahead order which would permit them to reserve their fire for any batteries which opened up on them. The Tennessee was quite deep at this point and wide enough to permit the tinclads to engage batteries as a fleet without risk of grounding.

When no sign of the enemy was found, Fitch ordered his craft to steam upriver the three or four miles to Paris Landing. Going ashore there, the tinclad warrior found a surgeon tending a number of wounded U.S. sailors from the *Undine*. Some of these men, all of whom were "suffering for want of medicines, etc.," reported that Forrest's Cavalry Corps was en route toward Johnsonville. They were reported to have some 18 to 20 artillery pieces which they were hauling overland, as well as the undamaged *Venus* and *Undine*.[30]

By noon on November 3, Forrest's cavalry and the *Undine*, last remaining vessel of the Tennessee River Navy, had reached the vicinity of Reynoldsburg Island, 3.5 miles below Johnsonville. The island was a major navigational feature that split the river flow and forced upstream traffic to pass it through a narrow chute that hugged the Tennessee's west bank. The river's main channel cut abruptly to the east bank south of the island and impassable shoal water lay to its east. Confederate artillery was placed at the head and foot of the atoll and a new trap was laid for the Union navy.[31]

In an effort to draw Acting Volunteer Lt. King's tinclads from Johnsonville into an ambush, Capt. Gracey's *Undine*, still loaded with grayclad troops, twice boldly sortied toward the Yankee depot. On each occasion, King was tempted to go after her, moving the *Key West* down a mile to a point where she came under intense volleys of musketry from the head of Reynoldsburg Island. Sensing his peril, the lieutenant refused both times to commit to further pursuit. Rather, he retired to the Johnsonville levee and, in the end, elected to anchor and station the *Tawah* with her head downstream, so as to command the channel with her 30-pounders.

Having in the meantime received a telegram of encouragement from Lt. Cmdr.

Shirk, King returned the wire, reporting that he had the *Undine* in sight below the island and that a battery of Rebel 10-pounders was reported on the adjacent western river bank. Believing the outpost surrounded and that his boats might be subjected to a "commando" raid after dark, he once again pleaded: "Send large fleet of gunboats at once, if possible."

In the early afternoon, the King relief force, *Moose, Brilliant, Victory, Paw Paw, Fairy,* and *Curlew.* departed Paris Island for up the river. At the Memphis and Clarksville Railroad crossing, the six came upon a force of 40 or 50 cavalry foraging. "They were shelled and soon disappeared."

Back at Johnsonville around 4 P.M., Acting Volunteer Lt. King met with the local assistant quartermaster in charge of the port's logistical machinery and advised him what action should be taken with regards to the tied-up steamers in the event of a surprise night attack on the gunboats. It was particularly recommended that the officer make plans to fire all of the transports to keep them out of Forrest's hands should the Rebels attempt to board and take the navy craft. The message was passed to all of the steamboat masters at the levee along with a warning not to destroy any of the boats until their takeover was imminent.

As the afternoon waned, Maj. Gen. Forrest and his artillery chief, Capt. Morton, stealthily examined the area across the river from Johnsonville, seeking firing locations from which to bombard the depot. The western shore was boggy, with only a few bad roads, much underbrush, and a surprisingly wide variety of wildlife. Working covertly in daylight, the two chose behind the levee and east of the low crest on the earthen tongue which separated Trace Creek and the Tennessee.

The Confederates could plainly see every detail of the base, 800 yards away, and hear every noise from horses to lifting machinery. Several boats and barges had yet to be unloaded because there wasn't room. The landing and banks were piled high with freight destined for Maj. Gen. Sherman. Indeed, all of the warehouses were full and trains were running "incessantly night and day in removing" the goods. The Federals had no pickets across the river and did not know they were under close surveillance.[32]

Above Turkey Island — or just below Green Bottom Bar — about 30 miles above Fort Heiman, the task group led by Lt. Cmdr. Fitch came upon a large Rebel encampment about 9:30 P.M. The gunboats opened fire in the dark and the shelling, which went on for a time, caused the soldiers to extinguish their campfires. The Indiana sailor believed they might have been driven back, but perhaps "not entirely away, as they could be heard during the night."

Given the narrow places, bad bars, and other navigational difficulties known to be ahead and unsure whether or not any Southern artillery awaited him, Fitch elected not to advance further. Instead, he dropped down a little below the camp he had been shelling and located a point where there was no road by which the enemy could bring cannon on the bank abreast his boats. There, six miles below Johnsonville, his flotilla anchored for the night.

By dark, all of Forrest's troops had arrived, and he began to dispose them at key points from which they could bombard the Union depot across the Tennessee. As he later wrote in his official report, the Yankees commanded the position he designed to occupy and so he was necessarily compelled to act with great caution. Having chosen his artillery loca-

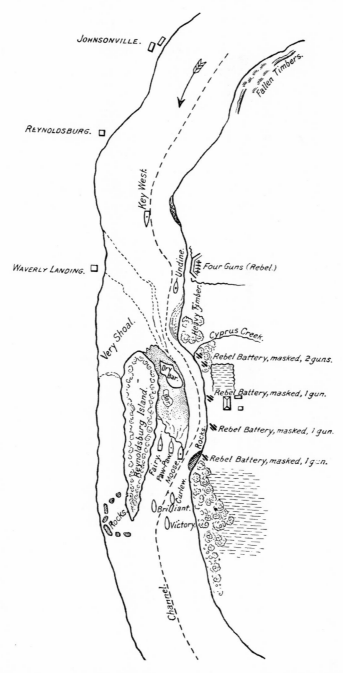

A rescue force sent up the Tennessee River to rescue besieged Johnsonville on November 4 could not get past Confederate gunners overlooking the northern approach. This map, drawn after the destruction of the supply depot, demonstrates the obstacles blocking six Federal tinclads from breaking through. (*Official Records of the Union and Confederate Navies* vol. 26).

tions that afternoon, the "Wizard" set to work that night planting his guns. Brig. Gen. Chalmers recorded the disposition:

> Colonel Mabry, with his brigade and Thrall's battery, on the right immediately above and opposite to Johnsonville; Colonel Rucker, with Morton's battery and
>
>> the Seventh Alabama Cavalry, immediately below and opposite to that place; Lieu-tenant Colonel Kelley, with the Twenty-Sixth Tennessee Battalion and two guns of Rice's battery, opposite to Reynoldsburg, and Lieutenant Colonel Logwood, of the Fifteenth Tennessee Cavalry, with his regiment and a section of Hudson's battery, at Clark's House, still further down the river and about two miles below Johnsonville.

Captain Thrall's howitzers, at their location about a half mile above the landing, were tasked with resisting Union attacks from upriver, while Capt. Hudson's two guns would hopefully beat back any assault from downstream. The others would smash the Northern depot when the attack began at noon sharp.

While his officers and men worked on their surprise, Maj. Gen. Forrest wrote a dispatch to his commander, Lt. Gen. Richard Taylor, now come east from the Trans-Mississippi Department. In it, he revealed that he was in front of Johnsonville, where he could see three gunboats, seven transports, "and quite a number of barges." Batteries had been placed above and below the boats and the night was being spent fortifying and placing a battery straight across from them. On the morrow, he would "endeavor to sink or destroy them."

Forrest, almost prophetically, offered his thoughts on the *Undine*. "We still have the gunboat," he noted, "but she is out of coal." As her furnaces required coal and he was unable to obtain any or run her by Johnsonville, "I may have to burn her." Even if he did not need to do so next day, he would certainly do so "day after tomorrow" before moving off to join General Hood.

When Capt. Morton arrived on the scene early on the morning of November 4, he found the secret work of clearing away the undergrowth and placing the guns well advanced. With Forrest's permission, Morton made a final check of possible positions and found a very suitable spot higher up. The scene which unfolded below him was animated with an "air of complete security." Two gunboats with steam up were moored at the landing, while another plied directly beneath the bluff on which the Confederate Chief of Artillery stood. He could, he remembered, "almost have dropped a stone upon it." Two freight trains were being made up, and a number of barges were being loaded by African-Americans.

Morton hastened back to detail his findings to Forrest. The spot was ideal, Morton pleaded. It was too high for the gunboats to reach without firing over it and the Yankee fort stood on a ridge that was so elevated that its guns could not be depressed sufficiently to hit any Rebel guns. A skeptical general permitted his artillery man to move two 3-inch guns to his "comparatively safe" location. The task, undertaken by Morton's men through mud and thick underbrush, required two hours of backbreaking hand transport to accomplish. Once the pair were placed, Forrest had eleven cannon in proximity to the huge base and no enemy the wiser. None of the gunboats or transports at Johnsonville or downriver from them would be able to pass Reynoldsburg Island either to escape or to help.[33]

While Capt. Morton was making his reconnaissance, Lt. Cmdr. Fitch got his task group underway and proceeded up the river in the rain the six miles from his night anchorage at the foot of Green Bottom Bar to a position off Reynoldsburg Island. From this vantage point, he could see the three Ninth District gunboats above, *Tawah, Key West,* and *Elfin.* The *Moose,* followed by the *Paw Paw* and *Fairy,* chosen because they had the guns with the longest range, moved up to the foot of the chute separating the island from the shore.

As they paddled up, a battery was spotted at the head of the chute. It was taken under fire in order to test the caliber of the Rebel cannon. The bombardment could be heard at Johnsonville. The Southerners refused to respond; rather, they moved their guns around into a small ravine or behind an embankment.

In late morning, as the three gunboats below the island were attempting by their fire to draw out the Confederate horse artillery, one of the gunboats above moved down and made its number, identifying itself as the *Key West.* Acting Volunteer Lt. King's flag boat was prevented from making a rendezvous by a heavy battery placed in the false bend of the Tennessee just above the point. The battery commanded the upper end of the chute and was protected from the *Moose, Paw Paw,* and *Fairy* by a skirt of heavy timber on the point below. Tragically, the three boats below also held additional ammunition and stores now desperately needed by the Johnsonville flotilla and the Rebel guns forbad a transfer. Acting Master's Mate Morse aboard the *Curlew* later remembered that "seeing the *Key West* stand toward us reminded me of a drowning man reaching out his hand to an idle crowd of cowards...."

Perhaps as cover for the Confederates' final bombardment preparations, particularly Morton's activities in digging his battery into a small enclosure, "Commodore" Dawson and Capt. Gracey now chose to run the *Undine* up toward Reynoldsburg Island in another attempt to lure the Johnsonville-based gunboats under the shore batteries of their land-based comrades, Rice and Hudson. Located as she was on the river below Pilot Knob, the highest point on the west bank of the Tennessee, the former Union gunboat, after shooting a few shells toward Johnsonville, succeeded in provoking the *Key West, Tawah,* and *Elfin* to cast off after her. As the three Union Navy tinclads chugged toward him, Gracey ordered his vessel backed downstream under the protection of the Southern land cannon.

The soldier-captain later recalled in a statement quoted in John Latham's book that his attention was drawn astern by wild gestures and the noise made by Ohio River pilot William Weaver in the pilothouse. Walking to the other side of the pilothouse, Gracey "saw a sight to make him gesticulate. There were seven of the latest Ohio River gunboats within easy gunshot range." The *Undine* was caught between the guns of Fitch's task group and King's task group, with the former blocking her escape downriver. Gracey and his crew fully realized, as Forrest's own admission had confirmed, that they were expendable, but, just maybe before her loss, a price might first be extracted from the enemy.

The *Key West* and *Tawah* came up with their former consort and, in a brief engagement, the amateur Confederate sailors were easily outmaneuvered. Still, *Undine* gave as good as she got — for a little while. Then, out of coal, Dawson and Gracey decided the game was over. As they ran the tinclad for shore under the Rebel batteries two and a half miles below Johnsonville, they knew they had accomplished something — the three Yankee boats were drawn within range of Hudson's and Rice's gunners.

When the *Key West* approached the battery in pursuit of the *Undine*, she was taken under fire by the shore-based artillerists who pumped thirty-odd shots at her in a space of 20 minutes, two-thirds for effect. The gunboat suffered ten hits through her upper works, seven through her berth deck, and two through the hull, with several guns disabled. Additionally, the *Tawah's* hull began to open along her stem as the result of the concussion of her bow guns. *Elfin* was also damaged, and the *Tawah* was largely ineffectual because her newly-received ammunition, obtained from Nashville a day earlier, proved too large. The shelling forced King to back up and return above, with the *Key West* assisted by the *Tawah*.

At the same time that the *Moose* started up the chute and the *Key West* started down, Capt. Gracey and several men spread torn-up straw mattresses around the deck and engineering spaces of the *Undine*, and sprinkled oil over them. The boat was headed hard for shore and struck a sandbar in three feet of water, about 75 yards from the head of the island. Gracey and several others applied the torches and jumped into the water. The *Undine* quickly burned down to the waterline, her magazine exploded spectacularly, and what was left of her lodged in the false bend above Reynoldsburg Island. The saga of the Tennessee River Navy was over. All of its surviving volunteer sailors were now soldiers once more.

Aware of the gunfire clash between King and the *Undine*, sailors aboard the tinclads above Reynoldsburg Island pondered whether a push through its chute, maybe reminiscent of the *Moose's* rush up the Buffington Island slot after Morgan in 1863, might be attempted. "We were every moment expecting orders to advance," Mate Morse later recalled. Capt. Gracey on the *Undine* later wondered: "Why they [Fitch's boats] did not shoot I could not say, unless they were afraid of striking their friends who were in easy range just above me."

Those aboard the *Curlew*, "both officers and men," were particularly anxious to assist, "Gunboat" recalled. Lt. Cmdr. Fitch himself was initially inclined "to try to run the batteries and get above," but soon changed his mind. In operational control of most of the tinclads remaining in the Mississippi Squadron's Ninth and Tenth Districts, Fitch was realized the stakes he faced and the potential for disaster that awaited any nautical charge. The enemy batteries, narrowness of the channel, shoal water, and the possibility of a damaged vessel blocking the passage militated against any decision to proceed. Forrest had outmaneuvered the USN and the Tenth District commander knew it. Historian Latham later confirmed Fitch's situation: "At the same time, the *Paw Paw*, *Fairy*, and *Moose* were engaging a Confederate battery at the head of the chute, thus making it impossible for them to ascend the river."

Afterwards, the task group skipper outlined the difficulties he thought he faced in a report to Rear Admiral Lee. The document, reproduced in the Navy *Official Records*, is accompanied by a map, which is not reproduced in the online version of the navy documents provided by Cornell University. Lee was advised that, to pass through the narrow channel to the right of the bar, the tinclads would have had to go single file within 50 yards of Hudson's battery. If any one of them was disabled in the swift shoal water, she would lodge on the head of the bar directly under the Rebel guns, less than 100 yards away. If such occurred, none of the other boats could steam to her assistance, as there was insufficient space to pass up alongside to go on ahead.

"Had there been a chance of my getting through with the loss of only one or two boats and then dislodging the enemy," perhaps remembering the exploit of Capt. Henry Walke at Island No. 10 in 1862 when the ironclad *Carondelet* and the following U.S.S. *Pittsburgh* had accomplished a similar goal, "I should have attempted it." Unlike Walke's exploit, however, Fitch had no land force to render assistance or gain advantage from any success the tinclads might realize and keep the Rebels away permanently.

Even if all or any of his six boats got through, they still had to return below again past Reynoldsburg Island by the same chute, at which time it could be expected that Forrest's guns would have been sited to fire into their sterns. "After considering everything and seeing what little chance there was for any of my boats getting through," he later wrote, "I thought it mere folly to attempt such a hazardous move...." Indeed, the task group commander believed that, if he made the effort, "not a single boat would have got out of the river." Thus it was that the hoped-for rescue attempt did not come off.

Hoping to save ammunition and suspecting that he could not "do much execution" due to the intervening heavy timber, Fitch, nevertheless, ordered his three vessels to open a deliberate fire on the offending gunners. This heavy shoot continued without result "until about 11 o'clock, when it ceased."

Though not as physically uncomfortable as Capt. Gracey, who was then hiding in the canebrakes along the river bank with the survivors of the *Undine*, the task group commander and his sailors were also unable to take any active part in the events that occurred after lunch.[34]

Following the *Undine* engagement, Acting Volunteer Lt. King's three gunboats retired to a position off Johnsonville to protect the transports and supplies. Many in the town, including those aboard King's craft, believed — in error — that the morning's triumph had caused Forrest's people to hesitate or perhaps withdraw.

The *Key West, Tawah, and Elfin*, moored at the landing, kept steam up, even as their officers and men attended to such regular duties as clothes washing and deck scrubbing. Just to be certain that the Rebels were departed, the damaged *Key West* and *Tawah*, lashed together, pushed off from the dock shortly before 2 P.M. to investigate a report that the enemy was "planting batteries directly opposite, also above and below, our warehouses and levee." As they swung out, ten hidden Confederate cannon, all carefully trained on them, "were discharged with such harmony that it could not be discerned there was more than one report — one heavy gun."

When Forrest opened fire, the *Key West* and *Tawah* were headed toward a Tennessee River bend above Johnsonville. The peaceful scene changed, as Capt. Morton later put it, "as if a magician's wand had been suddenly waved over it." The cannonade "continued with one unceasing roar" and, according to Maj. Gen. Forrest, quickly disabled King's two boats. "In fifteen minutes after the engagement commenced," he remembered, they "were set on fire and made rapidly for the shore, where they were consumed."

Tied to several flatboats, the *Elfin* was able to get off a number of rounds. Return fire badly damaged her paddle wheel, making it impossible for her to move. When the "abandon ship" order was received, the crew scrambled ashore. Her officers and men joined those from the other two boats in seeking the safety of Fort Johnson. Then, a young man from Chicago, Spencer A. Wright, to quote the correspondent from his hometown newspaper, "walked on board with the greatest coolness, set it afire, threw a shovelful of coal into the magazine, and then left." The *Elfin*, abandoned and ablaze, burned to the water's edge.

Forrest's batteries, having disposed of the USN guard, "next opened upon the eight transports, and in a short time, they were in flames." Among those thus destroyed were the *Anna*, which Forrest had nearly nabbed earlier, and the prize *Venus*.

The cannonade that followed against the river craft and depot facilities was the "most terrific" the port quartermaster, Capt. Henry Howland, had ever witnessed, and was accompanied by volleys of rifle fire. The *Louisville Journal* later reported that the "great fury" with which the Rebels shelled the town "created a panic among the citizens and government employees." Maj. Gen. Forrest observed that King's gunboats (28 guns) and Fort Johnson (14 guns) returned fire, and that about 50 guns were "thus engaged at the same time." Like Howland, the "Wizard" found that "the firing was terrific."

The racket from all this gunfire was easily heard by Fitch's task group above. About 2:30 P.M., as the din increased, the *Moose* paddled up into the Reynoldsburg Island chute; her commander thought that Hudson's battery might have been removed and that he might somehow assist King. It had not, and it opened on the Tenth District flagboat. After an uneventful 15-minute engagement during which she was unable to dislodge the Southern guns, the *Moose* returned and tied up at foot of island. Smoke and the din of combat continued from the direction of Johnsonville throughout the afternoon.

At some point, a messenger from Johnsonville reached Fitch with word that King's gunboats were actively engaged and fighting desperately. Thus it was believed on the boats above, but without conclusive visual collaboration, that the *Key West*, *Tawah*, and *Elfin* were having somewhat more success against the Rebel batteries than was actually the case. Still attempting to assert some control over the situation, Fitch penned an order to King directing him to "get the transports and the gunboats together, and as a last resort to run the batteries and get below to me, but above all not to let any of the transports fall into the enemy's hands." Fort Johnson telegraphed Nashville, which promised that the entire XXIII Corps under Maj. Gen. John M. Schofield would soon arrive.

At 4 P.M., Acting Volunteer Lt. King wired Lt. Cmdr. Shirk at Paducah advising him of the disaster. The *Paw Paw* and other boats were below, with batteries above and below them, and unable to intervene. Johnsonville, he warned, could only be saved by a large land force and ironclads. Shirk did not receive the telegraph until next day.

When it was nearly dark, observers reported Johnsonville ablaze and that all of the boats along the levee were on fire. It was impossible for Fitch to determine "whether the shell fired them or they were set on fire by our forces." It was, however, fairly certain that "the gunboats were among the number we saw on fire." In a report to Acting Rear Adm. Lee, Lt. Cmdr. Fitch expressed a belief that Forrest probably couldn't take Fort Johnson, "but his shell or our forces have undoubtedly destroyed everything." How accurate he was would shortly be revealed.[35]

Maj. Gen. Forrest did not know in real time that most of the transports and barges were purposefully put to the torch under the earlier contingency plan designed to prevent their capture agreed to by King and Fort Johnson's commander. The 10-foot high stacks of provisions stored in the open and on the levee, warehouses, and other facilities were shot up and, by nightfall, "the wharf for nearly one mile up and down the river presented one solid sheet of flame."

At Nashville, Capt. John C. Van Duzer wired a summary of the latest news to Maj. Thomas Eckert, head of the Federal telegraph service at the War Department and, after the war, Assistant Secretary of War. The news from the Tennessee capital was bleak. There was no definite information concerning the movement of Hood's main body. Additionally and bluntly, Van Duzer noted, that Forrest had "repulsed five gunboats which attacked him and compelled them to fall back down the river," in addition to destroying three gunboats and at least two transports at Johnsonville.[36]

Two days later, a leading Kentucky newspaper told its readers that this encounter between the Confederate batteries and King's light-draughts was, in fact, a duel between six Rebel batteries and four USN gunboats, convoying a fleet of 14 transports. "Their shot and shell crashed through our boats, wrecking them in a fearsome manner and completely disabling them. The gunboat No. 32 [*Key West*] received 35 cannon shot through her."

Fewer than 10 men altogether on both sides were killed in action at Johnsonville. The Federal loss in material was estimated at $2.2 million, though one modern historian has estimated that, in terms of the early 21st century value of the dollar, the goods destroyed could not be duplicated for less than $20 million. Not counting the value of the *Mazeppa*, Forrest was proud of the fact that, during the course of this unique raid, he had destroyed four gunboats, numerous steamers and barges, the 33 artillery pieces on the navy warships, and quartermaster's stores estimated at between 75,000 and 120,000 tons, while capturing 9,000 pairs of shoes, a thousand blankets, and 150 prisoners.

Nearly every history of the Johnsonville campaign suggests that the Union commanders in the town, both naval and military, acted too quickly to destroy the boats and supplies. Lt. Cmdr. Fitch, "whose judgment and courage were well proved," according to Admiral Mahan, said that King's three gunboats had been well handled, but could not stand up to the heavy guns firing upon them in the uncertain channel. Admiral Porter agreed on the bravery exhibited, but added that "they had been sent on duty that more properly belong to ironclads, and in contending against the enemy's works, their ardor eclipsed their judgment." Mahan, after reviewing the events of the day and noting that Johnsonville was relieved 24 hours later by elements from Schofield's corps, was blunt: "...if King had patiently held on a little longer, his pluck and skill would have been rewarded by saving his vessels."

Forrest, a master of placing the "skeert" into his enemy, outfoxed his opponents. "It was fear," Thomas Van Horne, biographer of Maj. Gen. George Thomas later admitted, "rather than necessity that caused this waste." Porter, when he wrote of the matter two decades later, was equally blunt. "Had he [Lt. Cmdr. Fitch] been present [in Johnsonville], his good judgment would have led to a different result."

The real story of the Johnsonville operation was, for the South, one of an opportunity seized too late and, for the North, the loss of a facility that, in the end, didn't mat-

The Union Army depot at Johnsonville, Tennessee, on the Tennessee River, had become an important supply hub by the fall of 1864. On November 4, Confederate forces under Maj. Gen. Nathan Bedford Forrest attacked and destroyed much of the center and numerous vessels, including three tinclads, at its levee. It was later estimated that the value of goods lost was approximately $2.2 million (approximately $20 million in today's money). The station was not reopened (Miller's *Photographic History of the Civil War,* v. 1).

ter all that much. Maj. Gen. Sherman had already assembled all of the supplies required for his sortie from Atlanta to Savannah. Indeed, in less than a week, he would cut himself off entirely from the North and "live off the land" of the Georgia countryside.

At Nashville, Maj. Gen. Thomas, who received "the truth on the disgraceful affair" from Schofield a few days later, could depend upon both the Louisville & Nashville Railroad and the Cumberland River. The attacking Southern troops hoped to sever Sherman's supply lines, forcing him to abandon the forthcoming March across Georgia. Able to grasp the big picture, Sherman, in a message to Lt. Gen. Grant, was not overly upset even as he noted "that devil Forrest was down about Johnsonville making havoc among the gunboats and transports." Johnsonville was not rebuilt as a depot; in fact, it was abandoned on November 30. Its wreckage would not be cleaned up for months.

Forrest's audacity did not change the Northern logistical situation one iota, but it did further enhance its author's legend. It was marked the largest loss of USN light-draughts in any single campaign of the Western war. The next time they were placed into the same arena with Forrest's gunners, they would be covered by ironclads.[37]

Because most of the depot's goods plus the gunboats and transports were destroyed, Maj. Gen. Forrest did not cross the river in force and capture Johnsonville. He had orders to rejoin Hood and could not have gotten over anyway, having only two small boats from the *Undine*. Besides, "the work designed by the expedition" was substantially completed; there was nothing to be gained by ransacking the blazing ruins of the depot or attacking Fort Johnson. Pleased with their success, the Confederates marched six miles away from the depot during the night "by the light of the enemy's burning property." The weather remained wretched, with rain falling heavily and mud everywhere, especially on the roads.

The following morning, November 5, Maj. Gen. Forrest returned to the Tennessee opposite Johnsonville to personally observe his success by daylight. After a brief artillery and rifle exchange with African-American troops across the stream, the butternut contingent headed off to the southwest to join the rest of the cavalry group as it moved toward Corinth, five days away.

At Cairo before lunch, Acting Rear Adm. Lee sent the first of many wires to Maj. Gen. Thomas. Written in cipher, the telegram announced his assumption of squadron command and promised to always cooperate cordially with the Nashville-based Army boss. The message also recapped what was known of Johnsonville area activities and preparations the navy was making to help prevent enemy reinforcements from reaching Hood from over the Mississippi.

Thomas at Nashville finally received Acting Rear Admiral Lee's dispatch 11 hours after it was sent. The theater commander replied immediately, noting that the Johnsonville garrison had reported being able to see the smoke from Fitch's task group, but was unable to communicate with it. On November 6, the rains came and there was hope that depths in the rivers would increase.

The general, too, asked the navy boss to assign some ironclads to the Tennessee "when the river gets high enough." Ever optimistic, he prophesied that, together, they would be able to "clear the enemy entirely out of west Tennessee." Even after almost four years of war, the word "ironclad" still had magic, even if "tinclad" did not.[38]

12

Nashville and Beyond, December 1864–April 1865

While Maj. Gen. Nathan Bedford Forrest was away burning Johnsonville, Gen. John Bell Hood's advance into Middle Tennessee was delayed by three weeks. After leaving the environs of unfriendly Decatur, the Army of Tennessee occupied Florence and Tuscumbia and then paused to gather and ensure its supplies. There it was joined by Forrest's command. Simultaneously, Union Maj. Gen. George ("Old Pap") Thomas was reinforced with several corps and cavalry.

On November 12, Maj. Gen. William Tecumseh Sherman cut himself off from the North and marched off toward the Atlantic. Two days later, 25,000 men from the Federal IV and XXIII Corps were at Pulaski to oppose Hood. Confederate forces, beginning on November 19, started toward Columbia, planning to turn the Yankees out of Pulaski. The Northern field commander, Maj. Gen. John Schofield, evacuated that place on November 22 and moved back toward Columbia, entrenching south of the Duck River.

Hood's soldiers came upon Columbia five days later, at which point Schofield moved across the river, destroying its bridges. The gallant Southern campaigner, with help from Forrest and Maj. Gen. Stephen D. Lee among others, managed to turn the Federals over the next four days so that, by November 29, Schofield was nearly cut off, reaching Franklin only through good luck on November 30.[1]

The convergence of the blue- and gray-uniformed soldiers in middle Tennessee, though occurring in late fall and early winter, was not unlike the coming of a summer thunderstorm to areas of the Volunteer State. Even today, the threatening clouds of such a local tempest can be seen well ahead of time by any attentive person, and most folks, after some residence, can almost tell how long it will be from first sightings of various thunderheads until the wind and rain arrives. Unlike the rapid thrust of a raider or guerrilla squall, the movement of the armies of Hood and Thomas was as ominous as such a gathering storm. Telegraph wires, scouts, patrols, shippers, journalists and civilians, like modern-day electronic and communications media, all contributed to the pool of threat intelligence and assessment available for review.

As Hood, Thomas, their lieutenants, and others near and far made and remade their observations and preparations for the military deluge on land, the sailors of the Ninth and Tenth Districts, Mississippi Squadron, led by Acting Rear Adm. Samuel P. Lee, made every effort to control the Cumberland and Lower Tennessee Rivers. The seamen knew a gale of Confederate iron was blowing and that it was their duty to help protect against it.

Through close coordination with the army, the Navy could best accomplish its duty by blockading the use of the twin rivers to Union purpose. Specifically, district vessels were tasked to prohibit their crossing or other use by Southern forces, to detect and, whenever possible, defeat Rebel movements, and to guard and facilitate the continuing transfer of men and supplies. The last-named goal included the protection of key ports and rendezvous as well as coordination with army quartermasters and railroad chiefs.

As November advanced, the riverine navy's mission intensified. As historian Byrd Douglas later commented, the arrival of Maj. Gen. A.J. Smith's army from Missouri remained "of utmost importance." Nearly every steamer coming up the Cumberland brought a few advance units of Smith's force. It now became obvious at both army and navy headquarters that a blocking assault on the Cumberland could be disastrous. If Maj. Gen. Forrest or one of his lieutenants could blockade transportation there as he had on the Tennessee, "it might result in the loss of the impending battle with Hood before it was fought."

The on-scene Mississippi Squadron operational commanders and their army counterparts continued to push, directly and indirectly, the buildup of the Tenth District flotilla; "above all," this growth "indicates the respect that Thomas, Sherman and Admiral Lee had for Forrest." In order to cope with powerful rifled batteries the Confederates could be expected to erect along the Cumberland River, Acting Rear Adm. Lee wisely strengthened the forces of Lt. Cmdr. Le Roy Fitch with ironclads. The two that would see action in the waters near Nashville were the *Carondelet*[2] and the *Neosho*.[3]

None of the local Union leadership could, however, know that the "devil's" role would be confined to support of Hood's main force inland of the rivers. Only a small portion of Forrest's command would threaten Cumberland transportation during the upcoming battle.

While the Ninth and Tenth district prepared for the anticipated, the gunboats of the Eleventh District remained alert to what had passed. The question of reinforcements for Hood crossing the Upper Tennessee remained constant. Not only that, but the possibility of local insurgents providing aid and comfort remained.

One of the most notorious Confederate sympathizers on Hood's invasion path was Cauis G. Fennel, who lived with his sons on the south side of the Tennessee in Guntersville, AL. On the night of November 14, a landing party from the *General Sherman* was sent ashore, surrounded Fennel's house, and moved in, capturing two Southern soldiers given shelter plus 33 bales of cotton. Also confiscated were all the cattle and hogs on the property.

A few days later at dusk, a lookout aboard one of the tinclads spied what appeared to be suspicious activity again taking place at the Fennel homestead. A telescope revealed what appeared to be a Confederate officer; perhaps he was leading a raiding party. The young man was, in fact, a wounded soldier attempting to reach his local residence, and being aided across the yard by Fennell.

As Fennel later reported, the "gunboat sneaked up without attracting our attention."

Given the noises made by approaching steamboats, such a claim seems rather far-fetched, but, in any event, as Fennel continued, the boat "immediately opened fire with two 32-pounders." The first shot was long, but the second landed between the men, making "a ditch that would hold a wagon and team." Neither was, fortunately for them, killed.

It would also prove fortunate for Union arms that other Confederate activity further south and west during these colder months was muted. The number of attacks on Mississippi River transportation was down, but still occurred. It remained dangerous to be aboard or from either a transport or a gunboat.

An example of these sporadic and uncoordinated assaults occurred on Saturday, November 19. Approximately 40 butternut irregulars hiding on the bank below Randolph, TN, fired into the steamer *Golden Eagle*,[4] en route to Memphis from Cincinnati. Passengers later reported that only three balls entered the boat, including one each through the pilothouse and skylight and a third that struck the leg of a porter but fell "at his feet without otherwise injuring him." Supposedly, the chief of the "bandits" hailed the craft before his men opened fire.

A half hour later, the 418-ton packet *Southwestern*[5] passed the same spot below Island 35, but was not molested. Arriving at Memphis, passengers told the always-ready newspaper correspondents that three guerrillas were seen lurking on the bank as the boat passed.[6]

While ashore at Raccourci, near Williamsport, LA, in the Tunica Bend area, on November 25, a party led by Acting Volunteer Lt. Charles Thatcher, captain of the tinclad *Gazelle*,[7] was surprised by Rebel insurgents. In the firefight between the four Navymen and an unknown number of the enemy, Thatcher was killed. The *New Orleans Daily True Delta* reported the Federals were "duck hunting."[8]

Through the month of November the Union divisions of Maj. Gen. Smith, fresh from their victory over Maj. Gen. Sterling Price at Westport on October 23, marched across Missouri to St. Louis. Early on November 24, Smith wired Paducah advising that lead elements of his corps were embarking for departure next day. Hood was now threatening Columbia, and according to Col. Henry Stone of Thomas's staff, it now became "an open question whether he would not reach Nashville before the reinforcements from Missouri."

The watch for waterborne reinforcements got underway in earnest on both the Ohio and Cumberland. In addition to convoys guarded by the USN, numerous steamers operated independently on the Cumberland, a few with protection from army gunboats. Near Cumberland City during the day, one of these lone sailors, the *Nannie*, was fired into by "guerrillas" hidden along the river bank. About thirty rounds struck the boat, but no one was hurt and there was no damage. As preparations for impending battle intensified, 738 penniless evacuees from Nashville arrived at Louisville aboard the transports *J.K. Baldwin* and *Irene*.

Hood continued to press into Tennessee. On November 25, Brig. Gen. Robert S. Granger, the Union Army's commander of the District of North Alabama, ordered the pontoon bridge at Decatur taken up. Protection for the engineers from Confederate sharpshooters was provided by the tinclad *General Grant*.

By the last week of November, the troop boats from St. Louis and Acting Rear Adm.

Lee's escorts were converging upon Smithland, KY, at the head of the Cumberland River. Ninth District Commander Lt. Cmdr. James Shirk, being too ill to participate in the upcoming campaign, was temporarily superseded by the Tenth District chief. So it was that Le Roy Fitch now assumed tactical command of the USN ironclads *Carondelet* and *Neosho*, as well as the heavy gunboat *Peosta*, the tinclads Moose (flagboat), *Fairplay, Silver Lake, Brilliant, Springfield, Reindeer,* and *Victory*, plus at least one auxiliary.

As the river's historian Douglas confirmed, "these constituted the greatest fleet of gunboats ever to appear on the Cumberland during the War." Although it is not generally recognized, Fitch could, if desired, also call upon available army gunboats, such as the *Silver Lake No. 2* and *Newsboy*. Although he did not hold elevated rank, Lt. Cmdr. Fitch now had more operational authority over more heavy vessels than any Mississippi Squadron junior officer since Capt. Henry Walke commanded the squadron's lower division at Vicksburg in the fall of 1862.

The *Carondelet* and *Neosho*, together with the last of Smith's transports, arrived at Smithland early on November 29. Lt. Cmdr. Fitch and his subordinate captains, in accordance with orders from Acting Rear Adm. Lee, quickly organized a water advance to the Tennessee capital and communicated the sailing order to the transport captains and affected military personnel.

Nashville army headquarters was notified that the transports would steam from Smithland next morning as soon as they had coaled. The major general commanding was also pleased to inform Lt. Gen. Grant at City Point, VA, that the usual "skeert" of Maj. Gen. Forrest, was evaporating. Although there was no positive news that the Confederate "devil" had departed Tennessee, he was "closely watched," and Thomas intended to move against Hood as soon as possible "whether Forrest leaves Tennessee or not."

At 10 A.M., just over two hours following the arrival of the ironclads, the *Moose* started up the Cumberland leading the grand parade of troop steamers. Among these were a significant number of craft impressed "from numerous small steamboat runners who lacked the means or influence to rescue their boats." Interspersed among the transports were the tinclad gunboats, acting as both shepherds and, on occasion, as towboats.

Every available light-draught of the Ninth and Tenth District was assigned to this expedition, except the *Paw Paw* and *Peosta*. The leading *Neosho* and the *Carondelet*, which brought up the rear, made their best speed; the sureness of their size and armament, if not their immediate proximity to the steamers, made them a viable "distant cover," a term later used for Allied battleship protection of convoys in the Atlantic during World War II.

Trailing huge clouds of smoke from over 50 chimneys, the steamboat procession stretched out over miles of river length and proceeded without incident throughout the day and into the evening. This was the largest troop convoy the Mosquito Flotilla had escorted to Nashville since that of Maj. Gen. Gordon Granger at the beginning of 1863. Numerous steamers were passed moving downstream and for the most part the weather was pleasant.[9]

On November 30, Gen. Hood's army, numbering something less than 16,000 effectives, attacked the 22,000 entrenched Union defenders of Franklin, losing 6,252 men, including six general officers killed. The five-hour battle cost the Northerners approximately 2,300 soldiers. Writing on "the five tragic hours" years later, historian Fisher opined that "Hood had virtually destroyed his army."

Before midnight, Maj. Gen. Schofield started yet another forced march, leaving his dead and wounded on the battlefield. All in the XXIII Corps who were able set off for Nashville, 18 miles away, arriving by noon the next day. There behind fortified lines they were joined by Maj. Gen. Frank Stanley's IV Army Corps, led by Brig. Gen. Thomas J. Wood. As the day wore on, more men arrived from various Tennessee locations, including Maj. Gen. James B. Steedman's Provisional Detachment of the District of the Etowah from Chattanooga.

As the Franklin bloodbath continued, the stretched-out Smith convoy puffed up the Cumberland. The heavier vessels steamed more slowly and were often overtaken by lighter units; all were regularly passed by vessels traveling in the other direction. Among the boats making the swiftest upriver passage was a specially-commissioned hospital boat, the *D.A. January*.

In Nashville while en route to a reception, Col. James F. Rusling, Acting Chief Quartermaster of the Department of the Cumberland, stopped by to see Maj. Gen. Thomas. The latter happily showed his supply officer a telegram from Schofield claiming to have defeated Hood at Franklin and reporting his withdrawal. Was there news of Smith, Thomas wondered? No, Rusling replied, though he had sent a steamer (probably the army gunboat *Newsboy*) down the Cumberland earlier in the afternoon to hurry the fleet. "Well," the commanding general replied, "if Smith does not get up here tonight, he will not get here at all; for tomorrow, Hood will strike the Cumberland and close it against all transports."

It was around midnight when the first couple of troop transports, encouraged ahead by Rusling's steamer and speeding in advance, came to off the city levee. Maj. Gen. Thomas was in a meeting with Maj. Gen. Schofield, who had himself just arrived, and Brig. Gen. Wood at Department of the Cumberland headquarters in the St. Cloud Hotel when the news arrived. The quartermaster colonel had hurried back from his engagement and burst into the room to announce that Smith had at long last come.

Rusling, like many other Nashvillians, had heard the joyful whistle calls of the advance steamers. Not long thereafter, the veteran infantryman Smith walked in and was immediately given a bear hug of welcome by the usually undemonstrative Thomas. Following brief handshakes, Rusling departed about 1 A.M., leaving his four superiors on their knees reviewing maps spread over the floor. Smith and several of his officers were among the few coming ashore. Most of the soldiers remained on their troop boats overnight.

With whistles and horns sounding in a continuous din to alert all that the long-awaited reinforcement was at hand, the remaining elements of the nautical procession slowly paddled the final few miles to the Nashville wharves. The *Moose* escorted in the final boats with 5,000 men just before late afternoon darkness. The ironclads *Neosho* and *Carondelet* tied up to the bank below Fitch's tinclad about 8 P.M.

An hour later, the Nashville chief telegraphed Maj. Gen. Henry Halleck at Washington, D.C.: "I have two ironclads here, with several gunboats, and Commander Fitch assures me that Hood can neither cross the Cumberland or blockade it. I therefore think it best to wait here until Wilson can equip all his cavalry." In one of the more famous quotes of the campaign, Thomas went on to size up his enemy's chances: "If Hood attacks me here, he will be more seriously damaged than he was yesterday; if he remains, ... I can whip him and will move against him at once."[10]

The Cumberland River leading into Nashville remained busy over the next two days as steamers brought in additional goods, men and horses. When not themselves being replenished in supplies or coal, Fitch's light-draughts were constantly in motion. The *Neosho* and *Carondelet* remained tied to the bank, their watch officers duly noting every witnessed activity in their logbooks.

Meanwhile, Gen. Hood's 25,000 men were almost at Nashville. Thinking he might draw Thomas into battle, the Southern commander considered that the possibility of a demonstration against the Union garrison at Murfreesboro was in order. This Rebel compulsion would remove one infantry division and all but a few of the men Thomas feared most — those from Forrest's Cavalry Corps.

The rest of the Southern army soon began establishing its line. Unhappily for the Rebels, Hood's four-mile line when in place was three miles shorter than the outer defenses built by the Nationals around the Tennessee capital. Specifically, the line halted two miles from the Cumberland River in the east and four in the west, leaving four of the eight roads into the city wide open.

To help alleviate this deficiency, the 1,500 men of Brig. Gen. James Chalmers's division were ordered by Forrest to operate in the unclaimed spaces that ran about four miles south between the Cumberland River below Nashville and Hood's anchor on the Hillsboro Pike. Specifically, the men were to patrol the Charlotte, Harding, and Hillsboro pikes on the left flank of the army. As part of this deployment, Chalmers now made one of the most important dispositions of any Rebel commander in the Nashville campaign.

Late in the afternoon, Col. David C. Kelley was sent to blockade the Cumberland. Kelley, who had bombarded river traffic twice in the last two months, positioned 300 men of Col. Edmund W. Rucker's brigade and two Parrott rifles of Lt. H.H. Brigg's section of Capt. T.W. Rice's artillery near Davidson's house on a ridge beyond a little creek that emptied at Davidson's Landing into the Cumberland opposite Bell's Mills. The Mills and Bell's Landing lay four miles below the town by land. By river, they were, depending upon who is providing directions, anywhere from 12 to 18 miles below. The spots were (and are) located at the nearest point to the city in the large bend in the Cumberland the comes nearly back of Nashville.

Soon reinforced with another two guns, Kelley had a pair in a lower battery and two in an upper emplacement. Marksmen were detailed in support from points in the hills above and below the artillery. This Johnsonville-like arrangement allowed the "fighting parson" to be largely successful in his mission, even though he had already missed the biggest target of all — A.J. Smith's troop convoy. Still, as historian Byrd Douglas noted, Kelley in the days ahead proved "what even a small force in gifted hands could do to supply lines and all the fine gunboats sent up the Cumberland."

In a 10 P.M. wire to Maj. Gen. Halleck, "Old Pap" Thomas outlined his defensive plans for Nashville. As part of that arrangement, the ironclads and gunboats were so disposed as to prevent Hood from crossing the Cumberland. "Captain Fitch," he added, "assures me that he can safely convoy steamers up and down the river." According to

Earlier a portion of a larger 60-acre tract where, in 2007, giant Lowe's and Wal-Mart outlets stood, the 6-acre Kelley's Point Battlefield is part of a 13-acre parcel nine miles west of Nashville in the Bellevue community. It was here that Confederate Col. David C. Kelley stationed his cannon and battled ironclads and tinclads of the Mississippi Squadron during the December 1864 Battle of Nashville (courtesy Robert Henderson).

Durham, Thomas had two major concerns about the river: that Confederates be neither able to cross it or cut off his supplies from below with mobile artillery. Neither the general or his top local Navy man knew for certain that old foe Kelley was even then endeavoring to ensure the latter, though rumors were beginning to come in that the Confederates were putting up cannon along the river in preparation for a night attack.[11]

While the tinclads plied the Cumberland guarding steamers, Nashville army headquarters remained nervous concerning Hood's intentions and grew concerned about the possibility that the Rebels might attempt to cross the Cumberland above Nashville. Feeling it unsafe to trust the courier line between Gallatin and Carthage for information, the commanding general asked Lt. Cmdr. Fitch, if the river level permitted, to institute a patrol to Carthage "with at least one ironclad and two gunboats."

Acting Volunteer Lt. Edmund Morgan of the U.S.S. *Springfield* was delegated to undertake the spy mission, in concert with the most famous member of the army's Cumberland River gunboat service, the *Newsboy*. That afternoon, the towboat *N.J. Bigley*, chartered to the USQMD, was convoyed upstream by the *Springfield* and the *Newsboy*. Their destination was Young's Point, 100 miles above Nashville near Hartsville. The former boat was to retrieve a number of workers from the area, while the others were to note Rebel activities.

While those craft paddled back and forth on the river, Col. Kelley's battery, further down, made its inaugural attacks. Responding to warning shots from the bluffs above the Cumberland, the contract steamers *Prairie State* and *Prima Donna* put into the bank, tied up and surrendered themselves into Confederate hands. Immediately the two boats, loaded with grain and cavalry animals, were taken and 56 aboard the two were made prisoner. Grayclad soldiers scrambled aboard and led off almost 200 horses and mules; they also pressed "into service the colored women on board who were employed as cooks and chambermaids," to help "liberate" items of value and to scatter and destroy the grain.

The naval supply steamer *Magnet* was fired into as she passed and was hit several times. Her captain, a man named Harrol, proceeded beyond the first battery, but, finding another below, gave up and ran his craft into shore, tying up at a point about eight miles below Hyde's Ferry. In darkness, Capt. Harrol traveled back to Hyde's Ferry, arriving where the ironclad *Carondelet* was stationed, and he was allowed to board about 7:30 P.M. Unable to move on his own without orders, her skipper sent the steamboat master with a naval rating up to Nashville, where they could raise the alarm with Lt. Cmdr. Fitch.

The *Moose* had not been moored long at Nashville when Harrol and his escort came aboard. By the time the contract skipper repeated his story the strength of the audacious Confederates had grown from a few guns to elements of the enemy's entire left wing. This body had, according to Harrol, struck the river and planted multiple batteries on its south side across from the Mills. Fitch, who had passed the location on many occasions over the past several years, was keenly aware of the location and knew it took far longer to reach by water than by land.

Even though it was very cloudy and threatening more rain, Fitch immediately determined to launch a night strike to wrest the two captured boats back from the enemy. He quickly stopped in to see Maj. Gen. Thomas and won his support to either recapture them or force their destruction — in either event, taking the steamers away from the Southerners. A signal was made to the captains of the *Neosho, Brilliant, Fairplay, Reindeer,* and *Silver Lake* at 9:30 P.M. to get up steam and follow the *Moose* downriver at best speed.

Fitch's task group hove to near the *Carondelet* and the Pook turtle was invited to join the parade. A few minutes later, the boats steamed on in this order: *Carondelet, Fairplay, Moose, Reindeer,* and *Silver Lake.* The four tinclads were about to engage in the most significant action by units of their class during the entire Nashville campaign.

At 12:30 A.M. December 4, as the ironclad and four mosquito boats approached Bell's Mills, all hands aboard the warships were called to quarters. Aboard the light-draughts, captains and pilots made close observation from their pilothouses. Down on the gun-decks, the eight men of each 24-pdr. crew looked to their executive officer for orders and for the young boys or "power monkeys" that brought them ammunition from the magazine. They did not have long to wait. The boats moved down, as Lt. Cmdr. Fitch put it later, "perfectly quiet, with no lights visible."

The Tenth District commander might be excused for that turn of phrase; steam-boats were not quiet, but made puffing and chugging noises which were usually quite audible. There is no record that the engineers aboard the tinclads or the ironclad had time to reroute the steam pipes. Before her run past Island No. 10 in April 1862, the engineers aboard Capt. Henry Walke's *Carondelet* had rerouted her exhaust steam aft into her wheelhouse rather than the chimneys. This had the effect of eliminating the puffing sound. What probably masked their approach was the mired of noise associated with a large city, sounds from the competing armies, general river traffic not yet completely stopped, and the crying of stolen livestock.

Coming down darkened, the *Carondelet,* closely followed by the *Fairplay,* steamed towards Kelley's batteries. The night was cool, cloudy and devoid of natural light, and hence the Confederates did not spot the Yankee craft, even though one was as big as a house.

About 12:45 A.M., the *Carondelet* opened with a hail of grape and canister as she passed the main Rebel camp in a hollow on the south side of the river opposite Bell's Mills. As her guns came to bear, a number of the men aboard could clearly see the *Prairie State* and *Prima Donna* tied up at the bank at Hillsboro Landing, two miles below. When the ironclad initiated the battle, the *Fairplay* was a little below the upper battery, with the *Moose* abreast of it, the *Reindeer* about 50 yards above, and the *Silver Lake* behind. As soon as the *Carondelet* started the fight, Kelley's musketmen poured a heavy volley into all of the boats and began a responsive cannonade. Rebel fire, in the words of Acting Volunteer Lt. Henry Glassford, "was rapid and warm."

The Pook turtle steamed slowly by the lower battery. After passing, she rounded to and came up within about 300 yards of the Confederates, fired a few shots, then passed up abreast, before dropping back again. The Southerners returned the ironclad's fire for about 20 minutes before falling back; *Carondelet* pumped occasional shells toward the last known Rebel locations until 2:30 A.M. When her gunners took stock of the magazine later in the morning, it would be found that 26 rounds had been expended.

The thinly-protected *Fairplay* could not possibly stand up to Kelley's rifled field guns and made no offensive effort to do so. Acting in concert with the ironclad, her job was to get quickly past the Rebel gunners and to ensure the recapture the transports at Hillsboro Landing. She fired rapidly in passing and turned the bend below out of range. The veteran tinclad did not get by entirely unscathed. One 12-pdr. shell passed through the boat, between the main and boiler decks, flying a few inches above the forward part of the boilers and damaging the port engine's escape pipe. The other projectile went straight through the cabin directly beneath the pilothouse. Fortunately neither shell exploded and both exited without causing serious damage. Despite her short time in battle, the *Fairplay* fired a total of 37 rounds of grape and canister.

The smoke from the guns and chimneys, combined with steam and the darkness of a starless night, quickly cut visibility for the mosquito boats. In this most literal "fog of war," the flag boat, in the narrow river bend, was hidden from the craft above and below her. Pilots and officers could see virtually nothing and the fear of collision became palpable, particularly aboard the *Moose* and *Reindeer*. On top of this, the smoke was so thick that, occasionally, the river surface could not be seen from their upper decks.

Lt. Cmdr. Fitch, fearful of ramming the *Fairplay*, ordered the *Moose* stopped quickly. That boat also halted briefly before following the *Carondelet* below the bend. At this point, the *Moose* was becoming a plum target for the Confederate gunners, who were firing at her from so far on her port quarter that her guns could not be brought to bear to fire back. In great danger, the *Moose* simply could not stay where she was long enough for the smoke to lift. It would also be very dangerous for her to attempt to round to. There was only one option and thus her pilots began to back up to a clear spot above the batteries and get out of the thick smoke below.

Fitch's tinclad had to move slowly while backing up, but the craft was so well handled that her guns could be worked "with marked rapidity and precision." The naval chief believed the *Moose*'s gunnery was the major reason "that in a great measure they [the Southern guns] were kept silent." Adm. Porter afterwards attributed the success to the "great judgement and coolness" of the vessel's management. Most Southern participants attribute the silence to the fact that "Kelley's artillery ammunition was, unhappily, exhausted."

If the *Carondelet* and *Fairplay* had passed down, rounded to, and were on their way back up, the danger of their running into the out-of-position flagboat was great. At this time, the *Moose* lay at a spot in the river not over 75 to 80 yards wide and directly under the Rebel guns. The Confederates, thankful for such a sitting duck, now gave her their full attention. Although the musketry along the bank and on the hillside was rather "annoying," the enemy artillery fire, though rapid, was not very telling because it was not well aimed. Still, Fitch admitted in his after-action report, it was a miracle "that amid so many shots and volleys of musketry, we should escape without the loss of a single man and no injury to the boats."

The lucky *Moose* was, in fact, hit three times by shells, two of which could have sunk her. One ploughed into the bread room, close to the magazine, but did not explode. A second, which also did not explode, "struck us fair," her commander later reported. The bullet would have passed out through the bottom, but was deflected by a deck beam and lodged in the rake. Another hit the paddle wheel, but did no damage. As might be expected, when the battle was over, the flag boat had flung 59 rounds toward the banks of the Cumberland.

During the few moments the shore was hidden from the *Reindeer* by the smoke, that tinclad went broadside to the current and drifted downstream toward the flag boat. To avoid a collision, Glassford immediately ordered her bow run ashore and then swerved round, stern downstream. Although badly exposed to a raking Rebel fire, the *Reindeer* was lucky as Kelley's men, in their excitement, were shooting high and only managed to knock a few splinters off her paddle wheel. As soon as he could get clear, Glassford ran his tinclad upstream and rounded to, resuming his place behind the *Moose*. By the time these maneuvers were completed, the hour-and-a-half-action was over. A check of the *Reindeer*'s magazine showed 19 rounds fired.

The *Silver Lake* did not get close enough to actually engage the batteries. She did fire six rounds of canister and that helped keep the musketry "silent along the bank above." Perhaps this explains how Landsman Rowland S. True confused the actions of December 4 and 6 in his later account. Still, the Pennsylvanian witnessed what he later called "a grand display of fireworks." He would always remember the "thundering of the mighty guns, the shells screeching through the air back and forth, from one side to the other; sometimes bursting in the air, sometimes in the water throwing the water high in the air...."

This Bell's Mills engagement, the first of several, was not a great victory for either side. It is true that Fitch's task group was able to recapture the two steamers before they were destroyed. The gunboatman claimed his boats drove the Rebel guns back from the river and that it was his intervention which forced Kelley to destroy most of the prized grain before it could be transported and to free some of their crews.

The thunder of the guns had ceased by 2:30 A.M. and the Union craft returned to Nashville, arriving several hours later. The night fight was something of a tradeoff, but, in the end, the Rebels stayed away for less than a day and then, despite several more visits in the next week by the *Carondelet* and *Neosho*, closed the Cumberland tight for a week.

Not to be forgotten in the excitement of the Bell's Mills rescue was the joint Army-Navy expedition above Nashville started the previous day. The *N. J. Bigley*, the *Springfield*, and the U.S. Army gunboat *Newsboy* reached Young's Point, near Hartsville, about 11 A.M. Sunday morning. There the *Bigley* took aboard a party of timbercutters and then returned downstream, reaching Tennessee's capital about 7 P.M. These largely unreported waterborne reconnaissance missions would continue off and on for the remainder of the campaign.[12]

Soldiers near Nashville continued to waltz towards combat for much of the next fortnight. "Commodore Fitch," as Benjamin Truman told readers of the *New York Times*, "commands upon the Cumberland and assists in protecting our banks to a considerable extent." Noting the presence of two ironclads, the journalist reported there were "also several other gunboats, of various shapes and sizes, patrolling the river...." Another writer also praised the gunboats, asserting that "those who man them are celebrated in this section for their skill, bravery, and promptness in executing the part assigned them."

The opening of what all suspected to be the climactic ball was postponed for the better part of a week during that time by one of the most severe winters in memory. The suffering from the cold, snow, and rain was intense among troops and civilians alike, though many sailors were warm aboard their boats. When the weather broke, there was much fog and mist.

The tinclad *General Grant*, operating on the Upper Tennessee, visited Decatur on December 12 and hurled 52 shells against Confederate positions around the town.

Under cover of poor visibility, the Federal army of Maj. Gen. Thomas launched a counterattack out of Nashville on December 15 against the lines of Gen. Hood. The bluecoats were supported on the Cumberland at Bell's Mills by the *Carondelet* and *Neosho*, whose heavy shell firing actually opened the contest. Within a day, the Rebels were in full flight south.

The situation with Gen. Hood's main army deteriorated throughout the 16th to a point where the shattered graycoats rushed pell-mell in sleet and rain, not stopping until they were south of Brentwood after dark. Only then, in terrible weather that spared them instant Union pursuit, were scattered units able to commence their regrouping process. "The night that followed was strangely silent," wrote Walter Durham in 1987, "the last cannonading having stopped at dark with the flight of the rebels." As occasional lightning flashes rent the darkness, stragglers could be seen exiting the battlefield, either south or toward Nashville.[13]

On the evening of December 17, with Gen. Hood in full retreat and the bluecoats in pursuit from several points, Maj. Gen. Thomas, from the field near Franklin, wrote to Acting Rear Adm. Lee asking for help in another direction. If feasible, could the Navy send one or two ironclads and several gunboats up the Tennessee to destroy the pre-positioned Confederate pontoon bridge believed functional at Florence? If the Federal gunboats could make it by Christmas Eve, Thomas reasoned, they had a good chance of intercepting the arriving Confederates and preventing their escape over the Tennessee. Upon receipt of the message next morning, Lee, who had been detained by low water at Clarksville for almost two weeks, quickly consulted a chart. Geography dictated that he would be in a better position to oversee such an advance from Paducah and took fast passage downriver.

Witnessed by a good crowd of dockworkers and others watching from the bank, the first post-battle return convoy from Nashville to Smithland departed in two waves beginning at 11:30 A.M. The parade was led by the *Neosho*, under tow of the supply boat *Magnet*. The monitor was followed ten minutes later by the *Moose and Reindeer*, which led 11 transports and a hospital boat. The tinclad *Fairplay* brought up the rear.

"We open the Cumberland today," Nashville quartermaster Col. James L. Donaldson cheerfully wrote to Quartermaster General Montgomery C. Meigs after witnessing the departure. "Transports here have left under convoy of the gunboats." The weather was cloudy, threatening rain.

While Lt. Cmdr. Fitch was supervising this return convoy out on the river, Acting Rear Adm. Lee wired Maj. Gen. Thomas agreeing to push a suitable naval force up the Tennessee River as soon as the boats arrived and the thick fog dissipated. If there was water enough in the river, it was anticipated that the gunboats could help cut off Hood's retreat. At the same time, he promised, in response to a morning wire, to have Lt. Moreau Forrest, commander of the Eleventh District, support the reoccupation of Decatur by troops under Brig. Gen. Robert S. Granger.

After battling rain, wind, and the shifting currents of the Cumberland for 18 hours, the Smithland-bound convoy reached Clarksville at dark on December 19. There, Lt. Cmdr. Fitch learned that Lee had gone after Hood and wanted him and several of his tinclads, including the *Silver Lake* and *Reindeer*, detached as soon as possible to aid in the strenuous pursuit. Appreciating the continuing necessity for well-organized and -conducted Upper River convoys, Fitch asked to stay behind. Agreeing, Acting Rear Adm. Lee jumped at the chance to participate, operationally, in the final pursuit of Gen. Hood. Sensing he might have the chance at combat that eluded him while stranded at Clarksville, Lee seized a possible opportunity to impress his Navy Department superiors.

At the same time, Fitch, from his knowledge of the rivers gained in two years of war, might have suspected that, based on intelligence reports, Hood was heading for Alabama via Great Muscle Shoals. Water levels over the obstruction would probably prevent any naval pursuit into the Upper Tennessee.[14]

Also on December 19, Confederate Brig. Gen. Philip D. Roddy, commanding at Decatur, was ordered to uniquely participate in Hood's rescue. The 15 pontoon bridges he had found when occupying the town of Decatur at the end of November were to be floated down the Tennessee to Bainbridge, a village on the river at the foot of Muscle Shoals, 6 miles above Florence. Bainbridge was not a regular ferry location, but it was hoped that the gunboats could or would not chance steaming over the shoals to interfere with any crossing. Thus the floating bridge would be thrown across with a reasonable expectation of being able to accommodating the retreating butternuts.

Thomas and Lee, urged on by Washington, D.C., generals and other leaders, pursued the retreating Confederates as they sped back to Alabama. Two days into Hood's retreat, Maj. Gen. Nathan Bedford Forrest took over as Confederate rear guard and provided spirited cover as the Rebels moved toward the bridge across the Tennessee at Florence, the head of steamboat navigation at that time. According to Stanley Horn, the butternut soldiers sang a parody of "The Yellow Rose of Texas":

> But now I'm going to leave you;
> My heart is full of woe.
> I'm going back to Georgia to see my Uncle Joe.
> You may talk about your Beauregards and sing of General Lee
> But the gallant Hood of Texas played hell in Tennessee.

Acting Rear Adm. Lee's expedition departed from Paducah up the Tennessee on December 20, a day after Roddy began shifting his pontoons to Bainbridge. Over the next week, the lead five gunboats proceeded with speed, destroying flatboats and ferries en route. Others followed, convoying troop boats. As Lee's craft dropped anchor off

Opposite: **During the Union Army pursuit of Confederate forces retreating from Nashville in January 1865, elements of the Mississippi Squadron under Acting Rear Adm. Samuel Phillips Lee provided active assistance, much of it centered on the Tennessee River town of Eastport, Mississippi. At least three ironclads and numerous tinclads gathered here, both to protect arriving Federal convoys and to mount ultimately ineffective attacks on Rebel pontoon bridges located above. As no photographs exist of the Rebel pontoon over the Tennessee, the reader may gain some idea of the structure from this 1864 Union bridge over the James River (Miller's *Photographic History of the Civil War*, v. 5).**

Chickasaw, above Eastport but below Florence, on Christmas Eve, a message was dispatched from Maj. Gen. Thomas recommending that the follow-on boats, which he expected to convoy troop transports to Eastport, remain at that point until Hood's intentions were clearly known.

Drawing from all squadron boats available, Lee's task force was far larger and more formidable, gun-for-gun, than that which Fitch had at Nashville. Still, many of the units were the same: *Neosho*, *Pittsburg*, and *Carondelet*, the timberclad *Lexington*, as well as the tinclads *Naumkeag*, *Peosta*, *St. Clair*, *Fairplay*, *Reindeer*, *Silver Lake*, and *Fairy*. Additionally, the dreadful wet weather had increased the water depth somewhat, making operations further up the river at least feasible. The possibility of the craft reaching the butternuts "was thought not improbable" even by the Confederates themselves.

Meanwhile, Brig. Gen. Roddy's pontoons arrived at Bainbridge in the cold and drizzle, having been easily floated over the shoals due to somewhat deeper water levels. Here, engineer units were assembled to get a bridge across the swift-flowing Tennessee. Additionally, as other Southerners crossed Shoal Creek, about two miles from the river, they threw up primitive earthworks "to protect the bridge in case the enemy should move on us from below." Other Confederate cannon were mounted at Florence, also prepared to contest Lee's passage. Inland of the Tennessee, Forrest's valiant command delayed the Federal pursuit as long as possible, allowing grayclad soldiers (many barefoot) a chance to retreat.

On Christmas Day, the survivors of Maj. Gen. Benjamin F. Cheatham's corps reached the Tennessee River. Work was intensified that Sunday on refurbishing, assembling, and deploying Roddy's pontoon or floating bridge across the Tennessee. For protection, light gun emplacements and field entrenchments were dug at the north end of the bridge.

As the Rebels labored, the *Neosho*, *Reindeer*, and *Fairy* advanced upon Florence, intent upon destroying gun emplacements reported at that town. The *Carondelet* and *Pittsburg* drew too much water to accompany the light-draught vessels and were left at Eastport.

From the bluff opposite Florence, Rebel infantry opened upon the Federal boats with musketry, while from the city side, they were targeted by two four-gun batteries. After a half-hour cannonade from both parties, the Southerners ceased shooting and the Union craft returned downstream. They were unable to interfere with Cheatham's work even though the butternuts "heard the gunboats all day in the direction of Florence."

Work continued on the Bainbridge bridge all night and at sunrise, supply wagons and artillery began to cross. By Boxing Day afternoon, the *Neosho* and several of her tinclad consorts had steamed slowly up the river, once more intent upon attacking enemy batteries. As they advanced, it was found that only the tinclads could proceed.

When within two to three miles of their goal, the light-draughts were assaulted by three Confederate batteries. Lee now headed back downriver, rejoining the *Neosho*. The trio moved only a few more miles when they were again pounded, this time by two masked batteries. As in the duel she fought with Col. Kelley at Bell's Mills in early December, the *Neosho* received much attention, being hit 27 times. When the contest closed, a total of three Federal sailors were killed aboard the gunboats, with five others wounded.

There were no Rebel casualties in this fight and the vessels did not return upriver that day. This respite, plus the addition of more pontoons that arrived by wagon, allowed the bulk of Hood's saved transport and cannon to get across. Having held off the gunboats, Cheatham moved his troops across the pontoon bridge, beginning at 3 A.M. Toward morning on December 27, Maj. Gen. Forrest and his rear guard marched across, unmolested. By evening, all of the Confederates would be safely across the Tennessee.

As daylight approached, Acting Rear Adm. Lee once more intended to disrupt the Confederate evacuation, this time by taking the monitor over the shoals. The squadron commander's chief pilot had said earlier this was impossible for any of the boats due to the swift water flowing in the Bainbridge stretch, and he offered no encouragement now. The same man had earlier advised the eastern officer that the *Neosho*, drawing as she did five feet of water, could not make it through for much the same reason. The swift and shallow waters of Little Mussel Shoals were too rocky, too uneven, and too dangerous, and so the *Neosho* had remained downstream during the ineffective tinclad attack the previous day.

Determined not to be turned back again, Lee ordered a reconnaissance in force undertaken. At this point, thick fog and a "sudden and rapid fall of the river," conspired, however, to convince his pilot to refuse going on the shoals, a decision that was within his right to make. The squadron commander later suggested that, but for these misfortunes, he could "have succeeded in reaching Bainbridge with an effective force, capable of destroying Hood's pontoons...."

In approximately the same mid–December timeframe during which he had requested assistance from Acting Rear Adm. Lee, Maj. Gen. Thomas put another plan into action designed to cut off Hood's retreat. The Provisional Corps, under Brig. Gen. James B. Steedman, was ordered to Decatur, via Murfreesboro and Stevenson. Once on the Tennessee River, it was to capture the town that Union forces had evacuated a month earlier. While the admiral was engaged at Florence-Bainbridge, the Eleventh District tinclads *General Sherman*, *General Burnside*, and *General Thomas* were fully engaged assisting Steedman. Having arrived two miles above the town on the north side of the river that morning, the 2nd Brigade of the Provisional Corps awaited the arrival of additional troops coming by water under gunboat escort.

When the troop boats arrived with the 2nd Brigade, their men, primarily African-Americans, "landed in fine style" on the south side of the river opposite the 1st Brigade. The latter was soon thereafter ferried across. As soon as these men began to go ashore, they were taken under fire by a section of Confederate artillery. While the Rebel shells fell near or burst over the Union landing beaches, Lt. Forrest ordered his gunboats to move up and provide close gunfire support. As the Federals advanced upon Decatur, the Confederate shore batteries engaged the Eleventh District gunboats in a noisy duel. The *General Burnside* and the *General Thomas* were each hulled at least twice, with three sailors killed and several wounded between them.

Taking Decatur was a tougher nut, it turned out, than many had expected. In the end, however, Confederate forces evacuated the town. Acting Master Morton next day attempted to take the *General Thomas* over the Elk River Shoals to further interfere with any Rebel crossing plans. Unhappily, the Tennessee had by now fallen and become too low to allow Tinclad No. 61 across.

Between December 25 and 28, the remnants of the Confederate Army of Tennessee

The tinclads of the Mississippi Squadron's 11th District provided direct riverine assistance to the Federal Army as it chased the defeated Confederates away from Nashville in December 1864 and January 1865. Just after Christmas, three District tinclads, including the *General Sherman* (bottom), provided gunfire support for Northern soldiers landing at Decatur, Alabama. In mid–January, the *General Grant* (top) and *General Thomas* assaulted a Rebel camp at Guntersville, Alabama (*General Grant*, National Archives; *General Sherman*, Naval Historical Center).

managed to cross over and make for its final rendezvous at Tupelo, MS. The Federal army, in warm if not hot pursuit, could not catch up, though it did manage to pick up many prisoners and much Confederate supply. The tinclads of the Eleventh District retired from the chase on December 30, coming to anchor as a group off Bridgeport, AL.

The frustrated Union generals were, with the exception of Thomas, not particularly happy with the role played by the Mississippi Squadron in this campaign. Cavalry chief Maj. Gen. James Wilson, who led the charge against Forrest, was told by local people that "the gunboats were within a mile of the Rebel bridge at Bainbridge and ... could have reached it without trouble." Federal horse soldiers, he claimed, "reached the north bank of the river just as the bridge had been swung to the south side and the last of the Rebels were disappearing in the distance."

In his memoirs, Wilson pinned the failure of the *Neosho* and her consorts to reach and destroy the pontoon bridge on "the independence of the navy and the natural timidity of a deep-water sailor in a shoal-water river." In his contribution to the *Battles & Leaders* series, he was far blunter. "The failure of the light-draught gunboats on the Tennessee River to reach and destroy the pontoon bridge which Hood had kept in position," he wrote, "ensured his safe retreat."

Writing to Maj. Gen. Thomas from Eastport on January 2, 1865, Acting Rear Adm. Lee confirmed that Hood had crossed Great Muscle Shoals. The Confederates, he suggested, were nearing Corinth, 30 miles west of his anchorage. What did the theater commander require of the USN at this point? he wondered. Writing back from Pulaski, TN, Thomas prioritized a need for convoys and for "keeping the river open if possible."[15]

Lee remained on the Tennessee in support of "Old Pap" Thomas through mid–January 1865. With the close of the Nashville campaign, Lee reported to Navy Secretary Gideon Welles that army-navy cooperation in the recent operation had "been of a most pleasing and cordial character." Saluting the admiral with kind remarks, Lee's recent biographers conclude: "It is difficult to find anywhere in the history of the American Civil War a better demonstration of combined operations in which the army and the navy worked together with fewer problems and more impressive results." On the other hand, Craig Symonds reminds us that Lee "never won his great victory or obtained the formal thanks of Congress, and remained an acting rear-admiral until the end of the war."

Military action along the western waters subsided almost daily from this time on through the conclusion of the war in April. Just as it was reported that Confederate soldiers were deserting from the lines in the east, so too did many disappear from duty in the Tennessee Valley — but not all. "The guerrilla war continued," observed Gildrie, "having a logic of its own, even though the military purposes were negligible."

While maintaining often minimal patrols, the Mississippi Squadron was gradually altered from a war fighting command to a coast guard force, which handled various police duties, some counterinsurgency activities, and customs inspections. When 1865 began, the U.S. Navy Department, believing that the Rebellion would soon be over, began seeking significant economy in its operations.

Though they were not as ferocious as in previous years, the need to interrupt or counter partisan and guerrilla activities still remained a major concern for the Federal gunboatmen. Rebel hit-and-run attacks continued to be made on shipping plying the

Mississippi, White, Tennessee, and Cumberland. On the latter, bushwhackers remained dangerous near Harpeth Shoals and from the banks near Palmyra's ruins. Many of the raids originated out of western Kentucky and were aimed at rail connections

Guerrillas continued to operate in or near towns and communities up and down the Western streams. Outrages, such as robberies and shootings, continued. Although a number of boats were shot up, only two more were actually destroyed by their enterprise before the end of February. Repaired after sinking at the Scuffletown Bar loaded for the Cumberland in July 1862, the 170-ton stern-wheeler *Venango*[16] entered the cotton trade in 1864. While on an expedition to gather the precious commodity, the craft was captured at Pilcher's Point, LA, below Lake Providence, on December 31. Although there were no casualties, the boat was burned to the water's edge, a $15,000 loss for her Vicksburg owners.[17] Owned by Capt. Luster P. Chester, son of the legendary steamboat master Capt. Thomas Chester, the *Grampus No. 2* was en route past Memphis in January 1865 when she was captured at Little Chicken Island and burned. She was insured for $6,500.[18]

While landing to wood at Tiptonville, TN, on the Mississippi on December 31, the steamer *Silver Moon* was fired into by 15 "guerrillas" lurking behind the fuel near a warehouse. She escaped capture by immediately backing out into the stream and heading away. When this matter was reported to Columbus, KY, the tinclad *New Era* steamed down on the first day of January to investigate. Putting into shore, the gunboat's commander informed the local town solons that he was going to burn the town in retaliation for the insurgent attack. When the leaders protested, the officer pointed out that the perpetrators had hidden behind a woodpile at their river bank and nearly took the boat. The disloyal community was home to guerrillas and deserved to be destroyed, he continued. Finally, after he was done venting, the skipper's temper cooled and he relented. Only two small houses and the offending woodpile were torched.[19]

On January 11, Thomas wrote to Lt. Moreau Forrest asking that his tinclads mount a new and vigorous patrol of the Upper Tennessee River to catch remnants of the escaping 6th Kentucky Cavalry (C.S.A.), under Brig. Gen. Hylan B. Lyon, that had been raiding in the Cumberland River region during the Nashville campaign. The *General Grant* and *General Thomas* were sent to assist.

Over the next several days, Lyon and his men reached Deposit Ferry, AL, where they took shelter on the property of Confederate sympathizer Cauis G. Fennel, recently of Guntersville, AL. On the night of January 14–15, a battalion of Federal cavalry surrounded the Rebel camp, charged, and captured 100 graycoats and their equipment. While escaping, Brig. Gen. Lyon shot and killed Sgt. Arthur Lyon of the 15th Pennsylvania Cavalry. The news of the sergeant's death brought Northern sadness and anger both afloat and ashore. The gunboatmen readily raised steam and proceeded in vengeance with the horse soldiers.

In conjunction with the cavalry, the two gunboats supposedly happened upon the Rebel raiders on January 15 at the town of Guntersville. What was reported as a spirited engagement followed, during which the tinclads pounded the town with over 50 explosive shells. The *General Grant* was hit once, but suffered no damage. After the bombardment and with the Federal cavalry surrounding the town, Acting Ensign Richard McAllister, executive officer of the *General Sherman*, led a large landing party of 125 bluejackets ashore to extract revenge for the killing of Sgt. Lyon. Despite appeals from two Union sympathizers whose houses were spared, the "hotbed of rebellion" was torched. Only seven buildings remained standing, all damaged.

Confederate Gen. John Bell Hood's Army of Tennessee completed its retreat back across the Tennessee River into Mississippi by the end of January. Pursuing Union forces, knowing that it was spent, allowed it to melt away, content in the knowledge that their actions since mid–December had all but finished the campaign in the west. Indeed, as historian Richard Gildrie has put it, the massive Union victory "effectively ended the war between the Mississippi River and the Appalachian Mountains."

While Hood was in Tennessee, Maj. Gen. Sherman's march to the sea virtually destroyed Rebel ability to send food and fuel to Virginia from the lower South via Georgia. The focus for Civil War military action now turned east, where Lt. Gen. Ulysses S. Grant had besieged the Army of Northern Virginia at Petersburg while Sherman and Rear Adm. David Dixon Porter set about shutting down Confederate succor from the sea by capturing Fort Fisher and Wilmington.[20]

Much further south, planning was underway for a campaign to capture Mobile, AL, as soon as sufficient forces could be assembled for the task. On January 26, Navy Secretary Welles wired Acting Rear Adm. Lee requiring that he forward two of his best light-draught ironclads to New Orleans for use in the upcoming campaign.

In late January, Lee traveled to New Orleans on a downriver inspection tour and also for a meeting with his West Gulf Coast Blockading Squadron (WGCBS) counterparts. In the Crescent City on February 1, he cut orders for the reinforcements ordered by Welles, detailing the Eads monitors *Neosho* and *Osage* to undertake the requested duty. Four days later, while traveling north, he detailed the *Naiad*, then at Bayou Sara, to serve as escort down for the former. As needed, the accompanying tinclad would also tow the ironclad.

At Natchez on February 8, the *Peri* was ordered to perform the same service for the *Osage*. Arriving at Skipwith's Landing next day, Acting Rear Adm. Lee reviewed and revoked his earlier order sending the *Juliet* south, leaving her in the Sixth District. Back at Mound City by February 14, the Mississippi Squadron boss again revised his contribution to the WGCBS. It was confirmed that the Eads monitor *Osage*, from the Eighth District, would proceed to New Orleans, escorted by the tinclad *Siren*. The same requirement was sent to Sixth District headquarters at Greenville, MS, dispatching the Pook turtle *Cincinnati*, accompanied by the *Marmora*.

Next day, the order sending the *Neosho* was canceled. On February 16, Lee was able to telegraph Secretary Welles that he had, indeed, "sent two light-draft ironclads and four tinclads" to New Orleans. The heavy units were, as he pointed out to his Gulf colleagues, "the very best I had, all of the few others are in such very bad condition as to be wholly useless in your operations."

In responding so rapidly, it was not possible to send any of the latest class of tinclads even then undergoing modification. A few last newly-finished tinclads would soon be accepted, with some told to wear the identification numbers of lost predecessors; the presence of all would be brief. Converted too late to be canceled or sent to New Orleans, ten tinclads would be commissioned before April 26, beginning with the *Grosbeak*[21] on February 24.

It was also impossible to retrofit for ocean service the offered in-service tinclads. To get the quartet away quickly, there was insufficient time to fit them with fresh-water condensers, chain down their boilers, or attend to their hulls below the waterline. These, like the *Osage* and *Cincinnati*, were the best available of his craft not purposefully repaired or strengthened for WGCBS service.

Freshly documented at New Orleans in mid–June 1864, the 224-ton *Mittie Stephens*[22] put into the east bank of the Mississippi, near Cole's Creek, MS, on February 18, to pick up a load of legally-permitted cotton. As the stages dropped away from the 170-foot-long side-wheeler and the deckhands prepared to take aboard the first of 100 bales, a group of partisan scouts under Confederate Lt. B.B. Paddock sprang up and began shooting. As they volleyed, several men split off to fire the produce. As soon as the steamer backed out, the tinclad *Prairie Bird*, providing escort, opened up on the graycoated riflemen. Unable to withstand 10 rounds of shrapnel sent their way from the light-draught, the scoundrels scampered off. Once they were gone, an armed party was sent ashore to extinguish the cotton fire, and all but five bales were saved.

The Upper Tennessee was now largely clear of organized Confederate resistance, though several large Southern groups were known to be in the area, including the command of Brig. Gen. Philip Roddy, the one-time commander at Decatur. Taking advantage of unusually high water, the *General Burnside* (flag) and *General Thomas* crossed the Elk River Shoals on February 26 and moved down to Mussel Shoals. One of Roddy's smaller camps was located near the giant natural river obstruction and when it was found by Lt. Forrest and his gunboatmen, it contained horses, wagons, and even baled cotton. Landing parties from the light-draughts were able to drive away the butternut defenders and captured several of the animals, along with seven cotton bales.

As part of this late winter expedition, the *General Burnside* and *General Thomas* also penetrated Elk River. During a brief cruise through the end of the month, the sailors believed themselves "meeting with a great deal of success in endeavoring to encourage loyal feelings on the south side of the river."

As winter turned into spring, the Mississippi and its tributaries appeared more pacified. Acting Rear Adm. Lee informed Secretary Welles on February 16 that "quiet prevails on the river," while "trading under Treasury permits is largely increasing." Only scattered incidents excited the tinclad sailors of the Western rivers from this point on. Although irregular attacks continued, the gunboats of the Mississippi Squadron held open the logistical lifelines of the Mississippi and its tributaries for the remainder of the war. Even though the Trans-Mississippi area west of the great river was still held largely intact by the Confederates, the Federal Navy blockaded it tightly.

For Acting Rear Adm. Lee's counterparts with the West Gulf Coast Blockading Squadron (WGCBS), the matter of capturing Mobile on the Gulf of Mexico to the east did, however, remain. As the troops of Maj. Gen. Thomas pursued Hood south after the Battle of Nashville, it was anticipated that they would continue toward the Gulf and join the forces of Maj. Gen. Edward R.S. Canby at New Orleans. Once in place, the enlarged Federal force could shift from New Orleans and attack the crumbling defenses of Mobile, the Confederacy's last remaining seaport, now manned by 10,000 Southerners under Confederate District of the Gulf commander Maj. Gen. Dabney H. Maury.

Bad weather and a shallow Tennessee River ended Thomas's pursuit of his defeated foe. There was no way that the conquering Nashville army would be joining Canby anytime soon. On January 18, Lt. Gen. Grant ordered the latter to capture Mobile. To boost his troop level to some 45,000 men, the XVI Corps of Maj. Gen. A.J. Smith was detached from Thomas and sent to New Orleans. Smith's 18,000 soldiers arrived at New Orleans aboard 43 tinclad-escorted transports on February 21. Two weeks later, ocean-going vessels would take them to Dauphin Island, Mobile Bay.

In February, the command of the WGCBS was changed. Commodore James S. Palmer, who had overseen USN activities in Mobile Bay since the departure of Rear Adm. Farragut the previous September, was relieved by Acting Rear Adm. Henry K. Thatcher, fresh from the conquest of Fort Fisher under Rear Adm. Porter. Additionally, the number of fighting ships and boats dedicated to the support of a land attack on the coastal city was enhanced.

The *Osage, Cincinnati,* and the four tinclads dispatched by Acting Rear Adm. Lee in mid–February arrived at the Crescent City, give or take a day or two, around February 24. At that point, they were inspected by the WGCBS fleet engineer, who found fault with all of them. Thatcher, who had authority to dispose of the vessels, returned the light-draughts to their previous upriver posts. He also caused Commodore Palmer to inform Acting Rear Adm. Lee of his decision to do so, believing that it would "require a great deal of time and expense to repair them." Stung, Lee replied in letters to both Thatcher and Welles, justifying his decision to send the boats that had been returned, noting that the "transfer of the four tinclads was only for a temporary emergency."

By the end of the month, four double-turreted monitors, the *Winnebago, Chickasaw, Milwaukee,* and *Kickapoo* were available to the WGCBS. Rear Adm. Thatcher kept the river monitor *Osage* and the Pook turtle *Cincinnati,* and was also joined by two wooden gunboats, the *Itasca* and *Scioto,* and four double-ender ocean-going wooden gunboats, the *Genesee, Octorara, Sebago,* and *Metacomet.* Thatcher chose the *Stockdale* to be his close-in flagboat. She and the *Rodolph* were joined in time by four other tinclads, including the *Nyanza,*[23] *Elk,*[24] *Meteor,*[25] and *Tallahatchie.*[26] Several of these vessels had departed New Orleans for the Alabama Bay via Mississippi Sound at the beginning of March after serving as guard and patrol boats on the Lower Mississippi or at Head of Passes and Pass a l'Outre.

While Northern preparations were underway for a mid–March advance, Maury's Rebel defenders at Mobile were not idle. Everything possible was done to augment the city's eastern bay shore guardians, Spanish Fort, located at the mouth of the Appalachee River, and Fort Blakely, at that river's head, where the Tensas River departed. The former had two major river batteries, but its two-mile long earthworks on the land side were incomplete at the northern end; its garrison comprised 3,500 soldiers. Fort Blakely was a connected entrenchment of nine artillery redoubts mounting 41 cannon; 4,000 Rebel soldiers manned this bastion.

Of particular interest to our story was the work of the Confederate torpedo service, which sowed the upper waters of Mobile Bay with large numbers (at least 150) of stationary underwater torpedoes (mines). By the beginning of March, "every avenue of approach to the outworks or to the city of Mobile was guarded by submarine torpedoes," wrote Brig. Gen. Maury later, "so that it was impossible for any vessel drawing three feet of water to get within effective cannon range of any part of our defenses."[27]

Stealing away from these events, we take the chronological opportunity to insert here an account of Henry Glassford's last nautical scout into the wilds of the Upper Cumberland River. Fresh from a Mound City overhaul following her participation in the January chase of Gen. Hood up the Tennessee, the super light-draught *Reindeer* was permitted to transfer back from the Ninth District to the Tenth.

Acting Volunteer Lt. Glassford was hardly back on the Lower Cumberland before learned during the month's first week that he had been chosen to run a special patrol as soon as the tinclad *Victory* arrived at Nashville. Maj. Gen. Thomas wanted the USN to undertake a scout as far up the Cumberland as possible to check on the depth of the river and the peace of the shoreline population.

On March 8, Glassford, who seemingly owned a patent on such Upper Cumberland investigations, officially received the job. Guerrilla activity in the areas above and below Tennessee's capital remained a topic of concern, he was told, though details of actual attacks or gatherings remained scarce. The commanding general would like the navy to take a look. Next day, the *Reindeer* and *Victory* departed upriver.

At Louisville during an upriver visit at this time, Acting Rear Adm. Lee had a meeting with Maj. Gen. John M. Palmer. The Department of Kentucky commander asked if it would be possible for a gunboat to escort a supply convoy up the Cumberland to Burkesville. Lee agreed to request the cover and sent an order to Tenth District commander Lt. Commander Fitch at Smithland ordering him to handle the matter. Fitch was to wire Palmer at Louisville in cipher and inform him whether the depth of the Upper Cumberland would permit such a trip and whether or not any gunboats were available to provide cover. He was also to inform the admiral as to what action, if any, was taken.

While Palmer, Lee, and Fitch were exchanging wires, the *Reindeer* and *Victory* steamed to Wolf Creek Shoals, a point about 40 miles below Camp Burnside, the name given the army camp at Big South Fork. When the two tinclads arrived, they found only five feet of water on the obstructions. With the river rapidly falling, Glassford determined it would be imprudent to proceed further and his little task unit started to descend.

Lt. Cmdr. Fitch received Lee's orders at Fort Donelson on March 13 and immediately informed his superior that Thomas had already sent Glassford upstream. On March 15, Lee informed Fitch that the decision to send Glassford up the Cumberland was sound. Neither man knew then that their subordinate had found the Upper Cumberland so shallow.

Now, all the way back, the *Reindeer* and *Victory*, as they had on the way up, stopped at all of the important towns and landings on the Upper Cumberland, as well as many farmhouses, to impress upon the people the benevolent intentions of the United States government so long as attacks were avoided. It was expected that a good opinion would be carried back inland.

At one point, Acting Volunteer Lt. Glassford was informed that a force of 200 irregulars had crossed the river near Celina, at the mouth of Obey's River, on Sunday, March 12, for unknown reasons. That intelligence was passed to the army commander at Carthage and to a camp of woodcutters at Dixon's Springs, 30 miles lower.

Upon his return to Nashville on March 17, the *Reindeer's* skipper reported to Thomas that there was a good deal of suspicion on the north side of the Cumberland that the guerrillas that crossed at Celina, as if they had plans to attack the woodmen. Glassford also reported his findings on civilian sentiment, the lack of irregular activity, and the stages of the upper steam to Lee and Fitch. The squadron commander, in turn, sent a letter with the dispatch boat mail from Mound City to Louisville telling Maj. Gen. Palmer that his Burkesville supply petition could not be honored.[28]

Hundreds of miles further south, on March 16, Maj. Gen. Canby requested that Rear Adm. Thatcher provide direct naval gunfire and transport support to the landing and movement of Federal troops against Mobile. Several of the tinclads had already undertaken missions against targets of opportunity, but these were rather isolated operations. For example, on March 11, the *Elk* and *Meteor* had turned their cannon upon Rebel troops behind Dog River Bar.

Maj. Gen. Canby was particularly hopeful that the heavy 1st Division monitors now led by Commodore Palmer might provide a distracting demonstration while the lighter craft provided both convoy and transport. Thatcher replied: "I shall be most happy and ready to give you all the assistance in my power. Six tinclads are all the light-draft vessels at my disposal. They will be ready at any moment."

The Federal land offensive against Mobile was launched early on March 17. With difficulty, 32,000 U.S. XIII Corps troops under Maj. Gen. Gordon Granger marched eastward from Fort Morgan overland across the swamps and woods, first along the peninsula and then north,

Meanwhile, Smith's XVI Corps departed Fort Gaines aboard transports and the USN tinclads, including the *Elk* and *Meteor*, which steamed across Mobile Bay and six miles up on the right bank of Fish River. Disembarkation occurred at Dannelly's Mills, about 17 miles above Mobile Bay. Such additional troop lifts were repeated on March 21 and 22.

Spanish Fort, across the bay directly east of Mobile and key to the city's defense, was invested by March 21. As a diversion, the monitors shelled the woods from Point Clear to Blakely River Bar. It was hoped that their huge 11-inch and 15-inch cannon would discourage the movement of additional Confederate troops to Mobile during the week prior to the full-scale opening of the Federal attack.

The many torpedoes in adjacent waters were a major concern and rigorous minesweeping operations were undertaken by men in small boats directed by Cmdr. Peirce Crosby of the double-ender *Metacomet*. Large numbers of infernal machines were found and destroyed and it was hoped that the threat was neutralized. However, as fast as the mines were pulled out, they were replaced in what turned out to be an around-the-clock dance of sow and sweep.

The "ball was opened" on March 27 as several of the tinclads and other supporting gunboats steamed up into Blakely River to cut Mobile's communications and help cover the Army's advance on the fort's outer works. The monitors also engaged, shelling both the fort and targets of opportunity. Ordnance mounted in all Confederate fortifications replied with vigor, but neither side harmed the other.

The first naval casualty of Canby's campaign was the 970-ton monitor *Milwaukee*.

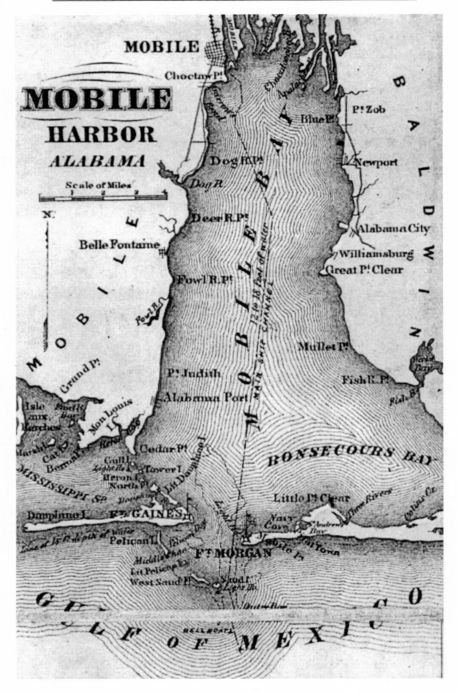

Although the Union owned the entrance into Mobile Bay at the beginning of 1865, the Confederacy still controlled the defenses around the city itself. Once the Confederate thrust into Tennessee was thrown back, these became a Northern objective (Alexander Stephens, *History of the United States,* 1882).

Late in the afternoon on March 28, she, together with the *Winnebago*, ascended the Blakely River to a point about a mile and a half from Spanish Fort and began dropping 11-inch shells around a Rebel supply transport from Mobile attempting to reach the defenders. Steaming in as far as the channel was buoyed, the two ships soon aborted their mission. The double-turreted monitors then started back toward what was believed to be "safer waters."

As the double-turreted *Milwaukee* passed over a spot in the Blakely River swept for torpedoes just the night before and deemed safe, her skipper, Lt. Cmdr. James H. Gillis, learned the opposite was true. He "felt a shock," as he later reported, "and saw at once that a torpedo had exploded on the port side of the vessel." Her stern sank to a depth of 10 feet within three minutes. Fortunately, it took almost an hour for the forward part of the hull to sink, thus no lives were lost. Gillis was immediately sent to Pensacola for a steam pump and diving gear with which to raise his sunken command.[29]

The low-intensity toll of Federal warships continued next day. After lunch on March 29, a gale-force wind from the east hit the monitor anchorage off Belle Rose Landing, inside the Blakely River Bar, forcing the *Winnebago* to drift away from her assigned location. To prevent a collision he could see coming, Lt. Cmdr. William M. Gamble ordered his river monitor *Osage* to hoist her anchor and steam forward slightly. As she did so, a torpedo exploded under the bow of this veteran of the Blair's Landing fight during the Red River campaign. The skipper of the *Osage* reported, "The vessel immediately com-

The Federal land offensive against Mobile, launched on March 17, 1865, featured an amphibious landing by elements of the U.S. XVI Corps on the Fish River. Lift from Fort Gaines to the debarkation point at Dannelly's Mills was provided by transports and a number of U.S. Navy tinclads attached to the West Gulf Coast Blockading Squadron (*Harper's Weekly*, March 29, 1865).

menced sinking." *Osage*, the second turret vessel lost in two days, was less lucky than the *Milwaukee*, suffering four men dead and eight wounded as the craft sank to a depth of 12 feet.

Later on that afternoon, the *Stockdale* also nearly became a casualty. One of the deadly Confederate instruments had been fished out of the water earlier and was supposedly "cleaned of its deadly content." It was then sent aboard the tinclad for the personal inspection of Acting Rear Adm. Thatcher. There, with the squadron commander observing from less than five yards away, two seamen who were extracting the percussion caps made a mistake. One of the torpedo nibbles exploded, badly hurting the ratings. Surprisingly, Thatcher was uninjured.

Cmdr. Crosby intensified his minesweeping activities next day, sending out a swarm of 20 cutters to traverse the river with nets dragging between them. When missiles were found, they were taken into the marshes and detonated by marksmen shooting them with muskets. On March 30, Maj. Gen. Canby was informed that the USN moved its monitors up "as far as is considered safe from torpedoes."

Despite these operational nautical setbacks, plans were in place to finish the Mobile campaign even as the collapse of the Confederacy and end of the war appeared imminent. As the year had begun in Washington, D.C., Navy Secretary Gideon Welles was among a host of government and political leaders looking ahead not only to peace but to a reduction in the huge Union military and naval force. Soon after the Federal victory at Fort Fisher in January, orders went out beginning the retrenchment of the naval establishment. Similar requirements would soon affect the Union army.

The directives from the Navy Department were sent out in stages with an overall goal of cutting costs wherever possible. For example, on March 30, Acting Rear Adm. Lee received a communication from Welles ordering that all vessels chartered by the Mississippi Squadron be immediately discharged. In future, their duties would be carried out by squadron boats "least serviceable as gunboats."

The final push by the Army of the Potomac against Gen. Robert E. Lee's lines began southwest of Petersburg on April 1. Unaware of these developments, the sailors of the WGCBS continued to support the army investment of Mobile.

Early that afternoon, Acting Master N. Mayo Dyer, having been requested aboard the *Metacomet*, turned the light-draught *Rodolph* over to her executive officer, Acting Ensign James F. Thompson. Shortly thereafter, the tinclad, anchored just inside the Blakely River Bar, was ordered to come out alongside the double-ender and take in tow a barge containing salvage apparatus. This equipment, which Acting Rear Adm. Thatcher had requested from Pensacola, was to be employed to raise the monitor *Milwaukee*.

Taking the barge in charge, the *Rodolph* steamed toward the *Milwaukee* wreck-site. As she passed inside the bar and directly between the *Chickasaw* and *Winnebago*, a torpedo exploded under her starboard bow. A hole 10 feet in diameter was blown in her bow back below the location of the starboard Parrott rifle. The little craft was not designed to withstand such a blast and sank quickly in 12 feet of water. Four sailors were lost and 11 wounded. She was the third WGCBS vessel destroyed by mine warfare in a week. Sailors in picket boats from the ironclad *Cincinnati* saw a torpedo floating near the *Chickasaw* and alertly swept it up before it could do any damage.

Confederate torpedoes employed at Mobile. While transporting gear with which to salvage the monitor *Milwaukee*, already lost to one of the hundreds of Confederate torpedoes that defended Mobile's approaches, the tinclad *Rodolph* became a victim of a torpedo on April 1, 1865. Not designed to withstand such a blast, she sank quickly, losing four sailors dead and 11 wounded. (*Harper's Weekly*, April 29, 1865).

Richmond fell on April 4, but word of the Union victory was not received in the west until late in the day. At noon the next day, a 36-gun salute was fired in honor of the triumph. Two days later, the Cumberland River gunboats *Reindeer* and *Victory* were ordered to report to Mound City, followed by the newer *Sibyl*, "a former towboat," on April 9. These light-draughts would be among the first tinclads demilitarized and turned into transports or employed on other duties.

Invested by Union soldiers and bombarded heavily by the big guns of the monitors, Spanish Fort finally fell on April 8. In reporting the capture to Secretary Welles, Acting Rear Adm. Thatcher noted that the Confederate underwater mines were still troublesome, concluding with his most famous quote. "Eighteen large submerged torpedoes were taken by our boats from Apalachee or Blakely River last night in the immediate vicinity of our gunboats," he wrote. "These are the only enemies that we regard."

At 5:30 P.M. on April 9, 16,000 Federal soldiers simultaneously charged three miles of Fort Blakely breastworks. When the dust settled, 250 Confederate defenders were dead, 200 had escaped, and all the rest were POWs.

The anti-torpedo war continued with the final stages of the siege of Mobile. "The channel is lined with torpedoes of the most explosive and dangerous character," wrote a correspondent imbedded with the XIII Corps. "These infernal machines," he continued," are one of the greatest barriers to our movements. But we are fast removing them." A reporter for *Harper's Weekly* wrote that the Union push was "probably the last charge of this war [and] it was as gallant as any on record."

Batteries Tracy and Huger, up the Blakely River from Spanish Fort, were now targeted. Between April 8 and 11, they were pounded by every Federal gun available, including the howitzers of the tinclads. Once those roadblocks fell to the Union forces on April 11, it was time for the final act to unfold.

On April 9, Gen. Lee surrendered to Lt. Gen. Grant at Appomattox Court House, VA, a fact soon communicated to friend and foe alike. That day and next, the monitors and tinclads steamed up the Blakely River to its intersection with the Tensas River and then down the latter to Mobile, where they assumed bombardment positions.

Union celebrations of Appomattox Court House began as appropriate all over the North. At precisely 12 P.M. on April 10, a 100-gun salute was fired in honor of the Appomattox ceremony. It was repeated at sunset. At this point, no one knew precisely where Confederate President Jefferson Davis and his followers were, least of all the men of the WGCBS or the Mississippi Squadron. A belief would soon take hold that they were trying to escape west to continue the war from Texas.

While these events unfolded, the tasked Union tinclads and other gunboats and transports were conveying 8,000 troops across the head of Mobile Bay for the final attack on the city. Unable to resist, the Confederate defenders evacuated the seaport on April 12 and declared it an open city. With the butternut defenders having retreated north, the town itself was surrendered by its mayor.

Two days later, the wooden gunboat *Sciota*, en route to transfer men to the tinclad *Elk*, hit one of the underwater weapons. The explosion on her starboard side ripped her apart, killing five men and wounding six.[30]

After the fall of Richmond and Mobile, it was only a matter of time before the Northern victory signified by Appomattox spread across the land. In these heady early days of Union victory, unregulated navigation on the Western rivers was fully reopened and military responsibility to police them was significantly reduced.

Resources devoted to war were now reduced by the Federals accordingly. On Good Friday, April 14, General Order 60 was received by district commanders of the Mississippi Squadron. Henceforth, the remaining gunboats were not required to cover the landings by steamboats engaged in lawful trade unless desired by military authorities or the parties making the landings. In short, convoy escort was ended and any conflicting squadron orders on this point were revoked. In general, the tinclads were to specifically concentrate on coast guard duties. To save fuel costs, all of the boats were to be kept underway "under easy steam to preserve a vigilant police of the rivers and protect public and private interests as required." With their guns and casemates removed, the *Reindeer* and *Victory* began temporary careers as naval transports on April 15, replacing several withdrawn chartered steamers.

By late Saturday evening or early on Sunday morning everyone in the Mississippi Squadron, as in every other naval squadron or shore base, had heard the awful news from the east. President Lincoln was shot shortly after 10 P.M. on April 14 while watching *Our American Cousin* at Ford's Theatre. He died at 7:22 A.M. the next morning. While the nation came to grips with the enormity of the assassination and Vice President Andrew Johnson became president, plans were put in place to honor the late chief executive.

On Sunday, Navy Secretary Welles wired all of his squadron commanders requiring them to observe the funeral with appropriate respect. More complete special orders were sent by mail. Commanders of the various squadrons passed word of Lincoln's death to all of their commanders. On most ships and boats, crews were assembled and the official announcement was read, along with the order for mourning. All officers began to wear crape, something which would adorn their uniforms for the next six months.

Sporadic outrages continued on the Western waters. These were now more often than not the result of crimes by lawless guerrilla bands or just plain outlaws than by regular military personnel. One such example was brought to the attention of Acting Rear Adm. Lee on April 16.

Writing from his flag boat, the new tinclad *Tempest*,[31] the Mississippi Squadron commander informed Secretary Welles that three steamers had been captured up Tennessee's Hatchie River during the previous week and all were probably burned. The information had been sent to Mound City from the tinclad *Siren*, then lying off Randolph, on the south side of the Hatchie's mouth. A few days later, Lee, employing another *Siren* report, was able to clarify his earlier message to the Navy Department. The three boats had indeed been captured by a band of renegades, led by one Mat Luxton, who posed as one of Brig. Gen. Jo Shelby's staff officers, but only one was destroyed.

A Federal army expedition, under the command of Brig. Gen. E.D. Osband, was loaded aboard two transports and sent down to Fulton (on the north side of the mouth of the Hatchie River) and Randolph. Under cover of the *Siren*, troops disembarked and went inland, with the column from Randolph shortly thereafter engaging the Rebel perpetrators near Brownsville, TN. Among the prisoners taken was the Shelby imposter. As soon as Luxton was brought back to Randolph, Brig. Gen. Osband immediately assembled a court-martial in the cabin of his transport and within an hour it found the man guilty and a sentence was passed. As the covering tinclad's captain wrote: "General Osband hung him from a cotton wood tree at this place this evening; his body is still hanging from the tree."[32]

In response to an April 23 telegram from Secretary Welles to his squadron commanders urging the utmost vigilance to prevent the escape of Jefferson Davis and his cabinet across the Mississippi, Acting Rear Adm. Lee, commanding, directed: "The immediate engrossing and important duty is to capture Jeff. Davis and his Cabinet and plunder. To accomplish this, all available means and every effort must be made to the exclusion of all interfering calls." This was, in fact, the second such fugitive alert within two weeks, coming upon the heels of a short-lived watch for Lincoln's assassin, John Wilkes Booth.

Next day, Lee, by special dispatch boats, ordered that each divisional officer was to "live aboard of a gunboat in which he can quickly and readily move about within the limits of his command, to see that orders are properly attended to, and that the duties required of the different vessels of his district are well performed." In the event that any of them picked up Davis or any of his followers, they were not to be turned over to military, but were to be immediately sent to Mound City aboard a gunboat.

Gen. Joseph Johnston surrendered in North Carolina to Maj. Gen. Sherman on April 26, thereby ending the war in the east. That night America's most horrific maritime tragedy occurred in the west.

As after every war through the Vietnam conflict a hundred years later, the U.S. accelerated the downsizing of its large military establishment. The Army and the USN rapidly consolidated the divisions of their organization and made plans to sell weapons and equipment stockpiles or sell ships and surplus goods.

Primary emphasis was given to manpower demobilization as the triumphant Union almost immediately started to release most of its soldiers and sailors from service and rapidly return them to their states of residence. Rescue, relief, and repatriation of POWs from both sides received early attention, with immediate succor to those from the North.

Vicksburg was chosen as a center for the return home of western POWs and men released from such Southern camps as Andersonville and Cahawba. As the result of USQMD contracts with shipowners and shipping combines, numerous steamboats landed at the town levee to board former prisoners for trips upriver and home.[33] Among the vessels participating in this repatriation program was the *Sultana*.[34]

Carrying somewhere between 75 and 100 passengers, plus her regular 85-man crew, the *Sultana* cleared New Orleans for up the river on April 21. She put into Vicksburg to make repairs to one of her leaky boilers[35] and to board additional people. During her stay, new lift papers were signed with the local quartermaster and over 2,000 ex–POWs, mostly from Ohio, many of whom were sick or weak from exposure, crowded aboard, taking up every berth or other space. To accommodate this gross overload (her legal capacity was 376 souls), the decks were strengthened with supporting stanchions, but still they sagged.

Severely overloaded, the *Sultana* paddled up the Mississippi, making intermediate stops at Helena, AR, and reached Memphis about 7 P.M. on April 26. With a thunderstorm gathering, she coaled and departed, working her way north against a stiff spring current. At Redman Point, on the Arkansas shore between Harrison's and Bradley's landings, approximately seven to nine miles above the city at Paddy's Hen and Chickens, the *Sultana* exploded at about 2 A.M., April 27.[36] Numerous passengers were thrown into the churning waters as hot coals turned the boat into a blazing torch. It was recorded that the disaster "torched a ruddy glare among the cottonwoods of Tennessee and Arkansas and a dull rumble shook the countryside." The thunderstorm broke at the same time.[37]

The glare from the burning *Sultana* could be seen at Memphis and numerous boats and vessels put out to the scene to learn what had occurred and to rescue survivors. In the hour before the first rescue boat arrived (the steamer *Bostona II*[38]), many not already dead died from burns or hypothermia or could no longer remain afloat in the icy water and drowned.

Among the craft lying at the U.S. Navy yard just north of Memphis that morning were the repairing timberclad *Tyler* and the idle tinclad *Grosbeak*. Aboard the latter, an Acting Master's Mate William B. Floyd had witnessed the *Sultana* depart the coal yard and then, not long after, "noticed a red glow in the sky, which very soon showed plainly as a fire." This development was pointed out to the senior master's mate of the boat, in command in the temporary absence ashore of Acting Master Thomas Burns. Unwilling to assume responsibility for firing up the boiler, he ordered that the tinclad not speed to the rescue.

When "faint cries for help" were heard echoing over the water sometime after 3 A.M., Pilot Karnes, awakened by Floyd, overrode the master's mate and sent the crew of the *Grosbeak* into action. Quickly, the tinclad's cutters were launched and began rowing toward the sound of the cries. Over a dozen survivors were quickly rescued. About this same time, small boats also set out from the *Tyler* and the ironclad *Essex*.

Within a short time, both the *Grosbeak* and the *Essex* were, themselves, underway, picking up people as they proceeded, including men (sometimes naked) along the shore. The *Essex* halted her effort at Fort Pickering; however, the *Grosbeak* continued, going as far as the other side of President's Island. When she returned to Memphis about 11 A.M., the tinclad had approximately 90 survivors on board.

The hulk of the devastated steamboat drifted to the west bank of the Mississippi at Hen Island, off the tiny settlement of Mound City, AR, where it sank about dawn. Bodies would be recovered for months, but altogether, some 700 to 800 people survived the *Sultana* disaster. Of the 1,700 to 1,800 who perished (no one knew how many were aboard, so an accurate count is impossible), many were buried in the Memphis National Cemetery.

Also on April 27, Maj. Gen. Thomas at Nashville wrote to Lee to say that he had received information that Davis and his followers were planning to make their escape across the Mississippi. The squadron commander laid the highest priority on effecting a capture and ordered all of his divisional commanders "to make a minute report of the dispositions made" to accomplish the "great object."

The following afternoon Secretary Welles and Lt. Gen. Grant forwarded hearsay information on the Confederate president's escape route. Welles advised Lee to continue to watch the Mississippi and its tributaries, while Grant thought Davis was headed to South Carolina and eventual escape out of the U.S., maybe via the great river.

Lee now began sending reinforcements from the upper flotillas to Memphis and lower points where it was realistically expected that the Davis party might make a run. Among the boats transferred to the pursuit were the *Silver Lake, Brilliant, Ozark, Naumkeag, Tyler, Victory, Neosho, Ibex,*[39] *Kate*[40] (on her first duty), *Juliet, Marmora, Colossus,*[41] *Louisville, Romeo,* and *Abeona.*[42] The acting rear admiral took personal charge from the *Tempest* (No. 1), off the mouth of the White River. Over the next few days, the target search area shifted gradually south to the regions near Grand Gulf, Rodney, or Bruinsburg.

No Mississippi Squadron boat ever came close to intercepting the Confederate president, who never actually made it very far west at all. Jefferson Davis, with members of his Cabinet, reached Abbeville, SC, on May 2. After several more days of fruitless running, Davis, his family, and part of his Cabinet were arrested at Irwinville, some 15 miles from Macon, GA, on May 18. Acting Rear Adm. Lee received a telegram from Maj. Gen Thomas on May 15 announcing the capture.[43]

As the death throes of the Confederacy continued, so to did the police work of the tinclads on the Western waters. Taking into account occasional dustups such as the Davis chase, the rivers were now mostly pacific and fully open to commercial steamboat traffic. Spring was upon the land and with it the certainty that the water stage was in decline. On the upper rivers, as was now customary, planning started to transfer naval operations from the Cumberland and Tennessee to the Ohio from a temporary base at Evansville, IN.

Toward the end of April, Acting Master Washington C. Coulson, the executive officer, assumed acting command of the Cumberland River flagboat *Moose*. On April 29, she was lying at the Tennessee Rolling Mills, not far from Eddyville, KY. At 6 A.M. Coulson was hailed by Acting Master Hall of the *Abeona* and told that 16 guerrillas were reported at Center Furnace, about two miles from the river. Some time later, a courier arrived with additional information concerning an even larger group. Supposedly, 150 to 200 Rebels, armed mostly with revolvers, were moving on Eddyville, with the intention of crossing the river and sacking the town.

The group was supposedly led by a Maj. Hopkins of Brig. Gen. Abraham Buford's Second Division, a part of the Cavalry Corps of Lt. Gen. Nathan Bedford Forrest. This report was not correct; a review of the officer roster for Forrest's entire command published as the appendix to Jordan and Pryor shows no leader down to company level named Hopkins. This may have been another case of outlaws masquerading as military officers and intent on doing mischief for their own personal gain.

Even though the Cumberland was falling, Coulson got the *Moose* immediately underway and started down the river. Nothing was seen until she reached the head of Big Eddy where, on rounding the point, a large body of armed butternuts was discovered on shore, with two troop-laden boats shoving off for the opposite bank. Upon seeing the tinclad, the men in the small boats began jumping overboard. To halt the *Moose's* way, Coulson stopped her engines and began backing. At the same time, he ordered the forward gun on the upper deck fired and sailors to volley with rifles. Few of the men caught in the boats reached shore; most were wounded, killed, or drowned as the craft were destroyed.

The flag boat's party of "small-arms men" was then landed and these engaged the disorganized Confederate survivors. Armed only with revolvers, these were no match for the landing force, which dispersed most of the party, killing or wounding 20 men and taking six captives. Additionally, 19 horses, three mules, saddles, bridles, accoutrements, and numerous pistols were also taken.

About 60 Southerners and their leader managed to escape into the woods on the north side of the Cumberland. Deciding it was not prudent to chase them too far inland, Coulson recalled his landing party, took his prisoners and plunder aboard, including the animals, and proceeded to Eddytown. There he informed the local post commander of the crossing and then returned to Smithland.

Although he was not aboard the *Moose* for this fight, Tenth District Commander Lt. Cmdr. Le Roy Fitch received Coulson's report and gained some satisfaction in knowing that his flagboat had emerged triumphant in the last significant naval counterinsurgency engagement on the western rivers during the Civil War. Having returned from Mound City duty to Smithland, Fitch reviewed with Coulson the particulars of the operation and spoke with some of the prisoners. It was found that two of those under guard had been impressed by the Confederates as guides. These, together with their mule, were released. The others were retained aboard the *Moose* subject to a decision on their fate by Acting Rear Adm. Lee. The horses, also subject to a disposition decision, were pastured. It was later learned that some of the men who survived and made it across the river were taken by Federal land forces.

Acting Master Coulson's full report of the *Moose's* last fight was forwarded to Acting Rear Adm. Lee on May 4, along with a covering letter from the Tenth District commander which summarized the combat and praised the officers and men of the *Moose*. On May 15, Lee forwarded a paraphrased copy of Coulson's written report to Secretary Welles.[44]

13

Winding Down,
May to the Fall of 1865

When 1865 began, the U.S. Navy Department, believing that the Rebellion would soon be over, began seeking significant economy in its operations. As winter turned into spring, this movement intensified. Several months earlier, Navy Secretary Gideon Welles, together with others in the Cabinet of President Abraham Lincoln, sensed that the failure of the Confederacy was at hand. Given this, the mood in Washington towards additional military spending shifted toward one of restraint.

As the civilian leader of the naval establishment, Welles, a fiscal conservative, "determined to dismantle the Navy as efficiently as it had been built up." This would, however, be no haphazard enterprise. Care had to be taken to scale back in such a fashion as to not harm material and human requirements. Eventually, however, the number of vessels would be reduced from several thousand to no more than 100.

In Chapter 12, we noted that, as early as March 30, Welles had called upon Acting Rear Admiral Samuel P. Lee, commander of the Mississippi Squadron, to begin the reduction of his fleet through the withdrawal of contract vessels. These were replaced with tinclads no longer considered vital, including the noted super-light-draught *Reindeer*.

Implementation of plans to reduce the overall size of the U.S. Navy were in full swing by the start of May. On the third day of the month, Secretary Welles ordered the expenses of the Mississippi Squadron, the major organization we consider here, reduced as far as possible. To start with, only 25 vessels of all types were to be kept in commission. Any units that belonged to the army or USQMD were to be dismantled of naval property and returned. These specifically included the four chartered Upper Tennessee gunboats. The resignations of any officers who wished to leave the service were to be approved. Requests for leave or transfer would also be considered, as long as a sufficient number of officers were retained to man the dwindling number of boats.

Almost two weeks later, after returning to Mound City from New Orleans, Acting Rear Adm. Lee sent Washington a list of vessels to be retained in the Mississippi Squadron long-term, with a secondary bill showing those that needed to be retained for the present. The tinclads on the first register included the *Ouachita, Fort Hindman, Tempest, Hastings, Grosbeak, Gazelle, Ibex, St. Clair, Abeona, Gamage, Collier,*[1] *Oriole,*[2] *Moose,* and *Sibyl.* The second register included the *Argosy, Colossus, Exchange, Forest Rose, Fairplay,*

Fairy, Kate, Kenwood, Little Rebel, Mist,[3] *Naumkeag, Prairie Bird, Alfred Robb, Reindeer, Siren, Silver Lake,* and *Silver Cloud.*

Lee took the opportunity on May 19 to pen a long report that provided his recommendations "regarding the reduction of the squadron." From his desk aboard the *Tempest,* the last boss of the Mississippi flotilla recommended that most of the ironclads be laid up in ordinary and all withdrawn once the last Confederate Trans-Mississippi area forces surrendered. Lee also pointed out that only a handful of craft needed to be retained for service work and that all of the others could be brought to a central location. Mound City was desired, not only because it had workmen and facilities, but would be convenient for later civilian surplus purchasers.

Given an anticipated demand, it was recommended that the withdrawn light-draughts be readied for disposal as soon as possible. Armor from their casemates could be quickly and easily removed by the boats' crews for separate sale or storage. The guns could similarly be withdrawn, along with the heavy anchors, cables, and other items not required for commercial purposes. Indeed, some of the anchors and cable could be shipped to New York for storage or use by other squadrons.

After the vessels were stripped, a grand public sale (terms cash) should be held to gain as much return as possible on their original purchase prices. Given the expected early opening of trade on the tributaries of regions lately in secession, it was suggested that the light-draughts could be converted within a short time, perhaps by June 20.

Acting Rear Admiral Lee also recommended that, for 15 days in advance of whatever auction date was chosen, newspaper advertisements be placed in the daily newspapers of the principal river cities, including Pittsburgh, Cincinnati, Louisville, Cairo, St. Louis, Memphis, and New Orleans. For a week or so prior to the sale, prospective buyers would be allowed to inspect the boats.

Assuming that this procedure would be approved, the squadron commander also issued orders the same day for the selected sale vessels to turn over to remaining district boats necessary crews and supplies. As this downsizing occurred, the craft were to steam to Mound City for demobilization. This information and direction was prepared in a series of dispatches that Acting Rear Adm. Lee ordered delivered by the *Sibyl* to "every gunboat on the river." Welles, in general, agreed with Lee's proposals for squadron downsizing. In responding on May 22, he noted that the surplus tinclads and other vessels would be sold under the direction of the Department's Bureau of Construction.[4]

Although it was anticipated that the sale of some of the boats could occur as early as the end of June, removal of the guns from the tinclads, as well as other units of the fleet, took more time, as did the dismantlement of their military bulwarks, casemates and other protections. Additionally, there remained a few police and surrender tasks yet to finish. The first of these, detailed here, was the last major tinclad operation associated with the Civil War.

Throughout the Civil War, in a development far outside the scope of our story until now, French forces under Emperor Maximilian occupied and attempted to fully subject Mexico. During the final days of the Confederacy, a number of Southern commands or parts of Rebel outfits, notably that of Brig. Gen. Joseph O. ("Jo") Shelby, refused to quit and either threatened to remove to Mexico or actually did so. These actions, plus the general threat posed by Maximilian to the U.S. southwestern border, caused President Andrew Johnson to order to Texas an expedition under Maj. Gen. Philip H. Sheridan.

Although most of the soldiers would be sent by sea, a number would go up the Red River. On May 24, Acting Rear Adm. Lee wrote to Lt. Cmdr. James P. Foster,[5] commander of his Third District, to say that, in the process of moving into Texas, Maj. Gen. Sheridan intended to garrison Shreveport and Alexandria with part of the troops sent into the Lone Star State from Louisiana. At least two light-draughts were sought to patrol the Red River between those communities. Foster was expected to cooperate with Sheridan in whatever manner was desired, and to do so, Lee was making available to him the tinclads *St. Clair, Fort Hindman, Collier, Gamage,* and *Little Rebel.*

Acting Rear Adm. Samuel Phillips Lee (1812–1897) succeeded Rear Adm. David D. Porter in command of the Mississippi Squadron during October 1864. Lee arrived just as Johnsonville was lost and was prevented by low water from direct participation in the Battle of Nashville prior to the Confederate retreat. He pushed up the Tennessee River after the retreating Rebels in January 1865 but was unable to come to grips with the Southerners, many of whom escaped via the shoals. He was subsequently blamed in certain Union army circles for letting Gen. John Bell Hood escape. It fell to Lee to disband the squadron in April through August 1865, an unhappy task he performed with great efficiency (Naval Historical Center).

Having learned the tricks of the Red a year earlier, the leaders of the Mississippi Squadron knew that the water in that stream would now be low, too low for ironclads. As a result, the number of tinclads, including the big gun *Fort Hindman,* was large. In addition, a last Confederate ironclad caused concern.[6] Though not high now, the water level upstream at Shreveport was up sufficiently at the end of March to allow the *Missouri*[7] to come down to Alexandria. Arriving on April 4, she anchored opposite Fort Randolph above the falls that had blocked the gunboat fleet of Rear Adm. David D. Porter. The reader will recall, from Chapter 10, that the gunboat's builder, CSN Lt. Jonathan H. Carter, and members of his crew were involved in the abortive September 1864 plot to seize the tinclad *Rattler.* Back at Shreveport following that adventure, they were idled until late spring.

Also on May 24, Lt. Cmdr. Foster sent, by Army request, the tinclad *Gazelle* to Baton Rouge to embark the Confederate generals Simon Bolivar Buckner and Sterling Price, who, on behalf of Trans-Mississippi Department commander Gen. Edmund Kirby Smith, were being sent to

New Orleans to negotiate surrender terms with Federal Military District of West Mississippi commander Maj. Gen. Edward R.S. Canby. On May 26, the two sides entered into a "military convention" which extended to Kirby Smith's command (army and navy) the same generous terms as given by Lt. Gen. Ulysses S. Grant to Gen. Robert E. Lee at Appomattox.

Next day, Canby's headquarters informed Foster of the surrender and asked that two or three gunboats be made available to convoy Federal occupation troops from the mouth of the Red River to garrison the various former Confederate posts on that stream. The expedition would depart early the following week.

The news of the Buckner-Price accord was wired to Rear Adm. Henry K. Thatcher of the West Gulf Coast Blockading Squadron (WGCBS) and Acting Rear Adm. Lee. Also on May 27, Maj. Gen. Sheridan met with Lee at Cairo, explaining his requirements for the forthcoming Texas operation. The next morning, the famed cavalry leader departed south, his transport being escorted to Memphis by the tinclad *Abeona*.

In the absence of Foster, who had traveled up to Mound City, Lee delegated the new Third District commander Lt. Cmdr. William E. Fitzhugh[8] to temporarily act as Mississippi Squadron liaison with Maj. Gen. Canby's command. At the same time, Fitzhugh's force was enhanced by assignment of the ironclads *Lafayette* and *Benton*, plus the *Argosy* and *Kenwood*, the latter substituted for the *St. Clair*. Though he led the last large inland USN operation associated with the conclusion of the Civil War, this officer, who would retire as a Commodore, has never appeared in a Civil War naval history before.

On May 28, Fitzhugh informed Canby that he had three gunboats at the mouth of the Red River ready to accompany his force. Consequently, and before the day was over, the *Benton*, *Ouachita*, and *Fort Hindman* were sent up the river leading the steamer *Ida May*, transporting Maj. Gen. Francis J. Herron and his staff. They were followed by eight troop transports loaded with 8,000 soldiers, with their rear protected by the *Lafayette*, *Gamage*, and *Little Rebel*.

The prompt beginning of the Herron mission brought another request from Canby on May 30 for a tinclad to ascend the Ouachita. Exhibiting complete cooperation, the Third District commander let it be known that he had "seven wooden and two ironclad vessels in readiness" for whatever the commanding general desired. This was the last large Union naval force assembled for operations on the Western waters.

For several days, Fitzhugh and Herron retraced the route taken by Rear Adm. Porter and Department of the Gulf troops in early 1864, arriving below Alexandria on the evening of June 2. Early next morning, Lt. James Carter presented himself and surrendered the *Missouri*, its 42 officers and crew. In conversation, the intrepid builder-skipper reported that his was the only Southern naval vessel left on the Red River or its tributaries. The last Rebel ironclad to capitulate in home waters was moved below the falls, cleaned up, and sent down the river to Memphis on June 4 under escort of the *Benton*.

Also on June 4, the *Gamage*, with both Fitzhugh and Carter embarked, escorted Maj. Gen. Herron and his steamers to Shreveport, arriving, via Grand Ecore, three days later. The city and countryside on the way up were destitute of supplies, but large quantities of cotton were found along the riverbanks. It was hoped that it could be pushed out while the river was still high. No Rebel navy yards, ordnance, or supplies of consequence were found at Shreveport, just as none were discovered earlier at Alexandria. Carter did turn over a pair of small supply steamers to Herron.

While Fitzhugh was up the Red, the *Kenwood* and *Collier*, in accordance with Canby's request, ascended the Ouachita River as far as Monroe. A flag of truce was met at one point and those holding it represented "the lawless condition of the soldiers and others" on and inland of the riverbanks.

Having resumed command of the Third District, Lt. Cmdr. Foster traveled up the Red River aboard a USQMD steamer, ordering back downstream the ironclads and most of the tinclads encountered at various points en route. About 70 miles below Shreveport, he met and conferred with Lt. Cmdr. Fitzhugh, whom he ordered to steam to Mound City aboard the *Ouachita* and report on his mission to Acting Rear Adm. Lee. Returning down the river, Foster left the *Gamage* and *Fort Hindman* to patrol and act in support of the Army. It being found unnecessary to run two boats, a few days later, on June 13, the *Fort Hindman* was withdrawn.[9]

As the Sheridan-Canby-Herron expeditions unfolded, commanders of Union Navy squadrons continued to downsize. Secretary Welles was determined to reduce his several fleets both efficiently and rapidly.

To expedite matters from an administrative viewpoint, Acting Rear Adm. Lee consolidated the Mississippi River districts of his command on May 29. Where there were previously eleven, now there were but three: First, "from White River, inclusive, as far up the Mississippi and its tributaries as naval operations extend"; Second, "from White River to Grand Gulf"; and Third, "from Grand Gulf to New Orleans." Five tinclads were assigned to the First, four to the Second, and five to the Third.

At the same time, he wrote to the Navy Department asking to retain thirteen light-draughts. "Gunboat protection for our trading vessels against guerrillas will be required up the tributaries — the Yazoo, Red, and Arkansas rivers — for some little time to come," Lee opined. He would, however, "reduce the batteries and crews of the vessels retained."

If his recommendation were accepted, three dozen light-draughts would be withdrawn, demobilized, and made ready for sale. These included the *Alfred*

Maj. Gen. Edward R.S. Canby (1817–1873), Federal commander of the Military Division of Western Mississippi, commanded U.S. Army forces in the battle for Mobile in March through May 1865 and accepted the surrender of Lt. Gen. Edmund Kirby Smith and Richard Taylor of the Confederate Trans-Mississippi Department in June (*Harper's Weekly*, April 15, 1865).

A tinclad with three names, the *Fort Hindman* was commissioned in April 1863 as the *James Thompson* and was renamed *Manitou* that June. Heavily armed, she was renamed five months later. Her big guns ensured she was always welcome on Federal expeditions and she served on many, including those up the Red, Black, and Ouachita Rivers. Stranded above the Red River dam, she was, like the ironclads, saved by Col. Bailey's dam. Her cannon were required up the Red again in June 1865, when she steamed to participate in the seizure of the *Missouri*, the last inland Confederate ironclad (Naval Historical Center).

Robb, Argosy, Alexandria, Brilliant, Colossus, Curlew, Cricket, Champion, Exchange, Fawn, Forest Rose, Fairplay, Fairy, General Pillow, Gazelle, Huntress,[10] *Juliet, Kate, Kenwood, Mist, Marmora, New Era, Nymph, Naiad, Naumkeag, Paw Paw, Peosta, Peri,*[11] *Romeo, Reindeer, Springfield, Siren, Silver Lake, Silver Cloud, Tensas,*[12] and *Victory.*

Such retention did not fit into Washington's cost-cutting plan and, on June 2, Assistant Secretary of the Navy Gustavus Vasa Fox wrote giving Lee the opportunity to choose and retain 15 vessels overall, plus store ships. Additionally, he was to economize wherever possible, especially in the use of coal. All vessels were "to keep steam down, except in an emergency...." These restrictions were noted by the admiral in a June 12 general order. Not only was fuel economy emphasized, but the use of coal oil was prohibited and all coal oil and lamps were to be immediately turned in to storage. "Vessels retained in commission," Lee directed, "will immediately obtain lard-oil lamps." There would be no more destroyed by fire in the manner of the *Black Hawk.*

A direct result of the Fox requirement communicated in this message to district and vessel commanders was the withdrawal from active service of the tinclads *Moose* and *Prairie Bird*. Those remaining were reshuffled, with three assigned to the First Division; three to the Second Division; and four to the Third Division. The *Tempest* continued as flag boat.

As the withdrawn tinclads reported to Mound City, they were taken in hand by laborers contracted for by Com. John W. Livingston[13] under order of the Bureau of Construction. In an orderly manner, the casemates were removed, along with all other protections, and the guns taken out. Small arms and powder were dispatched to magazines and basic engine repairs completed. Most of the light-draughts remained fully functional as steamboats and could soon again serve as transports.

Occasionally, the smaller warcraft provided special services. For example, one of services provided by the tinclads during the war often received little notice: the towing of ironclads. Most of the heavy gunboats had great difficulty making way against the currents of the rivers and often required assistance, which was usually provided by civilian craft or, when available, the tinclads. In keeping with Navy Department orders that a large number of the ironclads of the Mississippi Squadron be laid up at Mound City, it became necessary for several of the tinclads to assist in helping the larger boats reach their destination. It was particularly important that, in the process, they were not grounded on sandbars or other obstructions.

For example, on June 19, the tinclads *Argosy* and *Forest Rose* were dispatched to Memphis to tow up the veteran ironclad *Essex*. Although all practical dispatch was to be employed in accomplishing the mission, the pilots of the light-draughts were specifically ordered to "pass no doubtful place until you have thoroughly sounded and buoyed them in [small] boats."

Another difficulty facing Lee as he dismantled the Mississippi Squadron was finding a place to stow the guns, carriages, stores, and gunpowder taken off the boats. Also, on June 19, a telegram arrived from Washington, D.C., that seemed to solve this problem. The admiral was authorized to occupy the grounds of the Jefferson Barracks Reserve near St. Louis. The War Department, to whom Secretary Welles had turned for assistance in the matter, had even agreed to permit the USN to erect temporary sheds, storehouses, and a magazine.

As it turned out, the Mississippi Squadron did not require all of the Jefferson Barracks storage that Welles obtained. Indeed, all Acting Rear Adm. Lee really needed was a place to send his powder and loaded shell. There was plenty of covered room at Mound City, he wrote his civilian superior, to accommodate everything else. As soon as possible, the necessary buildings and sheds would be constructed at the Reserve, and then a "few navy transports will readily convey all material from here...." The required structures were in place at Jefferson Barracks by the end of June. At this point, Lt. Cmdr. Fitzhugh was detailed to Missouri to take charge of the unloading and storage operation, making certain that vessels were returned to Mound City as quickly as possible.

On July 2, the *Moose*, her casemate gone and her guns removed, received orders to steam to Jefferson Barracks with the first load of ordnance to be stored under the arrangement with the War Department. Within days, the famed veteran of Morgan's Raid and the Battle of Nashville would be joined in this transport duty by sixteen other demilita-

Mound City and Cairo, Illinois, were the operational and support centers of the Mississippi Squadron, with the former station center for the dissolution of the command in July and August 1865. The identity of the vessel pictured in the foreground is unknown (Miller's *Photographic History of the Civil War*).

rized light-draughts. Thereafter, every available demilitarized light-draught was engaged in moving ammunition to Jefferson Barracks, "which we did, trip after trip, working day and night till the task was done." Not only did crewmen have to oversee delivery of shot and shell, they had to participate in its loading, and often its unloading.

A large percentage of the ammunition, the so-called "fixed ammunition," was stowed in wooden boxes with rope handles, each of which weighed between 100 and 300 pounds. It required two men to carry one of the boxes, and they did so as gingerly as possible so as to avoid explosions. Solid shot was somewhat easier. The loading process was so arranged that it could be rolled right to the gangplank down a trench shoveled out of the river bank. Men were stationed along the trench, and if a ball stopped, it could be started again with a kick.[14]

Another requirement of squadron demobilization was recovery, where possible, of lost ordnance. On June 20, Acting Volunteer Lt. George W. Rogers,[15] the last commander of the tinclad *Kate*, was ordered to the Tennessee River to "raise or wreck, as the case may require, the gunboats *Undine*, *Key West*, *Elfin*, and *Tawah* at or near Johnsonville." He was also to raise a sunken coal barge there and two at Smithland. It took over two weeks for Rogers to handle his Johnsonville mission, recovering a total of nine howitzers. The wrecks themselves would gradually be consumed by the river.

On June 27, Lt. Moreau Forrest, late commander of the Eleventh District, was given final instructions by Maj. Gen. George Thomas in a Nashville interview concerning the procedure for turning back to the War Department the four chartered Upper Tennessee gunboats *General Thomas*, *General Grant*, *General Burnside*, and *General Sherman*. Returning to Bridgeport, AL, where the boats were homeported, he turned them over to the local Army quartermaster and was given a $76,000 receipt for each. Forrest also returned and received receipts for all leased property, which consisted primarily of a few buildings and sheds where his paymaster stored provisions and clothing.

Even as the tinclads and other squadron vessels were being retired, the Navy Department, appreciating the fact that it needed to unload a large number of surplus river naval vessels, settled upon a traditional American plan for liquidation. The boats would, as Acting Rear Adm. Lee had earlier suggested, be auctioned. Beginning in late June, advertisements were placed by Department officials in all of the leading newspapers from the East Coast through the Midwest and down to New Orleans for a "Large Sale of Gunboats." Noting that over 50 craft were available, officials submitting the notices anticipated that all of them would be sold in a giant one-day sale overseen by Com. Livingston at Mound City on August 17.

On July 3, Lee sent the Navy Department a report concerning his progress with squadron demobilization. So far as the tinclads were concerned, the work had gone smoothly. One was transporting paymasters' stores to New Orleans; one was temporarily stationed at Jefferson Barracks; eight were transporting ordnance stores to Jefferson Barracks; seven were on the Mississippi River proceeding under orders to Mound City; thirteen were at Mound City being dismantled; and sixteen were at Mound City, dismantled and about to be put out of commission.

Three days later, Secretary Welles, flogging his squadron commanders hard under "the stern injunction of economy," bluntly informed Lee that the "Department intends to break up the Mississippi Squadron." Consequently, all bases and stations other than the one at Mound City were to be closed and their functions transferred to Illinois. Additionally, only five active vessels could be retained, in addition to those temporarily moving stores, especially to Jefferson Barracks.

Far to the South at New Orleans, Acting Rear Adm. Henry K. Thatcher was also tasked with force reduction. On May 31, he had received an order from Assistant Navy Secretary Fox ordering that the WGCBS be reduced to fifteen steamers and one monitor. On July 13, the WGCBS was combined with the East Gulf Coast Blockading Squadron into a single Gulf Squadron. Thatcher had far fewer tinclads to dispose of than Lee and did so promptly and without press coverage other than the newspaper advertisements that provided particulars of disposal. In accordance with the same directive from Washington, D.C., that permitted the Bureau of Construction to organize a sale for his Mississippi Squadron counterpart, the New Orleans–based leader withdrew his vessels. Rather than selling off his craft in one gigantic offering, however, he chose to offer them in several.

Acting Rear Adm. Lee meanwhile had borne down heavily upon his task of downsizing the Mississippi Squadron. As the flow to Jefferson Barracks slowed, men from the unneeded boats were transferred to the receiving ship *Great Western*. The growing number of men awaiting detachment required that barge after barge, with tents, be lashed side-by-side to each other and to the *Great Western* with strong lines. It also required Acting Rear Adm. Lee and his personnel officers to turn over multiple and very specific manpower lists to the Bureau of Navigation and to the Office of Detail. Each morning, a boatswain sounded his whistle and men listened to learn if their boat was being called for what were becoming mass discharges by vessel. When it was, the bluejackets from a given craft assembled, signed and received the necessary papers, and were provided funds in payment or for passage home.

By July 27, Lee was able to report that most of the men on the receiving ship or the barges were discharged and 25 vessels were "anchored, generally in pairs, in the bend above Cairo. Many had been decommissioned, stripped of their protections, and turned over to Com. Livingston for sale. Five tinclads were yet on duty, and most of the others were employed as transports on the Jefferson Barracks run. It was hoped that all could be "thoroughly stripped and out of commission" within ten days.

The last two tinclads, and what little remained of the organ-

Acting Rear Adm. Henry Knox Thatcher (1806–1880) commanded the West Gulf Coast Blockading Squadron during the 1865 Mobile campaign from the ocean-going tinclad *Stockdale*. Like his Mississippi Squadron counterpart Acting Rear Adm. Lee, Thatcher was charged with the reduction, in April through July 1865, of his command, which was renamed the Gulf Squadron (Naval Historical Center).

ization, were surrendered to Commodore Livingston on August 12. Two days later, Acting Rear Adm. Lee hauled down his flag and the Mississippi Squadron ceased to exist.[16]

At New Orleans on August 12, four of the seven remaining Gulf Coast Squadron tinclads were sold at auction. Without fanfare, the *Carrabasset*,[17] *Glide II*,[18] *Nyanza*, and *Tallahatchie* went under the auctioneer's gavel, bringing in a combined $89,000. The others would go later: the *Elk* and *Stockdale* on August 24 and the *Meteor* on September

12. They brought in another combined $38,000. The $127,000 paid for all seven together by their new civilian owners was far less than the government paid for them in time of need.[19]

From its practice of covering large absolute sales, the editors of the Chicago *Daily Tribune* appreciated the impact that Com. Livingston's forthcoming large auction of tinclads, tugs, and support craft could have. Consequently, they sent one of their better-known war correspondents, J.A. Austen, to Mound City about a fortnight ahead of the sale. Austen was asked to review the atmosphere of the community, examine the mechanics of the sale, and take the pulse of potential buyers. As it turned out, according to Austen, the Navy's sale was probably one of the largest meetings of steamboatmen in a generation. It was even possible, he suggested, that "so great a meeting of boatmen was never before held in the West."

Austen found a total of 63 boats (timberclads, tinclads, support craft) and tugs anchored in the Ohio River between Mound City and Cairo, "nearly filing the bend between the two places." Many were, as Lee had reported earlier, tied up in pairs, both for maintenance and for security purposes. At night, lights and lanterns were hung aboard, sparkling on the water. All who saw this illuminated parade perceived it a most beautiful and striking sight, reminiscent of the myriad lights of a large town or city.

In the week before the August 17 sale, earnest buyers and the idly curious took passage aboard every small craft available to examine the merchandise, both from the water and by inspections aboard. Potential purchasers were encouraged to seek every nugget of information available on those boats of interest and to ply their sometimes immense knowledge in gauging their value. So thorough was this process, Austen believed, that "if any buyer paid more than his boat was worth, he did so with full knowledge of what he was doing."

The arrangements for the sale were familiar to all then and to anyone today who has ever attended the auction of a house, automobile, or farm animals. A large stand was placed in the center of the naval station ordnance building, "handsomely decorated with national ensigns." Here space and every convenience was afforded to clerks, reporters, and purchasers.

At exactly noon on that sweltering Thursday, Solomon A. Silver of Cairo took the stand and began the alphabetical disposal with the tinclad *Argosy*. She was quickly "knocked down" to U.P. Schenck for $10,000. The sale proceeded rapidly and the light-draughts, because of their future trading value, brought the highest bids.

Other sale examples include James Kenison's pickup of the *Fairy* for $9,600; John Gilbert's acquisition of the *Gazelle* for $10,850; and Thomas Scott's buy of the *Oriole* for $17,000. The sale price of some of the more historic included W. Thatcher's purchase of the *Cricket* for $6,050; David White's buy of the *Moose* for $10,100; the $7,100 pickup of the *Romeo* by Edward Williams; and the $8,650 sale of the *Marmora* to D.D. Barry.

After three hours of "good and spirited" bidding, the sale was over and $625,000 was earned for the Federal coffers, $491,018 of which was gained from selling the tinclads. The only interruption during the auction was a protest by the former owners of the *Little Rebel*, who interjected that the sale of that boat could not go forward because they had a suit pending in the U.S. Circuit Court at Springfield over her ownership. They claimed the boat was still theirs because it had been taken from them by the Rebels and converted to war purposes.

"Thus ended the great Government sale," reporter Austen wrote as the auction concluded around dusk, "and with it vanished the Mississippi Squadron...." Only the monitors and other ironclads remained to be sold, plus three tinclads yet retained.[20]

Most of the tinclads were reconverted to civilian use and many served their new owners long and with distinction. A number, as can be tracked in the compilations of Way and Silverstone, met violent ends, by snagging, boiler explosion, or ice. Others were broken up when their useful lives were over.

Three light-draughts escaped the August 17 auction as they were required to complete a variety of final tasks required by the Mound City naval station. Meanwhile, another great sale was authorized by the Bureau of Construction for November 29, at which time the demobilized ironclads were sold.

Four days before the November auction, the *General Pillow*, Tinclad No. 20, was sold to Wetzel and Hallerberg for $2,000. The former Mississippi Squadron flag boat *Tempest*, Tinclad No. 1, was sold under the gavel of auctioneer Silver to Robert Carns for $12,300. She actually went out of commission the following morning. Tinclad No. 55, the *Kate*, was the last of her type withdrawn from service. Decommissioned on March 25, 1866, she was sold at Mound City to James H. Trover four days later for $10,350.[21]

Regardless of their individual fates, collectively, the tinclads were among the most important vessels of the Civil War. Their activities reinforced the claims of the North to an undivided Union through incessant probing into the heartland via the Western rivers, helping to keep open the great Midwestern communication lines by convoy, patrol, and direct support of National military action. Unable to defeat the Federals on "its streams," the Confederacy resorted to operating both an organized and a disorganized ("guerrilla") antishipping campaign, hoping to dissuade the enemy. As one writer noted, these "tactics caused the Union some concern, but did little more than increase the barbarity of an already vicious war."[22]

Despite hundreds of attacks by Southerners on river transport during the war (only of a fraction of which have been reviewed within these pages), the overall number of U.S. civilian and commercial steamboats sunk by military action was surprisingly few. Bvt. Brig. Gen. Lewis B. Parsons, USQMD river transport czar, later reported that direct "guerrilla" action against river transports on all of the Western streams from 1861 to1865 resulted in 28 vessels of 7,065 tons sunk for a loss of $355,000. Regular Confederate forces sank another 19 craft of 7,925 tons valued at $518,500. Confederate secret agents using incendiaries sank double the tonnage (18,500) of either Rebel cavalry or irregulars, 29 boats worth $891,000.[23]

As part of their often mundane patrols and occasionally spirited actions in direct support of military activities, the 60 tinclads protected all Western river steamers either compelled to or willing to have their cover. This duty was often performed with very slight naval concentrations. For most of the time after August 1862, Lt. Cmdr. Le Roy Fitch operated all Cumberland River escort and patrol with fewer than eight light-draughts and often stretched this slight chain into the Ohio and Tennessee Rivers as well. Often there were no more than four boats available to Lt. Cmdr. S. Ledyard Phelps and Lt.

George Bache on the White River of Arkansas. A number of steamers lost were steaming independently when hit.

The tinclads also interrupted Confederate communications, blockaded the huge Trans-Mississippi area, and sailed into harm's way in the bays and rivers surrounding New Orleans. There were far fewer mundane moments aboard a light-draught than a larger ironclad. Rowland Stafford True, who served aboard the *Silver Lake*, remembered how the time passed: "One day lying peacefully at anchor, and the next, off on some expedition up or down the river." He continued: "Up the Cumberland today, up the Tennessee tomorrow, down the Mississippi the next — here and there wherever needed."

In three years of conflict, surprisingly few (13) were lost, though many were damaged by nature or gunfire. One was burnt out (*Glide I*), one was snagged and lost (*Linden*), and one was destroyed by a storm (*Rattler*). Nine were direct or indirect victims of Confederate shore batteries (*Covington, Elfin, Key West, Petrel, Queen City, Signal, Tawah, Undine*, and *Wave*), and one was sunk by an underwater torpedo (Rodolph).

Years later, a British historian stated the worth of the tinclad in a single long sentence. "All in all these tinclad river gunboats were ungainly, slow and unprepossessing," wrote Angus Konstam in 2002, "but without them the Union would never have managed to supply its field armies in the West, or keep them in communication with each other."

Acting Volunteer Lt. George W. Brown, the first commander of the light-draught *Forest Rose*, has summed up the tinclad value better than most and we conclude our tale of their service with this quote from his contemporary recollections:

> Like cavalry, we, the light-draft fleet, were kept on the go, never at rest. Our dutries on the river were severe; we were never out of rifle-range, and often our men were picked off by sharpshooters from behind the levee. There seemed to be something about us, perchance it was our activity, that made the army like to have us around; and I believe, if they could have put us upon wheels, "Uncle Billy" would have taken us on his "March to the Sea."[24]

APPENDIX I

Tinclad Acquisition Chronology,
1862–1865

The chart that follows provides acquisition data for the light-draught vessels added to the Mississippi Squadron. Information, with notes where necessary, is offered chronologically by commissioning or transfer date, and includes: name; number; rig (C=Center-wheeler; S=Side-wheeler; SW=Stern-wheeler; Sc=Screw); date purchased/captured; date commissioned/placed in service/transferred; and initial armament (r=rifled; SB=smoothbore; 12pdr & 24pdr=howitzer). Several tinclads were transferred to the West Gulf Coast Blockading Squadron (WGCBS).

1862

Name & No	Rig	Purchased/ Captured	Commissioned	Armament
Alfred Robb 21	SW	4–21–62	6–2–62	2 12pdr-r; 2 12pdr-SB
Little Rebel 16	Sc	6–6–62	8–21–62	3 12pdr-SB
Genl Pillow 20	S	6–9–62	8–23–62	2 12pdr-SB
Fairplay 17	S	8–18–62	9–6–62	4 12pdr-SB
St. Clair 19	SW	8–13–62	9–24–62	2 12pdr-r; 2 12pdr-SB
Brilliant 18	SW	8–13–62	10–1–62	2 12pdr-r; 2 12pdr-SB
Marmora 2	SW	9–17–62	10–21–62	2 12pdr-r; 2 12pdr-SB
Signal 8	SW	9–22–62	10–2?–62	2 30pdr-r; 4 24pdr-SB
Forest Rose 9	SW	11–15–62	12–3–62	2 30pdr-r; 4 24pdr-SB
Glide I	SW	11–17–62	12–3–62	6 24pdr-SB
Romeo 3	SW	10–31–62	12–11–62	6 24pdr-SB
Juliet 4	SW	11–1–62	12–14–62	6 24pdr-SB
New Era 7	SW	10–27–62	12–1?–62	6 24pdr-SB

Name & No	Rig	Purchased/ Captured	Commissioned	Armament
Rattler 1	S	11–11–62	12–19–62	2 30pdr-r; 4 24dr-SB
Silver Lake 23	SW	11–15–62	12–24–62	6 24dr-SB

1863

Name & No	Rig	Purchased/ Captured	Commissioned	Armament
Linden 10	S	11–20–62	1–3–63	6 24dr-SB
Springfield 22	S	11–20–62	1–12–63	6 24dr-SB
Cricket 6	SW	11–18–62	1–19–63	6 24dr-SB
Prairie Bird 11	SW	12–19–62	1–2?–63	8 24dr-SB
Curlew 12	SW	12–17–62	2–16–63	8 24dr-SB
Covington 25	S	2–13–62	3–?–63	2 30pdr-r; 2 50pdr-r
Argosy 27	SW	3–24–62	3–29–63	6 24dr-SB; 2 12-pdr-r
Hastings 15	S	3–24–63	4–?–63	2–32pdr-SB; 3 24dr-SB
Petrel 5	SW	12–22–62	4–?–62	8–24dr-SB
Fort Hindman 13	S	3–14–63	4–?–63	6 8"-SB
Queen City 26	S	2–13–63	4–1–63	2 32pdr-SB; 4 24dr-SB
Naumkeag 37	SW	4–14–63	4–16–63	2 30pdr-r; 4 24dr-SB
Champion 24	SW	3–14–63	4–26–63	2 30pdr-r; 1 24dr-SB; 1 12pdr-SB
Silver Cloud 28	SW	4–1–63	5–4–63	6 24dr-SB
Fawn 30	SW	5–13–63	5–11–63	6 24dr-SB
Kenwood 14	SW	4–3–63	5–24–63	2 32-pdr-SB; 4 24dr-SB
Key West 32	SW	5–16–63	5–26–63	6 24dr-SB
Exchange 38	SW	4–6–63	6–?–63	2 32pdr-SB; 4 24dr-SB; 1 12pdr-SB
Moose 34	SW	5–20–63	6–15–63	6 24dr-SB
Tawah 29	S	6–19–63	6–21–63	2 30pdr-r; 4 24dr-SB; 2 12pdr-r
Victory 33	S	7–14–63	7–8–63	6 24dr-SB
Reindeer 35	SW	6–13–63	7–25–63	6 24dr-SB

Name & No	Rig	Purchased/ Captured	Commissioned	Armament
Paw Paw 31	C	4–9–63	7–25–63	2 30pdr-r; 6 24pdr-SB
Peosta 36	S	6–13–63	10–2–63	3 30pdr-r; 3 32pdr-SB; 2 12pdr-SB; 6 24pdr-SB
Wave 45	S	11–14–63	WGCBS	6 24pdr-SB
Glide II 43	S	11–30–63	WGCBS	4 24pdr-SB
Stockdale 42	SW	11–13–63	WGCBS	4 24pdr-SB
Nyanza 41	S	11–4–63	WGCBS	6 24pdr-SB
Alexandria 40	S	7–13–63	12–12–63	2 12-pdr-SB

1864

Name & No	Rig	Purchased/ Captured	Commissioned	Armament
Tensas 39	S	8–14–63	1–1–64	2 24pdr-SB
Gazelle 50	S	11–21–63	WGCBS	6 12pdr-r
Elfin 52	SW	2–23–64	3–?–64	8 24pdr-SB
Fairy 51	SW	2–10–64	3–10–64	8 24pdr-SB
Meteor 44	SW	1–23–64	WGCBS	2 32pdr-SB; 2 24pdr-SB
Undine 55	SW	3–7–64	4–?–64	8 24pdr-SB
Tallahatchie 46	SW	1–23–64	WGCBS	4 24-pdr SB
Naiad 53	SW	3–3–64	4–3–64	8 24pdr SB
Nymph 54	SW	3–8–64	4–11–64	8 24pdr SB
Carrabasset 49	S	1–23–64	WGCBS	2 32pdr-SB; 4 24pdr-SB
Elk 47	S	12–8–63	WGCBS	2 32pdr-SB; 4 24pdr-SB
Rodolph 48	SW	12–31–63	WGCBS	2 32pdr-SB; 2 24-pdr-SB
Huntress 58	SW	5–?–64	6–10–64	2 30pdr-r; 4 24pdr-SB
Peri 57	SW	4–30–64	6–20–64	1 30pdr-r; 6 24pdr-SB
Sibyl 59	S	4–27–64	6–26–64	2 30pdr-r; 2 24pdr-SB
Gen'l Grant 62	S	1864	7–20–64	2 30pdr-r; 2 24pdr-SB
Gen'l Sherman 60	S	1864	7–27–64	2 20pdr-r; 3 24pdr-SB

Name & No	Rig	Purchased/ Captured	Commissioned	Armament
Gen'l Burnside 63	S	1864	8–8–64	2 20pdr-r; 3 24pdr-SB
Gen'l Thomas 61	S	1864	8–8–64	2 20pdr-r; 4 24pdr-SB
Siren 56	SW	3–11–64	8–30–64	2 24pdr-SB

1865

Name & No	Rig	Purchased/ Captured	Commissioned	Armament
Grosbeak 8	S	2–3–65	2–24–65	2 30pdr-r; 1 12pdr-SB
Colossus 25	SW	12–6–64	2–24–65	2 30pdr-r; 4 24pdr-SB; 1 12pdr-SB
Mist 26	SW	12–23–64	3–3–65	2 20pdr-r; 4 24pdr-SB; 1 12pdr-SB
Collier 29	SW	12–7–64	3–18–65	2 20pdr-r; 6 24pdr-SB; 1 12pdr-SB
Oriole 52	SW	12–7–64	3–22–65	2 30pdr-r; 6 24pdr-SB; 1 12pdr-SB
Gamage 60	SW	12–22–64	3–23–65	2 20pdr-r; 1 12pdr-SB
Kate 55	SW	12–23–64	4–2–65	2 20pdr-r; 6 24pdr-SB; 2 12pdr-SB
Ibex 10	S	12–10–64	4–4–65	2 30pdr-r; 4 24pdr-SB; 2 12pdr-SB
Abeona 32	S	12–21–64	4–10–65	2 30pdr-SB; 2 24pdr-SB; 2 12pdr-SB
Tempest 1	SW	12–30–64	4–26–65	2 30pdr-r; 2 24pdr-SB; 2 12pdr-SB

Sources: U.S. Navy Department, Official Records of the Union and Confederate Navies in the War of the Rebellion, *31 vols. (Washington, D.C.: GPO, 1894–1922), Series II, Vol. 1, pp. 27–246; Paul H. Silverstone,* Warships of the Civil War Navies *(Annapolis, MD: Naval Institute Press, 1989), pp. 164–180.*

Appendix II

Tinclad Postwar History, 1865–1876

The chart that follows provides basic postwar data for the light-draught vessels added to the Mississippi Squadron. Information, with notes where necessary, is offered chronologically by wartime acquisition date, and includes: name; number; date sold out of service or lost in service; later name; fate/last known service, breakup or writeoff; and date of fate/last known service, breakup or writeoff.

Abbreviations: BO = Burned Out; BU=Broken Up; DBE = Destroyed By Explosion; DBF = Destroyed By Fire; DBI = Destroyed by Ice; FU = Fate Unknown; RR = Removed from Records; W = Wrecked (by snag, grounding, foundering, storm, etc.).

1862

Name & No		Sale/Loss	Later Name	Fate	Date
Alfred Robb	21	8–17–1865	Robb	BU	1873
Little Rebel	16	11–29–1865	Spy	RR	1874
Genl Pillow	20	11–26–1863	FU	FU	FU
Fairplay	17	8–17–1865	Cotile	BU	1871
St. Clair	19	8–17–1865	St. Clair	RR	1869
Brilliant	18	8–17–1865	John S. McCune	BO	12–6–1867
Marmora	2	8–17–1865	FU	FU	FU
Signal	8	5–5–1864			
Forest Rose	9	8–17–1865	Anna White	DBI	2–4–1868
Glide I		2–7–1863			
Romeo	3	8–17–1865	Romeo	RR	1870
Juliet	4	8–17–1865	Goldena	W	12–31–1865
New Era	7	8–17–1865	Goldfinch	DBF	6–3–1868
Rattler	1	12–30–1864			
Silver Lake	23	8–17–1865	Mary Hein	DBF	2–28–1866
Linden	10	2–22–1864			

1863

Name & No	Sale/Loss	Later Name	Fate	Date
Springfield 22	8–17–1865	Jennie D	RR	1875
Cricket 6	8–17–1865	Cricket No. 2	BU	1867
Prairie Bird 11	8–17–1865	FU	FU	FU
Curlew 12	8–17–1865	FU	FU	FU
Covington 25	5–5–1864			
Argosy 27	8–17–1864	Argosy	DBF	3–7–1872
Hastings 15	8–17–1865	Dora	RR	1872
Petrel 5	4–22–1864			
Fort Hindman 13	8–17–1864	James Thompson	RR	1874
Queen City 26	6–24–1864			
Naumkeag 37	8–17–1864	Montgomery	DBF	1–19–1867
Champion 24	11–29–1865	Champion No. 4	RR	1868
Silver Cloud 28	8–17–1865	Silver Cloud	W	10–2–1868
Fawn 30	8–17–1865	Fanny Barker	W	3–24–1873
Kenwood 14	8–17–1865	Cumberland	DBE	8–14–1868
Key West 32	11–4–1864			
Exchange 38	8–17–1864	Tennessee	W	4–25–1869
Moose 34	8–17–1865	Little Rock	DBF	12–29–1867
Victory 33	8–17–1865	Lizzie Tate	W	2–8–1866
Reindeer 35	8–17–1865	Mariner	W	5–9–1867
Paw Paw 31	8–17–1865		BU	1865
Peosta 36	8–17–1865	Peosta	DBF	12–15–1870
Tawah 29	11–4–1864			
Wave 45	5–6–1864			
Glide II 43	8–12–1865	Glide	DBE	1–13–1869
Stockdale 42	8–24–1865	Caddo	RR	1871
Nyanza 41	8–17–1865	Nyanza	RR	1873
Alexandria 40	8–17–1865	Alexandria	W	10–5–1867

1864

Name & No	Sale/Loss	Later Name	Fate	Date
Tensas 39	8–17–1865	Teche	W	1868
Gazelle 50	8–17–1865	Plain City	BU	1869
Elfin 52	11–4–1864			
Fairy 51	8–17–1865	FU	FU	FU
Meteor 44	10–5–1865	De Sot	RR	1869
Undine 55	11–4–1864			
Tallahatchie 46	8–12–1865	Coosa	DBF	9–7–1869

Name & No	Sale/Loss	Later Name	Fate	Date
Naiad 53	8–17–1865	*Princess*	W	6–1–1868
Nymph 54	8–17–1865	*Cricket No. 3*	FU	FU
Carrabasset 49	8–12–1865	*Annie Wagley*	W	5–1–1870
Elk 47	8–24–1865	*Countess*	W	1868
Rodolph 48	4–1–1865			
Huntress 58	8–17–1865	*Huntress*	W	12–30–1865
Peri 57	8–17–1865	*Marietta*	W	1–8–1868
Sibyl 59	8–17–1865	*Comet*	RR	1876
Gen'l Grant 62	Returned 6–2–1865	FU	FU	FU
Gen'l Sherman 60	Returned 6–3–1865	FU	FU	FU
Gen'l Burnside 63	Returned 6–1–1865	FU	FU	FU
Gen'l Thomas 61	Returned 6–3–1865, Sold 1866	*Ingomar*	W, Raised, W	3–24–1868 12–31–1868
Siren 56	8–17–1865	*White Rose*	RR	1867

1865

Name & No	Sale/Loss	Later Name	Fate	Date
Grosbeak 8	8–17–1865	*Mollie Hambleton*	W	6–9–1871
Colossus 25	8–17–1865	*Memphis*	W	12–17–1866
Mist 26	8–17–1865	*Mist*	RR	1874
Collier 29	9–17–1865	*Imperial*	RR	1867
Oriole 52	8–17–1865	*Agnes*	W	3–3–1869
Gamage 60	8–17–1865	*Southern Belle*	DBF	10–11–1876
Kate 55	3–29–1866	*James H. Trover*	W	
Ibex 10	8–17–1865	*Harry Dean*	DBE	1–3–1868
Abeona 32	8–17–1865	*Abeona*	DBF	3–7–1872
Tempest 1	11–29–1865	*Tempest*	DBF	12–27–1869

Sources: U.S. Navy Department, Official Records of the Union and Confederate Navies in the War of the Rebellion, *31 vols. (Washington, D.C.: GPO, 1894–1922), Series II, Vol. 1, pp. 27–246; Paul H. Silverstone,* Warships of the Civil War Navies *(Annapolis, MD: Naval Institute Press, 1989), pp. 164–180.*

Chapter Notes

Introduction

1. Bobby Roberts, "Rivers of No Return," in Mark K. Christ, ed., *The Earth Reeled and Trees Trembled: Civil War Arkansas, 1863–1864* (Little Rock, AR: Old State House Museum, 2007), p. 87.

2. Lewis B. Parsons, *Reports to the War Department* (St. Louis, MO: George Knapp & Co., 1867), p. 40.

3. Rowland Stafford True, "Life Aboard a Gunboat [U.S.S. *Silver Lake*, No. 23]: A First-Person Account," *Civil War Times Illustrated* 9 (February 1971): p. 41.

4. Angus Konstam and Tony Bryan, *Mississippi River Gunboats of the American Civil War, 1861–1865* (New Vanguard Series; London, Eng.: Osprey Publishing, 2002), p. 11; George W. Brown, "Service in the Mississippi Squadron and Its Connection with the Siege and Capture of Vicksburg," in Vol. I of James Grant Wilson and Titus Munson Con, eds., *Personal Recollections of the War of the Rebellion: Addresses Delivered Before the New York Commandery of the Loyal Legion of the United States, 1883–1891* (New York: Published by the Commandery, 1891), p. 313.

Chapter 1

1. Charles B. Boynton, *History of the Navy During the Rebellion*, 2 vols. (New York: D. Appleton and Company, 1867–1868), Vol.1, pp. 497, 500. The West and Western Rivers in Civil War literature refers generally to the Western theatre of operations, which encompassed the area beyond the Allegheny Mountains. See Bruce Catton, "Glory Road Began in the West," *Civil War History* 6 (June 1960): pp. 229–237. Indeed, at this time, southern Illinois and the area south of St. Louis were known as the "Southwest." Many of the details and observations regarding the rivers and 1861–1862 period are based upon the opening chapters of my *Timberclads in the Civil War: The Lexington, Conestoga and Tyler on the Western Waters* (Jefferson, NC: McFarland, 2008), pp. 11–189.

2. Adam I. Kane, *The Western River Steamboat* (College Station: Texas A&M University Press, 2004), p. 6–7, 16; Louis C. Hunter, *Steamboats on the Western Rivers: An Economic and Technological History* (Cambridge, MA: Harvard University Press, 1949), pp. 484–485, 547–556; Richard W. Kaeuper, "The Civil War on the Fringe: Tinclad Navy," JCS Group Homepage, *http://www.jcs-group.org/military/war1861f ringle/navytinclad.html*, (September 8, 2008); James Mak and Gary M. Walton, "Steamboats and the Great Productivity Surge in River Transportation," *Journal of Economic History* 3 (September 1972): p. 623; Erick F. Haites and James Mak, "The Decline of Steamboating on the Antebellum Western Rivers: Some New Evidence and an Alternative Hypothesis," *Explorations in Economic History* 11 (Fall 1973): pp.

25–36; Haites, Mak, and Gary M. Walton, *Western River Transportation: The Era of Early Internal Development, 1810–1860* (Baltimore, MD: The Johns Hopkins University Press, 1975), p. 120; Charles Dana Gibson, with E. Kay Gibson, *Assault and Logistics,* Vol. 2: *Union Army Coastal and River Operations, 1861–1866* (Camden, ME: Ensign Press, 1995), pp. 615–616; Ron Powers, *Mark Twain: A Life* (New York: Free Press, 2005), pp. 76–77; U.S. War Department, *The War of the Rebellion: A Compilation of the Official Records of the Union and Confederate Armies,* 128 vols. (Washington, D.C.: GPO, 1880–1901), Series I, Vol. 52, pp. 707–708 (cited hereafter as, e.g., OR, I, 52: 707–708); U.S. Navy Department, *Official Records of the Union and Confederate Navies in the War of the Rebellion,* 31 vols. (Washington, D.C.: GPO, 1894–1922), Series I, Vol. 25, p. 474 (cited hereafter as, e.g., ORN, I, 25: 474); Alan Aronson, "Strategic Supply of Civil War Armies," *General Histories of the American Civil War, http:// members.cox.net/rb2307/content/STRATEGIC_SUP PLY_OF_CIVIL_WAR_ARMIES.htm* (March 30, 2000); Lawrence M. Smith, "Rise and Fall of the Strategy of Exhaustion," *Army Logistician* (November–December 2004): p. 35; Benjamin W. Bacon, *Sinews of War: How Technology, Industry and Transportation Won the Civil War* (Novato, CA: Presidio Press, 1997), pp. 75–97.

3. Irwin Anthony, *Paddle Wheels and Pistols* (New York: The Children's Book Club, 1930), p. 282; Hunter, *op. cit.,* pp. 219–236; OR, I, 51: 158, 164; ORN, I, 23: 360; Mark Twain, *Life on the Mississippi* (Modern Classics; New York: Harper & Brothers, 1950), p. 83; *New York Times,* May 2, 1861; Uriah Pierson James, *James' River Guide* (Cincinnati, OH: U.P. James, 1866), pp. 92–97; Marion Bragg, *Historic Names and Places on the Lower Mississippi River* (Vicksburg, MS: Mississippi River Commission, 1977), pp. 1–267; Grant Foreman, "River Navigation in the Early Southwest," *The Mississippi Valley Historical Review* 15 (June 1928): pp. 39+; Bobby Roberts, "Rivers of No Return," in Mark K. Christ, ed., *"The Earth Reeled and Trees Trembled": Civil War Arkansas, 1863–1864* (Little Rock, AR: The Old State House Museum, 2007), pp. 74–76.

4. ORN, I, 22: 318; Mark Twain, *Life on the Mississippi* (New York: Harper & Brothers, 1950), pp. 33–34; George Ward Nichols, "Down the Mississippi," *Harper's New Monthly Magazine* 41 (November 1870): p. 839; "Alex," "Our Western Letter," *Philadelphia Inquirer,* August 30, 1861; Edmund J. Huling, *Reminiscences of Gunboat Life in the Mississippi Squadron* (Saratoga Springs, NY: Sentinel Print, 1881), pp. 31–32; Kane, *op. cit.,* pp. 91–93; Hunter, *op. cit.,* pp. 81, 111, 160; Denys P. Myers, "The Architectural Development of the Western Floating Palace," *Journal of the Society of Architectural Historians* 11 (December 1952): pp. 25–26; Paul H. Silverstone, *Warships of the Civil War Navies* (Annapolis, MD: Naval Institute Press, 1989), pp.151, 155; William C. Lytle,

comp., *Merchant Steam Vessels of the United States, 1807–1868 "The Lytle List"* (Publication No. 6; Mystic, CT: The Steamship Historical Society of America, 1952), p. 180; Carl D. Lane, *American Paddle Steamboats* (New York: Coward–McCann, 1943), p. 33. Interestingly, "Alex" claimed in his newspaper piece to have sought the derivation of his host vessel's name, *Sucker State*. No one knew for certain, but most believed it referred to Illinois and her fiscal condition, allegedly formed by the many wildcat bankers who had moved there.

5. Kane, *op. cit.*, pp. 67–80; Slagle, *op. cit.*, p. 118; Hunter, *op. cit.*, pp. 133–142; Silverstone, *op. cit.*, pp. 172–173; Huling, *op. cit.*, p. 29; Fred Brown, "*Sultana* Burning," *Appalachian Life*, no. 41 (March 2000): pp. 3–4, 8; Canney, *op. cit.*, p. 36; "Alex," "Our Western Letter," *Philadelphia Inquirer*, August 30, 1861; William H. King, *Lessons and Practical Notes on Steam*, revised by James W. King (New York: D. Van Nostrand, 1864), pp.159–170; John D. Milligan, ed., *From the Fresh Water Navy, 1861–1864: The Letters of Acting Master's Mate Henry R. Browne and Acting Ensign Symmes E. Brown* (Naval Letters Series, Volume 3; Annapolis, MD: Naval Institute Press, 1970), p. 111. Coal was the preferred fuel of the Union gunboats, though the timberclads and later the tinclads could use wood if necessary. Early in the war it was pointed out that "Pittsburgh coal is the best. Pomeroy coal nearly if not quite as good (Pomeroy is half way between Pittsburgh and Cincinnati.)" The naval base at Cairo did not have a significant coal depot and the "nearest considerable coal supply above Cairo" was at Caseyville, about 120 miles up the Ohio River. OR, I, 52, 1: 164.

6. Kane, *op. cit.*, pp. 81–82; Hunter, *op. cit.*, pp. 72, 167–172, 219; Huling, *op. cit.*, pp. 30–31; ORN, I, 25: 681; Gary Matthews, "'Tinclad'—In Response to: Re: Tinclad (Terry Foenander),'" *Civil War Navies Message Board http://historysites.com/mb/cw/cwnavy/index.cgi?noframes;read=1314* (December 7, 2005); Richard W. Kaeuper, "The Civil War on the Fringe: Tinclad Navy," JCS Group Homepage. *http://www.jcs-group.org/military/war1861fringe/navytinclad.html* (September 8, 2008).

Chapter 2

1. ORN I, 23: 245, 262–265, 305, 474; Benjamin Franklin Cooling, *Fort Donelson's Legacy: War and Society in Kentucky and Tennessee, 1862–1863* (Knoxville: University of Tennessee Press, 1997), pp. 70–73, 219–222; Daniel E. Sutherland, "Guerrilla Warfare, Democracy, and the Fate of the Confederacy," *Journal of Southern History* 68 (May 2002): pp. 259, 287–288; Lattern to Harris, June 14, 1861, Isham G. Harris Papers, Papers of the Governors of Tennessee, Tennessee State Library and Archives; George Fitzhugh, "The Times and the War," *De Bow's Review* 32 (July 1861): pp. 2–3; Philip Shaw Paludan, *A People's Contest: The Union and Civil War, 1861–1865* (New York: Harper & Row, 1988), p. 452; Noel C. Fisher, "'Prepare Them For My Coming': General William T. Sherman, Total War, and the Pacification of West Tennessee," *Tennessee Historical Quarterly* 51 (1992): p. 77; J. Cutler Andrews, *The South Reports the Civil War* (Pittsburgh, PA: University of Pittsburgh Press, 1985), pp. 156–157; Donald Davidson, *The Tennessee*, Vol. 2: *The New River, Civil War to TVA* (New York: Rinehart & Co., 1948), pp. 77–85; J.F.C. Fuller quoted in Richard P. Gildrie, "Guerrilla Warfare in the Lower Cumberland River Valley, 1862–1865," *Tennessee Historical Quarterly* 49 (Fall 1990): 161; *Arkansas True Democrat*, July 18, 1861; *Memphis Daily Avalanche*, February 16, 1862; in his widely respected recent study *The Uncivil War: Irregular Warfare in the Upper South, 1861–1865* (Norman: University of Oklahoma Press, 2004), pp. 6–7, Robert M. Mackey reviews the fine points in the differences between guerrillas, partisans, and raiders, all of whom have existed, sometimes simultaneously, in history going back thousands

of years, quoting Lieber as necessary. The "Lieber Code," reprinted in War Department General Orders 100 (April 24, 1863), *Instructions for the Government of Armies of the United States in the Field,* is found in OR, III, 3: 148–164. The literature concerning the "wizards of the saddle," or "guerrillas," the misused term for insurgents in the "low intensity conflict" of 1861–1865 that came to stick, is immense; for a sampling, see Daniel E. Sutherland, "Sideshow No Longer: A Historiographical Review of the Guerrilla War," *Civil War History* 46 (March 2000): p. 5–23.

2. Mackey, *op. cit.*, pp. 28–31; Memphis *Daily Avalanche*, February 26, 1862; OR, I, 8: 28, 814–815; OR, I, 13: 831–832; OR, I, 16, 1: 300; Gildrie, *op. cit.*, p. 162; Fisher, *Ibid.*; Davidson, *op. cit.*, p. 85; Stephen V. Ash, "Sharks in an Angry Sea: Civilian Resistance and Guerrilla Warfare in Occupied Middle Tennessee, 1862–1865," *Tennessee Historical Quarterly* 45 (Fall 1986): pp. 226–227; Diane Neal and Thomas W. Kremm, *Lion of the South: General Thomas C. Hindman* (Macon, GA: Mercer University Press, 1993), pp. 116–119; Daniel E Sutherland, "Guerrillas: The Real War in Arkansas," *Arkansas Historical Quarterly* 52 (Autumn 1993): pp. 257–285; Roberts, *op. cit.*, pp. 78–80. General Order No. 17 is cited in OR, I, 13: 835 and Mackey, *op. cit.*, pp. 207–208.

3. *Louisville Democrat*, as quoted in the *Chicago Daily Tribune*, June 14, 1862. The *Autocrat* was later purchased by the U.S. Quartermaster Corps and converted into a hospital boat. Following the war, she was sold out of service, becoming the *Southerner*, under which name she steamed until burnt out in 1868. Frederick Way Jr., comp., *Way's Packet Directory, 1848–1994*, 2nd ed. (Athens, OH: Ohio University Press, 1994): pp. 34, 430.

4. OR, I, 10: 2: 69; Cooling, *op. cit.*, p. 75; Cornelia and Jac Weller, "The Logistics of Bedford Forrest, Part Two: A Leader of Men," *The Army Quarterly* 121 (October 1991): p. 429; Beringer, *op. cit.*, p. 189; Mackey, *op. cit.*, pp. 32–33, 35–36, 170–171; Mark Grimsley, "'Rebels' and 'Redskins': U.S. Military Conduct toward White Southerners and Native Americans in Comparative Perspective," in Mark Grimsley and Clifford J. Rogers, eds., *Civilians in the Path of War* (Lincoln, NE: University of Nebraska Press, 2002), pp. 143–150; R. Blake Dunnavent, *Brown Water Warfare: The U.S. Navy in Riverine Warfare and the Emergence of a Tactical Doctrine, 1775–1970* (New Perspectives on Maritime History and Nautical Archaeology; Gainesville, FL: University of Florida Press, 2003), p. 70; Carole Bucy, *A Path Divided: Tennessee's Civil War Years* (Nashville, TN: Tennessee 200, 1996), p. 5. For a lengthy discussion of Maj. Gen. Hindman and Col. Graham Newell Fitch in the formulation of a primitive counterinsurgency doctrine, see my *Timberclads in the Civil War: The Lexington, Tyler and Conestoga on Western Waters*, pp. 335–338. As the Civil War continued, the Western brown-water navy's timberclads and tinclads introduced a new tactical doctrine to riverine warfare—the patrol. Three kinds were initially executed: "day or night general patrols, reconnaissance patrols, or interdiction forays." R. Blake Dunnavent, *op. cit.*, p. 78.

5. Ordered by Capt. George W. Evans, the *Sallie Wood* was constructed at Paducah, KY, in 1860. She was 160 feet long, with a 31-foot beam. Two engines powered her great wheel. Before her capture, she was sometimes also known as the *Sallie Ward*. Way, *op. cit.*, p. 415.

6. OR, I, 16, 2: 136, 197, 727; OR, I, 31, 1: 781; OR, I, 13: 553; OR, I, 32, 2: 137; OR, I, 34, 4: 410; OR, I, 39, 2: 27, 27–28, 60–61; OR, I, 47, 3: 593, 602; OR, I, 41, 4: 663; Ash, *op cit.*, 227–229; ORN, I, 8: 647–649; ORN, I, 23: 272–273, 508, 687–688; ORN, I, 26: 344–346; ORN, I, 27: 293–294; *Chicago Daily Tribune*, August 4, 1862, January 5, 1863; *New York Times*, April 26, 1863; *New York Herald*, May 20, 1863; Lafayette C. Baker, *History of the United States Secret Service* (Philadelphia, PA: L.C. Baker, 1867), p. 368; Way, *op. cit.*, p. 415; Mackey, *op. cit.*, pp. 131–135; Cooling, *op. cit.*, pp. 70–72, 85–91; Gildrie, *op. cit.*, 163; E. Mer-

ton Coulter, "Commercial Intercourse with the Confederacy in the Mississippi Valley, 1861–1865," *Mississippi Valley Historical Review* 5 (March 1919): pp. 378, 381–383; Craig L. Symonds, *Lincoln and His Admirals: Abraham Lincoln, the U.S. Navy, and the Civil War* (New York: Oxford University Press, 2008), pp. 280–281, 284; Charles E. Wilcox, "Diary of Captain Charles E. Wilcox," *The Journal of Southern History* 4 (November 1938): 513; Chris Wehner, "The Burning of Prentiss, Mississippi, 1862: A Case Study in Total War," *Blog4 History: American History & Civil War History, http://www.blog4history.com/?m=200607* (May 3, 2007); A. Sellew Roberts, "The Federal Government and Confederate Cotton," *American Historical Review* 32 (January 1927): pp. 266–267; Joseph H. Parks, "A Confederate Trade Center Under Federal Occupation: Memphis, 1862 to 1865," *Journal of Southern History* 5 (August 1941): p. 309; for a look at late war illegal trading, see Ludwell H. Johnson, "Contraband Trade During the Last Year of the Civil War," *Mississippi Valley Historical Review* 49 (March 1963): pp. 635–652; James A. Ramage, *Rebel Raider: The Life of General John Hunt Morgan* (Lexington: University Press of Kentucky, 1986), pp. 91–107; John Allan Wyeth, *Life of General Nathan Bedford Forrest* (New York: Harper & Bros., 1904), pp. 83–103; *Evansville Daily Journal*, July 18, 1862; *Cincinnati Daily Commercial*, July 20, 1862; *Chicago Daily Tribune*, July 21, 25, 1862; *Natchez Weekly Courier*, August 6, 1862; Walter T. Durham, *Nashville: The Occupied City — the First Seventeen Months — February 16, 1862–June 30, 1863* (Nashville: The Tennessee Historical Society, 1985), pp. 104–107; Richard Troutman, ed., *The Heavens are Weeping: The Diaries of George R. Browder, 1852–1886* (Grand Rapids, MI: Zondervan Publishing House, 1987), pp. 119, 122; Marion Bragg, *Historic Names and Places on the Lower Mississippi River* (Vicksburg, MS: Mississippi River Commission, 1977), p. 130; Bobby Roberts, "Rivers of No Return," in Mark K. Christ, ed., *The Earth Reeled and Trees Trembled: Civil War Arkansas, 1863–1864* (Little Rock, AR: Old State House Museum, 2007), p. 82; Adam R. "Stovepipe" Johnson, *The Partisan Rangers of the Confederate Army*, edited by William J. Davis (Louisville, KY: George G Fetter, 1904; reprinted, Austin, TX: State House Press, 1995), pp. 112–125; Raymond Mulesky, *Thunder from a Clear Sky: Stovepipe Johnson's Confederate Raid on Newburgh, Indiana* (New York: iUniverse, Inc., 2005); Michael J. Bennett, *Union Jacks: Yankee Sailors in the Civil War* (Chapel Hill: University of North Carolina Press, 2004), pp. 85–88; Governor Johnson's edict on guerrilla suppression measures is found in LeRoy P. Graf and Ralph W. Haskins, eds., *The Papers of Andrew Johnson* (Knoxville: University of Tennessee Press, 1976), Vol. 5, p. 374.

7. ORN, I, 23: 245, 262–265, 305; Milford M. Miller, "Evansville Steamboats During the Civil War," *Indiana Magazine of History* 37 (December 1941): p. 373; *New York Times*, April 26, 1863; Myron J. Smith Jr., *Le Roy Fitch: The Civil War Career of a Union River Gunboat Commander* (Jefferson, N.C.: McFarland, 2007), pp. 93–94.

8. Owned by the Shinkle family and originally designed for harbor and ferry work, the *New Champion* was constructed at Cincinnati in 1856. The veteran was 160 feet long, with a 29.5-foot beam and a 4.7-foot draft. She would undertake numerous USQMD charters during the war, eventually being taken over by the government. Way, *op. cit.*, p. 77.

9. The 133-ton side-wheel ferry *Hamilton Belle* was built at Cincinnati in 1857, but her first home port was Keokuk, Iowa. She steamed independently and could be found at various points on the Mississippi during the war. Way, *op. cit.*, p. 206.

10. Charles H. Davis, *Charles H. Davis: Life of Charles Henry Davis, Rear Admiral, 1807–1877* (Boston and New York: Houghton, Mifflin and Company, 1899), p. 274; *Chicago Daily Tribune*, August 4, 25, 1862; Cooling, *op. cit.*, pp. 96–102; OR, 16, 1: 862–870; OR, I, 17, 1: 34; OR, I, 17, 2: 202; Johnson, *The Partisan Rangers, op. cit.*, pp. 104–108,

112–15; ORN, I, 23: 209, 307–309; Miller, *op. cit.*, p. 373; Smith, *op. cit.*, p. 95 . Information is absent for a number of the steamers appearing in Civil War accounts, including this one. Of the four boats noted attacked on August 18, Capt. Way, for example, reports on only one, the 371-ton contract side-wheeler *Skylark* skippered by Capt. William Blake. Way, *op. cit*, pp. 206, 429, 439. The younger half brother of Col. Graham Newell Fitch of Logansport, IN, and an 1856 USNA graduate, Le Roy Fitch (1835–1875), spent most of the war in command of the tinclads operating on the Upper Rivers, particularly the Ohio and Cumberland. He is remembered for blocking Maj. Gen. John Hunt Morgan's return south from his great Indiana–Ohio Raid (1863), his aggressive duels with MG Nathan Bedford Forrest and his several combats with Rebel gunners during the Battle of Nashville (1864). Fitch died of a mysterious illness at home just before his 40th birthday. He is profiled in my *Le Roy Fitch: The Civil War Career of a Union Gunboat Commander* (Jefferson, NC: McFarland, 2007).

Chapter 3

1. ORN I, 23: 77; "Springtime on the Tennessee" in *Cruising America-Halcyon Days http://www.geocities.com/bill_fiero/tenn05.htm* (December 11, 2007); "Spring on the Cumberland" in *Cruising America-Halcyon Days http://www.geocities.com/bill_fiero/tenn05.htm* (December 10, 2007). Hoosier Lt. Cmdr. William Gwin (1832–1863) was regarded as one of the most promising junior officers in the service prior to his death. Transferred west from the U.S.S. *Susquehanna*, he would command the flotilla's timberclad division in early 1862, gaining its greatest laurels. Transferred to the flag boat *Benton*, he was wounded in action at Haines Bluff on December 27, 1862 and died a week later. Born in Pennsylvania, Lt. Cmdr. James W. Shirk (1832–1873) was a midshipman aboard Com. Perry's *Mississippi* during the 1850s opening of Japan and was promoted to Lt. in 1856. Constantly at sea prior to his Western Flotilla assignment, he would later serve as commander of the Tennessee River district, eventually becoming the longest-serving junior officer in the Mississippi Squadron. Commissioned a Cmdr. on July 25, 1866, he died on February 10, 1873. Lt. Cmdr. Seth Ledyard Phelps (1824–1885) was appointed a Midshipman from Ohio in 1841 and prior to the Civil War served primarily in the Atlantic, including a stint aboard the sloop-of-war *St. Mary's* and with the squadron assigned to lay a great cable from the U.S. to the U.K. On June 19, the 105th ranking sea service lieutenant received orders from the Navy Secretary, Gideon Welles, to proceed west and join Cmdr. John Rodgers at Cincinnati. The appointment came with some pleasure to both Phelps and Rodgers; the two men were friends because the former was a cousin of Anne Rodgers. From the time he reached the Queen City until well into 1864 when he resigned, Phelps was involved in one significant Western Flotilla/Mississippi Squadron role after another, winning acclaim from its commanders. After the Rebellion, the former Buckeye naval commander was involved with steamship companies and in activities surrounding a possible Nicaraguan canal. He also served as ambassador to Peru. "Sketches of the Officers of the Fort Donelson Fleet," *Philadelphia Inquirer*, February 18, 1862; William B. Cogar, *Dictionary of Admirals of the U.S. Navy*, 2 vols. (Annapolis, MD: Naval Institute Press, 1989), Vol. 1, p. 179; Edward W. Callahan, *List of Officers of the Navy of the United States and of the Marine Corps, from 1775 to 1900, Comprising a Complete Register of All Present and Former Commissioned, Warranted, and Appointed Officers of the United States Navy, and of the Marine Corps, Regular and Volunteer. Compiled from the Official Records of the Navy Department* (New York: L.R. Hamersly & Co., 1901; reprinted, New York: Haskell House, 1969), pp. 111, 178–179; Lewis R. Hamersly, *The Records of Living Officers of the U.S. Navy and*

Marine Corps, Compiled from Official Sources, rev. ed. (Philadelphia, PA: J.B. Lippincott, 1870), p. 169; Jay Slagle profiled Phelps in his *Ironclad Captain: Seth Ledyard Phelps and the U.S. Navy* (Kent, OH: Kent State University Press, 1996).

2. Named for noted Pittsburgh-area boat builder James Dunbar, the 213-ton side-wheeler *Dunbar* was constructed at Brownsville, PA, in 1859 and purchased new by Capt. Gus Fowler for the Paducah-Evansville trade. A Confederate sympathizer, Fowler and his brothers took the boat up the Tennessee in 1861 and thereafter performed several missions on behalf of the Southern cause. She was scuttled to avoid capture. Frederick Way Jr., comp., *Way's Packet Directory, 1848–1994*, 2nd ed. (Athens, OH: Ohio University Press, 1994), p. 134; Myron J. Smith Jr., *The Timberclads in the Civil War: Lexington, Tyler and Conestoga on the Western Waters* (Jefferson, N.C.: McFarland, 2008), pp. 65, 90–91.

3. The *Robb* was a relatively new craft, having been constructed at Pittsburg in 1860 (the Pennsylvania community did not add an "h" to its name until after the Civil War). She was 114 feet long, with a 20-foot beam and a four-foot draft. Equipped with three boilers, she was propelled by two engines, each with a cylinder diameter of 16 inches and a five-foot stroke. Way, *op. cit.,* p. 10; *"Alfred Robb,"* in U.S. Navy Department, Naval Historical Center, *Dictionary of American Naval Fighting Ships*, http://www.history.navy.mil/danfs/a 6/alfred_robb.htm (accessed February 9, 2008). After administering the Federal oath to the boat's pilot, Joseph N. Smith, Lt. Cmdr. Gwin placed an 11-man prize crew, under Second Master Jason Goudy, on the vessel. That evening, Smith and Goudy departed Florence for Cairo with dispatches. There the *Robb* would face disposition, though Lt. Cmdr. Gwin hoped she could return with provisions for his boat and the *Lexington* and then stay on as a tender or armed auxiliary.

4. Alfred T. Mahan, *The Gulf and Inland Waters*, Vol. 3 of the *Navy in the Civil War* (New York: Scribner's, 1883), p 51; Paul H. Silverstone, *Warships of the Civil War Navies* (Annapolis, MD: Naval Institute Press, 1989), p. 159; ORN, I, 23: 76–77, 91, 93, 98; ORN, II, 1: 32; Smith, *The Timberclads, op. cit.,* p. 313; *Philadelphia Inquirer*, April 24, 1862; Gershom Bradford, *The Mariner's Dictionary* (New York: Weathervane Books, 1970), p. 126; Spencer C. Tucker, *Andrew Foote: Civil War Admiral on Western Waters* (Annapolis, MD: Naval Institute Press, 2000), pp. 194–196; Junius Henri Browne, *Four Years in Secessia: Adventures Within and Without the Union Lines* (Hartford, CT: O. D. Case and Company, 1865), pp. 147–149, 165–168. With the heavy units of the Western Flotilla engaged in the campaign against Fort Pillow, Capt. Charles H. Davis (1807–1877) temporarily assumed squadron command on May 9 from the injured Flag Officer Andrew Hull Foote. Foote's choice to act as his deputy (and successor, if need be) was a year younger than his friend and, in the Antebellum period, developed an enviable reputation, like Cmdr. John Rodgers, as a scientific officer. Born in Boston, he earned a degree from Harvard University, becoming superintendent of the Nautical Almanac Office located there. With sea service during the expedition to capture filibuster William Walker in Nicaragua and with the South Atlantic Blockading Squadron, Davis would succeed Foote in June 1862, only to be himself succeeded in command of the Mississippi Squadron by David Dixon Porter in October (effective July). Constantly on duty ashore and afloat, he would die at his desk as superintendent of the Naval Observatory. Our profile of Rear Adm. Davis is taken from Cogar, *op. cit.,* vol. 1, pp. 41–43 and Charles Henry Davis, *Life of Charles Henry Davis, Rear Admiral, 1807–1877* (Boston and New York: Houghton, Mifflin and Company, 1899). Years after the war, Capt. Fowler's son Saunders revealed to Capt. Way how the wreck of the *Dunbar* was raised and restored to service by the Federals during the siege of Chattanooga in 1863 and ended her postwar civilian days as a covered barge. Way, *op. cit.,* p. 134.

5. ORN, I, 23: 98–99, 102–103, 115–116; Smith, *Timber-*

clads, op. cit., pp. 314, 317; Richard W. Kaeuper, "The Civil War on the Fringe: Tinclad Navy," JCS Group Homepage, *http://www.jcs-group.org/military/war1861fringe/ navytinclad.html* (September 8, 2008). When the Mississippi Squadron adopted its now famous tinclad numbering system on June 19, 1863, the number 21 was painted in large black letters on the pilothouse of the *Alfred Robb*. Silverstone, *op. cit.* p. 165. Named an acting volunteer lieutenant on October 1, 1862, Cincinnatian Goudy would rise to command the ironclad U.S.S. *Cincinnati*. He died at Paducah, KY, on March 28, 1865 and was buried with full honors. Cmdr. Pennock was a native of Virginia. Like Tennessee's David Farragut, he had remained loyal to the Union. After years at sea (1828–1859), Pennock served as a lighthouse inspector in New York State. Plucked back into the mainstream by the Navy Department in September 1861, he was sent west with Flag Officer Foote to help oversee the construction of the Pook Turtles, to handle flotilla equipment, and became fleet captain that October 20. In January 1862, he took over command of the Cairo naval station. Pennock would hold his post through 1864, gaining during his tenure "a reputation as one of the best wartime executives of the navy." While serving at Cairo, Pennock, who had brought out his wife to be with him, lived in quarters on the receiving ship, where he frequently enjoyed the company of junior officers and visitors at dinner. His friend and colleague Quartermaster George D. Wise would confide to Flag Officer Foote at the end of July 1862 that Pennock "is a good officer for equipment and repairs, and his health is suffering from continued residence in this part of the country." ORN, I, 24, 74; ORN, I, 27: 125; Callahan, *op. cit.* , p. 225; *New York Herald*, February 16, 1863; Alan Westcott, "Alexander Mosely Pennock," in vol. 14 of *Dictionary of American Biography*, 10 vols. (New York: C. Scribner's, 1937), p. 444; Cogar, *op. cit.,* I, pp. 126–127; Hamersly, *op. cit.,* p. 54. Pennock deserves a full-scale biography.

6. Donald L. Canney, *Lincoln's Navy: The Ships, Men and Organization, 1861–65* (London: Conway Maritime Press, 1998), p. 76; Rowland Stafford True, "Life Aboard a Gunboat [U.S.S. *Silver Lake*, No. 23]: A First-Person Account," *Civil War Times Illustrated* 9 (February 1971): 39; *Macon Weekly Telegraph*, December 19, 1864. The U.S. Army also maintained a number of *ersatz* gunboats on the Upper Rivers, most of which were basically steamers protected by cotton bales and armed with field cannons. Interestingly, in a June 24, 1862, telegraph to Maj. Gen. Halleck, Maj. Gen. Ulysses S. Grant weighed in with his own opinion on light-draught gunboats. "Two or there light steamers might be fitted up with howitzers in front," he wrote, "to clear the banks of White River.... The boilers should be protected from musket balls with sheet iron." Ulysses S. Grant, *The Papers of Ulysses S. Grant*, Vol. 5: *April 1–August 31, 1862*, edited by John Y. Simon, 24 vols. to date (Edwardsville, IL: Southern Illinois University Press, 1973), p. 152.

7. ORN, I, 23: 245–246, 251, 307; Myron J. Smith Jr., *Le Roy Fitch: The Civil War Career of a Union River Gunboat Commander* (Jefferson, N.C.: McFarland, 2007), pp. 65–69, 76–78; Silverstone, *Ibid*. For two years before entering the Confederate River Defense Force, the 161-ton *Little Rebel*, built at Belle Verne, PA, was known in civilian life as the *R.E. & A.H. Watson*. She was a screw steamer (an unusual type on the upper rivers) with one engine and two boilers. Union workers at Cairo armed her with two 24-lb. howitzers and two 12-lb. rifled howitzers. She actually entered service before her purchase from the Illinois Prize Court in January 1863. The 38-ton side-wheeler *General Pillow* was captured on the Hatchee River on June 9, 1862. She had two engines and two boilers and was outfitted with a pair of 12-lb. smoothbore howitzers. Silverstone, *op. cit.,* pp. 167, 180; *"Little Rebel,"* in U.S. Navy Department, Naval Historical Center, *Dictionary of American Naval Fighting Ships*, http://www. history.navy.mil/danfs/l7/little_rebel.htm (accessed February 9, 2008).

8. Hunter, *op. cit.,* pp. 548–550; St. Louis *Daily Missouri Democrat,* June 2, 1862.

9. Hamersly, *op. cit.,* pp. 63–64; ORN, I, 23: 98, 290, 292–293, 307, 353–354, 379–380; ORN, II, 1: 47, 197; ORN, I, 23: 309; Paul H. Silverstone, *Warships of the Civil War Navies* (Annapolis, Md.: Naval Institute Press, 1989), p. 166; "Fairplay," in U.S. Navy Department, Naval Historical Center, *Dictionary of American Naval Fighting Ships, http://www.history.navy.mil/danfs/f1/fairplay.htm* (accessed February 9, 2008); ORN, I, 23: 294–304, 333; Jay Slagle, *Ironclad Captain: Seth Ledyard Phelps and the U.S. Navy* (Kent, OH: Kent State University Press, 1996), p. 283–286; Edwin C. Bearss, "The Union Raid Down the Mississippi and Up the Yazoo — August 16–27, 1862," in Editors of *Military Affairs, Military Analysis of the Civil War: An Anthology* (Millwood, NY: KTO, 1977), pp. 213–224.

10. ORN, I, 23: 342, 348, 353–354, 360; ORN, II, 1: 137, 208; James Edwin Campbell, "The Mississippi Squadron." *Ohio Archaeological and Historical Quarterly* 34 (January 1925): 60; Edmund J. Huling, *Reminiscences of Gunboat Life in the Mississippi Squadron* (Saratoga Springs, NY: Sentinel Print, 1881), pp. 5–7; True, *loc. cit.*; Milligan, ed. *From the Fresh Water Navy, 1861–1864, op. cit.,* p. 175; Mark F. Jenkins, "Tinclads," *Ironclads and Blockade Runners of the Civil War homepage, http://www.wideopenwest.com/~jenkins/ironclads/tinclads.htm,* (July 29, 2005); "A Tale of Three Tinclads, All Named *Argosy," Mid Missouri Civil War Roundtable Homepage,* 2005, *http://www.mmcwrt.org/2005/default0501.htm* (July 29, 2005). Pilot Bixby was a real person, a "small, sturdy man" who ruled his craft "dressed in high starched collars, silk neckties, and stickpins." He died in 1912, two years after Mark Twain. Ron Powers, *Mark Twain: a Life* (New York: Free Press, 2005), p. 78; "Brilliant," in U.S. Navy Department, Naval Historical Center, *Dictionary of American Naval Fighting Ships, http://www.history.navy.mil/danfs/b9/brilliant-i.htm* (accessed February 9, 2008); "St. Clair," in U.S. Navy Department, Naval Historical Center, *Dictionary of American Naval Fighting Ships, http://www.history.navy.mil/danfs/s17/st_clair.htm* (accessed February 9, 2008).

11. ORN, I, 23: 367, 371, 374, 379–380, 386; ORN, II, 1: 197; Bruce D. Liddell, "U.S.S. *Rattler* at Rodney, Sunday, September 13, 1863," *Jefferson County MSGenWeb Project homepage, http://jeffersoncountyms.org/USSRattler.htm* (August 18, 2008); Silverstone, *op. cit.,* pp. 169, 178; "Brilliant," *Ibid.;* "St. Clair," *Ibid.* In accordance with the transfer of the Western Flotilla to the Navy on October 1, first masters such as Kentuckian Hurd and Cincinnatian Perkins were appointed acting volunteer lieutenants. Jacob Hurd resigned on April 13, 1864; Charles Perkins would follow on March 25, 1865. Callahan, *op. cit.,* pp. 286, 430; *New York Herald,* February 16, 1863.

12. ORN, I, 23: 373, 379–380, 388–390, 394–395, 449 451–452, 472, 630; Cogar, *op. cit.,* Vol. 1, pp. 131–133; Chester G. Hearn, *Admiral David Dixon Porter: The Civil War Years* (Annapolis, MD: Naval Institute Press, 1996), pp. 145, 151–152; William H. Roberts, *Civil War Ironclads: The U.S. Navy and Industrial Mobilization* (Baltimore, Md.: The Johns Hopkins University Press, 2002), p. 52; Silverstone, *op. cit.,* pp. 169, 178; Donald L. Canney, *The Old Steam Navy,* Vol. 2: *The Ironclads, 1842–1885* (Annapolis, MD: Naval Institute Press, 1993), p. 95; Gustavus Vasa Fox, *Confidential Correspondence of Gustavus Vasa Fox, Assistant Secretary of the Navy, 1861–1865,* edited by Robert Means Thompson and Richard Wainwright, 2 vols. (New York: De Vinne Press, 1918–1919; reprinted, Freeport, NY: Books for Libraries, 1971), Vol. 2, pp. 137–138; James R. Soley, *Admiral Porter* (New York: D. Appleton, 1903), p. 239.

13. Charles G. Brewer, "African-American Sailors and the Unvexing of the Mississippi River," *Prologue: The Journal of the National Archives* 30 (Winter 1998): p. 280; Herbert Aptheker, "The Negro in the Union Navy," *Journal of Negro History* 32 (April 1947): p. 182. Appointed a midshipman from New Jersey on October 19, 1841, Watson Smith progressed up through the ranks, becoming a Lt. Cmdr. with the institu-

tion of that rank in July 1862. Shortly after Acting Rear Adm. Porter was ordered west, Smith, who had captained one of his mortarboat divisions at New Orleans, was assigned to supervise naval activities at Cincinnati, Ohio. During the fall, the task of helping to scout out light-draught vessels that might be converted into tinclads also fell to him. A light-draught task group commander from 1863, Smith would become ill and die at his Trenton home on Dec. 19, 1864. "Officers of the United States Navy During the War Period Appointed from New Jersey," *New Jersey Civil War Record Page 1600, http://www.njstatelib.org/NJ_Information/Searchable_Publications/civilwar/NJCWn1600.html* (July 4, 2008); Callahan, *op. cit.,* p. 508; Hearn, Porter, pp. 170–171. Born in New Hampshire but recruited from New York, Brown was named an Acting Master in July 1861. He commanded the mortar schooner *Dan Smith* through the New Orleans campaign and was posted to the Mississippi Squadron in October 1862. Promoted to Acting Volunteer Lt. in January 1863, the veteran tinclad commander was honorably discharged on September 3, 1865. Edmund Wheeler, *The History of Newport, New Hampshire, From 1766 to 1878* (Newport, N.H.: The Republican Press Association, 1879), p. 36; George W. Brown, "Service in the Mississippi Squadron and Its Connection with the Siege and Capture of Vicksburg," in Vol. 1 of James Grant Wilson and Titus Munson Con, eds., *Personal Recollections of the War of the Rebellion: Addresses Delivered Before the New York Commandery of the Loyal Legion of the United States, 1883–1891* (New York: Published by the Commandery, 1891), p. 303; Callahan, *op. cit.,* p. 81.

14. ORN, I, 21: 14; ORN, I, 23: 444, 477, 487, 494; ORN, I, 24: 164–165, 417, 440–441, 466, 468, 470–471, 505, 540, 571, 634, 670, 677; ORN, I, 25: 596–596, 681, 698–700, 733, 741; ORN, I, 26: 476, 488, 566, 573, 577, 724, 738–741; ORN, I, 27: 3–4; ORN, II, 1: 55, 67, 86, 92–93, 100, 172, 187; "The Archaeological Investigations of the Battle of Johnsonville," *PanAm Consultants Homepage, http://www.panamconsultants.com/PAGE* (June 8, 2004); John M. Latham, *Raising the Civil War Gunboats and Building the Magic Valley History Tower* (Camden, TN: J.M. Latham : Press Pros, 1997), pp. 172–173, 180; *Chicago Daily Tribune,* December 1, 1863; Silverstone, *op. cit.,* pp. 166–168, 170, 174, 178–179; Way, *op. cit.,* p. 77; Slagle, *op. cit.,* p. 328; Canney, *loc. cit.;* Porter to Phelps, February 14, March 6, May 2, 1863, *Seth Ledyard Phelps Papers,* Missouri Historical Society, St. Louis (hereafter cited as SLPC, with date); James A. Dickinson, *Diary* (photocopy), June 11, 16–21, 1863; *James A. Dickinson Papers,* Rutherford B. Hayes Presidential Center, Fremont (cited hereafter as Dickinson Diary, with date); Pennock to Phelps, March 12, 19, 1863, SLPC; Phelps to Porter, March 14, 1863, SLPC; OR I, 20, 2: 332, 338–339; OR, I, 31, 2: 56; OR, I, 32, 1: 21; OR, I, 32, 2: 104–105; OR, I, 52, 1: 713; Myron J. Smith, Jr., *Le Roy Fitch: The Civil War Career of a Union River Gunboat Commander* (Jefferson, N.C.: McFarland, 2007), pp. 242–244, 246–249, 257–261; Donald Davidson, *The Tennessee,* Vol. 2: *The New River, Civil War to TVA* (New York: Rinehart, 1948), pp. 64–67. Once the *Tuscumbia* was commissioned on March 12, 1863, Joseph Brown turned almost his entire attention to tinclad conversions. A former steamboat captain, Acting Volunteer Lt. Riley resigned on February 16, 1863. Callahan, *op. cit.,* p. 463. Shipboard routine, including daily tasks, is covered in, among others, Michael J. Bennett, *Union Jacks: Yankee Sailors in the Civil War* (Chapel Hill: University of North Carolina Press, 2004), pp. 28–53; Dennis J. Ringle, *Life in Mr. Lincoln's Navy* (Annapolis, MD: Naval Institute Press, 1998), pp. 57–63; and Rowland Stafford True, "Life Aboard a Gunboat [U.S.S. *Silver Lake,* No. 23]: A First-Person Account," *Civil War Times Illustrated* 9 (February 1971): pp. 37–39.

Chapter 4

1. Constructed at Belle Vernon, PA, in 1856, the 175-ton

stern-wheeler *W.B. Terry* ran the Paducah-Eastport route prior to the war. Caught trafficking with the enemy, the steamer was seized by the timberclad *Lexington* in August 1861. Frederick Way Jr., comp., *Way's Packet Directory, 1848–1994*, 2nd ed. (Athens, OH: Ohio University Press, 1994), p. 474; Myron J. Smith Jr., *The Timberclads in the Civil War: Lexington, Tyler and Conestoga on the Western Waters* (Jefferson, N.C.: McFarland, 2008), pp. 90–91.

2. OR I, 17, 1: 34; ORN I, XXIII: 332–333; *Boston Daily Advertiser*, September 10, 1862; Lewis B. Parsons, *Reports to the War Department* (St. Louis, MO: George Knapp & Co., 1867), p. 32; Benjamin Franklin Cooling, *Fort Donelson's Legacy: War and Society in Kentucky and Tennessee, 1862–1863* (Knoxville: University of Tennessee Press, 1997), p. 114. Certain Ohio outfits were not faring too well at this time; it was elements of the 71st Ohio which had surrendered at Clarksville two weeks earlier. Richard P. Gildrie, Philip Kemmerly, and Thomas H. Winn, *Clarksville, Tennessee, in the Civil War: A Chronology* (Clarksville, TN: Montgomery County Historical Society, 1984), p. 165. The term "mosquito" was applied to small craft designed to afflict an enemy and was rapidly applied to the tinclads. Famed correspondent Junius H. Browne of the *Cincinnati Daily Times* noted on November 11 that "in addition to the gunboats, there are at Cairo, a number of small craft known there as the mosquito fleet." *Cincinnati Daily Times*, quoted in the *Philadelphia Inquirer*, November 17, 1862.

3. ORN, I, 23: 309; Paul H. Silverstone, *Warships of the Civil War Navies* (Annapolis, Md.: Naval Institute Press, 1989), p. 166; "Fairplay," in U.S. Navy Department, Naval Historical Center, *Dictionary of American Naval Fighting Ships, http://www.history.navy.mil/danfs/f1/fairplay.htm* (accessed February 9, 2008); Myron J. Smith, Jr., *Le Roy Fitch: The Civil War Career of a Union River Gunboat Commander* (Jefferson, N.C.: McFarland, 2007), p. 95. A joint Army-Navy expedition under Lt. Commander S. Ledyard Phelps captured the Confederate transport *Fairplay* at Milliken's Bend on August 18 before she could offload a large cargo of rifles, cannon, and ammunition. ORN, I, 23: 294–304, 333; Milford M. Miller, "Evansville Steamboats During the Civil War," *Indiana Magazine of History* 37 (December 1941): p. 373; Jay Slagle, *Ironclad Captain: Seth Ledyard Phelps and the U.S. Navy* (Kent, OH: Kent State University Press, 1996), pp. 283–286; Edwin C. Bearss, "The Union Raid Down the Mississippi and Up the Yazoo — August 16–27, 1862," in Editors of *Military Affairs, Military Analysis of the Civil War: An Anthology* (Millwood, NY: KTO, 1977), pp. 213–224.

4. The 80-ton *Lou Eaves* was constructed at Evansville, IN, in 1859. Prior to the war, she operated from that town across the Ohio to and up the Green River. She was never actually turned into a tinclad as Way suggests. Way, *op. cit.*, p. 298.

5. Owner-operator Capt. Thompson constructed this stern-wheeler at Paducah earlier in the year and named it for his wife. The craft was 110 feet long, with a beam of 24.1 feet and a three-foot draft. She normally operated the route from Louisville to Cairo. Way, *op. cit.*, p. 111.

6. Constructed at Madison, IN, in 1860 for the Evansville-Green River trade, the vessel was jointly owned, with her captain, Adam Liter, a partner. Named for a Bowling Green, KY, girl, the 120-ton stern-wheeler was 124.2 feet long, with a 23.8-foot beam and a 4.5-foot draft. Although she escaped this assault, she was captured on September 16. Way, *op. cit.*, p. 316.

7. This small stern-wheeler was built at New Albany earlier in the year. When not under USQMD charter, she, too, operated the Evansville-Green River route. Way, *op. cit.*, p. 355.

8. The 217-ton stern-wheeler *Henry Fitzhugh* was constructed at Cincinnati in 1857. A veteran of the Ohio River trade, the craft would spend most of her war under USQMD contract. Way, *op cit.*, p. 211.

9. ORN, I, 23: 310, 322, 359–360; *Evansville Daily Jour-*

nal, September 10, 1862; *Milwaukee Daily Sentinel*, September 16, 1862; Parsons, *Ibid.*; Donald Davidson, *The Tennessee*, Vol. 2: *The New River, Civil War to TVA* (New York: Rinehart & Co., 1948), p. 80; Miller, *op. cit.*, pp. 364, 369, 373; Smith, *op. cit.*, pp. 95–97; Richard P. Gildrie, Philip Kemmerly, and Thomas H. Winn, *Ibid.* The Federal army often placed field pieces on chartered shallow-draft steamers, turning them into *ersatz* gunboats. Crewed by civilians with Army gun crews detailed, the vessels served at the pleasure of district commanders or even the Quartermaster Department. Generally, the ranking military officer aboard set the mission, leaving the master, pilots, and crew to operate the vessel accordingly. For example, several were employed from Nashville and Clarksville to guard that stretch of the Cumberland River between Nashville and Harpeth Shoals. These craft were served on the Upper Mississippi and the Ohio. Although these were not under Navy command, they did, as we shall see, occasionally participate in Navy-led expeditions. The five-year-old Evansville-Green River packet *Lou Eaves* is one of the first of these improvised Army gunboats about which we have much information. Civilian mail boats were also occasionally armed. There is almost no information on this topic in print (books, magazine articles, dissertations, etc.) and it is one of the few Civil War military topics upon which an enterprising writer or graduate student might yet conduct reputation-building original research. Charles Dana Gibson, with E. Kay Gibson, *Assault and Logistics*, Vol. 2: *Union Army Coastal and River Operations, 1861–1866* (Camden, ME: Ensign Press, 1995), p. 321; OR, I, 52, 1: 281–282; ORN, I, 24: 19.

10. Under Capt. Anson Ballard, this 298-ton side-wheeler was constructed at Parkersburg, VA/WV in 1860. Part of the Louisville & Henderson Mail Line, she was 183 feet long, with a beam of 32 feet and a 5.5-foot draft. Often under USQMD, the craft was the first from Louisville to visit Memphis after its recapture in June She would hit a snag and sink near Fort Pillow in November. Way, *op. cit.*, p. 155.

11. Built for her commander, the big 419-ton side-wheeler was constructed at Madison, IN, in 1858 for the Madison-Cincinnati trade. She was often under USQMD contract during the war and won accolades for her passing of the Vicksburg batteries in April 1863. Way, *op. cit.*, p. 169.

12. The *Sunshine* was built at Elizabeth, PA, in 1860 for the St. Louis-St. Paul trade. Captured by Confederate forces in late summer 1861, the 354-ton *Sunshine* was recovered. Like hundreds of other boats, she often executed wartime USQMD contracts. Way, *op. cit.*, pp. 437–438.

13. The *Roe* was built at Cincinnati in 1856 as a freight boat with little passenger accommodation. The 691-ton side-wheeler was 270 feet long, with a beam of 40 feet and an eight-foot draft. Her two huge paddle wheels were powered by steam from three boilers. Among her prewar pilots was Samuel Clemens ("Mark Twain"). Capt. Ben Taber was in command during the war and she was often in use as a Federal troop transport. Way, *op. cit.*, p. 252.

14. OR, I, 17, 1, 144–145, 201; OR, I, 17, 2: 235–236, 280–281, 285; *Evansville Daily Journal*, September 30, 1862; *Memphis Daily Bulletin*, September 27, 1862; *Nashville Daily Dispatch*, October 10, 1862; Noel C. Fisher, "'Prepare Them For My Coming': General William T. Sherman, Total War, and the Pacification of West Tennessee," *Tennessee Historical Quarterly* 51 (1992): pp. 78–79; William T. Sherman, *Sherman's Civil War: Selected Correspondence of William T. Sherman, 1860–1865*, edited by Brooks D. Simpson and Jean V. Berlin (Chapel Hill, NC: University of North Carolina Press, 1999), pp. 305–310; Mark Grimsley, *The Hard Hand of War: Union Military Policy Toward Southern Civilians, 1861–1865* (New York: Cambridge University Press, 1995), pp. 114–119; Cooling, *op. cit.*, pp. 72, 321.

15. U.S. Navy Department, Naval History Division, *Civil War Naval Chronology, 1861–1865*, Part 2: *1862* (Washington, D.C.: GPO, 1962), p. 100; *Evansville Daily Journal*,

September 16, 18–19, October 18, 1862; Miller, *Ibid.;* "David Dixon Porter," in William B. Cogar, *Dictionary of Admirals of the U.S. Navy*, 2 vols. (Annapolis, Md.: Naval Institute Press, 1989), Vol. 1, pp. 131–133; Chester G. Hearn, *Admiral David Dixon Porter: The Civil War Years* (Annapolis, MD: Naval Institute Press, 1996), pp. 145, 151–152; ORN, I, 23: 379–380, 390, 394, 451–452, 348–352, 388,395–396, 449. 472,630; ORN, I, 25, 372; Cooling, *op. cit.,* p. 115; Smith, *op. cit.,* pp. 97–98; Silverstone, *op. cit.,* pp. 169, 178 OR, 1, 20, 2: 102–103, 187–188; OR, 1, 52, 1: 10–11; *New York Herald,* October 28, 1862; Richard P. Gildrie, "Guerrilla Warfare in the Lower Cumberland River Valley, 1862–1865," *Tennessee Historical Quarterly* 49 (Fall 1990): p. 167; The Battle of Perryville is covered in most civil war military histories. Our review was taken from Thomas L. Connelly, *Army of the Heartland* (Baton Rouge, LA: Louisiana State University Press, 1967), pp. 243–270, and Stanley F. Horn, "The Battle of Perryville," *Civil War Times Illustrated* 5 (February 1966): pp. 4–11, 42–47. General Rosecrans is the subject of William M. Lamers's *The Edge of Glory: A Biography of General William S. Rosecrans, USA* (New York: Harcourt, Brace, 1961); Charles G. Brewer, "African-American Sailors and the Unvexing of the Mississippi River," *Prologue: The Journal of the National Archives* 30 (Winter 1998): p. 280; Herbert Aptheker, "The Negro in the Union Navy," *Journal of Negro History* 32 (April 1947): p. 182.

16. Principally owned by Francis Pratt, the *Campbell* was constructed at Louisville in 1859. The stern-wheel ferry was 109.8 feet long, with a beam of 21 feet and a 4.2-foot draft. Way, *op. cit.,* p. 117.

17. Owned by the Rees family plus two Pittsburgh businessmen, the *Hazel Dell* was built at California, PA, in 1857 to operate on the Pittsburgh-Cincinnati route. The vessel was 148.5 feet long, with a 29.8-foot beam and a 4.4-foot draft. During the war, she served as a mail boat and, under USQMD contract, a troop transport. Way, *op. cit.,* p.209.

18. Begun at Shoustetown, PA, and completed at Pittsburgh in 1860, this large side-wheeler received her power from four boilers. The *Continental* was 282 feet long, with a beam of 41 feet and an 8.5-foot draft. Capt. Ben F. Hutchinson's packet originally operated the St. Louis-New Orleans route, but was impressed into Federal service early in the war. Way, *op. cit.,* p. 109.

19. Constructed at Madison, IN, in 1858, the huge 403-ton side-wheeler was one of six boats originally built for the Missouri River fleet of the Great Mail and Transportation Company of the West During the war, Capt. Dan Able's craft would operate a number of USQMD contracts before she was almost destroyed by a boiler explosion in November. The ill-starred steamer would be repaired, only to be badly damaged again when another vessel collided with her in January 1865. Way, *op. cit.,* p.251.

20. ORN, I, 23: 311, 437; *Daily Cleveland Herald,* October 17, 1862; *Savannah (GA) Daily Morning News,* October 20, 1862; *Evansville Daily Journal,* October 23, 1862; Smith, *Le Roy Fitch, op. cit.,* pp. 101–102; Henry Walke, *Naval Scenes and Reminiscences of the Civil War in the United States on the Southern and Western Waters During the Years 1861, 1862 and 1863 with the History of That Period Compared and Corrected from Authentic Sources* (New York: F.R. Reed and Company, 1877), pp. 333–334. Known as something of a maverick and a great artist, the taciturn Virginian Henry A. Walke (1808–1896) was, arguments to the contrary accepted, one of the most successful and under-celebrated of all Civil War naval officers. A midshipman with Capt. Foote on the U.S.S. *Natchez* in 1827, Walke served in numerous ships and squadrons and was promoted to the rank of Cmdr. in 1855. One of many officers involuntarily retired by the infamous Naval Retiring Board set up under Congressional legislation of that year, he was eventually returned to duty. Like all "restored officers," he was placed on half pay and throughout the Civil War received only 50 per cent of the income his rank would ordinarily provide. In early 1861, while commanding

the store ship *Supply* off Pensacola, he elected to remove personnel from the guardian forts and the navy yard rather than allow them to become POWs. His actions, technically violating previous orders, resulted in his court-martial, a "complimentary reprimand," and temporary banishment to the post of lighthouse inspector at Williamsport, NY. On September 6, Secretary Welles ordered Walke to St. Louis. Later, in command of the famous Pook turtle *Carondelet,* he fought at Forts Henry and Donelson and ran the batteries at Island No. 10. Walke commanded several other vessels during the war, was promoted to Capt. in 1862 and Com. in 1866. He commanded the Mound City naval station 1868–1870, where he was joined by his former colleague Capt. Egbert Thompson. After becoming a Rear Adm. in 1870, he retired in 1871, contributing his drawings and memories to books and articles on the conflict. Walke died in New York in early 1896. Edward W. Callahan, *List of Officers of the Navy of the United States and of the Marine Corps, from 1775 to 1900, Comprising a Complete Register of All Present and Former Commissioned, Warranted, and Appointed Officers of the United States Navy, and of the Marine Corps, Regular and Volunteer. Compiled from the Official Records of the Navy Department* (New York: L.R. Hamersly & Co., 1901; reprinted, New York: Haskell House, 1969), pp. 236, 496, 541, 564, 594; Lewis R. Hamersly, *The Records of Living Officers of the U.S. Navy and Marine Corps, Compiled from Official Sources,* rev. ed. (Philadelphia, PA: J.B. Lippincott, 1870), pp. 45, 111, 178–179; 201; William B. Cogar, *Dictionary of Admirals of the U.S. Navy,* 2 vols. (Annapolis, MD: Naval Institute Press, 1989), Vol. 1, pp. 200–201.

21. Started at Belle Vernon, PA, and completed at Pittsburgh in 1857, the 425-ton *Gladiator* was built for a syndicate headed by Capt. George D. Moore. The big side-wheeler was 227 feet long, with a beam of 34 feet and a 5.8-foot draft. Capt. John Simpson Klinefelter took stock in 1858 and became the boat's master. The vessel became a regular USQMD contract vessel during the winter of 1861–1862. Way, *op. cit.,* p. 188.

22. Constructed for Capt. J.D. Walker at Murraysville, VA, in 1858, the *Catahoula* was 137 feet long, with a beam of 33 feet and a five-foot draft. When the war broke out, she was plying the New Orleans-to-Ouachita River route. The vessel was seized by the Confederacy, but was regained by the Union during the June 1862 Battle of Memphis. Way, *op. cit.,* p. 75.

23. The 211-ton *Nashville* was constructed at Cincinnati in 1860 to operate a service from the Queen City to Nashville. Following Fort Sumter, she was often employed in contract work by the USQMD. Way, *op. cit.,* p. 336.

24. ORN, I, 23: 311, 417–423; 426, 431–432, 434–438, 454–455; ORN, I, 8: 647–649; OR, I, 13, 742; OR, 17, 2, 280–281, 285; Grimsley, *The Hard Hand of War, op. cit.,* p. 117; Cooling, *op. cit.,* pp. 115, 163; *Evansville Daily Journal,* October 23, 27, 1862; *Memphis Daily Bulletin,* October 19, 1862; Davidson, *Ibid.;* Alfred T. Mahan, *The Gulf and Inland Waters,* Vol. 3 of the *Navy in the Civil War* (New York: Scribner's, 1883), p.179; Craig L. Symonds, *Lincoln and His Admirals: Abraham Lincoln, the U.S. Navy, and the Civil War* (New York: Oxford University Press, 2008), pp. 280–281, 284; Smith, *op. cit.,* pp 100–102; Gibson, *op. cit.,* pp. 245–247. The Caseyville assessment, paid largely in goods, was picked up in installments over the next three months. ORN, I, 23: 311, 530–531. There were two steamers named *Nashville* operating at this time: Capt. Barclay's two-year-old Cincinnati-built stern-wheeler and Capt. Thomas Bellanyder's much larger (497 tons, 250-foot length) side-wheeler, constructed at New Albany, IN, in 1847. Although both were plying the Cincinnati-to-Nashville route when war erupted, the former was home-ported at Cincinnati and the latter at Tennessee's capital. The big boat would soon become a thousand-berth Army hospital boat. Way, *op. cit,* p. 336.

25. ORN, I, 23: 439; ORN, II, 1, 137, 208; Way, *op. cit.,* pp. 309, 425; Paul H. Silverstone, *Warships of the Civil War*

Navies (Annapolis, MD: Naval Institute Press, 1989), pp. 173, 178. The 190-ton stern-wheeler *Signal* was a new boat, built at Wheeling, WV, earlier in the year. Eventually given the recognition number 8, the 157-foot craft had a beam of 30 feet and an overall depth of hold of 4.4 feet. Master Scott's tinclad was initially provided with two 30-pdr. Parrott rifles forward and four 24-pdr. smoothbore and two 12-pdr. rifled Dahlgren boat howitzers in broadside. The *Signal* was lost during the Red River campaign of 1864 and so little more has been recorded about her except that her armament was modified several times by addition or subtraction of the Parrott rifles. The total cost of her repairs while in service was $2,664.71. The 207-ton stern-wheeler *Marmora No. 2* was constructed at the William Latta yards at Monongahela, PA, at the beginning of 1862. She was 155 feet long, with a beam of 33.4 feet and an overall hold depth of 4.8 feet. The craft had two engines, with a cylinder diameter of 15? inches each and a 5.6-foot stroke. The *Marmora No. 2's* two Watson & Monroe-built boilers were quite innovative. Each was equipped with six flues, three 11" and three 8." The steamer's 20-foot diameter paddle wheel worked 24-foot buckets and pushed the sternwheeler along at a maximum upstream speed of 6 miles per hour. Built to the specifications of Capt. James McDonald, who had skippered a first *Marmora*, the vessel was only able to complete a few Pittsburgh-Cincinnati trips before she was acquired by the U.S. Navy for conversion into a tinclad with a shortened name. Later designated Tinclad No. 2, Lt. Getty's *Marmora* was initially armed with two 24-pdr. smoothbore Dahlgren howitzers and two 12-pdr. Dahlgren rifled howitzers. This battery would not be changed until June 1864, when she received four more 24-pdr. smoothbores. Her total service life repair bill would run to $15,107.40. Apparently something of a favorite with the compilers of the Navy *Official Records*, she is the tinclad with the most published logbook extracts. During November, tinclad modification was launched full-bore at the Cincinnati shipyards of Joseph Brown. Seven tinclads were commissioned in December: *Forest Rose and Glide I* (December 3), *Romeo* (December 11), *Juliet* (December 14), *New Era* (December 1?), *Rattler* (December 19), and *Silver Lake* (December 24). Particulars on these individual boats and their commanders are berthed in footnotes following their first textual mention.

26. Constructed at the Jeffersonville, IN, yards of Howard in 1850, the 170-ton side-wheeler *Blue Wing No. 2* was successor to a boat built in 1845 and later dismantled. She was 150 feet long, with a 30-foot beam and a 6.5-foot draft. Three boilers provided the steam for her paddle wheels. Way, *op. cit.,* pp. 55–56.

27. Built at Brownsville, PA, in 1857, the 171-ton *Lake City* initially served on the Upper Mississippi, running service out of St. Paul. During the war, the stern-wheeler often steamed independently in the dangerous waters below St. Louis. Way, *op. cit.,* p. 276.

28. The *Clarabell* would be nearly destroyed by Confederate artillery on the Mississippi, July 24, 1864. For details on the boat and the action, see Chapter 10.

29. Constructed at Cincinnati in 1860, the 207-ton stern-wheeler *Lady Pike* was designed as a low-water boat and ordinarily operated from the Queen City to Memphis. Way, *op. cit.,* p. 276.

30. The 176-ton *Rocket* was constructed by Capt. William Dean at Brownsville, PA, in 1856 for the Rochester-Wellsville trade on the upper Ohio River. She also ran round trips from Pittsburgh to Cincinnati, via Gallipolis, into 1861. The stern-wheeler was under USQMD contract for most of the Civil War and was a particular favorite of Maj. Gen. George H. Thomas. Way, *op. cit.,* p. 400.

31. *New York Times,* December 15, 1862; OR, I, 20, 2: 213, 229, 237–238; ORN, I, 23: 311–312, 626–629, 631, 659; ORN, I, 24: 56–57; Ebenezer Hannaford, *The Story of a Regiment: A History of the Campaigns and Associations in the Field of the Sixth Regiment Ohio Volunteer Infant*ry (Cincinnati, OH: privately printed, 1868), p. 390; ORN, I, 23: 309,

311–312, 446, 459, 463–465, 472, 474–476, 478–479, 481, 492, 494–498, 507–508, 515–518, 522; 524, 528–530, 536, 617–623, 626–629, 631, 659, 688–689; ORN, I, 24: 56–57; OR, I, 17, 2: 508–516; OR, I, 20, 1: 15–23; OR, I, 20, 2: 77, 100–108, 213, 229, 237–238; OR, II, 5: 774; *Cincinnati Times,* November 11, 1862, reprinted in *Philadelphia Inquirer,* November 17, 1862; Louisville *Daily Journal,* December 11, 1862–January 5, 1863; Nashville *Daily Union,* December 25, 1862; *Evansville Daily Journal,* November 23, 1862; *Chicago Daily Tribune,* December 2, 1862; *New York Times,* December 15, 1862, January 19, 1863; *Milwaukee Daily Sentinel,* December 17, 1862; *Savannah Daily Morning News,* December 25, 1862; Logbooks of the U.S.S. *Carondelet,* May 1862–June 1865; Records of the Bureau of Navigation, Record Group 19, U.S. National Archives, Washington, D.C., November 23–December 1, 1862 (cited hereafter as Logbook of the U.S.S. *Carondelet,* with date); Walke, *op. cit.,* pp. 334–335; Parsons, *Ibid.*; Charles E. Wilcox, "Diary of Captain Charles E. Wilcox," *The Journal of Southern History* 4 (November 1938): p. 513; Chris Wehner, "The Burning of Prentiss, Mississippi, 1862: A Case Study in Total War," *Blog4 History: American History & Civil War History http://www.blog4history.com/?m=200607* (May 3, 2007); Ronald S. Mangum, "The Vicksburg Campaign: A Study in Joint Operations," *Parameters* 21 (Autumn 1991): p. 75; William C. Lytle, comp., *Merchant Steam Vessels of the United States, 1807–1868 "The Lytle List"* (Publication No. 6; Mystic, CT: The Steamship Historical Society of America, 1952), p. 127; Silverstone, *op. cit.,* p. 180; John D. Milligan, ed., *From the Fresh Water Navy, 1861–1864: The Letters of Acting Master's Mate Henry R. Browne and Acting Ensign Symmes E. Brown* (Naval Letters Series, Volume 3; Annapolis, MD: Naval Institute Press, 1970), p. 117; Buell's Nashville quote is from Lenette S. Taylor's *"The Supply for Tomorrow Must Not Fail": The Civil War of Captain Simon Perkins, Jr., a Union Quartermaster* (Kent, OH: Kent State University Press, 2004), p. 22, while other details on the city are taken from the *Nashville Dispatch* of August 14 and 22, 1862, the Louisville *Daily Journal,* November 15, 1862, Walter T. Durham, *Nashville: The Occupied City—the First Seventeen Months—February 16, 1862–June 30, 1863* (Nashville: The Tennessee Historical Society, 1985), pp. 206–207, and Mark Zimmerman, *Battle of Nashville Preservation Society Guide to Civil War Nashville* (Nashville, TN: Lithographics, Inc., 2004), pp. 8–11, 25; Byrd Douglas, *Steamboatin' on the Cumberland* (Nashville, TN: Tennessee Book Company, 1961), p. 138; William M. Lamers' *The Edge of Glory: A Biography of General William S. Rosecrans, USA* (New York: Harcourt, Brace, 1961), pp. 192–194, 202–243; William Bickman, *Rosecrans' Campaigns with the 14th Army Corps; or, the Army of the Cumberland: A Narrative of Personal Observations* (Cincinnati, OH: Moore, Wilstach, Keys, 1863), p. 121; Smith, *Le Roy Fitch, op. cit.,* pp. 100–111. Born at Columbus, IN, December 5, 1832, William Gwin was commissioned a Midshipman in 1847 and a lieutenant in 1855. At the outbreak of the war, he was assigned to the blockade duty before assuming command of *Commodore Perry* in October 1861. Always remembered for his service at Shiloh and the running battle with the *Arkansas,* Gwin, promoted that July, would command the U.S.S. *Benton* in the December 27, 1862, battle at Haines Bluff on the Yazoo River. Mortally wounded there, he died on January 3, 1863. "William Gwin," in Vol. 3 of James Grant Wilson and John Fiske, eds. *Appleton's Cyclopaedia of American Biography,* 5 vols. (New York: D. Appleton & Co., 1888), p. 19. An informative Gwin tribute was published in the *Chicago Daily Tribune,* February 19, 1863. New aboard the *Marmora* upon her commissioning, Acting Ensign Walker was forced by his wound to resign, effective November 29. Callahan, *op. cit.,* p. 565. Promoted to the rank of acting volunteer master on October 1, 1862, George Groves would later command the *Fairplay* and be honorably discharged on December 11, 1865. Callahan, *op. cit.,* p. 235. Appointed Acting Master on October 1, John Neeld was sent aboard the *General Lyon* upon her renaming. He would later become executive officer of the ironclad *Lafayette*. Promoted to Acting Volunteer Lt. in May 1865, he was honorably discharged that November. Callahan, *op. cit.*, p. 401.

32. ORN, I, 24: 93, 154–159, 184, 194; OR, I, 22, 1: 886–887; OR, I, 22, 2: 11; Edwin C. Bearss, "The Battle of the Post of Arkansas," *Arkansas Historical Quarterly* 18 (Autumn 1959): pp. 244–245; Arthur Marvin Shaw, ed., "A Texas Ranger Company at the Battle of Arkansas Post," *Arkansas Historical Quarterly* 9 (Winter 1950): p. 281; Lamers, *op. cit.*, pp. 202–243; Smith, *Le Roy Fitch, op. cit.*, p. 111; James Lee McDonough, *Stones River: Bloody Winter in Tennessee* (Knoxville: University of Tennessee Press, 1980), pp. 81–216; Bickham, *op. cit.*, pp. 150–307; Larry J. Daniel, *Days of Glory: The Army of the Cumberland, 1861–1865* (Baton Rouge: Louisiana State University Press, 2004), pp. 201–224; G.C. Kniffin, "The Battle of Stones River," in *Battles and Leaders of the Civil War*, edited by Robert U. Johnson and Clarence C. Buel, 4 vols. (New York: The Century Company, 1884–1887; reprinted, Thomas Yoseloff, 1956), Vol. 3, pp. 613–632 (cited hereafter as B&L, followed by a comma, the volume number in Roman numerals, a comma, and the page numbers). Maj. Gen. Rosecrans was a careful and deliberate man. Steven E. Woodworth wrote of him that "he would, over the course of the war, prove himself to be an excellent general as long as his enemy gave him plenty of time to prepare and did nothing unexpected." *Nothing But Victory: The Army of the Tennessee, 1861–1865* (New York: Alfred A. Knopf, 2005), p. 246. The *Blue Wing No. 2* was subsequently burned at Pocahontas, on the White River, to prevent her recapture. Way, *op. cit.*, p. 56; Parsons, *op. cit.*, p. 33.

Chapter 5

1. OR, I, 22, 1: 232; OR, I, 17, 1: 709–710; ORN, I, XXIV: 124, 134; James M. McPherson, *Battle Cry of Freedom: The Civil War Era* (New York: Oxford University Press, 1988), pp. 582–583; *New York Herald*, January 21, 1863; Charles Dana Gibson, with E. Kay Gibson, *Assault and Logistics*, Vol. 2: *Union Army Coastal and River Operations, 1861–1866* (Camden, ME: Ensign Press, 1995), p. 228; Robert L. Kerby, *Kirby Smith's Confederacy: The Trans-Mississippi South, 1863–1864* (New York: Columbia University Press, 1972), pp. 28–29; Richard L. Kiper, *Major General John Alexander McClernand: Politician in Uniform* (Kent, OH: Kent State University Press, 1999), pp. 158–162; Milford M. Miller, "Evansville Steamboats During the Civil War," *Indiana Magazine of History* 37 (December 1941): pp. 374–375; Myron J. Smith Jr., *Le Roy Fitch: The Civil War Career of a Union River Gunboat Commander* (Jefferson, N.C.: McFarland, 2007), pp. 112–114; Smith, *Timberclads in the Civil War: The Lexington, Tyler and Conestoga on the Western Waters* (Jefferson, N.C.: McFarland, 2008), pp. 385–388. On December 29–30, 1862, several thousand butternut riders under Wheeler rode completely around the Army of the Cumberland as it marched toward Murfreesboro, wreaking destruction on its supply train. The 26-year-old Wheeler was able to destroy parts of four wagon convoys, obtain fresh remounts for his men, and carry off enough arms to outfit an infantry brigade. "Seven hundred prisoners and nearly a million dollars' worth of property was the penalty paid....," wrote a later reviewer. Joseph P. Dyer, *From Shiloh to San Juan: The Life of "Fighting Joe" Wheeler* (Baton Rouge: Louisiana State University Press, 1961), pp. 65–68.

2. ORN, I, 23: 312; ORN, I, 24: 5–9, 57; OR, I, 17, 2: 832; OR, I, 20, 2: 296–297, 307–308, 313, 317, 322–323; Robert R. Mackey, *The Uncivil War: Irregular Warfare in the Upper South, 1861–1865* (Norman: University of Oklahoma Press, 2004), p. 173; Miller, *op. cit.*, p. 375; Thomas L. Connelly, *Autumn of Glory: The Army of Tennessee, 1862–1863* (Baton Rouge: Louisiana State University Press, 1971), pp.

69–79; William M. Lamers' *The Edge of Glory: A Biography of General William S. Rosecrans, USA* (New York: Harcourt, Brace, 1961), pp. 248–249; William H. Howard to wife, March 9, 1863, William H. Howard Papers, University of Tennessee Library, Knoxville (cited hereafter as Howard Papers, with date). Howard would be honorably discharged on December 9, 1865 while Ensign Moyer was honorably discharged on October 12. Edward W. Callahan, *List of Officers of the Navy of the United States and of the Marine Corps, from 1775 to 1900, Comprising a Complete Register of All Present and Former Commissioned, Warranted, and Appointed Officers of the United States Navy, and of the Marine Corps, Regular and Volunteer. Compiled from the Official Records of the Navy Department* (New York: L.R. Hamersly & Co., 1901; reprinted, New York: Haskell House, 1969), p. 278.

3. ORN, I, 24, 134; Memphis *Daily Argus*, January 9, 1863; *Chicago Daily Tribune*, January 12, 1863; Kiper, *op. cit.*, p. 162; William C. Lytle, comp., *Merchant Steam Vessels of the United States, 1807–1868 "The Lytle List"* (Publication No. 6; Mystic, CT: The Steamship Historical Society of America, 1952), p. 95; Lewis B. Parsons, *Reports to the War Department* (St. Louis, MO: George Knapp & Co., 1867), p. 33. Way does not list the *Musselman*; our data here come from Lytle and Parsons.

4. ORN, I, 24: 107–108, 110, 113, 119, 126, 154–155; OR, I, 17, 1: 706–708, 721, 752, 781–782, 792; OR, I, 17, 2: 553, 559, 757; *New York Herald*, January 8, 1863; *New York Times*, January 18, 24, 29, 1863; Alfred T. Mahan, *The Gulf and Inland Waters*, Vol. 3 of the *Navy in the Civil War* (New York: Scribner's, 1883), p. 122; Chester G. Hearn, *Admiral David Dixon Porter: The Civil War Years* (Annapolis, MD: Naval Institute Press, 1996), pp. 168–175; Edwin C. Bearss, "The Battle of the Post of Arkansas," *Arkansas Historical Quarterly* 18 (Autumn 1959): pp. 247–264, 274–276, 279; Arthur Marvin Shaw, ed., "A Texas Ranger Company at the Battle of Arkansas Post," *Arkansas Historical Quarterly* 9 (Winter 1950): p. 283; Arthur F. Surovic, "Union Assault on Arkansas Post, " *Military History* 12 (March 1996): pp. 34–40; Thomas A. DeBlack, *With Fire and Sword: Arkansas, 1861–1874* (Histories of Arkansas; Fayetteville, AR: University of Arkansas Press, 2003), pp. 79–81; Smith, *The Timberclads, op. cit.*, pp. 387–394.

5. Constructed at Cincinnati during the summer of 1862, the future Tinclad No. 1 was originally named the *Florence Miller*. Purchased into the Mississippi Squadron on November 24, she was renamed *Rattler* on December 5. The 165-ton stern-wheel gunboat was modified by Joseph Brown and sent to Cairo for outfitting. Because she was lost, information on her dimensions and power plant was not retained. Acting Master Amos Longthorne and his crew commissioned their light-draught on December 19 after first having placed aboard a battery of two 30-pdr. Parrott rifles and four 24-pdr. smoothbore Dahlgren howitzers. ORN, II, 1: 189; Frederick Way Jr., comp., *Way's Packet Directory, 1848–1994*, 2nd ed. (Athens, OH: Ohio University Press, 1994), pp. 168, 388; Paul H. Silverstone, *Warships of the Civil War Navies* (Annapolis, Md.: Naval Institute Press, 1989), p. 176; "*Rattler*," in U.S. Navy Department, Naval Historical Center, *Dictionary of American Naval Fighting Ships*, *http://www. history.navy.mil/danfs/r3/rattler-i.htm* (accessed February 9, 2008). Amos Longthorne's service record is not recorded.

6. The 137-ton stern-wheeler *Glide* was commissioned at Cairo on December 3. She too was modified at Cincinnati and sent to Cairo for final outfitting, perhaps about the same time as the *Rattler*. At Cairo, Capt. Pennock found her two bow gunports unacceptable and ordered his carpenters to rebuild them. Captained by Lt. Selim E. Woodworth, she was armed with six 24-pdr. smoothbore Dahlgren howitzers. ORN, II, 1: 96; Way, *op cit.*, p. 189; Silverstone, *op. cit.*, p. 172; "*Glide I*," in U.S. Navy Department, Naval Historical Center, *Dictionary of American Naval Fighting Ships*, *http://www.history.navy.mil/danfs/g6/glide-i.htm* (accessed February 9, 2008). Former commander of the *John P. Jack-*

son in the West Gulf Coast Blockading Squadron, Lt. Cmdr. Selim E. Woodworth was named to take over the *Conestoga*, but Acting Rear Adm. Porter, needing a warship for Lt. Thomas O. Selfridge Jr. after the loss of the *Cairo*, gave Woodworth the tinclad *Glide*. Woodworth, first appointed a midshipman in 1838, resigned in early 1866. ORN, I, 23: 635; Callahan, *op. cit.*, p. 603.

7. The 117-ton second *Grampus* was constructed at Brownsville, PA, in the summer of 1862. Way suspects that she, like the previous unit, was actually a primitive towboat built packet style. With such a rig, she could push and guide coal south and return north loaded with or towing other pay cargo. Way, *op. cit.*, p. 195.

8. ORN, I, 24: 134–135, 696; OR, I, 22, 1: 233; Smith, *Timberclads, passim*; Kiper, *Ibid.* Although the list provided to the USQMD after the war by Maj. Gen. Parsons and cited throughout this study is very complete, it omits the loss of the *Grampus No. 2*.

9. The *Linden* was constructed at Belle Vernon, PA, during 1860 for Capt. T.M. Harton, who employed her in the Pittsburgh-Cincinnati trade in 1861. Beginning in January 1862, she was chartered by the USQD, initially hauling wagons from Cincinnati to Louisville. The 177-ton stern-wheeler was purchased at Cincinnati on November 20 for $19,000 and sent to Joseph Brown for alteration. With a length of 154 feet and a beam of 31 feet, the upgraded craft, soon to be known as Tinclad No. 10, had a 4-foot depth of hold. The modified *Linden*, with a skeleton crew, steamed to Cairo in mid–December for outfitting and victualling. There, she received her regular crew and an initial armament of six 24-pdr. smoothbore Dahlgren howitzers. An Acting Master since October 1861, Thomas E. Smith was named her captain and placed the vessel into commission on January 3. Six days later the *Linden* departed for the lower fleet to begin her career as a dispatch and escort vessel. En route, she stopped at Memphis and was thus drawn into the cases of the *Jacob Musselman* and *Grampus No. 2*. ORN, II, 1: 128; Way, *op. cit.*, p. 287; Silverstone, *op. cit.*, p. 173; "*Linden*," in U.S. Navy Department, Naval Historical Center, *Dictionary of American Naval Fighting Ships*, http://www.history.navy.mil/danfs/l6/linden-i.htm (accessed February 9, 2008). Smith was promoted to Acting Volunteer Lt. on January 29 and would be honorably discharged on February 28, 1869. Callahan, *op. cit.*, p. 508.

10. ORN, I, 24: 135.

11. *Nashville Daily Union,* January 11, 1863; *Evansville Daily Journal,* January 13–14, 17, 1863; Gibson, *Ibid*; Miller, *loc. cit.*

12. The 114-ton stern-wheeler *Charter* was constructed at Paducah in 1856. She entered USQMD contract service early in the war. Way, *op. cit.*, p. 82.

13. The 191-ton stern-wheeler *Hastings* was built at Shousetown, PA, in 1857 for the Upper Mississippi River trade. She was based at St. Paul, MN, prior to the war. Way, *op. cit.*, p. 82.

14. The 216-ton *Parthena* was built for a syndicate headed by Capt. Perry Brown at Freedom, PA, at the beginning of 1862. Way, *op. cit.*, p. 363.

15. The 150-ton *Trio* was built at Louisville in 1858 and prior to Fort Sumter made trips from that Kentucky city to Madison, up the Red River. Her first captain was John A. Dickinson. Way, *op. cit.*, p. 459.

16. OR, I, 20, 1: 980–984; OR, I, 20, 2: 322–323, 326, 328; *Nashville Daily Dispatch*, January 14, 17, 1863; *Nashville Daily Union*, January 14, 1863; *Chicago Daily Tribune*, January 22, 1863; *New York Herald*, January 15, 18, 1863; *New Haven Daily Palladium*, January 17, 1863; ORN, I, 24: 15, 19; Kenneth W. Noe, ed., *A Southern Boy in Blue: The Memoir of Marcus Woodcock, 9th Kentucky Infantry* (U.S.A.) (Knoxville, TN: University of Tennessee Press, 1996), p. 143; Gibson, *op. cit.*, pp. 228–230; Smith, *Le Roy Fitch, op. cit.*, pp. 116–119. The owners of the *Parthenia* would receive a $32,500 payment for their loss from the U.S. government in

April 1864. The *Trio's* machinery was salvaged during the summer of 1863 and shipped to Pittsburgh for reuse. The Lucy French quote can be found in Greg Poole's "The Affair at Harpeth Shoals," *Cheatham County Historical and Genealogical Association CCHGA Bytes* (February 2006), p. 6. On January 14, one of the *Sidell's* gunners made it back to Nashville, where he reported that the disaster to his craft had been caused by the pilot leaving his wheel. Lt. Van Dorn was taken prisoner and the rest of the men, himself included, were paroled.

17. ORN, I, 24: 156–157, 163, 192.

18. On December 4, Naval Constructor Hartt proudly reported to Com. Hull at St. Louis that the steamer *Romeo*, having a draft of 22 inches, had departed the waters of Carondelet for Cairo at 3 P.M. She had been purchased in Cincinnati on October 31, 1862, for $17,459 and sent up to the boatyard of James B. Eads for modification. The 175-ton stern-wheeler was built at Brownsville, PA, in August for Capt. John I. Rhoads, who also owned the *Juliet*. Intended for the Wabash River trade before she was sold, the 154.1-foot craft had a beam of 31.2 feet and a depth of four feet. *Romeo* was outfitted with two boilers and her two engines had a 1-foot cylinder diameter and a 4-foot stroke. She could steam 5 mph upstream. Arriving at Cairo under the command of her captain Acting Ensign Robert B. Smith, the future Tinclad No. 3 was given an initial battery of six 24-pdr. smoothbore Dahlgren howitzers and commissioned on December 11. ORN, II, 1: 194; Way, *op. cit.*, p. 401; Silverstone, *op. cit.*, p. 178; "*Romeo*," in U.S. Navy Department, Naval Historical Center, *Dictionary of American Naval Fighting Ships*, http://www.history.navy.mil/danfs/r8/romeo.htm (accessed February 9, 2008). A former mate, Robert B. Smith was appointed Acting Ensign on October 1, 1862. Promoted Acting Volunteer Lt. in December 1863, Smith reached the highest possible rank in the naval volunteer service on April 29, 1865, when he was named an Acting Volunteer Lt. Cmdr. He was honorably discharged on January 1, 1866. Callahan, *op. cit.*, p. 507; ORN, I, 23:622.

19. The brand-new *Forest Rose* was constructed at Freedom, PA, during the fall of 1862 for Capt. Frank Maratta, who planned to employ her in the Pittsburgh-St. Louis trade. Before this employment could begin, the 203-ton stern-wheeler was purchased at Pittsburgh on November 5 for $22,000 and sent to Cincinnati for alteration. With a length of 155 feet and a beam of 32.2 feet, the upgraded craft, soon to be known as Tinclad No. 9, had a 4.7-foot depth of hold. Her power plant comprised three boilers and two engines. Cylinder diameter of the latter was 16 inches and the stroke was five feet. She was said to be able to make 6 mph against the current. Although her modifications were completed by Joseph Brown's workmen toward the end of November, the *Forest Rose*, like the others modified at the Cincinnati yards, had first to visit Cairo for her crew and armament. The gunboat's new captain, Acting Master George W. Brown, was told by project supervisor Lt. Cmdr. Watson Smith to get his vessel down the Ohio as quickly as possible, as she was badly needed by Acting Rear Admiral Porter below. Underway with a skeleton working crew, Brown arrived at the locks of the Portland and Louisville Canal on a bitterly cold night, well after midnight. Those in charge had turned in and, once the tinclad was in the basin, there was no one to let her through. Brown went ashore and sought out the superintendent, who, within earshot of the vessel, promptly informed the young officer that he would have to wait until morning. Not so inclined, Brown hailed his executive officer and ordered him to run out his No. 1 gun and train it on the crew house. Shortly thereafter, an ominous black cylinder appeared out of the forward gun port and the superintendent was given 10 minutes to get his crews working on the gates. Within five minutes, the *Forest Rose* was through and on her way to Cairo. Master Brown's gunboat was without armament, having not even a musket aboard. The cannon with which she had fooled the workers at the Falls of the Ohio was a short log painted black.

At Cairo, the *Forest Rose* received her crew and an initial armament, later slightly altered, of two 30-pdr. Parrott rifles forward and four 24-pdr. smoothbore Dahlgren howitzers. She was placed into commission on December 3 and immediately sent down the Mississippi to join the main elements of Rear Adm. Porter's squadron. ORN, II, 1: 85; Way, *op. cit.,* p. 169; "Forest Rose," "in U.S. Navy Department, Naval Historical Center, *Dictionary of American Naval Fighting Ships, http://www.history.navy.mil/danfs/f3/forest_rose.htm* (accessed February 9, 2008); Silverstone, *op. cit.,* pp. 171–173; George W. Brown, "Service in the Mississippi Squadron and Its Connection with the Siege and Capture of Vicksburg," in Vol. 1 of James Grant Wilson and Titus Munson Con, eds., *Personal Recollections of the War of the Rebellion: Addresses Delivered Before the New York Commandery of the Loyal Legion of the United States, 1883–1891* (New York: Published by the Commandery, 1891), p. 303. Born in New Hampshire but recruited from New York, Brown was named an Acting Master in July 1861. Her commanded the mortar schooner *Dan Smith* through the New Orleans campaign and was posted to the Mississippi Squadron in October 1862. Promoted to Acting Volunteer Lt. in January 1863, the veteran tinclad commander was honorably discharged on September 3, 1865. Edmund Wheeler, *The History of Newport, New Hampshire, From 1766 to 1878* (Newport, N.H.: The Republican Press Association, 1879), p. 36; George W. Brown, "Service in the Mississippi Squadron and Its Connection with the Siege and Capture of Vicksburg," *Ibid.*; Callahan, *op. cit.,* p. 81.

20. ORN, I, 24: 156–160, 179–180, 185–190; OR, I, 17, 2: 563–564; Bearss, *op. cit.,* p. 277–279.

21. The hull of the small 111-ton stern-wheeler *Mary Crane* was finished at Madison, IN, in summer 1862. Her upper works were finished at Evansville, where her machinery was installed. Like many others, she was soon loaded with USQMD supplies and regularly steamed up the Cumberland. Way, *op. cit.,* p. 311; Miller, *loc. cit.*

22. ORN, I, 24: 9–10; *Nashville Daily Union,* January 20, 1863; *Evansville Daily Journal,* January 23–24, 1863; *New York Herald,* January 26, 1863; Benjamin Franklin Cooling, *Fort Donelson's Legacy: War and Society in Kentucky and Tennessee, 1862–1863* (Knoxville: University of Tennessee Press, 1997), p. 190; Smith, *Le Roy Fitch, op. cit.,* p. 121; Miller, *loc. cit.;* Howard Papers, January 20, 1863. The 19th of January was an important, if little appreciated, day in the annals of the Middle Tennessee conflict. That day, the *New York Tribune* reported that Lt. Gen. James Longstreet had arrived at Shelbyville, TN, with 13 brigades and had succeeded Bragg as Army of Tennessee commander. This "confirmation" by a respected Yankee newspaper of a series of rumors circulating since the beginning of the year caused the Federal War Department to concentrate 32,000 troops for the defense of key points in Kentucky, Indiana, and Ohio and to send a three-division corps under Maj. Gen. Gordon Granger to reinforce Rosecrans. Preparations to hire the 55 steamboats necessary for transport and worries over the safe arrival of the 12,000 battle-untested men would occupy Union military leadership and quartermasters for the rest of the month. Claire E. Swedberg, ed., *Three Years with the 92nd Illinois: The Civil War Diary of John M. King* (Mechanicsburg, PA: Stackpole Books, 1999), pp. 64–74.

23. Often spelled *Mill Boy*, this little 86-ton side-wheeler was built at Brownsville, PA, in 1857. Capt. Josiah Cornwall of Chambersburg, OH, had her constructed as a floating grist mill. The craft was steed-driven until 1860, when a boiler and small engine were installed that gave her the mobility to ply her trade up and down the rivers. Way, *op. cit.,* pp. 321–322.

24. Rod Paschall, "Tactical Exercises — Mission: Protection," *MHQ: The Quarterly Journal of Military History* 4 (Spring 1992): pp. 56–58; U. S. Navy Department, Naval Historical Center, Navy Department Library, "Chapter 6: Dispositions and Instructions," *War Instructions United States Navy 1944, http://www.history.navy.mil/library/online/warinst-*

6.htm (accessed March 13, 2006); ORN, I, 24: 24, 38–39, 61, 66; OR, I, 23, 2: 32; Smith, *Le Roy Fitch, op. cit.,* pp. 124–125; Howard Papers, April 6, 1863.

25. In 1858, the 175-ton stern-wheeler *R.B. Hamilton* was built at Symmes Creek, OH, to operate local services on the Upper Ohio. Impressed into USQMD operations during the summer of 1862, she was released that November. After that, she chose to operate independent contracts on behalf of the U.S. Army. Way, *op. cit.,* p. 382.

26. *New York Herald,* January 25–26, February 5, 1863; *Nashville Daily Dispatch,* January 30, 1863; Howard Papers, *Ibid.*

27. ORN, I, 24: 12–14, 192. In his January 24 follow-up letter to his January 23 telegram, Secretary Welles let Capt. Pennock know in no uncertain terms that "the Department" was not pleased with the way in which the station chief was handling relations with Rosecrans's prickly Murfreesboro-based army leadership. The hard-pressed Pennock, disappointed with the reprimand but who, nevertheless, carbon-copied his immediate superior with that and all correspondence, would be buoyed a week later by a letter from David Porter. The rear admiral, more knowledgeable of the local scene than the Washington establishment, expressed his complete confidence in his subordinate's ability to "always do what is right." Besides, Porter added, he hoped that Pennock would "take every opportunity to write these army officials and inform them" that the Cairo office did not have information to disseminate concerning squadron activities, that "General Halleck has no control here," and that he [Porter], and nobody else in country, disposed of western navy assets. ORN, I, 24: 13–14, 18.

28. ORN, I, 24: 14, 199. The *Silver Lake,* Tinclad No. 23, had her named shortened from *Silver Lake No. 3* upon her purchase (for $21,000) at Cincinnati on November 15. The craft was built earlier in the year at California, PA, for Capt. Henry Willoughby and Thomas M. Rees of Pittsburgh. Employed in transporting ordnance between Pittsburgh and St. Louis prior to her sale, the vessel had its superstructure improved in July by the addition of a Texas deck. With a length of 155.1 feet, the vessel had a beam of 32.2 feet and a depth of hold of 5.2 feet. Her power plant consisted of two boilers and two engines, with a cylinder diameter of 15 inches and a stroke of five feet. Her single stern wheel could drive her upstream at 7 mph against the current. The *Silver Lake* was altered by Joseph Brown and commissioned at his yard on Christmas Eve. Prior to that event, Acting Volunteer Lt. Robert K. Riley and the crew oversaw the installation of six 24-pdr. smoothbore Dahlgren howitzers. The vessel arrived at Cairo on Boxing Day evening. There, Capt. Pennock found her two bow gunports unacceptable and ordered his carpenters to rebuild them. Few crewmen could be found to man the new vessel and those shipped came down with plague. Through thick and thin, the vessel would remain on the Cumberland or Tennessee throughout the war. ORN, II, 1: 209; Way, *op. cit.,* p. 426; Silverstone, *op. cit.,* p.179; "Silver Lake," in U.S. Navy Department, Naval Historical Center, *Dictionary of American Naval Fighting Ships, http://www.history.navy.mil/danfs/s12/silver_lake.htm* (accessed February 9, 2008). Appointed Acting Volunteer Lt. on October 1, Pennsylvanian Robert K. Riley resigned on February 16, 1863. Callahan, *op. cit.,* p. 463; *New York Herald,* February 16, 1863.

29. ORN, I, 24: 14–15, 192, 472; Jay Slagle, *Ironclad Captain: Seth Ledyard Phelps and the U.S. Navy* (Kent, OH: Kent State University Press, 1996), p. 322. No sooner had the *Silver Lake* arrived at the mouth of the Cumberland River than her "doctor" engine broke down, requiring her return to Illinois. Fleet Captain Pennock in Cairo immediately ordered its repair. ORN, I, 24: 200.

30. ORN, I, 23: 312; ORN, I, 24: 15–17, 19, 21–22; *Nashville Dispatch,* January 30, 1863; *New York Herald,* February 5, 1863; Thomas Jordan and J.P. Pryor, *The Campaigns of Lieut. Gen. N.B. Forrest and of Forrest's Cavalry* (New Or-

leans and New York: Blelock & Co., 1868; reprinted, New York: DaCapo Press, 1996), p. 224; Smith, *Le Roy Fitch, op. cit.,* pp. 125–128; Slagle, *Ibid.* Acting Rear Adm. Porter had also anticipated, given the flurry of communications between Washington, Murfreesboro, and Cairo, the need for additional gunboats on the upper rivers. On January 28, he wrote Pennock from the Yazoo River authorizing his retention of the *Lexington* and two light-draught gunboats then at Cairo. "If the army officers would only notify us when they want a convoy, there would be no trouble," he lamented. Next day, 200 replacement sailors arrived at Cairo from New York City; all were ordered to crew the ironclads, with none left over for any of the hard-pressed light-draughts anywhere. ORN, I, 24: 18, 216.

31. ORN, I, 24: 20, 31; *New York Times,* January 31, 1863; *New York Herald,* January 25–26, February 2, 1863; *Raleigh Weekly Register,* February 3, 1863; Smith, *Le Roy Fitch,* op. cit., p. 129; Howard Papers, *Ibid.*; Walter T. Durham, *Nashville — the Occupied City: The First Seventeen Months, February 16, 1862–June 30, 1863* (Nashville: The Tennessee Historical Society, 1985), p. 219.

32. OR, I, 20, 2: 342; OR, I, 23, 2: 38–39; ORN, I, 24: 20–24; Swedberg, *op. cit.,* pp. 40–42. Although Fitch had the *Lexington,* he exercised his right to maintain his command chair and writing desk on the *Fairplay.* In working the convoys, he would put the big timberclad, under command of Acting Master James Marshall, in the lead and himself occupy a shepherding position with the smaller side-wheeler further back. Acting Master Marshall would go on to command the tinclad *New Era* and was involved in the April 1864 defense of Fort Pillow against forces led by Maj. Gen. Forrest. He resigned from the service on September 14 of that year. Callahan, *op. cit.,* p. 352.

33. OR, I, 23, 1: 40; Jordan and Pryor, *op. cit.,* pp. 225–227; Thomas B. Van Horne, *History of the Army of the Cumberland,* 2 vols. (Wilmington, NC: Broadfoot, 1988), Vol. 1, 289; John Allan Wyeth, *Life of General Nathan Bedford Forrest* (New York: Harper & Bros., 1904), p. 146; Benjamin Franklin Cooling, "The Battle of Dover, February 3, 1863," *Tennessee Historical Quarterly* 22 (June 1963): pp. 143–144; Cooling, *Fort Donelson's Legacy, op. cit.,* pp. 192–196; Terry Wilson, "'Against Such Powerful Odds': The 83rd Illinois Infantry at the Battle of Dover, Tennessee, February 1863," *Tennessee Historical Quarterly* 53 (December 1994): pp. 261–264; John E. Fisher, *They Rode with Forrest and Wheeler: A Chronicle of Five Tennessee Brothers' Service in the Confederate Western Cavalry* (Jefferson, NC: McFarland, 1995), p. 29; Smith, *Le Roy Fitch, op. cit.,* p. 130.

34. Not recorded by Way.

35. Cooling, "Battle of Dover," *op. cit.,* p. 145; Smith, *Le Roy Fitch, op. cit.,* p. 131 ; Cooling, *Legacy, op. cit.,* p. 195; Wilson, *op. cit.,* p. 265; OR, I, 23, 1:34. Fort Donelson, the scene of the great battle of February 1862, was a year later still covered by leavings from that miserable fight and for that reason, the fortifications were abandoned. Dover was easier and more attractive for Union forces to maintain, though newspapermen and gunboatmen alike would continue to call it Fort Donelson.

36. OR, I, 23, 1: 32–41; OR, I, 23, 2: 41–42; ORN, I, 24: 15; Robert Selph Henry, "*First with the Most*" *Forrest* (Indianapolis, IN: Bobbs-Merrill, 1944), p. 123; Miller, *Ibid.*; Swedberg, *op. cit.,* p. 46–47; Cooling, "Battle of Dover," *op. cit.,* p. 147; Cooling, *Legacy, op. cit.,* pp. 196–199; Jordan and Pryor, *op. cit.,* pp. 228–229; Wyeth, *op. cit.,* pp. 147–150; Van Horne, Vol. 1, pp. 289–290; Wilson, *op. cit.,* pp. 266–268; Smith, *Le Roy Fitch, op. cit.,* pp. 131–132; *Nashville Daily Union,* February 4, 1863.

37. OR, I, 23, 1: 146–147; OR, I, 23, 2: 31–45; ORN, I, 23: 313–314; ORN, I, 24: 25–27, 30; *Nashville Daily Union,* February 4–6, 1863; *New York Herald,* February 16, 1863; *Milwaukee Daily Sentinel,* February 5, 1863; Cooling, "Battle of Dover," *op. cit.,* p. 150; Cooling, *Legacy of Fort Donelson, op. cit.,* pp. 202–204; Wilson, *op. cit.,* p. 268; Richard

P. Gildrie, "Guerrilla Warfare in the Lower Cumberland River Valley, 1862–1865," *Tennessee Historical Quarterly* 49 (Fall 1990): p. 168; Wyeth, *op. cit.,* pp. 154, 161; Jordan and Pryor, *op. cit.,* pp. 229–230; Swedberg, *op. cit.,* pp. 47–52; Howard Papers, February 5, 1863; Mahan, *op. cit.,* p. 181; Henry M. Cist, *Army of the Cumberland,* Campaigns of the Civil War (New York: Charles Scribner's Sons, 1892), p. 141; Mary Bess McCain Henderson, Evelyn Janet McCain Young, and Anna Irene McCain McCain Naheloffer, *"Dear Eliza": The Letters of Michel Andrew Thompson* (Ames, IA: Carter Press, 1976), p. 23; Byrd Douglas, *Steamboatin' on the Cumberland* (Nashville, TN: Tennessee Book Company, 1961), pp. 139–140; Mackey, *op. cit.,* p. 171; Smith, *Le Roy Fitch, op. cit.,* pp. 134–135. My Fitch biography reviews the various claims concerning the effectiveness of the Cumberland River flotilla in the Dover action. Having returned to Smithland on February 9, Fitch wired Fleet Captain Pennock: "I have the honor to report my return from Nashville," he wrote, "having landed in safety at that place with some 45 steamers. This makes 73 steamers and 16 barges we have convoyed safely to Nashville since the river has been navigable for our boats." If the first convoy, which had to be offloaded at Harpeth Shoals, were counted, "we have taken through to Nashville over 100 steamers, all deeply loaded." This was, indeed, a remarkable achievement; not one vessel in the Hoosier's care had been lost or even badly damaged. ORN, I, 23: 30.

38. The literature on the Yazoo Pass Expedition is contained in those campaign histories, biographies, and unit chronicles touching in whole or in part upon the Vicksburg campaign. Of particular interest are Richard S. West, Jr., "Gunboats in the Swamps: The Yazoo Pass Expedition," *Civil War History* 9 (1963): pp. 157–166, and Frank "Galway" Wilkie's contemporary revelation of the failure in his "Details of the Yazoo Expedition Via the Sunflower," in the *New York Times,* April 4, 1863.

39. ORN, I, 23: 305–310; *New York Herald,* February 8, 1863; *New York Times,* February 20, 1863. The official report noted that the gunboat's crew comprised eight Caucasian and 30 African-American contrabands and blamed the latter for being "sensitive to the cold and reckless of the consequences of building a fire anywhere." De Soto, in reporting the event for the *Times,* stated quite frankly that the contrabands had "received permission to build a fire in the ash-pan in front of the boiler to warm themselves." The failure to control the blaze, the correspondent believed, was due to the "bungling use of the [fire-fighting] water." ORN, I, 23: 310; *New York Times,* February 20, 1863.

40. Built at Wellesville, OH, in the fall of 1862, the *New Era* was purchased at Cincinnati on October 27 for $14,238.73. Like other steamers acquired at this time, she, too, would be altered at Carondelet. With a length of 137.1 feet, the future Tinclad No. 7 had a beam of 29.6 feet and a depth of hold of 4.6 feet. The craft was powered by two boilers and two engines, the latter with cylinder diameters of 14 inches and a stroke of 4.6 feet. Brought to Cairo by her new captain, Acting Master Frank W.F. Flanner, on December 19, the gunboat took aboard her crew and an initial battery of six 24-pdr. smoothbore Dahlgren howitzers. Although the exact commissioning date is unknown, it was most likely during the same week as the *Romeo* and *Juliet.* "New Era," in U.S. Navy Department, Naval Historical Center, *Dictionary of American Naval Fighting Ships,* http://www.histo ry.navy.mil/danfs/n4/new_era.htm (accessed February 9, 2008); ORN, II, 1: 159; Way, *op. cit.,* p. 343; Silverstone, *op. cit.,* p. 175. Frank W.F. Flanner was appointed Acting Master on October 1, 1862, and sent to Carondelet, MO, two months to the day later to assume command of the *New Era.* He was dismissed the following March 2. William C. Hanford was first appointed a mate in April 1862 and was advanced to the rank of Acting Ensign in December. He would be "condemned" by medical survey at the end of February, but recovered sufficiently to assume command of the tinclad *Alfred Robb* on the Tennessee River. Renewed health prob-

lems caused him to lose his appointment on August 10. After recovering, he would be reinstated on September 2, but would have to resign on June 10, 1864. ORN, I, 23: 449; Callahan, *op. cit.*, pp. 196, 243.

41. The *Knapp* is not listed by Way, but is found in Lytle, *op. cit.*, p. 202.

42. With a reputation for speed, the 345-ton *White Cloud* was built at McKeesport, PA, in 1857 for the Upper Mississippi trade. She was 200 feet long, with a beam of 35 feet and a 5.5-foot draft, and was outfitted with double rudders. She was later operated up the Missouri River and acquired as part of the Great Mail and Transportation Co. She began service as a USQMD transport in time for the campaign against Fort Donelson in February 1862. Way, *op. cit.*, p. 485.

43. The giant packet *Rowena* was constructed at Elizabeth, PA, in 1858. The side-wheeler was 225 feet long, with a beam of 33.5 feet and a six-foot draft. Her four boilers provided sufficient power to drive her two paddle wheels smartly. Way, *op. cit.*, p. 403; "The *White Cloud* & *Rowena*: The Paths of Robert Louden and James Cass Mason Cross," *Civil War St. Louis: The Boatburners, http://www.civilwarstlouis.com/boatburners/whitecloud.htm* (June 30, 2008); Marion Bragg, *Historic Names and Places on the Lower Mississippi River* (Vicksburg, MS: Mississippi River Commission, 1977), p. 50.

44. The *Curlew* was constructed at Paducah, KY, in 1860 for Capt. Paul F. Semonin of Henderson, KY, for the Lower Ohio and Green River trade. She was 150 feet long, with a beam of 26.5 feet. She steamed as in independent until impressed into the Federal Yazoo Pass expedition later in the spring of 1863. She returned from that adventure in a most "dilapidated condition." Way, *op. cit.*, p. 116.

45. ORN, I, 23: 195, 236–238, 349–350, 546; Miller *op. cit.*, p. 377; *Wisconsin State Register*, February 7, 1863.

46. ORN, I, 23: 314–315; ORN, I, 24: 30–46, 57–58, 318; OR, I, 23, 1: 152–160, 215–239, 359–362; *Chicago Daily Tribune*, February 26, 1863; Robert G. Hartje, *Van Dorn: The Life and Times of a Confederate General* (Nashville, TN: Vanderbilt University Press, 1967), p. 274; Howard Papers, January 20, February 18, 20, 24, 1863; Samuel B. Barron, *The Lone Star Defenders: A Chronicle of the Third Texas Cavalry, Ross' Brigade* (New York and Washington, D.C.: The Neale Publishing Co., 1908), p. 144–145; Jordan and Pryor, *op. cit.*, pp. 246–248; William R. Morris, "The Burning of Clifton," *Wayne County Historian* 2 (June 1989), reprinted on the *Civil War Page http://www.netease.net/wayne/burningclifton.htm* (March 3, 2004); "*Dunbar*," in U.S. Navy Department, Naval History Division, *Civil War Naval Chronology, 1861–1865*, 6 vols. (Washington, D.C.: GPO, 1962–1966), Vol. 1, p. 223; Ben Earl Kitchens, *Gunboats and Cavalry: A History of Eastport, Mississippi, with Special Emphasis on Events of the War Between the States* (Florence, AL: Thornwood Book Publishers, 1985), p. 103; Smith, Le Roy Fitch, *op. cit.*, pp. 140–141; Woodward, *Ibid.*

47. The engines of the newly-available stern-wheeler, *Springfield*, or Tinclad No. 22, were originally deemed of "such small capacity" that the tinclad could not stem the current. Built at Cincinnati during the summer of 1862, the *W.A. Healy* was purchased for the U.S. Navy at that city on November 20 for the price of $13,000. The wooden, 146-ton craft was renamed *Springfield* on December 5, while she was undergoing conversion, probably at the shipyard of Joseph Brown. *Springfield* was 134.9' long, with a beam of 26.11' and a depth of hold of 4.4'. Equipped with two engines, each with a diameter of cylinder of 10" and a stroke of 3.6', plus two boilers, she could reportedly steam upstream at 5 mph — a figure Capt. Pennock soon disputed when he informed Admiral Porter, "she is slow, but will do something." On January 8, the new warship received her armament of six 24-pound brass Dahlgren howitzers and, on January 12, she was commissioned, Acting Volunteer Lt. Henry A. Glassford in command. Like the *Silver Lake*, she would remain on the upper rivers throughout the remainder of the war. ORN, II, 1: 213; Silverstone, *op. cit.*, p. 169; Way, *op. cit.*, pp. 431, 473. Henry A. Glassford was born in Montreal, Canada, in 1827 and immigrated to Albany, New York, at least a decade prior to Fort Sumter. In October 1861, he joined the staff of Brig. Gen. Alexander Asboth at St. Louis and, when the opportunity presented itself the following February, transferred to the Western Flotilla. Glassford was appointed an Acting Volunteer Lt. on December 3, 1862. He would succeed the ill Acting Ensign Hanford on the *New Era* on March 4 and in late spring would commission the new tinclad *Reindeer*, which he would command for the remainder of the war. Following his honorable discharge on November 29, 1865, Glassford returned to the New York capital, where he continued a career in finance and served as president of various social clubs and orders. In 1888, he moved to New York, becoming a senior member in the Wall Street banking concern Charles T. Wing & Co. The Senior Vice President of the Loyal Legion of the United States was a life-long bachelor who died alone at home on April 11, 1900. Callahan, *op. cit.*, p. 220; *New York Times*, April 12, 1900; ORN, I, 23: 449, 526.

48. One of the largest packets of her day, the 702-ton *Ruth* was constructed at Jeffersonville, IN, by Howard in 1862. She was 270 feet long, with a beam of 27.5 feet and a nine-foot draft. Just prior to her January 1, 1863, entry into service, giant pictures of the Biblical Ruth were painted on both wheelhouses. She was almost immediately contracted as a USQMD transport. Way, *op. cit.*, p. 405.

49. 34 The 178-ton sternwheeler *Cricket No. 2* was constructed at California, PA, in 1860. One of the most famous of the tinclads, she was 154.1' long, with a beam of 28.2' and a draft of just four feet. She was equipped with two engines, each with a diameter of cylinder of 13" and a stroke of 4.5', powered by two boilers, and was said to be able to steam at 6 mph. Owned by R. Hamilton of Hanging Rock, OH, and John Kyle of Cincinnati, she was operated on the Pittsburgh-Cincinnati-Louisville trade under Capt. S.B. Hempstead. The boat, whose name was immediately shortened to *Cricket*, was sold to the Navy at Cincinnati on November 18, 1862. Her conversion at Cairo was completed at the beginning of 1863 and she was armed with six 24-pounder smoothbore Dahlgren howitzers on January 6. Later given the ID number 6, the *Cricket* was commissioned 13 days later, Acting Master Langhorne in command. Between February 4 and April 7, she served as guard ship at Memphis, engaging in several contraband sweeps of the river below the city. Way, *op. cit.*, p. 115; ORN, II, 1:68; "*Cricket*," in U.S. Navy Department, Naval Historical Center, *Dictionary of American Naval Fighting Ships, http://www.history.navy.mil/danfs/c15/cricket.htm* (accessed February 9, 2008).

50. Little is known about this *Delta* (there were six, according to Way), other than that she was a 119-ton side-wheeler built at Chester, IL, in 1856. Home-ported at St. Louis, she disappeared from all listing after 1865. Way, *op. cit.*, p. 123.

51. 36 The 419-ton side-wheeler *Forest Queen* was constructed at Madison, IN, in 1858 for the Ohio River trade between that town and Cincinnati. During the war, she not only operated privately but accepted U.S. government transport contracts from time to time, operating both kinds of work with her own crew and management. Less than a month after her run in with the *Cricket*, she was one of the transports that ran the Vicksburg batteries on April 17. Way, *op. cit.*, p. 169.

52. ORN, I, 23: 449, 469, 503, 505–508, 534; Way, *op cit*, pp. 405. Glassford's assertive efforts elicited numerous complaints to a point where Acting Rear Admiral Porter asked him to respond to concerns that he had mistreated steamboat passengers and did "other things unbecoming an officer." Glassford's spirited response had the effect of winning his appointment to the *Springfield* and later to the new tinclad *Reindeer*. ORN, I, 23: 525, 672–673.

53. Ordered by a syndicate led by Capt. George D.

Moore, the 223-ton stern-wheeler *Eclipse* was constructed at Elizabeth, PA, in early 1862. She was almost immediately purchased by Capt. William G. Vohris to operate contract service for the USQMD. Although she escaped Palmyra, she was lost at Johnsonville, TN, on January 27, 1865, when her boiler blew up. Way, *op. cit.,* p. 140.

54. The 164-ton sternwheeler *Lizzie Martin* was constructed at Belle Vernon, PA in 1857. Under Capt. David T. Brown, she was a regular on the Upper Ohio River, particularly the route from Parkersburg to Zanesville. Later, in 1862, she extended her service to Pittsburgh and also undertook USQMD charters. Way, *op. cit.,* p. 291.

55. Constructed at Cincinnati at the beginning of 1863, the 1,023-ton *Luminary* was 260 feet long, with a beam of 42 feet and a seven-foot draft. Four boilers provided the power to propel her two big side wheels. She immediately entered into USQMD contract service from the Queen City to Nashville. Way, *op. cit.,* p. 299.

56. Constructed at Elizabeth, PA, in 1860, the small 93-ton *Charles Miller,* owned by the brothers Capt. Pink Varable and W. Varable, specialized in trips from Louisville to Nashville. Although she survived Palmyra, she was caught in a storm 12 miles below Nashville, capsized, and sunk. Way, *op. cit.,* p. 80.

57. Constructed at Brownsville, PA, in 1859, the 193-ton *Kellogg* was home-ported at Pittsburgh. Lytle, *op. cit.,* p. 94.

58. Lamers, *op cit.,* p. 257; Durham, *op. cit.,* pp. 221–222; OR, I, 23, 2: 200, 204, 208; ORN, I, 24: 66–71; *Chicago Daily Tribune,* April 8, 1863; *Cincinnati Daily Gazette,* April 6, 1863; *New York Herald,* April 7, 1863; *Milwaukee Daily Sentinel,* April 9, 1863; *Chicago Daily Tribune,* April 8, 1863; Robert Brandt, *Touring the Middle Tennessee Backroads* (Winston-Salem, NC: John F. Blair, Publisher, 1995), p. 82; Howard Papers, April 4–6, 1863; Cooling, *Fort Donelson's Legacy,* pp. 226–227; Smith, *Le Roy Fitch, op. cit.,* pp. 152–154. Fouty's leg was amputated, but he died at the Fort Donelson hospital on April 10. Callahan, *op. cit.,* p. 202.

59. ORN, I, 23: 317; *Chicago Daily Tribune,* April 8, 1863; Cooling, *Fort Donelson's Legacy, op. cit.,* pp. 227–228; Howard Papers, April 4–5, 1863; Smith, *Le Roy Fitch, op. cit.,* pp. 155–156; Brandt, *Ibid.* Fitzpatrick would go on to command the monitor *Chickasaw* and the tinclad *Signal* and would be honorably discharged on December 30, 1865. Callahan, *op. cit.,* p. 196.

60. ORN, I, 23: 317; ORN, I, 24: 71–72, 75, 78; OR, I, 23, 1, 333, 346–347; OR, I, 23, 2: 212, 219, 240, 253; Cooling, *Fort Donelson's Legacy, Ibid.*; Howard Papers, April 5–6, 1863; Gildrie, *op. cit.,* pp. 168–169. Back at Smithland on April 6, Fitch wrote out a full report of the Palmyra incident for Admiral Porter. He concluded it with the observation that contingency plans made earlier for the concentration of his entire upper fleet at any one point during an emergency had worked in this case. It was hoped they would be equally successful should the need arise in the future. On April 8, Capt. Pennock bundled up all of Cairo's telegrams relative to the Palmyra episode and forwarded them down to Admiral Porter; four days later, Porter reshipped them Secretary Welles in Washington. ORN, I, 24: 72–73, 78.

61. The towboat *Saxonia* was constructed Nelsonville, OH, at the beginning of the year. Contract USQMD charters took her up and down all of the upper rivers. Lytle, op. cit., p. 173.

62. The *R.M.C. Lovell* is not listed in any of the standard steamboat directories, probably because her name was changed. The *Granada (MS) Appeal* (formerly the *Memphis Daily Appeal*), portraying the *Lovell* as a "gunboat." *Granada (MS) Appeal,* April 14, 1863.

63. ORN, I, 24: 66, 77; Howard Papers, April 10, 1863; Parsons, *loc. cit.*; *Granada (MS) Appeal,* April 14, 1863; *Daily Mississippian,* April 16, 1863. Needing more gunboat assistance than was then available, officers of the U.S. Army continued to take it upon themselves to send out their own makeshift gunboats. The army leadership at Clarksville, no

doubt impressed with the work of Fitch's flotilla in the recent pursuit of the Palmyra belligerents, decided it needed an armed craft to check those Rebel troops marauding around Harpeth Shoals. Consequently, the old 162-ton ferryboat *Excelsior* (built at Brownsville, PA, in 1849 — Lytle, *op. cit.,* p. 60) was taken in hand, its vitals were barricaded with hay bales, and a couple of field pieces with their gun crews were posted aboard. The soldiers then "used her as a gunboat." During the week of April 10, the steamer convoyed part of a transport fleet above the Shoals. It also stopped to recover a cannon from the wreck of the military gunboat *W.H. Sidell* and dispersed a rebel band that was waiting at the shoals to fire on any unprotected boats, even managing to capture several of its men. There is no further mention of the *Excelsior* in the OR; however, at least three army gunboats were active on the Cumberland during the year and she may have been one of them. OR, I, 23, 2: 240.

64. OR, I, 24, 3: 152, 168; *New York Times,* April 16, 1863; Hearn, *Admiral David Dixon Porter, op cit.,* pp. 177–219; Steven E. Woodworth, *Nothing But Victory: The Army of the Tennessee, 1861–1865* (New York: Alfred A. Knopf, 2005), pp. 298–331; Michael B. Ballard, *Vicksburg: The Campaign That Opened the Mississippi* (Chapel Hill, NC: University of North Carolina Press, 2004), 168–203. The literature on the bayou expeditions and the task group's passing of Vicksburg (all of which is outside the scope of this title) is quite large; the Official Records, memoirs, and periodical literature record them in great detail. The passages noted in the following general works are recommended: Mahan, *op. cit.,* pp. 123–158; John D. Milligan, *Gunboats Down the Mississippi* (Annapolis, MD: Naval Institute Press, 1965), pp. 121–161; Jack D. Coombe, *Thunder Along the Mississippi: The River Battles That Split the Confederacy* (New York: Sarpedon Publishers, 1996), pp. 193–214; Spencer C. Tucker, *Blue & Gray Navies: The Civil War Afloat* (Annapolis, MD: Naval Institute Press, 2006), pp. 222–230; Bern Anderson, *By Sea and By River: The Naval History of the Civil War.* (New York: Knopf, 1962), pp. 141–143, 148.

65. OR, I, 23, 1: 281–294; Wyeth, *op. cit.,* pp. 185–187; Gibson, *op. cit.,* p. 304; Cooling, *Fort Donelson's Legacy, op. cit.,* p. 251; Lamers, *op. cit.,* p. 257; Smith, *Le Roy Fitch, op. cit.,* pp. 147–158; David Stanley, *Personal Memoirs of Major-General D.S. Stanley, U.S.A.* (Cambridge, MA: Harvard University Press, 1917), pp. 131–132; Kitchens, *op. cit.,* p. 105. Also at this time, a highly successful Union cavalry raid through Mississippi was planned and undertaken by the Michigan schoolmaster Col. Benjamin H. Grierson; the strike, as celebrated as Streight's was ridiculed, was the inspiration for the 1959 John Wayne motion picture, *The Horse Soldiers.* Another Yankee gambit, the equally-inspired Andrews raid, was a tragic-ending covert raid; it too got a movie, Fess Parker's 1956 *The Great Locomotive Chase.*

66. Built at Monongahela, PA, during the fall of 1862 for Capt. George W. Reed, the *Argosy* entered Ohio River service just before Christmas. The river correspondent of the *Pittsburgh Daily Gazette* was initially puzzled: "This is a queer name but appropriate," he wrote. "*Argosy* means a large vessel for the transportation of merchandise." Reed sold his new boat to Cmdr. J.P. Sanford at Cincinnati on March 10, 1863, for $35,000 and sent to Cairo for alteration next day. The wooden, 219-ton stern-wheeler retained her original moniker. *Argosy* was 156.4' long, with a beam of 33' and a depth of hold of 4.8'. She was equipped with two engines, each with a diameter of cylinder of 15" and a stroke of 5', powered by three boilers. Finished on March 24, the new Tinclad No. 27 received her armament of six 24-pounder brass Dahlgren howitzers and two 12-pounder rifled Dahlgren howitzers two days later and was commissioned on March 19, Acting Master William N. Griswold in command. ORN, I, 23: 468, 542; ORN, II, 1: 37; Silverstone, *op. cit.,* p. 169; Way, *op. cit.,* p. 28; Pittsburgh *Daily Gazette,* December 25, 1862; "*Argosy*" in U.S. Navy Department, Naval Historical Center, *Dictionary of American Naval Fighting Ships,*

http://www.history.navy.mil/danfs/a1l/argosy.htm (accessed February 8, 2008); "A Tale of Three Tinclads, All Named *Argosy*," *Mid Missouri Civil War Roundtable Homepage, 2005, http://www.mmcwrt.org/2005/default0501.htm* (accessed July 29, 2005). William N. Griswold was named an Acting Master on July 9, 1861, and would, within weeks, assume command of the tinclad *Hastings*. He was honorably discharged on Sept. 18, 1865. *Argosy's* new commander was Acting Volunteer Lt. Edward M. King. He would remain on the Tennessee River and be caught in command at Johnsonville, TN, when the supply depot there was burned by Forrest late in 1864. Though court-martialed, he was honorably discharged on July 18, 1867. Callahan, *op. cit.,* pp. 234, 314.

67. Much information was presented earlier in Chapter 3 for the side-wheelers *Covington* and *Queen City.* The former received her battery of four 24-pounder smoothbore Dahlgren howitzers, two 30-pounder Parrott rifles, and two 50-pounder Dahlgren rifles at Cairo on April 1, 1863, and was commissioned within days, Acting Volunteer Lt. Jacob S. Hurd in command. The conversion of the latter was finished on April 1 and she was placed into commission, Acting Master Jason Goudy in command. The battery was sent aboard on April 9 and comprised four 24-pounder smoothbore Dahlgren howitzers, two 30-pounder Parrott rifles, and two 32-pounder smoothbores. ORN, II, 1: 67, 187; "*Covington*" in U.S. Navy Department, Naval Historical Center, *Dictionary of American Naval Fighting Ships, http://www.history.navy.mil/danfs/c14/covington-i.htm* (accessed February 8, 2008); "*Queen City*" in U.S. Navy Department, Naval Historical Center, *Dictionary of American Naval Fighting Ships, http://www.history.navy.mil/danfs/q1/queen_city.htm* (accessed February 8, 2008).

68. OR, I, 24, 3, 246–261; Wyeth, *op. cit.,* pp. 190–222; Cooling, *Fort Donelson's Legacy, op. cit,* p. 253; ORN, I, 24: 87; Stanley, *Ibid.;* Jordan and Pryor, *op. cit.,* pp. 278–279; Grenville M. Dodge, *The Battle of Atlanta and Other Campaigns, Addresses, Etc.* (Council Bluffs, IA: The Monarch Printing Company, 1911; reprint, Denver, CO: Sage Books, 1965), pp. 118–119; Kitchens, *op. cit.,* pp. 107–108; Smith, *Le Roy Fitch, op. cit.,* pp. 160–162. Streight's report is found in OR, I, 23, 1: 281–294, while Forrest's account is in the same volume, pp. 120–121. Gen. Dodge, who reprinted both his official report and Streight's in his 1911 book, meanwhile, fell back after taking Tuscumbia Landing and Florence on April 29–30, believing his part of the expedition a success. Also on May 3, Grierson's raiders, pursued but not by the likes of Forrest, made it safely to Union lines at Baton Rouge, LA.

69. The *Emma Duncan* once had a field piece aboard and served briefly as a quasi-army gunboat in 1862. Built at Monongahela, PA, in 1860 and named for the daughter of a Cincinnati furniture maker, Capt. F.Y. Batchelor's packet was operated on the Pittsburgh-Cincinnati trade in 1861–1862. She was purchased from the captain and his brother, J. Batchelor, at Cairo on March 12 for $39,000. The 293-ton side-wheeler was 173 feet long, with a beam of 34.2 feet and a hold depth of 5.4 feet. She possessed two engines, three boilers, and was armed with two 30-pdr. Parrott rifles forward, two 32-pdrs. aft, and four 24-pdr. brass Dahlgren howitzers in broadside. On April 7, her name was officially changed to *Hastings*; however, she would continue to be known by her civilian name for some time to come. Later designated Tinclad No. 15, she was commissioned in mid–April under Acting Master Griswold. ORN, I, 23: 468; ORN, II, 1: 100; Way, *op cit.,* pp. 149–150, 208; Silverstone, *op cit,* p. 169; "*Hastings*," in U.S. Navy Department, Naval Historical Center, *Dictionary of American Naval Fighting Ships, http://www.history.navy.mil/danfs/h3/hastings.htm* (accessed February 8, 2008).

70. *New York Herald,* May 1, 1863; Silverstone, *op. cit.,* p. 107; Smith, *Le Roy Fitch, op. cit.,* pp. 162–163; Gibson, *op cit.,* p. 231; Hiram H. Martin, "Service Afield and Afloat: A Reminiscence of the Civil War Edited by Guy R. Everson," *Indiana Magazine of History* 89 (March 1993): pp. 44.

71. OR, 23, 1, 1: 278–280; ORN, I, 24: 86–88, 90–91, 636; Smith, *Le Roy Fitch, op. cit.,* pp. 163–164; Chester G. Hearn, *Ellet's Brigade: The Strangest Outfit of All* (Baton Rouge: Louisiana State University Press, 2000), pp. 156–159; Martin, *op cit.,* pp. 45–47; Warren D. Crandall and Isaac D. Newell, *History of the Ram Fleet and Mississippi Marine Brigade* (St. Louis, MO: Buschart Brothers, 1907), pp. 277–281. The three men wounded on the *Emma Duncan* on April 24 were later sent to the naval hospital at Memphis. ORN, I, 24: 636.

72. ORN, I, 24: 85–88; Smith, *Le Roy Fitch, op. cit.,* pp. 164–165; Dodge, *Ibid.*

Chapter 6

1. Although her $33,500 acquisition was not officially completed until May 19, Barker, Hart & Cook agreed to sell their year-old stern-wheeler, *Silver Cloud,* to the U.S. Navy at Cairo on April 1. Immediately taken in hand by Capt. Pennock's workmen, the 236-ton was altered into Tinclad No. 28 within a month. The boat was 155 feet long, with a beam of 33.5 feet and a hold depth of 5.3 feet. She possessed two engines and two boilers, which could power her to a top speed of 7 mph against the current. On May 1, she received her armament of six 24-pdr. brass Dahlgren howitzers, all mounted in broadside. Next day, her new commander, Acting Master Augustus F. Thompson, appointed to his rank on April 9, received orders for Paducah. Thompson would not remain with the boat long, being posted to the newly converted *Paw Paw* in July. He would be honorably discharged on October 20, 1865. Paul H. Silverstone, *Warships of the Civil War Navies* (Annapolis, Md.: Naval Institute Press, 1989), p. 178; "*Silver Cloud*," in U.S. Navy Department, Naval Historical Center, *Dictionary of American Naval Fighting Ships, http://www.history.navy.mil/danfs/s-12/silver_cloud-i.htm* (accessed February 9, 2008); ORN, II, 1: 209; Frederick Way Jr., comp., *Way's Packet Directory, 1848–1994,* 2nd ed. (Athens, OH: Ohio University Press, 1994), p. 425; Edward W. Callahan, *List of Officers of the Navy of the United States and of the Marine Corps, from 1775 to 1900, Comprising a Complete Register of All Present and Former Commissioned, Warranted, and Appointed Officers of the United States Navy, and of the Marine Corps, Regular and Volunteer. Compiled from the Official Records of the Navy Department* (New York: L.R. Hamersly & Co., 1901; reprinted, New York: Haskell House, 1969), p. 541.

2. Benjamin Franklin Cooling, *Fort Donelson's Legacy: War and Society in Kentucky and Tennessee, 1862–1863* (Knoxville: University of Tennessee Press, 1997), pp. 258–264; Myron J. Smith Jr., *Le Roy Fitch: The Civil War Career of a Union River Gunboat Commander* (Jefferson, N.C.: McFarland, 2007), pp. 165–166; Jay Slagle, *Ironclad Captain: Seth Ledyard Phelps and the U.S. Navy* (Kent, OH: Kent State University Press, 1996), pp. 329–330; ORN, I, 24: 658.

3. The 249-ton *Golden Era* was constructed at Wheeling, VA/WV, in 1852 for the Galena, Dunleith & Minnesota Packet Co. The side-wheeler was 178 feet long, with a beam of 29 feet and a 5.1-foot draft. Early in the war she became a USQMD transport and she would complete at least three visits to Vicksburg in 1863. Way, *op. cit.,* p. 191.

4. *New York Herald,* May 20, 1863; Way, *op. cit.,* p. 191; ORN, I, 24: 636–639; Michael B. Ballard, *Vicksburg: The Campaign that Opened the Mississippi* (Chapel Hill, NC: University of North Carolina Press, 2004), pp. 186–187, 209–211, 319; Marion Bragg, *Historic Names and Places on the Lower Mississippi River* (Vicksburg, MS: Mississippi River Commission, 1977), p. 130. Bragg tells us that the Greenville bends were artificially altered after the Civil War.

5. The *Minnesota* was built at California, PA, in 1857 for Capt. Charles A. Hay. The towboat was 131 feet long, with a beam of 30 feet and a four-foot draft. Her prewar

route often included the Mississippi and Red Rivers, from New Orleans to Alexandria. Way, *op. cit.*, p. 323.

6. ORN, I, 24: 636–369; Way, *op. cit.*, p. 77, 323; *New York Herald,* May 20, 1863; Lewis B. Parsons, *Reports to the War Department* (St. Louis, MO: George Knapp & Co., 1867), p. 34. At the end of May, Langthorne was relieved of command and required to face a court of inquiry concerning his station departure. His defense was successful and, on January 25, 1864, Rear Adm. Porter appointed him commander of the ironclad *Mound City.* ORN, I, 25: 140, 715.

7. Walter E.H. Fentress joined the Western Flotilla as a mate in December 1861. He was promoted to Acting Ensign in August 1862 and Acting Master in January 1863. As the *Rattler's* executive officer, Fentress impressed many with his command of a land-based mortar battery during the Yazoo Pass attacks on Fort Pemberton. He was elevated to the boat's captaincy on March 17, succeeding Acting Volunteer Lt. Langthorne, who was posted to the *Cricket.* Fentress would return to command another tinclad late in the war and was honorably discharged in September 1867. ORN, I, 24: 247, 286–287; Callahan, *op. cit.,* p. 191.

8. ORN, I, 24: 639.

9. Salvaged after her capture during the June 1862 Battle of Memphis, the 840-ton side-wheeler *General Bragg* was refurbished into Union service during that fall. Possessing a formidable 12-foot draft, she was anything but a light-draught. Still, her single engine and boiler gave her a reported top speed of 10 knots. Her armament comprised one each 30-pounder Parrott rifle, 32-pounder smoothbore, and 12-pounder brass Dahlgren howitzer. A native of Missouri, Bishop was commissioned a Passed Midshipman in 1858, a Master in February 1861, and a Lieutenant two months later. Active with the Mississippi naval establishment, he would attain the rank of Lt. Cmdr. in 1865. He retired with the rank of Cmdr. in 1896. Bishop would be one of the few USN officers to have certain details of a court-martial case against him heard by the U.S. Supreme Court. Dismissed from the service after an 1868 finding of drunkenness and neglect of duty, he was restored to duty at his old rank in 1871 by a special Act of Congress, his career essentially ruined. His appeal for back pay, made through the courts, failed. It is ironic that Bishop owed his initial appointment as a lieutenant to the dismissal of another officer, Lt. William B. Fitzgerald, who "went South." ORN, II, 1: 91; "Sketches of the Officers of the Fort Donelson Fleet," *Philadelphia Inquirer,* February 18, 1862; Callahan, *op. cit.,* p. 58; Lewis R. Hamersly, *The Records of Living Officers of the U.S. Navy and Marine Corps, Compiled from Official Sources,* rev. ed. (Philadelphia, PA: J.B. Lippincott, 1870), p. 90. Bishop's legal case, *Bishop v U.S., 197 U.S. 334 (1905),* was decided on April 3, 1905, and is printed on the Internet's *Find Law* site *http://caselaw.lp.findlaw.com/scripts/getcase.pl?navby=case&court=us&vol=197&invol=334* (October 1, 2006) while his lieutenant appointment is noted in the July 26, 1861, issue of the U.S. Senate's *Executive Journal, American Memory Homepage http://memory.loc.gov/cgi-bin/query/r?ammem/hlaw:@field(DOCID+@lit(ej011131)* (October 1, 2006).

10. Minted an Acting Ensign in January 1863, Ferguson would be appointed Acting Master a year later. As commander of the tinclad *Silver Cloud,* he would participate in events surrounding Maj. Gen. Forrest's capture of Fort Pillow in the fall of 1864. Ferguson was honorably discharged in November 1865. Callahan, *Ibid.*

11. ORN, I, 24: 640–642.

12. The 688-ton *Crescent City* was constructed at Cincinnati in 1854; the veteran side-wheel packet served extensively on the New Orleans–St. Louis route prior to the war and as a troop transport for the USQMD during the conflict. Way, *op. cit.,* p. 114.

13. ORN, I, 25: 4; Way, *op. cit.,* p. 114, 287; OR, I, 24, 2: 143–144.

14. ORN, I, 24: 674; Slagle, *op. cit.,* pp. 329–330; William H. Howard to wife, May 6, 10, 1863, William H.

Howard Papers, University of Tennessee Library, Knoxville (cited hereafter as Howard Papers, with date).

15. ORN, I, 24: 672; ORN, I, 25: 124–125; *Chicago Daily Tribune,* November 22, 1863; Richard E. Beringer, Herman Hattaway, Archer Jones, and William N. Still, Jr., *Why the South Lost the Civil War* (Athens: The University of Georgia Press, 1986), pp. 191–192; Gary D. Joiner, *Mr. Lincoln's Brown Water Navy: The Mississippi Squadron* (Lanham, MD: Rowman and Littlefield, 2007), p. 173; David Dixon Porter, *Naval History of the Civil War* (New York: Sherman Publishing Company, 1886; reprinted, Secaucus, N.J.: Castle Books, 1984), p. 339. The district scheme was first modified in mid–August, when a new disposition was announced:

District #	Location
1	New Orleans to Donaldsonville, LA
2	Donaldsonville to Red River
3	Red River to Natchez, MS
4	Natchez, MS, to Vicksburg, MS
5	Vicksburg, MS, to White River
6	White River to Cairo, IL
7	Cairo, IL, to head of Tennessee River
8	Cumberland River to its source + Upper Ohio River

Creation and administration of the district arrangement of the Mississippi Squadron is worthy of further study, perhaps a lengthy article or PhD. Dissertation.

16. Later designated Tinclad No. 38, the 211-ton stern-wheeler *Exchange* was built by Capt. John W. Anawalt at Brownsville, PA, in 1862. The boat's hull was constructed by Cox and Williams and her engines came from Snowden & Sons. The new vessel was 155.2 feet long, with a beam of 33.4 feet and a depth of hold of 4.9 feet. Her three boilers sent sufficient power to her two engines to permit a maximum upstream speed of 6 mph as she engaged in the Pittsburgh–St. Louis packet trade. On May 13, Henry B. Cock, on behalf of her owner, sold the *Exchange* to the USN for $30,000 and she was sent to Joseph Brown's yards for modification. Completed but without armament, the modified vessel was employed in Maj. Gen. Burnside's secret scheme. When that duty was completed, the Exchange steamed to Cairo, where, on June 8–9, she received a battery comprising two 32-pounder smoothbores, four 24-pounder brass Dahlgren smoothbore howitzers and one 12-pdr. rifled howitzer. Within days, the new boat joined Lt. Cmdr. Phelps's Tennessee River division, serving under command of the veteran Acting Volunteer Lt. J.S. Hurd. Way, *op. cit.,* p. 157; Silverstone, *op. cit.,* p. 171; ORN, II, I: 81; "*Exchange,*" in U.S. Navy Department, Naval Historical Center, *Dictionary of American Naval Fighting Ships, http://www.history.navy.mil/danfs/e6/exchange.htm* (accessed February 9, 2008).

17. ORN, I, 25: 140; *Boston Daily Advertiser,* May 21, 1863; Jennifer L. Weber, *Copperheads: The Rise and Fall of Lincoln's Opponents in the North* (New York: Oxford University Press, 2006), pp. 95–99 ; Frank L. Klement, "Clement L. Vallandigham's Exile in the Confederacy, May 25–June 17, 1863," *Journal of Southern History* 31 (1965): pp. 150–152. Pennock wrote Rear Adm. Porter a few days after the event confessing that he did not know what the *Exchange's* mission was until he "learned it from the public prints...."

18. Constructed at Cincinnati in 1854, the huge *Nebraska* was 285 feet long, with a beam of 38 feet and an eight-foot draft. Her paddle wheels were serviced by six boilers, each 32 feet long. A veteran of the New Orleans & Memphis Packet Line, the craft became a USQMD troop transport early in the war. Way, *op. cit.,* p. 341.

19. A veteran of the prewar Cincinnati-New Orleans run, the 406-ton *Ohio Belle* was built at the Queen City in 1855. Just after the Federal victory at Island No. 10, Capt. John Sebastian and his crew began operating contract troop services

on behalf of the USQMD, which would take over the boat in 1864. Way, *op. cit.*, p. 354.

20. The noted Howard shipyard at Jeffersonville, IN, constructed the *Platte Valley* in 1857. The giant 394-ton side-wheeler was 220 feet long, with a beam of 33 feet and a five-foot draft. Three boilers powered her two side paddle wheels, each of which was 32 feet in diameter with eight-foot buckets. The craft operated independently from St. Louis south and was often sought for USQMD charters. Way, *op. cit.*, p. 374.

21. Way, *op. cit.*, pp. 341, 374, 405; OR, I, 24, 2: 507–508; ORN, I, 25: 173–174, 187, 193; Bragg, *op. cit.*, p. 126; James A. Ramage, *Rebel Raider: The Life of General John Hunt Morgan* (Lexington: The University Press of Kentucky, 1986), p. 158. In his after-action report, Col. Campbell informed Col. Greene of his belief that "our guns are entirely too light to do much damage.... If the enemy's communications are to be embarrassed, we must have heavy guns." OR, I, 24, 2: 508.

22. ORN, I, 25: 170, 183. When in mid–June, the geographical boundaries of the Fifth District were extended into the Mississippi, the number of boats available for the Tennessee occasionally slipped below the six thought minimal.

23. ORN, I, 25: 188–189, 205; Porter, *op. cit.*, pp. 34–335.

24. The 232-ton *Kenwood* was launched at Cincinnati on April 3, 1863; as soon as she was finished and before her owner, H.A. Jones, had her documented, he instead sold her to the USN for $28,000. The formal purchase contract would not, however, be signed until July 15. The new stern-wheeler was powered by two engines and three boilers and was said to have a maximum speed of 7 mph. Following her initial alteration by Joseph Brown, Tinclad No. 14 was sent to Cairo, where she received her armament of two 30-pounder Parrott rifles and four 24-pounder Dahlgren howitzers. She was commissioned on May 24, under Acting Master John Swaney in command. ORN, II, 1: 120; Way, *op. cit.*, p. 270; "*Kenwood*," in U.S. Navy Department, Naval Historical Center, *Dictionary of American Naval Fighting Ships, http://www.history.navy.mil/danfs/k3/kenwood-i.htm* (accessed February 9, 2008); Silverstone, *op. cit.*, p. 173. Swaney joined the Mississippi Squadron as an Acting Ensign in October 1862. He was promoted to the rank of Acting Master in January 1863 and would become an Acting Volunteer Lt. in March 1864. He would be honorably discharged in December 1865. Callahan, *op. cit.*, p. 530.

25. The 390-ton *Silver Moon* was constructed at Cincinnati in 1859 for the Cincinnati & Memphis Packet Co. The big side-wheeler was the last Northern steamboat to freely depart Memphis in 1861 and was chartered for service at Shiloh a year later. She then resumed service between the Queen City and Memphis with occasional trips south beyond the Tennessee city. Way, *op. cit.*, p. 427.

26. ORN, I, 25: 200–201.

27. The 368-ton *Iberville* was built at New Albany, IN, in 1859 for the Bayou Sara Mail Co., Eugene Lanone, president. The side-wheeler was 179 feet long, with a beam of 35 feet and a 6.3-foot draft. Four boilers provided the power for her paddle wheels. Capt. J.J. Brown's craft was captured by Federal forces at New Orleans and placed into service as a USQMD transport. Way, *op. cit.*, p. 220.

28. Another captured Confederate-registered steamer, the 267-ton *Sallie Robinson* was constructed at Cincinnati in 1856. The side-wheeler was 160 feet long, with a 33-foot beam and a 5.5-foot draft. She was owned in part by her master, Capt. Power, who often operated her up the Red and Yazoo rivers. Way, *op. cit.*, p. 415.

29. The 175-ton stern-wheeler *Romeo* was built at Brownsville, PA, in August for Capt. John I. Rhoads. Intended for the Wabash River trade before she was sold to the USN for $17,459 on October 31, 1862, the 154.1-foot craft had a beam of 31.2 feet and a depth of four feet. *Romeo* was outfitted with two boilers and her two engines had a 1-foot

cylinder diameter and a 4-foot stroke. She could steam 5 mph upstream. Arriving at Cairo under the command of her captain Acting Ensign Robert B. Smith, the future Tinclad No. 3 was given an initial battery of six 24-pdr. smoothbore Dahlgren howitzers. She was commissioned on December 11. Way, *op. cit.*, p. 401; ORN, II, 1: 116; Silverstone, *op. cit.*, p. 178; "*Romeo*," in U.S. Navy Department, Naval Historical Center, *Dictionary of American Naval Fighting Ships, http://www.history.navy.mil/danfs/r8/romeo.htm* (accessed February 9, 2008). A former mate, Robert B. Smith was appointed Acting Ensign on October 1, 1862. Promoted Acting Volunteer Lt. in December 1863, Smith reached the highest possible rank in the naval volunteer service on April 29, 1865, when he was named an Acting Volunteer Lt. Cmdr. He was honorably discharged on January 1, 1866. Callahan, *op. cit.*, p. 507; ORN, I, 23: 622.

30. *New York Times,* July 11, 1863. No record of this *Zephyr* has been seen.

31. Lester V. Horwitz, *The Longest Raid of the War: Little Known and Untold Stories of Morgan's Raid Into Kentucky, Indiana, and Ohio* (Cincinnati, OH: Farmcourt Publishing, 1999), p. 2; Basil W. Duke, *A History of Morgan's Cavalry* (Civil War Centennial Series; Bloomington, IN: Indiana University Press, 1960), pp. 410–411; Duke, "The Raid," *The Century Magazine* 41 (January 1891): pp. 404; Cecil Fletcher Holland, *Morgan and His Raiders: A Biography of the Confederate General* (New York: The Macmillan Company, 1942), p. 217; Myron J. Smith, Jr., "Gunboats at Buffington: The U.S. Navy and Morgan's Raid, 1863," *West Virginia History* 44 (Winter 1983): pp. 98–99; Smith, *Le Roy Fitch, op. cit.,* pp. 167–168. A brief summary of "Morgan's Ohio Raid," appears in *Battles and Leaders of the Civil War,* edited by Robert U. Johnson and Clarence C. Buel, 4 vols. (New York: The Century Company, 1884–1887; reprinted, Thomas Yoseloff, 1956), Vol. 3, pp. 634–635. The temporary "Acting" was dropped from Porter's rank, effective July 4, in honor of his part in the Vicksburg success. ORN, I, 26: 316.

32. Watson was appointed Acting Ensign in October 1862 and was honorably discharged in September 1865. Callahan, *op. cit.*, p. 572.

33. ORN, I, 25: 240–246; *Chicago Daily Tribune,* July 10, 1863; Holland, *op. cit.*, pp. 232–233; William E. Wilson, "Thunderbolt of the Confederacy; or, King of Horse Thieves," *Indiana Magazine of History* 54 (June 1958): p. 125; Duke, *A History of Morgan's Cavalry, op. cit.*, pp. 432–434; Taylor, *op. cit.*, p. 37; Arville L. Funk, *The Morgan Raid in Indiana and Ohio (1863)* (Corydon, IN: ALFCO Publications, 1971), p. 5; David L. Taylor, *With Bowie Knives and Pistols: Morgan's Raid in Indiana* (Lexington, IN: Taylor-Made Write, 1993), pp. 36–43; Fred W. Conway, *Corydon: The Forgotten Battle of the Civil War* (New Albany, IN : FBH Publishers, 1991), pp. 8–10; Brandenburg Methodist Church Men's Club, *The Brandenburg Story: With Particular Reference to John Hunt Morgan's Crossing of the Ohio July 8, 1863* (Brandenburg, KY, 1963), pp. 19–20, 23–24; Smith, *Le Roy Fitch, op. cit.*, pp. 181–183.

34. The 375-ton *Magnolia* was constructed for her owner-captain, James H. Prather, at Cincinnati in 1859. The side-wheeler was 200 feet long, with a 31-foot beam and a 5.5-foot draft. She was engaged in the Cincinnati-Maysville trade. Although she survived the Civil War, the steamer was lost (with 35 lives) when her boilers exploded at California, OH, in March 1868. Way, *op. cit.*, p. 303.

35. The 143-ton *Allegheny Belle No. 4* (as she was officially known) was constructed at Pittsburgh in 1859 for the Hanna family of steamboat operators. The vessel was engaged in the Allegheny River oil trade, having a carrying capacity of 500–600 barrels of crude and then served as a U.S. mail packet. On April 16, 1863, she was sold to Com. William J. Kountz, *et al.*, for $21,000. Way, *op. cit.*, p. 14.

36. ORN, I, 25: 246–253, 277; Porter, *op. cit.*, p. 338; Horwitz, *op. cit.*, pp. 40, 55–57, 114–166, 193, 204–205, 208, 210; Ramage, *op. cit.*, p. 173–176; *Cincinnati Daily Commer-*

cial, July 13–20, 1863; OR, I, 23, 1: 747, 760, 766; *New York Herald,* July 23, 1863; Smith, *Le Roy Fitch, op. cit.,* pp. 184–196. Because of state boundaries, Buffington Island is officially part of West Virginia; thus both jurisdictions are able to claim "ownership" of the Battle of Buffington Island, as I learned when I penned my article for *West Virginia History* years ago. The best photographic review of the area and the island remains B. Kevin Bennet and Dave Roth, "The General's Tour: The Battle of Buffington Island," *Blue & Gray Magazine* 15 (April 1998): pp. 60–65.

37. Weighing in at 160 tons, the *Victory* was the smallest of the three Queen City–constructed boats acquired in May. Having been obtained for $25,000—though the contract would not be inked until July 15—she was also the least expensive. The craft, originally to have been documented as the *Banker,* was 157 feet long, with a 30.3-foot beam. Her depth of hold was 4.2 feet and her deeply-laden draft was just five feet. Equipped with two boilers, she also had two engines, each with a 1.1-foot cylinder diameter and a 4.6-foot stroke. The warship wore No. 33 on her pilothouse and carried six 24-pdr. smoothbore Dahlgren howitzers on her gun deck. ORN, II, 1: 232; Way, *op. cit.,* 469; Silverstone, *op. cit.,* p. 169; "Victory," in U.S. Navy Department, Naval Historical Center, *Dictionary of American Naval Fighting Ships, http://www.history.navy.mil/danfs/v3/victory.htm* (accessed February 9, 2008). The *Victory* was commanded by Acting Ensign Frederick Read. Holding that rank since the previous Christmas Eve, he was named an Acting Master on March 5, 1864, and was honorably discharged on September 16, 1865. Callahan, *op. cit.,* p. 453.

38. The *Naumkeag* was one of a group of light-draughts acquired at the beginning of the second quarter for service on the twin rivers of Kentucky and Tennessee. Constructed at Cincinnati early in 1863, the 148-ton stern-wheeler was purchased from her owner, Allen Collier, for $32,000. The new squadron addition was 154.4 feet long, with a beam of 30.5 feet. Her depth of hold was 4.6 foot and deeply laden, her draft was 5.6 feet. *Naumkeag* was powered by two engines, with a cylinder diameter of 14.5 feet and a stroke of 3.6 feet. Her armament comprised two 30-pdr. Parrott rifles in the bow and four 24-pdr. brass howitzers in broadside. The tinclad's conversion at Cincinnati, under the direction of Acting Chief Engineer Samuel Bickerstaff, was completed at the time of her commissioning on April 16. ORN, II, 1: 156; Way, *op. cit.,* p. 340; Silverstone, *op. cit.,* p. 175; "Naumkeag," in U.S. Navy Department, Naval Historical Center, *Dictionary of American Naval Fighting Ships, http://www.history.navy.mil/danfs/n2/naumkeag.htm* (accessed February 9, 2008).

39. Wearing the number 35 on her pilothouse, the 212-ton *Reindeer* was a new Cincinnati-built stern-wheeler purchased into the northern navy for $29,750. Although she would not officially be commissioned until July 25, the boat was available in time for the Morgan chase. *Reindeer* was 154 feet long, with a beam of 32.9 feet. Her depth of hold was five feet and, deeply laden, her draft came to six feet even. She was powered by two engines, each with a 16-inch cylinder diameter and a five-foot stroke; steam came from three boilers. Under the command of Acting Ensign Amasa C. Sears, the craft was the "racehorse" of Fitch's three Cincinnati boats; her official speed was listed at eight knots, two knots faster than the *Moose* and three quicker than the *Victory.* Six 24-pdr. smoothbore Dahlgren howitzers comprised her battery; much later she would also be given a pair of 30-pdr. Parrott rifles. ORN, II, 1: 190; Way, *op. cit.,* p. 390; Silverstone, *op. cit.,* p. 178; "Reindeer," in U.S. Navy Department, Naval Historical Center, *Dictionary of American Naval Fighting Ships, http://www.history.navy.mil/danfs/r4/reindeer-i.htm* (accessed February 9, 2008). Appointed to his rank on January 3, 1863, Sears would become an Acting Master on March 7, 1864, and would be honorably discharged on August 10, 1865. Sears would also command the tinclad *New Era.* Callahan, *op. cit.,* p. 488.

40. The *Moose,* Lt. Cmdr. Fitch's flag boat for the remainder of the war, was a new locally-constructed 189-ton stern-wheel steamboat purchased into the USN on May 20 for $32,000. Briefly documented as *Florence Miller II* before her acquisition, the vessel was 154 feet, 8 inches long and 32 feet, 2 inches wide at the beam and had a 5-foot draught. Her depth of hold was 4.6 feet and, deeply laden, her draft was five feet. The *Moose* was powered by two engines, each with a 14-inch cylinder diameter and a stroke of 4.6 feet, and two boilers. Once outfitted with armor and six 24-pounder smoothbore Dahlgren howitzers, she could reportedly produce a flank speed of six knots in calm waters. ORN, II, 1: 151; Silverstone, *op. cit,* p. 174; Way, *op. cit.,* p. 331; "Moose," in U.S. Navy Department, Naval Historical Center, *Dictionary of American Naval Fighting Ships, http://www.history. navy.mil/danfs/m14/moose-i.htm* (accessed February 9, 2008).

41. The 286-ton stern-wheel dispatch boat Imperial, under Capt. T.J. Oakes, was constructed at Cincinnati earlier in the year. Outfitted with three boilers, she was chosen for her mission due to her speed. Way, *op. cit.,* p. 223.

42. ORN, I, 25: 256, 656; OR, I, 23, 1: 641; 677; OR, I, 51, 1: 207; Boyd B. Stutler, *West Virginia in the Civil War* (Charleston, WV: Education Foundation, Inc., 1963), pp. 232–233; *Cincinnati Daily Gazette,* July 20, 1863; *New York Herald,* July 23, 1863; Duke, *A History of Morgan's Cavalry, op. cit.,* pp. 445–446; Horwitz, *Ibid.;* Smith, *Le Roy Fitch, op. cit.,* pp. 196–200. General's aide, Lt. Weaver, later reported that the Union field commanders were as ignorant of the naval officer's location was Fitch was of theirs. They "supposed he has jealously patrolling the river." Henry C. Weaver, "Morgan's Raid in Kentucky, Indiana, and Ohio, July 1863," in William H. Chamberlain, ed., *Sketches of War History, 1861–1865: Papers Prepared for the Ohio Commandery of the Military Order of the Loyal Legion of the United States,* 6 vols. (Cincinnati, OH: R. Clarke & Co., 1890–1908), Vol. 5, p. 304.

43. ORN, I, 25: 318; Duke, *A History of Morgan's Cavalry, op. cit.,* pp. 450–452; Weaver, "Morgan's Raid in Kentucky, Indiana, and Ohio, July 1863, *Ibid.;* Horwitz, *op. cit.,* pp. 215, 420; *Cincinnati Daily Gazette,* July 20, 1863; *Chicago Daily Tribune,* July 20, 23, 1863; *New York Herald,* July 23, 1863. Captain Oakes of the *Imperial* later wrote of the battle to a colleague; his July 21 letter was reprinted in Vol. 4 of Moore, Frank, ed. *The Rebellion Record: A Diary of American Events,* 11 vols. (New York: G.P. Putnam and D. Van Nostrand, 1861–1868), pp. 391–392. A concise review of the entire episode is Mark F. Jenkins's "Operations of the Mississippi Squadron During Morgan's Raid," *Ironclads and Blockade Runners of the American Civil War Homepage, www.wideopenwest.com/~jenkins/ironclads/buffingt.htm* (November 11, 2005) which has appeared at several URLs since it was first published in 1999.

44. OR, I, 23, 1: 14, 640–645, 656–657, 660–662, 667–668, 774, 776–777, 781, 788; OR, I, 30, 2: 547–552; OR, I, 51, 1: 207; ORN, I, 25: 256–257, 315; Horwitz, op cit., pp. 195–248; Keller, *op. cit.,* pp. 162–178; Smith, *Le Roy Fitch, op. cit.,* pp. 200–205; Oakes Letter, *Ibid.; Cincinnati Daily Gazette,* July 20, 1863; *New York Herald,* July 23, 1863; *Indianapolis Journal,* July 15, 1863; *Louisville Daily Journal,* July 21, 27, 1863; *Nashville Daily Union,* July 30, 1863; Ramage, *op. cit.,* p. 178–179, 183; Duke, *A History of Morgan's Cavalry, op. cit.,* pp. 453–454, 464; Andrew R. L. Cayton, *Ohio: The History of a People* (Columbus: The Ohio State University Press, 2002), p. 130; Bern Anderson, *By Sea and By River: The Naval History of the Civil War* (New York: Knopf, 1962), p. 155.

45. Finished for Capt. John L. Rhoads, at Brownsville, PA, on December 10, 1862, Capt. J.H. Lightner's 226-ton stern-wheeler *Duchess* completed her first and only packet run from Pittsburgh to Cincinnati on December 22. There she was purchased into the USN as tinclad No. 5, the *Petrel,* for $26,000 and, after modifications, steamed up to Cairo, where she received her battery of eight 24-pounder smoothbore Dahlgren howitzers. Placed into commission under Act-

ing Volunteer Lt. John Pearce, she was dispatched downriver to join those units of the main squadron remaining above Vicksburg following the passage of the city's guns by Rear Adm. Porter in mid–April. Because she was later lost, few details concerning the vessel remain. ORN, II, 1: 176; Way, *op. cit.,* pp. 133, 369; Silverstone, *op. cit.,* p. 176; "Petrel," in U.S. Navy Department, Naval Historical Center, *Dictionary of American Naval Fighting Ships, http://www.history.navy.mil/danfs/p5/petrel-ii.htm* (accessed February 9, 2008). By the time of the Selfridge expedition, Peace had moved over to command the *Manitou* and was succeeded in command of the *Petrel* by Acting Master Charles S. Kendrick. Pearce was appointed an Acting Master on October 1, 1862, and an Acting Volunteer Lt. on April 16; he would be honorably discharged on December 19, 1865. Named an Acting Master on October 1, 1862, the fatally ill Kendrick died on August 13, 1863. ORN, I, 25: 264, 369; Callahan, *op. cit.,* pp. 310, 426.

46. The 286-ton *James Thompson* was launched by Howard at Jeffersonville, IN, on November 1, 1862, she entered service with the Jeffersonville Ferry Company before the end of the year. Officially purchased by the USN from H. Marbury *et al.* for $35,000 on April 16, 1863, the future Tinclad No. 13 was actually taken in hand for modification somewhat earlier; she would have more name changes than any other tinclad. The side-wheeler was 150 feet long, with a beam of 37 feet. Her draft was 20 inches forward and 26 inches aft. She was powered by two direct engines and received power from two boilers, with four flues in each. Once her conversion was completed, the craft received an initial armament, later changed, of two 8-inch 55 cwt. smoothbore cannon forward and four 80-inch 63 cwt. smoothbores in broadside. She was renamed *Manitou* on March 23, 1863, and *Fort Hindman* on November 8, 1863. Way, *op. cit.,* 243, 170, 306; ORN, II, 1: 86; Silverstone, *op. cit.,* p. 164; "Fort Hindman," in U.S. Navy Department, Naval Historical Center, *Dictionary of American Naval Fighting Ships, http://www.history.navy.mil/danfs/f4/fort_hindman.htm* (accessed February 9, 2008). The *Manitou* was renamed *Fort Hindman* on November 5, 1863. ORN, I, 25: 533. The *Manitou's* first commander was Lt. Cmdr. Selfridge, but he was later succeeded by Acting Volunteer Lt. John Pearce of the *Petrel.*

47. This 281-ton side-wheeler was originally constructed at Louisville, KY. in 1850 and served on the New Orleans trade until early in the Civil War. In 1861, the 171-foot-long craft, whose name has been spelled differently in various accounts, was taken to Shreveport to serve Confederate interests. Way, *op. cit.,* p. 130.

48. No vessel by the name of *Nelson* was recorded by either Lytle or Way.

49. Constructed at New Albany, IN, in early 1861, the *Louisville* was powered by five boilers. Her machinery, however, was salvaged from another boat. The giant 572-ton packet entered the Louisville-New Orleans trade on February 9, but soon thereafter found herself employed as a Confederate transport. Way, *op. cit.,* p. 296.

50. This 139-ton packet was built at Pittsburgh, PA, in 1859 for Capt. James J. Smith of New Orleans. The following year, the *Elmira* was sold to Nathaniel and William Offutt of Washington, LA, who, a year later, placed her into service on behalf of the Confederacy, Capt. B.P. Stinson commanding. Way, *op. cit.,* p. 147.

51. ORN, I, 25: 264–271; *Chicago Daily Tribune,* November 22, 1863; Thomas O. Selfridge, *Memoirs of Thomas O. Selfridge, Jr., Rear Admiral, U.S.N.* (New York: Knickerbocker Press, 1924; reprinted, Columbia, University of South Carolina Press, 1987), pp. 84–86; Porter, *Naval History of the Civil War,* pp. 332–333; .Alfred T. Mahan, *The Gulf and Inland Waters,* Vol. 3 of the *Navy in the Civil War* (New York: Scribner's, 1883), pp. 177–178; Grant to Porter, July 19, 1863, *David Dixon Porter Papers,* Missouri Historical Society, St. Louis (here after cited as DDPC).

52. Built at Cincinnati in 1861, the *Hambleton* was a 154-ton side-wheel packet. Way, *op. cit.,* p. 402.

53. *New York Herald,* August 10, 1863; *Memphis Daily Bulletin,* August 11, 1863.

54. OR, I, 22, 1: 472–476, 511; *St. Louis Daily Missouri Democrat,* quoted in the *Chicago Daily Tribune,* August 27, 1863; Thomas A. DeBlack, *With Fire and Sword: Arkansas, 1861–1874* (Histories of Arkansas; Fayetteville, AR: University of Arkansas Press, 2003), p. 93; Albert G. Castel, *General Sterling Price and the Civil War in the West* (Baton Rouge, LA: Louisiana State University Press, 1968), pp. 152–155.

55. Little is known about the *Kaskaskia,* a 49-ton side-wheeler built at Cincinnati in 1859 and initially home-ported at Evansville, IN. Following her Federal capture, she returned to the Ohio River trade, where she was lost in the Grand Chain in February 1864. Way, *op. cit.,* p. 263.

56. The *Tom Sugg* was also a small side-wheeler. The 62-ton vessel was built at Cincinnati in 1860. Way, *op. cit.,* p. 458.

57. OR, I, 22, 1: 511–512; ORN, I, 25: 352–363, 367; *St. Louis Daily Missouri Democrat,* quoted in the *Chicago Daily Tribune,* August 27, 1863; *Chicago Daily Tribune,* September 19, 1863; Castel, *op. cit.,* pp. 154, 158; DeBlack, *op. cit.,* pp. 92–98. The entire Little Rock campaign is covered in Leo E. Huff, "The Union Expedition Against Little Rock, August–September 1863," *Arkansas Historical Quarterly* 22 (Fall 1963): pp. 223–237.

58. ORN, I, 25: 404–412, 419; Chicago *Daily Tribune,* November 22, 1863; David Knapp, Jr., "The Rodney Church Incident," *Journal of Mississippi History* 32 (July 1970): pp. 245–249; Bruce D. Liddell, "U.S.S. *Rattler* at Rodney, Sunday, September 13, 1863," *Jefferson County MSGenWeb Project homepage, http://jeffersoncountyms.org/USSRattler.htm* (accessed August 18, 2008); "Ghost Town of Rodney, Mississippi: The 'Almost' Capital of Mississippi," *Southpoint Travel Guide http://www.southpoint.com/states/ms/rodney.htm* (September 12, 2008). Fentress holds the unique Civil War record of being the only USN ship's captain captured by Confederate cavalry. A new round of shore visit rules was imposed after this fiasco; officers and men from gunboats at Donaldsonville, Baton Rouge, Bayou Sara, the mouth of the Red River, Natchez, Skipwith's Landing, Carthage, and Memphis were the only ones allowed off their boats except on raids.

59. *Memphis Daily Bulletin,* September 22, 1863.

60. Although her name was shortened from the original, *Key West No. 3,* the 207-ton stern-wheel Tinclad No. 32 was ideally suited to become a gunboat. Purchased into the USN at Cairo on April 16, 1863, her original owners, Capt. William S. Evans and associates, received for her the tidy sum of $33,800. Modified at Mound City, the *Key West* was 156 feet long, with a beam of 32 feet and a hold depth of 4.6 feet. Acting Master King was named her captain and he supervised the installation of her main armament of six 24-pounder smooth bore Dahlgren howitzers on April 11. Five days later, the vessel was commissioned and assigned to Lt. Cmdr. Phelps's Tennessee River division. ORN, II, 1: 121; Way, *op. cit.,* p. 271; Silverstone, *op. cit.,* p. 173; "Key West," in U.S. Navy Department, Naval Historical Center, *Dictionary of American Naval Fighting Ships, http://www.history.navy.mil/danfs/k3/key_west-i.htm* (accessed February 9, 2008). Acting Master King was named an Acting Volunteer Lt. in October 1863. Although court-martialed for the November 1864 Johnsonville fiasco (q.v.), he was acquitted and honorably discharged in July 1867. Callahan, *op. cit.,* p. 314.

61. ORN, I, 25: 466–475; Slagle, *op. cit.,* pp. 338–341; David Dixon Porter, *Incidents and Anecdotes of the Civil War* (New York: D. Appleton and Co., 1885; reprinted, Harrisburg, PA: The Archive Society, 1997), pp. 210–211; Henry R. and Symmes E. Browne, *From the Fresh Water Navy, 1861–1864: Letters of Acting Master's Mate Henry R. Browne and Acting Ensign Symmes E. Browne,* edited by John D. Milligan (Naval Letters Series, Vol. 3; Annapolis, MD: Naval Institute Press, 1970), p. 225.

62. Named for the Native American wife of John Dubuque, the 204-ton side-wheeler was constructed at

Cincinnati in 1857 and then home-ported at the Iowa city. She was purchased by the USN on June 13, 1863 for $22,000 and taken to Mound City for modifications. *Peosta* was 151.2 feet long, with a beam of 34.3 feet and a deeply laden draft of just six inches. Her two engines, powered by two boilers, gave her a maximum speed of 5 mph. Tinclad No. 36 was commissioned at Cairo on October 2, Acting Volunteer Lt. Thomas E. Smith. Her armament of three 30-pounder Parrott rifles, three 32-pounder Navy smoothbore cannon, six 24-pounder smoothbore Dahlgren howitzers, and two heavy smoothbore 12-pounder Dahlgren howitzers was mounted six days later. The light-draught was assigned to the Tennessee River, where she would remain for the rest of the war. ORN, II, 1: 174–175; Way, *op. cit.*, p. 367; Silverstone, *op. cit.*, p. 168; "*Peosta*," in U.S. Navy Department, Naval Historical Center, *Dictionary of American Naval Fighting Ships, http://www.history.navy.mil/danfs/p4/peosta.htm* (accessed February 9, 2008). Appointed Acting Master in October 1861, Smith became an Acting Volunteer Lt. in January 1863. He was honorably discharged in February 1869. Callahan, *op. cit.*, p. 508.

63. "A miserable little ferry boat," in the words of Acting Ensign Symmes Brown, the center-wheel *St. Charles* was built at St. Louis in 1862 and christened as *Fanny*. With a length of 120 feet and a 34-foot beam, the craft, with a depth of 3.7 feet, was powered by two engines and two boilers and was said to have a maximum upstream speed of 4 mph. She was purchased for the USN from J. Van Vortwick at Chicago on April 9, 1863, for $8,000 and was sent for conversion from St. Joseph, MO, to Cairo four days later. Her name was changed to *Paw Paw* on May 12 and she was designated tinclad No. 31 on June 19. A battery of two 30-pounder Parrott rifles and six 24-pounder smoothbore Dahlgren howitzers was mounted on July 24 and she was commissioned on July 25, Acting Master Augustus F. Thompson commanding. Way, *op. cit.*, 365; Silverstone, *op. cit.*, p. 180; ORN, II, 1: 172; "*Paw Paw*," in U.S. Navy Department, Naval Historical Center, *Dictionary of American Naval Fighting Ships, http://www.history.navy.mil/danfs/p3/paw_paw.htm* (accessed February 9, 2008); Brown, *op. cit.*, p 211. Thompson had previously commanded the tinclad *Silver Cloud*.

64. Named for her owner Ebenezer Blackstone, the 108-ton side-wheeler *Ebenezer* was built at Brownsville, PA. Like the *Paw Paw*, she was serving as a ferry at St. Joseph, MO, when purchased into the USN for $11,000 from Blackstone on June 19. With a length of 114 feet and a beam of 33 feet, the craft had a 3.9-foot hold depth. She was powered by two engines and at least two boilers. Also taken to Cairo for conversion, the modification of the new Tinclad No. 29 was very rapid and she mounted her battery of two 30-pounder Parrott rifles, four 24-pounder smoothbore Dahlgren howitzers, and two rifled 12-pounder Wiard steel guns on June 17. Commissioned on June 21, her first captain was Acting Master Alfred Phelps, Jr., brother of Lt. Cmdr. S. Ledyard Phelps. Holding his rank only since April, the younger Phelps had served in the *Conestoga* with his commissioned sibling for almost two years. He left the new tinclad when she reached Memphis on June 30 and was succeeded by Acting Master Jason Goudy. With a crew of 77 officers and men, the *Tawah* departed for the elder Phelps's Tennessee River district next day. Alfred Phelps would resign in February 1864, much to his brother's displeasure. Way, *op. cit.*, pp. 138, 445; ORN, II, 1: 220; Silverstone, *op. cit.*, p. 169; ; "*Tawah*," in U.S. Navy Department, Naval Historical Center, *Dictionary of American Naval Fighting Ships, http://www.history.navy.mil/danfs/t3/tawah.htm* (accessed February 9, 2008); Callahan, *op. cit.*, p. 433; Slagle, *op. cit.*, p. 354; James A. Dickinson, Diary (photocopy), June 17, 21, 30, July 1, 5, 1863, *James A. Dickinson Papers*, Rutherford B. Hayes Presidential Center, Fremont (cited hereafter as *Dickinson Diary*, with date). The *Tawah* would be destroyed at Johnsonville, TN, in November 1864.

65. ORN, I, 25: 477–496, 614–615; *Dickinson Diary*, November 18–27, 1863; *Nashville Daily Press*, November 3,

7, 1863; Slagle, *op. cit.*, pp. 338–341; Walter T. Durham, *Reluctant Partners: Nashville and the Union—July 1, 1863, to June 30, 1865* (Nashville: The Tennessee Historical Society, 1987), p. 16; Way, *op. cit.*, p. 249.

66. Constructed at Freedom, PA, in 1862, the *Emma No. 2*, now a veteran of the Memphis–White River trade, was 156.7 feet long, with a beam of 33.7 feet and a five-foot draft. Way, *op. cit.*, p. 149.

67. Built at Shousetown, PA in 1854, the *Adriatic* was one of the more unusual craft then operating on the rivers. With a length of 200 feet, a 45-foot beam, and a 6.5-foot draft, she was propelled by two stern wheels, each handled by two engines. Only four other four-engine stern-wheelers were constructed. Way, *op. cit.*, p. 6.

68. The small stern-wheeler *Allen Collier* was built at Cincinnati in 1860 for the Cincinnati-Kanawha river trade. She was not the same vessel as the *Allen Collier* constructed by John Swasey & Co. in the fall of 1864, which became the tinclad *Collier*. Way, *op. cit.*, p. 14.

69. ORN, I, 26: 705; *Chicago Daily Tribune*, November 4, 1863; Bragg, *op. cit.*, p. 110.

70. The *Neosho* was one of two stern-wheel light-draught river monitors completed by James B. Eads earlier in the year. The 523-ton craft featured a single turret forward that, like the one aboard the famous type namesake *Monitor*, protected a pair of 11-inch Dahlgren smoothbores. Unlike the Ericsson vessel, the boat's profile was broken aft by her covered wheelbox. Silverstone, *op. cit.*, p. 149.

71. Peoria, Illinois-born steamboatman and Western Flotilla volunteer Cyrenius Dominy (1829–1907) was the only *Mound City* officer to escape the June 17, 1862, White River disaster unhurt, though he was shaken. After some relief, he was given command of the tinclad *Signal*. Callahan, *op. cit.*, p. 166.

72. USNA 1856 graduate Francis M. ("Frank") Ramsay (1835–1914) served afloat and ashore in the east, including the Africa Squadron, until 1862; upon his promotion, he was given the new ironclad *Choctaw*, which he skippered up the Yazoo and at Milliken's Bend in May–June. He received his district after the fall of Vicksburg, but would depart to the North Atlantic Blockading Squadron in the fall. He participated in the capture of Fort Fisher and, after the war, continued a long career leading to his promotion to the rank of Rear Admiral in 1894. Lewis B. Hamersly, *The Records of Living Officers of the U.S. Navy and Marine Corps* (Philadelphia, PA: J.B. Lippincott & Co., 1870), p, 171; Callahan, *op. cit.*, p. 451; William B. Cogar, *Dictionary of Admirals of the U.S. Navy*, 2 vols. (Annapolis, MD: Naval Institute Press, 1989), Vol. 1, 139–140.

73. A former river steamer built in September 1862, the 1,004-ton *Choctaw* was converted into a giant 260-foot-long ironclad according to plans drawn by Acting Rear Adm. Porter's brother, Lt. Cmdr. William D. Porter. When commissioned in late March 1863, it was found that her armor and armament (one 100-pounder rifle, one nine-inch smoothbore, two 30-pounder Parrott rifles, and two 24-pounder smoothbore Dahlgren howitzers) were too heavy. Nevertheless, she was a welcome reinforcement for the Mississippi Squadron. Silverstone, *op. cit.*, p. 157.

74. ORN, I, 25: 570–573, 614–615. Low water presented a significant logistical concern seldom mentioned in river war histories. On November 20, the *Wheeling Daily Register* reported that bids were being accepted at Cairo for half a million bushels of coal for the Mississippi Squadron. The newspaper opined that, unless the river rose soon, the government would not be able to retrieve much Appalachian coal and where it was "to come from is more than we can clearly see."

75. Constructed at New Albany, IN, in 1859, the 211-ton side-wheeler *Black Hawk* was active on the upper rivers in the early 1860s. She was confiscated at Port Hudson, LA, during November. Way, *op. cit.*, p. 54.

76. ORN, I, 25: 573–575.

77. The 214-foot-long *Welcome*, having spurned the op-

portunity in this case to steam in a convoy, survived only another year before she was lost in a July 1864 St. Louis fire. Way, *op. cit.,* p. 483.

78. The stern-wheeler *Florence* was built at Elizabeth, PA, in late 1861. With a displacement of 196 tons, the steamer was 159 feet long, with a beam of 32.1 feet and a 4.6-foot draft. Equipped with two boilers and two engines, she was said to be able to make 4 mph upstream. When completed, she was placed on the Pittsburgh to St. Louis trade in March 1862. In June, she was sold by her original owners to Capt. Will Kyle and associates, who sold her to the USN on December 17 for $21,500. When she was taken over, her name was changed to *Curlew* and she was later assigned the No. 12. Toward the end of her two-month conversion, she was armed with eight 24-pounder Dahlgren boat howitzers. The *Curlew* was commissioned at Cairo on February 16, 1863, Acting Master George Hentig in command. ORN, II, 1: 69; Way, *op. cit.,* pp. 116, 167; Silverstone, *op. cit.,* p. 171; "*Curlew*" in U.S. Navy Department, Naval Historical Center, *Dictionary of American Naval Fighting Ships, http://www.histo ry.navy.mil/danfs/c16/curlew-i.htm* (accessed February 9, 2008). Named to his rank on October 1, 1862, Hentig was dismissed the following June. Acting Ensign H.B. O'Neill, who would resign in March 1865, was the boat's commander in November–December. Callahan, *op. cit.,* pp. 262, 415.

79. Browne, *op. cit.,* p. 235; ORN, I, 25: 589, 628.

80. Having served the St. Louis–New Orleans route prior to the war, the side-wheeler *Von Phul* was constructed at Paducah in 1860. The packet was 249 feet long, with a beam of 39 feet and a 7.2-foot draft. Although she survived her wartime duty as a troop transport, the vessel caught fire while passing near Donaldsonville, LA, in November 1866 and was destroyed. Way, *op. cit.,* p. 213.

81. The 684-ton *Atlantic* was built for J.B. Ford of New Albany at the Jeffersonville yards in 1859. The giant side-wheeler was 275 feet long, with a 39-foot beam and a 6.8-foot draft. Five boilers provided the steam required to drive her huge paddle wheels. A veteran of the Louisville–New Orleans prewar service, she served as a Federal troop transport for much of the war. Way, *op. cit.,* p. 32.

82. Built for Capt. Redmund J. Grace, the 211-ton *Brazil* was constructed at McKeesport, PA, in 1854. The stern-wheeler was 150 feet long, with a beam of 31 feet and a four-foot draft. Her stern wheel received steam via two engines and three boilers. Prior to the war, the craft served the Upper Mississippi and Illinois Rivers. Independent and USQMD contracts were operated during the war. Way, *op. cit.,* p. 60.

83. *Nashville Daily Union,* December 15, 1863; ORN, I, 25: 624–626, 636; *Dickinson Diary,* December 5, 1863; Browne, *op. cit.,* p. 239; Smith, *Le Roy Fitch, op. cit.,* p. 234.

84. ORN, I, 25: 657–659; Smith, *Le Roy Fitch, op. cit.,* p. 238; the Barry quote appears in Michael J. Bennett, *Union Jacks: Yankee Sailors in the Civil War* (Chapel Hill, NC: University of North Carolina Press, 2004), p. 79.

85. The 129-ton *Silver Lake No. 2* was constructed at Wellsville, OH, in early 1861 and was almost immediately sold to the USQMD. After the "liberation" of Nashville, she was sent to that city, where she was converted into an *ersatz* gunboat. Outfitted with field cannon (usually howitzers similar to those aboard the USN tinclads), she served on the Cumberland between Carthage and Clarksville until sold out of service in October 1865. Way, *op. cit.,* p. 426.

86. ORN, I, 25: 647–651; OR, I, 31, 1: 644–645; Byrd Douglas, *Steamboatin' on the Cumberland* (Nashville, TN: Tennessee Book Company, 1961), p. 149; Ulysses S. Grant, *The Papers of Ulysses S. Grant,* Vol. 9: *July 7–December 31, 1863,* edited by John Y. Simon, 24 vols. to date (Edwardsville, IL: Southern Illinois University Press, 1967), p. 549; John W. Donn, "War Record of J.W. Donn, Including Reminiscences of Frederick W. Dorr, July 1861 to June 1865," NOAA History Homepage, *http://www.history.noaa.gov/stories_tales/donn.html* (accessed April 4, 2005); Smith, *Le Roy*

Fitch, *op. cit.,* pp. 237–238; *Dickinson Diary,* December 31, 1863.

Chapter 7

1. Ulysses S. Grant, *Personal Memoirs of U.S. Grant: A Modern Abridgment* (New York: Premier Books, 1962), pp. 264–265; OR, I, 32, 2: 99–101; James A. Dickinson, *Diary* (photocopy), January 1–5,1864, *James A. Dickinson Papers,* Rutherford B. Hayes Presidential Center, Fremont (cited hereafter as Dickinson Diary, with date); Herbert Saunders, "The Civil War Letters of Herbert Saunders," edited by Ronald K. Huch, *Register of the Kentucky Historical Society* 69 (January 1971): p. 18; William R. Morris, "The Tennessee River Voyages of the U.S.S. *Peosta," Morris homepage, http://www.cen turyinter.net/nacent/bs/peosta.htm* (accessed March 3, 1997); Myron J. Smith Jr., *Le Roy Fitch: The Civil War Career of a Union River Gunboat Commander* (Jefferson, N.C.: McFarland, 2007), pp. 239–240. On January 11, Brig. Gen. Eleazer Paine, headquartered at Gallatin and charged with guarding the Louisville and Nashville railroad from Nashville to Kentucky, made an aggressive proposal to Governor Andrew Johnson. It was suggested, that his infantry and Col. William B. Stokes's 5th Tennessee Cavalry (U.S.) be allowed to accompany the *Newsboy* and the next USN convoy to clear out the guerrillas all the way up the Cumberland to Burkesville. The sortie was sanctioned. Walter T. Durham, *Reluctant Partners: Nashville and the Union—July 1, 1863, to June 30, 1865* (Nashville: The Tennessee Historical Society, 1987), p. 83.

2. Acquired by the USQMD in 1862 for use as an *ersatz* Cumberland River gunboat between Nashville and Clarksville, the 53-ton stern-wheeler *Newsboy* was constructed at Brownsville, PA, early in the year. Her armament while in government service included several field pieces, including at least one 12-pounder. Frederick Way Jr., comp., *Way's Packet Directory, 1848–1994,* 2nd ed. (Athens, OH: Ohio University Press, 1994), p. 347.

3. ORN, I, XXV: 714, 716–717, 720–721; Smith, *Ibid.,* pp. 240–241; Logbooks of the U.S.S. *Moose,* June 15, 1863–August 10, 1865, Records of the Bureau of Navigation, Record Group 19, U.S. National Archives, Washington, D.C., January 1–January 31, 1864 (cited hereafter as Logbook of the U.S.S. *Moose,* with date).

4. The 250-foot-long side-wheeler *Belle Creole* would serve as a troop transport during the Red River expedition. Way, *op. cit.,* pp. 41, 123.

5. The *Gilburn* is not listed in the standard steamboat directories and may have been a local ferry.

6. The 150-ton stern-wheeler *Freestone* was constructed for Garrett & Co. at Murraysville, VA, in 1858. Prewar, she ran on the Upper Ohio and Kanawha Rivers. Numerous USQMD contracts were accepted which took her up and down the Mississippi and its tributaries during the conflict. Way, *op. cit.,* pp. 173–174.

7. Constructed at Freedom, PA, in 1863, the 220-ton stern-wheeler *Lillie Martin* was 159 feet long, with a beam of 33 feet and a four-foot draft. Way, *op. cit.,* p. 287.

8. The four-year-old 163-ton *Shreveport,* with a 155.6-foot-long deck, was a side-wheeler built at Louisville. Way, *op. cit.,* p. 424.

9. ORN, I, 25: 678, 737; *Chicago Daily Tribune,* January 21, 29, 1864; *North American and United States Gazette,* February 10, 1864; *Chicago Daily Tribune,* March 2, 1864.

10. Later designated *Prairie Bird* or Tinclad No. 11, the 171-ton stern-wheeler *Mary Miller* was constructed by Joel Wall at Millersport, OH, and completed at Pittsburgh, PA, in April 1862. The new vessel was 159.10 feet long, with a beam of 29.3 feet and a depth of hold of 4.2 feet. Her two boilers sent sufficient power to her two engines to permit a maximum up stream speed of 6 mph. On December 19, the Ohio River packet was sold to the USN at Cincinnati for

$17,500 and she was sent to Joseph Brown's yards for modification. Completed but without armament, the *Prairie Bird* steamed to Cairo, where, at the beginning of February 1863, she received a battery of eight 24-pounder brass Dahlgren smoothbore howitzers and one 12-pdr. rifled howitzer. Within days, the new boat, under command of Acting Master J.C. Moore, was en route down the Mississippi. Way, *op. cit.,* pp. 314, 376; Paul H. Silverstone, *Warships of the Civil War Navies* (Annapolis, Md.: Naval Institute Press, 1989), p.176; ORN, II, I: 184; "*Prairie Bird*," in U.S. Navy Department, Naval Historical Center, *Dictionary of American Naval Fighting Ships, http://www.history.navy.mil/danfs/p10/prairie_bird.htm* (accessed February 9, 2008). Though noted in the index of ORN, 25, Master Moore is not listed in the standard biographical reference, Edward W. Callahan, *List of Officers of the Navy of the United States and of the Marine Corps, from 1775 to 1900, Comprising a Complete Register of All Present and Former Commissioned, Warranted, and Appointed Officers of the United States Navy, and of the Marine Corps, Regular and Volunteer. Compiled from the Official Records of the Navy Department* (New York: L.R. Hamersly & Co., 1901; reprinted, New York: Haskell House, 1969). On the other hand, Illinois-born Lt. Cmdr. Owen was promoted to the rank of Cmdr. in 1866. He retired a decade later and died in 1877. Lewis R. Hamersly, *The Records of Living Officers of the U.S. Navy and Marine Corps, Compiled from Official Sources* (Rev. ed.; Philadelphia, PA: J.B. Lippincott, 1870), p 165.

11. ORN, I, 25: 715, 722, 725–726; Philip L. Bolte, "Up the Yazoo River: A Riverine Diversion," *Periodical: Journal of America's Military Past,* XXII (1995), 18; Jim Huffstodt, *Hard Dying Men* (Bowie, MD: Heritage Books, 1991), pp. 196–197; Huffstodt, "River of Death," *Lincoln Herald* 84 (1982): pp. 70–71.

12. ORN, I, 25: 763–764; OR, I, 32, 1: 387–389; OR, I, 32, 2: 583; Bolte, *op. cit.,* pp. 20–23; Huffstodt, *Hard Dying Men, op. cit.,* pp. 198–202; Huffstodt, "River of Death," *op. cit.,* 71–76.

13. ORN, I, 25: 730, 745; OR, I, 32, 1: 162; OR, I, 32, 2: 22, 30, 32, 100, 103, 365–366; *Dickinson Diary,* February 3–6, 1864; *Evansville Daily Journal,* January 11–13, 1864; *Nashville Daily Union,* February 10, 1864; *Nashville Dispatch,* February 24, 27, 1864. Ulysses S. Grant, *The Papers of Ulysses S. Grant,* Vol. 10: *January 1–May 31, 1864,* edited by John Y. Simon, 24 vols. to date (Edwardsville, IL: Southern Illinois University Press, 1967), p. 104, 536; Smith, *Le Roy Fitch, op. cit.,* pp. 241, 247–248; Richard P. Gildrie, "Guerrilla Warfare in the Lower Cumberland River Valley, 1862–1865," *Tennessee Historical Quarterly* 49 (Fall 1990): p. 170. Brig. Gen. Paine's punitive expedition also got off into the overlooking steep terrain; it would eventually kill about 33 Rebels and capture 63, but most of the butternut irregulars chose to hide in the hills rather than fight.

14. ORN, I, 25: 755–756, 763–764; OR, I, 32, 1: 322,349; Bolte, *op. cit.,* pp. 23–24; Huffstodt, *Hard Dying Men, op. cit.,* p. 198–202; Huffstodt, "River of Death," *op. cit.,* 76–78.

15. Completed at Pittsburgh, PA, in 1858, the *Ida May* was 157 feet in length, with a 32-foot beam and a 4.8-foot draft. She provided packet service between Pittsburgh and Cincinnati until sold to the government in December 1862. Way, *op. cit.,* pp. 220–221.

16. ORN, I, 25: 748–751; OR, I, 32, 1: 157–159; *Chicago Daily Tribune,* March 2, 1864; Henry R. and Symmes E. Browne, *From the Fresh Water Navy, 1861–1864: Letters of Acting Master's Mate Henry R. Browne and Acting Ensign Symmes E. Browne,* edited by John D. Milligan (Naval Letters Series, Vol. 3; Annapolis, MD: Naval Institute Press, 1970), pp. 244–248; *North American and United States Gazette,* February 12, 1864. Former skipper of the tinclad *Romeo,* John V. Johnston was shipped at this rank in August 1862; he would resign on June 23. Callahan, *op. cit.,* p. 300, ORN, I, 25: 562.

17. OR, I, 26, 1: 384, 559, 653, 673; ORN, I, 25: 734–

736, 770–773; U. S. Congress, Joint Committee on the Conduct of the War, *Report: Red River* (38th Cong., 2nd sess.; Washington, D.C.: GPO, 1864; reprinted, Greenwood Press, 1971), p. 5, cited hereafter as *Joint Committee,* with page number in Arabic; Gary D. Joiner, *Through the Howling Wilderness: The 1864 Red River Campaign and Union Failure in the West* (Knoxville, TN: University of Tennessee Press, 2006), p. 52; Thomas O. Selfridge, *Memoirs of Thomas O. Selfridge, Jr., Rear Admiral, U.S.N.* (New York: Knickerbocker Press, 1924; reprinted, Columbia, University of South Carolina Press, 1987), pp. 87–88; William Riley Brooksher, *War Along the Bayous: The 1864 Red River Campaign in Louisiana* (Washington, D.C.: Brassey's, 1998), pp. xi–xii, 1–24; Myron J. Smith, Jr., *The Timberclads in the Civil War: The Lexington, Conestoga and Tyler on the Western Rivers* (Jefferson, N.C.: McFarland, 2008), p. 432.

18. Joiner, *op. cit.,* pp. 24–26, 52–53; ORN, I, 25: 787–788; ORN, I, 26: 747–748, 783, 788; OR, I, 34, 1: 155–160; *New York Times,* March 15, 17, 1864; *Philadelphia Inquirer,* March 15, 1864; *Chicago Daily Tribune,* March 15, 1864; Smith, *The Timberclads in the Civil War, op. cit.,* pp. 433–440; Silverstone, *op. cit.,* p. 149; "Surgeon Mixer's Account, March 2, 1864," in Frank Moore, ed., *The Rebellion Record: A Diary of American Events,* 12 vols. (New York: G.P. Putnam, 1861–1863; D. Van Nostrand, 1864–1868; reprinted, Arno, 1977), Vol. 8, 445–446; Hiram H. Martin, "Service Afield and Afloat: A Reminiscence of the Civil War, Edited by Guy R. Everson," *Indiana Magazine of History* 89 (March 1993): pp. 52–53; David Dixon Porter, *Naval History of the Civil War* (New York: Sherman Publishing Company, 1886; reprinted, Secaucus, N.J.: Castle Books, 1984), p. 556; Richard Taylor, *Destruction and Reconstruction: Personal Experiences of the Late War* (New York: D. Appleton and Company, 1879), pp. 153–154; Alwyn Barr, *Polignac's Texas Brigade,* 2nd ed. (College Station, TX: Texas A&M University Press, 1998), pp. 1–30; Mark M. Boatner III, *The Civil War Dictionary* (New York: David McKay, 1959), p. 657. Forgetting about leap year, Surgeon Henry M. Mixer dated his account of Ramsay's reconnaissance off by one day. The *Conestoga* was lost when accidentally rammed by the *General Price* on March 10. *New York Times,* March 17, 1864.

19. ORN, I, 26: 14–17; OR, I, 32, 1: 320–330; Bolte, *op. cit.,* pp. 24–28; *Memphis Daily Bulletin,* March 12, 1864; *New York Times,* March 17, 1864; Huffstodt, *Hard Dying Men, op. cit.,* pp. 206–212. McElroy, who joined the flotilla from New Jersey as a gunner in September 1861, was captured with the *Petrel* in April and remained a POW until October. The loss of the tinclad did not damage his naval career and he was returned to duty. On August 2, 1865, squadron commander, Acting Rear Adm. Samuel P. Lee, reviewed his volunteer officers in order to determine which would be kept on. McElroy was determined to be "a good officer." The former commander of the *Petrel* was honorably discharged in March 1868. His petition for a pension 40 years later was denied; however, his descendant, Verna McElroy Werlock, published a 114-page biography, *The Civil War Record of Thomas McElroy, Acting Master, United States Navy, 1861–1868* (Woodbridge, NJ: V.M. Werlock, 1986). Callahan, *op. cit.,* p. 366; ORN, I, 27: 320; "Thomas McElroy," in "Officers of the United States Navy During the War Period Appointed from New Jersey," *New Jersey Civil War Record http://www.njstatelib.org/NJ_Information/Searchable_Publications/civilwar/NJCWn1602.html* (accessed November 1, 2008); "For the Relief of Thomas McElroy-Department Letter," in U.S. Congress, House Committee on Naval Affairs, *Hearings* (60th Cong., 1st sess.; Washington, D.C.: GPO, 1908), p. 1069. Named an Acting Ensign in October 1863, Holmes was dismissed from the service on April 13, 1864. In the wake of the *Petrel's* loss, he was arrested "for drunkenness, disobedience of orders, and scandalous conduct," and held in confinement until these charges were forwarded to Porter for disposition. Callahan, *op. cit.,* p. 272; ORN, I, 26: 258.

20. Begun at Shousetown, PA, and completed at Pittsburgh in 1860, the 420-ton side-wheeler *C.E. Hillman* was 230 feet long, with a beam of 35 feet and a six-foot draft. Placed on the Cincinnati-to-Nashville trade, she was briefly detained by Southern interests at the beginning of the war but was recaptured. The huge steamer served under contract to the USQMD throughout the conflict. Way, *op. cit.*, p. 65.

21. The 97-ton stern-wheeler *S.C. Baker* was built at Industry, PA, in 1860 for the Upper Ohio. The towboat was 133 feet long, with a beam of 32 feet and a 3.7-foot draft. During the war, she towed loads all over the Upper Rivers. The stern-wheeler *Ella Faber* was built at California, PA, in 1862 for the Louisville-Henderson route. The 198-ton craft was 150 feet long, with a beam of 32 feet and a 4.5-foot draft. The *World* is not mentioned in Way. The *Nettie Hartupee* was a diminutive 81-ton stern-wheeler constructed at Allegheny, PA, the previous year. Way, *op. cit.*, pp. 146, 342, 406.

22. OR, I, 34, 1: 168, 304, 476; OR, I, 34, 2: 448–449, 494–496, 554, 616; ORN, I, 26: 23–26, 789; *Dickinson Diary*, March 16–17, 1864; *Chicago Daily Tribune*, March 13, 19, 1864; *New York Tribune*, March 28, 1864; *St. Louis Daily Missouri Republican*, March 28, 1864; *Philadelphia Inquirer*, March 30, 1864; U.S., Congress, Joint Committee on the Conduct of the War, *Report: Red River* (38th Cong., 2nd sess.; Washington, D.C.: GPO, 1864; reprint, Greenwood Press, 1971), p. 21 cited hereafter as *Joint Committee*, with page number in Arabic; Alfred T. Mahan, *The Gulf and Inland Waters*, Vol. 3 of the *Navy in the Civil War* (New York: Scribner's, 1883), pp. 189–190; Porter, *Naval History, op. cit.*, pp. 494–496, 559–560; Porter, *Incidents and Anecdotes of the Civil War* (New York: D. Appleton and Co, 1885; reprinted, Harrisburg, PA: The Archive Society, 1997), p. 213; Taylor, *op. cit.*, pp. 180–181; Richard B. Irwin, "The Red River Campaign," in *Battles and Leaders of the Civil War*, edited by Robert U. Johnson and Clarence C. Buel, 4 vols. (New York: The Century Company, 1884–1887, reprinted Thomas Yoseloff, 1956), Vol. 5, 349–351; Thomas O. Selfridge, Jr., "The Navy in the Red River," *B & L*, Vol. 5, 362; Smith, *The Timberclads in the Civil War, op. cit.*, pp. 443–444; David Dixon Porter, "The Mississippi Flotilla in the Red River Expedition," *B & L*, Vol. 4, 367; Walter G. Smith, ed., *Life and Letters of Thomas Kilby Smith* (New York: G.P. Putnam, 1898), p. 356; Joiner, *Through the Howling Wilderness, op. cit.*, pp. 54–57; Joiner and Charles E. Vetter, "The Union Naval Expedition on the Red River, March 12–May 22, 1864," *Civil War Regiments: A Journal of the American Civil War* 4 (1994): pp. 26–41; Curtis Milbourn and Gary D. Joiner, "The Battle of Blair's Landing," *North and South* 9 (February 2007): p. 12; Chester G. Hearn, *Admiral David Dixon Porter: The Civil War Years* (Annapolis, MD: Naval Institute Press, 1996), pp. 245–246; Saunders, *op. cit.*, 20–21; Morris, *loc. cit.*; Mahan, *op. cit.*, pp. 190–191. Way, undoubtedly quoting local newspapers, tells an entirely different story of the plight of the *Nettie Hartupee*. In this version, the craft was hijacked near Nashville by "pirates," who took off with her to the upper Cumberland. The *Newsboy* was sent in pursuit and as she began to overhaul the thieves, they landed their prize ashore and "leaped in the woods and vamoosed." Upon her arrival, the gunboat "shelled the vicinity to no effect." Way, *op. cit.*, p. 342.

23. The 198-ton *Countess* was built at Cincinnati in 1860. Owned by Capt. William C. Harrison, the side-wheeler was 150 feet long, with a beam of 30 feet and a 4.8-foot draft. She operated out of New Orleans, often providing Confederate service up the Red River to Alexandria. Way, *op. cit.*, p. 113.

24. OR, 34, 1: 305, 313, 338–339, 500, 506, 561; OR, I, 34, 2: 494, 610–611; ORN, I, 26: 29–31, 35, 41, 50, 781, 784–785, 789; Mahan, *op. cit.*, pp. 190–191; Smith, *The Timberclads in the Civil War, op. cit.*, pp. 444–445; *Chicago Daily Tribune*, March 29 and April 1, 1864; *New York Daily Tribune*, April 4, 1864; *St. Louis Daily Missouri Republican*, March 26, 1864; *Columbus (WI) Democrat*, May 29, 1895; Porter, *Naval History, op. cit.*, p. 499–500; Taylor, *op. cit.*, pp. 156, 181–183;

Joint Committee, *op. cit.*, pp. 8–9, 18, 71, 74, 224–225; Joiner and Vetter, *op. cit.*, 41–49; Selfridge, "The Navy in the Red River," *B & L*, Vol. 4, *Ibid.*; Selfridge, *Memoirs, op. cit.*, pp. 96–98; Mahan, *op. cit.*, p. 193–194; Harris H. Beecher, *Record of the 114th Regiment, New York State Volunteer Infantry* (Norwich, NY: J.F. Hubbard, Jr., 1866), pp. 299–300; John D. Winters, *The Civil War in Louisiana* (Baton Rouge, LA: Louisiana State University Press, 1963), pp. 330–331; Ludwell H. Johnson, *Red River Campaign: Politics & Cotton in the Civil War* (Kent, OH: Kent State University Press, 1993), p. 99–105; Ivan Musicant, *Divided Waters: The Naval History of the Civil War* (New York: HarperCollins, 1995), pp. 295–296; Irwin, "The Red River Campaign," *B & L*, Vol. 4, 349–350; Robert L. Kerby, *Kirby Smith's Confederacy: The Trans-Mississippi South, 1863–1865* (New York: Columbia University Press, 1972), p. 297; Hearn, *Admiral David Dixon Porter, op. cit.*, p. 246–248. Born at Barbados in the West Indies on August 11, 1841, Gorringe was a remarkable Union navy success story whose profile is missing from published naval histories. Immigrating to the U.S. at an early age to join the merchant marine, he joined the navy as an able-bodied seaman from New York in July 1862 and was transferred as a mate to Western fleet shortly thereafter. He was named an Acting Ensign when the Mississippi Squadron was created that October and an Acting Volunteer Lt. by Porter personally on April 27. Thrice promoted for gallantry, Gorringe was one of the few appointed an Acting Volunteer Lt. Cmdr. (in 1865). He was kept on in the peacetime fleet and commanded the steamer *Memphis* in the Atlantic Squadron in 1867. In 1868, he managed the truly remarkable feat of transferring from the volunteer ranks and was commissioned a Lt. Cmdr. of the regular USN on December 18, 1868. After service at the New York Navy Yard, he was posted to the sloop *Portsmouth* of the South Atlantic Squadron, 1869–1871. After four years at the USN Hydrographic Office, he spent two years on special duty commanding the *Gettysburg* in the Mediterranean. Gorringe's greatest fame came in 1880 when he delivered the Suez Canal–opening commemorative Egyptian obelisk "Cleopatra's Needle" to New York, where it was erected in Central Park and remains today. He resigned in February 1883, published a history of Egyptian obelisks, and died on July 6, 1885, from injuries sustained while hopping a train at a Philadelphia station. Callahan, *op. cit.*, p. 224; Lewis R. Hamersly, *The Records of Living Officers of the U.S. Navy and Marine Corps, Compiled from Official Sources*, rev. ed. (Philadelphia, PA: J.B. Lippincott, 1870), p. 241; *New York Times*, July 7, 1885; John T. Chiarella, "Henry Honeychurch Gorringe," Find a Grave Memorial homepage *http://www.findagrave.com/cgi-bin/fg.cgi?page=gr&GRid =6926925* (accessed November 3, 2008). Pearce was named an Acting Master at the same time as Gorringe and became an Acting Volunteer Lt. on April 16, 1864. He was honorably discharged in December 1865. Callahan, *op. cit.*, p. 426.

25. Constructed for the Memphis-to-Cairo trade in 1862, the 276-ton side-wheeler packet *Des Arc* was 205 feet long, with a 31-foot beam and a 6-foot draft. Owned by Capt. Hicks King for the Archer Line, she transferred to the Memphis-Duball's Bluff (White River) route in 1863, carrying general cargo, passengers, and the U.S. mail under contract. By 1864, she was owned by Champion & Ogden. In the spring, the machinery of the burned boat was salvaged and taken to Cincinnati. Way, *op. cit.*, p. 125.

26. Held by parties in St. Louis, the 176-foot long *Arago* was a side-wheeler constructed at Brownsville, PA, in 1860. She had originally served on the Pittsburgh-St. Louis trade. Way, *op. cit.*, p. 26.

27. *Memphis Daily Bulletin*, March 26, 1864; *Chicago Daily Tribune*, March 28, 1864; *Pittsburgh Daily Commercial*, March 31, 1864. Valued at $50,000 and insured for $20,000, the *Des Arc*, owned by Champion & Ogden, had $70,000 worth of cotton aboard, all of which was uninsured when lost. About 300 bales were saved and later sold in damaged condition.

28. Constructed at Jeffersonville, IN, by Howard in 1858, the side-wheeler *John D. Perry* was 220 feet long, with a beam of 33 feet and a six-foot draft. She was owned during the war by the St. Louis-Memphis Packet Company and served largely on that firm's namesake route. Way, *op. cit.,* p. 250.

29. Constructed at Augusta, KY, in 1856, the *Columbia* had a displacement of 164 tons. Way, *op. cit.,* p. 105.

30. OR, I, 32, 1: 504–505, 547–552, 607–608, 611–612; ORN, I, 26: 183, 195–207; Charleston *Mercury,* May 2, 1864; *New York Times,* April 1, 1864; *New York Tribune,* April 2, 1864; *Chicago Times,* March 29, 1864; *Memphis Daily Bulletin,* March 31, 1864; *Chicago Daily Tribune,* March 28–29 and April 6, 1864; *Indianapolis Daily Journal,* April 2, 1864; *Wisconsin State Register,* April 2, 1864; *Ripley Bee,* March 31, 1864; Ronald K. Huch, "Fort Pillow Massacre: The Aftermath of Paducah," *Journal of the Illinois State Historical Society* 66 (1973): pp. 62–70; *Nashville Times,* March 9, 1864; William Tecumseh Sherman, *Memoirs* (Penguin Classics; New York: Penguin Books, 2000), pp. 365, 379, 382; John Allan Wyeth, *Life of General Nathan Bedford Forrest* (New York: Harper & Bros., 1904; reprinted, New York: Harper and Brothers, 1959), pp. 315–319, 326–330; Saunders, *op. cit.,* 22–24; Robert S. Henry, *"First with the Most" Forrest* (Indianapolis, IN: Bobbs-Merrill, 1944; reprinted, New York: Mallard Press, 1991), p. 251; Thomas Jordan and J.P. Pryor, *The Campaigns of Lieut. Gen. N. B. Forrest and of Forrest's Cavalry.* (New Orleans and New York: Blelock & Co., 1868; reprint, New York: DaCapo Press, 1996), pp. 412–414; Lonnie E. Maness, *An Untutored Genius: The Military Career of General Nathan Bedford Forrest* (Oxford, MS: The Guild Bindery Press, 1990), pp. 224–227; Andrew Ward, *River Run Red: The Fort Pillow Massacre in the American Civil War* (New York: Viking Press, 2005), pp. 102–125; Byrd Douglas, *Steamboatin' on the Cumberland* (Nashville: The Tennessee Book Company, 1961), p. 159.

Chapter 8

1. Built as the *Maria* at Cincinnati in 1863, Capt. Eugene Bowers had originally intended his new boat to ply the more shallow streams. Owned by Thomas Sherlock and others, the 211-ton side-wheeler was 157 feet long, with a beam of 31.6 feet and a depth of hold of 5 feet. Purchased into the navy for $32,000 on March 7, 1864, her name was changed to *Fairy* and she was designated Tinclad No. 51. Supposedly, the craft was able to steam at six knots. Armed with eight 24-pdr. howitzers, she began service under Acting Master Henry S. Wetmore on March 10. Way, *op. cit.,* p. 159, 307; Paul H. Silverstone, *Warships of the Civil War Navies* (Annapolis, Md.: Naval Institute Press, 1989), p.171; ORN, II, I: 82; "Fairy," in U.S. Navy Department Naval Historical Center, *Dictionary of American Naval Fighting Ships, http://www.history.navy.mil/danfs/f1/fairy.htm* (accessed February 9, 2008). Wetmore was trice rated a mate, being discharged the first time (1858), resigning the second (1862), and returning to that rank on October 1, 1862. He was promoted to Acting Master on December 14, 1863, became an Acting Volunteer Lt. on July 9, 1864, and was honorably discharged on Dec. 29, 1865. Callahan, *op. cit.,* p. 415.

2. James A. Dickinson, *Diary* (photocopy), April 2, 16, 1864, *James A. Dickinson Papers,* Rutherford B. Hayes Presidential Center, Fremont (cited hereafter as *Dickinson Diary,* with date); ORN, I, 26: 214–216, 219–226; OR, I, 32, 1: 553, 556, 558–563, 568, 571–574, 595–597, 609, 612–614, 621; OR, I, 32, 3: 520; U.S. Congress, Joint Committee on the Conduct of the War, *Fort Pillow Massacre* (38th Cong., 1st sess., House Report 65; Washington, D.C.: GPO, 1864), pp.3–4, 85–89; *St. Louis Daily Missouri Democrat,* April 16, 1864; *St. Louis Daily Union,* April 16, 1864; *Cincinnati Daily Commercial,* April 20, 1864; *Chicago Daily Tribune,* April 17, 1864; *Memphis Argus,* April 14, 1864; *New York Times,* April

16, 20, 24, and May 3, 1864; *New York Evening Post,* April 15, 21, 1864; Frederick Way, Jr., comp., *Way's Packet Directory, 1848–1994,* 2nd ed. (Athens, OH: Ohio University Press, 1994), pp. 217, 276, 286, 354–355; Andrew Ward, *River Run Red: The Fort Pillow Massacre in the American Civil War* (New York: Viking Press, 2005), pp. 157–158, 176–182; Richard L. Fuchs, *An Unerring Fire: The Massacre at Fort Pillow* (Mechanicsburg, PA: Stackpole Books, 2002), pp. 46–49, 51–53,81–83; Logbook of the U.S.S. *Moose,* April 1–12, 1864; "Logbook of the U.S.S. *New Era,* April 12, 1864," quoted in John Cimprich and Robert C. Mamfort, Jr., "Fort Pillow Revisited: New Evidence About an Old Controversy," *Civil War History* 28 (December 1982): pp. 294–295; Cimprich and Mamfort, "Dr. Fitch's Report on the Fort Pillow Massacre," *Tennessee Historical Quarterly* 44 (Spring 1985): pp. 30–31; John Allan Wyeth, *Life of General Nathan Bedford Forrest* (New York: Harper & Bros., 1904), pp. 319–349, 373, 380,589; Robert S. Henry, *"First with the Most" Forrest* (Indianapolis, IN: Bobbs-Merrill, 1944; reprinted, New York: Smithmark, 1991), pp. 254–260; Charles W. Anderson, "The True Story of Fort Pillow," *Confederate Veteran* 3 (November 1895): p. 323; E.J. Huling, *Reminiscences of Gunboat Life in the Mississippi Squadron* (Saratoga Springs, NY: Sentinel Print, 1881), p. 7; James Dinkins, "The Capture of Fort Pillow," *Confederate Veteran* 33 (December 1925): p. 461; Thomas Jordan and J.P. Pryor, *The Campaigns of Lieut. Gen. N.B. Forrest and of Forrest's Cavalry* (New Orleans and New York: Blelock & Co., 1868, reprinted, New York: DaCapo Press, 1996), pp. 424–446; Brian S. Wills, *A Battle From the Start: The Life of Nathan Bedford Forrest* (New York: HarperCollins, 1992), pp. 174–177; Lonnie E. Maness, *An Untutored Genius: The Military Career of General Nathan Bedford Forrest* (Oxford, MS: The Guild Bindery Press, 1990), pp. 229–260.

3. OR, I, 32, 1: 556–614; ORN, I, 215–218, 226–233; Logbook of the U.S.S. *Moose,* April 1–16, 1864; Wyeth, *op. cit.,* pp. 333–361; Thomas Jordan and J.P. Pryor, *op. cit.,* 424–454; Porter, *Naval History, op. cit.,* pp. 518–519; Ward, *op. cit.,* pp. 280–282. It is not our purpose to review the charges of a Fort Pillow massacre, a matter which has been hashed and rehashed in the nearly 150 years since. We have noted several titles in our bibliography and call the reader's attention to Robert C. Mainfort Jr., "Fort Pillow Massacre: A Statistical Note," *Journal of American History* 76 (December 1989): pp. 836–837 and John Cimprich, "The Fort Pillow Massacre: Assessing the Evidence," in John David Smith, ed., *Black Soldiers in Blue: African American Troops in the Civil War Era* (Chapel Hill, NC: University of North Carolina Press, 2002), pp. 150–168.

4. ORN, I, 26: 38–39, 42–43, 46, 49–52, 54–55, 60–61, 777–778, 781, 785, 789; OR, I, 34, 1: 172–204, 282, 308–309, 322, 324, 331, 341, 380–385, 388–393, 407, 428, 445, 452, 468, 471–472, 570–571, 633–634; OR, I, 34, 2: 610–611; OR, I, 34, 3: 98–99, 174; U.S. Congress, Joint Committee on the Conduct of the War, *Report: Red River* (38th Cong., 2nd sess.; Washington, D.C.: GPO, 1864; reprint, Greenwood Press, 1971), pp. 35, 210, 275–276, 282, 286–287, 323; *New York World,* April 16, 1864; *Columbus (WI) Democrat,* May 29, 1895; Robert L. Kerby, *Kirby Smith's Confederacy: The Trans-Mississippi South, 1863–1865* (New York: Columbia University Press, 1972), p. 309; Richard B. Irwin, "The Red River Campaign," in *Battles and Leaders of the Civil War,* edited by Robert U. Johnson and Clarence C. Buel, 4 vols. (New York: The Century Company, 1884–1887, reprinted Thomas Yoseloff, 1956), Vol. 4, pp. 351–358; Thomas O. Selfridge Jr., "The Navy in the Red River," *B & L,* Vol. 4, pp. 363–364; Thomas O. Selfridge, *Memoirs of Thomas O. Selfridge Jr., Rear Admiral, U.S.N.* (New York: Knickerbocker Press, 1924; reprinted, Columbia, SC: University of South Carolina Press, 1987), pp. 99–106; Chester G. Hearn, *Admiral David Dixon Porter: The Civil War Years* (Annapolis, MD: Naval Institute Press, 1996), pp. 248–251; David Dixon Porter, *Naval History of the Civil War* (New

York: Sherman Publishing Company, 1886; reprinted, Secaucus, N.J.: Castle Books, 1984), pp. 512–513; Richard Taylor, *Destruction and Reconstruction: Personal Experiences of the Late War* (New York: D. Appleton and Company, 1879), pp. 177–178, 212; Gary D. Joiner, *Through the Howling Wilderness: The 1864 Red River Campaign and Union Failure in the West* (Knoxville, TN: University of Tennessee Press, 2006), pp. 32, 131–137; Joiner and Charles E. Vetter, "The Union Naval Expedition on the Red River, March 12–May 22, 1864," *Civil War Regiments: A Journal of the American Civil War* 4 (1994): pp. 26–41, 59–51, 55–59; Curtis Milbourn and Gary D. Joiner, "The Battle of Blair's Landing," *North and South* 9 (February 2007): pp. 12–21; William Riley Brooksher, *War Along the Bayous: The 1864 Red River Campaign in Louisiana* (Washington, D.C.: Brassey's, 1998), pp. 69–78, 153–157; Way, *op. cit.,* p. 257; Alfred T. Mahan, *The Gulf and Inland Waters,* Vol. 3 of *The Navy in the Civil War* (New York: Scribner's, 1883), pp. 194–198; Anne J. Bailey, "Chasing Banks Out of Louisiana: Parsons' Texas Cavalry in the Red River Campaign, " *Civil War Regiments: A Journal of the American Civil War* 2 (1992): pp. 219–221; Rebecca W. Smith and Marion Mullins, eds., "The Diary of H.C. Medford, Confederate Soldier, 1864," *Southwestern Historical Quarterly Online* 34, no. 2, *http://www.tsha.utexas.edu/publications/journals/shq/online/v034/n2/contrib_DIVL1540.html* (July 22, 2007); H.P. Gallaway, *Ragged Rebel: A Common Soldier in W.H. Parsons' Texas Cavalry, 1861–1865* (Austin, TX: University of Texas Press, 1988), pp. 97–100; Odie Faulk, *General Tom Green, Fightin' Texan* (Waco, TX: Texian Press, 1963), p. 62; Carl L. Duaine, *The Dead Men Wore Boots: An Account of the 32nd Texas Volunteer Cavalry, CSA, 1862–1865* (Austin, TX: San Felipe Press, 1966), p. 63; Hearn, *Admiral David Dixon Porter, op. cit.,* pp. 248–250; Myron J. Smith Jr., *The Timberclads in the Civil War: The Lexington, Conestoga and Tyler on the Western Rivers* (Jefferson, N.C.: McFarland, 2008), pp. 444–457; Bruce S. Allardice, "Curious Clash at Blair's Landing," *America's Civil War 9* (July 1997): pp. 60–64; Alwyn Barr, "The Battle of Blair's Landing." *Louisiana Studies* 2 (Winter 1963): pp. 204–212.

5. Destined to spend much of her naval career as a dispatch boat, the 157-ton *Juliet,* Tinclad No. 4, was built at Brownsville, PA, in 1862 and was almost identical in physical size to the *Romeo.* With a length of 155.6 feet, her beam was 30.2 feet and her depth when sold to the Mississippi Squadron on November 1 was five feet. The gunboat's power plant would also allow her to steam 5 mph against the current. It comprised two boilers and two engines. The latter had a cylinder diameter of 13 inches and a 3.6-foot stroke. At Cairo, Acting Volunteer Lt. Edward Shaw oversaw the berthing of her crew and the installation of a battery of six 24-pdr. smoothbore Dahlgren boat howitzers. She was commissioned on December 14. ORN, II, 1: 116; Silverstone, *op. cit.,* p. 173; Way, *op. cit.,* p. 261; "*Juliet,*" in U.S. Navy Department, Naval Historical Center, *Dictionary of American Naval Fighting Ships, http://www.history.navy.mil/danfs/j4/juliet.htm* (accessed February 9, 2008). While lying at the upper part of the Memphis landing at 3 A.M. on January 11, the tinclad's pilothouse caught fire and before the flames could be contained, a large portion of the upper superstructure was consumed. She was out of service for some weeks. *Chicago Daily Tribune,* January 15, 1864. As a result of damage sustained in the tale related here, the gunboat was subsequently towed to Cairo for repairs and was out of service until September 6. Acting Master John S. Watson had succeeded Shaw the previous fall and would be named an Acting Volunteer Lt. in June. He would be honorably discharged in October 1865. Edward W. Callahan, *List of Officers of the Navy of the United States and of the Marine Corps, from 1775 to 1900, Comprising a Complete Register of All Present and Former Commissioned, Warranted, and Appointed Officers of the United States Navy, and of the Marine Corps, Regular and Volunteer. Compiled from the Official Records of the Navy Department* (New York: L.R. Hamersly & Co., 1901; reprinted, New York: Haskell House, 1969), p. 572.

6. OR, I, 34, 1: 310, 382–383; ORN, I, 26: 66, 69, 72–78; 790; *Philadelphia Press,* April 29, 1864; *St. Louis Daily Missouri Democrat,* May 10, 1864; *Columbus (WI) Democrat,* May 29, 1895; Mahan, *op. cit.,* p. 198; Brooksher, *op. cit.,* pp. 158–159; Joiner and Vetter, *op. cit.,* 58–59; Selfridge, Jr., "The Navy in the Red River," *B & L,* Vol. 4, p. 364; Selfridge, *Memoirs, op. cit., Ibid.*; Jay Slagle, *Ironclad Captain: Seth Ledyard Phelps and the U.S. Navy* (Kent, OH: Kent State University Press, 1996), pp. 365–367; Hearn, *op. cit.,* pp. 253–254; Smith, *The Timberclads, op. cit.,* pp. 457–459; Porter, *Naval History, op. cit.,* p. 515–519; Porter, *Incidents and Anecdotes of the Civil War* (New York: D. Appleton and Co, 1885; reprinted, Harrisburg, PA: The Archive Society, 1997), pp. 235–239; Pellet, *op. cit.,* p. 222; *Joint Committee,* pp. 247–248. The unique *Ozark* was an unsuccessful 578-ton river monitor that featured a single turret with two 11-inch guns forward and a casemate with four cannon aft. Silverstone, *op. cit,* pp. 147–148.

7. Captured after her loss in the Battle of Memphis on June 6, 1862, the Confederate ram *General Sterling Price* was salvaged, repaired, and commissioned into the Union Navy in March 1863. The 483-ton gunboat was armed with four 9-inch smoothbores. Silverstone, *op. cit.,* p. 162.

8. The 417-ton *Superior* was constructed at Cincinnati in 1856 for a syndicate headed by her master, Capt. Henry T. Dexter. Operated in the U.S. Mail Line Co., the side-wheeler steamed primarily between the Queen City and Louisville. Capt. Dexter purchased the steamer from his partners in February 1863, added iron plating to her pilothouse, and began to operate on the Evansville to Memphis route, often with contracts for the USQMD. Way, *op. cit.,* p. 438; Milford M. Miller, "Evansville Steamboats During the Civil War," *Indiana Magazine of History* 37 (December 1941): p. 380.

9. ORN, I, 26: 311; Miller, *op. cit.,* pp. 379–380; *Cairo City Weekly Gazette,* May 19, 1864. Later in November, Capt. Dexter, an avid horse racing fan, attended the races at St. Louis and supposedly won sufficient funds to purchase a replacement for the *Superior. Evansville Daily Journal,* November 15, 1864.

10. OR, I, 32, 3: 348, 394–395, 463–464, 796–797, 825–826; OR, I, 32, 1: 674–675; OR, I, 44, 1: 675–676; ORN, I, 26: 246–260; *Chicago Daily Tribune,* May 2, 1864; Porter, *Naval History, op. cit.,* pp. 560–561; Edwin C. Bearss, "Wirt Adams Repels Yankee Task Force at Yazoo City," *Morningside Notes, http://www.morningsidebooks.com/notes/yazoo.htm* (April 10, 2000); Robert Bowman, "Yazoo City in the Civil War," in *Publications of the Mississippi Historical Society,* Vol. 7 (Oxford, Ms.: Published for the Society, 1903), pp. 71–72; Benjamin P. Jett, "Capture of the Gun Boat *Petrel* in 1864," in Charlean Moss Williams, *The Old Town Speaks: Washington, Hempstead County, Arkansas; Gateway to Texas, 1835, Confederate Capital 1863* (Houston, TX: Anson Jones Press, 1951), pp. 99–102; Herbert Aptheker, "The Negro in the Union Navy," *The Journal of Negro History* 32 (April 1947): pp. 190–191. Acting Master Chambers joined the service in April 1863 and was honorably discharged in September 1865. Acting Ensign Flanigan was recruited the previous April, but would resign on June 14. Callahan, *op. cit.,* pp. 108, 196. Born in Hamburg, Germany, in 1847, Nibbe joined the merchant marine when he was 14 and jumped ship to enlist in the Union Navy three years later. He was honorably discharged in January 1865 and received his award four months later. After the war, he moved to Bremerton, WA, where he became a successful businessman and died in 1902. Fredi Perry, "John H. Nibbe," in *Bremerton and the Puget Sound Naval Yard* (Bremerton, WA: Perry Publishing, 2002), pp. 33–34. The MOH citation can be found in U.S. Congress, Senate, Committee on Veterans Affairs, "Civil War Medal of Honor Citations," in *Medal of Honor Recipients: 1863–1973 http://americancivilwar.com/medal_of_honor6.html* (accessed November 1, 2008).

11. ORN, I, 26: 61, 68–87, 166–169, 176–177, 781–782 787–787, 790–791; OR, I, 34,1, 583–584, 632, 634. 782,

790–791; *Chicago Daily Tribune,* May 8, 1864; *Milwaukee Daily Sentinel,* May 9, 1864; *Columbus (WI) Democrat,* May 29, 1895; Chuck Veit, "Engagement at Deloges Bluff," *Navy and Marine Homepage, http://www.navyandmarine.org/ond eck/1862delogesbluff.htm* (July 24, 2007); Taylor, *op. cit.,* pp. 183–185, 218; Hearn, *op. cit.,* pp. 255–257; Slagle, *op. cit.,* pp. 367–378; Joiner, *Through the Howling Wilderness, op. cit.,* pp. 138–140; Joiner and Vetter, *op. cit.,* 60–62; Mahan, *op. cit.,* pp. 198–203; Selfridge Jr., "The Navy in the Red River," *B & L,* Vol. 4, pp. 364–365; Smith, *The Timberclads, op. cit.,* pp. 460–463; Selfridge, *Memoirs, op. cit., Ibid.;* Brooksher, *op. cit.,* pp. 190–193; Joint Committee, pp. 245–248; Porter, *Naval History, op. cit.,* pp. 520–524; Porter, *Incidents and Anecdotes, op. cit.,* pp. 239–243; Frank L. Church, *Civil War Marine: A Diary of the Red River Expedition, 1864,* edited and annotated by James P. Jones and Edward F. Keuchel (Washington, D.C.: History and Museums Division, Headquarters, U.S. Marine Corps, 1975), pp. 20, 53; Herbert Saunders, "The Civil War Letters of Herbert Saunders," edited by Ronald K. Huch, *Register of the Kentucky Historical Society* 69 (January 1971): p. 26. Like Viet, Brooksher also disputes the number of cannon involved in the Deloges Bluff battle, suggesting the 18 Porter claimed was a stretch. Brooksher, *op. cit.,* p. 253. Surprisingly, *Osage* captain Selfridge does not mention steaming to meet the *Eastport* rescue group in his Deloges Bluff report, his *B & L* article, or his *Memoirs.* The best and most accurate contemporary newspaper account of the escape of the *Cricket, Juliet,* and *Fort Hindman* appeared in the Philadelphia-based *North American and United States Gazette* of May 12, 1864; Pilot Maitland recovered from his wounds and was released two months later. Eighteen months earlier, Porter, who was not initially in favor of employing African-Americans in his river fleet, had a severe manpower shortage. "I could get no men," he wrote to Rear Adm. Andrew H. Foote, "so I work in the darkies." Perhaps his ordeal aboard the *Cricket* caused him to inwardly if not publicly relent somewhat, and confirm his original sentiment to Foote concerning the use of contraband sailors: "They do first-rate, and are far better behaved than their masters." ORN, I, 23: 603.

Chapter 9

1. Constructed at Cincinnati in 1856, the 211-foot-long 750-ton side-wheeler *Emma* had served the USQMD as a transport since September 1861. One of her crewmen, John Price, escaped captivity in November 1864 and made it back to St. Louis where he sued for the wages he would have earned while in prison. Frederick Way Jr., *Way's Packet Directory, 1848–1994,* 2nd ed. (Athens, OH: Ohio University Press, 1994), p. 148.

2. Built at Paducah a year before the *Emma,* the 153-ton *City Belle* was also taken into the U.S. Quartermaster service in late 1861, serving initially as a hospital steamer. The noted St. Louis river reporter and songwriter Will S. Hays served as clerk aboard as the 179-foot side-wheeler made several Louisville-Memphis round trips in early 1864. Way, *op. cit.,* p. 88.

3. A side-wheeler built at Jeffersonville, IN, at the noted Howard yards, the 199-foot long *Laurel Hill* was employed on the New Orleans-Bayou Sara service before passing to U.S. government ownership. Way, *op. cit.,* p. 280.

4. The second steamer by this name, the 199-ton *Rob Roy* was constructed at Cincinnati earlier in the year. Way, *op. cit.,* p. 394.

5. The 220-foot long *John Warner* was constructed at New Albany, IN, in 1856 and served the U.S. government for much of the war. Way, *op. cit.,* p. 257.

6. OR, I, 34, 1: 442, 474–475, 587–588, 589, 621–623; ORN, I, XXVI: 104–105, 112–124, 134, 174–175; Way, *op. cit.,* p. 257, 424; *Chicago Daily Tribune,* May 24, 1864;

Harper's Weekly, June 18, 1864; *Columbus (WI) Democrat,* May 29, 1895; *New York Times,* May 29, 1864; *Ironton (OH) Register,* January 19, 1888; *New Orleans Era,* May 17, 1864; *New Orleans Times,* May 18, 1864; J. Thomas Scharf, *History of the Confederate Navy from Its Organization to the Surrender of Its Last Vessel* (New York: Rodgers and Sherwood, 1887; reprinted; New York: Fairfax Press, 1977), pp. 520–521; Thomas J. Williams, *An Historical Sketch of the 56th Ohio Volunteer Infantry* (Columbus, OH: Lawrence Press, 1899), pp. 73–78; Henry R. and Symmes E. Browne, *From the Fresh Water Navy, 1861–1864: Letters of Acting Master's Mate Henry R. Browne and Acting Ensign Symmes E. Browne,* edited by John D. Milligan (Naval Letters Series, Volume 3: Annapolis, MD: Naval Institute Press, 1970), pp. 272–275; Alfred T. Mahan, *The Gulf and Inland Waters,* Vol. 3 of the *Navy in the Civil War* (New York: Scribner's, 1883), pp. 209–210; Gary D. Joiner, *Through the Howling Wilderness: The 1864 Red River Campaign and Union Failure in the West* (Knoxville, TN: University of Tennessee Press, 2006), pp. 149–150, 194; Dave Page, *Ships versus Shore: Engagements Along Southern Shores and Rivers* (Nashville TN: Rutledge Hill Press, 1994), p. 330; Joiner and Charles E. Vetter, "The Union Naval Expedition on the Red River, March 12–May 22, 1864," *Civil War Regiments: A Journal of the American Civil War* 4 (1994): pp. 63–64; Richard Taylor, *Destruction and Reconstruction: Personal Experiences of the Late War* (New York: D. Appleton and Company, 1879), pp. 185–186; Lewis B. Parsons, *Reports to the War Department* (St. Louis, MO: George Knapp & Co., 1867), p. 36; David Dixon Porter, *Naval History of the Civil War* (New York: Sherman Publishing Company, 1886; reprinted, Secaucus, N.J.: Castle Books, 1984), pp. 528–529. The MOH citations for the six *Signal* crewmen can be found in U.S. Congress, Senate, Committee on Veterans Affairs, "Civil War Medal of Honor Citations," in: its *Medal of Honor Recipients: 1863–1973 http://americancivilwar.com/medal_of_honor6.html* (accessed November 1, 2008). Burial and minor life profiles for Wilkes, Asten, Butts, Hyland, and McCormick may be accessed at the Find-a-Grave website, *http://www.findagrave.com.* Many of the lads in the 120th Ohio came from the author's home Buckeye County and this disaster to their regiment is noted in Ben Douglass's *History of Wayne County, Ohio* (Indianapolis, IN: Robert Douglass, Publisher, 1878), p.756.

7. The *Argosy No. 2* was constructed for Capt. George W. Reed at Monongahela, PA, after his first *Argosy,* constructed the previous year, was sold to the USN in March 1863, becoming Tinclad No. 27. There is some dispute between Way and Silverstone on the one hand and the USN on the other as to the second vessel's propulsion unit. We will agree with the former and suggest that the 229-ton second vessel was also a stern-wheeler. *Argosy No. 2* was 154 feet long with a beam of 31 feet and a draft of 4.5 feet. Reed sold his latest interest to the Mississippi Squadron on November 14 for $34,000. At that point the boat's name was changed to avoid confusion on the rolls with the earlier craft. Refitted at Cincinnati, where the No. 45 was painted on the side of her pilothouse, she was dispatched to Cairo at year's end to take on her armament, comprising one each 20-pounder Parrott rifle, one 32-pounder smoothbore, and four 24-pounder Dahlgren boat howitzers. Acting Volunteer Lt. Commander Benjamin W. Loring was placed in command and delivered the *Wave* down the Mississippi to New Orleans. Loring had originally been appointed an Acting Master in February 1862 and was promoted on June 29, 1863. After the loss of the *Wave,* the remainder of his war was spent either as a POW or in preparation for a court of inquiry. He was honorably discharged in February 1866. Way, *op. cit.,* pp. 28, 482; ORN, II, 1: 238; Paul H. Silverstone, *Warships of the Civil War Navies* (Annapolis, Md.: Naval Institute Press, 1989), p.179; "*Wave,*" in U.S. Navy Department, Naval Historical Center, *Dictionary of American Naval Fighting Ships, http://www.history.navy.mil/danfs/w4/wave.htm* (accessed February 9, 2008); *Houston Daily Telegraph Supplement,* May 11, 1864; Edward

W. Callahan, *List of Officers of the Navy of the United States and of the Marine Corps, from 1775 to 1900, Comprising a Complete Register of All Present and Former Commissioned, Warranted, and Appointed Officers of the United States Navy, and of the Marine Corps, Regular and Volunteer. Compiled from the Official Records of the Navy Department* (New York: L.R. Hamersly & Co., 1901; reprinted, New York: Haskell House, 1969), p. 338.

8. Originally captured and purchased into the USN from a New York prize court, the light-draught *Granite City* was 160 feet long with an armament that included six 24-pounder Dahlgren howitzers, one 12-pounder Dahlgren rifled howitzer, and a 20-pounder Parrott rifle. She was commanded by Acting Master Charles W. Lamson, whose July 1861 appointment would, as a result of the Calcasieu action, be revoked in February 1865. ORN, II, 1: 97; Callahan, *op. cit.*, p. 320.

9. ORN, I, 21: 246–259, 324–325, 816, 893, 897; OR, I, 34, 3: 806–813; OR, I, 34, 1: 912–914; *Houston Daily Telegraph,* May 4, 1864; *Houston Daily Telegraph Supplement,* May 11, 1864; *Galveston Tri-Weekly News,* May 8, June 20, 1864; *Galveston Weekly News,* May 9–10 and June 22, 1864; *Beaumont Enterprise,* May 9, 1909; Scharf, *op. cit.*, pp. 527–528; Alwyn, Barr, "The Battle of Calcasieu Pass," *Southwestern Historical Quarterly* 66 (July 1962): pp. 59–67; "A Tale of Three Tinclads, All Named *Argosy*," *Mid-Missouri Civil War Round Table Homepage, http://www.mmcwrt.org* (accessed April 6, 2005); William T. Block, "The Battle of Calcasieu Pass, Louisiana: Reprinted from the *Beaumont Enterprise,* May 6, 1977," *W.T. Block Homepage http://www.wtblock.com/wtblockjr/calcasie.htm* (accessed November 1, 2007); C. Walter von Rosenburg to William C. von Rosenburg, "Battle of Calcasieu Pass," *Confederate Veteran* 26 (1918): p. 516. The stealthy lead-ups to the attacks by Brig. Gen. Jo Shelby on the *Queen City* in June and Nathan B. Forrest's assault on Johnsonville, TN, in November were very similar to the silent preparations made before Griffith's assault on the *Wave.* Both Calcasieu-captured vessels were later employed to transport cargo, but the fate of the tinclad is unknown.

10. ORN, I, 26: 92–95, 102,123, 130–132; OR, I, 34, 1: 209, 310, 402–406, 491, 585–586, 621; *New York Times,* May 13, 29, 1864; *New Orleans Era,* May 17, 1864; *New Orleans Times,* May 18, 1864; *Columbus (WI) Democrat,* May 29, 1895; *Ironton (OH) Register,* January 19, 1888; *Harper's Weekly,* June 18, 1864; Mahan, *op. cit.*, pp. 203–207; Steven D. Smith and George J. Castille III, "Bailey's Dam," *Louisiana, Department of Culture, Recreation and Tourism Anthropological Study* No. 8, March 1986, *http://www.crt.state.la.us/archaeology/BAILEYS/baileys.htm* (August 7, 2006); David Dixon Porter, *Incidents and Anecdotes of the Civil War* (New York: D. Appleton and Co, 1885; reprinted, Harrisburg, PA: The Archive Society, 1997), pp. 248–249; Porter, *Naval History, op. cit.*, pp. 525–534; Johnson, *op. cit.*, pp. 254–262; Robert L. Kerby, *Kirby Smith's Confederacy: The Trans-Mississippi South, 1863–1865* (New York: Columbia University Press, 1972), p. 318; Frank L. Church, *Civil War Marine: A Diary of the Red River Expedition, 1864,* edited and annotated by James P. Jones and Edward F. Keuchel (Washington, D.C.: History and Museums Division, Headquarters, U.S. Marine Corps, 1975), p. 54; Taylor, *op. cit.*, pp. 186–189; Richard B. Irwin, "The Red River Campaign," in *Battles and Leaders of the Civil War,* edited by Robert U. Johnson and Clarence C. Buel, 4 vols. (New York: The Century Company, 1884–1887; reprinted, Thomas Yoseloff, 1956), Vol. 4, pp. 358–362; Chester G. Hearn, *Admiral David Dixon Porter: The Civil War Years* (Annapolis, MD: Naval Institute Press, 1996), pp. 258–265; Jay Slagle, *Ironclad Captain: Seth Ledyard Phelps and the U.S. Navy* (Kent, OH: Kent State University Press, 1996), pp. 378–381; Myron J. Smith Jr., *The Timberclads in the Civil War: The Lexington, Conestoga and Tyler on the Western Rivers* (Jefferson, N.C.: McFarland, 2008), pp. 463–464; Gary D. Joiner, *One Damn Blunder From Beginning to End: The Red River Campaign of*

1864 (Lanham, MD: Rowman and Littlefield, 2003), pp. 161–162; Joiner and Vetter, *op. cit.*, pp. 63–67; Henry R. and Symmes E. Browne, *From the Fresh Water Navy, 1861–1864: Letters of Acting Master's Mate Henry R. Browne and Acting Ensign Symmes E. Browne,* edited by John D. Milligan (Naval Letters Series, Vol. 3; Annapolis, MD: Naval Institute Press, 1970), pp.177–179; Thomas O. Selfridge, Jr., "The Navy in the Red River," *B & L* 4, pp. 365–366; Selfridge, *Memoirs of Thomas O. Selfridge, Jr., Rear Admiral, U.S.N.* (New York: Knickerbocker Press, 1924; reprinted, Columbia, SC: University of South Carolina Press, 1987), pp. 109–111; William Riley Brooksher, *War Along the Bayous: The 1864 Red River Campaign in Louisiana* (Washington, D.C.: Brassey's, 1998), pp. 209–215. Lt. Col. Bailey received the thanks of Congress for saving the fleet. OR, I, 34: 586. Both the *Cricket* and the *Juliet* had to be towed to Cairo for repairs. Acting Master's Mate De Witt C. Morse noticed the progress of the latter from the deck of the tinclad *Curlew* off St. Joseph, LA, in late May and wrote home that she "passed up yesterday in tow of the steamer *Benefit,* from the scene of action up Red River; she was well riddled on all sides, and her machinery was disabled." Jeffrey L. Patrick, "A Fighting Sailor on the Western Rivers: The Civil War Letters of 'Gunboat,'" *The Journal of Mississippi History* 58 (Fall 1996): pp. 268–269.

11. ORN, I, 26: 329–330.

12. A Kentuckian like John Hunt Morgan and a wealthy slave-holder like Nathan Bedford Forrest, Jo Shelby (1830–1897) joined the CSA cavalry under Sterling Price in 1861. Rising to the rank of colonel, he raised his own cavalry brigade, sometimes called the "Iron Brigade," and led it throughout the Trans-Mississippi Theater for the remainder of the war. Refusing to surrender, he led his brigade into Mexico to support Maximilian, returning to Missouri after the end of the French adventure. He was appointed a U.S. marshal in 1893. Mark M. Boatner III, *The Civil War Dictionary* (New York: David McKay, 1959), p. 737. In addition to the work of his colleague, John Edwards, cited in footnote no. 14, see also Daniel O'Flaherty and Daniel E. Sutherland, *General Jo Shelby: Undefeated Rebel* (Chapel Hill, NC: University of North Carolina Press, 2000).

13. Though petitions were signed by nearly every commander in the Trans-Mississippi including Marmaduke and Shelby, South Carolina-born Col. Greene (1832–1900) was never promoted to the rank of Brig. Gen. He was one of the most engaged and capable officers of the Confederacy from the beginning of the conflict, a man of whom Shelby's wartime biographer, Edwards, would write: "No braver or better officer ever drew a sword." Following the conflict, he lived and died in Memphis. Charles Steven Palmer, "'Our Most Noble Stranger': The Mystery, Gallantry, and Civicism of Colton Greene," unpublished MA thesis, University of Oklahoma, 1995; John W. Coltern, *Confederates of Elmwood* (Westminster, MD: Heritage Books, 2001), p. 183; Edwards, *op. cit.*, p. 251; Bruce S. Allardice, *More Generals in Gray* (Baton Route, LA: Louisiana State University Press, 1995), pp. 104–105.

14. OR, I, 34, 1: 486–487; OR, I, 34, 3: 828–829; OR, I, 41, 1: 191–192; OR, I, 41, 4: 1068–1069; John Swift, "Letters from a Sailor on a Tinclad," edited by Lester L. Swift, *Civil War History* 10 (March 1961): pp. 55–56; Benson J. Lossing, *Pictorial Field Book of the Civil War: Journeys Through the Battlefields in the Wake of Conflict,* 3 vols. (Hartford, CT: T. Belknap, 1874; reprinted, The Johns Hopkins University Press, 1997), Vol. 3, p. 274; Thomas A. DeBlack, *With Fire and Sword: Arkansas, 1861–1874* (Histories of Arkansas; Fayetteville, AR: University of Arkansas Press, 2003), p. 119; Albert G. Castel, *General Sterling Price and the Civil War in the West* (Baton Rouge, LA: Louisiana State University Press, 1968), pp. 196–197; William L. Shea, "Battle at Ditch Bayou," *Arkansas Historical Quarterly* 39 (Autumn 1980): pp. 195–196; John N. Edwards, *Shelby and His Men; or, The War in the West* (Cincinnati, OH: Miami Printing and Publishing Co., 1867; reprinted, Waverly, MO: Gen-

eral J.O. Shelby Memorial, 1993), pp. 363–366; Kerby, *op. cit.*, p. 323; Mahan, *op. cit.*, p. 212; Smith, *The Timberclads, op. cit.*, p. 467. Shelby himself estimated that, at this time, there were over 10,000 draft-dodgers and bushwhackers in the White River Valley. OR, I, 34, 1: 660.

15. The 225-ton *Lebanon* was constructed at Brownsville, PA, in 1855 and was impressed by the USQMD in early 1862. She had been carrying military supplies up and down the Mississippi ever since. Col. Parsons was blunt in stating the reason for her presence at Ford's: she was "captured and burned by guerrillas while in pursuit of cotton," he wrote. Way, *op. cit.*, p. 281; *Chicago Daily Tribune*, June 2, 1864; Lewis B. Parsons, *Reports to the War Department* (St. Louis, MO: George Knapp & Co., 1867), p. 36; Edwards, *op. cit.*, p. 364–366; Stephen B. Oates, *Confederate Cavalry West of the River* (Austin, TX: University of Texas Press, 1961; reprinted, 1992), pp. 182–183.

16. The brand-new 534-ton *Nicholas Longworth* was constructed at Cincinnati earlier in the year to run between the Queen City and New Orleans. For defense, she was armed with a single 6-pounder fieldpiece on her main deck and a howitzer on her hurricane deck, both manned by volunteers. Way, *op. cit.*, p. 347; *Chicago Daily Tribune*, June 5, 1864.

17. ORN, I, 26: 305, 317, 323–324, 805; Chester G. Hearn, *Ellet's Brigade: The Strangest Outfit of All* (Baton Rouge, LA: Louisiana State University Press, 2000), pp. 232–233; Shea, *loc. cit.*; Patrick, *op. cit.*, 269–271; Don R. Simon, "Engagement at Old River Lake," *The Encyclopedia of Arkansas History and Culture* http://www.encycopediaofarkansas.net/encyclopedia/entry-detail.aspx?entryID=1120 (accessed November 10, 2008). Greene informed Brig. Gen. Marmaduke that the *Curlew* was "towed up to Napoleon seriously damaged." This was not accurate. ORN, I, 26: 803, 805.

18. OR, I, 34, 1: 946–947; ORN, I, 26: 803, 805; Patrick, *op. cit.*, 271–272; *Chicago Daily Tribune*, June 2, 5, 1864; *New York Times*, June 4, 1864; Way, *loc. cit.*; Hearn, *op. cit.*, p. 233. Both the Chicago and copying New York newspapers incorrectly informed their readers that the battle was between 12 of Marmaduke's fieldpieces and the tinclads *Marmora*, *Juliet*, and *Prairie Bird*, with the latter struck 30 times before the trio "succeeded in driving them away."

19. The 406-ton *Monarch* was constructed at Fulton, OH, near Cincinnati, in 1853; during the June 1862 naval battle of Memphis, she was particularly effective against the Confederate cottonclad gunboats. Way, *op. cit.*, pp. 328–329.

20. In USQMD service during most of the Civil War, the *Rocket* was constructed at Brownsville, PA, in 1856. Way, *op. cit.*, p. 400.

21. OR, I, 34, 1: 946–947, 951; ORN, I, 26: 326–327, 331, 335, 339, 803, 805–806; Hearn, *op. cit.*, pp. 233–235; *Chicago Daily Tribune*, June 5, 1864; *St. Louis Daily Missouri Democrat*, May 30, 1864. Acting Ensign Dwyer of the *Romeo*, appointed to his rank in December 1862, resigned from the service on May 30. Callahan *op. cit.*, p. 175.

22. Parsons, loc. cit.

23. ORN, I, 26: 806; *Chicago Daily Tribune*, June 7, 1864; Hearn, *op. cit.*, p. 235. When Currie returned to Greenville, he sent a message to Owen at Skipwith's Landing informing him that Greene was at Sunnyside. Owen was reluctant to leave his anchorage for fear that Rebel cavalry would strike the naval anchorage and sink his barges and tugboats. ORN, I, 26: 339.

24. Named for the daughter of her owner, Capt. John Carroll, the huge new side-wheeler *Pauline Carroll* was constructed at Cannelton, IN, earlier in the year. With a displacement of 714 tons, the big St. Louis-New Orleans packet was 256 feet long, with a beam of 42 feet and a 7.7-foot draft. Way, *op. cit.*, p. 364.

25. ORN, I, 26: 804, 806; *Memphis Evening Times*, July 28, 1864; Shea, *op. cit.*, pp. 196–197; Edwards, *op. cit.*, pp. 366–370. There was no ironclad involved in this exchange. Though nowhere referenced, the vessel involved could have been the 410-ton side-wheel ram *Avenger*, which had just ar-

rived at Greenville from Vicksburg. Constructed at New Albany, IN, earlier in the year, the craft was 210 feet long with a 41.5-foot beam and a 6-foot draft. She was armed with one 100-pounder Parrott rifle, one 12-pounder Parrott rifle, and three 24-pounder smoothbore howitzers. ORN, II, 1: 41; Way, *op. cit.*, p 34.

26. Named an Acting Ensign in October 1862, Gipson received his current rank a year later. His gallantry aboard the *Exchange* would be rewarded on July 9 with a promotion to the rank of Acting Volunteer Lt. He was honorably discharged in November 1865. Callahan, *op. cit.*, p. 220.

27. ORN, I, 26: 354–355; *Chicago Daily Tribune*, June 7, 1864; Edwards, *op. cit.*, p. 368; David Dixon Porter, *Naval History of the Civil War* (New York: Sherman Publishing Company, 1886; reprinted, Secaucus, N.J.: Castle Books, 1984), pp. 560–561. Gipson remained aboard the *Exchange* making a slow recovery over the next several days. When Lt. Cmdr. Owen arrived off Columbia the next day, he found her "pretty badly cut up," but except for her inability to make full speed, she was ready for action. ORN, I, 26: 353.

28. OR, I, 34, 1: 947–953, 971–985; OR, I, 34, 4: 137–138, 230–231, 368; ORN, I, 26: 355–356, 364, 383–384, 407–408; *Chicago Daily Tribune*, June 7, 1864; Edwards, *op. cit.*, pp. 368–377; Shea, *op. cit.*, 197–207; Browne, *From the Fresh Water Navy, op. cit.*, pp. 288–289; Hearn, *op. cit.*, pp. 234–243; Charles Dana Gibson, with E. Kay Gibson, *Assault and Logistics*, Vol. 2: *Union Army Coastal and River Operations, 1861–1866* (Camden, ME: Ensign Press, 1995), pp. 78–79.

Chapter 10

1. The 174-ton stern-wheeler *Fanny Barker* was constructed for Barker, Hart & Cook at Cincinnati early in 1863. Negotiations for her sale to the Mississippi Squadron began on April 10 and her sale to the government, for $28,000, was completed on May 13. Tinclad no. 30 was 158.8 feet long, with a beam of 20.5 feet and a 4.3-foot depth of hold. Her wheel was powered by two engines and two boilers. At Cairo, the new gunboat received her armament of six 24-pounder smoothbore Dahlgren howitzers. It took just over a month for the vessel to be converted into a light-draught. She was commissioned on May 11, Acting Master John R. Grace in command, and, by order of the Navy Department, her name was changed to *Fawn* on June 19. ORN, II, 1: 83; Frederick Way Jr., comp., *Way's Packet Directory, 1848–1994*, 2nd ed. (Athens, OH: Ohio University Press, 1994), pp. 162, 164; Paul H. Silverstone, *Warships of the Civil War Navies* (Annapolis, MD: Naval Institute Press, 1989), p. 171; "*Fawn*," in U.S. Navy Department, Naval Historical Center, *Dictionary of American Naval Fighting Ships*, http://www.history.navy. mil/danfs/f/fawn.htm (accessed February 9, 2008). Grace held his rank from the time he joined the Western Flotilla in November 1861 until his honorable discharge in January 1866. Edward W. Callahan, *List of Officers of the Navy of the United States and of the Marine Corps, from 1775 to 1900, Comprising a Complete Register of All Present and Former Commissioned, Warranted, and Appointed Officers of the United States Navy, and of the Marine Corps, Regular and Volunteer. Compiled from the Official Records of the Navy Department* (New York: L.R. Hamersly & Co., 1901; reprinted, New York: Haskell House, 1969), p. 225.

2. Washingtonian and 1860 Naval Academy graduate Bache (1840–1896) was commissioned a lieutenant in July 1862, the same month he was posted to the ironclad *Cincinnati*. He would command her until she was sunk off Vicksburg in May 1863. Porter next gave Bache—who, Like Lt. Cmdr. Selfridge, also lost a Pook turtle—a timberclad, the *Lexington*, which he would skipper into summer 1864. He finished the war in the North Atlantic Blockading Squadron. Serving afloat and ashore after the war, he was commissioned

a Lt. Cmdr. in 1866 and a Cmdr. on April 5, 1875, the same day he retired. Callahan, *op. cit.,* p. 33; Lewis R. Hamersly, *The Records of Living Officers of the U.S. Navy and Marine Corps, Compiled from Official Sources,* rev. ed. (Philadelphia, PA: J.B. Lippincott, 1870), p. 214.

3. ORN, I, 26: 392–393, 414, 464, 562, 791; OR, I, 34, 1: 783, 946–953; OR, I, 41, 1: 191–192; "Where We've Been: U.S.S. *Queen City* Sinking," *Clarendon Arkansas Homepage http://www.clarendon-ar.com/been/uss_queen_city/index.html* (July 6, 2007); Thomas A. DeBlack, *With Fire and Sword: Arkansas, 1861–1874* (Histories of Arkansas; Fayetteville, AR: University of Arkansas Press, 2003), pp. 66–67, 118; David Dixon Porter, *Naval History of the Civil War* (New York: Sherman Publishing Company, 1886; reprinted, Secaucus, N.J.: Castle Books, 1984), p. 562; Jay Slagle, *Ironclad Captain: Seth Ledyard Phelps and the U.S. Navy* (Kent, OH: Kent State University Press, 1996), pp. 383–384; John N. Edwards, *Shelby and His Men; or, The War in the West* (Cincinnati, OH: Miami Printing and Publishing Co., 1867; reprinted, Waverly, MO: General J.O. Shelby Memorial, 1993), pp. 317–318; Myron J. Smith, Jr., *The Timberclads in the Civil War: The Lexington, Conestoga and Tyler on the Western Rivers* (Jefferson, N.C.: McFarland, 2008), pp. 465–469. The *Tyler,* in company with the tinclads *Fawn* and *Naumkeag,* steamed up the Arkansas next morning with Col. Fenn's nine transports, leaving the *Lexington* to literally hold the little fort at White River Station. The *Queen City* was shifted up to guard Clarendon.

4. OR, I, 34, 1: 1044–1045; ORN, I, 26: 402–403, 415–417, 791; Slagle, *op. cit.,* p. 385; Smith, *The Timberclads, op. cit.,* pp. 469–470; *New York Times,* June 29, 1864.

5. The *Queen City's* commander joined the Western Flotilla as a mate in September 1861 and was promoted to his current rank in November 1863. Honorably discharged in December 1865, he returned to the lower deck, continuing his naval career as a master's mate from 1866 until his death in April 1876. Callahan, *op. cit.,* p. 264.

6. The long-time skipper of the *Naumkeag* was named an Acting Ensign in October 1862 and promoted to his current rank in July 1863. He would become an Acting Volunteer Lt. in July 1864 and be honorably discharged in September 1865. Callahan, *op. cit.,* p. 471.

7. ORN, I, 26: 417–433, 451–454, 461, 464; OR, I, 34, 1: 1051–1052; Edwards, *op. cit.,* pp. 321–326; *St. Louis Daily Missouri Democrat,* July 2, 1864; *Chicago Daily Tribune,* July 3–4, 1864; *Baltimore Sun,* July 4, 1864; *Cleveland Daily Herald,* July 5, 1864; *Chattanooga Daily Gazette,* July 12, 1864; *Memphis Argus,* July 12, 1864; "Where We've Been: U.S.S. *Queen City* Sinking," *Clarendon Arkansas Homepage http://www.clarendon-ar.com/been/uss_queen_city/index.html* (July 6, 2007); DeBlack, *op. cit.,* p. 118; Alfred T. Mahan, *The Gulf and Inland Waters,* Vol. 3 of the *Navy in the Civil War* (New York: Scribner's, 1883), pp. 212–213; Porter, *op. cit,* pp. 562–563; Duane Huddleston, Sammie Cantrell Rose, and Pat Taylor Wood, *Steamboats and Ferries on the White River: A Heritage Revisited* (Conway, AR: University of Central Arkansas Press, 1995; reprinted, Fayetteville, AR: University of Arkansas Press, 1998), p. 63; Smith, *The Timberclads, op. cit.,* pp. 470–477. Despite support from Rear Adm. Porter, Fitch, one of the most innovative convoy commanders of the Civil War, was regularly pilloried by army commanders for his tactics. His most famous dustup with the soldiers involved no less a figure than Lt. Gen. Ulysses S. Grant. Myron J. Smith Jr., *Le Roy Fitch: The Civil War Career of a Union Gunboat Commander* (Jefferson, NC: McFarland, 2007), pp. 221–226. There is a difference in the estimated length of the Clarendon battle. Bache claimed 45 minutes, Shelby in his OR report said an hour and a half, and Edwards reported that it took two hours. ORN, I, 26: 424; OR, I, 34, 1: 1050; Edwards, *op. cit.,* p. 325.

8. The 533-ton side-wheeler *Joseph Pierce* was finished at Pittsburgh for Capt. S.B. French at the beginning of the year. Powered by four boilers and four engines, the giant was

260 feet long, with a beam of 36 feet and a 6-foot draft. The first new packet to enter the New Orleans to Vicksburg trade since the beginning of the war, the vessel's captain as J.D. Pratt. Way, *op. cit.,* p. 258.

9. Tinclad No. 53 was constructed as the *Princess* for Capt. Frank Maratta and George W. Cullen at Freedom, PA, at the end of 1863. Powered by three boilers and two engines, the 185-ton stern-wheeler was 156.9 feet long, with a beam of 30.3 feet and a 4.4-foot depth of hold. After negotiations were completed, the USN officially purchased the vessel at Cincinnati on March 3, 1864, for $32.400. Modified before that by Joseph Brown, she was sent to Cairo for completion. Her battery of two 30-pounder Parrott rifles and six 24-pounder Dahlgren smoothbore howitzers was placed aboard, her name was changed, and she was placed into commission on April 3, Acting Master Henry T. Keene in command. ORN, II, 1: 154; Way, *op. cit.,* pp. 335, 379; "Naiad," in U.S. Navy Department, Naval Historical Center, *Dictionary of American Naval Fighting Ships, http://www.history. navy.mil/danfs/n1/naiad.htm* (accessed February 9, 2008); Silverstone, *op. cit.,* p 174. Harry Keene joined the Western Flotilla as a mate in February 1862 and was named an acting ensign a year later. He received his current rate and this command in March and was honorably discharged in January 1865. Callahan, *op. cit.,* p. 307.

10. Constructed by James B. Eads at the Carondelet, MO, yards, the 1,300-ton *Winnebago* was commissioned on April 27, the same day as her sister, the *Milwaukee.* Silverstone, *op. cit.,* p. 149.

11. ORN, I, 26: 395–400; *New York Times,* June 26, 1864; Porter, *op. cit.,* p. 562; Henry Walke, *Naval Scenes and Reminiscences of the Civil War in the United States on the Southern and Western Waters During the Years 1861, 1862 and 1863 with the History of That Period Compared and Corrected from Authentic Sources* (New York: F.R. Reed and Company, 1877), pp. 426–427.

12. ORN, I, 26: 463; Parsons, *loc. cit.* The 180-foot long *Mariner* was built at Belle Vernon, PA, in 1856. Way, *op. cit.,* p. 308.

13. The 266-ton Archer Line side-wheeler *Commercial* was constructed at Brownsville, PA, in 1860 operating on the Memphis-White River service since spring. Way, *op. cit.,* p. 107.

14. Employed as a troop transport to Vicksburg during much of 1863, the *Golden Era* was built at Galena, IL, in 1852. Displacing 24 tons, the craft was 178 feet long, with a beam of 29 feet and a 5.1-foot depth of hold. Way, *op. cit.,* p. 191.

15. ORN, I, 26: 472–473, 478, 482–484; *Memphis Daily Bulletin,* July 11, 1864; *Chicago Daily Tribune,* July 13, 1864. The 155-ton stern-wheeler *Reindeer* was constructed at Cincinnati in the fall of 1863 for the Ohio River trade. The merchantman was 147 feet long, with a 28.2-foot beam and a 4.6-foot draft. Two engines drove her wheel and gave her a top speed of 6 mph against the current. The packet was purchased into the USN at the Queen City on April 30, 1864, for $28,000 and immediately sent to the shipyards of Joseph Brown for conversion. With her name changed to avoid confusion with the super light-draught skippered by Acting Volunteer Lt. Henry Glassford, the *Peri* was finished at Mound City, where she was armed with one 30-pounder Parrott rifle (later swapped for two 20-pounders) and six 24-pounder smoothbore Dahlgren howitzers. The gunboat was commissioned on June 30, Acting Master Thomas M. Farrell, commanding, and on July 7, was dispatched to the Fourth District at the mouth of the Red River. ORN, I, 26: 466; ORN, II, 1, 175; Way, *op. cit.,* pp. 367, 391; Silverstone, *op. cit.,* p. 176. Farrell joined the squadron as an Acting Ensign in December 1862 and was given his current rank on June 29, 1863. He would be honorably discharged in December 1865. Callahan, *op. cit.,* p. 189.

16. *Indianapolis Journal,* July 22, 1864; *Chicago Daily Tribune,* July 24, 1864.

17. Powered by four boilers and four engines, the 230-foot long *Runyan* was constructed at Cincinnati in 1858. She had originally served on the Nashville-New Orleans and St. Louis-Alton trade, but since her return to service, had largely operated from St. Louis to New Orleans. Way, *op. cit.*, pp 35–36

18. ORN, I, 26: 470, 485; *New York Times,* July 27, 1864; Marion Bragg, *Historic Names and Places on the Lower Mississippi River* (Vicksburg, MS: Mississippi River Commission, 1977), p. 134; Lewis B. Parsons, *Reports to the War Department* (St. Louis, MO: George Knapp & Co., 1867), p. 36.

19. The *Clarabell* was constructed at Louisville in 1860 and employed, off and on, under government contract so far in the war. Way, *op. cit.,* p. 100.

20. *Memphis Evening Times,* July 28, 1864; *New York Times,* August 5, 9, 1864; *Wisconsin Daily Patriot,* July 30, 1864; *St. Louis Daily Missouri Democrat,* July 30, 1864; Bragg, *op. cit.,* p. 141; Parsons, *loc. cit.*

21. Tinclad No. 42, the 188-ton *J.T. Stockdale,* was constructed at West Brownsville, PA, in the summer of 1863 and named for Allegheny, PA steamboat captain Jackman T. Stockdale. The stern-wheeler entered the Pittsburgh-Cincinnati trade on October 26, but was sold to the U.S. Navy at the Queen City on November 13 for $32,500. One of the first tinclads to be completed for Rear Adm. Farragut, the vessel's armament comprised two 30-pounder Parrott rifles and four 24-pounder Dahlgren howitzers. Her name was changed at her December 26 commissioning, when Acting Ensign John Lowrie assumed temporary command. Acting Volunteer Lt. Thomas Edwards became the 63-man *Stockdale's* regular commander in January 1864. ORN, I, 21: 18; ORN, II, 1: 215; Way, *op. cit.,* pp. 237. 434; Silverstone, *op. cit.,* p. 179; "*Stockdale,*" in U.S. Navy Department, Naval Historical Center, *Dictionary of American Naval Fighting Ships, http://www.history.navy.mil/danfs/s18/stockdale-i.htm* (accessed February 9, 2008). Edwards was originally named an Acting Master in October 1861 and was promoted to his present rank in April 1864. He would be honorably discharged in February 1866. Callahan, *op. cit.,* p. 179.

22. Tinclad No. 48, the 217-ton *Rodolph* was completed at Cincinnati in late 1863 and sold to the Federal Navy by H.A. Jones and T. Sherlock on December 31, 1863, for $34,900. Completion of the stern-wheeler's casemate lagged into the spring. Finally, with her armament of two 30-pounder Parrott rifles and four 24-pounder Dahlgren howitzers installed and crewed by 60 sailors, she was commissioned on May 18, 1864, Acting Volunteer Lt. George D. Upham commanding. Silverstone, *op. cit.,* p. 178; Way, *op. cit.,* p. 401; "*Rodolph,*" in U.S. Navy Department, Naval Historical Center, *Dictionary of American Naval Fighting Ships, http://www.history.navy.mil/danfs/r8/rodolph.htm* (accessed February 9, 2008). George Upham was appointed an Acting Master in September 1861 and promoted into his present rank in April 1864. He would resign in May 1865. Callahan, *op. cit.,* p. 556.

23. The operations culminating in the Battle of Mobile Bay represent one of the great naval campaigns of the Civil War. The most complete recent account is Jack Friend's *West Wind, Flood Tide: The Battle of Mobile Bay* (Annapolis, MD: Naval Institute Press, 2004).

24. ORN, I, 21: 502–503, 629–638, 854–855; Friend, *op. cit.,* pp. 126, 135, 163, 228–229; *Mobile Advertiser and Register,* August 9, 11, 1864; Foxhall A. Parker, *The Battle of Mobile Bay and the Capture of Forts Morgan, Gaines, and Powell* (Boston, MA: Boston Stereotype Foundry, 1878), p. 22; Jack D. Coombe, *Gunfire Around the Gulf: The Last Major Naval Campaigns of the Civil War* (New York: Bantam Books, 1999), pp. 153, 162, 173, 189; William H. Roberts, *Now for the Contest: Coastal & Oceanic Naval Operations in the Civil War* (Lincoln: University of Nebraska Press, 2004), pp. 146–150; Dave Page, *Ships versus Shore: Engagements Along Southern Shores and Rivers* (Nashville TN: Rutledge Hill Press, 1994), pp. 215–216; Hurieosco Austill, "Fort Morgan in the Confederacy-August 1864," *Alabama Historical Quarterly* 7 (Summer 1945): p. 259 ; Mahan, *op. cit.,* pp. 219, 245; "*Stockdale,*" in U.S. Navy Department, Naval Historical Center, *Dictionary of American Naval Fighting Ships, http://www.history.navy.mil/danfs/s18/stockdale-i.htm* (accessed February 9, 2008).

25. King remain on the Tennessee River and be caught in command at Johnsonville, TN, when the supply depot there was burned to prevent its capture by Forrest late in 1864. Though court-martialed, he was honorably discharged on July 18, 1867. Callahan, *op. cit.,* p. 314.

26. Purchased new from her owners by Capt. James L. Wise of Cincinnati in 1862, the stern-wheeler *Eclipse* was constructed at Elizabeth, PA. She provided USQMD service throughout the war. Way, *op. cit.,* p. 140.

27. *Philadelphia Inquirer,* August 10, 1864; Christopher S. Dwyer, "Raiding Strategy: As Applied to the Western Confederate Cavalry in the American Civil War," *The Journal of Military History* 63 (April 1999): p. 275; Thomas Weber, *The Northern Railroads in the Civil War, 1861–1865* (New York: King's Crown Press, 1952), pp. 202–203; Archer Jones, *Confederate Strategy from Shiloh to Vicksburg* (Baton Rouge, LA: Louisiana State University Pres, 1961), pp. 27–28. Two days later, Lt. Cmdr. Shirk was forced to inform Rear Adm. Porter that he shared a problem common to the several district commanders. The enlistments of many gunboatmen were simultaneously expiring and they wished to return home. Reminding his chief how important it was to have the Tennessee patrolled in order to "protect the large amount of supplies going to General Sherman's army," the Shiloh veteran succinctly noted that "if the vessels have no crews, they can not be of use." ORN, I, 26: 508.

28. The giant side-wheeler *Empress* was constructed at Madison, IN, in 1861. At the time of the Shiloh campaign, she served as a hospital boat on the Tennessee River. Way, *op. cit.,* p. 152.

29. ORN, I, 26: 503–504; *Chicago Daily Tribune,* August 16, 1864; Cleveland *Daily Herald,* August 19, 1864; *New York Times,* August 21, 1864. Acting Master Baldwin's fears, later expressed to Lt. Cmdr. Owen, concerning the possible fate of the *Empress* had she been taken were not shared by the Sixth District boss. In fact, rather than praising the *Romeo's* skipper, the regular officer wrote his own superior: "...I am of the opinion a more competent person ought to be placed in command of the *Romeo.*" Owen believed that Baldwin was "entirely too old and too unused to a naval life to render him an efficient commander of an active vessel." ORN, I, 26: 504.

30. ORN, I, 26: 504–505. It is unknown for certain which battery had conducted the shoots of August 10–11. On August 20, the *Memphis Daily Bulletin* reported that all steamboats from below were obliged to pass Gaines Landing by night with all lights out. This was because there was a Rebel battery there, "at last accounts commanded by Capt. Pratt ... supported by Colton Greene's brigade of Marmaduke's division."

31. The *Henry Chouteau* was constructed at Cincinnati in 1853 and was one of the largest and oldest vessels plying the rivers. The side-wheeler was 263 feet long, with a beam of 35 feet and a 7-foot draft; six boilers were required to provide power. Way, *op. cit.,* p. 211.

32. Tinclad No. 54 was constructed at Cincinnati, OH, in 1863 and originally documented as *Cricket No. 3.* The 171-ton stern-wheeler was 161.1 feet long, with a beam of 30.3 feet and a 4.1-foot draft. She was powered by two engines and two boilers and was said to be capable of 4 mph against the current. The third *Cricket* was purchased by the USN at the Queen City for $32,000 on March 8, 1864, at which point her name was changed. Her alterations were completed at Mound City, where she received her armament of eight 24-pounder smoothbore Dahlgren howitzers. The light-draught was commissioned on April 11, Acting Master Patrick Don-

nelly in command. ORN, II, 1: 163; *Way, op. cit.,* pp. 115, 351; "*Nymph,*" in U.S. Navy Department, Naval Historical Center, *Dictionary of American Naval Fighting Ships,* http://www.history.navy.mil/danfs/n6/nymph.htm (accessed February 9, 2008); Silverstone, *op. cit.,* p. 175. Irishman Donnelly was appointed an Acting Ensign in April 1863 and was promoted into his current rank in January 1864. He would be honorably discharged in November 1865. Callahan, *op. cit.,* p. 166.

33. ORN, I, 26: 525; *Chicago Daily Tribune,* September 8, 1864.

34. The Johnson incursion is covered in my *Le Roy Fitch, op. cit.,* pp. 264–266; *Chicago Daily Tribune,* August 16, 19, 1864.

35. OR, I, 52, 1, 619; *Nashville Daily Press,* August 26, October 11, 1864.

36. The 232-ton stern-wheel transport *White Rose* was constructed at Parkersburg, VA/WV, in the summer of 1862. When finished, the vessel was 154.7 feet long, with a beam of 32.3 feet and a 5.1-foot draft. The *Rose* was sent to Pittsburgh, whence she began round trips to St. Louis in October. Powered by two engines and two boilers, she was said to be able to make 7 mph against the current. After purchasing her in February 1864, Capt. Mirah Shinkle completed one more Missouri trip before selling the craft to the USN on March 11 for $34,500. The *White Rose* was transferred to Mound City to serve as that station's temporary receiving ship. During the summer, workmen at the Illinois facility took her in hand and modified her into a tinclad, arming her with two 30-pounders, while four more 24-pounder smoothbore Dahlgren howitzers joined the two employed aboard earlier for training purposes. Renamed *Siren,* Tinclad No.56 was commissioned on August 30, Acting Master James Fitzpatrick commanding. ORN, II, 1: 209; *Way, op. cit.,* pp. 428, 485; "*Siren,*" in U.S. Navy Department, Naval Historical Center, *Dictionary of American Naval Fighting Ships,* http://www.history.navy.mil/danfs/s13/siren-1.htm (accessed February 9, 2008); Silverstone, *op. cit.,* p. 179. Fitzpatrick held this rank from his initial appointment in October 1862 through his honorable discharge on December 30, 1865. Callahan, *op. cit.,* p. 196.

37. ORN, I, 26: 535.

38. Daniel Glenney was appointed an Acting Ensign in October 1862 and an Acting Master a year later. He was officially listed as Deserted, November 4, 1864. Although there were several sightings of him late in the war, he was never apprehended. Callahan, *op. cit.,* p. 221. Interestingly enough, there is a lengthy article by a Daniel W. Glenney (whether this officer or someone assuming that name, maybe a relative) of interest: "Attempted Sale of the Federal Fleet," in *Southern Historical Society Papers* 32 (1904): pp. 58–67.

39. A member of the first graduating class of the U.S. Naval Academy, North Carolinian Jonathan H. Carter (?–1887) resigned his USN commission in April 1861. Sent west, he commanded the CSN gunboat *Polk* on the Mississippi through June 1862. Carter was then ordered to Shreveport to build the ironclad C.S.S. *Missouri,* which project occupied him for the remainder of the war. Promoted to the rank of CSN captain, Carter and the *Missouri* surrendered in June 1865. After the war, he married and became a cotton plantation owner in Louisiana. A full profile of this enterprising but forgotten officer is Katherine Brash Jeter, *A Man and His Boat: The Civil War Career and Correspondence of Lieutenant Jonathan H. Carter, CSN* (Baton Rouge, LA: Center for Louisiana Studies, 1996).

40. Wells was originally posted to the Western Flotilla as a mate in April 1863 and was promoted to his current position in February 1864. Unstained by the *Rattler* incident, he was honorably discharged in June 1866. Callahan, *op. cit.,* p. 577.

41. ORN, I, 26: 536–551, 794–802; ORN, I, 27: 177–178; OR, I, 41,1: 110, 112; William N. Bock to Mother, May 5, 1864, William N. Bock Papers, Illinois State Historical

Society, Springfield (cited hereafter as Bock Papers, with date); *New York Times,* November 17, 1864; *Chicago Daily Tribune,* November 17, 1864; Robert L. Kerby, *Kirby Smith's Confederacy: The Trans-Mississippi South, 1863–1865* (New York: Columbia University Press, 1972), pp. 323–330; Jeffrey S. Prushankin, *A Crisis in Confederate Command: Edmund Kirby Smith, Richard Taylor, and the Army of the Trans-Mississippi* (Baton Rouge, LA: Louisiana State University Press, 2005), 175–197; Terry Foenander, "Treachery of a Union Gunboat Commander," *Foenander Home Page,* http://www.tfoenander.com/treachery.htm (accessed December 1, 2008). After losing two skippers under unique circumstances, the *Rattler* herself was struck by an uncommonly heavy winter gale off Grand Gulf, MS, on December 30. Her anchor cable parted and she was driven onto shore, where she hit a snag and sank. The gunboat was abandoned and left for the Rebels to finally capture. Once all of her stores and guns were removed, the Confederates torched her and she was destroyed. ORN, I, 26: 769–771.

42. Capt. J.C. Dowty's 140-foot stern-wheeler *Celeste* was a new boat completed at Cincinnati early in the year. She was often employed on the New Orleans-to-Red River route, particularly at times of low water. *Way, op. cit.,* p. 76.

43. Constructed at Belle Vernon, PA, in 1863, the 299-ton *Nevada* was owned in Pittsburgh and usually ran between that city and St. Louis. She was occasionally employed on USQMD charters, of which this was one. *Way, op. cit.,* p. 343.

44. ORN, I, 26: 529–532; *Chicago Daily Tribune,* September 16, 1864.

45. ORN, I, 26: 565.

46. The 160-foot long *Melnotte* was built at California, PA, in 1856 and went through a series of ownership changes during the war. *Way, op. cit.,* pp. 318.

47. *Chicago Daily Tribune,* October 2, 1864.

48. The 231-foot-long *Adam Jacobs* was constructed at Brownsville, PA, earlier in the year. The vessel was not owned by a shipping concern, but steamed as an independent. *Way, op. cit.,* p. 5.

49. *Chicago Daily Tribune,* October 3, 1864; *New York Times,* October 4, 1864.

50. The 180-foot-long side-wheeler *Darling* was completed at McKeesport, PA, in 1863 to run the Cincinnati-Memphis trade and was taken over by the Dean Line at the end of September 1864 to operate over the same route. *Way, op. cit.,* p. 120.

51. *Chicago Daily Tribune,* October 2, 1864.

52. *Chicago Daily Tribune,* October 3, 1864; *New York Times,* October 4, 1864.

53. The 156.7-foot long *Emma No. 2* was constructed at Freedom, PA, in 1862. In the spring of 1864 she began serving the Memphis-White River route. *Way, op. cit.,* p. 149.

54. *Chicago Daily Tribune,* October 3, 1864; *New York Times,* October 4, 1864.

55. *Chicago Daily Tribune,* October 14, 17, 1864.

Chapter 11

1. William Tecumseh Sherman, *Memoirs* (Penguin Classics; New York: Penguin Books, 2000), p. 519; OR, I, 39, 3: 162; Lloyd Lewis, *Sherman: Fighting Prophet* (New York: Harcourt, Brace and World, 1960), p. 430.

2. Bruce Catton, *Never Call Retreat* (New York: Pocket Books, 1973), p. 388; John Bell Hood, *Advance and Retreat: Personal Experiences in the United States and Confederate States Armies* (New Orleans, LA: Pub. For the Hood Orphan Memorial Fund, 1880), pp. 263–269; Hood, "The Invasion of Tennessee," in *Battles and Leaders of the Civil War,* edited by Robert U. Johnson and Clarence C. Buel, 4 vols. (New York: The Century Company, 1884–1887; reprinted, Thomas Yoseloff, 1956), Vol. 4, p. 425; OR, I, 39, 2: 121; Lonnie E.

Maness, *An Untutored Genius: The Military Career of General Nathan Bedford Forrest* (Oxford, MS: The Guild Bindery Press, 1990), pp. 317–322; Benson J. Lossing, *Pictorial Field Book of the Civil War: Journeys Through the Battlefields in the Wake of Conflict*, 3 vols. (Hartford, CT: T. Belknap, 1874; reprinted, The Johns Hopkins University Press, 1997), Vol. 3, pp. 398–399; "Decatur and the Civil War," *Nostagiaville*, *http://travel.nostalgiaville.com/Alabama/Decatur/decatur%20ci vil%20war.htm* (accessed December 1, 2008);Myron J. Smith, Jr., *Le Roy Fitch: The Civil War Career of a Union Gunboat Commander* (Jefferson, NC: McFarland, 2007), pp. 267–268.

3. Rev. Dr. David Campbell Kelley was born at Leeville, TN, on Christmas Day, 1833. An 1851 graduate of Cumberland University, he became a medical doctor, graduating from the University of Nashville. That same year he traveled to China as a Methodist medical minister. Nicknamed "the Parson," Kelley began his war service at Huntsville, AL, as captain of "The Kelly Rangers/Kelly Troopers," Company F, Forrest's Battalion (3d Tennessee Cavalry). It was Kelley whom Forrest asked to pray for the troops at Fort Donelson in February 1862, becoming thereafter, according to Dr. Wyeth, one of the cavalry leader's intimate associates. After the Civil War, the colonel took a D.D. degree from Cumberland University in 1868 and served the Methodist Episcopal Church at Gallatin, TN, and at other towns thereafter in the Nashville area. Kelley was one of the founders of Vanderbilt University in 1873 and served on its board of trustees from 1875 to 1891. Fitch's wartime opponent held numerous posts within his church hierarchy and ran (unsuccessfully) as Prohibition Party candidate for Governor of Tennessee in 1890. Kelley, who died at Nashville on May 14, 1909, "was a vocal force," according to John E. Fisher, "in urging upon whites reasoned and informed views of blacks and relations between the races." W. Calvin Dickinson, "Temperance," in Carroll Van West, ed., *The Tennessee Encyclopedia of History and Culture* (Nashville, TN: Rutledge Hill Press for the Tennessee Historical Society, 1998), p. 913; "'The Kelly Rangers/ Kelly Troopers," Company F, Forrest's Battalion (3d Tennessee Cavalry) and Company K, 4th Alabama Cavalry Regiment," *Confederate Units of Madison County* homepage, *http://www.rootsweb.com/~almadiso/confunit.htm* (March 4, 2006); John E. Fisher, *They Rode with Forrest and Wheeler: A Chronicle of Five Tennessee Brothers' Service in the Confederate Western Cavalry* (Jefferson, NC: McFarland, 1995), pp. 244–245, 250; "Reverent Dr. D.C. Kelley," *The Vanderbilt University Quarterly* 9 (October 1909): p. 236; Teresa Gray, Public Services Archivist, Special Collections and University Archives, Jean and Alexander Heard Library, Vanderbilt University, "Re: David Campbell Kelley," March 13, 2006, Personal email, March 13, 2006; Myron J. Smith Jr., "Le Roy Fitch Meets the Devil's Parson: The Battle of Bell's Mills, December 4–6, 1864," *North & South* 10 (January 2008): p. 43.

4. The stern-wheeler *City of Pekin* was constructed at Elizabeth, PA, in 1863 for the Illinois River-to-St. Louis trade; like other vessels, she also served under USQMD contracts. Frederick Way Jr., comp., *Way's Packet Directory, 1848–1994*, 2nd ed. (Athens, OH: Ohio University Press, 1994), p. 96.

5. Capt. J.H. Dunlap's 215-ton stern-wheeler *Kenton* was built at Shousetown, PA, in 1860. Previously on the Pittsburgh-Cincinnati-Louisville route, Dunlap purchased her in October 1863 to employ on government contracts. Way, *op. cit.*, p. 269

6. Built at Brownsville, PA, in 1857, the 151-foot long stern-wheeler *Aurora* was owned by David Gibson & Co. of Aurora, IN, after which town she took her name. Way, *op. cit.*, p. 33.

7. Tinclad No. 55 was constructed as the *Ben Gaylord* at Cincinnati in 1863 by Capt. Uriah B. Scott. Originally placed on the Ohio River trade between Portsmouth and Parkersburg, the vessel was purchased at the Queen City by the USN on March 7, 1864 for $35,000. Renamed *Undine*, she was finished at Mound City and armed with eight 24-pounder Dahlgren smoothbore howitzers. The tinclad was commissioned there in April, Acting Master John L. Bryant in command. On July 25 she hit a snag and sank near Clifton, but was raised a week later and repaired. Way, *op. cit.*, pp. 48, 463; ORN, II, 1: 229; Paul H. Silverstone, *Warships of the Civil War Navies* (Annapolis, MD: Naval Institute Press, 1989), p. 179; "Undine," in U.S. Navy Department, Naval Historical Center, *Dictionary of American Naval Fighting Ships*, *http://www.history.navy.mil/danfs/u/undine-i.htm* (accessed February 9, 2008); Donald H. Steenburn, "The United States Ship *Undine*," *Civil War Times Illustrated* 35 (August 1996): p. 27. Acting Master John L. Bryant was appointed an Acting Ensign in December 1862 and to his present rank in February 1864. He would be honorably discharged in February 1868. Edward W. Callahan, *List of Officers of the Navy of the United States and of the Marine Corps, from 1775 to 1900, Comprising a Complete Register of All Present and Former Commissioned, Warranted, and Appointed Officers of the United States Navy, and of the Marine Corps, Regular and Volunteer. Compiled from the Official Records of the Navy Department* (New York: L.R. Hamersly & Co., 1901; reprinted, New York: Haskell House, 1969), p. 86.

8. The 192-ton stern-wheeler *W.C. Mann* was constructed at Cincinnati, OH, in 1863 for her owner/master, Capt. John M. Shunk. The craft was 155 feet long, with a beam of 31 feet and a 3.10-foot depth of hold. The future Tinclad No. 52 was purchased for $29,500 by the USN in the Queen City on February 23, 1864, at which point her name was changed. Moved to Mound City, the gunboat was armed with eight 24-pounder Dahlgren howitzers and was commissioned in April, Acting Master Augustus F. Thompson commanding. Following a month patrolling in the Seventh District, she was permanently assigned to the Ninth. ORN, II, 1: 77; Way, *op. cit.*, pp. 144, 474; Silverstone, *op. cit.*, p. 171; "Elfin," in U.S. Navy Department, Naval Historical Center, *Dictionary of American Naval Fighting Ships*, *http://www.history.navy.mil/danfs/u2/elfin-i.htm* (accessed February 9, 2008). Acting Master Thompson joined the Mississippi Squadron at that rank in April 1863. The former skipper of the *Paw Paw* would be honorably discharged in October 1865. Callahan, *op. cit.*, p. 541.

9. OR, I, 39,1, 539–541, 546–549; OR, I, 39, 3: 238–239, 815–817; Way, *op. cit.*, pp. 33, 269; ORN, I, 26: 582–583, 587; *Chicago Daily Tribune*, October 15, 21, 1864; *Charleston Mercury*, November 1, 1864; *Macon Weekly Telegraph*, November 11, 1864; Brian Steel Wills, *A Battle From the Start: The Life of Nathan Bedford Forrest* (New York: HarperCollins, 1992), pp. 260–261; "Battle of Eastport," *Confederate Veteran* 5 (January 1897): p. 13; Maness, *op. cit.*, p. 304; David Dixon Porter, *Naval History of the Civil War* (New York: Sherman, 1886; reprinted, Mineola, NY: Dover Publications, 1998), p. 563; William C. Lytle, comp., *Merchant Steam Vessels of the United States, 1807–1868 "The Lytle List"* (Mystic, CT: The Steamship Historical Society of America, 1952), pp. 18, 107; Jacob D. Cox, *March to the Sea: Franklin and Nashville*, Campaigns of the Civil War, no. 10 (New York: Scribner's, 1882), p. 12; Thomas Jordan and J.P. Pryor, *The Campaigns of Lieut. Gen. N.B. Forrest and of Forrest's Cavalry* (New Orleans and New York: Blelock & Co., 1868, reprinted, New York: DaCapo Press, 1996), pp. 575, 584–586; Donald H. Steenburn, *loc. cit.*; John Allan Wyeth, *Life of General Nathan Bedford Forrest* (New York: Harper & Bros., 1904), pp. 47, 50; Robert Selph Henry, "*First with the Most" Forrest* (Indianapolis, IN: Bobbs-Merrill, 1944), pp. 364–365, 368–369; Ben Earl Kitchens, *Gunboats and Cavalry: A History of Eastport, Mississippi* (Florence, AL: Thornwood Book Publishers, 1985), pp. 119–124; Herschel K. Smith Jr., *Some Encounters with General Forrest* (McKenzie, TN: privately printed, 1959?), p. 3; John Watson Morton, *The Artillery of Nathan Bedford Forrest's Cavalry* (Nashville, TN: Publishing House of the Methodist Episcopal Church, South, 1909), p. 252; Edward F. Williams III and H.K. Humphreys,

eds., *Gunboats and Cavalry: The Story of Forrest's 1864 John-sonville Campaign, as Told to J.P. Pryor and Thomas Jordan, by Nathan Bedford Forrest* (Memphis, TN: Nathan Bedford Forrest Trail Committee, 1965), p. 6; "The Battle of East-port," *Confederate Veteran* 5 (January 1897): p. 13; Smith, *Le Roy Fitch, op. cit.,* pp. 268–271; Edward F. Williams, 3rd, "The Johnsonville Raid and Nathan Bedford Forrest State Park," *Tennessee Historical Quarterly* 28 (Fall 1969): p. 227; Campbell H. Brown, "Forrest's Johnsonville Raid," *Civil War Times Illustrated* 4 (June 1965): p. 53; Norman R. Denny, "The Devil's Navy," *Civil War Times Illustrated* 35 (August 1996): p. 28; Mark Zimmerman, *Guide to Civil War Nashville* (Nashville, TN: Battle of Nashville Preservation Society, 2004), p. 14. The literature on Forrest vs. the gunboats in Oc-tober–November 1864 is huge, largely because the cavalry-naval aspect of the adventure is so unusual. Donald H. Steen-burn's recent work is very helpful, *Silent Echoes of Johnsonville: Rebel Cavalry and Yankee Gunboats* (Rogersville, AL: Elk River Press, 1994).

10. The 184-ton *General Thomas* was one of four side-wheel wooden gunboats built by the War Department's USQMD at Bridgeport, AL, for use on the upper Tennessee River. The $19,000 construction was undertaken by Capt. Arthur Edwards, with supervision and support from Lt. Cmdr. Fitch and Acting Volunteer Lt. Henry Glassford. When completed, the vessel was 165 feet long, with a beam of 26 feet and a 4.6-foot depth of hold. Once her armament of two 20-pounder Parrott rifles and four 24-pounder Dahlgren howitzers was aboard, she was officially leased to the USN and commissioned August 8, 1864, Acting Master Gilbert Morton in command. Way, *op. cit.,* p. 184; ORN, II, 1: 93; Silverstone, *op. cit.,* p. 166; "*General Thomas*" in U.S. Navy Department, Naval Historical Center, *Dictionary of American Naval Fighting Ships, http://www.history.navy.mil/d anfs/g3/general_thomas.htm* (accessed February 9, 2008). Gilbert Morton (?–1890) joined the Mississippi Squadron as an Acting Gunner on October 1, 1862, being promoted to his present rank five days later. He would be honorably dis-charged in October 1865. One of the few volunteer inland officers to transition back into the regular USN, he was reap-pointed an Acting Master in May 1867 and an Ensign in March 1868. Morton retired in 1874 and died June 26, 1890. Callahan, *op. cit.,* p. 394.

11. The 214-ton *Stone River* was also built by Capt. Ed-wards at Bridgeport 1864, originally as one of the ten con-structed as part of the famed "Cracker Line" designed to en-sure the supply of Chattanooga. When it was determined that insufficient light-draught gunboat capability was avail-able on the upper Tennessee, the decision was taken to con-vert the *Stone River* into a light army gunboat. She was lightly armored, equipped with cannon (most likely howitzers) served by military gun crews, and provided with a civilian crew commanded by Capt. William A. Naylor. Charles Dana Gibson and E. Kay Gibson, comps., *The Army's Navy Series,* Vol. I: *Dictionary of Transports and Combat Vessels, Steam and Sail, Employed by the Union Army, 1861–1868* (Camden, ME: Ensign Press, 1995), p. 305; Gibson, comp., *The Army's Navy Series,* Vol. II: *Assault and Logistics, Union Army Coastal and River Operations, 1861–1868* (Camden, ME: Ensign Press, 1995), p. 380, 386. Naylor was commander of the 10th In-diana Battery, stationed with the reserve at Nashville on Au-gust 10, when he received orders to turn over his battery and "proceed with his company to Chattanooga, Tenn, where he will embark upon a gunboat to be there furnished him and proceed with it to Decatur, Ala., and report to Brig. Gen. Granger." OR, I, 52, 1: 573.

12. The 201-ton *General Grant* was one of four side-wheel wooden gunboats built by the War Department's USQMD at Bridgeport, AL, for use on the upper Tennessee River. The $19,000 construction was undertaken by Capt. Arthur Edwards, with supervision and support from Lt. Cmdr. Fitch and Acting Volunteer Lt. Henry Glassford. When completed, the vessel was 171 feet long, with a beam

of 26 feet and a 4.7-foot depth of hold. Once her armament of two 20-pounder Parrott rifles and three 24-pounder Dahlgren howitzers was aboard, she was officially leased to the USN and commissioned July 20, 1864, Acting Ensign Joseph Watson in command. Way, *op. cit.,* p. 181; ORN, II, 1: 92; Silverstone, *op. cit.,* p. 166; "*General Grant*" in U.S. Navy Department, Naval Historical Center, *Dictionary of American Naval Fighting Ships, http://www.history.navy. mill/danfs/g3/general_grant.htm* (accessed February 9, 2008). Remembered for his initial role in the Morgan Raid incident a year earlier, Watson was the successful skipper of the Cum-berland River tinclad *Springfield.* His transfer to the *Thomas* was arranged by Fitch at the end of July 1864. Callahan, *op. cit.,* p. 572.

13. The 201-ton *General Burnside* was one of four side-wheel wooden gunboats built by the War Department's USQMD at Bridgeport, AL, for use on the upper Tennessee River. The $19,000 construction was undertaken by Capt. Arthur Edwards, with supervision and support from Lt. Cmdr. Fitch and Acting Volunteer Lt. Henry Glassford. When completed, the vessel was 171 feet long, with a beam of 26 feet and a 4.9-foot depth of hold. Once her armament of two 20-pounder Parrott rifles and three 24-pounder Dahlgren howitzers was aboard, she was officially leased to the USN and commissioned August 8, 1864, Acting Volun-teer Lt. Glassford in command. Way, *op. cit.,* p. 171; ORN, II, 1: 92; Silverstone, *loc. cit.;* "*General Burnside*" in U.S. Navy Department, Naval Historical Center, *Dictionary of American Naval Fighting Ships, http://www.history.navy.mil/ danfs/g2/general_burnside.htm* (accessed February 9, 2008). When Lt. Forrest took over the Eleventh District, he made the *Burnside* his flag boat on October 15.

14. The 187-ton *General Sherman* was one of four side-wheel wooden gunboats built by the War Department's USQMD at Bridgeport, AL, for use on the upper Tennessee River. The $19,000 construction was undertaken by Capt. Arthur Edwards, with supervision and support from Lt. Cmdr. Fitch and Acting Volunteer Lt. Henry Glassford. When completed, the vessel was 168 feet long, with a beam of 26 feet and a 4.6-foot depth of hold. Once her armament of two 20-pounder Parrott rifles and three 24-pounder Dahlgren howitzers was aboard, she was officially leased to the USN and commissioned July 27, 1864, Acting Master Joseph W. Morehead in command. Way, *op. cit.,* p. 181; ORN, II, 1: 93; Silverstone, *loc. cit.;* "*General Sherman*" in U.S. Navy Department, Naval Historical Center, *Dictionary of American Naval Fighting Ships, http://www.history.navy.mil/da nfs/g3/general_sherman.htm* (accessed February 9, 2008). Joseph W. Morehead was appointed an Acting Ensign in Jan-uary 1863 and was awarded promotion to his current rank in December. Previously executive officer of the tinclad *Cricket,* he would be honorably discharged in September 1865. Calla-han, *op. cit.,* p. 390.

15. OR, I, 39, 1: 694–695; OR, I, 39, 3: 810, 815–816, 841; OR, I, 45, 1: 647; ORN, I, 26: 589–592; Hood, *op. cit.,* p. 269; Wyeth, *op. cit.,* pp. 453, 456, 516; Maness, *op. cit.,* pp. 305, 322; Jordan and Pryor, *The Campaigns, op. cit.,* pp. 589–590; Brown, *op. cit.,* p. 49; Henry, *op. cit.,* p. 371; Wills, *op. cit.,* p. 263; ORN, I, 26: 693, 699–700; "*Nashville,*" in *Major General George Thomas Blog Site, http://home.earth-line.net/~oneplez/majorgeneral georgehthomasblogsite/id20.html* (February 28, 2006), which is cited hereafter as Thomas Blog Site; "Decatur and the Civil War," Nostagiaville *http://travel.nostalgiaville.com/Alabama/Decatur/decatur %20civil%20war.htm* (accessed December 1, 2008); Wiley Sword, *Embrace an Angry Wind—The Confederacy's Last Hur-rah: Spring Hill, Franklin & Nashville* (New York: Harper-Collins, 1992), pp. 56–58, 63–65. In Washington, D.C. U.S. Navy Secretary Gideon Welles infused his Mississippi Squadron with new leadership. On October 19, he turned the unit over to Acting Rear Adm. Samuel Phillips Lee. Lee had recently been relieved from command of the North Atlantic Blockading Squadron that was going to Porter. Dudley Tay-

lor Cornish and Virginia Jeans Laas, *Lincoln's Lee: The Life of Samuel Phillips Lee, United States Navy, 1812–1897* (Lawrence, KS: University Press of Kansas, 1986), p. 140; Johnny H. Whisenant, "Samuel Phillips Lee, U.S.N.: Commander, Mississippi Squadron (October 19, 1864–August 14, 1865)," (Unpublished MS Thesis; Pittsburg, KS: Kansas State College of Pittsburg, 1968), pp. 12–20; "Samuel Phillips Lee," in William B. Cogar, *Dictionary of Admirals of the U.S. Navy*, 2 vols. (Annapolis, Md.: Naval Institute Press, 1989), Vol. 1, pp. 96–97. On October 26, Gen. Thomas received a warning from Memphis: "It is reported that Forrest has sent to Mobile for a battery of heavy guns to plant on the Tennessee River." OR, I, 39, 3: 459.

16. The hull of the first *Belle Saint Louis* was built at Metropolis, IL, in early 1864; the side-wheel boat was then completed at St. Louis. A unit in the early Anchor Line, she was 277 feet long, with a beam of 38.5 feet and a 7.5-foot draft. Way, *op. cit.*, p. 46.

17. OR, I, 39, 1: 879–882.

18. The 184-ton *Mazeppa* was a new boat constructed at Cincinnati earlier in the year. Under Capt. Lee Pettit, she was contracted to the USQMD for cargo services between Louisville and Johnsonville. Surviving members of the crew reached Cincinnati on November 6, save Capt. Pettit and mate Sam Pence from Middleport, OH, who were "last seen going up over the bank on the opposite shore amid a rain of shot." Way, *op. cit.*, p. 318; Lewis B. Parsons, *Reports to the War Department* (St. Louis, MO: George Knapp & Co., 1867), p. 37.

19. The *Anna* was built at Cincinnati in 1860. Way, *op. cit.*, p. 23; Parsons, *loc. cit.*

20. Constructed at Cincinnati during the summer, the 157-foot-long stern-wheeler *Naugatuck* was completed in September. Under the command of Capt. A.Q. Ross, she entered the Cincinnati-to-Memphis or Nashville trade. She was released by her captors and survived the war. Way, *op. cit.*, p. 340.

21. The 234-ton *Alice* was constructed at Pittsburgh, PA, in early 1864 for Capt. S.B. French. The *Pittsburgh Commercial* on August 4 called her "a nice looking craft." She also survived her holdup and was sold for parts in 1866. Way, *op. cit.*, p. 11.

22. OR, I, 39, 1: 695–701, 870; OR, I, 39, 3: 282, 302–303, 343, 345, 357, 524; OR, I, 41, 4: 427–428, 431, 452, 469; OR, I, 45, 1: 648; ORN, I, 26: 591–594; *St. Louis Daily Missouri Republican*, November 6, 1864; Sword, *op. cit.*, pp. 65, 416; Hood, *op. cit.*, pp. 259, 270–271; *Chicago Daily Tribune*, November 2, 1864; *New York Times*, November 7, 1864; "Decatur and the Civil War," Nostagiaville *http://travel.nostalgiaville.com/Alabama/Decatur/decatur%20civil%20war.htm* (accessed December 1, 2008); Brown, "Forrest's Johnsonville Raid," *op. cit.*, 50–53; Henry, *op. cit.*, pp. 369–372; R.R. Hancock, *Hancock's Diary; or, a History of the Second Tennessee Confederate Cavalry....* (Dayton, OH: Press of Morningstar Bookshop, 1981), p. 495; John W. Morton, "Raid of Forrest's Cavalry on the Tennessee River in 1864," *Southern Historical Society Papers* 10 (1882): pp. 261–268; Maness, *op. cit.*, pp. 309–310; Wills, *loc. cit.*, pp. 263–265; Morton, *The Artillery of Nathan Bedford Forrest's Cavalry, op. cit.*, pp. 245–248; Jordan and Pryor, *op. cit.*, pp. 592–593; Julius F. Gracey, "Capture of the *Mazeppa*," *Confederate Veteran* 13 (December 1905): pp. 566–570; J.F. Orr, "Capture of the *Undine* and *Mazappa*," *Confederate Veteran* 18 (July 1910): p. 323; Smith, *Le Roy Fitch, op. cit.*, pp. 274–275. Brig. Gen. Granger would evacuate Decatur on November 25, leaving behind 15 pontoon boats. Shortly thereafter, these were among the items found when Confederate Brig. Gen. Philip D. Roddy occupied the town. OR, I, 45,1: 673, OR, I, 34, 2: 729.

23. The 235-ton stern-wheeler *Venus* was constructed at Carondelet, MO, in 1863. Way, *op. cit.*, p. 467; Parsons, *op. cit.*, p. 38.

24. Constructed at Cincinnati in 1856, the 165-foot-long

J.W. Cheeseman had already had a major close call while under government contract. Her captain, Jacob Ketchum, was shot during a passage up the Yazoo River in April 1863. This time, her crew was taken prisoner and did not return to the Queen City until March 1865. Way, *op. cit.*, p. 237; Parsons, *loc. cit.*

25. James B. Williams was named an Acting Ensign on March 11, 1863 and was reinstated as an acting master on September 1, 1864; he would be honorably discharged on December 20, 1865. Callahan, *op. cit.*, p. 591.

26. OR, I, 39, 1: 860, 863; ORN, I, 26: 594–595, 598–607; ORN, II, 220; *Chicago Daily Tribune*, November 3, 6, 1864; *Paducah Federal Union*, November 3, 1864; *St. Louis Daily Missouri Republican*, November 6, 1864; *Louisville Democrat*, November 8, 1864; *Cleveland Daily Herald*, November 11, 1864; Washington, D.C. *Daily National Intelligencer*, November 11, 1864; Brown, "Forrest's Johnsonville Raid," *op. cit.*, pp. 51–52; Wills, *op. cit.*, pp. 264–267; Way, *op. cit.*, p. 467; John W. Morton, "Raid of Forrest's Cavalry," *Ibid.;* Maness, *op. cit.*, pp. 310–312; Morton, *The Artillery of Nathan Bedford Forrest's Cavalry, op. cit.*, pp. 248–249; Gracey, *op. cit.*, 566; Wyeth, *op. cit.*, pp. 522–526; Henry, *op. cit.*, p. 374; John A. Eisterhold, "Fort Heiman, Forgotten Fortress," *West Tennessee Historical Society Papers* 38 (1974): p. 53.; Steenburn, "The United States Ship *Undine*," *Ibid.;* Smith, *Le Roy Fitch, op. cit.*, pp. 275–276. After the Civil War, Capt. Gracey became a distinguished Clarksville citizen "very active in the affairs of the Cumberland." Byrd Douglas, *Steamboatin' on the Cumberland* (Nashville: The Tennessee Book Company, 1961), p. 158. Certain aspects of the *Undine* and *Pueblo* captures are eerily similar as testimony at the respective inquiries demonstrates. I look at the literature of the *Pueblo* incident in my *The United States Navy and Coast Guard, 1946–1983* (Jefferson, NC: McFarland, 1984), pp. 294–296.

27. Way does not list the *David Hughes*. Our information comes from Parsons, *op. cit.*, p. 37, who lists her as the *Dave Hughes*.

28. ORN, I, 26: 594, 604,706–707; OR, I, 39, 1: 867–869; OR, I, 39, 3: 548, 602; OR, I, 52, 1: 120–122; *Louisville Democrat*, November 8, 1864; *Cleveland Daily Herald*, November 11, 1864; Wills, *loc. cit.*; Stanley F. Horn, *The Decisive Battle of Nashville* (Baton Rouge, LA: Louisiana State University Press, 1956), p. 30; Gibson, *Dictionary, op. cit.*, p. 81; Whisenant, *op. cit.*, pp. 43–44; Williams, *op. cit.*, 237; James Dinkins, *1861 to 1865, by an Old Johnnie: Personal Recollections and Experiences in the Confederate Army* (Cincinnati, OH: The Robert Clarke, Co., 1897), p. 205; Morton, *The Artillery of Nathan Bedford Forrest's Cavalry, loc. cit.*; Wyeth, *op. cit.*, pp. 524–525; Jordan and Pryor, *op. cit.*, pp. 597–598; Brown, *op. cit.*, 53–54; Smith, *Le Roy Fitch, op. cit.*, pp. 277–278.

29. ORN, I, 26: 600–605, 611–612; OR, I, 39, 3: 590, 611; Smith, *Le Roy Fitch, op. cit.*, pp. 278–279; Logbooks of the U.S.S. *Moose*, June 15, 1863–August 10, 1865, Records of the Bureau of Navigation, Record Group 19, U.S. National Archives, Washington, D.C., November 1–2, 1864 (cited hereafter as Logbook of the U.S.S. *Moose*, with date). The *Undine*'s captain was "severely chastised" by the investigating board for loss of the tinclad's signal book; still, he was not cashiered. Thereafter, all vessels were to be issued weighted bags for quick disposal in times of emergency. The Fitch-Shirk strategy has been criticized as an "over-cautious approach." Williams, *op. cit.*, 238.

30. ORN, I, 26: 611, 615; OR, I, 52, 1: 122; OR, I, 39, 1: 861, 869, 874; Wyeth, *op. cit.*, p. 525; Jordan and Pryor, *The Campaigns, op. cit.*, p. 598; Maness, *op. cit.*, pp. 312–313; Jeffrey L. Patrick, "A Fighting Sailor on the Western Rivers: The Civil War Letters of 'Gunboat,'" *The Journal of Mississippi History* 58 (Fall 1996): p. 279. The *Paw Paw* could barely make four mph steaming upstream. Robert W. Kaeuper, "The Forgotten Triumph of the *Paw Paw*." *American Heritage* 46 (October 1995): p. 88; Wills, *loc. cit.*; Smith, *Le Roy Fitch, op. cit.*, pp. 279–280; Stephen E. Ambrose, *Halleck:*

Lincoln's Chief of Staff (Baton Rouge: Louisiana State University Press, 1962), pp. 190–191; Logbook of the U.S.S. *Moose*, November 3, 1864. The last Confederate elements to leave Paris were Col. Hinchie P. Mabry's cavalry brigade and the 12-lb. howitzers from Capt. John C. Thrall's battery, nicknamed "The Arkansas Rats." These took position above Johnsonville later in the day. OR, I, 39, 1: 874–875; Wyeth, *op. cit.*, p. 527.

31. ORN, I, 26: 630; Maness, *loc. cit.*; Williams, *op. cit.*, 239; J.B. Irion and D.V. Beard, *Underwater Archaeological Assessment of Civil War Shipwrecks in Kentucky Lake, Benton and Humphreys Counties, Tennessee* (New Orleans, LA: R. Christopher Goodwin & Associates, Inc., for the Tennessee Division of Archaeology, Department of Environment and Conservation, State of Tennessee, 1993), p. 3. The island, Johnsonville, Reynoldsburg, and the surrounding area were covered by the TVA's Kentucky Lake in 1944. "The Archaeological Investigations of the Battle of Johnsonville," *PanAm Consultants Homepage, http://www.panamconsultants.com/P AGE* (accessed June 8, 2004).

32. OR, I, 39, 1: 861, 871,874; ORN, I, 26: 612–616; OR, I, 39, 1: 122, 124, 869; Henry, *op. cit.*, p. 375; Brown, *op. cit.*, p. 54; Wills, *op. cit.*, pp. 268–269; Smith, *Le Roy Fitch, op. cit.*, pp. 281–282; Morton, *The Artillery of Nathan Bedford Forrest's Cavalry, op. cit.*, pp. 249–253.

33. ORN, I, 26: 612; OR, I, 39, 1: 869, 871, 875; *New York Times*, November 7, 1864; Wills, *loc. cit.*; Henry, *loc. cit.*; Smith, *Le Roy Fitch, loc. cit.*; Brown, *op. cit.*, Ibid.; Morton, *The Artillery of Nathan Bedford Forrest's Cavalry, loc. cit*; Logbook of the U.S.S. *Moose, Ibid.* The Johnsonville bombardment, and specifically the location of the Confederate cannon, was the topic of much debate in Tennessee newspapers 30 years later; see the *Dyer County Herald* (March 19, 1896) and *Memphis Commercial Appeal* (March 23 and April 12, 1896).

34. ORN, I, 26: 612–613; OR, I, 39, 1: 861, 869; OR, I, 52, 1: 123; *New York Times*, November 7, 1864; *Louisville Democrat*, November 8, 1864; *Cleveland Daily Herald*, November 11, 1864; *Chicago Daily Tribune*, November 11, 1864; Henry, *op. cit.*, pp. 376–377; Jordan and Pryor, *op. cit.*, pp. 600–601; Wills, *op. cit.*, pp. 269–270; John M. Latham, *Raising the Civil War Gunboats and Building the Magic Valley History Tower* (Camden, TN: J.M. Latham: Press Pro, 1997), pp. 161–162; Logbook of the U.S.S. *Moose*, November 4, 1864; Brown, *op. cit.*, pp. 55–56; Denny, *op. cit.*, p. 29; Patrick, *op. cit.*, pp. 280–281; Kaeuper, *op. cit.*, p. 92. Maness, *op. cit.*, pp. 313–314; Morton, *The Artillery of Nathan Bedford Forrest's Cavalry, op. cit.*, p. 251; Williams, *op. cit.*, pp. 239–240; Smith, *Le Roy Fitch, op. cit.*, pp. 282–286. The loss of the *Undine* was reported in the *New York Times* on November 7.

35. OR, I, 39, 1: 861–862, 866–867, 871; OR, I, 52, 1: 123; ORN, I, 26: 614; *New York Times*, November 7, 1864; *Charleston Mercury*, November 8, 1864; *Louisville Journal*, November 8–9, 1864; *Louisville Democrat*, November 8, 1864; *Cleveland Daily Herald*, November 11, 1864; Wills, *op. cit.*, pp. 270–272; Maness, *op. cit.*, pp. 314–315; Jordan and Pryor, *The Campaigns, op. cit.*, p. 602; Morton, *The Artillery of Nathan Bedford Forrest's Cavalry, op. cit.*, pp. 253–254; Smith, *Le Roy Fitch, op. cit.*, pp. 286–287; Logbook of the U.S.S. *Moose, Ibid.*. Fitch sent a written report of the day's activities by dispatch boat to Paducah for Lt. Cmdr. Shirk to forward on to Rear Admiral Lee. In his endorsement, Shirk was complementary of his colleagues Fitch and King, pointing out that both "have done all that men could do to defeat the plans of the enemy and to uphold the honor of the flag." He went on to add: "If they were not successful, it was not because they were not brave, prudent, and faithful officers, but because they were met by an overwhelming force of the enemy." ORN, I, 26: 615.

36. OR, I, 39, 1: 871; OR, I, 52, 1: 123–124; ORN, I, 26: 610–611, 620; *New York Times*, November 7, 1864; *Democrat*, November 8, 1864; *Louisville Journal*, November 8–9, 1864; *Cleveland Daily Herald*, November 11, 1864; *Charleston*

Mercury, November 8, 1864; *Chicago Daily Tribune*, November 10, 1864; Wills, *loc. cit.*; Maness, *loc. cit.*; Morton, *The Artillery of Nathan Bedford Forrest's Cavalry, op. cit.*, p. 255; Smith, *Le Roy Fitch, op. cit.*, pp. 287–288; Brown, *op. cit.*, p. 57; E.G. Cowen, "Battle of Johnsonville," *Confederate Veteran* 22 (April 1914): pp. 174–175; "The Archaeological Investigations of the Battle of Johnsonville," *PanAm Consultants Homepage, http://www.panamconsultants.com/PAGE* (accessed June 8, 2004). The hulls of the sunken gunboats were, according to John W. Morton, still visible at the beginning of the 20th century when, "on a subsequent visit," he inspected them and "discovered a shell from one of his guns" in one of the hulls. Morton withdrew "this shell which had failed to explode" and turned it into a curio, "together with a fragment of the hull of the vessel where it was found." Morton, *The Artillery of Nathan Bedford Forrest's Cavalry, op. cit.*, p. 266.

37. OR, I, 39, 1: 853, 856, 858,862; 870–872; OR, I, 45, 1, 751; OR, I, 52, 1: 682–683, 777; OR, I, 52, 2: 774; ORN, I, 26: 622–626; *Charleston Mercury*, November 8, 1864; *Louisville Democrat*, November 8, 1864; *Cleveland Daily Herald*, November 11, 1864; Wyeth, *op. cit.*, p. 528; Henry, *op. cit.*, pp. 377–378; Denny, *op. cit.*, p. 30; Brown, *Ibid.*; Williams, *op. cit.*, pp. 243–244; Maness, *op. cit.*, pp. 315–316; Alfred T. Mahan, *The Gulf and Inland Waters*, Vol. 3 of the *Navy in the Civil War* (New York: Scribner's, 1883), pp. 214–215; Cox, *op. cit.*, p. 18; Williams and Humphreys, *Gunboats and Cavalry, op. cit.*, p. 24; Morton, *The Artillery of Nathan Bedford Forrest's Cavalry, op. cit.*, pp. 255–265; Thomas Van Horne, ed., *History of the Army of the Cumberland: Its Organization, Campaigns, and Battles, Written at the Request of Major General George H. Thomas Chiefly from His Private Military Journal and Official and Other Documents Furnished by Him*, 2 vols. (Cincinnati, OH: R. Clarke & Co., 1875; reprinted, Wilmington, NC: Broadfoot, 1988), Vol. 2, p. 484; Smith, *Le Roy Fitch, op. cit.*, pp. 288–289; Porter, *Ibid.* Acting Volunteer Lt. King was court-martialed on May 8, 1865, for ordering the burning of the Johnsonville gunboats, but was found not guilty. Witness after witness pointed out that, had the naval craft been scuttled rather than destroyed, the water, only five feet deep, would not have covered their gun decks, and had Forrest occupied the depot, as many feared possible, veterans of his Tennessee River Navy could have raised them in six hours' time. Latham, *op. cit.*, p. 166–167. The King court-martial proceedings are one of the great untapped sources on the entire campaign. U.S. Navy Department, *Records of General Courts-Martial and Courts of Inquiry of the Navy Department*, "Case of Acting Vol. Lieut. E.M. King, Lately of the U.S.S. *Key West*," Microfilm Publications, M273, National Archives, Washington, D.C.

38. OR, I, 39, 1: 871; OR, I, 45, 1: 752; ORN, I, 26: 614, 616, 629, 717–718; *Chicago Daily Tribune*, November 12, 1864; Logbook of the U.S.S. *Moose*, November 4–6, 1864; Jordan and Pryor, *op. cit.*, pp. 604–606; Sword, *op. cit.*, pp. 67–68; Patrick, *op. cit.*, pp. 280–281; Smith, *Le Roy Fitch, op. cit.*, pp. 289–290; Cornish and Laas, *op. cit.*, pp. 142–145; *Nashville Daily Press*, November 7–8, 1864; *Nashville Dispatch*, November 8–10, 1864; *New York Times*, November 10, 1864.

Chapter 12

1. Mark M. Boatner III, *The Civil War Dictionary* (New York: David McKay, 1959), pp. 308–309; OR, I, 45, 1: 32–34; Wiley Sword, *Embrace an Angry Wind—The Confederacy's Last Hurrah: Spring Hill, Franklin & Nashville* (New York: HarperCollins, 1992), pp. 84–120; Myron J. Smith Jr., *Le Roy Fitch: The Civil War Career of a Union Gunboat Commander* (Jefferson, NC: McFarland, 2007), pp. 291–296.

2. The *Carondelet* was one of the seven Pook turtles (designed by Samuel Pook) constructed at Carondelet, MO, in 1861. The sisters were all but identical, except for the different colored identification bands on their chimneys. By late

1864, all were pretty well worn out, having been in most of the heavy combats of the river war since Fort Henry in February 1862. Taking the *Carondelet* as our example, we find a 512-ton steamer that was 175 feet long, with a beam of 51.2 feet and a depth of six feet. She possessed a rectangular casemate with sloped armor (thickest at the front) and a single paddle wheel located amidships toward the stern. Powered by two horizontal high-pressure engines, with a 22" cylinder and six-foot stroke, and five boilers, she could supposedly make a top speed of nine mph. The 251 officers and men aboard were responsible at this time for working a battery that comprised two 100-pdr. Parrott rifles, one-each 50-pdr. and 30-pdr. Dahlgren rifles, and three Dahlgren nine-inch smoothbores. Capt. Henry Walke's boat at Island No. 10, *Carondelet* was the "most famous of all the river gunboats of the Civil War" and "was in more battles and encounters with the enemy (about fourteen or fifteen times; and under fire, it is believed, longer and oftener) than any other vessel in the Navy," including those which went to sea. She was the only one of her class to directly engage a Confederate armorclad, the C.S.S. *Arkansas*, in July 1862. ORN, I, XXVI, 627, 717, 719; ORN, II, 1: 52; OR, I, 52, 1: 712. Logbooks of the U.S.S. *Carondelet*, May 1862–June 1865, Records of the Bureau of Navigation, Record Group 19, U.S. National Archives, Washington, D.C., November 15, 1864 (cited hereafter as Logbook of the U.S.S. *Carondelet*, with date); John Hagerty, "Letter, November 15, 1864," in "Dear Maggie…The Letters of John Hagerty, 1st Class Fireman, U.S.S. *Carondolet* to Margaret 'Maggie' O'Neil, September 8, 1864–May 28, 1865," *Letters of John Hagerty* homepage, *http://www.webnation.com/~spectrum/usn-cw/diaries/HagertyJohnHome.htm* (accessed April 10, 2000); Logbooks of the U.S.S. *Moose*, June 15, 1863–August 10, 1865, Records of the Bureau of Navigation, Record Group 19, U.S. National Archives, Washington, D.C., November 7, 1864 (cited hereafter as Logbook of the U.S.S. *Moose*, with date). Lucius F. Hubbard, "Minnesota in the Battles of Nashville, December 15 and 16, 1864: Read Before the Minnesota Commandery of the Loyal Legion of the United States, March 14, 1905," Collections of the Minnesota Historical Society, Volume 12 *http://memory.loc.gov/cgi-bin/query/r?ammem/lhbum:@field%28DOCID+@lit%28lhbum0* (accessed January 9, 2006); Paul H. Silverstone, *Warships of the Civil War Navies* (Annapolis, MD: Naval Institute Press, 1989), pp. 151–153; H. Allen Gosnell, *Guns on the Western Waters: The Story of the River Gunboats in the Civil War* (Baton Rouge, LA: Louisiana State University Press, 1949), p. ii; Henry Walke, *Naval Scenes and Reminiscences of the Civil War in the United States on the Southern and Western Waters During the Years 1861, 1862 and 1863 with the History of That Period Compared and Corrected from Authentic Sources* (New York: F.R. Reed and Company, 1877), p. 53; Myron J. Smith Jr., "A Construction and Recruiting History of the U.S. Steam Gunboat *Carondelet*, 1861–1862," Unpublished MA Thesis, Shippensburg State University, 1969, p. iv; Donald L. Canney, *The Old Steam Navy*, Vol. 2: *The Ironclads, 1842–1885* (Annapolis, MD: Naval Institute Press, 1993), pp. 47–55..

3. Designed by James B. Eads, the *Neosho*, and her sister the *Osage*, were the only stern-wheel monitors. Both were laid down at Carondelet, MO, in 1862; the former cost $194,757.67 and was commissioned in May 1863. With a "turtleback" design on wooden hulls, both came in at 523 tons. The pair, which both participated in the Red River Expedition, measured 180 feet, with beams of 45 feet and depths of hold of 4.6 feet; each had a single forward-mounted revolving turret and one tall chimney amidships. The two were each powered with a pair of horizontal high-pressure engines and four boilers and were designed to steam at a top speed of 12 mph. Armament comprised two 11-inch Dahlgren smoothbores in the turrets, which were shielded by six inches of armor. Armor protection on the sides was 2.5" thick, with 1.25" on the deck. ORN, II, 1: 157; Silverstone, *op. cit.* p. 149; Canney, *op. cit.*, pp. 107–110. Acting Volunteer Lt. Samuel

Howard, *Neosho*'s captain, remained with the USN until honorably discharged on November 4, 1868. Edward W. Callahan, *List of Officers of the Navy of the United States and of the Marine Corps, from 1775 to 1900, Comprising a Complete Register of All Present and Former Commissioned, Warranted, and Appointed Officers of the United States Navy, and of the Marine Corps, Regular and Volunteer. Compiled from the Official Records of the Navy Department* (New York: L.R. Hamersly & Co., 1901; reprinted, New York: Haskell House, 1969), p. 278.

4. The 506-ton stern-wheeler *Golden Eagle* was built at Freedom, PA, and completed at Pittsburgh during the spring of 1864. Owner Capt. William B. Donaldson sold his new stern-wheeler to the Dean Line within a few months to run on the Cincinnati-Memphis trade. Frederick Way Jr., comp., *Way's Packet Directory, 1848–1994*, 2nd ed. (Athens, OH: Ohio University Press, 1994), p. 190.

5. Constructed by Howard at Jeffersonville, IN, in 1857, the side-wheeler *Southwestern* (also known as the *South Western*) was 217 feet long, with a beam of 36 feet and a 6.5-foot draft. *Ibid.*, p. 430.

6. Donald H. Steenburn, "Gunboats of the Upper Tennessee," *Civil War Times Illustrated* 32 (May 1993): p. 42; Byrd Douglas, *Steamboatin' on the Cumberland* (Nashville, TN: Tennessee Book Company, 1961), pp. 162–163; *Chicago Daily Tribune*, November 24, 1864. Luckily for the Union, Gen. Hood elected to keep Forrest with him, allowing only a few mounted units to be split off and sent against logistical targets along the Cumberland. "No longer would this ingenious leader be left," wrote Douglas, "to harass Thomas." On the other hand, Maj. Gen. Thomas would continue to overestimate Forrest's strength and threat, with his concern for "the devil" a major reason Nashville was placed into a defensive position. Douglas, *op. cit.*, p. 164; Sword, *op. cit.*, p. 278.

7. Constructed at Madison, IN, in the fall of 1863 for Brown-Dunkerson & Co. of Evansville, the future Tinclad No. 50 was named Emma Duncan for the young daughter of William Brown. The 117-ton side-wheeler was acquired by the USN at Cincinnati on November 21 for $30,150. Modified by Joseph Brown, the craft was 135 feet long, with a beam of 23 feet and a 4-foot draft. Her two engines provided sufficient power to drive her at 5 mph against the current. Upon her arrival at Mound City on January 26, 1864, her name was changed. After her battery of six 12-pounder rifled howitzers was mounted aboard, the *Gazelle* was commissioned in February, Acting Master Charles Thatcher in command. Paul H. Silverstone, *Warships of the Civil War Navies* (Annapolis, MD: Naval Institute Press, 1989), p. 166; "Gazelle," in U.S. Navy Department, Naval Historical Center, *Dictionary of American Naval Fighting Ships*, *http://www.history.navy.mil/danfs/g2/gazelle-i.htm* (accessed February 9, 2008); ORN, II, 1: 91; Way, *op. cit.*, pp. 149, 178. Thatcher joined the Mississippi Squadron as an Acting Ensign in March 1863 and was promoted in December. Callahan, *op. cit.*, p. 539.

8. ORN, I, 26: 745–746, 762; ORN, I, 27: 21; *New Orleans Daily True Delta*, November 27, 1864. Accompanied by three tinclads and two U.S. Army transports with a thousand troops, the *Gazelle* returned to Williamsport on December 16. There, in retaliation for Thatcher's death, a number of plantation buildings were burned and large quantities of sugar, corn, and molasses destroyed. ORN, I, 26: 762.

9. ORN, I, 26: 632–635, 647, 746; Logbook of the *Carondelet*, November 27–29, 1864; Logbook of the U.S.S. *Moose*, November 25–29, 1864; OR, I, 45, 1, 1031–1033, 1104; *Nashville Daily Union*, November 25, 1864; *Nashville Dispatch*, November 26, 1864; Walter T. Durham, *Reluctant Partners: Nashville and the Union—July 1, 1863, to June 30, 1865* (Nashville: The Tennessee Historical Society, 1987), pp. 205–206; Henry Stone, "Repelling Hood's Invasion of Tennessee," in *Battles and Leaders of the Civil War*, edited by Robert U. Johnson and Clarence C. Buel, 4 vols. (New York: The Century Company, 1884–1887, cited hereafter as *B & L*;

reprinted, New York: Thomas Yoseloff, 1956), p. 443; Smith, *Le Roy Fitch, op. cit.*, pp. 297–300; Smith, "Le Roy Fitch Meets the Devil's Parson: The Battle of Bell's Mills, December 4–6, 1864," *North & South* 10 (January 2008): p. 43; Minnesota Board of Commissioners on Publication of History of Minnesota in the Civil and Indian Wars, *Minnesota in the Civil and Indian Wars, 1861–1865*, 2 vols. (St. Paul, MN: Printed for the State of Minnesota by the Pioneer Press Company, 1889), Vol. 1, p. 274. The manner by which Col. Lewis B. Parsons and the USQMD obtained its charters was a matter of considerable controversy during the conflict, often being portrayed as "the strong, but not entirely impartial hand of the Government," *Washington (D.C.) Daily National Intelligencer*, December 5, 1864.

10. ORN, I, 26: 636–637, 647–648; OR, I, 45, 1: 34; OR, I, 45, 2: 3, 17; Hubbard, *Ibid.;* Minnesota, *Ibid.;* Edwin G. Huddleston, *The Civil War in Middle Tennessee* (Nashville, TN: Nashville Banner, 1965), pp. 118–119; Logbook of the U.S.S. *Moose,* November 30–December 1, 1864; Logbook of the U.S.S. *Carondelet,* November 30–December 1, 1864; Nashville *Daily Press,* November 30–December 2, 1864; Fisher, *op. cit.,* p. 161; Smith, *Le Roy Fitch, op. cit.,* pp. 300–303; Henry, *op. cit.,* pp. 399–400; Stanley F. Horn, *The Army of Tennessee: A Military History* (Indianapolis, IN: Bobbs-Merrill, 1941; reprinted, Norman, OK: University of Oklahoma Press, 1968), p. 404; Horn, *The Decisive Battle of Nashville* (Baton Rouge, LA: Louisiana State University Press, 1956), pp. 30–31; James F. Rusling, *Men and Things I Saw in Civil War Days* (new ed.; New York: The Methodist Book Concern, 1914), pp. 87–88; Stanley F. Horn, comp., *Tennessee's War, 1861–1865: Described by Participants* (Nashville: Tennessee Civil War Centennial Commission, 1965), pp. 321–322; Sword, *op. cit.,* pp. 272–274; Durham, *op. cit.,* pp. 211–214. Smith's units, now collectively named with several other provisional groups as the Army of the Tennessee Detachment, were debarked from their boats on December 1–2 and were moved into line of battle on a range of hills two miles southwest of town. There they threw up earthworks and settled down to wait, guarding the right of the Union defense. The center was held by the IV Corps under Wood, while Schofield's XXIII Corps was on the left.

11. OR, I, 45, 1: 79–83, 764; OR, I, 45, 2: 18, 27, 191; ORN, I, 26: 636–639, 646; Sword, *op. cit.,* p. 281; Henry, *op. cit.,* p. 401; Logbook of the U.S.S. *Moose,* December 2, 1864; Logbook of the U.S.S. *Carondelet,* December 2, 1864; Mark Zimmerman, *Battle of Nashville Preservation Society Guide to Civil War Nashville* (Nashville, TN: Lithographics, Inc., 2004), p. 49; Stanley F. Horn, "Nashville During the Civil War," *Tennessee Historical Quarterly* 4 (March 1945): p. 19; Thomas L. Connelly, *Autumn of Glory: The Army of Tennessee, 1862–1865* (Baton Rouge: LA: Louisiana State University Press, 1971), p. 508; James Lee McDonough, *Nashville: The Western Confederacy's Final Gamble* (Knoxville, TN: The University of Tennessee Press, 2004), pp. 141–142; Steven E Woodward, *Jefferson Davis and His Generals: The Failure of Confederate Command in the West* (Lawrence, KS: University Press of Kansas, 1990), p. 301; Byrd Douglas, *Steamboatin' on the Cumberland* (Nashville: The Tennessee Book Company, 1961), p. 165; Smith, *Le Roy Fitch, op. cit.,* pp. 303–305; Durham, *op. cit.,* p. 214–215; John E. Fisher, *They Rode with Forrest and Wheeler: A Chronicle of Five Tennessee Brothers' Service in the Confederate Western Cavalry* (Jefferson, NC: McFarland, 1995), p. 162; John Allan Wyeth, *Life of General Nathan Bedford Forrest* (New York: Harper & Bros., 1904), p. 547; Thomas Jordan and J. P. Pryor, *The Campaigns of Lieut. Gen. N.B. Forrest and of Forrest's Cavalry* (New Orleans and New York: Blelock & Co., 1868; reprinted, New York: DaCapo Press, 1996), p. 636; Smith, "Le Roy Fitch Meets the Devil's Parson," *op. cit.,* 44. One reporter characterized Kelley as "a bold, desperate, and notorious partisan." He was a man who "threatened to blow every gunboat out of the river, whenever the opportunity presented itself." *Cincinnati Daily Gazette,* December 8, 1864.

12. Logbook of the U.S.S. *Carondelet,* December 3–4, 1864; *Nashville Daily Dispatch,* December 6, 1864; *Cincinnati Daily Gazette,* December 8, 1864; *Milwaukee Daily Sentinel,* December 14, 1864; Logbook of the U.S.S. *Moose,* December 3–4, 1864; David Dixon Porter, *Naval History of the Civil War* (New York: Sherman, 1886; reprinted, Mineola, NY: Dover Publications, 1998), pp. 803–804; Alfred T. Mahan, *The Gulf and Inland Waters,* Vol. 3 of *The Navy in the Civil War* (New York: Scribner's, 1883), pp. 215–216; Starr, *op. cit.,* p. 284; ORN, I, 26: 639–647; OR, I, 45, 2: 30–31, 36–37, 43, 48–49, 52, 54; *New York Times,* December 8, 1864; *Chicago Daily Tribune,* December 8, 1864; Rowland Stafford True, "Life Aboard a Gunboat," *Civil War Times Illustrated* 9 (February 1971): pp. 39–40; Jordan and Pryor, *op. cit.,* p. 636; Wyeth, *op. cit.,* pp. 547–548; OR, I, 45, 2: 51–52; Henry Walke, *Naval Scenes and Reminiscences of the Civil War in the United States on the Southern and Western Waters During the Years 1861, 1862 and 1863 with the History of That Period Compared and Corrected from Authentic Sources* (New York: F.R. Reed and Company, 1877), p. 124; Smith, *Le Roy Fitch, op. cit.,* pp. 305–310; Smith, "Le Roy Fitch Meets the Devil's Parson," *op. cit.,* 45–48. In a followup report, it was reported that the Confederates had "established a battery on a bluff 14 miles down the river." It continued: "Seven gunboats went down and engaged this battery without dislodging the rebels from their position. The gunboats returned…, one of them considerably damaged." *New York Times,* December 9, 1864.

13. ORN, I, 26: 184, 650–651, 653, 661–662, 668; ORN, I, 27: 153; OR, I,45, 1: 37–39, 45, 128, 599–601, 606,765; OR, I, 45, 2: 117, 154, 160, 180–185, 191–192, 194, 196–197, 205–206, 210, 213, 231, 245; *Nashville Daily Union,* December 20, 22, 1864; *Cincinnati Daily Gazette,* December 8, 1864; *Milwaukee Daily Sentinel,* December 14, 24, 1864; *Nashville Daily Press,* December 12, 14, 1864; *New York Times,* December 12, 18–19, 24–25, 1864; *Chicago Daily Tribune,* December 16, 19, 1864; James H. Wilson, *Under the Old Flag,* 2 vols. (New York: D. Appleton & Co., 1912), Vol. 2, pp. 109–112; Wyeth, *op. cit.,* pp. 555–559; Isaac R. Sherwood, *Memories of the War* (Toledo, OH: The H.J. Crittenden Co., 1923), p. 149; Logbook of the U.S.S. *Carondelet,* December 8–179, 1864; Logbook of the U.S.S. *Moose,* December 8–17, 1864; Durham, *op. cit.,* pp. 237, 245, 261, 266, 268; Starr, *op. cit.,* pp. 317–318; McDonough, *op. cit.,* pp. 149–151, 157,176–177; Horn, *The Decisive Battle of Nashville, op. cit.,* pp. 39, 84, 150–152; Sword, *op. cit.,* pp. 319–350; Zimmerman, *op. cit.,* p. 69; Smith, *Le Roy Fitch, op. cit.,* pp. 310–331; Colleen Creamer, "Civil War Battle Site Gets Commemorative Marker: Reprinted from The City Paper, Nashville Tennessee, n.d.," American Civil War Round Table of the United Kingdom homepage, *http://www.americancivilwar.org.uk/preservaton/city_paper_nashville.htm* (accessed April 1, 2006).

14. OR, I, 45, 1: 618–619, 632, 755; OR, I, 45, 2: 231, 251; ORN, I, 26: 670–673; *Nashville Daily Union,* December 17, 1864; Logbook of the U.S.S. *Moose,* December 18–19, 1864; Logbook of the U.S.S. *Carondelet,* December 18–19, 1864; Sword, *op. cit.,* p. 401, 416; Sword, *op. cit.,* p. 416; Smith, *Le Roy Fitch, op. cit.,* pp. 331–333; Dudley Taylor Cornish and Virginia Jeans Laas, *Lincoln's Lee: The Life of Samuel Phillips Lee, United States Navy, 1812–1897* (Lawrence, KS: University Press of Kansas, 1986), p. 148. Lee did not engender the same spirit among his inherited divisional officers as Porter when he took over from Davis. After sending his December 19 telegram turning down the Lee assignment, Fitch, the senior and most active of all district commanders, largely disappeared, his name seldom thereafter appearing in official dispatches or records, including even those not destroyed in the 1865 fire aboard the *Black Hawk.* For an account of the loss of the flag boat, see B.F. Clough's "The Burning of the Flagship *Black Hawk*" in the September 3, 1885, issue of the *National Tribune.*

15. OR, I, 45, 1: 674, 732; OR, I, 45, 2: 357,371, 507, 731;

ORN, I, 26: 672–679. 690; ORN, I, 27: 9–28; *Chicago Daily Tribune,* January 10, 1865; McDonough, *op. cit.,* pp. 273–274; Sword, *op. cit.,* pp. 401, 421, 423; Starr, *op. cit.,* pp. 421, 423; Wyeth, *op. cit.,* pp. 564–575; Smith, *Le Roy Fitch, op. cit.,* pp. 333–334; Robert Selph Henry, *"First with the Most" Forrest* (Indianapolis, IN: Bobbs-Merrill, 1944), p. 416; Stanley F. Horn, *The Army of Tennessee* (Indianapolis, IN: Bobbs-Merrill, 1941), pp. 420–421; Wilson, *op. cit.,* Vol. 2, 142; Wilson, "The Union Cavalry in the Hood Campaign," in *Battles and Leaders of the Civil War,* edited by Robert U. Johnson and Clarence C. Buel, 4 vols. (New York: The Century Company, 1884–1887; reprinted Thomas Yoseloff, 1956), Vol. 4, p. 471; Donald Davidson, *The Tennessee,* Vol. 2: *The New River, Civil War to TVA* (Rivers of America; New York: Rinehart & Co., 1948), p. 106; Cornish and Laas, *op. cit.,* p. 149.

16. Constructed at California, PA, in 1858, the *Venango* was one of the first vessels to engage in the petroleum trade out of Pittsburgh. Way, *op. cit.,* p. 466.

17. Lewis B. Parsons, *Reports to the War Department* (St. Louis, MO: George Knapp & Co., 1867), p. 38; Cornish and Laas, *op. cit.,* pp. 149–150; Craig L. Symonds, *Lincoln and His Admirals: Abraham Lincoln, the U.S. Navy, and the Civil War* (New York: Oxford University Press, 2008), p. 33. Between mid–February and mid–March, Gen. Robert E. Lee, for example, lost 8 percent of his army "either into the Union lines or into North Carolina."

18. Parsons, *op. cit.,* p. 39. The 117-ton second *Grampus* was built at Brownsville, PA, in late 1862. Way believed her a primitive towboat possibly built packet-style. Way, *op. cit.,* p. 195.

19. ORN, I, 27: 7–9; Marion Bragg, *Historic Names and Places on the Lower Mississippi River* (Vicksburg, MS: Mississippi River Commission, 1977), p. 37.

20. ORN, I, 27: 15–16, 36, 41, 47–53, 85; Thomas Connelly, *Autumn of Glory: The Army of Tennessee, 1862–1865* (Baton Rouge, LA: Louisiana State University Press, 1971), p. 513; Allen C. Guelzo, *The Crisis of the American Republic: A History of the Civil War and Reconstruction* (New York: St. Martin's Press, 1995), pp. 368–369; Richard P. Gildrie, "Guerrilla Warfare in the Lower Cumberland River Valley, 1862–1865." *Tennessee Historical Quarterly* 49 (Fall 1990): p. 173; Way, *op. cit.,* p. 327; Steenburn, *op. cit.,* p. 43.

21. Tinclad No. 8 was originally constructed as the *Fanny* at Cincinnati for Capt. Albert Stein during the spring of 1864. The 195-ton side-wheeler was 179 feet long, with a beam of 27 feet and a 5.5-foot draft. She was powered by two 40-inch diameter tubular boilers, each 18 feet long, and her flues were 15 inches. The 20-foot diameter paddle wheels each worked 6.5-foot buckets. Upon completion, she operated service from the Queen City to Pittsburgh. The vessel was purchased into the USN on December 3 for $33,500 and was sent to Joseph Brown's yards for modification. Dispatched to Mound City for final outfitting, the craft was renamed *Grosbeak* on February 3. Armed with two 20-pounder and two 30-pounder Parrotts and two 24-pounder smoothbore Dahlgren howitzers, she was commissioned on February 24, Acting Master Thomas Burns commanding. Her first mission was to convoy several unarmed monitors from Cincinnati to Mound City. ORN, I, 27: 64; ORN, II, 1: 98; Way, *op. cit.,* pp. 162, 201; "*Grosbeak,*" in U.S. Navy Department, Naval Historical Center, *Dictionary of American Naval Fighting Ships,* http://www.history.navy.mil/danfs/g8/grosbeck–i.htm (accessed February 9, 2008); Silverstone, *op. cit.,* p. 167.

22. Way, *op. cit.,* p. 327.

23. Tinclad No. 41 was built at Belle Vernon, PA, during the summer of 1863 and was purchased into the USN at Cincinnati on November 4 for $33,500. The dimensions of the 203-ton side-wheeler were not recorded. Converted with speed, the vessel was armed at Mound City with six 24-pounder smoothbore Dahlgren howitzers. *Nyanza* was commissioned there on December 21, Acting Master Samuel B. Washburn in command. Sent to the West Gulf Coast Blockading Squadron, she had some success in Louisiana's

Atchafalaya River and Atchafalaya Bay, capturing prizes in March and April 1864. Way, *op. cit.,* pp. 331; Silverstone, *op. cit.,* p. 168; ORN, II, 1: 163; "*Nyanza,*" in U.S. Navy Department, Naval Historical Center, *Dictionary of American Naval Fighting Ships,* http://www.history.navy.mil/danfs/n6/nyanza.htm (accessed February 9, 2008). One of the earliest recruits to the U.S. Army's Western Flotilla, Washburn was initially appointed an Acting Master in November 1861, but for infractions, got himself dismissed on December 30. He was reappointed in January 1862 and, befitting his new WGCBS command, was promoted to the rank of Acting Volunteer Lt. in January 1864. He would be honorably discharged in October 1865. Callahan, *op. cit.,* p. 570.

24. Constructed at Cincinnati in the fall of 1863, the 162-ton *Countess* was purchased into the USN at the Queen City on December 8, 1863, for $29,500. While undergoing conversion, the name of the side-wheeler was changed to *Elk* on January 26, 1864. Tinclad No. 47 was 155 feet long, with a beam of 31 feet and a depth of 4.4 feet. Even though a battery of two 32-pounders and four 24-pound smoothbore howitzers was mounted, final alterations took longer than expected. The *Elk* was commissioned on May 6, Lt. Cmdr. James H. Gillis in command. Gillis would soon depart for the new monitor *Milwaukee.* As late as mid–March 1865, the craft was on patrol off Cedar Point, FL. Way, *op. cit.,* pp. 113, 145; Silverstone, *op. cit.,* p. 166; ORN, II, 1: 77; "*Elk,*" U.S. Navy Department, Naval Historical Center, *Dictionary of American Naval Fighting Ships,* http://www.history.navy. mil/danfs/e3/elk.htm (accessed February 9, 2008).

25. Tinclad No. 44 was built as the *Scioto* at Portsmouth, OH, in late 1863 and was sold to the USN at Cincinnati in late December, her name being changed to *Meteor* on the 21st while she was undergoing conversion. *Meteor* was formally taken over from her owner, Washington Houshell, on January 23, 1864, upon Treasury Department payment of her $34,000 asking price. The new acquisition was 156 feet long, with a 33-foot beam and 4.3-foot draft. Always intended for the West Gulf Coast Blockading Squadron (WGCBS), the craft was armed with two 32-pounds and four 24-pound smoothbore Dahlgren howitzers and sent off to New Orleans. There she was commissioned on March 8, Acting Master Meletiah Jordan commanding. Way, *op. cit.,* pp. 320, 420; Silverstone, *op. cit.,* p. 174; ORN, II, 1: 77; "*Meteor,*" in U.S. Navy Department, Naval Historical Center, *Dictionary of American Naval Fighting Ships,* http://www.history.navy. mil/danfs/m9/meteor-ii.htm (accessed February 9, 2008). Like Saunders of the *Tallahatchie,* Jordan remained an Acting Master from the day of his appointment in February 1862 until his honorable discharge in August 1865. Callahan, *op. cit.,* p. 304.

26. Built for Stephen Morse and others at Cincinnati in the fall of 1863 as the *Cricket No. 4,* this 171-ton stern-wheeler was sold to the USN at Cincinnati on January 23, 1864, for $32,000. Two days later, Tinclad No. 46 was renamed *Tallahatchie.* After a two-week departure delay caused by ice in the Ohio River, the new acquisition was sent out to Mound City for modification into a tinclad suitable for the West Gulf Coast Blockading Squadron (WGCBS). Armed with two 32-pounders and four 24-pounder smoothbore Dahlgren howitzers and with a temporary crew, she departed down the Mississippi on March 9. Arriving at New Orleans, she, like other WGCBS tinclads, was taken in hand and her bottom was covered with copper to protect her during saltwater operations. She was commissioned at the Crescent City on April 19, Acting Master J.W. Saunders commanding. Way, *op. cit.,* pp. 115, 443; Silverstone, *op. cit.,* p. 179; ORN, II, 1: 219; "*Tallahatchie,*" in U.S. Navy Department, Naval Historical Center, *Dictionary of American Naval Fighting Ships,* http://www.history.navy.mil/danfs/t1/tallahatchie.htm (accessed February 9, 2008). Like Jordan of the *Meteor,* Saunders remained an Acting Master from the day of his appointment in February 1862 until his honorable discharge in October 1865. Callahan, *op. cit.,* p.483.

27. ORN, I, 22: 54–55; ORN, I, 27: 28, 89, 96–97, 116–118; Richard B. Irwin, "Land Operations Against Mobile," *B & L* 4, pp. 410–411; James Russell Soley, "Closing Operations in the Gulf and Western Waters," *B & L*, 4, p. 412; Sean Michael O'Brien, *Mobile, 1865: Last Stand of the Confederacy* (Westport, CT: Praeger, 2001), pp. 1–167; Joe A. Mobley, "The Siege of Mobile, August 1864–April 1865," *Alabama Historical Quarterly* 38 (1976): p. 269; Chester G. Hearn, *Mobile Bay and the Mobile Campaign: The Last Great Battles of the Civil War* (Jefferson, NC: McFarland, 1993), pp. 1–145, 148; Milton F. Perry, *Infernal Machines: The Story of Confederate Submarine and Mine Warfare* (Baton Rouge, LA: Louisiana State University Press, 1965), pp. 183–184; Dabney H. Maury, "Defense of Mobile," *Southern Historical Society Papers* 3 (1877): p. 11; Norman A. Nicholson, "The Mobile Campaign: Battle of Fort Blakely and Spanish Fort," *Blakeley State Park: Civil War Memorial Site and Scenic Nature Trails http://new.siteone.com/sites/blakeleypark/com/battlehistory.htm* (accessed December 17, 2008); Louis S. Schafer, *Confederate Underwater Warfare: An Illustrated History* (Jefferson, NC: McFarland, 1996), p. 176. New Jerseyan James S. Palmer (1810–1867) joined the USN as a ship's boy in 1824 and worked his way up through the ranks, becoming captain of Rear Adm. Farragut's flagship *Hartford* in 1862. Taking over the *Pensacola* and *Monongahela* in 1864, he found himself a commodore in command of the West Gulf Coast Blockading Squadron (WGCBS) following Farragut's withdrawal in August of that year. When the WGCBS passed to Rear Adm. Thatcher (q.v.), Palmer stayed on as 1st division commander, frequently commanding the *Richmond* through the end of the war. Promoted to Rear Adm. in 1866, he died of yellow fever at St. Thomas, Virgin Islands. A native of Maine, Henry Knox Thatcher (1806–1880) was the grandson of Revolutionary War hero Henry Knox. Joining the USN a year before James S. Palmer (q.v.), Knox also grew in rank, becoming skipper of the *Colorado* in the North Atlantic Blockading Squadron in 1864. Sent to relieve Palmer of the WGCBS in February 1865, Thatcher held that command until July, when he took over the Gulf Squadron. He retired in 1868. William B. Cogar, *Dictionary of Admirals of the U.S. Navy*, 2 vols. (Annapolis, MD: Naval Institute Press, 1989), Vol. 1, p. 120–121, 192–193.

28. ORN, I, 27: 78, 86–87, 92–93, 102, 104–105; Cornish and Laas, *op. cit.*, p. 151; Logbook of the U.S.S. *Moose*, March 8–18, 1864; *Louisville Journal*, March 9, 1864.

29. ORN, I, 22: 65–71; Soley, *loc. cit.*; O'Brien, *op. cit.*, pp. 37, 167–168, Nicholson, *loc. cit.*; Perry, *op. cit.*, p. 185; Schaefer, *op. cit.*, pp. 177–178. A reporter later claimed that "a hole was blown in her amidships about the size of the bore of a 10-inch mortar." *Milwaukee Daily Sentinel*, April 14, 1865.

30. ORN, I, 11: 164; ORN, I, 22: 70, 72–75, 87–89; ORN, I, 27: 4, 40, 125, 131, 135–137; OR, I, 49, 1: 320–321; *Milwaukee Daily Sentinel*, April 14, 1865; *Harper's Weekly*, May 27, 1865; Nicholson, *loc. cit.*; Irwin, *op. cit.*, p. 411; Soley, *loc. cit.*; Hearn, *op. cit.*, pp. 169–170; Perry, *op cit.*, pp. 185–188; O'Brien, *op. cit.*, pp. 169–170; Schaefer, *op. cit.*, pp. 178–179; J. Thomas Scharf, *History of the Confederate States Navy* (New York: Rogers & Sherwood, 1887), p. 594; Christopher C. Andrews, *History of the Campaign of Mobile, Including the Cooperative Operations of Gen. Wilson's Cavalry in Alabama* (New York: Van Nostrand, 1867), pp. 94, 132–133; Charles Oscar Paullin, *Paullin's History of Naval Administration, 1775–1911* (Annapolis, MD: U.S. Naval Institute, 1968), p. 312.. At the end of April, the tinclad *Meteor* was assigned to raise the *Osage*, a task not accomplished until mid–August. Torpedoes were still sinking vessels as late as the end of May, well after the conflict was over.

31. The last tinclad placed into service was constructed at Louisville, KY, in 1862. During the war the *Tempest* (original name) was owned by Cincinnati boat builder Joseph Brown, who operated her locally. The 161-ton stern-wheeler was 162 feet long, with a beam of 32.8 feet and a 5.8-foot draft. In a transaction completed on February 10, 1865, Brown sold her to the USN on December 30, 1864 for $55,000 and then modified her into Tinclad No. 1. Transferred west, she was taken in hand for her final outfit and armed with two each 30-pounder Parrott rifles, 24-pounder smoothbore Dahlgren howitzers, and 12-pounder rifled Dahlgren howitzers. Commissioned at Cairo on April 26, the *Tempest* replaced as command ship the flag boat *Black Hawk* lost four days earlier. ORN, II, 1: 221; Way, *op. cit.*, p. 448; Silverstone, *op. cit.*, p. 179; "*Tempest*," in U.S. Navy Department, Naval Historical Center, *Dictionary of American Naval Fighting Ships, http://www.history.navy.mil/danfs/t3/tempest.htm* (accessed February 9, 2008).

32. ORN, I, 27: 141, 148–149, 711; Guelzo, *op. cit.*, pp. 377–379; Edmund J. Huling, *Reminiscences of Gunboat Life in the Mississippi Squadron* (Saratoga Springs, NY: Sentinel Print, 1881), pp. 57–58. The literature surrounding Lincoln's assassination is enormous. The details may be found in any recent biography of the 16th president. Osband left the body swing in the breeze for 24 hours when, after having returned to Memphis, he granted permission to the stepfather of the dead man to remove him for burial.

33. Lonnie R. Speer, *Portals to Hell: Military Prisoners in the Civil War* (Mechanicsburg, PA: Stackpole Books, 1997), pp. 287–289; William O. Bryant, *Cahaba Prison and the Sultana Disaster* (Tuscaloosa, AL: University of Alabama Press, 1990), pp. 127–128.

34. Constructed at John Litherbury's Cincinnati yards, the 660-ton side-wheeler was 260 feet long, with a 42-foot beam and a 7-foot draft. Four boilers were employed to provide the steam necessary to drive the 34-foot (diameter) paddle wheels, each of which worked 11-foot buckets. The boilers themselves were each 18 feet long by 46 inches wide and had 24 5-inch flues. After early service on the Ohio and Cumberland rivers, the vessel was sold by Capt. Pres Lodwick to a St. Louis consortium in early March 1864. Under her new skipper, Capt. J. Cass Mason, she launched New Orleans service, with intermediate stops, in August. During the remainder of the year and into 1865, she was often employed as a troop transport. On her last downriver trip in April 1865, she stopped at various isolated locations en route delivering the news of President Lincoln's murder. Way, *op. cit.*, p. 436; Margie Riddle Bearss, "Messenger of Lincoln Death Herself Doomed," *The Lincoln Herald* (Spring 1978): pp. 49–51; Gene Eric Salecker, *Disaster on the Mississippi: the Sultana Explosion, April 27, 1865* (Annapolis, MD: Naval Institute Press, 1996), pp. 1–7. Many brevetted regular army officers and those with acting rank in the Navy were soon to hold lesser titles (Acting Rear Adm. Lee, for example, would revert to his permanent rank of captain), while the majority of volunteer officers were discharged.

35. Time was money in the 1860s river shipping business just as it is today with modern transport. Rather than take three days to replace his troubled boiler, Capt. Mason ordered that workmen perform a hasty patch. As a result, a section of bulged boiler plate was removed and another, of less thickness than the parent plate, was welded into its place. Robert Frank Bennett, "A Case of Calculated Mischief," *United States Naval Institute Proceedings* (March 1976): pp. 77–83; Salecker, *op. cit.*, p. 40.

36. Bragg, *op. cit.*, p. 74. The official cause of the explosion was the combined effects of low water, careening due to overloading, and the faulty boiler repair. A conspiracy theory advanced during the 1880s concerning incendiary sabotage by a former Confederate agent has largely been discredited. Bennett, *loc. cit.*; William A. Tidwell, *April '65* (Kent, Ohio: The Kent State University Press, 1995), p. 52.

37. Way, *loc. cit.,*; Bennett, *loc. cit.*; Bearss, *loc. cit.*; Salecker, *op. cit.*, pp. 75–119; Bragg, *op. cit*, p. 75. Hunter tells us that the *Sultana* blast was the most tragic episode in the worst year for steamboat disasters, during which total casualties reached 2,050, or 13 times the average for the previous four years. Louis C. Hunter, *Steamboats on the Western Rivers:*

An Economic and Technological History (Cambridge, MA: Harvard University Press, 1949), p. 543.

38. *Bostonia II* was constructed at Cincinnati, OH, in 1860. The 304-ton side-wheeler was nearly finished herself when attacked at Carrollton, KY, by guerrillas in November 1864. The vessel managed to escape boarding "with but a few bullet holes in the pilothouse." Way, *op. cit.,* p. 60.

39. Constructed at the Knox Yard at Marietta, OH, as the *Ohio Valley* in 1863, the 232-ton side-wheeler was 157 feet long, with a 33-foot beam and a 4.6-foot draft. Upon completion, she undertook tramp service between towns on the Ohio and Cumberland Rivers under Capt. Amos Davis. The craft was sold by Theodore Johnson into the USN on December 10, 1864, for $41,950, becoming Tinclad No. 10, *Ibex.* Outfitted at Mound City, she was provided with an armament of two 30-pounder Parrott rifles, two 12-pounder rifled howitzers, and four smoothbore Dahlgren howitzers on March 31, 1865. The tinclad was commissioned on April 4, Lt. Cmdr. Robert L. May commanding. "*Ibex,*" in U.S. Navy Department, Naval Historical Center, *Dictionary of American Naval Fighting Ships, http://www.history.navy.mil/danfs/il/ibex-i.htm* (accessed February 9, 2008); ORN, II, 1: 106; Way, *op. cit.,* pp. 220, 354; Silverstone, *op. cit.,* p. 167. Commander of the Fifth and then the Fourth District since the fall of 1864, Lt. Cmdr. May had joined the service as a midshipman in November 1849. Moving up through the ranks, he obtained his current status in July 1862. Two days after taking formal command of the *Ibex,* he was tasked with overseeing the withdrawal of the squadron's chartered steamers. May retired on April 21, 1866. ORN, I, 27: 135; Callahan, *op. cit.,* p. 357.

40. The *Kate B. Porter* was built by J.B. Porter & Sons at the L.M. Speer yard at Belle Vernon, PA, in the summer of 1864. Construction was supervised by Nathan Porter, brother of co-owner Capt. Joseph H. Porter, the skipper designate. The 241-ton stern-wheeler was 160 feet long, with a beam of 31 feet and a 4.2-foot draft. Power was supplied by two boilers, each 40 inches wide and 20 feet long; she was said to be capable of 6 mph against the current. Upon arrival at Cincinnati on her first trip, she was commandeered by the USQMD to transport a shipment of goods to Nashville. Before that took place, the vessel was sold to the USN on December 23, 1864 for $37,500. Taken in hand by Joseph Brown, she was altered and her name was shortened as she became Tinclad No. 55. Once Brown's casemate was in place and his $24,500 worth of other repairs were completed, the *Kate* was sent to Mound City, where she received her armament on March 31, 1865: two 20-pounder Parrott rifles, two 12-pounder rifled howitzers, and six smoothbore Dahlgren howitzers. She was commissioned on April 2, Acting Volunteer Lt. W.R. Wells commanding. "*Kate,*" in U.S. Navy Department, Naval Historical Center, *Dictionary of American Naval Fighting Ships, http://www.history.navy.mil/danfs/k2/kate.htm* (accessed February 9, 2008); ORN, II, 1: 112; Way, *op. cit.,* pp. 263, 265; Silverstone, *op. cit.,* p. 173. Named an Acting Master in October 1862, Wells was elevated to his current rank in December 1863. He would be honorably discharged on September 5, 1865. Callahan, *op. cit.,* p. 578.

41. The 183-ton stern-wheeler *Colossus* was constructed at Brownsville, PA, in 1863. With a length of 155.2 feet, she had a 31.9-foot beam and a draft of 4.2 feet; her two engines gave her wheel sufficient power to push her upstream at 5 mph. After Ohio River service, she was purchased into the USN on December 6, 1864, for $32,900. Her name was not changed, but she was designated Tinclad No. 25 on February 24, 1865. Following a $24,550 refit at the Brown yards, she was commissioned the same day, Acting Master Frederick G. Sampson in command. The vessel departed the same day for Mound City, where she received her ordnance on March 31: two 30-pounder Parrott rifles, one 12-pounder rifled howitzer, and four smoothbore Dahlgren howitzers. "*Colossus,*" in U.S. Navy Department, Naval Historical Center, *Dictionary of American Naval Fighting Ships,*

http://www.history.navy.mil/danfs/cll/colossus.htm (accessed February 9, 2008); ORN, II, I: 61; Way, *op. cit.,* p. 105; Silverstone, *op. cit.,* p. 170. Sampson joined the squadron as an Acting Ensign in October 1862 and was promoted to his current rank in July 1864. He would be honorably discharged on November 20, 1865. Callahan, *op. cit.,* p. 481.

42. The 206-ton side-wheeler *Abeona* was built at Cincinnati in late 1864, She was 157.5 feet long, with a beam of 31.4 feet and a 4.5-foot draft. The new boat was sold to the USN on December 31 for $37,000, retaining her original name. It was ordered that the number 55, previously worn by the *Key West* sunk at Johnsonville, be painted on the sides of her pilothouse. Modified by Brown at Cincinnati, she, too, received her armament at Mound City on March 31, 1865: two 30-pounder Parrott rifles, two 12-pounder Parrott rifles, and two 24-pounder smoothbore Dahlgren howitzers. She was commissioned on April 10—the day after the surrender of Gen. Lee, Acting Master Samuel Hall commanding. "*Abeona,*" in U.S. Navy Department, Naval Historical Center, *Dictionary of American Naval Fighting Ships, http://www.history.navy.mil/danfs/al/abeona.htm* (accessed February 9, 2008); ORN, II, 1: 27; Way, *op. cit.,* p. 165. An Acting Master since January 1862, the veteran Hall would be honorably discharged in November 1865. Callahan, *op. cit.,* p. 239.

43. ORN, I, 27: 154, 160–184, 202–203; *Memphis Daily Argus,* April 28–29, 1865; *Memphis Daily Bulletin,* April 28, 1865; *Cincinnati Daily Gazette,* April 29, 1865; *St. Louis Daily Missouri Democrat,* April 28–May 1, 1865; *St. Louis Daily Missouri Republican,* April 28–May 1, 1865; Salecker, *op. cit.,* pp. 121, 140–142, 171–172; Bennett, *loc. cit.*; William B. Floyd, "The Burning of the *Sultana,*" *Wisconsin Magazine of History* 11 (September 1927): pp. 70–71; Joseph Taylor Elliott, "The *Sultana* Disaster," *Indiana Historical Society Publication* 5, no. 3 (1913): pp. 177–178; Speer, *op. cit.,* p. 289; *New York Times,* April 29, May 1–4, 1865; *New Orleans Daily Picayune,* May 5, 1865; *Chicago Daily Tribune,* May 13, 1865. As might be expected with such a gigantic disaster, the literature concerning the *Sultana* explosion is of significant size. We have noted here those publications directly bearing upon the USN involvement in the rescue effort. For the latest information, readers are directed to David Markland's blog *Sultana Disaster Online: Museum and Archives, http://sultanadisaster.com/blog* (accessed November 1, 2008).

44. ORN, I, 27: 185–187, 200; Logbook of the U.S.S. *Moose,* April 28–May 3, 1865; Thomas Jordan and J.P. Pryor, *The Campaigns of Lieut. Gen. N.B. Forrest and of Forrest's Cavalry* (New Orleans and New York: Blelock & Co., 1868, reprinted, New York: DaCapo Press, 1996), pp. 685–703; Cornish and Laas, *op. cit.,* p. 153.

Chapter 13

1. Not the same vessel constructed in 1860 for the Cincinnati-Kanawhwa River trade, the 176-ton stern-wheeler *Allen Collier* was built at Cincinnati in the fall of 1864 for John Swasey & Co. (which also owned the *Florence Miller*). The 161-foot-long craft was sold to the USN on December 8 (the same day as the *Miller*) for $35,000. Converted at the Queen City yards of Joseph Brown early in 1865, her name was shortened and she was dispatched to Mound City for final outfitting. On March 31, the *Collier* received her armament: two 20-pounder Parrott rifles, one 12-pounder Parrott rifle, and six 24-pounder smoothbore Dahlgren howitzers. Tinclad No. 29 was commissioned on March 18, Acting Master J. Frank Reed commanding. "*Collier,*" in U.S. Navy Department, Naval Historical Center, *Dictionary of American Naval Fighting Ships, http://www.history.navy.mil/danfs/cll/collier.htm* (accessed February 9, 2008); ORN, II, 1: 1; Frederick Way Jr., comp., *Way's Packet Directory, 1848–1994,* 2nd ed. (Athens, OH: Ohio University Press, 1994), pp. 14, 103; Paul H. Sil-

verstone, *Warships of the Civil War Navies* (Annapolis, MD: Naval Institute Press, 1989), p. 170. Skipper Reed became an Acting Ensign in September 1862 and was promoted to his present rank in June 1863. He would be honorably discharged in November 1865. Edward W. Callahan, *List of Officers of the Navy of the United States and of the Marine Corps, from 1775 to 1900, Comprising a Complete Register of All Present and Former Commissioned, Warranted, and Appointed Officers of the United States Navy, and of the Marine Corps, Regular and Volunteer. Compiled from the Official Records of the Navy Department* (New York: L.R. Hamersly & Co., 1901; reprinted, New York: Haskell House, 1969), p. 455.

2. Also held by John Swasey & Co. (which also owned the Allen Collier), the 236-ton *Florence Miller No. 3* was constructed at Cincinnati during the fall of 1864. The future Tinclad No. 52" was 160 feet long, with a beam of 33 feet and a 5.5-foot draft. The stern-wheeler was sold for $40,000 to the USN on December 8 (the same day as the *Allen Collier*). She was sent to Joseph Brown who converted her at a cost of $24,550. Assigned to the Mississippi Squadron on February 3, 1865, she was simultaneously renamed. Dispatched to Mound City, she received her final outfits and an armamentidentical to that of the Collier: two 20-pounder Parrott rifles, one 12-pounder Parrott rifle, and six 24-pounder smoothbore Dahlgren howitzers. She was commissioned on March 22, Acting Master Edward Alford commanding. "Oriole," in U.S. Navy Department, Naval Historical Center, *Dictionary of American Naval Fighting Ships, http://www.history.navy.mil/danfs/o3/oriole-i.htm* (accessed February 9, 2008); ORN, II, I: 166; Way, *op. cit.*, pp. 168, 357; Silverstone, *op. cit.*, p. 175. Named an Acting Ensign on October 1, 1862, Alford was promoted to his current rank in June 1864. He would be honorably discharged in April 1866. Callahan, *op. cit.*, p. 20.

3. Among the last light-draughts purchased, the 232-ton *Mist* was constructed at J.A. Williamson and J.G. Isham at Allegheny, PA, in the fall of 1864. With a beam of 30.2 feet and a 4.3-foot draft, the new stern-wheeler was 157.2 feet long. Her two engines with two boilers provided sufficient power to drive her against the current at 4.5 mph. Tinclad No. 26 was purchased at Cincinnati on January 21, 1865, for $38,500. Converted by Joseph Brown, she was outfitted at Mound City and received her armament there: two 20-pounder Parrott rifles, one 12-pounder Parrott rifle, and four 24-pounder smoothbore Dahlgren howitzers. The *Mist* was commissioned on March 3, 1865, Acting Master Walter E.H. Fentress in command. "*Mist*," in U.S. Navy Department, Naval Historical Center, *Dictionary of American Naval Fighting Ships, http://www.history.navy.mil/danfs/m12/mist-i.htm* (accessed February 9, 2008); ORN, II, I: 146; Way, *op. cit.*, p. 327; Silverstone, *op. cit.*, p. 174. Captured when ashore from the *Rattler* in September 1863, Fentress had returned to take command of this new boat.

4. ORN, I, XXVII, 185: 210–213, 217; John Niven, *Gideon Welles: Lincoln's Secretary of the Navy* (New York: Oxford University Press, 1973), pp. 506–507; Charles Oscar Paullin, *Paullin's History of Naval Administration, 1775–1911* (Annapolis, MD: U.S. Naval Institute, 1968), p. 312.

5. In the USN since his 1846 appointment as a Midshipman, Kentuckian James P. Foster (1827–1869) became a Lt. in 1855 and a Lt. Cmdr. in July 1862. He was promoted to rank of Cmdr. in July 1866. Callahan, *op. cit.*, p. 201.

6. ORN, I, 27: 216–217; OR, I, 48, 1: , 215, 297–303; OR, I, 48, 2: 908, 1141; Charles Dana Gibson, with E. Kay Gibson, *Assault and Logistics*, Vol. 2: *Union Army Coastal and River Operations, 1861–1866* (Camden, ME: Ensign Press, 1995), pp. 510–513; Robert L. Kerby, *Kirby Smith's Confederacy: The Trans-Mississippi South, 1863–1865* (New York: Columbia University Press, 1972), p. 415; Alfred Jackson and Kathryn Abbey Hanna, *Napoleon III and Mexico: American Triumph Over Monarchy* (Chapel Hill, NC: University of North Carolina Press, 1971), pp. 238–239; Philip H. Sheridan, *Personal Memoirs*, 2 vols. (New York. C.L. Webster &

Co., 1888), Vol. 2, pp. 223–226; Richard O'Connor, *Sheridan the Inevitable* (Indianapolis, IN: Bobbs-Merrill, 1953), pp. 278–281.

7. An April 1865 intelligence sighting from Alexandria reported that the *Missouri* appeared to have been built on the plan of the C.S.S. *Tennessee*, captured at Mobile Bay the previous August. Designed especially for river operations, she was 180 feet long, with a beam of 53.8 feet. Her casemate was sloped at 35 degrees and, although pierced for seven guns, she mounted only three. She was reported "very slow, not being able to stem the current alone." After her surrender, a survey was ordered and its results are printed in the Navy *Official Records*. ORN, I, 27: 142, 241–242; OR, I, 48, 2: 93; William N. Still, *Armor Afloat: The Story of the Confederate Armorclads* (Columbia, SC: University of South Carolina Press, 1985), pp. 148–149, 226.

8. Buckeye Fitzhugh was appointed a Midshipman in 1848 and a Lt. in 1855. Like James P. Foster, he was also named a Lt. Cmdr. In July 1862, while commander of the steam sloop *Iroquois* of the North Atlantic Blockading Squadron. Following service in the WGCBS, he was transferred to the Mississippi Squadron late in 1864 and given command of the large gunboat *Ouachita*. After the war, Fitzhugh was promoted to the ranks of Cmdr. (1866), Captain (1876), and Commodore (1887). Callahan, *op. cit.*, p. 196; *New York Times*, August 4, 1889.

9. ORN, I, 27: 219–237, 248–249; OR, I, 48, 2: 600–602; Kerby, *op. cit.*, p. 426; Albert Castel, *General Sterling Price and the Civil War in the West* (Baton Rouge, LA: Louisiana State University Press, 1968), p. 271; Joseph H. Parks, *General Edmund Kirby Smith, C.S.A.* (Baton Rouge, LA: Louisiana State University Press, 1954), pp. 476–477; Still, *loc. cit.*

10. The 138-ton *Huntress* was constructed at New Albany, IN, in late 1862. The stern-wheeler was 131.6 feet long, with a beam of 31.2 feet and a 4.1-foot draft. Her two engines and two boilers generated sufficient power to drive her upstream at 6 mph. Retaining her original name, the future Tinclad No. 58 was purchased at Louisville, KY, on June 9, 1864 for $33,000. She was commissioned a day later, Acting Master John S. Dennis in command. Modified at the Cincinnati yards of Joseph Brown, she was sent out to Mound City to complete her outfitting. There she received her ordnance: two 30-pounder Parrott rifles and four 24-pounder smoothbore Dahlgren howitzers. "*Huntress*," in U.S. Navy Department, Naval Historical Center, *Dictionary of American Naval Fighting Ships, http://www.history.navy.mil/danfs/h9/huntress-i.htm* (accessed February 9, 2008); ORN, II, I: 105; Way *op. cit.*, p. 219; Silverstone, *op. cit.*, pp. 174–175. Pennsylvanian Dennis had run away to sea while a boy to go whaling from New Bedford, MA. Beginning as a cabin boy, he rose to command a whaler. Dennis was a veteran volunteer officer, having signed on as an Acting Master in August 1861, and served at Hilton Head and before Charleston. The *Huntress* was his first command, but he did not live to see her decommission. He died of unspecified causes aboard the *Huntress* on February 27, 1865. Callahan, *op. cit.*, p. 159 Edmund J. Huling, *Reminiscences of Gunboat Life in the Mississippi Squadron* (Saratoga Springs, NY: Sentinel Print, 1881), pp.1, 38.

11. Built at Cincinnati in 1863, the 209-ton packet *Reindeer* was purchased there on April 28, 1864, for $28,000. Measuring 147.6 feet long, with a beam of 28.2 feet and a 4.65-foot draft, the stern-wheeler's two engines and two boilers provided sufficient power to drive her against the current at 6 mph. Renamed *Peri*, the craft was modified into Tinclad No. 57 at the shipyards of Joseph Brown before her dispatch to Mound City for final outfitting. There *Peri* received her ordnance: two 30-pounder Parrott rifles and six 24-pounder smoothbore Dahlgren howitzers. She was commissioned on June 20, Acting Master Thomas M. Farrell in command. ORN, II, I: 175; Way, *op. cit.*, pp. 367, 391; Silverstone, *op. cit.*, p. 176. Named an Acting Ensign in December 1862, Farrell was promoted to his current rank nine days after the *Peri*

was commissioned. He would be honorably discharged in December 1865. Callahan, *op. cit.,* p. 189.

12. As related in Chapter 6, the Confederate cottonclad *Tom Sugg* was captured by the tinclad *Cricket* on the White River in August 1863. Sent to Cairo, the prize was adjudicated by the Illinois Prize Court and sold to the USN on September 29 for $7,000. Sent over to Mound City for modification, Tinclad No. 39 was 91.8 feet long, with a 22.5-foot beam and a draft of 3.75 feet. The side-wheeler's two engines and two boilers provided sufficient power to drive her against the current at 4 mph. She was armed with two 24-pounder smoothbore Dahlgren howitzers and was commissioned on January 1, 1864, Acting Ensign Elbert C. Van Pelt in command. Thereafter, she served largely as a guard and picket boat at Cairo. "*Tensas,*" in U.S. Navy Department, Naval Historical Center, *Dictionary of American Naval Fighting Ships, http://www.history.navy.mil/danfs/t3/tensas.htm* (accessed February 9, 2008); ORN, II, I: 222; Way, *op. cit.,* pp. 449, 458; Silverstone, *op. cit.,* p. 169. Van Pelt was named an Acting Ensign in September 1862 and would resign in March 1865. Callahan, *op. cit.,* p. 559.

13. Son of a naval surgeon, New York City native Livingston (1804–1885) joined the Navy as a Midshipman in 1823, rising through the ranks to that of Cmdr. in 1855. In May 1862, he was placed in charge of the recaptured Norfolk Navy Yard and, two months later, was given the rank of Commodore. In December 1864, he took over command of the Mound City station, holding it for a year (he succeeded Lee in charge of naval affairs in the West); he was transferred to the retired list thereafter, being promoted to the rank of Rear Adm. in May 1868. William B. Cogar, *Dictionary of Admirals of the U.S. Navy,* 2 vols. (Annapolis, MD: Naval Institute Press, 1989), Vol. 1, pp. 98–99.

14. ORN, I, 27: 252–255, 257, 263, 272–274, 287–288; Logbooks of the U.S.S. *Moose,* June 15, 1863–August 10, 1865, Records of the Bureau of Navigation, Record Group 19, U.S. National Archives, Washington, D.C., July 2, 1865 (cited hereafter as Logbook of the U.S.S. *Moose,* with date). Rowland Stafford True, "Life Aboard a Gunboat [U.S.S. *Silver Lake,* No. 23]: A First-Person Account," *Civil War Times Illustrated* 9 (February 1971): pp. 42–43.

15. Rogers joined the squadron as an Acting Ensign on October 1, 1862, and was promoted an Acting Master in April 1863, assigned to the ironclad *Pittsburg.* In June 1864, he was given command of the tinclad *Forest Rose* and was promoted to his current rank the following month. He would be honorably discharged in December 1868. Callahan, *op. cit.,* p. 471; ORN, I, 26: 404.

16. True, *loc. cit.;* ORN, I, 17: 861; ORN, I, 22: 210, 217–218, 237, 253; ORN, I, 27: 275–276, 283, 285–288, 310,342–344; Niven, *op. cit.,* p. 507; Philadelphia *Inquirer,* June 24, 1865; Dudley Taylor Cornish and Virginia Jeans Laas, *Lincoln's Lee: The Life of Samuel Phillips Lee, United States Navy, 1812–1897* (Lawrence, KS: University Press of Kansas, 1986), p. 155. A large sale of coal and coal barges was held at Natchez on August 7.

17. The 202-ton side-wheeler *Carrabasset* was built at Louisville, KY, in late 1863. She was 155 feet long, with a beam of 31 feet and a 4.7-foot draft. The vessel was purchased at Cincinnati on January 23, 1864, and remodeled by Joseph Brown at a cost of $2,387.50. She picked up her armament at Mound City, consisting of two 32-pounders and four 24-pounder smoothbore Dahlgren howitzers, before she was sent to New Orleans. Serving mostly on Berwick Bay and the Atchafalaya River, Tinclad No. 49 was decommissioned on July 25, 1865. "*Carrabasset,*" in U.S. Navy Department, Naval Historical Center, *Dictionary of American Naval Fighting Ships, http://www.history.navy.mil/danfs/c4/carrabasset-i.htm* (accessed February 9, 2008); ORN, II, I: 52; Way, *op. cit.,* pp. 72–73; Silverstone, *op. cit.,* p. 165.

18. The second *Glide* was constructed at Murraysville, WV, in the summer 1863. The 232-ton stern-wheeler was 160.4 feet long, with a beam of 33 feet and a 5.1-foot draft. Purchased into the USN at Pittsburgh on November 30 for $33,800, the vessel was modified at the Cincinnati shipyards of Joseph Brown for another $3,306.72. Upon completion, she was sent to Mound City, where she received an armament comprising two 32-pounders and four 24-pounder smoothbore Dahlgren howitzers. Tinclad No. 43 was sent to New Orleans for service with the WGCBS. "*Glide II,*" in U.S. Navy Department, Naval Historical Center, *Dictionary of American Naval Fighting Ships, http://www.history.navy.mil/danfs/g6/glide-ii.htm* (accessed February 9, 2008); ORN, II, I: 96; Way, *op. cit.,* p. 189; Silverstone, *op. cit.,* p. 172.

19. ORN, II, I: 52, 77, 96, 143, 163, 215, 219.

20. *Chicago Daily Tribune,* August 18, 21, 1865; Myron J. Smith Jr., *The Timberclads in the Civil War: Lexington, Tyler and Conestoga on the Western Waters* (Jefferson, N.C.: McFarland, 2008), p. 490.

21. ORN,II,I: 92, 221, 118. The sale of the three final tinclads netted the U.S. Treasury Department a total of $24 650.

22. Bobby Roberts, "Rivers of No Return," in Mark K. Christ, ed., *The Earth Reeled and Trees Trembled: Civil War Arkansas, 1863–1864* (Little Rock, AR: Old State House Museum, 2007), p. 87.

23. Lewis B. Parsons, *Reports to the War Department* (St. Louis, MO: George Knapp & Co., 1867), p.40.

24. True, *op. cit.,* 41; Angus Konstam and Tony Bryan, *Mississippi River Gunboats of the American Civil War, 1861–1865* (New Vanguard Series; London, Eng.: Osprey Publishing, 2002), p. 11; George W. Brown, "Service in the Mississippi Squadron and Its Connection with the Siege and Capture of Vicksburg," in Vol. I of James Grant Wilson and Titus Munson Con, eds., *Personal Recollections of the War of the Rebellion: Addresses Delivered Before the New York Commandery of the Loyal Legion of the United States, 1883–1891* (New York: Published by the Commandery, 1891), p. 313.

Bibliography

Primary Sources

Bache, George M. *Collection.* Navy Department Library, Naval Historical Center, Washington, D.C.

Barry, William Wesley. *Papers.* New York Historical Society, New York City.

Bock, William N. *Papers.* Illinois State Historical Society, Springfield.

Browne, Symmes. *Papers.* Ohio Historical Society, Columbus.

Carondelet, U.S.S. Logbook: May 1862–June 1865. Record Group 24: U.S. Navy Department, Records of the Bureau of Naval Personnel. National Archives, Washington, D.C.

Civil War, Confederate and Federal. Collection. Tennessee State Library and Archives, Nashville.

Civil War Times Illustrated. Collection. U.S. Army Military History Institute, Carlisle Barracks, PA.

Confederate States of America. War Department. *Official Reports of Battles.* Richmond, VA, *Enquirer* Book & Job Press, 1862.

Davis, Frederic E. *Papers.* Emory University. Atlanta.

Dickerson, James A. *Diary* (photocopy). Rutherford B. Hayes Presidential Center, Fremont, OH.

Eads, James B. *Papers,* Missouri Historical Society, St. Louis.

Harris, Isham G. *Papers.* Papers of the Governors of Tennessee, Tennessee State Library and Archives, Nashville.

Howard, William H. *Papers.* University of Tennessee Library, Knoxville.

Indiana. Morgan Raid Commission. *Report of the Morgan Raid Commission to the Governor, December 31, 1867.* N.p., 1867.

Irion, Jack B., and David V. Beard. *Underwater Archaeological Assessment of Civil War Shipwrecks in Kentucky Lake, Benton and Humphreys Counties, Tennessee.* New Orleans, LA: R. Christopher Good-win & Associates, Inc., for the Tennessee Division of Archaeology, Department of Environment and Conservation, State of Tennessee, 1993.

James, Stephen R., Jr., Michael C. Tuttle, and Michael C. Krivor. *Remote Sensing Survey and Archaeological Assessment of Submerged Cultural Resources Associated with the Battle of Johnsonville.* Memphis, TN: Submitted to the Tennessee Historical Commission by Pan-American Maritime, L.L.C., 1999.

Johnson, Andrew. *The Papers of Andrew Johnson.* Vol. 5. Knoxville, TN: University of Tennessee Press, 1976.

Johnson, Robert U., and Clarence C. Buel, eds. *Battles and Leaders of the Civil War.* 4 vols. New York: The Century Company, 1884–1887, reprinted Thomas Yoseloff, 1956.

Meigs, Montgomery C. *Papers.* Manuscript Division, Library of Congress, Washington, D.C.

Pennock, Alexander Mosley. *Papers.* Illinois State Historical Society, Springfield.

Phelps, Seth Ledyard. *Papers.* Missouri Historical Society, St. Louis (SLPC).

Porter, David Dixon. *Papers.* Manuscript Division, Library of Congress, Washington, D.C. (LC).

_____. Missouri Historical Society, St. Louis. (DDPC).

United States Congress, Joint Committee on the Conduct of the War. *Report: Fort Pillow Massacre.* 38th Cong., 1st sess. Washington, D.C.: GPO, 1864.

_____. *Report: Red River.* 38th Cong., 2nd sess. Washington, D.C.: GPO, 1864; reprint, Greenwood Press, 1971.

United States Navy Department. *Official Records of the Union and Confederate Navies in the War of the Rebellion (ORN).* 31 vols. Washing-ton, D.C.: GPO, 1894–1922.

_____. Records of the Bureau of Naval Personnel: Record Group 24. National Archives, Washington, D.C.

_____. Records of the Office of Naval Records and Library, *Naval Records Collection:* Record Group 45. National Archives, Washington, D.C.

_____. *Tinclad Logbooks.* Record Group 24: U.S. Navy Department, Records of the Bureau of Naval Personnel. National Archives, Washington, D.C. (Not all of the logbooks kept on the tinclads have survived. Those available are here. Abstracts were taken from the deck logs of several ships; these appear in the Navy Official Records and include information for dates of deck logs no longer available, e.g., *Marmora.*)

U.S. War Department. *Atlas to Accompany the Official Records of the War of the Rebellion.* Compiled by Calvin D. Cowles. 3 vols. Washington, D.C.: GPO, 1891–1895.

_____. *The War of the Rebellion: A Compilation of the Official Records of the Union and Confederate Armies (OR).* 128 vols. Washington, D.C.: GPO, 1880–1901.

Watson, Theodore. *Letters.* The Newberry Library (Chicago).

Welles, Gideon. *Papers.* Manuscript Division, Library of Congress, Washington, D.C.

Newspapers

Arkansas True Democrat
Atlantic Democrat
Beaumont (TX) *Enterprise*
Boston Daily Advertiser
Boston Morning Journal
Cairo City Weekly Gazette
Charleston Daily Courier
Charleston Mercury
Chicago Daily Post

Chicago Daily Times
Chicago Daily Tribune
Chicago Evening Journal
Cincinnati Daily Commercial
Cincinnati Daily Enquirer
Cincinnati Daily Gazette
Cincinnati Daily Times
Clarksville Chronicle
Cleveland Daily Herald
Cleveland Daily Plain Dealer
Columbus (OH) Crisis
Columbus (GA) Daily Enquirer
Columbus (WI) Democrat
The Daily Mississippian
Dyer County (TN) Herald
Evansville Daily Journal
Florence (AL) Gazette
Frank Leslie's Illustrated Newspaper
Galveston Tri-Weekly News
Galveston Weekly News
Granada (MS) Appeal
Harper's Weekly
Houston Daily Telegraph
Illinois Weekly State Journal
Indiana Herald
Indianapolis Daily Journal
Indianapolis News
Ironton (OH) Register
Jackson Mississippian
Little Rock True Democrat
Louisville Courier
Louisville Daily Journal
Louisville Democrat
Macon Daily Telegraph
Macon Weekly Telegraph
Memphis Argus
Memphis Commercial Appeal
Memphis Daily Appeal
Memphis Daily Avalanche
Memphis Daily Bulletin
Memphis Evening Times
Milwaukee Daily Sentinel
Mobile Daily Advertiser & Register
Mobile Daily Tribune
Mobile Evening News
Nashville Banner
Nashville Daily Dispatch
Nashville Daily Patriot
Nashville Daily Union
Nashville Times
Nashville Union and American
National Intelligencer
Natchez Weekly Courier
Natchitoches (LA) Union
New Albany Ledger
New Haven Daily Palladium
New Orleans Daily Crescent
New Orleans Daily Delta
New Orleans Daily Picayune
New Orleans Era
New Orleans Times
New York Evening Post
New York Herald
New York Times
New York Tribune
New York World
North American and United States Gazette
Philadelphia Press

Pittsburgh Daily Commercial
Raleigh Weekly Register
Richmond Dispatch
Ripley (OH) Bee
Savannah Daily Morning News
St. Louis Daily Missouri Democrat
St. Louis Daily Missouri Republican
St. Louis Daily Union
Savannah Republican
The Tri-Weekly Telegraph (Houston, TX)
Vicksburg Evening Post
Vicksburg Sunday Post
Wheeling Daily Register
Wisconsin State Journal
Wisconsin State Register

Books

Abbott, John S.C. The History of the Civil War in America. Vol. 1. New York: H. Bill, 1863.

Abdill, George R. Civil War Railroads: Pictorial Story of the Iron Horse, 1861–1865. Seattle, WA: Superior Publishing Co., 1961.

Alden, Carroll Storrs, and Ralph Earle. Makers of Naval Tradition. Boston: Ginn and Company, 1925.

Allardice, Bruce S. More Generals in Gray. Baton Route, LA: Louisiana State University Press, 1995.

Alldredge, J. Haden, et al. A History of Navigation on the Tennessee River. Washington, D.C.: GPO, 1937.

Allen, David C. Winds of Change: Robertson County, Tennessee, in the Civil War. Nashville, TN: Land Yacht Press, 2000.

Allen, John W. Legends and Lore of Southern Illinois. Carbondale, IL: University Graphics, 1978.

Ambrose, Daniel L. History of the Seventh Regiment Illinois Volunteer Infantry. Springfield, IL: Illinois Journal Company, 1868.

Ambrose, Stephen E. Halleck: Lincoln's Chief of Staff. Baton Rouge, LA: Louisiana State University Press, 1962.

Anders, Curt. Disaster in Damp Sand: The Red River Expedition. Carmel, IN: Guild Press of Indiana, 1997.

_____. Henry Halleck's War: A Fresh Look at Lincoln's Controversial General-in-Chief. Indianapolis: Guild Press of Indiana, 1999.

Anderson, Bern. By Sea and By River: The Naval History of the Civil War. New York: Knopf, 1962.

Andrews, Christopher C. History of the Campaign of Mobile, Including the Cooperative Operations of Gen. Wilson's Cavalry in Alabama. New York: Van Nostrand, 1867.

Andrews, J. Cutler. The North Reports the Civil War. Pittsburgh, PA: University of Pittsburgh Press, 1985.

_____. The South Reports the Civil War. Pittsburgh, PA: University of Pittsburgh Press, 1985.

Angle, Paul M., ed. Illinois Guide and Gazetteer: Prepared Under the Supervision of the Illinois Sesquicentennial Commission. Chicago: Rand McNally & Company, 1969.

Anthony, Irwin. Paddle Wheels and Pistols. New York: The Chldren's Book Club, 1930.

Ash, Stephen V. Middle Tennessee Society Transformed, 1860–1870: War and Peace in the Upper South. Baton Rouge, LA: Louisiana State University Press, 1988.

_____. When the Yankees Came: Conflict and Chaos in the Occupied South, 1861–1865. Chapel Hill: University of North Carolina Press, 1995.

Asprey, Robert B. The War in the Shadows: The Guerrilla in History, Two Thousand Years of the Guerrilla at War from Ancient Persia to the Present. 2 vols. New York: William Morrow, 1975.

Aughey, John H. The Iron Furnance: or, Slavery and Secession. Philadelphia, PA: William S. and Alfred Martien, 1863.

Austin, J.P. The Blue and the Gray: Sketches of a Portion of the Unwritten History of the Great American Civil War. Atlanta, GA: Franklin Printing and Publishing Co., 1899.

Bacon, Benjamin W. Sinews of War: How Technology, Industry and Transportation Won the Civil War. Novato, CA: Presidio Press, 1997.

Badeau, Adam. Military History of Ulysses S. Grant. 3 vols. New York: D. Appleton and Co., 1868–1881.

Bailey, Anne J. Between the Enemy and Texas: Parsons's Texas Cavalry in the Civil War. Fort Worth: Texas Christian University Press, 1989.

_____. The Chessboard of War: Sherman and Hood in the Autumn Campaigns of 1864. Great Campaigns of the Civil War. Lincoln: University of Nebraska Press, 2000.

Baker, Lafayette C. History of the United States Secret Service. Philadelphia, PA: L.C. Baker, 1867.

Ballard, Michael B. Vicksburg: The Campaign that Opened the Mississippi. Chapel Hill, NC: University of North Carolina Press, 2004.

Banta, Richard E. The Ohio. Rivers of America. New York: Rinehard, 1949.

Barr, Alwyn. Polignac's Texas Brigade. 2nd ed. College Station, TX: Texas A & M University Press, 1998.

Barrett, Edward. Gunnery Instruction Simplified for the Volunteer Officers of the U.S. Navy, with Hints for Executive and Other Officers. New York: D. Van Nostrand, 1863.

Barron, Samuel B. *The Lone Star Defenders: A Chronicle of the Third Texas Cavalry, Ross' Brigade.* New York and Washington, D.C.: The Neale Publishing Co., 1908.

Bartols, Barnabas H. *A Treatise on the Marine Boilers of the United States.* Philadelphia, PA: R.W. Barnard, 1851.

Beach, Ursula Smith. *Along the Warioto; or, a History of Montgomery County, Tennessee.* Clarksville, TN: Clarksville Kiwanis Club and Tennessee Historical Commission, 1964.

Beale, Howard K., ed. *Diary of Gideon Welles: Secretary of the Navy Under Lincoln and Johnson.* 2 vols. New York: W.W. Norton, 1960.

Beard, William E. *The Battle of Nashville, Including an Outline of the Stirring Events Occurring in One of the Most Notable Movements of the Civil War — Hood's Invasion of Tennessee.* Nashville, TN: Marshall & Bruce, 1913.

Bearss, Edwin C. *Hardluck Ironclad: The Sinking and Salvage of the Cairo.* Baton Rouge: Louisiana State University, 1966.

_____. *The Vicksburg Campaign.* 3 vols. Dayton, OH: Morningside Book Shop, 1985–1986.

Beecher, Harris H. *Record of the 114th Regiment, New York State Volunteer Infantry.* Norwich, NY: J.F. Hubbard, Jr., 1866.

Bennett, Frank M. *Steam Navy of the United States: A History of the Growth of the Steam Vessel of War in the U.S. Navy, and of the Naval Engineer Corps,* etc. Pittsburgh: Warren, 1896; reprinted New York: Greenwood, 1970.

Bennett, Michael J. *Union Jacks: Yankee Sailors in the Civil War.* Chapel Hill: University of North Carolina Press, 2004.

Bergeron, Arthur W., Jr. *Confederate Mobile.* Jackson, MS: University Press of Mississippi, 1991.

Beringer, Richard E., Herman Hattaway, Archer Jones, and William N. Still Jr. *Why the South Lost the Civil War.* Athens: The University of Georgia Press, 1986.

Berry, Chester D. *Loss of the Sultana and Reminiscences of Survivors.* Lansing, MI: Darius D. Thorp, 1892.

Berry, Thomas Franklin. *Four Years with Morgan and Forrest.* Oklahoma City, OK: The Harlow-Ratliff Co., 1914.

Bickman, William. *Rosecrans' Campaigns with the 14th Army Corps; or, the Army of the Cumberland: A Narrative of Personal Observations.* Cincinnati, OH: Moore, Wilstach, Keys, 1863.

Birtle, Andrew J. *U.S. Army Counterinsurgency and Contingency Operations Doctrine, 1860–1941.* Washington, D.C.: GPO, 1998.

Blackburn, George M., ed. *Dear Carrie: The Civil War Letters of Thomas M. Stevens.* Mount Pleasant, MI: Central Michigan University Press, 1984.

Blessington, Joseph P. *The Campaigns of Walker's Texas Division.* Austin, TX: The Pemberton Press, 1968.

Boatner, Mark M. III. *The Civil War Dictionary.* New York: David McKay, 1959.

Bowers, John. *Chickamauga and Chattanooga: The Battles That Doomed the Confederacy.* New York: HarperPerennial, 1995.

Boynton, Charles B. *History of the Navy During the Rebellion.* 2 vols. New York: D. Appleton and Company, 1867–1868.

Bradford, Gershom. *The Mariner's Dictionary.* New York: Weathervane Books, 1970.

Bragg, Marion. *Historic Names and Places on the Lower Mississippi River.* Vicksburg, MS: Mississippi River Commission, 1977.

Brandenburg Methodist Church Men's Club. *The Brandenburg Story: With Particular Reference to John Hunt Morgan's Crossing of the Ohio July 8, 1863.* Brandenburg, KY: 1963.

Brandt, J.D. *Gunnery Catechism, As Applied To The Service Of Naval Ordnance.* New York: D. Van Nostrand, 1864.

Brandt, Robert. *Touring the Middle Tennessee Backroads.* Winston-Salem, NC: John F. Blair, Publisher, 1995.

Brazelton, B.G. *A History of Hardin County, Tennessee.* Nashville, TN: Cumberland Presbyterian Publishing House, 1885.

A Brief and Condensed History of Parsons' Texas Cavalry Brigade. Waxahachie, TX: J.M. Flemister, Printer, 1893.

Brock, Eric, and Gary D. Joiner. *Red River Steamboats.* Charleston, SC: Arcadia Publishing, 1999.

Brookshire, William Riley. *War Along the Bayous: The 1864 Red River Campaign in Louisiana.* Washington, D.C.: Brassey's, 1998.

Browne, Henry R., and Symmes E. Browne. *From the Fresh Water Navy, 1861–1864: Letters of Acting Master's Mate Henry R. Browne and Acting Ensign Symmes E. Browne.* Edited by John D. Milligan. Naval Letters Series, Vol. 3. Annapolis, MD: Naval Institute Press, 1970.

Browne, Junius Henri. *Four Years in Secessia: Adventures Within and Without the Union Lines.* Hartford, CT: O. D. Case and Company, 1865.

Brownlee, Richard S. III. *Gray Ghosts of the Confederacy: Guerrilla Warfare in the West, 1861–1865.* Baton Rouge, LA: Louisiana State University Press, 1958.

Bryant, William O. *Cahaba Prison and the Sultana Disaster.* Tuscaloosa, AL: University of Alabama Press, 1990.

Bucy, Carole. *A Path Divided: Tennessee's Civil War Years.* Nashville, TN: Tennessee 200, 1996.

Callahan, Edward W. *List of Officers of the Navy of the United States and of the Marine Corps, from 1775 to 1900, Comprising a Complete Register of All Present and Former Commissioned, Warranted, and Appointed Officers of the United States Navy, and of the Marine Corps, Regular and Volunteer. Compiled from the Official Records of the Navy Department.* New York: L.R. Hamersly & Co., 1901. Reprint: New York: Haskell House, 1969.

Calore, Paul. *Naval Campaigns of the Civil War.* Jefferson, NC: McFarland & Co., Inc., 2002.

Campbell, R. Thomas. *Confederate Naval Forces on Western Waters: The Defense of the Mississippi River and Its Tributaries.* Jefferson, NC: McFarland & Co., Inc., 2005.

_____. *Gray Thunder: Exploits of the Confederate States Navy.* New Orleans, LA: Burd Street Press, 1996.

_____. *Southern Thunder: Exploits of the Confederate States Navy.* New Orleans, LA: Burd Street Press, 1996.

Canfield, Eugene B. *Civil War Naval Ordnance.* Washington, D.C.: Naval History Division, U.S. Navy Department, 1969.

Canney, Donald L. *Lincoln's Navy: The Ships, Men and Organization, 1861–65.* London and New York: Conway Maritime Press, 1998.

_____. *The Old Steam Navy: Vol. 2, The Ironclads, 1842–1885.* Annapolis, MD: Naval Institute Press, 1993.

Capers, Gerald M. *The Biography of a River Town: Memphis — Its Heroic Age.* Chapel Hill: University of North Carolina Press, 1939.

Carter, Samuel III. *The Final Fortress: The Campaign for Vicksburg 1862–1863.* New York: St. Martin's Press, 1980.

Castel, Albert. *General Sterling Price and the Civil War in the West.* Baton Rouge, LA: Louisiana State University Press, 1968.

Castlen, Harriet (Gift). *Hope Bids Me Onward.* Savannah, GA: Chatham Printing Co., 1945.

Catton, Bruce. *The American Heritage Picture History of the Civil War.*

New York: American Heritage Publishing Co., 1960.

_____. *The Centennial History of the Civil War*. 3 vols. Garden City, NY: Doubleday, 1961–1965.

_____. *Grant Moves South*. Boston, MA: Little, Brown, 1960.

_____. *Never Call Retreat*. New York: Pocket Books, 1973.

_____. *This Hallowed Ground: The Story of the Union Side of the Civil War*. Garden City, N.Y.: Doubleday, 1956.

Cayton, Andrew R.L. *Ohio: The History of a People*. Columbus: The Ohio State University Press, 2002.

Chamberlain, William H., ed. *Sketches of War History, 1861–1865: Papers Prepared for the Ohio Commandery of the Military Order of the Loyal Legion of the United States*. 6 vols. Cincinnati, OH: R. Clarke & Co., 1890–1908.

Chappelle, Howard I. *History of the American Sailing Navy*. New York: W.W. Norton, 1935.

Christ, Mark K., ed. *Rugged and Sublime: The Civil War in Arkansas*. Fayetteville: University of Arkansas Press, 1994.

Church, Frank L. *Civil War Marine: A Diary of the Red River Expedition, 1864*. Edited and annotated by James P. Jones and Edward F. Keuchel. Washington, D.C.: History and Museums Division, Headquarters, U.S. Marine Corps, 1975.

Cist, Henry M. *Army of the Cumberland*. Campaigns of the Civil War. New York: Charles Scribner's Sons, 1892.

Clark, Orton. *The One Hundred and Sixteenth Regiment of New York Volunteers*. Buffalo, NY: Matthews & Warren, 1868.

Cleaves, Freeman. *Rock of Chickamauga: The Life of General George H. Thomas*. Norman, OK: University of Oklahoma Press, 1948.

Cogar, William B. *Dictionary of Admirals of the U.S. Navy*. 2 vols. Annapolis, MD: Naval Institute Press, 1989.

Coltern, John W. *Confederates of Elmwood*. Westminster, MD: Heritage Books, 2001.

Conger, Arthur L. *The Rise of U.S. Grant*. New York: Century, 1931.

Connelly, Thomas Lawrence. *Army of the Heartland: The Army of Tennessee, 1861–1862*. Baton Rouge, LA: Louisiana State University Press, 1967.

_____. *Autumn of Glory: The Army of Tennessee, 1862–1865*. Baton Rouge, LA: Louisiana State University Press, 1971.

_____. *Civil War Tennessee: Battles and Leaders*. Knoxville, TN: University of Tennessee Press, 1979.

Connelly, Thomas W. *History of the 70th Ohio Regiment: From Its Organization to Its Mustering Out*. Cincinnati, OH: Peak Bros., 1902.

Conway, Fred W. *Corydon: The Forgotten Battle of the Civil War*. New Albany, IN: FBH Publishers, 1991.

Coombe, Jack D. *Gunfire Around the Gulf: The Last Major Naval Campaigns of the Civil War*. New York: Bantam Books, 1999.

_____. *Thunder Along the Mississippi: The River Battles That Split the Confederacy*. New York: Sarpedon Publishers, 1996.

Cooling, Benjamin F. *Fort Donelson's Legacy: War and Society in Kentucky and Tennessee, 1862–1863*. Knoxville: University of Tennessee Press, 1997.

Cornish, Dudley Taylor, and Virginia Jeans Laas, *Lincoln's Lee: The Life of Samuel Phillips Lee, United States Navy, 1812–1897*. Lawrence, KS: University Press of Kansas, 1986.

Coulter, E. Merton. *The Civil War and Readjustment in Kentucky*. Chapel Hill, NC: University of North Carolina Press, 1926.

Cox, Jacob D. *March to the Sea: Franklin and Nashville*. Campaigns of the Civil War, no. 10. New York: Scribner's, 1882.

_____. *Military Reminiscences of the Civil War*. 2 vols. New York: Scribner's, 1900.

Cozzens, Peter. *The Battle of Stones River*. Civil War Series. Washington, D.C.: Eastern National Park and Monument Association, 1995.

_____. *No Better Place to Die: The Battle of Stones River*. Urbana: University of Illinois Press, 1990.

_____. *The Shipwreck of Their Hopes: The Battle of Chattanooga*. Urbana: University of Illinois Press, 1994.

Crandall, Warren D., and Isaac D. Newell. *History of the Ram Fleet and Mississippi Marine Brigade*. St. Louis, MO: Buschart Brothers, 1907.

Crocker, Helen B. *The Green River of Kentucky*. Lexington: University Press of Kentucky, 1976.

Crook, George. *General George Crook: His Autobiography*. Edited by Martin F. Schmitt. Norman, OK: University of Oklahoma Press, 1946.

Crooker, Lucien B., Henry S. Nourse, and John G. Brown. *The 55th Illinois, 1861–1865*. Huntington, WV: Blue Acorn Press, 1993.

Currie, George E. *Warfare Along the Mississippi: The Letters of Lieutenant Colonel George E. Currie*. Edited by Norman E. Clark. Mount Pleasant,

MI: Central Michigan University, 1861.

Curry, Jane. *The River's in My Blood: Riverboat Pilots Tell Their Story*. Lincoln, NE: University of Nebraska Press, 1983.

Daniel, Larry J. *Cannoneers in Gray: The Field Artillery of the Army of Tennessee, 1861–1865*. Birmingham, AL: University of Alabama Press, 1984.

_____. *Days of Glory: The Army of the Cumberland, 1861–1865*. Baton Rouge, LA: Louisiana State University Press, 2004.

Davidson, Alexander, and Bernard Stuve, *A Complete History of Illinois from 1673 to 1873*. Springfield, IL: Illinois Journal Company, 1874.

Davidson, Donald. *The Tennessee*. Vol. 2: *The New River, Civil War to TVA*. Rivers of America. New York: Rinehart & Co., 1948.

Davis, Charles H. *Charles H. Davis: Life of Charles Henry Davis, Rear Admiral, 1807–1877*. Boston and New York: Houghton, Mifflin and Company, 1899.

Davis, Jefferson. *Rise and Fall of the Confederate Government*. 2 vols. New York: D. Appleton and Company, 1881.

DeBlack, Thomas A. *With Fire and Sword: Arkansas, 1861–1874*. Histories of Arkansas. Fayetteville, AR: University of Arkansas Press, 2003.

Dewey, George. *Autobiography of George Dewey: Admiral of the Navy*. New York: Charles Scribner's Sons, 1913.

Dickey, Thomas S., and Peter C. George. *Field Artillery Projectiles of the American Civil War, Revised and Supplemented 1993 Edition*. Mechanicsville, VA: Arsenal Publications II, 1993.

Dictionary of American Naval Fighting Ships. 8 vols. Washington, D.C.: GPO, 1916–1981.

Dinkins, James. *1861 to 1865, by an Old Johnnie: Personal Recollections and Experiences in the Confederate Army*. Cincinnati, OH: The Robert Clarke, Co., 1897.

Dodge, Grenville M. *The Battle of Atlanta and Other Campaigns, Addresses, Etc.* Council Bluffs, IA: The Monarch Printing Company, 1911; reprint, Denver, CO: Sage Books, 1965.

Dodson, W.C. *Campaigns of Wheeler and His Cavalry*. Atlanta, GA: Hudgins, 1897.

Donald, David Herbert. *Lincoln*. New York: Simon and Schuster, 1995.

Douglas, Byrd. *Steamboatin' on the Cumberland*. Nashville: The Tennessee Book Company, 1961.

Douglass, Ben. *History of Wayne County, Ohio.* Indianapolis, IN: Robert Douglass, Publisher, 1878.

Driggs, George W. *Opening the Mississippi; Or, Two Years Campaigning in the Southwest.* Madison, WI: William J. Park Co., 1864.

Duaine, Carl L. *The Dead Men Wore Boots: An Account of the 32nd Texas Volunteer Cavalry, CSA, 1862–1865.* Austin, TX: San Felipe Press, 1966.

Du Bose, John W. *General Joseph Wheeler and the Army of Tennessee.* New York: Neale Publishing Co., 1912.

Duffy, James P. *Lincoln's Admiral: The Civil War Campaigns of David Farragut.* New York: Wiley, 1997.

Dugan, James. *History of Hurlbut's Fighting Fourth Division.* Cincinnati, OH: Morgan & Co., 1863.

Duke, Basil W. *The Great Indiana-Ohio Raid by Brig. Gen. John Hunt Morgan and His Men, July 1863.* Louisville, KY: Book Nook Press, 1956.

_____. *The History of Morgan's Cavalry.* New York: Neale Publishing Co., 1906. Reprint, Bloomington, IN: Indiana University Press, 1960.

_____. *Reminiscences of General Basil W. Duke.* Garden City, NY: Doubleday Page, 1911.

Dunnavent, R. Blake. *Brown Water Warfare: The U.S. Navy in Riverine Warfare and the Emergence of a Tactical Doctrine, 1775–1970.* New Perspectives on Maritime History and Nautical Archaeology. Gainesville, FL: University of Florida Press, 2003.

Durham, Walter T. *Nashville: The Occupied City—the First Seventeen Months—February 16, 1862–June 30, 1863.* Nashville: The Tennessee Historical Society, 1985.

_____. *Reluctant Partners: Nashville and the Union—July 1, 1863 to June 30, 1865.* Nashville: The Tennessee Historical Society, 1987.

Dyer, Frederick H. *A Compendium of the War of the Rebellion.* 3 vols. Des Moines, IA: Dyer Publishing Co., 1908. Reprint, New York: Thomas Yoseloff, 1959.

Dyer, Joseph P. *"Fightin' Joe" Wheeler.* Southern Biography Series. Baton Rouge, LA: Louisiana State University Press, 1941.

_____. *From Shiloh to San Juan: The Life of "Fighting Joe" Wheeler.* Baton Rouge, LA: Louisiana State University Press, 1961.

Eddy, T.M. *The Patriotism of Illinois: A Record of the Civil and Military History of the State in the War for the Union.* 2 vols. Chicago, IL: Clarke & Co., Publishers, 1865.

Edwards, John N. *Shelby and His Men; or, The War in the West.*

Cincinnati, OH: Miami Printing and Publishing Co., 1867; reprinted, Waverly, MO: General J.O. Shelby Memorial, 1993.

Ellicott, John M. *The Life of John Ancrum Winslow, Rear-Admiral, United States Navy, Who Commanded the U.S. Steamer Kearsarge in Her Action with the Confederate Cruiser Alabama.* New York: G.P. Putnam's Sons, 1905.

Elliott, James W. *Transport to Disaster: The Forgotten Story of the Sultana.* New York: Holt, Rinehart and Winston, 1962.

Evans, Robley D. *A Sailor's Log: Recollections of a Naval Life.* New York: D. Appleton, 1901.

Faulk, Odie. *General Tom Green, Fightin' Texan.* Waco, TX: Texian Press, 1963.

Faust, Patricia L. *Historical Times Illustrated Encyclopedia of the Civil War.* New York: Harper Collins Publishers, 1986.

Feis, William B. *Grant's Secret Service: The Intelligence War from Belmont to Appomattox.* Lincoln, NE: University of Nebraska Press, 2002.

Ferguson, John L., ed. *Arkansas and the Civil War.* Little Rock: Arkansas Historical Commission, 1962.

Fisher, John E. *They Rode with Forrest and Wheeler: A Chronicle of Five Tennessee Brothers' Service in the Confederate Western Cavalry.* Jefferson, NC: McFarland & Co., Inc., 1995.

Fisk, Harold. *Geological Investigations of the Alluvial Valley of the Lower Mississippi River.* Washington, D.C.: U.S. Army Corps of Engineers, 1944.

Fitzhugh, Lestern N. *Texas Batteries, Battalions, Regiments, Commanders and Field Officers, Confederate States Army, 1861–1865.* Midlothian, TX: Mirror Press, 1959.

Folmsbee, Stanley J., Robert E. Corlew, and Enoch L. Mitchell. *Tennessee: A Short History.* Knoxville: University of Tennessee Press, 1969.

Foote, Shelby. *The Civil War: A Narrative.* 3 vols. New York: Random House, 1958–1974; reprint, New York: Vintage Books, 1986.

Forsyth, Michael J. *The Red River Campaign of 1864 and the Loss by the Confederacy of the Civil War.* Jefferson, NC: McFarland, 2001.

Fowler, William H. *Under Two Flags: The American Navy in the Civil War.* New York: W.W. Norton, 1990.

Fox, Gustavus Vasa. *Confidential Correspondence of Gustavus Vasa Fox, Assistant Secretary of the Navy, 1861–1865.* Edited by Robert Means Thompson and Richard Wainwright. 2 vols. New York: De Vinne Press, 1918–1919.

Frankignoul, Daniel. *Prince Camille de Polignac, Major General, C.S.A. "The Lafayette of the South."* Brussels, Belgium: Confederate Historical Association of Belgium, 1999.

Franklin, Samuel R. *Memories of a Rear Admiral: Who Has Served for More Than Half a Century in the Navy of the United States.* New York: Harper and Brothers, 1898.

Freemon, Frank R. *Gangrene and Glory: Medical Care During the American Civil War.* Urbana: University of Illinois Press, 2001.

Friend, Jack. *West Wind, Flood Tide: The Battle of Mobile Bay.* Annapolis, MD: Naval Institute Press, 2004.

Fuchs, Richard L. *An Unerring Fire: The Massacre at Fort Pillow.* Mechanicsburg, PA: Stackpole Books, 2002.

Funk, Arville L. *The Morgan Raid in Indiana and Ohio (1863).* Corydon, IN: ALFCO Publications, 1971.

Gabel, Christopher R., and the Staff Ride Team. *Staff Ride Handbook for the Vicksburg Campaign, December 1862–July 1863.* Fort Leavenworth, KS: Combat Studies Institute, U.S. Army Command and General Staff College, 2001.

Gallaway, H.P. *Ragged Rebel: A Common Soldier in W.H. Parsons' Texas Cavalry, 1861–1865.* Austin, TX: University of Texas Press, 1988.

Geer, Allen Morgan. *The Civil War Diary of Allen Morgan Geer, 20th Regiment, Illinois Volunteers.* Edited by Mary Ann Anderson. Denver, CO: Robert C. Appleman, 1977.

Gerteis, Louis S. *Civil War St. Louis.* Lawrence, KS: University Press of Kansas, 2001.

Gibbons, Tony. *Warships and Naval Battles of the Civil War.* New York: Gallery Books, 1989.

Gibson, Charles Dana, with E. Kay Gibson. *Assault and Logistics.* Vol. 1: *Dictionary of Transports and Combat Vessels Steam and Sail Employed by the Union Army, 1861–1868.* Camden, ME: Ensign Press, 1995.

_____. *Assault and Logistics.* Vol. 2: *Union Army Coastal and River Operations, 1861–1866.* Camden, ME: Ensign Press, 1995.

Gildrie, Richard, Philip Kemmerly, and Thomas H. Winn. *Clarksville, Tennessee, in the Civil War: A Chronology.* Clarksville, TN: Montgomery County Historical Society, 1984.

Glazier, Willard. *Battles for the Union.* Hartford, CT: Dustin, Gilman & Co., 1875.

Goodspeed's General History of Tennessee. Chicago, IL: Goodspeed Publishers, 1887; reprinted, Nashville, C. and R. Elder, 1973.

Gosnell, H. Allen. *Guns on the Western Waters: The Story of the River Gunboats in the Civil War*. Baton Rouge, LA: Louisiana State University Press, 1949; reprinted, Louisiana State University Press, 1993.

Graf, LeRoy P., and Ralph W. Haskins, eds., *The Papers of Andrew Johnson*. Vol. 5. Knoxville: University of Tennessee Press, 1979.

Grant, Ulysses S. *The Papers of Ulysses S. Grant*. Edited by John Y. Simon. 24 vols. to date. Edwardsville, Southern Illinois University Press, 1967–.

_____. *Personal Memoirs of U.S. Grant*. 2 vols. New York: C.L. Webster & Co., 1885–1886. Reprint (2 vols. in 1), New York: Penguin Books, 1999.

_____. *Personal Memoirs of U.S. Grant: A Modern Abridgment*. New York: Premier Books, 1962.

Greeley, Horace. *The American Conflict: A History of the Great Rebellion in the United States of America, 1860–1865*. 2 vols. Hartford, CT: O.D. Case & Company, 1879.

Green, Francis Vinton. *The Mississippi*. Campaigns of the Civil War, vol. 8. New York: Charles Scribner's Sons, 1885. Reprint, The Blue & The Gray Press, n.d.

Griess, Thomas E., ed. *Atlas for the American Civil War*. The West Point Military History Series. Wayne, NJ: Avery Publishing Group, 1986.

Grimsley, Mark. *The Hard Hand of War: Union Military Policy Toward Southern Civilians*. New York: Cambridge University Press, 1995.

Grisamore, Silas T. *The Civil War Reminiscences of Major Silas T. Grisamore, C.S.A.* Edited by Arthur W. Bergeron, Jr. Baton Rouge, LA: Louisiana State University Press, 1993.

Groom, Winston. *Shrouds of Glory: From Atlanta to Nashville—The Last Great Campaign of the Civil War*. New York: Atlantic Monthly Press, 1995.

Guelzo, Allen C. *The Crisis of the American Republic: A History of the Civil War and Reconstruction*. New York: St. Martin's Press, 1995.

Hackemer, Kurt. *The U.S. Navy and the Origins of the Military-Industrial Complex, 1847–1883*. Annapolis MD: Naval Institute Press, 2001.

Haites, Erik F., James Mak, and Gary M. Walton, *Western River Transportation: The Era of Early Internal Developments, 1810–1860*. Baltimore, MD: The Johns Hopkins University Press, 1975.

Hallock, Judith Lee. *Braxton Bragg and Confederate Defeat*. Tuscaloosa, AL: University of Alabama Press, 1991.

Hamersly, Lewis B. *The Records of Living Officers of the U.S. Navy and Marine Corps*. Philadelphia, PA: J.B. Lippincott & Co., 1870.

Hancock, R.R. *Hancock's Diary; or, A History of the Second Tennessee Cavalry, with Sketches of the First and Seventh Battalions*. Nashville, TN: Brandon Printing Co., 1887.

Hannaford, Ebenezer. *The Story of a Regiment: A History of the Campaigns and Associations in the Field of the Sixth Regiment Ohio Volunteer Infantry*. Cincinnati, OH: privately printed, 1868.

Harrington, Fred Harvey. *Fighting Politician: Major General N.P. Banks*. Westport, CT: Greenwood Press, 1948.

Harris, NiNi. *History of Carondelet*. St. Louis, MO: Southern Commercial Bank, 1991.

Harrison, Lowell H. *The Civil War in Kentucky*. Lexington: The University Press of Kentucky, 1975.

Hartigen, Richard S. *Lieber's Code and the Law of War*. South Holland, IL: Precedent Publishing, 1983.

Hartjie, Robert C. *Van Dorn: Life and Times of a Confederate General*. Nashville, TN: Vanderbilt University Press, 1967.

Hay, Thomas Robson. *Hood's Tennessee Campaign*. New York: Neale, 1929.

Hearn, Chester G. *Admiral David Dixon Porter: The Civil War Years*. Annapolis, MD: Naval Institute Press, 1996.

_____. *Admiral David Glasgow Farragut: The Civil War Years*. Annapolis, MD: Naval Institute Press, 1998.

_____. *Ellet's Brigade: The Strangest Outfit of All*. Baton Rouge: Louisiana State University Press, 2000.

_____. *Mobile Bay and the Mobile Campaign: The Last Great Battles of the Civil War*. Jefferson, NC: McFarland & Co., Inc., 1993.

_____. *Rebels and Yankees: Naval Battles of the Civil War*. San Diego CA: Thunder Bay Press, 2000.

Hedley, F.Y. *Marching Through Georgia: Pen-Pictures of Every-Day Life in General Sherman's Army from the Beginning of the Atlanta Campaign Until the Closing of the War*. Chicago, IL: Donohue, Henneberry & Co., 1890.

Henderson, Mary Bess McCain, Evelyn Janet McCain Young, and Anna Irene McCain Naheloffer. *"Dear Eliza": The Letters of Michel Andrew Thompson*. Ames, IA: Carter Press, 1976.

Henry, James P. *Resources of the State of Arkansas; with Description of Counties, Railroads, Mines, and the City of Little Rock*. Little Rock, AK: Price & McClure, 1872.

Henry, Robert Selph. *"First with the Most" Forrest*. Indianapolis, IN: Bobbs-Merrill, 1944.

_____., ed. *As They Saw Forrest: Some Recollections and Comments of Contemporaries*. Jackson, TN: McCowat-Mercer, 1956.

Herr, Kincaid. *The Louisville and Nashville Railroad, 1850–1963*. Louisville, KY: Public Relations Department, L & N, 1964; reprinted, University of Kentucky Press, 2000.

Heyman, Max L., Jr. *Prudent Soldier: A Biography of Major General E.R.S. Canby, 1817–1873*. Glendale, CA: Arthur H. Clarke Co., 1959.

Hicken, Victor. *Illinois in the Civil War*. Urbana, IL: University of Illinois Press, 1991.

Hill, Jim Dan. *Sea Dogs of the Sixties*. Minneapolis MN: University of Minnesota, 1935; reprinted, New York: A.S. Barnes & Company, 1961.

Holland, Cecil Fletcher. *Morgan and His Raiders: A Biography of the Confederate General*. New York: The Macmillan Company, 1942.

Holllandsworth, James G., Jr. *Pretense of Glory: The Life of General Nathaniel P. Banks*. Baton Rouge, LA: Louisiana State University Press, 1998.

Hoobler, James A. *Cities Under the Gun: Images of Occupied Nashville and Chattanooga*. Nashville, TN: Rutledge Hill Press, 1986.

Hood, John Bell. *Advance and Retreat: Personal Experiences in the United States and Confederate States Armies*. New Orleans, LA: Pub. For the Hood Orphan Memorial Fund, 1880.

Horn, Stanley F. *The Army of Tennessee*. Indianapolis, IN: Bobbs-Merrill, 1941.

_____. *The Decisive Battle of Nashville*. Baton Rouge, LA: Louisiana State University Press, 1956.

_____., comp. *Tennessee's War, 1861–1865: Described by Participants*. Nashville: Tennessee Civil War Centennial Commission, 1965.

Horwitz, Lester V. *The Longest Raid of the War: Little Known and Untold Stories of Morgan's Raid Into Kentucky, Indiana, and Ohio*. Cincinnati, OH: Farmcourt Publishing, 1999.

Hosmer, James K. *A Short History of the Mississippi Valley*. New York: Houghton, Mifflin and Co., 1902.

Howard, Robert P. *Illinois: A History of the Prairie State*. Grand Rapids, MI: William B. Eerdmans Publishing Co., 1973.

Hubbard, John Milton. *Notes of a Private.* Memphis, TN: E.H. Clarke and Brother, 1909.

Hubbart, Henry Clyde. *The Older Middle West, 1840–1880: Its Social, Economic and Political Life and Sectional Tendencies Before, During and After the Civil War.* New York: Russell & Russell, 1963.

Hubbell, John T., and James W. Geary, eds. *Biographical Dictionary of the Union: Northern Leaders of the Civil War.* Westport, CT: Greenwood Press, 1995.

Hubert, Charles F. *History of the 50th Regiment, Illinois Volunteer Infantry in the War of the Union.* Kansas City, MO: Western Veteran Publishing Co., 1894.

Huddleston, Duane, Sammie Rose, and Pat Wood. *Steamboats and Ferries on White River: A Heritage Revisited.* Conway, AK: University of Central Arkansas Press, 1995; reprinted, Fayetteville, AK: University of Arkansas Press, 1998.

Huddleston, Edwin G. *The Civil War in Middle Tennessee.* Nashville, TN: Nashville Banner, 1965.

Huffstodt, Jim. *Hard Dying Men.* Bowie, MD: Heritage Books, 1991.

Huling, Edmund J. *Reminiscences of Gunboat Life in the Mississippi Squadron.* Saratoga Springs, NY: Sentinel Print, 1881.

Hunt, Roger D., and Jack R. Brown. *Brevet Brigadier Generals in Blue.* Gaithersburg, MD: Olde Soldier Books, 1997.

Hunter, Louis C. *Steamboats on the Western Waters: An Economic and Technological History.* Cambridge, MA: Harvard University Press, 1949; reprinted, New York: Dover Publications, 1993.

Huston, James A. *The Sinews of War: Army Logistics, 1775–1953.* Army Historical Series. Washington, D.C.: Office of the Chief of Military History, United States Army, 1966.

Jackson, Alfred, and Kathryn Abbey Hanna. *Napoleon III and Mexico: American Triumph Over Monarchy.* Chapel Hill, NC: University of North Carolina Press, 1971.

James, Uriah Pierson. *James' River Guide.* Cincinnati, OH: U.P. James, 1866.

Jessee, James W. *Civil War Diaries of James W. Jessee, 1861–1865, Company K, 8th Regiment of Illinois Volunteer Infantry.* Edited by William P. LaBounty. Normal, IL: McLean County Genealogical Society, 1997.

Jeter, Katherine Brash. *A Man and His Boat: The Civil War Career and Correspondence of Lieutenant Jonathan H. Carter, CSN.* Baton Rouge, LA: Center for Louisiana Studies, 1996.

Johnson, Adam R. "Stovepipe." *The Partisan Rangers of the Confederate Army.* Edited by William J. Davis. Louisville, KY: George G Fetter, 1904; reprinted, Austin, TX: State House Press, 1995.

Johnson, E. McCleod. *A History of Henry County, Tennessee.* Paris, TN: privately printed, 1958.

Johnson, Ludwell H. *Red River Campaign: Politics and Cotton in the Civil War.* Baltimore, MD: Johns Hopkins Press, 1958; reprinted, Kent State University Press, 1993.

Joiner, Gary. *Mr. Lincoln's Brown Water Navy: The Mississippi Squadron.* Lanham, MD: Rowman & Littlefield, 2007.

_____. *One Damn Blunder From Beginning to End: The Red River Campaign of 1864.* Lanham, MD: Rowman and Littlefield, 2003.

_____. *Through the Howling Wilderness: The 1864 Red River Campaign and Union Failure in the West.* Knoxville, TN: University of Tennessee Press, 2006.

_____., ed. *Little to Eat and Thin Mud to Drink: Letters, Diaries, and Memoirs from the Red River Campaigns, 1863–1864.* Knoxville, TN: University of Tennessee Press, 2007.

Jones, Archer. *Confederate Strategy: From Shiloh to Vicksburg.* Baton Rouge, LA: Louisiana State University Press, 1961.

Jones, James P., and Edward F. Keuchel, eds. *Civil War Marine: A Diary of the Red River Expedition, 1864.* Washington, D.C.: Naval History Division, Navy Department, 1975.

Jones, Virgil C. *Gray Ghosts and Rebel Raiders.* New York: Holt, 1956.

Jordan, Thomas, and J.P. Pryor. *The Campaigns of Lieut. Gen. N.B. Forrest and of Forrest's Cavalry.* New Orleans and New York: Blelock & Co., 1868; reprinted, New York: DaCapo Press, 1996.

Joyner, Elizabeth Hoxie. *The U.S.S. Cairo: History and Artifacts of a Civil War Gunboat.* Jefferson, NC: McFarland & Co., Inc., 2006.

Kane, Adam. *The Western River Steamboat.* College Station: Texas A & M University Press, 2004.

Keller, Allan. *Morgan's Raid.* New York: Collier, 1962.

Kerby, Robert L. *Kirby Smith's Confederacy: The Trans-Mississippi South, 1863–1865.* Tuscaloosa, AL: University of Alabama Press, 1972.

Killebrew, J.B. *Introduction to the Resources of Tennessee.* 2 vols. Nashville, TN: Tavel, Eastman, and Howell, 1874.

King, William H. *Lessons and Practical Notes on Steam.* Revised by James W. King. New York: D. Van Nostrand, 1864.

Kiper, Richard L. *Major General John Alexander McClernand: Politician in Uniform.* Kent, OH: Kent State University Press, 1999.

Kitchens, Ben Earl. *Gunboats and Cavalry: A History of Eastport, Mississippi, with Special Emphasis on Events of the War Between the States.* Florence, AL: Thornwood Book Publishers, 1985.

Klein, Benjamin F. *The Ohio River Atlas: A Collection of the Best Known Maps of the Ohio River, from 1713 to 1854.* Cincinnati, OH: Picture Marine, 1954.

Knapp, David. *The Confederate Horsemen.* New York: Vantage, 1966.

Konstam, Angus, and Tony Bryan. *Mississippi River Gunboats of the American Civil War, 1861–1865.* New Vanguard Series. London, Eng.: Osprey Publishing, 2002.

_____. *Union Monitor, 1861–1865.* New Vanguard Series. London, Eng.: Osprey Publishing, 2002.

_____. *Union River Ironclad, 1861–1865.* New Vanguard Series. London, Eng.: Osprey Publishing, 2002.

Lamers, William M. *The Edge of Glory: A Biography of General William S. Rosecrans, USA.* New York: Harcourt, Brace, 1961.

Lane, Carl D. *American Paddle Steamboats.* New York: Coward-McCann, 1943.

Lansden, John M. *History of the City of Cairo, Illinois.* Chicago: R.R. Donnelley, 1910.

Latham, John M. *Raising the Civil War Gunboats and Building the Magic Valley History Tower.* Camden, TN: J.M. Latham Press Pros, 1997.

Lee, Elizabeth Blair. *Wartime Washington: The Civil War Letters of Elizabeth Blair Lee.* Edited by Virginia Jeans Laas. Urbana, IL: University of Illinois Press, 1991.

Lemcke, Julius A. *Reminiscences of an Indianian: From the Sassafras Log Behind the Barn in Posey County to Broader Fields.* Indianapolis: Hollenbeck Press, 1905.

Lewis, Berkeley R. *Notes on Ammunition of the American Civil War, 1861–1865.* Washington, DC: American Ordnance Association, 1959.

_____. *Union River Ironclad, 1861–65.* Ill. by Tony Bryan. New Vanguard 56. Oxford, UK: Osprey Publishing, 2002.

Lewis, Charles Lee. *David Glasgow Farragut.* Annapolis, MD: Naval Institute Press, 1943.

Lewis, Lloyd. *Sherman: Fighting Prophet*. New York: Harcourt, Brace and World, 1960.

Lieber, Francis. *Guerrilla Parties Considered with Reference to the Laws and Usages of War*. New York: D. Van Nostrand, 1862.

Logan, Mrs. John A. *Reminiscences of a Soldier's Wife*. New York: Scribner's Sons, 1913.

Longacre, Edward G. *Mounted Raids of the Civil War*. New York: A.S. Barnes & Co., 1975.

Lonn, Ella. *Foreigners in the Union Army and Navy*. Baton Rouge, LA: Louisiana State University Press, 1951.

Lossing, Benson J. *Pictorial Field Book of the Civil War: Journeys Through the Battlefields in the Wake of Conflict*. 3 vols. Hartford, CT: T. Belknap, 1874; reprinted, The Johns Hopkins University Press, 1997.

Lowe, Richard. *Walker's Texas Division, C.S.A.: Greyhounds of the Trans-Mississippi*. Baton Rouge, LA: Louisiana State University Press, 2004.

Luraghi, Raimondo. *A History of the Confederate Navy*. Translated by Paolo E. Coletta.. Annapolis MD: Naval Institute Press, 1996.

Lytle, Andrew Nelson. *Bedford Forrest and His Critter Company*. New York: Milton, Balch, 1931; reprinted, Nashville, TN: J.S. Sanders & Co., 1992.

Lytle, William C., comp. *Merchant Steam Vessels of the United States, 1807–1868. "The Lytle List."* Publication No. 6. Mystic, CT: The Steamship Historical Society of America, 1952.

Macartney, Clarence Edward. *Mr. Lincoln's Admirals*. New York: Funk and Wagnalls, 1956.

Mackey, Robert M. *The Uncivil War: Irregular Warfare in the Upper South, 1861–1865*. Norman: University of Oklahoma Press, 2004.

Mahan, Alfred T. *The Gulf and Inland Waters*. Vol. 3 of the *Navy in the Civil War*. New York: Scribner's, 1883.

Maness, Lonnie E. *An Untutored Genius: The Military Career of General Nathan Bedford Forrest*. Oxford, MS: The Guild Bindery Press, 1990.

Marshall-Cornwall, James. *Grant as Military Commander*. New York: Van Nostrand Reinhold, 1970.

Marszalek, John F. *Commander of All Lincoln's Armies: A Life of General Henry W. Halleck*. Cambridge, MA: Belknap Press, 2004.

_____. *Sherman: A Soldier's Passion for Order*. New York: Free Press, 1993.

Marvel, William. *Burnside*. Chapel Hill: University of North Carolina Press, 1991.

Maslowski, Peter. *"Treason Must Be Made Odious": Military Occupation and Wartime Reconstruction in Nashville, Tennessee, 1862–1865*. New York: K.T.O. Press, 1978.

Mathes, Harvey J. *General Forrest*. New York: D. Appleton & Co., 1902.

Mayeux, Steven M. *Earthen Walls, Iron Men: Fort De Russy, Louisiana, and the Defense of Red River*. Knoxville, TN: University of Tennessee Press, 2006.

McCutchan, Kenneth P., ed. *"Dearest Lizzie": The Civil War as Seen Through the Eyes of Lieutenant Colonel James Maynard Shanklin, of Southwest Indiana's Own 42nd Regiment, Indiana Volunteer Infantry, and Recounted in Letters to His Wife*. Evansville, IN: Friends of Willard Library Press, 1988.

McDonough, James Lee. *Nashville: The Western Confederacy's Final Gamble*. Knoxville, TN: The University of Tennessee Press, 2004.

_____. *Stones River: Bloody Winter in Tennessee*. Knoxville: University of Tennessee Press, 1980.

McDowell, Robert Emmett. *City of Conflict: Louisville in the Civil War, 1861–1865*. Louisville, KY: Civil War Roundtable, 1962.

McFeely, William S. *Grant: A Biography*. New York: W.W. Norton, 1981.

McMurray, William J. *History of the Twentieth Tennessee Regiment Volunteer Infantry, C.S.A.* Nashville, TN: The Publication Committee, 1904.

McPherson, James M. *Battle Cry of Freedom: The Civil War Era*. New York: Oxford University Press, 1988.

_____. *The Negro's Civil War*. New York: Ballantine Books, 1991.

McWhitney, Grady. *Braxton Bragg and Confederate Defeat*. New York: Columbia University Press, 1969.

Merrill, James M. *Battle Flags South: The Story of the Civil War Navies on Western Waters*. Rutherford, NJ: Fairleigh Dickinson University Press, 1970.

_____. *The Rebel Shore: The Story of Union Sea Power in the Civil War*. Boston, MA: Little, Brown, 1957.

Miller, David W. *Second Only to Grant: Quartermaster General Montgomery C. Meigs*. Shippensburg, PA: White Mane Books, 2000.

Miller, Francis Trevelyan, ed. *The Photographic History of the Civil War*. Vol. 6: *The Navies*. New York: Castle Books, 1911; Reprint, New York: Thomas Yoseloff, 1957.

Milligan, John D. *Gunboats Down the Mississippi*. Annapolis, MD: Naval Institute Press, 1965.

Mitchell, Joseph B., ed. *The Badge of Gallantry: Recollections of Civil War Congressional Medal of Honor Winners*. New York: Macmillan, 1968.

Monaghan, James. *Civil War on the Western Border, 1854–1865*. Boston, MA: Little, Brown & Co., 1955.

Monaghan, Jay. *Swamp Fox of the Confederacy: The Life and Military Services of M. Jeff Thompson*. Tuscaloosa, AL: Confederate Publishing, 1956.

Montgomery, Frank A. *Reminiscences of a Mississippian in Peace and War*. Cincinnati, OH: The Robert Clarke Company Press, 1901.

Moore, Frank, ed. *The Rebellion Record: A Diary of American Events*. 12 vols. New York: G.P. Putnam, 1861–1863; D. Van Nostrand, 1864–1868; re-printed, Arno, 1977.

Morison, Samuel Eliot. *The Oxford History of the American People*. New York: Oxford University Press, 1965.

Morris, Richard B. *The Encyclopedia of American History*. Rev. ed. New York: Harper & Bros., 1961.

Morton, John Watson. *The Artillery of Nathan Bedford Forrest's Cavalry*. Paris, TN: The Guild Bindery Press, 1988.

Mulesky, Raymond. *Thunder from a Clear Sky: Stovepipe Johnson's Confederate Raid on Newburgh, Indiana*. New York: iUniverse, Inc., 2005.

Musgrove, George D. *Kentucky Cavaliers in Dixie: Reminiscences of a Confederate Cavalryman*. Edited by Bell I. Wiley. Jackson, TN: McCowat-Mercer Press, 1957; reprinted, Lincoln: University of Nebraska Press, 1999.

Musicant, Ivan. *Divided Waters: The Naval History of the Civil War*. New York: HarperCollins, 1995.

Musser, Charles O. *Soldier Boy: The Civil War Letters of Charles O. Musser, 29th Iowa*. Edited by Larry Popchock. Iowa City, IA: Iowa State University Press, 1995.

The Navigator, Containing Directions for Navigating the Monongahela, Allegheny, Ohio and Mississippi Rivers. 8th ed. Pittsburgh, PA: Cramer, Speark and Eichbau, 1814; reprinted, University of Michigan Press, 1966.

Neal, Diane, and Thomas W. Kremm, *Lion of the South: General Thomas C. Hindman*. Macon, GA: Mercer University Press, 1993.

Neuman, Frederick G. *The Story of Paducah, Kentucky*. Paducah: Young Printing, 1927.

Nevins, Allan. *The War for the Union: War The Improvised War*. New York: Charles Scribner's Sons, 1959.

Nichols, James L. *Confederate Engineers*. Tuscaloosa, AL: Confederate Publishing Company, 1957.

Niven, John. *Gideon Welles: Lincoln's Secretary of the Navy.* New York: Oxford University Press, 1973.

Noe, Kenneth W., ed. *A Southern Boy in Blue: The Memoir of Marcus Woodcock, 9th Kentucky Infantry* (U.S.A.). Knoxville, TN: University of Tennessee Press, 1996.

Northup, James E., and Samuel W. Northup. *"Drifting to an Unknown Future": The Civil War Letters of James E. Northup and Samuel W. Northup.* Edited by Robert C. Steensma. Sioux Falls, SD: Center for Western Studies, 2000.

Oates, Stephen B. *Confederate Cavalry West of the River.* Austin, TX: University of Texas Press, 1961.

O'Brien, Sean Michael. *Mobile, 1865: Last Stand of the Confederacy.* Westport, CT: Praeger, 2001.

O'Connor, Richard. *Sheridan the Inevitable.* Indianapolis, IN: Bobbs-Merrill, 1953.

O'Flaherty, Daniel. *General Jo Shelby: Undefeated Rebel.* Chapel Hill, NC: University of North Carolina Press, 1954.

Olmstead, Edwin, Wayne E. Stark, and Spencer C. Tucker. *The Big Guns: Civil War Siege, Seacoast and Naval Cannon.* Ontario, Bloomfield, New York, Alexandria Bay: Museum Restoration Service, 1997.

Owens, Harry P. *Steamboats and the Cotton Economy: River Trade in the Yazoo-Mississippi Delta.* Jackson, MS: University Press of Mississippi, 1990.

Page, Dave. *Ships versus Shore: Engagements Along Southern Shores and Rivers.* Nashville TN: Rutledge Hill Press, 1994.

Palmer, Patricia J. *Frederick Steele: Forgotten General.* Stanford, CA: Stanford University Press, 1971.

Paludan, Philip Shaw. *A People's Contest: The Union and Civil War, 1861–1865.* New York: Harper & Row, 1988.

_____. *Victims: A True Story of the Civil War.* Knoxville, TN: University of Tennessee Press, 1981.

Parker, Foxhall A. *The Battle of Mobile Bay and the Capture of Forts Morgan, Gaines, and Powell.* Boston, MA: Boston Stereotype Foundry, 1878.

_____. *The Naval Howitzer Afloat.* New York: D. Van Nostrand, 1866.

_____. *The Naval Howitzer Ashore.* New York: D. Van Nostrand, 1865.

Parks, Joseph H. *General Edmund Kirby Smith, C.S.A.* Baton Rouge, LA: Louisiana State University Press, 1954.

Parrish, T. Michael. *Richard Taylor: Soldier Prince of Dixie.* Chapel Hill,

NC: University of North Carolina Press, 1992.

Parsons, Lewis B. *Reports to the War Department.* St. Louis, MO: George Knapp & Co., 1867.

Paullin, Charles Oscar. *Paullin's History of Naval Administration, 1775–1911.* Annapolis, MD: Naval Institute Press, 1968.

Pellet, Elias P. *History of the 114th Regiment, New York State Volunteers.* Norwich, NY: Telegraph & Chronicle Power Press Print., 1866.

Perry, James M. *A Bohemian Brigade: The Civil War Correspondents, Mostly Rough, Sometimes Ready.* New York: John Wiley, 2000.

Perry, Milton F. *Infernal Machines: The Story of Confederate Submarine and Mine Warfare.* Baton Rouge, LA: Louisiana State University Press, 1965.

Peterson, Harold L. *Notes on Ordnance of the American Civil War, 1861–1865.* Washington, D.C.: American Ordnance Association, 1959.

Petrie, Donald A. *The Prize Game: Lawful Looting on the High Seas in the Days of Fighting Sail.* Annapolis, MD: Naval Institute Press, 1999.

Philadelphia Maritime Museum Library. *John Lenthall, Naval Architect: A Guide to Plans and Drawings of American Naval and Merchant Vessels, 1790–1874: With a Bibliography of Works on Shipbuilding ... Collected by John Lenthall (b. 1807–d.1882).* Philadelphia, PA: Philadelphia Maritime Museum, 1991.

Plum, William R. *The Military Telegraph During the Civil War in the United States.* 2 vols. Chicago: Jansen, McClurg, 1882.

Pollard, E.B. *The Lost Cause: A New Southern History of the War of the Confederates.* New York: E.B. Treat & Co., 1867.

Ponder, Jerry. *Major General John S. Marmaduke, C.S.A.* Mason, TX: Ponder Books, 1999.

Porter, David D. *Incidents and Anecdotes of the Civil War.* New York: D. Appleton and Co, 1885; reprinted, Harrisburg PA: The Archive Society, 1997.

_____. *Naval History of the Civil War.* New York: Sherman Publishing Company, 1886; reprinted, Secaucus, N.J.: Castle Books, 1984.

Powers, Ron. *Mark Twain: A Life.* New York: Free Press, 2005.

Pratt, Fletcher. *The Civil War on Western Waters.* New York: Holt, 1958.

_____. *The Navy — A History: The Story of a Service in Action.* Garden City, NY: Garden City Publishing Co., 1941.

Prushankin, Jeffrey S. *A Crisis in Confederate Command: Edmund Kirby Smith, Richard Taylor, and the Army of the Trans-Mississippi.* Baton Rouge, LA: Louisiana State University Press, 2005.

Putnam, A.W. *History of Middle Tennessee.* Knoxville, TN: University of Tennessee Press, 1971.

Rae, Ralph R. *Sterling Price: The Lee of the West.* Little Rock, AK: Pioneer Press, 1959.

Ramage, James A. *Rebel Raider: The Life of General John Hunt Morgan.* Lexington, KY: The University Press of Kentucky, 1986.

Ramold, Steven J. *Slaves, Sailors, Citizens: African Americans in the Union Navy.* DeKalb, IL: Northern Illinois University Press, 2002.

Reed, Rowena. *Combined Operations in the Civil War.* Annapolis, MD: Naval Institute Press, 1978.

Regimental Association. *History of the 46th Regiment, Indiana Volunteer Infantry, September 1861–September 1865.* Logansport, IN: Press of Wilson, Humphries & Co., 1888.

Reid, Whitelaw. *Ohio in the War: Her Statesmen, Her Generals, and Soldiers.* 2 vols. Cincinnati: Moore, Wilstach & Baldwin, 1868.

Rerick, John H. *The 44th Indiana Volunteer Infantry: History of Its Services in the War of the Rebellion.* Lagrange, IN: privately printed, 1880.

Rice, Ralsa C. *Yankee Tigers: Through the Civil War with the One Hundred and Twenty-Fifth Ohio.* Edited by Richard A. Baumgartner and Larry M. Strayer. Huntington, WV: Blue Acorn Press, 1992.

Richardson, Albert D. *A Personal History of Ulysses S. Grant.* Hartford, CT: Winter and Hatch, 1885.

_____. *The Secret Service: The Field, the Dungeon and the Escape.* Hartford, CT: American Publishing Company, 1866.

Ringle, Dennis J. *Life in Mr. Lincoln's Navy.* Annapolis, MD: Naval Institute Press, 1998.

Ritner, Jacob, and Emeline Ritner. *Love and Valor: The Intimate Civil War Letters Between Captain Jacob and Emeline Ritner.* Edited by Charles F. Larimer. Western Springs, IL: Sigourney Press, 2000.

Roberts, William H. *Civil War Ironclads: The U.S. Navy and Industrial Mobilization.* Baltimore, MD: Johns Hopkins University Press, 2002.

_____. *Now for the Contest: Coastal & Oceanic Naval Operations in the Civil War.* Lincoln: University of Nebraska Press, 2004

Roe, Francis Asbury. *Naval Duties and Discipline, with the Policy and*

Principles of Naval Organization. New York: D. Van Nostrand, 1865.

Rombauer, Robert J. *The Union Cause in St. Louis in 1862.* St. Louis, MO: Press of Nixon-Jones Printing Co., 1909.

Rusling, James F. *Men and Things I Saw in Civil War Days.* New ed. New York: The Methodist Book Concern, 1914.

Safford, James M. *Geology of Tennessee.* Nashville, TN: S.C. Mercer, 1869.

Sayers, Brian. *On Valor's Side: Tom Green and the Battles for Early Texas.* Hemphill, TX: Dogwood Press, 1999.

Schafer, Louis S. *Confederate Underwater Warfare: An Illustrated History.* Jefferson, NC: McFarland & Co., Inc., 1996.

Scharf, J. Thomas. *History of the Confederate Navy from Its Organization to the Surrender of Its Last Vessel.* New York: Rodgers and Sherwood, 1887; reprinted, New York: Fairfax Press, 1977.

Schlay, Cora R. *Alexandria in the Civil War: Four Louisiana Civil War Stories.* Baton Rouge, LA: Louisiana Civil War Centennial Commission, 1961.

Seitz, Don C. *Braxton Bragg: General of the Confederacy.* Columbia, SC: The State Co., 1924.

Selfridge, Thomas O., Jr. *Memoirs of Thomas O. Selfridge Jr., Rear Admiral, U.S.N.* New York: Knickerbocker Press, 1924; reprinted, Columbia, University of South Carolina Press, 1987.

Shalhope, Robert E. *Sterling Price: Portrait of a Southerner.* Columbia, MO: University of Missouri Press, 1971.

Shepard, Eric W. *Bedford Forrest: The Confederacy's Greatest Cavalryman.* New York: Dial Press, 1930.

Sheridan, Philip H. *Personal Memoirs.* 2 vols. New York. C.L. Webster & Co., 1888.

Sherman, William Tecumseh. *Memoirs.* 2 vols. New York: Appleton, 1875; reprinted, Penguin Classics. New York: Penguin Books, 2000.

_____. *Sherman's Civil War: Selected Correspondence of William T. Sherman, 1860–1865.* Edited by Brooks D. Simpson and Jean V. Berlin. Chapel Hill, NC: University of North Carolina Press, 1999.

Sherwood, Isaac R. *Memories of the War.* Toledo, OH: The H.J. Crittenden Co., 1923.

Silverstone, Paul H. *The Sailing Navy, 1775–1854.* Annapolis, MD: Naval Institute Press, 2001.

_____. *Warships of the Civil War Navies.* Annapolis, MD: Naval Institute Press, 1989.

Simpson, Brooks D. *Ulysses S. Grant: Triumph Over Adversity, 1822–1885.* New York: Houghton, Mifflin, 2000.

Simson, Jay W. *Naval Strategies of the Civil War: Confederate Innovations and Federal Opportunism.* Nashville TN: Cumberland House, 2001.

Slagle, Jay. *Ironclad Captain: Seth Ledyard Phelps and the U.S. Navy.* Kent, OH: Kent State University Press, 1996.

Smart, James G., ed. *A Radical View: The "Agate" Dispatches of Whitelaw Reid, 1861–1865.* 2 vols. Memphis, TN: Memphis State University Press, 1976.

Smith, Edward Conrad. *The Borderland in the Civil War.* New York: Macmillan, 1927.

Smith, Herschel K., Jr. *Some Encounters with General Forrest.* McKenzie, TN: privately printed, 1959(?).

Smith, Jean Edward. *Grant.* New York: Simon and Schuster, 2001.

Smith, Myron J., Jr. *Le Roy Fitch: The Civil War Career of a Union River Gunboat Commander.* Jefferson, NC: McFarland & Co., Inc., 2007.

_____. *The Timberclads in the Civil War: The Lexington, Tyler and Conestoga on the Western Waters, 1861–1865.* Jefferson, NC: McFarland & Co., Inc., 2008.

_____. *U.S.S. Carondelet, 1861–1865.* Manhattan, KS: MA/AH Publishing, 1982.

_____. *Volunteer State Battlewagon: U.S.S. Tennessee (BB-43).* Missoula, MT: Pictorial Histories Publishing Company, 1992.

Smith, Walter G., ed. *Life and Letters of Thomas Kilby Smith, Brevet Major General United States Volunteers.* New York: G. P. Putnam, 1898.

Soley, James R. *Admiral Porter.* New York: D. Appleton, 1903.

Speer, Lonnie R. *Portals to Hell: Military Prisons of the Civil War.* Mechanicsburg, PA: Stackpole Books, 1997.

Stanley, David. *Personal Memoirs of Major-General D.S. Stanley, U.S.A.* Cambridge, MA: Harvard University Press, 1917.

Stanley, Henry M. *The Autobiography of Sir Henry Morton Stanley.* Edited by Dorothy Stanley. Boston, MA: Houghton, Mifflin, 1909.

_____. *Sir Henry Morton Stanley, Confederate.* Edited by Nathaniel C. Hughes, Jr. Baton Rouge, LA: Louisiana State University Press, 2000.

Starr, Stephen. *The Union Cavalry in the Civil War.* Vol. 3. *The War in the West, 1861–1865.* Baton Rouge, LA: Louisiana State University Press, 1985.

Steenburn, Donald H. *Silent Echoes of Johnsonville: Rebel Cavalry and Yankee Gunboats.* Rogersville, AL: Elk River Press, 1994.

Stevenson, William G. *Thirteen Months in the Rebel Army, Being a Narrative of Personal Adventures,* etc. New York: A.S. Barnes & Burr, 1862.

Still, William N., Jr. *Confederate Shipbuilding.* Athens, GA: University of Georgia Press, 1969; reprinted, Columbia, SC: University of South Carolina Press, 1987.

_____. *Iron Afloat, The Story of Confederate Armorclads.* Nashville, TN: Vanderbilt University Press, 1971; reprinted, Columbia, SC: University of South Carolina Press, 1985.

_____., ed. *The Confederate Navy: The Ships, Men, and Organization, 1861–1865.* Annapolis, MD: Naval Institute Press, 1997.

The Story of the 55th Regiment Illinois Volunteer Infantry in the Civil War. Clinton, MA: W.J. Coulter, 1887.

Stotherd, R.H. *Notes on Torpedoes, Offensive and Defensive.* Washington, D.C.: Government Printing Office, 1872.

Stutler, Boyd B. *West Virginia in the Civil War.* Charleston, WV: Education Foundation, Inc., 1963.

Surdam, David G. *Northern Naval Superiority and the Economics of the American Civil War.* Columbia, SC: University of South Carolina, 2001.

Swedberg, Claire E., ed. *Three Years with the 92nd Illinois: The Civil War Diary of John M. King.* Mechanicsburg, PA: Stackpole Books, 1999.

Swiggert, Howard. *The Rebel Raider: A Life of John Hunt Morgan.* Indianapolis, IN: Bobbs-Merrill, 1934.

Sword, Wiley. *The Confederacy's Last Hurrah: Spring Hill, Franklin and Nashville.* Lawrence, KS: University Press of Kansas, 1993.

_____. *Embrace an Angry Wind—The Confederacy's Last Hurrah: Spring Hill, Franklin & Nashville.* New York: HarperCollins, 1992.

Symonds, Craig L. *Lincoln and His Admirals: Abraham Lincoln, the U.S. Navy, and the Civil War.* New York: Oxford University Press, 2008.

Taylor, David L. *With Bowie Knives and Pistols: Morgan's Raid in Indiana.* Lexington, IN: TaylorMade Write, 1993.

Taylor, Lenette S. *"The Supply for Tomorrow Must Not Fail": The Civil War of Captain Simon Perkins, Jr., a Union Quartermaster.* Kent, OH: Kent State University Press, 2004.

Taylor, Richard. *Destruction and Reconstruction: Personal Experiences of the Late War*. New York: D. Appleton and Company, 1879.

Thomas, David Y. *Arkansas in War and Reconstruction, 1861–1874*. Little Rock, AK: Central Printing Co., 1926.

Thomas, Dean S. *Cannons: Introduction to Civil War Artillery*. Arendtsville, PA: Thomas Publications, 1985.

Thomas, Edison H. *John Hunt Morgan and His Raiders*. Lexington: University Press of Kentucky, 1975.

Thompson, M. Jeff. *The Civil War Reminiscences of General M. Jeff Thompson*. Edited by Donal J. Stanton, Goodwin F. Berquist, and Paul C. Bowers. Dayton, OH: Morningside Bookshop, 1988.

Thompson, M.S., ed. *General Orders and Circulars Issued by the Navy Department from 1863 to 1887*. Washington DC: Government Printing Office, 1887.

Tidwell, William A. *April '65*. Kent, Ohio: The Kent State University Press, 1995.

Townsend, Edward. *Anecdotes of the Civil War in the United States*. New York: D. Appleton, 1884.

Troutman, Richard, ed. *The Heavens are Weeping: The Diaries of George R. Browder, 1852–1886*. Grand Rapids, MI: Zondervan Publishing House, 1987.

Trudeau, Noah Andre. *Like Men of War: Black Troops in the Civil War, 1862–1865*. Boston, MA: Little, Brown, 1998.

_____. *Out of the Storm: The End of the Civil War, April–June 1865*. Boston, MA: Little, Brown & Co., 1994.

Tucker, Louis L. *Cincinnati During the Civil War*. Publications of the Ohio Civil War Centennial Commission, no. 9. Columbus, OH: The Ohio State University Press, 1962.

Tucker, Spencer C. *Andrew Foote: Civil War Admiral on Western Waters*. Annapolis, MD: Naval Institute Press, 2000.

_____. *Arming the Fleet: U.S. Navy Ordnance in the Muzzle-Loading Era*. Annapolis, MD: Naval Institute Press, 1988

_____. *Blue & Gray Navies: The Civil War Afloat*. Annapolis, MD: U.S. Naval Institute, 2006.

Turner, George Edgar. *Victory Rode the Rails: The Strategic Place of Railroads in the Civil War*. Indianapolis: Bobbs-Merrill, 1953.

Twain, Mark. *Life on the Mississippi*. New York: Harper & Brothers, 1950.

U.S. Navy Department. *Laws of the United States Relating to the Navy*. Washington, D.C.: GPO, 1866.

_____. *Regulations for the Government of the United States Navy*. Washington, D.C.: GPO, 1865.

_____. Mississippi Squadron. *General Orders, Rear Adm. D.D. Porter, Commanding, From Oct. 16th 1862 to Oct. 26th 1864*. St. Louis, MO: R.P. Studley, 1864.

_____. Mississippi Squadron. *General Orders, Rear Adm. S.P. Lee, Commanding, From Nov. 1st 1864 to April 24th, 1865*. St. Louis, MO: R.P. Studley, 1865.

_____. Naval History Division. *Civil War Naval Chronology, 1861–1865*. 6 vols. Rev. ed. Washington, D.C.: GPO, 1966.

_____. Naval History Division. *Riverine Warfare: The United States Navy's Operations on Inland Waters*. Rev. ed. Washington, D.C.: GPO, 1968.

_____. Office of the Secretary of the Navy. *Report of the Secretary of the Navy*. 6 vols. Washington, D.C.: GPO, 1861–1866.

Valuska, David L. *The African-American in the Union Navy, 1861–1865*. New York: Garland, 1993.

Van Doren Stern, Philip. *The Confederate Navy: A Pictorial History*. New York: Bonanza Books, 1961.

_____., ed. *Soldier Life in the Union and Confederate Armies*. New York: Premier Books, 1961.

Van Horne, Thomas B., ed. *History of the Army of the Cumberland: Its Organization, Campaigns, and Battles, Written at the Request of Major General George H. Thomas Chiefly from His Private Military Journal and Official and Other Documents Furnished by Him*. 2 vols. Cincinnati, OH: R. Clarke & Co., 1875; reprinted, Wilmington, NC: Broadfoot, 1988.

Villard, Henry. *Memoirs of Henry Villard, Journalist and Financier, 1835–1900*. 2 vols. Boston, MA: Houghton, Mifflin, 1904.

Walke, Henry. *Naval Scenes and Reminiscences of the Civil War in the United States on the Southern and Western Waters During the Years 1861, 1862 and 1863 with the History of That Period Compared and Corrected from Authentic Sources*. New York: F.R. Reed and Company, 1877.

Wallace, Edward. *Destiny and Glory*. New York: Coward-McCann, 1957.

Wallace, Lew. *An Autobiography*. 2 vols. New York: Harper & Brothers, 1906.

_____. *Smoke, Sound & Fury: The Civil War Memoirs of Major General Lew Wallace, U.S. Volunteers*. Edited by Jim Leeke. Portland, OR: Strawberry Hill Press, 1998.

Ward, Andrew. *River Run Red: The Fort Pillow Massacre in the American Civil War*. New York: Viking Press, 2005.

Warner, Ezra. *Generals in Blue: Lives of Union Commanders*. Baton Rouge, LA: Louisiana State University Press, 1964; reprinted, 1993.

_____. *Generals in Gray. Lives of Confederate Commanders*. Baton Rouge, LA: Louisiana State University Press, 1959; reprinted, 1993.

Wash, W.A. *Camp, Field and Prison Life, Containing Sketches of Service in the South*, etc. St. Louis, MO: Southwestern Book and Pub. Co., 1870.

Waters, Charles M. *Historic Clarksville: The Bicentennial Story, 1784–1984*. Clarksville, TN: Historic Clarksville Publishing Co., 1983.

Way, Frederick, Jr. *Way's Packet Directory, 1848–1994: Passenger Steamboats of the Mississippi River System Since the Advent of Photography in Mid-Continent America*. Athens, OH: Ohio University Press, 1983; revised edition, Athens OH: Ohio University, 1994.

Weber, Jennifer L. *Copperheads: The Rise and Fall of Lincoln's Opponents in the North*. New York: Oxford University Press, 2006.

Weber, Thomas. *The Northern Railroads in the Civil War, 1861–1865*. New York: King's Crown Press, 1952.

Webster, William G. *The Army and Navy Pocket Dictionary*. Philadelphia, PA: J.B. Lippincott & Company, 1865.

Webster's Geographical Dictionary. Rev. ed. Springfield, MA: G. & C. Merriam Co., Publishers, 1966.

Weigley, Russell F. *Quartermaster General of the Union Army: A Biography of M.C. Meigs*. New York: Columbia University Press, 1959.

Welcher, Frank J. *The Union Army, 1861–1865: Organization and Operations*. Vol. 3: *The Western Theater*. Bloomington: Indiana University Press, 1993.

Welles, Gideon. *The Diary of Gideon Welles, Secretary of the Navy Under Lincoln and Johnson*. Edited by John T. Morse, Jr. 3 vols. Boston, MA: Houghton, Mifflin and Company, 1911; reprinted, New York: W.W. Norton, 1960.

Wells, Tom H. *The Confederate Navy: A Study in Organization*. University, AL: The University of Alabama Press, 1971.

Werlock, Verna McElroy. *The Civil War Record of Thomas McElroy, Acting Master, United States Navy, 1861–1868*. Woodbridge, NJ: V.M. Werlock, 1986.

West, Richard S. *Gideon Welles, Lincoln's Navy Department*. Indianapolis, IN: Bobbs-Merrill, 1943.

_____. *Mr. Lincoln's Navy*. New York: Longman's, Green, 1957.

_____. *The Second Admiral: A Life of David Dixon Porter, 1813–1891*. New York: Coward-McCann, 1937.

Wheeler, Edmund. *The History of Newport, New Hampshire, from 1766 to 1878*. Newport, N.H.: The Republican Press Association, 1879.

Wideman, John C. *The Sinking of the U.S.S. Cairo*. Jackson, MS: University Press of Mississippi, 1993.

Wiley, Bell I. *The Life of Billy Yank, the Common Soldier of the Union*. New York: Bobbs-Merrill, 1952; reprinted. Baton Rouge, LA: Louisiana State University Press, 1991.

_____. *The Life of Johnny Reb, the Common Soldier of the Confederacy*. New York: Bobbs-Merrill, 1943; reprinted. Baton Rouge, LA: Louisiana State University Press, 1990.

Wiley, William. *The Civil War Diary of a Common Soldier*. Edited by Terrence J. Winschel. Baton Rouge, LA: Louisiana University Press, 2001.

Wilkie, Franc B. *Pen and Powder*. Boston, MA: Ticknor and Company, 1888.

Williams, Edward F., III. *Fustest with the Mostest: The Military Career of Tennessee's Greatest Confederate, Lt. Gen. Nathan Bedford Forrest*. Memphis, TN: Southern Books, 1969; reprinted, Memphis, TN: Historical Hiking Trails, 1973.

_____, and H.K. Humphreys, eds., *Gunboats and Cavalry: The Story of Forrest's 1864 Johnsonville Campaign, as Told to J.P. Pryor and Thomas Jordan, by Nathan Bedford Forrest*. Memphis, TN: Nathan Bedford Forrest Trail Committee, 1965.

Williams, T. Harry. *Lincoln and His Generals*. New York: Alfred Knopf, 1952; reprinted, New York: Vintage Books, 1962.

Williams, Thomas J. *An Historical Sketch of the 56th Ohio Volunteer Infantry*. Columbus, OH: Lawrence Press, 1899.

Willison, Charles A. *Reminiscences of a Boy's Service with the 76th Ohio in the 15th Army Corps, Under General Sherman, During the Civil War, by That "Boy" at Three Score*. Menasha, WI: Press of The George Banta Publishing Co., 1908; reprinted, Huntington, WV: Blue Acorn Press, 1995.

Wills, Brian S. *A Battle from the Start: The Life of Nathan Bedford Forrest*. New York: HarperCollins, 1992.

_____. *The Confederacy's Greatest Cavalryman: Forrest*. Lawrence, KS: University Press of Kansas, 1992.

Wills, Charles Wright. *Army Life of an Illinois Soldier*. Compiled by Mary E. Kellogg. Washington, D.C.: Globe Printing Co., 1906.

Wilson, James Grant, and John Fiske, eds. *Appleton's Cyclopaedia of American Biography*. 5 vols. New York: D. Appleton & Co., 1888.

Wilson, James H. *The Life of John A. Rawlins*. New York: Neale, 1916.

Winters, John D. *The Civil War in Louisiana*. Baton Rouge, LA: Louisiana State University Press, 1963.

Winters, William. *The Musick of the Mocking Birds, the Roar of the Cannon: The Diary and Letters of William Winters*. Edited by Steven E. Woodworth. Lincoln, NE: University of Nebraska Press, 1998.

Woodall, Eliza B. *The Stevenson Story*. Stevenson, AL: Stevenson Depot Museum, 1982.

Woodworth, Steven E. *Jefferson Davis and His Generals: The Failure of Confederate Command in the West*. Lawrence, KS: University Press of Kansas, 1990.

_____. *Nothing But Victory: The Army of the Tennessee, 1861–1865*. New York: Alfred A. Knopf, 2005.

_____. *Six Armies in Tennessee: The Chickamauga and Chattanooga Campaigns*. Great Campaigns of the Civil War Series. Lincoln, NE: University of Nebraska Press, 1999.

_____., ed. *Grant's Lieutenants: From Cairo to Vicksburg*. Lawrence, KS: University Press of Kansas, 2001.

Wright, Charles. *A Corporal's Story: Experiences in the Ranks of Company C, 81st Ohio Vol. Infantry*. Edited by W.H. Chamberlain. Philadelphia, PA: James Beal, Printer, 1887.

Wyeth, John Allan. *Life of General Nathan Bedford Forrest*. New York: Harper & Bros., 1904; reprinted, New York: Harper, 1959.

Zimmerman, Mark. *Battle of Nashville Preservation Society Guide to Civil War Nashville*. Nashville, TN: Lithographics, Inc., 2004.

Articles or Essays in Books or Journals

Abbott, John S.C. "The Civil War in the Wilds of Arkansas." *Harper's New Monthly Magazine* 33 (October 1866): 581–601.

Allardice, Bruce S. "Curious Clash at Blair's Landing." *America's Civil War* 9 (July 1997): 60–64.

Anderson, Bern. "The Naval Strat-egy of the Civil War." *Military Affairs* 26 (Spring 1962): 11–21.

Anderson, Charles W. "The True Story of Fort Pillow." *Confederate Veteran* 3 (November 1895): 322–326.

Andrews, Peter. "The Rock of Chickamauga." *American Heritage* 41 (February 1990): 81–91.

Aptheker, Herbert. "The Negro in the Union Navy." *Journal of Negro History* 32 (April 1947): 169–200.

Ash, Stephen V. "A Community at War: Montgomery County, 1861–65." *Tennessee Historical Quarterly* 36 (Spring 1977); 30–43.

_____. "Sharks in an Angry Sea: Civilian Resistance and Guerrilla Warfare in Occupied Middle Tennessee, 1862–1865." *Tennessee Historical Quarterly* 45 (Fall 1986): 217–320.

Austill, Hurieosco. "Fort Morgan in the Confederacy — August 1864." *Alabama Historical Quarterly* 7 (Summer 1945): 254–268.

Bailey, Anne J. "Chasing Banks Out of Louisiana: Parson's Texas Cavalry in the Red River Campaign." *Civil War Regiments: A Journal of the American Civil War* 2 (1992): 212–233.

_____. "The Mississippi Marine Brigade: Fighting Rebel Guerrillas on Western Waters." *Military History of the Southwest* 22 (Spring 1992): 34–41.

Barr, Alwyn. "The Battle of Blair's Landing." *Louisiana Studies* 2 (Winter 1963): 204–212.

_____. "The Battle of Calcasieu Pass." *Southwestern Historical Quarterly* 66 (July 1962): 59–67.

_____. "Confederate Artillery in Arkansas." *Arkansas Historical Quarterly* 22 (Fall 1963): 238–272.

_____. "Confederate Artillery in the Trans-Mississippi." *Military Affairs* 27 (Summer 1963): 77–84.

_____. "Confederate Artillery in Western Louisiana, 1864." *Louisiana History* 5 (Winter 1964): 53–73.

_____. "Polignac's Texas Brigade." *Texas Gulf Coast Historical Association Publications* 8 (November 1964): 1–72.

Bastian, David F. "Opening of the Mississippi During the Civil War." In U.S. Navy Academy, Department of History, ed., *New Aspects of Naval History: Selected Papers from the Fifth Naval History Symposium*. Baltimore, MD: Nautical & Aviation Pub. Co., 1985, 129–136.

"Battle of Eastport." *Confederate Veteran* 5 (January 1897): 13.

Beard, Dan W. "With Forrest in West Tennessee." *Southern Historical Society Papers* 37 (1909): 304–308.

Bearss, Edwin C. "The Battle of the Post of Arkansas." *Arkansas Historical Quarterly* 18 (Autumn 1959): 237–279.

_____. "The Trans-Mississippi Confederates Attempt to Relieve Vicksburg." *McNeese Review* 15 (1964): 46–70.

_____. "The Union Raid Down the Mississippi and Up the Yazoo — August 16–27, 1862." In Editors of *Military Affairs, Military Analysis of the Civil War: An Anthology.* Millwood, NY: KTO, 1977, 213–224.

Benedict, James B., Jr. "General John Hunt Morgan: The Great Indiana-Ohio Raid." *Filson Club Historical Quarterly* 31 (April 1957): 147–171.

Bennet, B. Kevin, and Dave Roth. "The General's Tour: The Battle of Buffington Island." *Blue & Gray Magazine* 15 (April 1998): 60–65.

Bennett, Robert Frank. "A Case of Calculated Mischief." *United States Naval Institute Proceedings* (March 1976): 77–83.

Bergeron, Arthur W., Jr. "General Richard Taylor as a Military Commander." *Louisiana History* 23 (Winter 1982): 35–47.

Bigelow, Martha M. "The Significance of Milliken's Bend in the Civil War." *Journal of Negro History* 45 (Fall 1960): 156–163.

Billias, George A. "Maine Lumbermen Rescue the Red River Fleet." *New England Social Studies Bulletin* 16 (January 1958): 5–8.

Blair, John L. "Morgan's Ohio Raid." *Filson Club Historical Quarterly* 36 (July 1962): 242–271.

Blake, W.H. "Coal Barging in Wartime, 1861–1865." *Gulf States Historical Magazine* 1 (May 1903): 409–412.

Block, W.T. "Calcasieu Pass Victory, Heroism Equal Dowling's." *East Texas Historical Journal* 9, no. 2 (1971): 139–144.

Bolte, Philip L. "Up the Yazoo River: A Riverine Diversion," *Periodical: Journal of America's Military Past* 22 (1995): 18–30.

Blume, Kenneth J. "'Concessions Where Concessions Could Be Made': The Naval Efficiency Boards of 1855–1857." In Randy Carol Balano and Craig L. Symonds, eds., *New Interpretations in Naval History: Selected Papers form the 14th Naval History Symposium.* Annapolis, MD: Naval Institute Press, 2001, 147–159.

Bowman, Robert. "Yazoo City in the Civil War." In *Publications of the Mississippi Historical Society.* Vol. 7. Oxford, MS: Published for the Society, 1903, 71–72.

Brewer, Charles C. "African-American Sailors and the Unvexing of the Mississippi River." *Prologue* 30 (Winter 1996): 279–286.

Brown, Campbell H. "Forrest's Johnsonville Raid." *Civil War Times Illustrated* 4 (June 1965): 48–57.

Brown, Fred. "*Sultana* Burning." *Appalachian Life,* no. 41 (March 2000): 3–4, 8.

Brown, George W. "Service in the Mississippi Squadron and Its Connection with the Siege and Capture of Vicksburg." In Vol. 1 of James Grant Wilson and Titus Munson Con, eds., *Personal Recollections of the War of the Rebellion: Addresses Delivered Before the New York Commandery of the Loyal Legion of the United States, 1883–1891.* New York: Published by the Commandery, 1891, 303–312.

Brown, Henry. "The Dark and the Light Side of the River War." Edited by John D. Milligan. *Civil War Times Illustrated* 9 (December 1970): 12–18.

Burt, Jesse C., Jr. "Sherman's Logistics and Andrew Johnson." *Tennessee Historical Quarterly* 15 (1956): 195–215.

Campbell, James Edwin. "Recent Addresses of James Edwin Campbell: The Mississippi Squadron." *Ohio Archaeological and Historical Quarterly* 34 (January 1925): 29–64.

Carson, Kevin. "21 Days to Glory: The Saga of the Confederate Ram *Arkansas.*" *Sea Classics* 39 (July 2006): 38–41, 58–59.

Castel, Albert. "The Fort Pillow Massacre: A Fresh Examination of the Evidence." *Civil War History* 4 (March 1958): 37–50.

_____. "The Guerrilla War." *Civil War Times Illustrated* 34 (October 1974): 1–50.

Catton, Bruce. "Glory Road Began in the West," *Civil War History* 6 (June 1960): 229–237.

Chalmers, James R. "Forrest and His Campaigns." *Southern Historical Society Papers* 7 (1879): 451–486.

Chamberlain, S. "Opening of the Upper Mississippi and the Siege of Vicksburg." *Magazine of Western History* 5 (March 1887): 609–624.

Chandler, Walter. "The Memphis Navy Yard." *West Tennessee Historical Papers* 1 (1947): 68–72.

Cimprich, John. "The Fort Pillow Massacre: Assessing the Evidence." In John David Smith, ed., *Black Soldiers in Blue: African American Troops in the Civil War Era.* Chapel Hill, NC: University of North Carolina Press, 2002, 150–168.

_____, and Robert C. Mamfort, Jr. "Dr. Fitch's Report on the Fort Pil-low Massacre." *Tennessee Historical Quarterly* 44 (Spring 1985): 27–39.

_____. "Fort Pillow Revisited: New Evidence About an Old Controversy." *Civil War History* 28 (December 1982): 293–306.

Coggins, Jack. "Civil War Naval Ordnance: Weapons and Equipment." *Civil War Times Illustrated* 4 (November 1964): 16–20.

Cooling, Benjamin Franklin. "The Attack on Dover, Tenn." *Civil War Times Illustrated* 2 (August 1963): 10–13.

_____. "The Battle of Dover, February 3, 1863." *Tennessee Historical Quarterly* 22 (June 1963): 143–151.

Coulter, E. Merton. "Commercial Intercourse with the Confederacy in the Mississippi Valley, 1861–1865." *Mississippi Valley Historical Review* 5 (March 1919): 377–395.

_____. "Effects of Secession Upon the Commerce of the Mississippi Valley." *Mississippi Valley Historical Review* 3 (December 1916): 275–300.

Cowen, E.G. "The Battle of Johnsonville." *Confederate Veteran* 22 (1914): 174–175.

Cozzens, Peter. "Roadblock on the Mississippi." *Civil War Times Illustrated* 41 (March 2002): 40–49.

Crowley, R.O. "The Confederate Torpedo Service." *Century Illustrated Magazine* 56 (June 1898): 290–300.

Davidson, Hunter. "Mines and Torpedoes During the Rebellion." *Magazine of History* 8 (November 1908): 255–261.

Davis, Steven R. "Death Takes No Holiday." *America's Civil War* 5 (May 1993): 22–28, 74

DeBlack, Thomas A. "'We Must Stand of Fall Alone.'" In Mark K. Christ, ed., *Rugged and Sublime: The Civil War in Arkansas.* Fayetteville, AK: University of Arkansas Press, 1994, 59–104.

Denny, Norman R. "The Devil's Navy." *Civil War Times Illustrated* 35 (August 1996): 25–30.

Dinkins, James. "The Capture of Fort Pillow." *Confederate Veteran* 33 (December 1925): 460–462.

Duke, Basil W. "Morgan's Indiana and Ohio Raid." In *The Annals of the War: Written by Leading Participants North and South.* Philadelphia, PA: The Times Publishing Co., 1879, 241–256.

_____. "The Raid." *The Century Magazine* 41 (January 1891): 403–412.

Dwyer, Christopher S. "Raiding Strategy: As Applied to the Western Confederate Cavalry in the American Civil War." *The Journal of Mil-*

itary History 43 (April 1999): 263–281.

East, Sherrod E. "Montgomery C. Meigs and the Quartermaster Department." *Military Affairs* 25 (Winter 1961–1962): 183–196.

Eisterhold, John A. "Fort Heiman: Forgotten Fortress." *West Tennessee Historical Society Papers* 28 (1974): 43–54.

Elliott, Joseph Taylor. "The *Sultana* Disaster." *Indiana Historical Society Publication* 5, no. 3 (1913): 161–199.

Farrenholt, Oscar W. "The Volunteer Navy in the Civil War." *U.S. Naval Institute Proceedings* 45 (October 1919): 1691–1694.

Fisher, Noel C. "'Prepare Them for My Coming': General William T. Sherman, Total War, and Pacification in West Tennessee." *Tennessee Historical Quarterly* 51 (Summer 1992): 75–86.

Fitzhugh, George. "The Times and the War." *De Bow's Review* 32 (July 1861): 2–3.

Fitzhugh, Lester N. "Texas Forces in the Red River Campaign." *Texas Military History* 3 (Spring 1963): 15–22.

Floyd, William B. "The Burning of the *Sultana.*" *Wisconsin Magazine of History* 11 (September 1927): 70–76.

Foreman, Grant. "River Navigation in the Early Southwest." *The Mississippi Valley Historical Review* 15 (June 1928): 34–55.

Freidel, Frank. "General Orders 100 and Military Government." *Mississippi Valley Historical Review* 32 (March 1946): 541–546.

Gaden, Elmer L., Jr. "Eads and the Navy of the Mississippi." *American Heritage of Invention & Technology* 9 (Spring 1994): 24–31.

Gildrie, Richard P. "Guerrilla Warfare in the Lower Cumberland River Valley, 1862–1865." *Tennessee Historical Quarterly* 49 (Fall 1990): 161–176.

Glenney, Daniel W. "Attempted Sale of the Federal Fleet." *Southern Historical Society Papers* 32 (1904): 58–67.

Gracey, Julius F. "Capture of the *Mazappa.*" *Confederate Veteran* 13 (December 1905): 566–570.

Grimsley, Mark. "'Rebels' and 'Redskins': U.S. Military Conduct Toward White Southerners and Native Americans in Comparative Perspective." In Mark Grimsley and Clifford J. Rogers, eds., *Civilians in the Path of War.* Lincoln, NE: University of Nebraska Press, 2002, 137–162.

Hagerman, Edward. "Field Transportation and Strategic Mobility in the Union Armies." *Civil War History* 34 (June 1988): 143–171.

Haites, Erick F., and James Mak, "The Decline of Steamboating on the Antebellum Western Rivers: Some New Evidence and an Alternative Hypothesis." *Explorations in Economic History* 11 (Fall 1973): 25–36.

Hirsch, Charles B. "Gunboat Personnel on the Western Waters." *Mid-America* 34 (April 1952): 73–86.

Hogan, George M. "Parson's Brigade of Texas Cavalry." *Confederate Veteran* 33 (January 1925): 17–19.

Horn, Stanley F. "The Battle of Perryville." *Civil War Times Illustrated* 5 (February 1966): 4–11, 42–47.

_____. "Nashville During the Civil War." *Tennessee Historical Quarterly* 4 (March 1945): 3–22.

Huch, Ronald K. "Fort Pillow Massacre: The Aftermath of Paducah." *Journal of the Illinois State Historical Society* 66 (1973): 62–70.

Huff, Leo E. "The Union Expedition Against Little Rock, August–September 1863." *Arkansas Historical Quarterly* 22 (Fall 1963): 223–237.

Huffstodt, James. "The Last Great Assault: Campaigning for Mobile." *Civil War Times Illustrated* 21 (March 1982): 9–17.

_____. "River of Death." *Lincoln Herald* 84 (1982): 70–83.

Huston, James A. "Logistical Support of Federal Armies in the Field." *Civil War History* 7 (March 1961): 36–47.

Jett, Benjamin P. "Capture of the Gun Boat *Petrel* in 1864." In Charlean Moss Williams, *The Old Town Speaks: Washington, Hempstead County, Arkansas; Gateway to Texas, 1835, Confederate Capital 1863.* Houston, TX: Anson Jones Press, 1951, 99–102.

Johnson, Kenneth R. "Confederate Defense and Union Gunboats on the Tennessee River." *The Alabama Historical Quarterly* 64 (Summer 1968): 39–60.

Johnson, Ludwell H. "Contraband Trade During the Last Year of the Civil War." *Mississippi Valley Historical Review* 49 (March 1963): 635–652.

Joiner, Gary D. "The Congressional Investigation Following the Red River Campaign." *North Louisiana History* 35 (Fall 2004): 147–167.

_____. "The Red River Campaign." *Louisiana Cultural Vistas,* (Fall 2006), 58–69.

_____. "Up the Red River and Down to Defeat." *America's Civil War,* (March 2004), 22–29.

_____, and Charles E. Vetter. "The Union Naval Expedition on the Red River, March 12–May 22, 1864." *Civil War Regiments: A Journal of the American Civil War* 4, no. 2 (1994): 26–67.

Kaeuper, Robert W. "The Forgotten Triumph of the *Paw Paw.*" *American Heritage* 46 (October 1995): 88.

Kellar, Allan. "Morgan's Raid Across the Ohio." *Civil War Times Illustrated* 2 (June 1963): 6–10.

Klement, Frank L. "Clement L. Vallandigham's Exile in the Confederacy, May 25_June 17, 1863." *Journal of Southern History* 31 (1965): 149–163.

Knox, Dudley W. "River Navies in the Civil War." *Military Affairs* 8 (Spring 1954): 29–32.

Longnecker, Julie. "The *Sultana*: A Civil War Tragedy." *Arkansas Times,* X (September 1983), 88–91.

Mainfort, Robert C., Jr. "Fort Pillow Massacre: A Statistical Note." *Journal of American History* 76 (December 1989): 836–837.

Mak, James, and Gary M. Walton, "Steamboats and the Great Productivity Surge in River Transportation," *Journal of Economic History* 3 (September 1972): 619–640.

Maness, Lonnie E. "Fort Pillow Under Confederate and Union Control." *West Tennessee Historical Society Papers* 38 (1984): 84–98.

Mangum, Ronald S. "The Vicksburg Campaign: A Study in Joint Operations." *Parameters* 21 (Autumn 1991): 74–86.

Martin, David. "The Red River Campaign." *Strategy and Tactics,* no. 106 (1986): 11–20.

Martin, Hiram H. "Service Afield and Afloat: A Reminiscence of the Civil War, Edited by Guy R. Everson." *Indiana Magazine of History* 89 (March 1993): 35–56.

Maury, Dabney H. "Defense of Mobile in 1865." *Southern Historical Society Papers* 3 (1877): 1–13.

_____. "Defense of Spanish Fort." *Southern Historical Society Papers* 39 (1914): 130–136.

_____. "Sketch of General Richard Taylor." *Southern Historical Society Papers* 7 (1879): 343–345.

McCammack, Brian. "Competence, Power, and the Nostalgic Romance of Piloting in Mark Twain's *Life on the Mississippi.*" *The Southern Literary Journal* 38 (March 2006): 1–18.

McCreary, James Bennett. "Journal of My Soldier Life." *Register of the Kentucky State Historical Society* 33 (April_July 1935): 97–117, 191–211.

Merrill, James M. "Cairo, Illinois: Strategic Civil War River Port." *Journal of the Illinois State Historical Society* 76 (Winter 1983): 242–257.

_____. "Union Shipbuilding on Western Waters During the Civil War." *Smithsonian Journal of History* 3 (Winter 1968–1969): 17–44.

Michael, William H. "The Mississippi Squadron in the Civil War." In *Sketches and Incidents: Paper Read by Companions of the Commandery of the State of Nebraska, Military Order of the Loyal Legion of the United States.* Omaha, NE: The Commandery, 1902, 21–33.

Milbourn, Curtis, and Gary D. Joiner. "The Battle of Blair's Landing." *North and South* 9 (February 2007): 12–21.

Miller, Milford M. "Evansville Steamboats During the Civil War." *Indiana Magazine of History* 37 (December 1941): 359–381.

Milligan, John D. "Navy Life on the Mississippi River." *Civil War Times Illustrated* 33 (May_June 1994): 16, 66–73.

_____, ed. "The Dark and the Light Side of the River War." *Civil War Times Illustrated* 9 (December 1970): 12–19.

Mobley, Joe A. "The Siege of Mobile, August 1864_April 1865." *Alabama Historical Quarterly* 38 (1976): 250–270.

"*Moose* Chase: Morgan's Raid." *All Hands*, no. 519 (April 1960): 59–63.

"Morgan's Ohio Raid." In *Battles and Leaders of the Civil War*, Robert V. Johnson and Clarence C. Buel, eds. 4 vols. New York: The Century Company, 1884–1887; reprinted, Thomas Yoseloff, 1956. Vol. 3, 634–635.

Morton, John Watson. "The Battle of Johnsonville." *Southern Historical Society Papers* 10 (1882): 471–488.

_____. "Raid of Forrest's Cavalry on the Tennessee River in 1864." *Southern Historical Society Papers* 10 (1882): 261–268.

Musgrove, George D. "Last Raid of Morgan Through Indiana and Ohio." *Southern Historical Society Papers* 35 (1907): 110–121.

Myers, Denys P. "The Architectural Development of the Western Floating Palace." *Journal of the Society of Architectural Historians* 11 (December 1952): 25–31.

Nichols, George Ward. "Down the Mississippi." *Harper's New Monthly Magazine* 41 (November 1870): 836–845.

Orr, J.F. "Capture of the *Undine* and *Mazappa*." *Confederate Veteran* 18 (July 1910): 323.

Owens, Harry P. "Steamboat Landings on the Yazoo and Tallahatchie Rivers." *Journal of Mississippi History* 47 (November 1985): 266–283.

Parks, Joseph H. "A Confederate Trade Center Under Federal Occupation: Memphis, 1862 to 1865." *Journal of Southern History* 5 (August 1941): 289–314.

Paschall, Rod. "Tactical Exercises —

Mission: Protection." *MHQ: The Quarterly Journal of Military History* 4 (Spring 1992): 56–58.

Patrick, Jeffrey L., ed. "A Fighting Sailor on the Western Waters: The Civil War Letters of [De Witt C. Morse] 'Gunboat.'" *Journal of Mississippi History* 58 (September 1996): 255–283.

Perry, Fredi. "John H. Nibbe." In *Bremerton and the Puget Sound Naval Yard.* Bremerton, WA: Perry Publishing, 2002, 33–34.

Poole, Greg. "The Affair at Harpeth Shoals." *Cheatham County Historical and Genealogical Association CCHGA Bytes* (February 2006): 5–6.

Quisenberry, Anderson C. "Morgan's Men in Ohio." *Southern Historical Society Papers* 39 (1914): 91–99.

Read, Charles W. "Reminiscences of the Confederate States Navy." *Southern Historical Society Papers* 1 (1876): 333–362.

Rector, Charles R. "Morgan 'Goes A-Raiding' and Views West Virginia: A Bit of Civil War History." *West Virginia Review* 6 (May 1929): 310–311, 322.

"Reverend Dr. D.C. Kelley." *The Vanderbilt University Quarterly* 9 (October 1909): 236.

Roberts, A. Sellew. "The Federal Government and Confederate Cotton." *American Historical Review* 32 (January 1927): 262–275.

Roberts, Bobby. "Rivers of No Return." In Mark K. Christ, ed., "*'The Earth Reeled and Trees Trembled': Civil War Arkansas, 1863–1864.* Little Rock, AR: The Old State House Museum, 2007, 74–88.

Roberts, John C. "Gunboats in the River War, 1861–1865." *U.S. Naval Institute Proceedings* 91 (March 1965): 83–99.

Robertson, Middleton. "Recollections of Morgan's Raid." *Indiana Magazine of History* 34 (June 1938): 188–194.

Roth, David E. "The Civil War at the Confluence: Where the Ohio Meets the Mississippi." *Blue & Gray Magazine* 2 (July 1985): 6–20.

Sanger, D.B. "Red River: A Mercantile Expedition." *Tyler's Quarterly Historical and Genealogical Magazine* 17 (October 1935): 70–81.

Saunders, Herbert. "The Civil War Letters of Herbert Saunders." Edited by Ronald K. Hutch. *Register of the Kentucky Historical Society* 69 (March 1971): 17–29.

Sawyer, William D. "The Western River Engine." *Steamboat Bill* 35 (1978): 71–80.

Sharp, Arthur G. "War on the River: The Mississippi River Brigade at

Lake Chicot." *Civil War Times Illustrated* 21 (1982): 18–23.

Shaw, Arthur Marvin, ed. "A Texas Ranger Company at the Battle of Arkansas Post." *Arkansas Historical Quarterly* 9 (Winter 1950): 270–297.

Shea, William L. "Battle at Ditch Bayou." *Arkansas Historical Quarterly* 39 (Autumn 1980): 195–207.

_____. "The Confederate Defeat at Cache River." *Arkansas Historical Quarterly* 52 (Summer 1993): 129–155.

Siddali, Silvana R. "'The Sport of Folly and the Prize of Treason': Confederate Property Seizures and the Northern Home Front in the Secession Crisis." *Civil War History* 4 (Fall 2001): 310–333.

Smith, Lawrence M. "Rise and Fall of the Strategy of Exhaustion." *Army Logistician* (November_December 2004): 33–37.

Smith, Myron J., Jr. "Gunboats at Buffington: The U.S. Navy and Morgan's Raid, 1863." *West Virginia History* 44 (Winter 1983): 97–110.

_____. "Le Roy Fitch Meets the Devil's Parson: The Battle of Bell's Mills, December 4–6, 1864." *North & South* 10 (January 2008): 42–53.

Spenser, Kay Terry. "History of St. Charles During the Civil War." *Grand Prairie Historical Society Bulletin* 2 (January 1960): 29–32.

Steenburn, Donald H. "Gunboats of the Upper Tennessee." *Civil War Times Illustrated* 32 (May 1993): 38–43.

_____. "The United States Ship *Undine*." *Civil War Times Illustrated* 35 (August 1996): 27.

Still, John S. "Blitzkrieg, 1863, Morgan's Raid and Rout." *Civil War History* 3 (1957): 291–306.

Still, William N., Jr. "The Common Sailor — The Civil War's Uncommon Man: Part I, Yankee Blue Jackets." *Civil War Times Illustrated* 23 (February 1985): 25–39.

_____. "The Confederate Ironclad *Missouri*." *Louisiana Studies* 4 (Summer 1965): 101–110.

Stucky, Scott W. "Joint Operations in the Civil War." *Joint Forces Quarterly*, no. 6 (Autumn–Winter 1994–1995): 92–105.

Suhr, Robert C. "Personality: Charles Henry Davis' Brilliant U.S. Navy Career was Interrupted, Not Enhanced, by the Civil War." *Military History* 21 (January_February 2005): 74–75.

Surovic, Arthur F. "Union Assault on Arkansas Post." *Military History* 12 (March 1996): 34–40.

Sutherland, Daniel E. "Guerrillas: The Real War in Arkansas."

Arkansas Historical Quarterly 52 (Autumn 1993): 257–285.

_____. "Sideshow No Longer: A Historiographical Review of the Guerrilla War." *Civil War History* 46 (March 2000): 5–23.

Swift, John. "Letters from a Sailor on a Tinclad." Edited by Lester L. Swift. *Civil War History* 10 (March 1961): 48–62.

Thomas, Edison H. "The Long, Thin Supply Line." *L & N Magazine* (May 1964): 10–11.

Tomlin, Carolyn Ross. "Nathan Bedford Forrest and His 'Horse Marines.'" *Tennessee Conservationist* 61 (March 1995): 26–29.

Toplovich, Ann. "Cumberland River." In Carroll Van West, ed., *The Tennessee Encyclopedia of History and Culture*. Nashville, TN: Rutledge Hill Press for the Tennessee Historical Society, 1998, 227–228.

_____. "Tennessee River System." In Carroll Van West, ed., *The Tennessee Encyclopedia of History and Culture*. Nashville, TN: Rutledge Hill Press for the Tennessee Historical Society, 1998, 943–945.

True, Rowland Stafford. "Life Aboard a Gunboat [U.S.S. *Silver Lake*, No. 23]: A First-Person Account." *Civil War Times Illustrated* 9 (February 1971): 36–43.

Tucker, Spencer C. "Capturing the Confederacy's Western Waters." *Naval History* 20 (June 2006): 16–23.

Tyson, Carl P. "Highway to War." *Red River Valley Historical Review* 3 (Summer 1978): 28–51.

United States Naval Historical Foundation. "River Navies in the Civil War." *Military Affairs* 18 (Spring 1954): 29–32.

Vitz, Carl. "Cincinnati: Civil War Port." *Museum Echoes* 34 (July 1961): 51–54.

Von Rosenburg, William C. "Battle of Calcasieu Pass." *Confederate Veteran* 26 (1918): 516.

Walton, Gary M. "River Transportation and the Old Northwest Territory." In David C. Klingaman and Richard K. Vedder, eds. *Essays on the Economy of the Old Northwest*. Athens: Ohio University Press, 1987, 225–242.

Weaver, Henry C. "Morgan's Raid in Kentucky, Indiana, and Ohio, July 1863." In William H. Chamberlain, ed., *Sketches of War History, 1861–1865: Papers Prepared for the Ohio Commandery of the Military Order of the Loyal Legion of the United States*. 6 vols. Cincinnati, OH: R. Clarke & Co., 1890–1908. Vol. 5, 278–314.

Webber, Richard, and John C. Roberts. "James B. Eads: Master Builder." *The Navy* 8 (March 1965): 23–25.

Weigley, Russel F. "Montgomery C. Meigs: A Personality Profile." *Civil War Times Illustrated* 3 (November 1964): 42–48.

Weller, Cornelia, and Jac Weller. "The Logistics of Bedford Forrest, Part Two: A Leader of Men." *The Army Quarterly* 121 (October 1991): 423–429.

Weller, Jac. "Bedford Forrest: Tactical Teamwork was His Secret Weapon." *Ordnance* 38 (September–October 1953): 248–251.

_____. "Nathan Bedford Forrest: An Analysis of Untutored Military Genius." *Tennessee Historical Quarterly* 18 (1959): 213–259.

West, Richard S., Jr. "Gunboats in the Swamps: The Yazoo Pass Expedition." *Civil War History* 9 (1963): 157–166.

_____. "Lincoln's Hand in Naval Matters." *Civil War History* 4 (June 1958): 175–181.

Wilcox, Charles E. "Hunting for Cotton in Dixie: From the Diary of Captain Charles E. Wilcox." Edited by Edgar L. Erickson. *The Journal of Southern History* 4 (November 1938): 493–513.

Williams, Edward F., III. "The Johnsonville Raid and Nathan Bedford Forrest State Park." *Tennessee Historical Quarterly* 28 (Fall 1969): 225–251.

Wilson, Terry. "'Against Such Powerful Odds': The 83rd Illinois Infantry at the Battle of Dover, Tennessee, February 1863." *Tennessee Historical Quarterly* 53 (December 1994): 260–271.

Wilson, William E. "Thunderbolt of the Confederacy; or, King of Horse Thieves." *Indiana Magazine of History* 54 (June 1958): 119–130.

Unpublished Sources

Barksdale, Ethelbert. "Semi-Regular and Irregular Warfare in the Civil War." Unpublished PhD. Dissertation, University of Texas at Austin, 1941.

Barr, Alwyn. "Confederate Artillery in the Trans-Mississippi." Unpublished MA thesis, University of Texas, 1961.

Bogle, Victor M. "A 19th Century River Town: A Social-Economic Study of New Albany, Indiana." Unpublished PhD. Dissertation, Boston University, 1951.

Chapman, Jesse L. "The Ellet Family

and Riverine Warfare in the West, 1861–1865." Unpublished MA thesis, Old Dominion University, 1985.

Daniel, John S., Jr. "Special Warfare in Middle Tennessee and Surrounding Areas, 1861–1862." Unpublished MA thesis, University of Tennessee, 1971.

Getchll, Charles M., Jr. "Defender of Inland Waters: The Military Career of Isaac Newton Brown, Commander, Confederate States Navy, 1861–1865." Unpublished MA thesis, University of Mississippi, 1978.

Goodman, Michael Harris. "The Black Tar: Negro Seamen in the Union Navy." Unpublished PhD. Dissertation, University of Nottingham, 1975.

Grimsley, Mark. "A Directed Severity: The Evolution of Federal Policy Toward Southern Civilians and Property, 1861–1865." Unpublished PhD. Dissertation, The Ohio State University, 1992.

Hughes, Michael Anderson. "The Struggle for Chattanooga, 1862–1863." Unpublished PhD. Dissertation, University of Arkansas, 1991.

Lighthall, Laurence J. "John Hunt Morgan: A Confederate Asset or Liability?" Unpublished MA thesis, Georgia State University, 1996.

Palmer, Charles Steven. "Our Most Noble Stranger": The Mystery, Gallantry, and Civicism of Colton Greene." Unpublished MA thesis, University of Oklahoma, 1995.

Parker, Theodore R. "The Federal Gunboat Flotilla on the Western Waters During Its Administration by the War Department to October 1, 1862." Unpublished PhD. Dissertation, University of Pittsburgh, 1939.

Polser, Aubrey Henry. "The Administration of the United States Navy, 1861–1865." Unpublished PhD. Dissertation, University of Nebraska, 1975.

Sharpe, Hal F. "A Door Left Open: The Failure of the Confederate Government to Adequately Defend the Inland Rivers of Tennessee." Unpublished MA thesis, Austin Peay State University, 1981.

Smith, Myron J., Jr. "A Construction and Recruiting History of the U.S. Steam Gunboat *Carondelet*, 1861–1862." Unpublished MA Thesis, Shippensburg State University, 1969.

Stowe, John Joel, Jr. "The Military Career of Nathan Bedford Forrest." Unpublished MA thesis, George Peabody College, 1930.

Whisenant, Johnny H. "Samuel Phillips Lee, U.S.N.: Commander, Mississippi Squadron (October 19,

1864–August 14, 1865." Unpublished MS Thesis, Kansas State College of Pittsburg, 1968.

Wright, Aubrey Gardner. "Henry Walke, 1809–1896: Romantic Painter and Naval Hero." Unpublished MA thesis, The George Washington University, 1971.

Wynne, Robert Bruce. "Topographical Influences Upon the 1863 Campaigns in East Tennessee and North Georgia." Unpublished MA thesis, University of Tennessee, 1962.

Internet Sources

"The Archaeological Investigations of the Battle of Johnsonville." *PanAm Consultants Homepage, http://www. panamconsultants.com/PAGE* (accessed June 8, 2004).

Aronson, Alan. "Strategic Supply of Civil War Armies." *General Histories of the American Civil War, http:// members.cox.net/rb2307/content/ STRATEGIC_SUPPLY_OF_ CIVIL_WAR_ARMIES.htm* (accessed March 30, 2000).

"Arkansas River," *Wikipedia: The Free Encyclopedia,* en.wikipedia.org/wiki/Arkansas_River (accessed September 2, 2006).

Backs, Jean. "Morgan's Raid." *Explore Magazine* (Spring 2001), *Ohio Department of Natural Resources Home Page. http://www.dnr.state.oh. us/parks/explore/magazine/spru 2001/morgan.htm* (accessed November 14, 2005).

Bailey, Anne J. "Parson's Texas Cavalry." *Handbook of Texas Online. http://www.tsha.utexas.edu/handb ook/online/articles/PP/qkp1.html* (accessed July 22, 2007).

Bearss, Edwin C. "Wirt Adams Repels Yankee Task Force at Yazoo City." *Morningside Notes. http://w ww.morningsidebooks.com/notes/ yazoo.htm* (accessed April 10, 2000).

Bering, John A. and Thomas Montgomery, *History of the Forty-Eighth Ohio Vet. Vol. Inf., In Don Worth, 48th OVVI Home Page http://www. riovvi.org/oh48hist.html* (accessed January 25, 2007).

Biographical Directory of the United States Congress, 1774–Present, http:// bioguide.congress.gov/scripts/biodis play.pl?index=B000231 (accessed October 1, 2006).

Block, William T. "The Battle of Calcasieu Pass, Louisiana: Reprinted from the Beaumont *Enterprise,* May 6, 1977. *W. T. Block Homepage. http://www.wtblock.com/ wtblockjr/calcasie.htm* (accessed November 1, 2007).

_____. "Calcasieu Parish, LA: Hotbed of the Civil War Jayhawkers." *W.T. Block Homepage http://ww w.wtblock.com/wtblockjr/calcasie1. htm* (accessed November 1, 2007).

_____. "Calcasieu Pass Victory, Heroism 'Equal Dowling's': Reprinted from the *Port Arthur News,* January 3, 1971." *W.T. Block Homepage http://www.wtblock.com/ wtblockjr/calcasie4.htm* (accessed November 1, 2007).

Chiarella, John T. "Henry Honeychurch Gorringe." *Find a Grave Memorial http://www.findagrave. com/cgi-bin/fg.cgi?page=gr& GRid=6926925* (accessed November 3, 2008).

"The Civil War Diary of Michael Sweetman, Co. K 114th O.V.I.." Edited by Johnda T. Davis. *Fortunecity http://www.fortunecity.com/ westwood/makeover/347/id229.htm* (accessed May 5, 2007).

"Cumberland River." in *Wikipedia: The Free Encyclopedia, http://en. wikipedia.org/wiki/Cumberland_ River,* (August 6, 2005).

"Decatur and the Civil War," *Nostalgiaville http://travel.nostalgiaville. com/Alabama/Decatur/decatur%20 civil%20war.htm* (accessed December 1, 2008).

Donn, John W. "War Record of J. W. Donn, Including Reminiscences of Frederick W. Dorr, July 1861 to June 1865." *NOAA History Homepage, http://www.history.noaa.gov/stories_ tales/donn.html,* (accessed April 4, 2005).

Foenander, Terry. "Treachery of a Union Gunboat Commander." *Foenander Home Page. http://www.tfoe nander.com/treachery.htm* (accessed December 1, 2008).

"Ghost Town of Rodney, Mississippi: The 'Almost" Capital of Mississippi." Southpoint Travel Guide http://www. southpoint.com/states/ms/rodney.htm (accessed September 12, 2008).

Harris, Isham G. "Correspondence of Governor Isham Green Harris, 1861." TNGenWeb Project: The Biographies of Our Ancestors, *http:// www.tngenweb.org/bios/h/18610429. html* (accessed September 11, 2006).

History of the Val Verde Battery. http://www.geocities.com/valverde_ battery (accessed July 24, 2007).

Hogan, Brian, Conrad Bush and Mike Brown. "The 76th New York and the Navy." *76th New York Infantry Regiment Homepage http:// www.bpmlegal.com/76NY/76navy. html* (accessed July 12, 2005).

INGenWeb. "Madison City Directory, 1859–1860." *Madison and Jefferson County Directories, http://m yindianahome.net/gen/jeff/records/di rect/maddir.html* (accessed September 30, 2006).

"James Buchanan Eads." *University of Illinois at Urbana-Champaign Riverweb Site. http://www.riverweb. uiuc.edu/TECH/TECH20.htm* (accessed September 18, 2006).

Jenkins, Mark F. "Operations of the Mississippi Squadron During Morgan's Raid," *Ironclads and Blockade Runners of the American Civil War Homepage. www.wideopenwest.com/ ~jenkins/ironclads/buffingt.htm* (accessed November 11, 2005).

_____. "Tinclads," *Ironclads and Blockade Runners of the Civil War homepage. http://www.wideopenwest. com/~jenkins/ironclads/tinclads.htm* (accessed July 29, 2005).

"Jesse J. Phillips." *Illinois Courts homepage. http://www.state.il.us/Court/ SupremeCourt/Previous/Bio_JPhillips. asp* (accessed October 6, 2006).

Kaeuper, Richard W. "The Civil War on the Fringe: Tinclad Navy." JCS Group Homepage. *http://www.jcs- group.org/military/war1861fringe /navytinclad.html* (accessed September 8, 2008).

"'The Kelly Rangers/Kelly Troopers," Company F, Forrest's Battalion (3d Tennessee Cavalry) and Company K, 4th Alabama Cavalry Regiment," *Confederate Units of Madison County homepage, http://www.rootsweb.co m/~almadiso/confunit.htm* (accessed March 4, 2006).

Ledoux, Tom. "United States Navy Biographies: George M. Blodgett." *VermontCivilWar.Org http://ver- montcivilwar.org/units/navy/bios. php?input=33437* (accessed January 27, 2007).

Liddell, Bruce D. "U.S.S. *Rattler* at Rodney, Sunday, September 13, 1863." *Jefferson County MSGenWeb Project homepage.* http://jeffersonc ountyms.org/USSRattler.htm (accessed August 18, 2008).

Letters Home from an Iowa Soldier in the American Civil War. http://www. civilwarletters.com/scott_7_6_1863.h tml (accessed July 2, 2007).

Matthews, Gary. "'Tinclad'—In Response to: Re: Tinclad (Terry Foenander).'" *Civil War Navies Message Board http://history-sites.com/mb/acw cwnavy/index.cgi?noframes;read=1314* (accessed December 7, 2005).

"Mississippi River," in *Wikipedia: The Free Encyclopedia, http://en. wikipedia.org/wiki/Ohio_River* (accessed August 25, 2006).

Morris, William R. "The Burning of Clifton." *Wayne County Historian,* II (June 1989) reprinted on the *Civil War Page http://www.netease.net/ wayne/burningclifton.htm* (accessed March 3, 2004).

_____. "The Tennessee River Voyages of the U.S.S. *Peosta.*" Morris homepage, *http://www.centuryinter.net/nacent/bs/peosta.htm* (accessed March 3, 1997).

"My Pollard Family: Chapter 2 & Chapter 3, Daniel, the War Years." *My American Family, or ????* Homepage http://freepages.family.rootsweb.com/-ricksgenealogy/e_book.htm (accessed July 13, 2005).

Nicholson, Norman A. "The Mobile Campaign: Battle of Fort Blakely and Spanish Fort." *Blakeley State Park: Civil War Memorial Site and Scenic Nature Trails* http://new.siteone.com/sites/blakeleypark.com/battlehistory.htm (accessed December 17, 2008).

"Officers of the United States Navy During the War Period Appointed from New Jersey," *New Jersey Civil War Record Page 1600* http://www.njstatelib.org/NJ_Information/Searchable_Publications/civilwar/NJCWn1600.html (accessed July 4, 2008).

"Ohio River." in *Wikipedia: The Free Encyclopedia, http://en.wikipedia.org/wiki/Ohio_River* (accessed August 5, 2005).

"The Origin of the Ranks and Rank Insignia Now Used by the United States Armed Forces, Officers: Lieutenants." *Traditions of the Naval Service* http://www.history.navy.mil/trivia/triv4-5d.htm (accessed July 7, 2005).

"Red River." *LoveToKnow 1911,* http://www.1911encyclopedia.org/Red_River (accessed September 3, 2006).

"Red River (Mississippi Watershed)." *Wikipedia: The Free Encyclopedia,* http://en.wikipedia.org/wiki/Red_River_%28Mississippi_watershed%29 (accessed September 3, 2006).

Redington Papers, University of Wisconsin Digital Collections *http://digital.library.wisc.edu/1711.dl/WI.EdRed01* (accessed August 30, 2006).

Rice, Thomas E. "Managing the Mississippi," *The Nature of Illinois* homepage http://www.natureillinois.org/news/mississippi.html (accessed August 26, 2006).

Richard, Joseph. *The 18th Louisiana Infantry Regiment: A Brief History and Roster.* http://members.tripod.com/j_richard/ (accessed February 1, 2007).

Simon, Don R. "Engagement at Old River Lake." *The Encyclopedia of Arkansas History and Culture* http://www.encycopediaofarkansas.net/encyclopedia/entry-detail.aspx?entryID=1120 (accessed November 10, 2008).

Smith, David M. "The Defense of Cincinnati — The Battle That Never Was: Past Presentations of the Cincinnati Civil War Roundtable, January 15, 1998." Cincinnati Civil War Roundtable Homepage, *http://www.cincinnaticwrt.org/data/ccwrt_history/talks_text/smith_defense_cin.html* (accessed September 4, 2006).

Smith, Rebecca W., and Marion Mullins, eds. "The Diary of H.C. Medford, Confederate Soldier, 1864," Volume 34, Number 2, *Southwestern Historical Quarterly Online.* http://www.tsha.utexas.edu/publications/journals/shq/online/v034/n2/contrib_DIVL1540.html (accessed July 22, 2007).

Smith, Steven D., and George J. Castille III. "Bailey's Dam." *Louisiana, Department of Culture, Recreation and Tourism Anthropological Study No. 8,* March 1986, *http://www.crt.state.la.us/archaeology/BAILEYS/baileys.htm* (accessed August 7, 2006).

"Spring on the Cumberland" in *Cruising America-Halcyon Days* http://www.geocities.com/bill_fiero/tenn05.htm (accessed December 10, 2007).

"Springtime on the Tennessee" in *Cruising America-Halcyon Days* http://www.geocities.com/bill_fiero/tenn05.htm (accessed December 11, 2007).

"A Tale of Three Tinclads, All Named Argosy." *Mid Missouri Civil War Roundtable Homepage,* 2005. http://www.mmcwrt.org/2005/default0501.htm (accessed July 29, 2005).

"Tennessee River." in *Wikipedia: The Free Encyclopedia,* http://en.wikipedia.org/wiki/Tennessee_River (accessed August 5, 2005).

"Towns of the Cumberland." *Save the Cumberland Homepage,* http://www.savethecumberland.org/towns.htm (accessed July 21, 2005).

United States Congress. Senate Committee on Veterans Affairs. "Civil War Medal of Honor Citations." in: its *Medal of Honor Recipients: 1863–1973.* http://americancivilwar.com/medal_of_honor6.html (accessed November 1, 2008).

United States Navy Department. Naval Historical Center. *Dictionary of American Naval Fighting Ships,* http://www.history.navy.mil/danfs (accessed February 8–9, 2008).

_____. Naval Historical Center. *Frequently Asked Questions, No. 63: Ship Naming in the United States Navy, A Note on Navy Ship Name Prefixes* http://www.history.navy.mil/faqs/faq63-1.htm (accessed April 16, 2007).

_____. Navy Department Library. "Chapter 6: Dispositions and Instructions," *War Instructions United States Navy 1944.* http://www.history.navy.mil/library/online/warinst-6.htm (accessed March 13, 2006).

"The Valverde Battery." *The Road to Glorieta Readers Companion.* http://darkwing.uoregon.edu/-donh/page78.html (accessed July 24, 2007).

VandeCreek, Drew E. "And the War Came, 1861–1862." Illinois During the Civil War Homepage *http://dig.lib.niu.edu/civilwar/narrative2.html* (accessed August 30, 2006).

Veit, Chuck. "Engagement at Deloges Bluff." *Navy and Marine Homepage.* http://www.navyandmarine.org/ondeck/1862delogesbluff.htm (accessed July 24, 2007).

Weatherred, John. "Wartime Diary of John Weatherred, Bennett's Regiment or 9th Tennessee Cavalry, John Hunt Morgan's Command." Edited by Jack Masters. *The Wartime Diary of John Weatherred.* http://www.jackmasters.net/we1863.html (accessed April 11, 2005).

Wehner, Chris. "The Burning of Prentiss, Mississippi, 1862: A Case Study in Total War." *Blog4 History: American History & Civil War History* http://www.blog4history.com/?m=200607 (accessed May 3, 2007).

"Where We've Been: U.S.S. *Queen City* Sinking." *Clarendon Arkansas Homepage* http://www.clarendon-ar.com/been/uss_queen_city/index.html (accessed July 6, 2007).

"The *White Cloud* & *Rowena*: The Paths of Robert Louden and James Cass Mason Cross." *Civil War St. Louis: The Boatburners,* http://www.civilwarstlouis.com/boatburners/whitecloud.htm (accessed June 30, 2008).

"White River." *Wikipedia,* The Free Encyclopedia, http://en.wikipedia.org/wiki/White_River_%28Arkansas%29 (accessed September 2, 2006).

Wiener, James G., et al. "Mississippi River." *U.S. Geological Survey, Biological Resources Division homepage* <http://biology.usgs.gov/s+t/SNT/noframe/ms137.htm>, (accessed August 26, 2006).

Williams, Scott K. "St Louis' Ships of Iron: The Ironclads and Monitors of Carondelet (St. Louis), Missouri." *Missouri Civil War Museum Home Page,* http://www.moissouricivilwarmuseum.org/ironclads.htm (accessed July 12, 2005).

"Yazoo River." *Wikipedia: The Free Encyclopedia* en.wikipedia.org/wiki/Yazoo_River (accessed September 2, 2006).

Index

Numbers in **bold italics** indicate pages with photographs.